Date Due

APR 30 2010			

BRODART, INC. Cat. No. 23 233 Printed in U.S.A.

CRIME
AND
JUSTICE

CRIME AND JUSTICE

1970 - 1971

An AMS Anthology

edited by

Jackwell Susman
American University

AMS PRESS
NEW YORK
London   Toronto

Copyright © 1972 by AMS Press, Inc.

All rights reserved. Published in the United States by AMS Press, Inc., 56 East 13th Street, New York, N.Y. 10003, and distributed in England by AMS Press, Inc., 17 Conduit Street, London, W.1.; and in Canada by AMS Canada Library Services Ltd., Royal Trust Tower, Toronto 111, Ontario.

Library of Congress Catalog Card Number: 78-38401

International Standard Book Number:
Buckram-Bound   0-404-10201-8
Paper-Bound   0-404-10251-4

Manufactured in the United States of America.

TABLE OF CONTENTS

IV. DETERRING CRIMINAL BEHAVIOR

V. PLANNING FOR JUSTICE

VI. DIVERSION FROM THE CRIMINAL JUSTICE SYSTEM

VII. THE OPERATION OF THE CRIMINAL JUSTICE SYSTEM

The Police

Courts and Judges

ACKNOWLEDGMENTS

Acknowledgment is made to the authors and publishers below who have granted permission to reprint material and who reserve all rights in the articles appearing in this anthology.

Allen, "Freedom, Order and Justice," *Current History*, June, 1971, Vol. 60, pp. 321-326, 368.

Amir and Berman, "Chromosomal Deviation and Crime," *Federal Probation*, June, 1970, pp. 55-62.

Andenaes, "Deterrence and Specific Offenses," *University of Chicago Law Review*, Spring, 1971, Vol. 38, pp. 537-553.

Black, "Production of Crime Rates," *American Sociological Review*, August, 1970, pp. 733-748.

Bromberg, "Is Punishment Dead?," *American Journal of Psychiatry*, August, 1970, Vol. 127, pp. 245-248. Copyright ©1970, the American Psychiatric Association.

Brown, Gauvey, Meyers, Stark, "In Their Own Words: Addicts Reasons for Initiating and Withdrawing from Heroin," *International Journal of the Addictions*, 1971, Vol. 6. Reprinted with the permission of Marcel Dekker, Inc.

Christian, "Delay in Criminal Appeals: A Functional Analysis of One Court's Work," *Stanford Law Review*, April, 1971, Vol. 23, pp. 676-702. Copyright ©1971 by the Board of Trustees of the Leland Stanford Junior University.

Conklin, "Dimensions of Community Response to the Crime Problem," *Social Problems*, Winter, 1971, Vol. 18, pp. 373-385. Reprinted with the permission of The Society for the Study of Social Problems.

Cressey, "Bet Taking, Cosa Nostra, and Negotiated Social Order," *Journal of Public Law*, 1970, Vol. 19, pp. 13-22.

Ferdinand and Luchterhand, "Inner-City Youth, the Police, the Juvenile Court, and Justice," *Social Problems*, Spring, 1970, Vol. 17, pp. 510-527. Reprinted with the permission of The Society for the Study of Social Problems.

Fox, "Why Prisoners Riot," *Federal Probation*, March, 1971, pp. 9-14.

Gamson and McEvoy, "Police Violence and Its Public Support," *The Annals*,

The American Academy of Political and Social Science, September, 1970, Vol. 391, pp. 97-110.

Goode, "Marijuana and the Politics of Reality," from Smith (ed.): *The New Social Drug*, 1970, pp. 168-186. Reprinted by permission of the American Sociological Association.

Graham, "Police Eavesdropping: Law-Enforcement Revolution," *Criminal Law Bulletin*, June, 1971, Vol. 7, pp. 445-471.

Greider, "The Point Where War Becomes Murder," *The Washington Post*, October 11, 1970, pp. D1, D4.

Ianni, "The Mafia and the Web of Kinship," *The Public Interest*, Winter, 1971, pp. 78-100. Copyright©1970, National Affairs, Inc.

Jackson, "Letter, June 10, 1970," from *Soledad Brother: The Prison Letters of George Jackson*. Copyright©1970 by World Entertainers Limited. By permission of Bantam Books, Inc.

Katz, "A Psycho-Analytic Peek at Conspiracy," *Buffalo Law Review*, Fall, 1970, Vol. 20, pp. 239-251. Copyright©1970 by Buffalo Law Review.

Krantz and Kramer, "The Urban Crisis and Crime," *Boston University Law Review*. 50 B.U.L. Rev. 343 (1970).

Lejins, "Ideas Which Have Moved Corrections," *Proceedings of the Centennial Congress of the American Correctional Association*, 1970. Reprinted with the permission of the American Correctional Association.

Mendelsohn, "Police-Community Relations: A Need in Search of Police Support," *American Behavioral Scientist*, May-June-July-August, 1970, pp. 745-760. Reprinted by permission of the Publisher, Sage Publications, Inc.

Milner, "Comparative Analysis of Patterns of Compliance with Supreme Court Decisions: 'Miranda' and the Police in Four Communities," *Law and Society Review*, August, 1970, pp. 119-134.

Morris and Hawkins, "Rehabilitation: Rhetoric and Reality," *Federal Probation*, December, 1970, pp. 9-17.

Niederhoffer and Smith, "Power and Personality in the Courtroom: The Trial of the Chicago 7," *Connecticut Law Review*, Winter, 1970-1971, Vol. 3, pp. 233-243.

Nimmer, "St. Louis Diagnostic and Detoxification Center: An Experiment in

Non-Criminal Processing of Public Intoxicants," *Washington University Law Quarterly*, Winter, 1970, Vol. 1970, pp. 1-27.

Perkins and Bloch, "A Study of Some Failures in Methadone Treatment," *American Journal of Psychiatry*, July, 1971, Vol. 128, pp. 47-51. Copyright©1971, the American Psychiatric Association.

Sagalyn, "The Crime of Robbery in the U.S.," from *The Crime of Robbery in the U.S.*, Government Printing Office, 1971, pp. 6-16.

Salem and Bowers, "Severity of Formal Sanctions as a Deterrent to Deviant Behavior," *Law and Society Review*, August, 1970, Vol. 5, pp. 21-40.

Scanlan's Monthly, "The Student Who Burned Down the Bank of America," *Scanlan's Monthly*, January, 1971, Vol. 1, pp. 21-23.

Schoenfeld, "Psychoanalysis, Criminal Justice Planning and Reform, and the Law," *Criminal Law Bulletin*, May, 1971, Vol. 7, pp. 313-327.

Singer, B.D., "Violence, Protest, and War in Television News: The U.S. and Canada Compared," *Public Opinion Quarterly*, Winter, 1970-1971, Vol. 34, pp. 611-616.

Singer, B.F., "Psychological Studies of Punishment," *California Law Review*, March, 1970, Vol. 58, pp. 405-443. Copyright©1970, California Law Review, Inc. Reprinted by permission.

Singer, R.G., "Prison Conditions: An Unconstitutional Roadblock to Rehabilitation," *Catholic University Law Review*, Spring, 1971, Vol. 20, pp. 365-393.

Swados, "The City's Island of the Damned," *The New York Times Magazine*, April 26, 1970, pp. 25, 106, 108, 109, 111, 112. Copyright©1970, by the New York Times Company. Reprinted by permission.

Warren, "Classification of Offenders as an Aid to Efficient Management and Effective Treatment," *Journal of Criminal Law, Criminology and Police Science*. Reprinted by special permission of the Journal of Criminal Law, Criminology and Police Science (Northwestern University School of Law), copyright©1971, Vol. 62, pp. 239-258.

White, "A Proposal for Reform of the Plea Bargaining Process," *University of Pennsylvania Law Review*, January, 1971, Vol. 119, pp. 439-465.

Wolfgang, "Violent Crime in a Birth Cohort," from *Youth and Violence*, Government Printing Office, 1970, pp. 39-50.

INTRODUCTION

This volume, indeed the series which it initiates, appears at a propitious period in our social history. The movement to reconstruct criminal justice is gaining momentum. At various times in our history the legislative, judicial and executive branches of government have had a leading role to play in this development. The courts, especially the Supreme Court, have been leaders for the past few decades. But with the dramatic changes in personnel the Supreme Court has experienced recently, it seems clear that it will go into eclipse as an agent of change. While the President has given some indication of a willingness to introduce changes, it is Congress that seems destined to initiate those changes in criminal justice long overdue. What is the nature of these changes? They are twofold. First, we are reconsidering our social values and priorities. Secondly, we are reconsidering the scope of the criminal law. We, as a society, are examining our values and deciding which should be protected by the criminal law and which should be protected by other institutions. In some cases this could mean that new crimes are created, a process leading to "overcriminalization." But the wiser tendency, and more likely in the longer run, is to divest the criminal law, that is, remove from the reach of the criminal law certain behaviors that were once crimes. The successes and failures of this movement from year to year can be followed in this series of books.

Another tendency, which this book and its series will reflect, is the increasing awareness that a serious problem, that of "crime and justice," cannot be solved in a vacuum. We have abandoned the puerile hope for a dramatic intellectual breakthrough. "Crime and justice" includes a very broad area of society, one which desperately cries out for reform. As a problem, it encompasses many traditional professions and institutions. Similarly, at the university, there is evidence of a breaking up of traditional academic jurisdictions, of an academic reform movement which tries to understand and solve problems in their variegated reality. Professors and students alike are no longer content to see a problem from the narrow perspective of one discipline but are demanding that they be examined from a diversity of perspectives. The area of "crime and justice" is peculiarly susceptible to this demand, since it is a problem which must encroach on criminology, law, sociology, social psychology, and a variety of other fields of study. For these reasons, the collection of articles in this book are divergent in viewpoint and method. These divergences, however, are subordinate to a common concern, that of arriving at an understanding of crime and constructive reforms of justice.

In this sense the volume is inter-disciplinary; the authors are representative of a variety of disciplines. But it is not an attempt by them to pool their abstractions or to go their separate ways under a common heading. No one here speaks for a discipline or schoool of thought or set of techniques. As individual authors, they fall roughly into three categories. The first category comprises members of that rare group of scholarly practitioners who are equipped with academic training and have tested their knowledge against practice. The second set of contributions comes from scholars who attempt to bring to bear information, techniques, and thinking that can increase our understanding beyond the range of practical experience. The final category of contributors includes authors who, lacking the experience of practitioners and the knowledge of scholars, have with great insight reported on specific problems and needed reforms.

Despite the differences in their backgrounds, the contributors approach their subject from one of four orientations. Some have as their viewpoint the traditional concern of criminology for the causes of criminal behavior. Others seek to determine how some people come to be considered criminals by examining how and why criminal laws are created, what interests are represented and what interests are not represented, under what circumstances and against whom enforcement of the law occurs, etc. Still others use the traditional policy approach of rigorous logical and comparative analysis. Finally, there are those who approach justice and crime from a behavioral perspective and seek to describe justice in action.

The book is offered with a dual purpose: It seeks to provide the scholar, student, specialist and interested layman with facts about some of the social processes involved in crime and justice. Secondly, it is intended to challenge thinking and provoke argument about these facts. To fulfill the first objective, no effort has been spared to provide factual information, taking as little for granted as possible. In line with the second aim, several contributions were selected principally because they represent refreshing and challenging viewpoints.

The thirty-nine selections are organized into eight subdivisions: Section I puts the critical problem of crime and justice in the perspective of broader social processes; Section II and III respectively describe and analyze selected criminal activities; Section IV reviews current thinking on sanctions as a form of crime prevention; Section V looks at the increasingly influential field of criminal justice planning and presents some intelligent suggestions and criticisms; Section VI presents studies of three types of diversions from the criminal system; Section VII examines the operation of the criminal justice system as represented by some recent problems. The last section, appropriately enough, ends the book with a plea for justice.

In comparison with a book written by one author, a book of readings has both disadvantages and advantages. It lacks the continuity of a book written by one author but it has the inestimable advantage of placing before the reader exactly what an author had to say on his subject. A book of readings serves another purpose. It prolongs the time during which worthwhile articles are saved from the obscurity of the bound volumes of periodicals shelved in dark recesses in the library. It brings to the reader material he might never discover or would not take the trouble to locate as originally published.

Certain principles guided the selection of the thirty-nine articles. As indicated above, they delve into the fields of criminology, criminal justice and penology at critical points. They are current, having been published during 1970 and 1971. For the most part, simply descriptive articles have been omitted in favor of articles that deal with controversial aspects of the field. Controversies indicate the growing edge of the subject where thinking is needed. In order to reach a wide range of readers, articles written in highly technical phrases have been bypassed, although the articles selected rest firmly on sound theory or research. Articles that are primarily methodological have not been included; however, many of the articles detail the methods used in the research. The book therefore has been planned to stir the reader's critical faculties without diverting him into technical byways.

The editor thanks the many authors and publishers who consented to the reprinting of the material in this book.

Jackwell Susman
The American University

I.

THE SOCIAL
AND POLITICAL CONTEXT
OF CRIME AND JUSTICE

MARIJUANA AND
THE POLITICS OF REALITY

Erich Goode

Introduction

One of the more mystifying chapters in recent social research is the seemingly totally contradictory conclusions arrived at in regard to marijuana use. It is possible that no sector of social behavior is more disputed. To raise empirical questions concerning aspects of marijuana use is to arouse a hornet's nest of controversy. Even the fundamental question of the effects of the drug on the human mind and body is hotly disputed; two descriptions, both purporting to be equally "objective," often bear no relation to one another whatsoever.[1] Is marijuana a drug of "psychic dependence"? Or is it meaningless to speak of dependency in regard to marijuana? Does marijuana cause organic damage to the brain? Are its effects criminogenic? How does it influence the over-all output of activity—in popular terms, does it produce "lethargy" and "sloth"? Does it precipitate "psychotic episodes"? What, specifically, is its impact on artistic creativity? What is the drug's influence on mechanical skills, such as the ability to drive an automobile? Does the use of marijuana "lead to" heroin addiction?

These are questions which can be answered within the scope of empirical sociological, psychological and pharmacological scientific technique. Each query can be operationalized. Indices can be constructed; tests can be devised. Occasionally they are. Yet the zones of widespread agreement are narrow indeed. Surely this should puzzle the sociologist. We propose, therefore, to explore some of the likely sources of this controversy, and to attempt a partial explanation for this almost complete discord.

The Social Construction of Reality[2]

All civilizations set rules concerning what is "real" and what is not, what is "true" and what "false." All societies select out of the data before them a world, one world, the "world taken for granted," and declare that the "real world." Each one of these artificially constructed worlds is to some degree idiosyncratic, unique. No individual views reality directly, "in the raw," so to speak. Our perceptions are narrowly channeled through concepts and interpretations. What is commonly thought of as "reality," that which "exists," or simply "is," is a set of concepts, conceptual frames, assumptions, suppositions, rationalizations, justifications, defenses, all generally collectively agreed upon, which guide and channel each individual's perceptions in a specific and distinct direction. The specific rules governing the perception of the universe which man inhabits are more or less arbitrary, a matter of convention. Every society establishes a kind of *epistemological methodology.*

Meaning, then, does not automatically announce itself. Rather, it is *read into* every situation, event, entity, object, phenomenon. What one individual understands by a given phenomenon may be absolutely heterogenous to what another individual understands by it. In a sense, then, the reality itself is different. The only reality available to each individual consciousness is a subjective reality. Yet this insight poses a dilemma: we must see in a skewed manner or not at all. For, as Berger and Luckmann point out, "To include epistemological questions concerning the validity of sociological knowledge is like trying to push a bus in which one is riding" (Berger and Luckmann, 1966:13).

Sociologists, too, are implicated in this same process. But unless we wish to remain huddled in the blind cave of solipsism, the problem should not paralyze us. We leave the problem of the ultimate validity of sociological knowledge to the metaphysical philosophers.

If we wish to grasp the articulation between ideology and what Westerners call science, we must look to fundamental cultural beliefs which stimulate or inhibit the growth of scientific-empirical ideas. One form of this selection process, the course of defining the nature of the universe, involves *the rules of validating reality.* A procedure is established for accepting inferential evidence; some forms of evidence will be ruled out as irrelevant, while others will serve to negotiate and determine what is real. For instance, some religious systems have great faith in the validity of the message of the senses (Merton; Kennedy). Other civilizations give greater weight to mystical insight, to the reality beyond empirical reality (Needham: 417–422, 430–431).

The sociologist's task only begins on this vast cultural canvas. While the "major mode" of the epistemological selection and validation process involves the decision to accept or rule out the data of our senses, within this tradition, minor modes of variation will be noticed. Clearly, even societies with powerful scientific and empirical traditions will contain subcultures which have less faith in the logic of the senses than others. Moreover, all cultures have absorbed one or another mode of reasoning *differentially*, so that some institutions will typify the dominant mode more characteristically than others. Certainly few in even the most empirical of civilizations will apply the same rules of evidence in the theater of their family as in their workaday world.

The more complex the society, the greater the number of competing versions concerning reality. The Positivists were in error in assuming that greater knowledge would bring epistemological convergence. The arenas of controversy are more far-flung than ever before. Now, instead of societies differing as to how they view the real world, sub-segments of society differ. This poses a serious problem for those members of society who have an emotional investment in stability and in the legitimacy of their own special version of reality. The problem becomes, then, a matter of *moral hegemony*, of legitimating one distinctive view of the world, and of discrediting competing views. These rules of validating reality, and society's faith in them, may serve as *strategies* in ideological struggles. Contending parties will wish to establish veracity by means of the dominant cultural mode.

All societies invest this selection process with an air of *mystification,* to use Peter Berger's phrase (1967:90–91, 203): "Let the institutional order be so interpreted as to hide, as much as possible, its *constructed* character. . . . [The] humanly constructed nomoi are given a cosmic status. . . ." (1967:33, 36). This process must not, above all, be seen as whimsical and arbitrary; it must be grounded in the nature of reality itself. The one selected view of the world must be seen as the *only possible* view of the world; it must be identified with the real world. All other versions of reality must be seen as whimsical and arbitrary and, above all, *in error.* At one time, this twin mystification process was religious in character: views in competition with the dominant one were heretical and displeasing to the gods— hence, Galileo's "crime." Now, of course, the style is to cloak what Berger terms "fictitious necessities" with an aura of scientific validity. Nothing has greater discrediting power today than the demonstration that a given assertion has been "scientifically disproven." Our contemporary pawnbrokers of reality are scientists.

Value and Fact in Negotiating the Marijuana Reality

Probably no area of social life reflects this selective process more than drug use. Note the pharmacological definition of a "drug": ". . . a drug is broadly defined as any chemical agent that effects living protoplasm. . . ." (Fingl and Woodbury, 1965:1). Yet very few in our society will admit to the use of drugs, including the man who smokes two packs of cigarettes a day, the barbiturate-dependent housewife, and the near-alcoholic. Society has constructed the social concept (if not the pharmacological definition) in such a way that it excludes elements which are substantially identical to those it includes. What is seen as the essential reality of a given drug and its use, then, is a highly *contingent* event. What society selects as crucial to perceive about drugs, and what it ignores, tells us a great deal about its cultural fabric.

The scientist makes a clear distinction between those questions which can be tested empirically and those which are wholly in the realm of sentiment. A man may have an opinion about whether marijuana causes crime, but the question is, ideally at least, answerable. As long as the combatants agree on the rules of the road, there is supposedly a more or less clear right and wrong here. But the question of whether marijuana is *evil* or not is intrinsically unanswerable, within an empirical and scientific framework; it depends completely on one's perspective. However clear-cut this distinction is in the scientist's mind, as a tool for understanding the combatants' positions in this controversy it is specious and misleading, for a variety of reasons.

To begin with, the strands of value and fact intersect with one another so luxuriantly that in numerous reasoning sequences they are inseparable. What one society or group or individual takes for granted as self-evidently harmful, others view as obviously beneficial or even necessary. In crucial ways, the issue of harm or danger to society as a result of the drug pivots on moot points, totally unanswerable questions, issues that science is unable to resolve. Science requires that certain basic issues be resolved before any reasonable solution can be reached. And for many crucial debated marijuana questions, this modest requirement cannot be met. In other words, before we raise the question of whether marijuana has a "desirable" or a "noxious" effect, we would first have to establish the fact of the desirability or the noxiousness to whom. We must concern ourselves with the differential *evaluations* of the same "objective" consequences. Many of the drug's effects—agreed upon by friend and foe alike—will be regarded as reprehensible by some individuals and desirable or neutral by others. Often anti-marijuana forces will argue against the use of the drug, employing reasons which its supporters will also employ— in *favor* of its use. In other words, we have here not a disagreement in what the effects are, but in whether they are a "good" or a "bad" thing. This is probably the most transparently ideological of all of the platforms of debate over marijuana. Three illustrations of this orbit of disputation should suffice.

With marijuana use more prevalent than today would come the billowing of a distinct esthetic. The state of marijuana intoxication seems to be associated with, and even to touch off, a unique and peculiar vision of the world. That the marijuana-induced vision is distinctive seems to be beyond dispute (Anonymous, in Goode, 1969; Adler, 1968; Ginsberg, 1966; Ludlow, 1965); that it is rewarding or fatuous is a matter for endless disputation. Inexplicably, the drug seems to engender a mental state which is coming into vogue in today's art forms. An extraordinarily high proportion of today's young and avant-garde artists—film-makers, poets, painters, musicians, novelists, photographers, mixed media specialists—use the drug and are influenced by the marijuana "high" (Anonymous, in Goode). Some of the results seem to be an increasing irrelevance of realism; the loss of interest in plot in films and novels; a glorification of the irrational and the seemingly nonsensical; an increased faith in the logic of the viscera, rather than in the intellect; a heightened sense for the absurd; an abandonment of traditional and "linear" reasoning sequences, and the substitution of "mosaic" and fragmentary lines of attack; *bursts* of insight rather than *chains* of thought; connectives relying on internal relevance, rather than a commonly understood and widely accepted succession of events and thoughts; love of the paradoxical, the perverse, the contradictory, the incongruous; an "implosive" inward thrust, rather than an "explosive" outward thrust; instantaneous totality rather than specialization; the dynamic rather than the static; the unique rather than the general and the universal.[3]

Those with conventional, traditional and "classic" tastes in art will view these results in a dim light. A recent anti-marijuana tract, for instance, comments on the highly unconventional and antitraditionalist novelist William Burroughs' approval of marijuana's influence on his creative powers: "The irony is that Burroughs meant his remark as an endorsement" (Bloomquist, 1968:189). The sociologist of knowledge seeks to understand and explain the bases from which man's intellectual efforts spring. He will notice the prominent place in this debate of the manner in which matters of taste, such as artistic esthetics, are intimately and inseparably bound with views of the empirical reality of the drug. He who is opposed to the use of marijuana, and who believes that it is (empirically) harmful, is very likely to dislike contemporary art forms, and vice versa. The two are not, of course, necessarily causally related, but rather emerge out of the same matrix.

Marijuana's reputed impact on sexual behavior is all to the good to some who are comfortable with an unconventional view of sex. To the sexually traditional, the fact that marijuana could disrupt man's (and woman's) traditional patterns of sexuality is an out-of-hand condemnation of the drug. While marijuana's opponents would label any imputed increase in sexual activity as a result of the drug [4] "promiscuity"[5] and would roundly condemn it, the drug's apostles would cheer society's resurgant interest in the organic, the earthy, the sensual.

The argument that marijuana is a "mind altering" drug has discrediting power to him who thinks of the everyday workings of the mind as "normal" and desirable. But to the explorer of unusual and exotic mental realms, its mind-altering functions are an argument in its favor. The ideologues of the psychedelic movement—and marijuana is considered by most commentators as the weakest of the psychedelic or "hallucinogenic" drugs—claim that every member of society is lied to, frustrated, cheated, duped and cajoled, and thus grows up totally deceived. Barnacles of attitudes, values, beliefs, layer themselves upon the mind, making it impossible to see things as they truly are. This ideology maintains that far from offering an "escape from reality," the psychedelic drugs thrust man more intensely *into* reality. By suspending society's illusions, the "voyager" is able to see reality "in the raw," with greater verisimilitude. Aldous Huxley (1963:34) exclaimed, under the influence of mescaline, "This is how one ought to see, how things really are."

The anti-psychedelic stance will, of course, deny the validity of this process. What is "real" is the world as the undrugged person perceives it. Any alteration of the "normal" state of consciousness is destructive and inherently distorting. Drug use, it is claimed, is "a way to shut out the real world or enter a world of unreality"; the psychedelic drug user attempts to "take a trip away from the real world and to a society of his own making." (AMA, 1968, 6:1, 4). But what is astonishing about the controversy is that both sides presume to know precisely what *reality* is. Whichever version we choose to guide our senses, we should not fail to notice the ideological character of the controversy. Both orientations are to a large degree arbitrary, conventional. Epistemological questions cannot be resolved by fiat or empirical test. Even the natural sciences rest on faith, an unprovable assumption that the senses convey valid information. Yet each side insists that it alone has a monopoly on knowing what is true and what false, what is real and what illusory. Both sides attempt to mask the capricious nature of their decision with an air of legitimacy and absolute validity. Taking a relativistic stance toward both perspectives, we are forced to regard both to be statements of political persuasion.

An essential component of dominant medical and psychological thinking about illicit drug use is that it is undesirable, that the user should be "treated" in such a manner that he discontinues use. The user is felt, rightly or wrongly, to threaten some of the more strongly held cultural values of American society:

> In my opinion, psychopharmacologic agents may be divided into two major categories depending on the manner in which they either help or hinder the individual in his adaptation to society.

Drugs may be used in one of two ways to help relieve . . . tensions:
by sufficiently diminishing emotional tension to permit the individual
to function or by allowing the individual to totally escape from reality. Sedatives, tranquilizers, and antidepressants . . . often permit
an individual to function more effectively. Psychedelic drugs . . .
allow the individual to escape from reality so that he need not function at all. The first group of drugs is often useful to society; the
second group would only destroy it (Kissin, 1967:2).

Given the basic premises on which statements such as these are based,
it is difficult to understand just what the notion of detachment and
objectivity toward drug use might mean.

Another locus of unresolvable controversy, where value and fact
interlock inseparably, is the question of a *hierarchy of values.* An
impartial stance is claimed by combatants in a multitude of pseudo-
scientific questions. Here, even the value issues may be resolved.
Everyone agrees that marijuana may precipitate psychotic episodes,
and that, further, psychotic episodes are a "bad thing." The issue then
becomes not, does it occur, or, is it good or bad, but: Do marijuana's
claimed dangers outweigh its possible benefits? Should we restrict
society's right to access to drugs so that we may minimize the potential harm to society? How does one set of values stack up against
another? One might, by donning a white coat, pretend to scientific
objectivity in answering this question, but it might be wise to remember that even the emperor didn't succeed in the ruse.

The Logistics of Empirical Support

A second powerful reason why strictly empirical arguments seem
to have exerted relatively little hold in the marijuana controversy,
aside from the.intricate intertwining of value and fact, seems to be a
basic panhuman psychic process which leads to the need for the confirmation of our strongly held biases; moreover, empirical reality, being
staggeringly complex, permits and even *demands* factual selection.
We characteristically seek support for our views: contrary opinions and
facts are generally avoided. This opens the way for the maintenance of
points of view which are contradicted by empirical evidence. And
there is invariably a variety of facts to choose from. It is a comparatively simple matter to find what one is looking for in any moderately
complex issue. Each individual facing an emotionally charged issue
selects the facts which agree with his own opinions, supermarket-like.
Individuals do not judge marijuana to be "harmful" or "beneficial" as
a result of objective evidence, rationally weighed and judiciously
considered. The process, rather, works in the opposite direction: the
drug is considered harmful—as a result of customs which articulate
or clash with the use and the effect of the drug, as a result of the
kinds of people who use it, and the nature of the "reading" process

society applies to these individuals, and as a result of campaigns conducted by "moral entrepreneurs" (Becker, 1963), as well as innumerable other processes—and *then* positive and negative traits are attributed to the drug. The explanation for perceiving the drug in a specific manner *follows* attitudes about it. A man is not opposed to the use or the legalization of marijuana *because* (he thinks) it "leads to" the use of more dangerous drugs, because it "causes" crime, because it "produces" insanity and brain damage, because it "makes" a person unsafe behind the wheel, because it "creates" an unwillingness to work. *He believes these things because he thinks the drug is evil.* The negative consequences of the use of marijuana *are superadded to support a basically value position.* But everyone, Pareto says, seeks to cloak his prejudices in the garb of reason, especially in an empirical age, so that evidence to support them is dragged in *post hoc* to provide rational and concrete proof.[6]

Conceptions of true and false are extravagantly refracted through social and cultural lenses to such an extent that the entire notion of empirical truth becomes irrelevant. "True" and "false" become, in fact, what dominant groups define as true and false; its very collectivity establishes legitimacy. A pro- or anti-marijuana stance reflects a basic underlying attitudinal syndrome, ideological in character, which is consonant with its drug component. Prior to being exposed to attitudes or "facts" about marijuana, the individual has come to accept or reject fundamental points of view which already lead him to apprehend the reality of marijuana in a definite manner. These ideological slants are not merely *correlates* of related and parallel attitudes. They are also *perceptual screens* through which a person views empirically grounded facts. In other words, marijuana provides an *occasion* for ideological expression.

Perceptions of the very empirical reality of the drug are largely determined by prior ideological considerations. Almost everyone facing the issue already has an answer concerning its various aspects, because of his attitudes about related and prior issues. He finds facts to suit his predilections—whether supportive or critical—and commandeers them to suit his biases. The essential meaning of the marijuana issue is the meaning which each individual brings to it. The marijuana "reality" going on before us is a vast turmoil of events which, like all realities, demands factual selection. Yet the selection of facts is never random. It is always systematic, it always obeys a specific logic. Any message can be *read into* the impact of the drug; anything you wish to see is there. We support our predilections by seeing in the drug only that which supports them. If the critic wants to see in the drug and its use violence, sadism, rape and murder, they are there, buried in the reality of marijuana.[7] If the drug supporter wishes to see peace and serenity, it is no difficult job to find them.

This is not to say, of course, that no research has ever been conducted which approaches scientific objectivity. (Scientific objectivity is, as we pointed out above, one form of bias, but since on most issues all participants in the dispute pay their respects to it, this axiom is apolitical in its import). It is to say, however, that not all participants in the marijuana controversy have been trained as scientists, nor do they reason as scientists. *Interpretations* of the marijuana studies are more important to us here than the studies' findings themselves. Out of a multitude of findings a diversity of mutually exclusive conclusions can be reached. The multitude of results from the many marijuana reports forms a sea of ambiguity into which nearly any message may be read. The researcher's findings do not announce themselves to the reader. Any opinion may be verified by the scientific literature on marijuana. Mayor La Guardia's Report (The Mayor's Committee on Marihuana, 1944) rivals the Bible in the diversity of the many conclusions which have been drawn from it.

Marijuana's proponents take heart in its conclusions (Rosevear, 1967:111–112), and nearly all of the report has been reprinted in a recent pro-marijuana anthology (Solomon, 1966). Yet anti-marijuana forces find in the study solid evidence for the damaging effects of the drug (Bloomquist, 1968:122–126; Brill, 1968:20–21; Louria, 1968:105). Our point, then, is that drawing conclusions from even the most careful and parsimonious scientific study is itself a highly *selective* process. The welter of findings are subject to a systematic sifting process. Often the researcher finds it necessary to disassociate himself from the conclusions which others have reached on his work. For instance, a sensationalistic popular article on LSD (Davidson, 1967) was denounced as a "distortion" and "an atrocity" by the very scientists whose research it cited. More attention ought to be paid, therefore, to the "reading" process of drawing conclusions from scientific work, rather than the findings themselves. In fact, specifically what is meant by the "the findings themselves" is unclear, since they can be made to say so many different and contradictory things.

Strategies of Discreditation

Naming has political implications. By devising a linguistic category with specific connotations, one is designing armaments for a battle; by having it accepted and used, one has scored a major victory. For instance, the term "psychedelic" has a clear pro-drug bias: it announces that the mind works best when under the influence of a drug of this type. (Moreover, one of the psychedelic drug proselytizers, in search of a term which would describe the impact of these drugs, rejected "psychedelic" as having negative overtones of psychosis.) Equally biased is the term "hallucinogen," since an hallucination is, in our civilization at least, unreal, illusory and therefore undesirable; the same holds for the term "psychotomimetic": capable of producing a madness-like state. The semantics and linguistics of the drug issue form an essential component of the ideological skirmishes[8] (Fort, 1967:87–88; Goode, 1969).

Drug "abuse" is such a linguistic device. It is often used by physicians and by the medically related. Encountering the use of the term, one has the impression that something quite measurable is being referred to, something very much like a disease, an undesirable condition which is in need of remedy. The term, thus, simultaneously serves two functions: (1) it claims clinical objectivity; (2) it discredits the action which it categorizes. In fact, no such objectivity obtains in the term, and its use is baldly political. Drug abuse is the use of a drug in a way that influentials with legitimacy disapprove of. Their objections are on moral, not medical, grounds, although their argument will be cast in medical language. The American Medical Association, for instance, defines the term: "drug abuse [is] taking drugs without professional advice or direction" (AMA, 1967:2). Nonmedical drug use is, in the medical view, *by definition* abuse. *Any* use *of any* drug outside a medical context, regardless of its consequences, is *always* undesirable, i.e., is by definition, abuse.

A linguistic category both crystalizes and influences responses to, and postures toward, a phenomenon. The term "abuse" illustrates this axiom. It announces that nonmedical drug-taking is undesirable, that the benefits which the drug-using subculture proclaims for drug use are outweighed by the hard rock of medical damage. Yet, since the weighing of values is a moral, not a medical process, we are full-face against an ideological resolution of the issue, yet one cast in a scientific and empirical exoskeleton. Further: *the linguistic category demands verification.* By labeling a phenomenon "abuse," one is willy-nilly under pressure to *prove* that the label is valid. The term so structures our perceptions of the phenomenon that it is possible to see only "abusive" aspects in drug use. Therefore, data must be collected to discredit the beneficial claims of drug use.

Another strategy of disconfirming the marijuanists' claims to legitimacy is the notion, closely interconnected with drug use as "abuse," of marijuana use as being the manifestation of medical *pathology.* This thrust bears two prongs: (1) the *etiology* of marijuana use as an expression of, or an "acting out" of, a personality disturbance (Ausubel, 1958:98–100, 102–103, 106; AMA, 1967:369–370; AMA, 1968b:2, Halleck, 1967:4–5);[9] (2) the effects of the drug as a precipitator of temporary but potent *psychotic episodes* (Farnsworth, 1967:434–435; Farnsworth and Weiss, 1968; Isbell et al., 1967; Keeler, 1967 and 1968; Ungerleider et al., 1968:355).[10] By assigning marijuana use to the twilight world of psychic pathology, its moral and willful character has been neutralized. The labeled behavior has been removed from the arena of free will; its compulsive character effectively denies that it can be a viable alternative, freely chosen.[11] An act reduced to both symptom and cause of pathology has had its claims to moral rectitude neutralized and discredited. As a manifestation of illness, it calls for "treatment," not serious debate. In a sense, then, physicians and psychiatrists have partially replaced policemen as preservers of the social order, since attempts at internal controls have replaced external sanctions. Both presume to know for the subject how he "ought" to act. Yet the new sanctions, based on an ideology which the deviant partially believes in—scientific treatment of a medical illness—becomes a new and more powerful form of authoritarianism.

Generally, some sort of explanation, particularly one involving compulsion and pathology, is called for wherever it is not rationally understandable to the observer—that is, it "doesn't make sense." An anomalous and bizarre form of behavior demands an explanation. We can understand repeated dosages of poetry because we all approve of poetry, so that no special examination is necessitated. It is only where the behavior violates our value biases that we feel it necessary to construct an interpretation. There is the built-in assumption that the individual *should* be able to do without recreational drugs, that their use is *unnecessary*, and a life without them is the *normal* state of affairs. Violation of our expectations requires an explanation. No explanation for *abstinence from* drugs is necessary, since our biases tell us that that is the way one "ought" to live.

Looking at all of the actions of which society disapproves—"deviant" behavior—we notice that they share fundamental similarities. However, these similarities inhere not so much in the acts themselves as in the way society responds to them. One of the more interesting responses is the tendency to impute psychological abnormality to their authors. The issue of whether such judgments are "correct" or not is less relevant to us as in the nexus between the kinds of acts which attract such judgments, and the nature of the society in which they are made. It is said that Freud once had a patient who believed that the center of the earth was filled with jam. Freud was not concerned with the truth or falsity of that statement, but with the *kind of man* who made it. Similarly, the sociologist of knowledge concerns himself with the kinds of explanations a society fabricates about behavior in its midst, and what those explanations reveal about that society. It should be regarded as extremely significant that deviant behavior seems to have attracted explanations which activate a principle of psychological abnormality. The sociologist legitimately raises the question as to what it is about American society which begets a personality abnormality explanation for marijuana smokers, as well as heroin addicts (Chein et al., 1964), homosexuals (Bieber, 1962; New York Academy of Medicine, 1964), unwed mothers (Young, 1945 and 1954), criminals (Abrahamsen, 1960), juvenile delinquents (Grossbard, 1962), prostitutes, as well as a host of other deviant groups and activities. The fact that each of these social categories—and the activities associated with them—are severely condemned by American society makes the nature of the process of constructing pathology interpretations of deviance at least as interesting as the etiology of the deviant behavior itself. In all of these cases, adopting a medical approach to the deviant and his behavior effectively neutralizes his moral legitimacy, as well as the viability of his behavior. In this sense, the constructors of such theories serve to mirror the basic values of American society.

Overview

It is the sociologist's job to discover and explicate patterns in social life. When one side of a protracted and apparently insoluble controversy activates arguments that involve such putatively repugnant components as: "socially irresponsible," "vagabond existence," "outlandish fashions," "long hair," "lack of cleanliness," and "disdain for conventional values" (Farnsworth, 1967), while the other side emphasizes factors which it deems beneficial, and which sound very different: "discovery," "optical and aural aesthetic perceptions," "self-awareness," "insight," and "minute engagement" (Ginsberg, 1966), we are ineluctably lead to the conclusion that the controversy is a matter of taste and style of life, that it revolves about basically unanswerable issues, and its adjudication will take place on the basis of power and legitimacy, and not on the basis of scientific truth. In fact, given the nature of the disputation, it is difficult to know exactly what is meant by scientific truth. The problem becomes one of gathering support for one or another bias, rather than the empirical testing of specific propositions, whatever that might entail.

The American Medical Association urges educational programs as an "effective deterrent" to marijuana use (AMA, 1968a:92). It is not, however, the sheer accumulation of information about marijuana which the AMA is referring to, since any marijuana user knows more than the average nonuser about the effects of the drug. What is being referred to is *attitudes toward* the drug, not factual information:

> . . . district officials are so fired up, they'd interrupt the routine of the whole district just to make sure our kids hear a good speaker or see a movie that will teach them the basic fact: *stay away from drugs.*
>
> In order to know exactly what it is that they should stay away from, students must know the *nature* of drugs . . . they're provided with basic facts. These facts aren't given "objectively"—they're slanted, so there's not the slightest doubt that students understand just how dangerous drugs can be.
>
> You can call it brainwashing if you want to. We don't care what you call it—as long as these youngsters get the point. (School Management, 1966b:103).[12]

Not only is the "meaning in the response," but both meaning and response are structured by power and legitimacy hierarchies. Society calls upon certain status occupants to verify what we wish to hear. These statuses are protective in nature, and are especially designated to respond to certain issues in a predetermined manner. Threats to society's security must be discredited. An elaborate charade is played out, debating points are scored—with no acknowledgment from the other side—and no one is converted. Inexorably, American society undergoes massive social change, and the surface froth of marijuana changes with it.

Summary

1. Civilizations differ in their rules for validating reality.
2. The particular manner in which a given culture chooses to view the material world is an arbitrary and conventional decision.
3. Yet this decision must be, and generally is, accorded a semi-sacred status.
4. Empirical and scientific rules and statuses have become basic arbiters of reality for the recent West.
5. Yet, different subcultures within the same society vary in their conceptions of what is real.
6. Yet these subcultures also vary significantly in their access to power and legitimacy.
7. He who is dominant in a given society attempts to enforce his version of reality on the rest of society, both in terms of legitimacy (i.e., moral hegemony), and in terms of making sure that others who disagree with him do not do anything which he disapproves of. He generally believes that he does this for the good of society, for the good of the individual whose behavior is restricted, because it is both moral and scientifically sound. In other words, society is not merely an agglomeration of different individuals and social groups, each neutral to one another, getting "equal time," but is made up of elements which are differentially able to enforce and impose their own unique version of reality on others.
8. Imposing a dominant mode of thinking about reality—as well as behavioral compliance in correspondence with that definition—involves questions of strategy.
9. Thus, the scientific status of one or another version of reality becomes a political and a tactical issue.
10. Yet the complexity of empirical phenomena, along with widespread unfamiliarity with scientific reasoning processes, and the degree of emotion engaged by the issue, combine to make a "genuine" scientific adjudication of the debate spurious and nonexistent.
11. Moreover, many of the issues surrounding the controversy are ideological, matters of taste, beyond the test of scientific instruments (*de gustibus non est disputandum*); they sum up styles of life, ways

of viewing the universe. They represent inviolable cultural perspectives, attitudinal gestalts, outlooks on the world, which shape the individual's behavior patterns, which represent taken-for-granted realities, irrefutable and unquestionable.

12. These basically nonrational beliefs shape perceptions of empirically testable assumptions. He who thinks of marijuana use as morally wrong is likely to exaggerate its criminogenic effects; he who thinks of it as beneficial will minimize its impact on crime.

13. It is not uncommon to assume that from the acceptance of a particular empirically relevant belief that he who has a belief which is in disagreement with my own is *wrong*, ignorant, and possibly stupid as well.

14. The line between what can and cannot be tested empirically is fuzzy, nonexistent and irrelevant to most people. Therefore, not only is he who disagrees with me on scientific matters wrong and ignorant, but he who disagrees with me on matters of taste and style of life is also wrong and ignorant.

15. Marijuana can be thought of as a kind of *symbol* for a complex of other positions, beliefs and activities which are correlated with and compatible with its use. In other words, those who disapprove of marijuana use often feel that he who smokes must, of necessity, also be a political radical, engage in "loose" (from his point of view) sexual practices, and have a somewhat dim view of patriotism. Marijuana use is seen (whether rightly or wrongly) to sum up innumerable facts about the individual, facts which can clearly place him along the conservative-liberal-radical dimension in a number of areas of social and political life.

16. In view of these and other intricacies, the debate over marijuana use is unlikely to be solved in the foreseeable future.

Notes

[1] A recent anthology (Goode, 1969) includes sections which assert and supposedly demonstrate wholly contradictory answers to these questions.

[2] The title of this section is taken from a book of the same name (Berger and Luckmann, 1966).

[3] The parallel between the mental processes associated with the marijuana "high" and the "tribal" mind typified by McLuhan (1964) is too close to escape mention.

[4] There is some question about marijuana's sexual impact. Although pharmacologists today generally feel that marijuana is either non-sexual or even anti-sexual (anaphrodisiac) in its effects in the strict physiological sense, marijuana users often feel that the drug acts as a pleasure-stimulator. In a study by the author still in progress at the time of this writing, of 200 marijuana users, 44 percent said that marijuana increased their sexual *desire*, and 68 percent said that it increased their sexual *enjoyment*.

[5] A recent court ruling by Joseph Tauro (1967), Chief Justice of the Superior Court of Massachusetts, held that "sexual promiscuity" was one of the undesirable consequences of marijuana use; Justice Tauro rejected the defendants'

appeal. Strangely, *Time* magazine claimed that Tauro's ruling would be judged fair by even the staunchest of marijuana supporters.

[6] Clearly, not many interested participants in a given controversy are aware of the rules of the scientific method. They may feel that they are empirically proving a point by submitting concrete evidence, yet the mode of reasoning merely confirms their ideological biases. "Proof" by enumeration exemplifies this principle. The criminogenic effect of marijuana is "demonstrated" by a listing of individuals who smoke marijuana who also, either under the influence or not, committed a crime. Munch (1966) and Anslinger and Tompkins (1953: 23–25) exemplify this line of reasoning.

[7] In its Field Manual, the Federal Bureau of Narcotics requests district supervisors to obtain from state and local officials "reports in all cases . . . wherein crimes were committed under the influence of marijuana." To illustrate the selective process involved in this request, imagine the impressive dossier which might result from a request that reports be conveyed on anyone *wearing a hat* while committing a crime; a case could thus be made on the criminogenic effects of hat-wearing.

[8] As an example of how naming influences one's posture toward a phenomenon, note that the Bureau of Narcotics and Dangerous Drugs has jurisdiction over "addicting" drugs, which supposedly includes marijuana, while the Food and Drug Administration preside over "habit-forming" drugs. Because of this jurisdictional division, the bureau is forced into the absurd position of having to claim that marijuana is an "addicting" drug, and to shore up this contention, it supplies drug classifications which follow jurisdictional lines (School Management, 1966a), as if they had some sort of correspondence in the real world.

[9] Most formulations, however, include the important qualification that the more the user smokes, the greater is the likelihood of a personality disturbance; the less he smokes—the "experimenter" and the "occasional," as opposed to the "regular," smoker—the greater is the likelihood that accidental, cultural, social, contextual, factors play a role.

[10] Likewise, as above, the greater the dosage, the greater is the chance for such episodes to occur; at lower dosages, it is less likely.

[11] A recent discussion (Stone and Farberman, 1969) argues that assigning the status of medical pathology is an effective device for neutralizing the legitimacy of a political opponent's ideology.

[12] The interview is with Dr. Sidney Birnbach, director of school health, physical education and safety in the Yonkers, New York, school system.

References

ABRAHAMSEN, DAVID. 1960. The Psychology of Crime. New York: Columbia University Press.

ADLER, RENATA. 1968. "The screen: Head, monkees movie for a turned-on audience." The New York Times (November 7).

AMERICAN MEDICAL ASSOCIATION. 1967. "Dependence on cannabis (marijuana)." Journal of the American Medical Association 201 (August 7):368–371. 1968a. "Marihuana and society." JAMA 204 (June 24:1181–1182. 1968b. "The Crutch That Cripples: Drug Dependence." (a pamphlet)

ANSLINGER, HARRY J. and W. G. TOMPKINS. 1953. The Traffic in Narcotics. New York: Funk and Wagnalls.

AUSUBEL, DAVID P. 1958. Drug Addiction. New York: Random House.

BECKER, HOWARD S. 1963. Outsiders. New York: Free Press.

BERGER, PETER L. 1967. The Sacred Canopy. Garden City, New York: Doubleday.

BERGER, PETER L. and THOMAS LUCKMANN. 1966. The Social Construction of Reality. Doubleday.

BIEBER, IRVING et al., 1962. Homosexuality. New York: Basic Books.

BLOOMQUIST, EDWARD R. 1968. Marijuana. Beverly Hills, California: Glencoe Press.

BRILL, HENRY. 1968. "Why not pot now? Some questions and answers about marijuana." Psychiatric Opinion 5, no. 5 (October):16–21.

CHEIN, ISIDORE et al., 1964. The Road to H. New York: Basic Books.

DAVIDSON, BILL. 1967. "The hidden evils of LSD." The Saturday Evening Post (August 12):19–23.

FARNSWORTH, DANA. 1967. "The drug problem among young people." West Virginia Medical Journal 63 (December):433–437.

FARNSWORTH, DANA and SCOTT T. WEISS. 1969. "Marijuana: the conditions and consequences of use and the treatment of users." in Rutgers Symposium on Drug Use. New Brunswick, New Jersey: The State University.

FINGL, EDWARD and DIXON WOODBURY. 1965. "General principles." in Louis S. Goodman and Alfred Gilman (eds.), The Phamarcological Basis of Therapeutics. New York: Macmillan.

FORT, JOEL. 1967. "The semantics and logic of the drug scene." in Charles Hollander (ed.), Background Papers on Student Drug Involvement. Washington: National Student Association.

GINSBERG, ALLEN. 1966. "The great marijuana hoax: manifesto to end the bringdown." Atlantic (November):106–112.

GOODE, ERICH (ed.). 1969. Marijuana. New York: Atherton Press.

GROSSBARD, HYMAN. 1962. "Ego deficiency in delinquents." Social Casework 43 (April):171–178.

HALLECK, SEYMOUR. 1967. "Psychiatric treatment of the alienated college student." Paper presented at the annual meeting of the American Psychiatric Association.

HUXLEY, ALDOUS. 1963. The Doors of Perception (bound with Heaven and Hell). New York: Harper Colophon.

ISBELL, HARRIS et al. 1967. "Effects of $(-)\Delta^9$ trans-tetrahydrocannabinol in man." Psychopharmacologia 11:184–188.

KEELER, MARTIN. 1967. "Adverse reactions to marihuana." American Journal of Psychiatry 128 (November):674–677. 1968. "Marihuana induced hallucinations." Diseases of the Nervous System 29 (May):314–315.

KENNEDY, ROBERT E. 1962. "The protestant ethic and the parsis." The American Journal of Sociology (July):11–20.

KISSIN, BENJAMIN. 1967. "On marihuana." Downstate Medical Center Reporter 2, no. 7 (April):2.

LOURIA, DONALD B. 1968. "The great marihuana debate." The Drug Scene. New York: McGraw-Hill.

LUDLOW, PETER. 1965. "In Defence of pot: confessions of a Canadian marijuana smoker." Saturday Night (October):28–32.

MAYOR LAGUARDIA'S COMMITTEE ON MARIHUANA. 1944. The Marihuana Problem in the City of New York. Lancaster, Pennsylvania: Jacques Cattell Press.

MCLUHAN, MARSHALL. 1964. Understanding Media: The Extensions of Man. New York: McGraw-Hill.

MERTON, ROBERT K. 1968. "Puritanism, pietism and science." in Social Theory and Social Structure, 3rd ed. New York: Free Press.

MUNCH, JAMES. 1966. "Marihuana and Crime." United Nations Bulletin on Narcotics 18 (April–June):15–22.

NEEDHAM, JOSEPH. 1956. "Buddhism and chinese science." Science and Civilization in China, Volume 2, Cambridge: Cambridge University Press.

NEW YORK ACADEMY OF MEDICINE. 1964. "Homosexuality." Bulletin of the New York Academy of Medicine 40 (July):576–580.

ROSEVEAR, JOHN. 1967. Pot: A Handbook of Marihuana. New Hyde Park, New York: University Books.

SCHOOL MANAGEMENT. 1966a. "A schoolman's guide to illicit drugs." School Management (June):100–101. 1966b. "How one district combats the drug problem." School Management (June):102–106.

STONE, GREGORY and HARVEY A. FARBERMAN (eds.). 1969. Social Psychology Through Symbolic Interaction. Waltham, Massachusetts: Blaisdell.

TAURO, G. JOSEPH. 1967. Commonwealth v. Joseph D. Leis and Ivan Weiss, Findings, Rulings and Order on Defendants' Motion to Dismiss. Boston: Superior Court of the Commonwealth of Massachusetts.

UNGERLEIDER, J. THOMAS et al. 1968. "A statistical survey of adverse reactions to LSD in Los Angeles county." The American Journal of Psychiatry 125 (September):352–357.

YOUNG, LEONTYNE R. 1945. "Personality patterns in unmarried mothers." The Family 26 (December):296–303. 1954. Out of Wedlock. New York: McGraw-Hill.

VIOLENCE, PROTEST, AND WAR
IN TELEVISION NEWS:
THE U.S. AND CANADA COMPARED

Benjamin D. Singer

An analysis of the manner in which a nation's major news media portray the nation's events may tell us a great deal about the actual distribution of events in that nation; it may be a reflection of the values of the audience toward news; or it may reflect the social system of the medium itself.

Until now, there has been a great deal of attention paid to the role of television drama in presumably stimulating violence, while the newscasts, with their huge, heterogeneous audiences, have escaped close attention. Television news may be a more sensitive barometer of the central values of a culture than printed media because television time is scarce—a national news show may have the time to carry perhaps twenty items compared with several hundred by its news counterpart, the daily newspaper.

While an analysis of the content of popular American newscasts would provide us with some notion as to the kind of reality being portrayed to audiences, it would be of even greater interest if American newscasts could be compared with those of another society which possessed similarities. We could thus begin to find out if American newscasts tend to favor the presentation of violent news.

Canada is probably the ideal comparison society, for, in addition to being largely English-language speaking and possessing a similar social structure, Canada is a client of American news services, directly receiving American stations and rebroadcasting a substantial amount of American television material, both entertainment and news.

The "National News," a Canadian Broadcasting Company program, is received in London, Ontario at 11 P.M. The CBC has a purchase arrangement with CBS-TV and NBC-TV which permits them to pick up and use any news stories carried by either network. The CBC program does carry a substantial number of American stories. During the test period April 20 to May 10, 1970, approximately 20 per cent of all items carried on the CBC National News were stories about the United States. London, the site of the present research, receives seven American television stations by cable and three Canadian stations, two by cable.

The objective of the present research was to compare a leading American television news program, "CBS Evening News," with its Canadian counterpart, "National News," on a daily basis. While it could be argued that a comparison between two noncommercial news programs or two commercial programs would be more appropriate, the CBC National is the only Canada-wide television news program that represents all areas, and there is no equivalent American noncommercial national news program.

The research focuses upon three major areas of concern which have been the subject of a substantial amount of comment because of their purported influence on viewers: the presentation of material dealing with violence, protest, and war. The research attempts to provide a breakdown of the amount of such "aggression items" presented on a typical national news program in the U.S. and by its Canadian counterpart. The working hypothesis to be explored is that American television presents a higher proportion of news items of an aggressive nature, even where the foreign station has full access to the same materials and is accustomed to utilizing a substantial amount of American materials.

If the hypothesis is supported, it may be an indication that U.S. culture has a larger number of such events which the media rather passively reflect; that the culture's value system is such that there is more interest by the population in such items; or that American news institutions, particularly television, choose to emphasize these aspects of social reality. It cannot, of course, point up which of the factors is most responsible—a project far beyond the ability of the present research.

METHOD

The research was conducted between April 20 and May 10, 1970, the time being fortuitously chosen as a result of the availability of graduate student assistance. Research workers monitored the programs with the aid of tape recorders; the materials were then transcribed, coded, and tabulated. A test of coder disagreement based on a sample of several days was computed. The range of disagreement reported was from 2 to 11 per cent, with the mean being 4.6 per cent. The coding scheme involved the news locale (Canadian, U.S., international) as well as its substantive concern (labor, war, space, business, politics or government, protest, violence, etc.). The coding was straightforward with the exception that protest includes events of the contemparary protest variety—such as civil rights, women's liberation, anti-Vietnam, student protest—and excludes such labor activities as strikes. Because of the treatment of the latter, findings on aggression items ought to be considered conservative. The amount of time occupied by each news item was also recorded.

RESULTS

The major finding is indeed striking. The American television news show exceeds the Canadian program in aggression items for every one of the 21 consecutive days monitored. CBS-TV has carried as much as 78 per cent aggression items (on April 30), compared to 38 per cent for CBC-TV. The smallest differential was on May 2, when CBS-TV carried 50 per cent compared to 46 per cent for the CBC, but most typically the differential was on the order of more than twice as much.

The grand total for the three weeks indicates CBC with 25.9 per cent and CBS with 49.5 per cent, a nearly two-to-one difference in favor of the American news shows.

Comparative data were available for some days on NBC-TV. During the period April 20-April 25 inclusive and April 30-May 1 (a total of eight days), CBS-TV exceeded the NBC-TV aggression item percentage five days, was exceeded by NBC-TV two days, and tied one day. The summary total was: CBS-TV 53.4 per cent and NBC-TV 40.9 per cent.

Since item counts may be disputed as a measure of emphasis, the proportion of time spent on such stories was calculated. The daily pattern was much the same as for item counts. Table 1 summarizes the findings on a weekly basis (the daily basis was similar).

Some may argue that the war in Southeast Asia is of such overwhelming concern, is such a part of the inherent event environment in North America, that its coverage is mandatory, thus removing choice on the part of audience and medium. If this is true, it would be most true for the U.S. Thus, inclusion of the war in Southeast Asia may explain why so many more aggression items are found on the American program. To answer this argument, the tables have been reconstructed in order to cancel out the effects of the Southeast Asian war in both cases. Weekly summations are shown in Tables 2 and 3.

As can be seen from these tables, when war items are removed, not only do "aggression items" continue to represent a substantial proportion of CBS items and time (36 per cent and 40 per cent, respectively), but on a comparative basis the American station continues to be significantly ahead on such items—the CBC figures are 17.7 per cent and 19 per cent respectively.

In societies where the media are not controlled and news presentations are free to vary, periodic monitoring of such media as television

TABLE 1

AGGRESSION TIME TOTALS AND PERCENTAGE OF TOTAL TIME ON CBC
AND CBS TELEVISION NEWS SHOWS

		CBC		CBS	
			Per Cent		Per Cent
		Time in	of Total	Time in	of Total
Date	Subject	Minutes	Time	Minutes	Time
April 20–	Violence	12.5	11.2%	10.0	6.3%
April 26	Protest	8.0	7.2	11.25	7.1
	War	10.75	9.6	46.25	29.3
	Aggression Totals	31.25	28.0%	67.50	42.7%
	Total Newscast Minutes	111.75		158.00	
April 27–	Violence	4.7	4.7%	15.75	8.7%
May 3	Protest	0.2	0.0	17.25	9.5
	War	23.4	23.5	53.00	29.4
	Aggression Totals	28.3	28.3%	86.00	47.6%
	Total Newscast Minutes	133.25		180.50	
May 4–	Violence	12.25	11.1%	19.25	12.2%
May 10	Protest	16.25	14.7	49.75	31.4
	War	7.00	6.3	31.75	20.1
	Aggression Totals	35.50	32.1%	100.75	63.7%
	Total Newscast Minutes	110.75		158.25	

in a comparative perspective is important, particularly where scarcity of time intensifies the selective process. One of the assumptions underlying traditional press freedoms is that, within limits, all news will be published. This is hardly the case with our dominant medium, television; in fact, the reverse is true: very little of the news is used. Hence, such a medium has enormous power to affect the perceived en-

TABLE 2

AGGRESSION ITEMS ON CBC AND CBS TELEVISION NEWS SHOWS,
FREQUENCY AND PERCENTAGE OF ITEMS
(ITEMS ON WAR IN SOUTHEAST ASIA REMOVED)

Date	Subject	CBC		CBS	
		No. of Items	Per cent	No. of Items	Per cent
April 20–April 26	Violence	8	7.0%	18	18.8%
	Protest	4	3.5	8	8.3
	War	4	3.5	4	4.2
	Aggression Totals	16	14.0%	30	31.3%
	Total Newscast Items	114		96	
April 27–May 3	Violence	8	9.4%	14	13.8%
	Protest	1	1.2	12	11.8
	War	4	4.7	10	10.0
	Aggression Totals	13	15.3%	36	35.6%
	Total Newscast Items	85		101	
May 4–May 10	Violence	10	11.1%	16	16.2%
	Protest	12	13.3	19	19.2
	War	0	0.0	5	5.1
	Aggression Totals	22	24.4%	40	40.4%
	Total Newscast Items	90		99	
April 20–May 10 (TOTAL)	Violence	26	9.0%	48	16.2%
	Protest	17	5.9	39	13.2
	War	8	2.8	19	6.4
	Aggression Totals	51	17.7%	106	35.8%
	Total Newscast Items	289		296	

vironment of viewers through repeated emphasis of certain categories
of events. This process, by distorting the social reality perceived by
individuals in a society, alters their standards of judgment and hence
frame of reference toward what is normal and expected in such a
society.

The present research raises questions that are not easily answered.
The questions are relevant to much of the controversy that has
raged with increased vigor since the advent of television. It is of course
possible that such newscasts reflect a true state of affairs, i.e., differential amounts of violence in each social system. Another possibility
involves both differential rates of known occurrences along with
variations in selection, i.e. a system with greater violence may still
overreport it on television when compared to a system experiencing
less violence. It is possible, in addition, that a system whose television
newscasts report a higher number of such items, is, nevertheless, underreporting in terms of the population of known events.

TABLE 3

AGGRESSION TIME TOTALS AND PERCENTAGE OF TOTAL
TIME ON CBC AND CBS TELEVISION NEWS SHOWS
(ITEMS ON WAR IN SOUTHEAST ASIA REMOVED)

		CBC		CBS	
Date	Subject	Time in Minutes	Per cent of Total Time	Time in Minutes	Per cent of Total Time
April 20–	Violence	12.5	11.8%	10.0	14.1%
April 26	Protest	8.0	7.5	11.25	15.9
	War	5.0	4.7	0.0	0.0
	Aggression Totals	25.5	24.0%	21.25	30.0%
	Total Newcast Minutes	106.0		70.7	
April 27–	Violence	6.25	6.1%	15.75	11.5%
May 3	Protest	0.25	0.3	17.25	12.6
	War	0.0	0.0	9.25	6.8
	Aggression Totals	6.50	6.4%	42.25	30.9%
	Total Newcast Minutes	102.0		136.75	
May 4–	Violence	12.25	11.8%	19.25	14.7%
May 10	Protest	16.25	15.7	49.75	38.1
	War	0.0	0.0	4.0	3.1
	Aggression Totals	28.5	27.5%	73.0	55.9
	Total Newcast Minutes	103.75		130.50	
April 20–	Violence	31.0	9.9%	45.0	13.3%
May 10	Protest	24.5	7.9	78.25	23.2
(TOTAL)	War	5.0	1.6	13.25	3.9
	Aggression Totals	60.5	19.4%	136.5	40.4%
	Total Newcast Minutes	311.75		338.0	

There is also the policy question of whether it necessarily follows that a high incidence of violence need be reported if it is believed that reportage—particularly television reportage—plays a crucial causal role in serial violence. Some would and have argued that reportage of such events, particularly the dramatized reportage so prevalent on television, is a determinant of such serial events as air hijacking, arson, bombings, mass murders, campus disturbances, and urban riots. The policy implications of this question are enormous and ultimately become matters of political philosophy.

Some methodological issues may be answered in the future by the development of new and imaginative research designs, particularly dealing with the problem of ascertaining the relationship of reportage, viewed as a sample selected from a population of events, to the population of events. One purpose of the present research has been to establish a base from which such questions may be explored in the future.

DIMENSIONS OF COMMUNITY
RESPONSE TO THE CRIME PROBLEM

John E. Conklin

In recent years criminology has moved from an exclusive emphasis on the genesis of criminal behavior to a concern with other factors involved in the crime problem. Some have stressed the role of authorities in attaching the label of criminal to certain individuals (Becker, 1963; Turk, 1969). Others have examined the role of the victim of a crime, including both the contribution of the victim to a crime (Von Hentig, 1948; Wolfgang, 1958:203-265) and the loss suffered by the victim of a criminal act (President's Commission on Law Enforcement and Administration of Justice, 1967:42-59).

The victim of a crime may be regarded as victimized in two analytically distinct ways. *Direct victimization* refers to the loss incurred by the victim in such "crimes *with* victims" as murder, rape, robbery, and burglary. In these crimes the victim is directly affected by the criminal behavior of the offender. Although such direct victimization may result from contributory behavior by the victim, such as his own negligence (e.g., leaving a window open for a potential burglar to enter) or his own involvement in the social dynamics that culminate in the crime (e.g., arguing and fighting with a person who has a record of violent crime), the victim nevertheless clearly incurs a loss from the criminal act.

The second form of victimization might be called *indirect victimization*. This suggests that an individual may suffer a loss from a crime in which he is not directly involved. During a time of widespread social concern with the crime problem, it is likely that a larger proportion of all crimes that occur will become known to the public than would be the case during a time of less concern. To the extent that crimes do become known to the public, attitudes and behavior of individuals not directly victimized may be altered. When these changes are regarded negatively by the individuals themselves, indirect victimization occurs. The National Crime Commission did a substantial amount of research on the problem of such changes in attitudes and behavior, finding that people who fear crime sometimes change their behavior patterns by staying home at night, taking taxicabs rather than walking, avoiding strangers, and securing their homes with locks and watchdogs (President's Commission on Law Enforcement and Administration of Justice, 1967:87-88).

Such changes in attitudes and behavior—referred to here as indirect victimization—may or may not reflect changes in the actual amount of direct victimization occurring in society. If direct victimization is increasing and if it becomes known to the public (as it probably will if concern with the crime problem is great), then the indirect victimization of the public will also increase. However, it is also possible that behavior and attitudes may change because of a *perceived* increase in crime rates, without that perception necessarily reflecting a real increase. The mass media, politicians, and law enforcement officials are all capable of presenting crime statistics in such a way as to convince large segments of the public that crime rates are rising. Although a number of social changes—such as changing age distribution, increased affluence, and urbanization—provide reasons to believe that there has been some actual increase in crime rates over time (Ohlin, 1968:

834-846), changes and fluctuations in reporting practices and in attention given to the problem of crime in the mass media suggest that public perceptions of crime can increase without any real increase occurring (see Davis, 1952:325-330).

Although direct victimization is probably in part responsible for the current alarm over the crime problem, the effects that perceptions of crime have on the lives of individuals through indirect victimization may be even more important. One survey in Baltimore found a negative relationship between crime in one's neighborhood and fear of crime, suggesting that the attitudes and behavior of citizens may be changed not only by direct threat of criminal victimization (Rosenthal, 1969:16-23). It is this relationship between perception of crime in one's community and one's attitudes and behavior which is of central concern in this paper.

Fear of crime in a community not only affects the mental well-being of residents of the area, but it may also lead to isolation of strangers and new residents from those who have lived in the community for longer periods of time. Feelings of not being safe in the area may lead to a deterioration of social solidarity in the community, for residents may stay indoors rather than walk on the streets and interact with neighbors. Perceptions of crime may also affect attitudes toward the neighborhood as a whole, including loyalty to the community, desire to move elsewhere, and satisfaction with the area as a place to raise children.

This paper investigates some of these relationships between perceptions of crime and individuals' attitudes and behavior in two communities in a metropolitan area in the eastern United States. Ideally, data would have been collected from a larger number of communities with different crime rates and different perceptions of crime by local residents. Study of such communities at a number of points in time would also have been desirable, for it would then have been possible to determine if changes in perceptions of crime over time were related to changes in attitudes and behavior. However, limitations of time and resources made it necessary to carry out the study by interviewing a sample of residents of only two communities at one point in time. For this reason, the conclusions of the study should be validated for other communities at different points in time.

THE SAMPLES

A sample of 200 names was chosen from each of two communities in an eastern metropolitan area, the names being selected from listings of all residents of each community who were over the age of 20. Such listings are published annually by every town and city in the state for the purpose of providing an up-to-date list of persons eligible for voting. Every nth name was chosen from each list, n being chosen in each community so as to draw a total sample of 200. If it can be assumed that no bias is introduced by the fact that the lists are arranged by precinct, street within precinct, street number within street, and name at each number, then the samples may be referred to as systematic samples proportional to the population of the precincts of each town.

After sending a letter to each subject to inform him or her of the general nature of the study, either the writer or his wife approached the subject at his or her door. If the subject was willing to be interviewed, a questionnaire was administered by the interviewer and then a Likert-item battery was filled out by the subject. The entire procedure took about 45 minutes, an amount of time which did not seem to unduly tax respondents. Interviews were completed in the period from May to September 1968, a time of political campaigning and conventions and a time during which "law and order" and "crime in the streets" were widely discussed topics. This atmosphere may have sensitized the subjects to the issue of crime.

Interviews with 138 residents of a suburb about six miles from the central city were completed. This community is comprised of residents who are predominantly from middle-class backgrounds, engaged in white-collar occupations, well-educated, prosperous, and from various ethnic backgrounds. One in ten of the original sample of 200 could not be located, since they had died or moved since the town listing had been compiled. Another one in six gave outright refusals to participate, a number being persons of high socioeconomic status who felt their time was too valuable to spend being interviewed. Such outright refusals may have led to a slight underrepresentation of residents of the highest socioeconomic status (e.g., doctors and lawyers) in the community, but they did not introduce any bias by age or sex. One in 20 of the original sample could not be interviewed because of infirmity due to age or because of serious illness. This produced a slight under-representation of the elderly, but no bias by sex.

One hundred twenty-eight residents of an urban community were interviewed. This town is comprised of residents who are predominantly working class in background, engaged in blue-collar occupations, less well-educated, less prosperous and of Italian ancestry. One out of nine refused to be interviewed, a common reason being a suspicion of surveys in general. Such outright refusals did not lead to any bias by age or sex. The elderly were slightly under-represented in the sample of completed interviews, since one in 20 of the subjects could not be interviewed because of infirmity or illness and one in 15 could not be interviewed because of lack of fluency in English. As in the suburban sample, about one in ten of the original sample could not be located because of moving or dying since the list of residents had been compiled.

CRIME IN THE TWO COMMUNITIES

Examination of Federal Bureau of Investigation statistics suggested that the two areas would have different crime rates, although such statistics suffer from recording and reporting problems (see Beattie, 1955:178-186; Biderman and Reiss, 1967:1-15). However, it was felt that a high probability did exist that the two areas would in fact have different amounts of crime, even though official statistics imperfectly measured the actual amounts. One of the reasons for selection of the two communities was that from official data they appeared to have dissimilar crime problems.

Table 1 presents rates of F.B.I. Crime Index offenses per 100,000 of population averaged over the three year period prior to the study for each community, for the Standard Metropolitan Statistical Area (abbreviated SMSA) in which they are located, and for the nation as a whole. It can be seen from this table that the rate of property offenses is about three times as high in the urban area as in the suburb, while the rate for offenses against the person is about nine times as high in the urban community. This difference in ratios for the two categories of offenses is consistent with the finding of the Kerner Commission that rates of crimes against the person vary more from community to community than do rates of property offenses (National Advisory Commission on Civil Disorders, 1968:267). This may be because interpersonal relations vary more in their quality from community to community than do opportunities for property crimes. It may also be that in areas with lower amounts of actual property crimes (e.g., the suburbs), a higher proportion of such cases are reported, recorded and prosecuted because of a greater concern on the part of residents of such areas with the security of their property. However, explanations of differences in crime rates between communities are of less interest here than the examination of attitudes and behavior which are related to perceptions of crime in the community.

To test perceptions of crime among residents of the two communities, three questions about the relative size of local crime rates were asked. When asked to compare local rates with rates for the metropolitan area as a whole (see Table 1 for comparison of official statistics), 83.2 percent of the suburban sample but only 39.1 percent of

TABLE 1
AVERAGE CRIME RATES PER 100,000 FOR 1965-1967

Crime	United States	SMSA	Suburb	Urban area
Murder	5.6	2.9	0.0	2.5
Rape	12.8	6.5	1.2	5.9
Robbery	83.3	59.1	2.3	44.4
Aggravated assault	118.6	61.7	11.6	78.7
Burglary	718.1	609.7	439.9	686.9
Larceny over $50	464.9	369.2	280.2	207.7
Auto theft	289.9	724.6	97.2	1424.1
Crimes against persons	220.3	130.2	15.1	131.5
Crimes against property	1472.9	1703.5	817.3	2318.7
Total crime rate	1693.2	1833.7	832.4	2450.2

the urban sample stated that rates in their community were lower. More than nine out of ten (90.7 percent) of the suburban sample felt that their community had rates lower than those of the nation, but only 56.6 percent of the urban sample felt that way. Although 87.4 percent of the suburban sample described local rates as low, only 53.3 percent of the urban sample described rates in their community in that fashion. All three of these differences between samples are significant beyond the .001 level, with the suburban sample in all cases perceiving lower local crime rates than the urban sample. It will be assumed in this paper that these perceptions are perceptions of the crime problem in the community, rather than of what official statistics say the local crime problem is. While there is little direct exposure to official data among the general public, the media often allude to such data in pointing out the increasing crime problem. However, correlations in this study showed that the relationships between each of two measures of exposure to media news (one for television and radio news, the other for newspaper news) and a scale measuring perception of local crime rates

were not statistically significant in either sample.

A perception of crime scale was formed by summing the three items discussed above. They were summed because of the large and consistent differences between samples and because the correlations between pairs of the items were moderate (between .34 and .49) and significant at the .01 level. The difference between sample means on the scale was significant beyond the .001 level, with the urban residents seeing more crime in their community than the suburban residents. This large cross-sample difference held up when comparisons were made for various levels of the following control variables: age, sex, social background, income, education, occupational prestige, self-designated class, religion, and ethnicity. The difference between samples also obtained when a scale measuring general alienation was used as a control.[1] Although substantial differences existed between samples in terms of demographic composition and extent of alienation, such differences do not account for the great dissimilarity in perceptions of local crime rates; for the cross-sample differences on the perception of crime scale remained when such variables were used as controls.

A number of other differences exist between samples with respect to perception of the crime problem. Residents of the urban area are significantly more likely to say that most persons who commit crime in their community live in that community, are more apt to mention crime as either the first or second most important social problem to them, and are somewhat more likely to state that the crime problem in general has become greater in the past twenty years. A number of other indicators of dissimilar perceptions of crime in the two samples could be cited; but for the purposes of this paper, the perception of crime scale will be used as a measure of the crime problem to which individuals are responding.

PERCEIVED SAFETY IN THE COMMUNITY

Research by the National Crime Commission has documented widespread fear for personal safety among residents of American cities (President's Commission on Law Enforcement and Administration of Justice, 1967:87-88). The way in which such fear is related to perception of local crime rates will be examined.

A number of items were asked of subjects concerning their feelings of safety in their neighborhood. Three of these items were selected for analysis because they seemed to have face validity as measures of a sense of personal security in the community. The moderate (between .33 and .50) but significant correlations between pairs of the items also gave support to the impression that they were tapping the same underlying dimension. Table 2

shows the response of each sample to the three safety items.

For all three items the residents of the suburb expressed less fear for personal safety than did residents of the urban area; and in all three cases, responses by a national sample to the same questions fell between the responses of the two samples in this study. For all three items a t-test for differences between sample means showed the cross-sample difference to be significant at the .01 level. These differences remained large and in the same direction when the social background variables discussed above were used as controls, although in some cases the differences failed to reach the .05 level of significance.

The findings for the two samples on the safety items and on the perception of crime scale suggest that there is an inverse relationship between feelings of personal safety and perception of local crime rates: the more crime perceived by residents of a community, the less those residents will feel personally safe. It is necessary to test whether this relationship also obtains for subjects *within* each sample.

A regression analysis was performed for each of the three measures of personal safety on the perception of crime scale. Table 3 shows the regression coefficients (standardized)[2] and their levels of significance (p) for each of the three safety items regressed on the perception of crime scale for each sample. Each of the three coefficients in the urban sample is highly significant, and each of the three in the suburban sample is near zero and non-significant. This finding suggests a *threshold effect*, such that the *relationship* between perception of crime

TABLE 2
RESPONSES TO THREE SAFETY ITEMS

Question	Suburb	Urban area	National*
1. Some people worry a great deal about having their house broken into, and other people are not as concerned. Are you very concerned, somewhat concerned, or not at all concerned about this? (Percent not at all concerned)	51.1%	35.7%	50%
2. How safe do you feel walking alone in your neighborhood when it's dark? (Percent very safe and somewhat safe)	85.6%	63.1%	70%
3. How likely is it that a person walking around here at night will be held up or attacked? (Percent very unlikely and somewhat unlikely)	84.9%	65.8%	79%

* Ennis, (1967:73-75). Data in this column are only for white respondents, since the two samples in this study were almost all white.

TABLE 3
STANDARDIZED REGRESSION COEFFICIENTS FOR SAFETY ITEMS ON PERCEPTION OF CRIME SCALE

Safety item number	Suburb Coefficient	p	Urban area Coefficient	p
1	.07	NS	−.29	.001
2	−.08	NS	−.28	.002
3	−.06	NS	−.46	.001

and feelings of personal safety is *stronger* in the urban community than in the suburban community. In other words, residents of a community with a high crime rate, which is perceived to be high by those residents, will have their feelings of personal safety affected more by the amount of crime they perceive than will residents of a low crime rate area. This says more than that people in a high crime rate area are more afraid for their personal safety: it says that in such an area variation in feelings of safety will be tied to variation in perception of local crime rates, while such a relationship will not exist to as great a degree in a low crime rate area.

The relationship between feelings of personal safety and perception of local crime rates may be summarized as follows: more residents of the urban area than of the suburb *perceive high rates* in their community, and more residents of the high crime rate area *feel unsafe* in their community. *Within* the low crime rate area there is no significant relationship between three measures of personal safety and a perception of crime scale; but *within* the high crime rate area, all three relationships are statistically significant. One qualification must be added. Relationships between the three safety items and the perception of crime scale are probably attenuated because of the homogeneity of residents of each community. This problem is more acute in the suburb, where there is restricted variance on the perception of crime scale and on two of the three safety items. It is possible that with a wider range of responses to these items a stronger relationship between perception of crime and feelings of safety would have emerged in the suburb, diminishing the importance of the threshold effect interpretation of the difference in strength of relationships in the two samples.

INTERPERSONAL TRUST

A second dimension of response to local crime problems is an alteration of feelings of interpersonal trust among residents of a community. Perception of high crime rates may not only lead to feelings of insecurity and thus damage the mental state of well-being of residents of the area; but it may also produce a feeling that no one can be trusted. To the extent that individuals do not trust others, the social fabric of community life may be destroyed. Lack of trust can lead to reduced social interaction among residents of the area, particularly new residents and visitors to the area. Such attenuated social bonds may be related to a subsequent rise in crime rates, for social control may be diminished in effectiveness if social solidarity of residents is weakened.

To measure degree of interpersonal trust among residents of the two communities, four questions were asked. Table 4 shows responses of subjects in each sample to the four items. Correlations between pairs of items suggest that the four items may well form two dimensions of trust, the first two items measuring trust of others in the immediate neighborhood and the last two items measuring a more general type of trust. Each of the four items will be dealt with separately.

Subjects responded to each item by agreeing or disagreeing with it on a five-point scale ranging from strongly agree to strongly disagree. A mean value was calculated for each item for each sample, and a t-test for differences between sample means was used to test the significance of cross-sample differences. The difference between means on the second item was significant at the .05 level, but for the other three items the differences were significant beyond the .001 level. In all four cases the suburban sample expressed considerably more interpersonal trust—both of the specific and general varieties—than did the urban sample. Thus the community in which perception of crime rates is lower is the one in which there is more interpersonal trust. This difference cannot be attributed to differences between samples in social background characteristics, for the difference between sample means on each item remains strong and in the expected direction when the control variables mentioned above are employed; although in a few cases, the difference between means fails to reach the .05 level of significance. The cross-sample difference thus cannot be explained on the basis of different demographic compositions of the two samples.

Treating the perception of crime scale as an independent variable and calculating the standardized regression coefficients for each of the four dependent variables (the trust items) on the independent variable, the analysis again suggests a threshold effect, subject, of course, to the qualification noted previously about attenuation due to restricted variance. Table 5 shows that for the two trust items dealing with one's immediate neighbors (items 1 and 2), the regression coefficients for the urban sample are moderate in size but significant beyond the .001 level, while the coefficients for the suburban sample are near zero. In neither sample were the coefficients for the two global trust items (items 3 and 4) significant,

TABLE 4
RESPONSES TO FOUR TRUST ITEMS

Question	Suburb	Urban area
1. Most people in this neighborhood can be trusted. (Percent agree and strongly agree)	88.3%	67.2%
2. Most people in this neighborhood are truthful and dependable. (Percent agree and strongly agree)	83.9%	65.4%
3. Nice as it may be to have faith in your fellowman, it seldom pays off. (Percent disagree and strongly disagree)	70.8%	46.9%
4. The world is full of people who will take advantage of you if you give them the slightest opportunity. (Percent disagree and strongly disagree)	37.5%	15.6%

indicating that while trust of one's neighbors could be predicted to some extent from perception of crime in a high crime rate area, *general* trust of others could not be predicted from perception of crime in either the high rate area or the low rate area.

Again the relationship between perception of crime and a possible dimension of social response to such a perception, in this case interpersonal trust,

TABLE 5
STANDARDIZED REGRESSION COEFFICIENTS FOR TRUST ITEMS ON PERCEPTION OF CRIME SCALE

Trust item number	Suburb		Urban area	
	Coefficient	p	Coefficient	p
1	−.07	NS	−.35	.001
2	.01	NS	−.31	.001
3	−.10	NS	−.01	NS
4	−.05	NS	−.07	NS

of one's neighbors, is stronger in the community with a higher crime rate and a higher level of perceived crime. Within the high crime rate area, those who perceive more crime are more apt to be distrustful of their neighbors than are those who perceive less crime. Such a relationship does not emerge in the suburban sample, in which no

linear relationship exists between trust of neighbors and perception of local crime rates. In part, the lack of such a relationship may be a result of restricted variance on the two trust items and the perception of crime scale.

AFFECT FOR THE COMMUNITY

Perception of crime in the local community may produce another type of response in residents of the area—a diminished positive feeling for the community itself. This dimension will be called affect for the community, meaning the feeling of a resident of a community about how satisfactory a place to live in is his present place of residence. Not only may social bonds among residents of a community be reduced by diminished affect for the community, but lack of positive feeling for a community may also be related to the absence of certain types of social activity that are instrumental in maintaining the quality of life in the area, such as interest in local schools and support for higher taxes to improve the community.

Four items were used to tap this dimension of affect for the community. The four items, the responses to which are shown in Table 6, ask subjects if they would like to move someday, if

TABLE 6
RESPONSES TO FOUR AFFECT ITEMS

Question	Suburb	Urban area
1. Do you think that this community is a good place to bring up children? (Percent yes)	94.9%	47.7%
2. Would you someday like to move to another neighborhood? (Percent no)	55.1%	37.5%
3. On the whole, do you like living in this community or not? (Percent yes)	95.6%	61.7%
4. How would you describe the attitudes of your neighbors toward strangers from outside the neighborhood? (Percent very friendly or somewhat friendly)	51.6%	52.4%

they feel the area is suitable for raising children, if they think their neighbors are friendly to outsiders, and if they generally like their community. On the first three items in the table, the cross-sample differences in means were significant beyond the .001 level, with the suburban sample expressing more positive affect for their community than the urban sample. On the fourth item, that which measured perceived friendliness of neighbors toward outsiders, there was no difference between samples. The differences between sample means remained consistent in direction and in most cases significant beyond the .05 level when the various levels of the social background control variables were compared for each sample.

Table 7 shows the standardized regression coefficients for each of the four affect items regressed separately on the independent variable of the perception of crime scale. On the first item, suitability of the community for raising children, the coefficients for each sample are similar in magnitude and significance. Even with restricted variance on both this item and the perception of crime scale in the suburban sample, a moderate coefficient does emerge. However, before concluding that one can predict this particular aspect of affect for the community from perception of local crime rates, it would be necessary to have a low crime rate area in which there was more variance on both the independent and the dependent variables.

In neither sample is the desire to move someday predictable to a significant degree from perception of crime in the community. The reason for this may be that a number of factors other than perception of local crime rates influence one's wish to move—factors of social as well as physical mobility, desire to have one's children in a more adequate school system, and hope of having more spacious and pleasant living quarters.

General affect for the community (item 3) is more strongly related to perception of crime in the high rate area than in the low rate area. Not only is there a lower level of positive affect for the community in the urban sample than in the suburban sample, but the *relationship* between general affect and perception of crime is stronger in the high crime rate urban area than in the low crime rate suburb. This again suggests that a threshold effect may be operating, although the possibility of attenuation due to restricted variance is again present.

The difference between sample regression coefficients on item 4, which

TABLE 7
STANDARDIZED REGRESSION COEFFI-
CIENTS FOR AFFECT ITEMS ON
PERCEPTION OF CRIME SCALE

Affect item number	Suburb		Urban area	
	Coefficient	p	Coefficient	p
1	−.34	.001	−.33	.001
2	−.09	NS	−.13	NS
3	−.01	NS	−.28	.001
4	−.05	NS	−.17	.06

measures perception of neighbors' friendliness, is also consistent with the threshold effect, although the coefficient is significant only at the .06 level in the urban sample. Though the restricted variance problem again arises for the independent variable in the suburban sample, the problem in this case does not arise for the dependent variable (item 4). Both samples responded to this item in similar fashion, but the regression coefficient is still somewhat larger in the urban sample than in the suburban sample, suggesting a threshold effect.

For two of the affect items (items 3 and 4), there is, then, support for the idea of a threshold effect, subject to the qualification discussed above. For these two items, stronger relationships do exist between affect for the community and perception of local crime rates in the urban sample than in the suburban sample.

CONCLUSIONS

Two communities located in the metropolitan area of a large eastern city were selected for study on the basis of their contrasting official crime rates. Interviews with samples from each community showed a substantial difference between residents of the two areas in their perception of local crime

rates. This difference was not due to cross-sample differences in social background characteristics, although the two samples differed on such characteristics; for the difference in perception of crime between the urban sample and the suburban sample still held when such variables were controlled.

A number of dimensions of social response to the crime problem were explored, in particular, feelings of personal safety, degree of interpersonal trust, and extent of positive affect for the community. Residents of the high crime rate area, who perceived higher local rates than residents of the low crime rate area, felt less safe, were less trusting of others, and expressed less positive feeling for their community than did suburban residents.

The items measuring these three dimensions of social response to the crime problem were used as dependent variables and standardized regression coefficients were calculated, using a perception of crime scale as the independent variable. Although a problem of restricted variance on both the perception of crime scale and on a number of dependent variables arose in the suburban sample and thus limited the assurance with which conclusions might be drawn, the difference between samples in the magnitude of regression coefficients for a number of the dependent variables suggested that a threshold effect might be operating.

The threshold effect points to the magnitude of relationships between perception of crime and measures of social response and suggests that social response will be greater in certain social contexts than in others. The aspect of social context which was examined was the amount and perception of crime in the community. The evidence suggested that stronger relationships exist in the community characterized by a higher crime rate and a perception of a higher crime rate than in a low crime rate area with a perception of a larger number and more varied assortment of communities would permit a more conclusive test of the inferred threshold effect.

NOTES

[1] The eight Likert-items summed in the general alienation scale are:

1. Many times I feel that I have little influence over the things that happen to me.
2. Most people in our society are lonely and unrelated to their fellow human beings.
3. This country is run by politicians who do what they want, not what the people want.
4. I have very little in common with most people I meet.
5. There is nothing I can do to make anything better or worse in this country.
6. The average citizen in this country can't have much effect on politics.
7. I often feel lonely.
8. I think that life, as most men live it, is meaningless.

[2] Although the standardized regression coefficient for a dependent variable on one independent variable is the same as the correlation between the two variables, the asymmetry of the relationships under discussion here makes use of regression analysis proper.

REFERENCES

Beattie, Ronald H.
1955 "Problems of criminal statistics in the United States." Journal of Criminal Law, Criminology and Police Science 46(July-August): 178-186.

Becker, Howard S.
1963 Outsiders: Studies in the Sociology of Deviance. New York: The Free Press.

Biderman, Albert B. and Albert J. Reiss, Jr.
1967 "On exploring the 'dark figure' of crime." The Annals of the American Academy of Political and Social Science 374(November): 1-15.

Davis, F. James
1952 "Crime news in Colorado newspapers." American Journal of Sociology 57(January): 325-330.

Ennis, Philip H.
1967 Criminal Victimization in the United States: A Report of a National Survey. Field Surveys II of The President's Commission on Law Enforcement and Administration of Justice. Washington, D.C.: U.S. Government Printing Office.

National Advisory Commission on Civil Disorders
1968 Report of the National Advisory Commission on Civil Disorders. New York: Bantam Books, Inc.

Ohlin, Lloyd E.
1968 "The effect of social change on crime and law enforcement." Notre Dame Lawyer 43(1968): 834-846.

President's Commission on Law Enforcement and Administration of Justice
1967 Task Force Report: Crime and Its Impact—An Assessment. Washington, D.C.: U.S. Government Printing Office.

Rosenthal, Jack
1969 "The cage of fear in cities beset by crime." Life Magazine 67(July 11):16-23.

Turk, Austin T.
1969 Criminality and Legal Order. Chicago: Rand McNally & Company.

Von Hentig, Hans
1948 The Criminal and His Victim. New Haven: Yale University Press.

Wolfgang, Marvin E.
1958 Patterns in Criminal Homicide. Philadelphia: University of Pennsylvania Press.

II.

THE CRIMINAL NATURE
OF SOCIAL BEHAVIOR

VIOLENT CRIME IN
A BIRTH COHORT

Marvin E. Wolfgang

New kinds of evidence about juvenile crime are being analyzed by the Center for Studies in Criminology and Criminal Law at the University of Pennsylvania.[38] The data constitute a unique collection of information in the United States about a birth cohort of boys born in 1945. Approximately 10,000 males born in that year and who resided in Philadelphia at least from ages 10 to 18, have been analyzed in a variety of ways. Using school records, offense reports from the police, and some Selective Service information, the Center has, among other things, followed the delinquency careers of those boys in the cohort who *ever* had any contact with the police. Comparisons have been made between delinquents and nondelinquents on a wide variety of variables, thus yielding findings that are not tied to a single calendar year. The entire universe of cases is under review, not merely a group that happened to be processed at a given time by a juvenile court or some other agency. Computing a birth-cohort rate of delinquency as well as providing analyses of the dynamic flow of boys through their juvenile court years has been possible. The time analysis uses a stochastic model for tracing delinquency of the cohort and includes such factors as time intervals between offenses, offense type, race, social class, degree of seriousness of the offenses.

Some of the findings from this Philadelphia study are particularly pertinent for more understanding about youth and crimes of violence. Of the total birth cohort of 9,946 boys born in 1945, about 85 percent were born in Philadelphia and about 95 percent went through the Philadelphia school system from first grade. From the entire cohort, 3,475, or 35 percent, were delinquent, meaning that they had at least one contact with the police. Of the 7,043 white subjects, 2,017, or 28.64 percent were delinquent. Of the 2,902 nonwhites, 1,458, or 50.24 percent were delinquent. It is a dramatic and disturbing fact that just slightly more than half of all Negro boys born in the same year were delinquent, more than were nondelinquent. This higher proportion of nonwhite delinquents constitutes one of the major statistical dichotomies running throughout the analysis of the cohort, and particularly of the delinquent subset.

Some of the major variables examined in a detailed comparison of delinquents and nondelinquents—residential and school moves, highest grade completed, I.Q. and achievement level, all by delinquency status, race, and socio-economic status—indicate that values for each of these variables are most variant by race, are next most diverse by socio-economic status(SES), and finally by delinquency status. In eight-cell analyses of whites and nonwhites, delinquents and nondelinquents, lower and upper socio-economic status, the white upper SES nondelinquent, as might be expected, contrasts most with the nonwhite lower SES delinquent. The latter has the lowest I.Q., the lowest achievement level, makes the most residential and school moves, and least frequently completes the 12th grade.

The rate of delinquency of the birth cohort is 349.4 per thousand subjects. Slightly more than half of the 3,475 offenders—1,862 or 55 percent—were recidivists, while the remaining 1,613 were single, or one-time offenders. This distinction between one-time offenders and recidivists provided another major basis for splitting the delinquent cohort. Altogether, the boys who were delinquent committed 10,214 delinquent acts from age seven through 17. The offense rate (i.e., acts/cohort × 1000) was 1,027; nonwhites had a rate (1,983.5) three times higher than whites (633.0). The 1,862 recidivists were responsible for 8,601 of all offenses committed by the cohort. Nearly three-fourths of the offenses committed by one-time offenders were petty, including "juvenile status" offenses such as running away from home, being truant from school, or being listed as incorrigible. In general, only about 30 percent of the cohort's offenses were index crimes, defined in terms of the UCR system, or in terms of all acts of injury, theft, and damage.

Of special significance is the fact that only 627 boys were classified as chronic offenders, or heavy repeaters, meaning that they committed five or more offenses during their juvenile court ages. These chronic offenders represent only 6.3 percent of the entire birth cohort and 18 percent of the delinquent cohort. Yet, these 627 boys were responsible for 5,305 delinquencies, which is 52 percent of all the delinquencies committed by the entire birth cohort.

Chronic offenders are heavily represented among those who commit violent offenses. Of the 815 personal attacks (homicide, rape, aggravated and simple assaults), 450, or 53 percent were committed by chronic offenders; of the 2,257 property offenses, 1,397, or 62 percent were from chronic offenders; and of 193 robberies, 135, or 71 percent were from chronic offenders. Of all violent offenses committed by nonwhites, 70 percent were committed by chronic boys; of all violent acts committed by whites, 45 percent were performed by chronic boys. Clearly, these chronic offenders represent what is often referred to as the "hard core" delinquents. That such a high proportion of offenses—particularly serious acts of violence—are funnelled through a relatively small number of offenders, is a fact that loudly claims attention for a social action policy of intervention.

In order to determine the relationships between race, socio-economic status, and delinquency status (one-time v. recidivists) among offense types, we may concentrate on offenses involving assaults on the person, on property offenses, and robbery. The assault category collapses the sub-categories of homicide, rape, aggravated and simple assault and battery. Property offenses include burglary, larceny, and auto theft. We have retained robbery as a separate category.

Nonwhites (742.2) have higher rates than whites (157.7) for all three categories combined. Nonwhites (206.1) commit assault offenses six times the rate of whites (30.8) and are four times greater in property offenses (476.6 to 124.1). But clearly the highest difference is in robbery, for which nonwhites have a rate 20 times higher than whites (59.6 to 2.8). The SES levels, without regard to race, show similar but generally less pronounced differences. For example, the lower SES rate for robbery (35.3) is only about six times greater than the higher SES rate (5.8).

One-time delinquents commit relatively few index offenses compared to recidivists. In fact, recidivists committed over twice as many assaults alone (N = 726) as the total number of assaults, property offenses and robberies committed by single offenders (N = 330). One-time offenders were responsible for only ten robberies compared to recidivists who committed 183. All told there were nearly twice as many index offenses committed by recidivists as by one-time delinquents, but nearly ten times as many property offenses. The assault-property-robbery rate of offenses for one-time offenders was 204.5, and for recidivists was 1,039.

Table 7 shows race-SES-delinquency status-specified rates for each of the three offense types. It is clear from the rates shown that regardless of race or SES, juveniles who do not continue past their single offense have rarely committed the disturbing index offenses. Even usually poor positioned nonwhites in the lower SES, when they are one-time delinquents, have a rate (49.9) for these offenses that is only about half the rate for higher SES white recidivists (92.4). The nonwhite and white single offenders have rates not far apart when the boys are all from the lower SES.

This comparison of whites and nonwhites—when one-time offenders are also compared to recidivists—is considered a finding of social significance. It was the first point in the analysis of the cohort in which the variable of race yielded its position of statistical prominence. Socio-economic status also retreats as a major distinctive variable. It is still the case that race and SES show considerable differences among recidivists. But the greatest reduction in race and SES disparity occurs among one-time index offenders.

Under the generally accepted assumption that these index offenses are the most serious and the ones to reduce in any deterrence or prevention program, and that most of the other forms of delinquency are relatively trivial, the *pivotal point of social cost reduction* appears to be when juveniles have committed their *first* offense. To produce delinquency desisting at this stage in the biography of the child might thus be considered the most efficient procedure. More nonwhites go on after the first offense, and perhaps the major concern should be with this racial group. Of the 2,017 white delinquents, 55 percent were one-time offenders and desisted thereafter; whereas, of the 1,458 nonwhite delinquents only 35 percent were one-time offenders. At the other extreme, nearly 30 percent of the nonwhite boys, compared to only 10 percent of the white boys, fall into the chronic offender category of having committed five or more offenses.

By using the judgmental scale of seriousness described in the *Measurement of Delinquency,* a quantitative measure of the amount of social harm inflicted on the community by the birth cohort can be obtained. Assigning seriousness scores to each delinquent for each act committed during the age-span of exposure to potential delinquency provides the basis for the following discussion of the gravity of delinquency registered by the cohort.

TABLE 7. ASSAULT, PROPERTY AND ROBBERY OFFENSES BY DELINQUENCY STATUS, RACE, AND SOCIO-ECONOMIC STATUS:—NUMBER, PER CENT AND RATE PER 1,000 COHORT SUBJECTS

	Assaults			Property			Robbery			Total		
	N	%	R	N	%	R	N	%	R	N	%	R
One-Time Delinquents												
Lower SES												
Nonwhite	35	28.69	14.3	84	68.85	34.3	3	2.46	1.2	122	100.0	49.9
White	24	30.00	11.2	54	67.50	25.2	2	2.50	0.9	80	100.0	37.4
Total	59	29.21	12.9	138	68.32	30.1	5	2.48	1.1	202	100.0	44.1
Higher SES												
Nonwhite	5	23.81	10.9	13	61.90	28.4	3	14.29	6.6	21	100.0	45.9
White	25	23.36	5.1	80	74.77	16.3	2	1.87	0.4	107	100.0	21.8
Total	30	23.44	5.6	93	72.66	17.3	5	3.91	0.9	128	100.0	23.8
Recidivists												
Lower SES												
Nonwhite	509	27.68	208.3	1180	64.17	482.8	150	8.16	61.4	1839	100.0	752.5
White	85	18.05	39.7	379	80.47	177.1	7	1.49	3.3	471	100.0	220.1
Total	594	25.71	129.6	1559	67.49	340.1	157	6.80	34.2	2310	100.0	503.9
Higher SES												
Nonwhite	49	28.49	107.0	106	61.63	231.4	17	9.88	37.1	172	100.0	375.5
White	83	18.32	16.9	361	79.69	73.6	9	1.99	1.8	453	100.0	92.4
Total	132	21.12	24.6	467	74.72	87.1	26	4.16	4.8	625	100.0	116.6
Both SES												
Lower	653	26.00	142.4	1697	67.56	370.2	162	6.45	35.3	2512	100.0	548.0
Higher	162	21.51	30.2	560	74.37	104.5	31	4.12	5.8	753	100.0	140.5
Both Races												
Nonwhite	598	27.76	206.1	1383	64.20	476.6	173	8.03	59.6	2154	100.0	742.2
White	217	19.53	30.8	874	78.67	124.1	20	1.80	2.8	1111	100.0	157.7
Total	815	24.96	82.0	2257	62.13	226.9	193	5.91	19.4	3265	100.0	328.3

The following table shows weighted rates for the cohort, with race-specific weighted rates per 1,000 cohort subjects, as well as per 1,000 delinquents.

TABLE 8. *RACE-SPECIFIC RATES OF DELINQUENCY WEIGHTED BY SERIOUSNESS OF OFFENSE*

	Weighted Rate per 1,000 Cohort Subjects	Weighted Rate per 1,000 Delinquents
Both Races _____	1,172.4	3,365.5
Nonwhite _____	2,594.4	5,163.8
White _____	587.9	2,052.8

Most offenses of bodily injury are committed by delinquent repeaters. Less than 10 percent, or 117, of the 1,391 delinquencies with known physical injury involve one-time, or single, offenders despite the fact that one-time offenders were 45 percent of all delinquents. Nonwhite repeaters, particularly from the lower SES, are responsible for most of these offenses. Table 9 shows these various data by mean seriousness score and weighted rates. Perhaps the most striking conclusions revealed by the weighted injury offense rates on Table 9 are as follows:

(a) There are no significant race differences within each respective SES level for *one-time delinquents.* Thus, for example, among lower SES boys who committed only one injury offense and no further delinquency, the weighted rate is 35.2 for nonwhites and 31.8 for whites. Among higher SES boys who committed only one offense, nonwhites have a weighted rate of 17.5 and white boys a weighted rate of 14.7. These within-SES rates across racial groups are not significant.

(b) Significant race differences re-appear among *recidivists.* Within the lower SES, the nonwhite weighted rate (779.0) is 4.6 times greater than the white rate (169.4), and within the higher SES, nonwhites have a weighted rate (467.3) that is about 6.5 times higher than that for whites (72.0).

(c) The greatest difference is not between the races or between the SES levels, but between nonwhite one-time offensivity and nonwhite recidivism. The nonwhite lower SES boys have a weighted rate differential that shows recidivists (779.0) 22 times higher than one-time offenders (35.2), and nonwhite higher SES boys have a rate 26 times greater for recidivists (467.3) than for one-time delinquents (17.5).

TABLE 9. *INJURY OFFENSES: MEAN SERIOUSNESS SCORE, NUMBER, AND WEIGHTED RATE, BY DELINQUENCY STATUS, SES, AND RACE*

SES Level	One-Time Delinquents			Recidivists			Total		
	X	N	WR	X	N	WR	X	N	WR
Lower SES									
Both Races	220.00	70	33.6	240.60	942	494.4	239.18	1012	528.0
Nonwhite	209.76	41	35.2	241.93	787	779.0	240.34	828	814.2
White	234.48	29	31.8	233.87	155	169.4	233.97	184	201.2
Higher SES									
Both Races	170.21	47	14.9	172.34	329	105.8	172.07	376	120.7
Nonwhite	100.00	8	17.5	222.92	96	467.3	213.46	104	484.7
White	184.61	39	14.7	151.50	233	72.0	156.25	272	86.7

Once again our attention is mostly drawn to the delinquency status difference rather than to race or SES differences. The sheer size of offenses of bodily harm committed by nonwhite lower SES boys who are recidivists is alone a measure of their importance for promoting some kind of intervention as a basis for prevention. The 787 offenses of injury committed in this category alone constitute 56 percent of all 1,388 such offenses.

A further refinement in Table 10 shows the types of physical injury committed by each racial group. The frequency distributions as well as the weighted rates show that more *serious* forms of harm are committed by nonwhites. No whites were responsible for the 14 homicides. The modal weighted rate for nonwhites is to cause victims to be hospitalized (although the modal number is in the "minor harm" category). The modal weighted rate (WR) and number for white offenders is for minor harm. By using the weighted rate, based on the judgmental scale of the gravity of crime, the 14 homicides represent more social harm to the community during the juvenile life span (WR = 125.4) of nonwhite boys than all the combined 456 acts of physical injury committed by white boys during their juvenile years (WR = 119.3). The same can be said about the 59 acts of violence committed by nonwhites that resulted in hospitalization of the victims (WR = 142.3).

TABLE 10. *RACE OF DELINQUENT BY TYPE OF INJURY:*
NUMBER, PER CENT AND WEIGHTED RATE PER 1,000
COHORT SUBJECTS

Type of Injury	Race of Delinquent								
	Nonwhite			White			Total		
	N	%	WR	N	%	WR	N	%	WR
Number of Deaths ...	14	1.49	125.4	..	..	..	14	1.01	36.6
Hospitalized	59	6.31	142.3	22	4.82	21.9	81	5.82	57.0
Treated & Discharged	217	23.21	299.1	84	18.47	47.7	301	21.64	121.1
Minor Harm	645	68.98	222.3	350	76.75	49.7	995	71.53	100.0
Total	935	100.00	789.1	456	100.00	119.3	1391	100.00	314.71
Unknown	64			11			75		
Grand Total	999	68.14		467	31.86		1466	100.00	
Mean Seriousness .... Score		244.92			184.21			225.02	

Another way to view the weighted rates is in terms of total cumulative scores for the offenses and the total amount of social harm inflicted on the community. For example, nonwhites inflicted 750,433 units of social harm, or seriousness points, in the city, 639,445 of which were from index offenses and 110,988 from nonindex offenses. If there were a 10 percent reduction, not of all nonwhite offenses but of index offenses, that were shifted to a 10 percent increase in nonindex offenses, the corresponding reduction in seriousness units would amount to 72,777. That is, index gravity units would dip to 565,501, and nonindex gravity units would increase to 122,087, a socially favorable trade-off. The overall crude rate of 1,983 could remain the same, but the reduction of 72,777 seriousness units (or a weighted rate reduction from 2,585.91 to 2,403.81) would be equivalent to the elimination of 28 homicides, or 104 assaults that send victims to hospitals for treatment, or 181 assaults treated by physicians without hospitalization.

In short, if juveniles are to be delinquent, a major thrust of social action programs might be to cause a change in the *character* rather than in the absolute reduction of delinquent behavior. It could also be argued that concentration of social action programs on a 10 percent reduction of white *index* offenses (N = 1,400; WR = 483.63) would have a greater social payoff than a 10 percent reduction of nonwhite *nonindex* offenses (N = 3,343; WR = 382.45). To inculcate values against harm, in body or property, to others is obviously the major means to reduce the seriousness of delinquency, both among whites and nonwhites. We are simply faced with the fact that more social harm is committed by nonwhites, and the resources and energies of social harm nonindex offenses at age 17 (N = 591) is offset by the lower mean seriousness score of these offenses at age 16 (X = 19.7) compared to age 17 (X = 35.3).

The weighted rates help to make especially clear the fact that a relatively low incidence of serious offenses in the early ages can produce rates by the gravity of offenses that are higher than the weighted rates for a high incidence of minor offenses in the later ages. In short, many petty offenses may have a lower quantum of social harm than a few serious offenses. For example, at age 11, nonwhites committed 158 serious index offenses, had a crude rate of only 54.45 and a weighted, or seriousness, rate of 99.25 per 1,000. At age 16, nonwhites were picked up by the police on 890 quite minor offenses, had their highest crude rate of 278.77 but a weighted rate of only 94.23. Whites provide a similar example: at age 12, white boys committed 126 index offenses, had a low crude rate of 17.89 and a weighted rate of 35.17; at age 16 they committed 992 minor nonindex offenses, had their highest crude rate at 140.85 but a rate by degree of gravity that was only 27.75.

In summary, of the 9,945 boys in the birth cohort, 3,475, or 35 percent, were delinquent and responsible for 10,214 delinquent acts from age seven through age 17. Nonwhites have an offense rate that is three times higher than whites. In general, however, only about 30 percent of these offenses are index crimes, defined in terms of the FBI Standard Classification system or in terms of all acts of injury, theft, and damage.

Although nonwhites and lower socio-economic status boys have significantly higher crude rates and weighted rates based on the seriousness of their offenses, the differences between one-time offenders and recidivists are among the most striking of any of the multiple ways of analyzing the data. If a question about social intervention is posed in terms of the data available thus far from the cohort and in terms of the greatest amount of offense reduction registered between groups, it is clear that *preventing the group of nonwhite lower SES boys from continuing delinquency after their first offense would indeed produce the maximum delinquency reduction.* By focusing resources and attention on the lower SES nonwhite subset of a birth cohort who have a first delinquency, not only would the general rate of delinquency be affected; the most serious acts, those involving physical violence or assault on others, would be most *drastically decreased.*

VIOLENCE IN GANGS COMPARED TO SPONTANEOUS GROUPS OF DELINQUENTS

Another recent study adds information about youth violence in delinquent gangs and non-gang aggregates, or spontaneous groups of delinquents.[39] Using data from the Gang Control Unit of the Philadelphia Juvenile Aid Division, Bernard Cohen has produced some empirical data analysis in an area commonly devoid of good statistics but fortified with middle-range theory. Building upon the work of (Albert) Cohen, Cloward and Ohlin, Miller, and the more data-filled study of Short and Strodtbeck, this new analysis clearly distinguishes the more property-offense delinquent group from the more violent delinquent gang. Instead of examining a few gangs or individuals intensively, this research takes gangs or corporate entities as a base and is an investigation of all gang (217) and group (95) delinquent events between July 1965 and July 1966.

Gangs are readily identified as highly developed aggregates with relatively large memberships, elaborate organization, differentiated roles, names, and a sense of corporate identity, particularly with a circumscribed territory. The delinquent group is a relatively small clique of youth who coalesce sporadically, without apparent reason, and rather spontaneously violate the law. This group has no specific identity, no durability, no "turf," and if individuals in it are apprehended once, rarely are they arrested together again.

Although both gangs and groups engage in violent, aggresive behavior, 145, or 66 percent, of the gang events comprised offense categories of homicide, rape, aggravated and simple assault, compared to 50 or 53 percent of the group events. None of the simple aggregates committed rape, but one group and three gang events were homicides. Not only do gangs engage in more violent behavior than do the other groups, but, according to this study, the predominant activity of delinquent gangs centers around violence.

Property offenses present an interesting contrast. Fourteen percent of the group events consisted of property offenses (burglary, larceny, robbery, auto theft) compared to only one percent of gang events. Gangs were recorded for only one robbery during the year of study, compared to nine for the aggregates. No gang was apprehended (discovered?) for committing larceny or auto theft. The gang seems to *specialize*, while the group is more *versatile*.

With the Sellin-Wolfgang magnitude scale values used for scoring the seriousness of gang and group events, the study shows that 202, or 65 percent of the total 312 events (gang and group), involved various degrees of physical injury to 248 individual victims. Twice as many victims of gangs (44 percent) as of groups (19 percent) had injuries requiring hospitalization. On the other hand, more victims of groups (45 percent) than of gangs (15 percent) sustained minor harm (i.e., requiring no medical treatment). Gangs carry and use weapons. In 66 percent of their police-recorded offenses they carried weapons. Groups did too, but in fewer cases (37 percent). Gangs used knives (33 percent) and guns (23 percent) much more often than groups (20 and 7 percent).

There are many other interesting aspects to this study, but we have here focused on the amount and kinds of violence performed by delinquent gangs and simple groupings of delinquents. Perhaps the most striking observation from the study is that gangs are characterized by homogeneous patterns of offense behavior, which is mostly violent, while groups are more diverse, diffuse, and versatile.

In this section we have tried to give an overview of the amount of violence of youth reflected in official national police statistics. We have examined the effect which the changing age structure of our population has on producing an increase in the total volume of recorded crimes of violence. And we have briefly reviewed some new data and analyses of violent delinquency in a birth cohort and among delinquent gangs and unstructured groups of delinquent juveniles.

With these statistics we have meant to be illustrative rather than comprehensive. They are *provocative,* more than *profound,* because they rarely yield things that are now unexpected. But they do render more clear the issues with which society must cope and add meaningful information that can be used not only to comprehend but to *control* crimes of violence committed by youth.

NOTES (this article is part of a larger one)

38. The study has been supported by the National Institute of Mental Health and has been under the direction of Thorsten Sellin and Marvin E. Wolfgang. The new data represented in this section will appear in a forthcoming publication, *Delinquency in a Birth Cohort.*

39. Bernard Cohen, "The Delinquency of Gangs and Spontaneous Groups," a chapter in Thorsten Sellin and Marvin E. Wolfgang (eds.), *Selected Studies in Delinquency,* New York: John Wiley and Sons, Inc., in press.

THE STUDENT WHO BURNED DOWN
THE BANK OF AMERICA

Scanlan's Monthly

On the night of February 25, 1970, demonstrating students of the University of California at Santa Barbara started a fire which completely destroyed the Bank of America's Isla Vista branch. The demonstrations were the spontaneous result of the university's decision not to grant tenure to a popular, radical anthropology professor, Bill Allen.

Shortly after the bank burning, a member of the political underground arranged an interview between the student who was primarily responsible for the destruction and the editors of Scanlan's. Since that time, the State of California has indicted 12 people for the bank burning. The trial of 11 of the defendants is expected to conclude soon, and the twelfth, who was recently arrested in Oregon, will be brought to trial during the next month.

The details of the interview explain why those charged could not possibly be guilty.

What did this bank represent to you? This Bank of America branch?

Well, *this* Bank of America represented to me the same thing every Bank of America does. It's essentially the Bank of America which has its hand in everything all over the world. It's like the largest bank in the world, from what I understand. The people who sit on the board of directors of this bank, they're pigs! You know, it was more symbolic, because it's one bank and they've got so much fuckin' money. But we figured, you know, the Bank of America, let them feel the same fear they have to feel abroad. Like when guerillas in Lebanon, the next day, shot mortars through their windows. Let them feel that at home. They're not safe anywhere, and they shouldn't be. It was also an ugly building. Aesthetically, it was ugly. As one of my friends remarked: "That fuckin' thing was so ugly, it had to go anyway."

Tell us about the events which led up to your burning down the Bank of America at Isla Vista.

An anthropology professor named Bill Allen was fired for being cool. The Regents gave the excuse that he was being fired for not having done enough research, but in fact he had done more research than anyone else in his department. He's a noted California archaeologist. They threw him out because he had long hair and a beard and smoked dope.

He was very well-liked. He was pretty radical. He taught a class in Latin-American revolution. He had this picture on his wall that we all dug. The mouth was filled with a collage of poor people all over the world and it said: "U.S. imperialism swallows the globe." We dug him, because he was not making it into a student-teacher relationship, like a dictator to a dummy. He made it, you know, we're all in this together. So, the students got very upset when the Regents fired him.

Santa Barbara first became radicalized by the blacks who took over the university computer center. Then when the Regents dismissed Bill Allen, the whites began getting radicalized. The students requested an open hearing for Bill Allen. It was refused. This really solidified the campus because people actually knew what was going on. Over 7,000 students, over half the enrollment, signed a petition to keep him on. It was ignored by the administration and the Regents. Prior to this, most people were not aware of their roles as students. But, then, when all of a sudden, they were put in the role of niggers — having one of their teachers taken away — they became aware. This was such a needed kick to all of us.

How many demonstrations were there before the first attacks by the police?

It's pretty hard to remember exactly. But I do remember that we were gassed and beaten a few times. But overall they were, you know, typical average riots. There was nothing special about them. It's not even worth going into detail. But it was enough to make people pissed off at the police.

Then one day, the pigs decided to arrest these four people. They were walking down the street and a pig car pulls up. "You're under arrest," one pig says. And their immediate reaction was: "Well, what are we under arrest for?" The pig says: "Get in the car." And they give out the constitutional rights trip: "What are we being arrested for?" And the pig just said: "Resisting arrest." Okay. "Resisting arrest to what charge?" "Get in the car." So they pulled these four people in and while they were doing that, they tried to pull each other out. You know, when the pig was puttin' one in, they kept tryin' to get out. And they were struggling with the pigs right on the street. People saw this and they couldn't believe what was going on. So, pretty fast there was a bunch of us out on the street. The police got uptight and said, "This is an illegal assembly," and the people started throwing rocks at the police. It was really an incredible scene. People running all over the streets throwing rocks at the police. The police called in reinforcements, and there was this street fight going on. All of a sudden, all you heard out windows of the houses right next door was The Rolling Stones' Street Fighting Man. And people are going crazy when this comes on. Like the minute they heard that, they start throwing rocks in the realty office.

Were you throwing rocks?

Well, yes. To be precise, I hit one pig in the stomach. The fucker.

All right, so groups are running around throwing rocks at the police. The police, I presume, were making arrests?

No. The pigs were retreating. They were forced to retreat. We had militarily defeated them. One pig car was bombed. It was Molotov'd. The pigs weren't in it at the time. They were away. They couldn't make arrests because there were so few of them. They couldn't get enough reinforcements. So now the area was more or less ours, and at that point you could hear Jefferson Airplane singing Got A Revolution. People were all putting on like all revolutionary songs on their record players. It was just unbelievable.

Were you near the bank while all this was going on?

We were floating around on Embarcadero. That's where the bank is. We were deciding if there were any good targets and we saw some people congregating by the bank. The bank windows had already been broken the night before and the windows were boarded up. We'd beaten the pigs. We were all so happy we had finally beaten the pricks.

At this time I was wearing a green Army jacket. And the collar is big on it. So I pushed it up so you couldn't see my cheeks, or mouth. My hair was really long. So I'm pretty hard to tell in the midst of chaos and other friends of mine did typically the same thing with their coats. And we like pulled this trash can right in front of the boarded window of the bank. And what happened was people were talking in frenzied voices and saying beautiful, crazy things, like "I wish we would blow this fucking bank up." Just then some people started to rip down the boards from the window and, just out of inspiration, I threw a match in the trash can trying to start it, you know.

You had not planned anything prior to right then?

No. I planned to start a fire in the trash can, not before but right then. The inspiration was like, "Light this fuckin' trash can".

The inspiration must have hit all of us at once 'cause we pulled the sleeves of our jackets over our hands so we wouldn't leave fingerprints on the trash can handles, and then — WHAM! Right through the fuckin' open window. The trash splattered out all over the bank. Papers caught on fire. People were going wild, yelling out, "They're burning the bank!" The people started throwing matches and shit. Pieces of paper on fire.

What did you do after you threw the trash can through the window?

I split. We went and checked to see if there were any pigs in the area, if we were being followed. We were pretty sure we'd gotten away with it. So we went home and smoked some more dope and relaxed and waited to see the outcome. Actually, it was rather tense after we smoked the dope. We were elated and then we settled down for our one paranoia stretch. We got the guns out of the closet and just loaded . . .

You had guns in your closet?

Yeah, I mean, fuck it. Like when you do this stuff, you should generally be prepared to die right then and there. My politics are I believe in armed self-defense. I believe in having guns in your house. 'Cause I believe there is so much repression that you never know who they're going to get. And, like, I was once formerly an SDS member, so my name is on lists. They know who the fuck I am. So, I'm not taking any chances. Any time repression can hit. It's not something you should laugh and play about.

Why did you split? Were there still other people left out on the street?

There were people outside the bank when we left, chanting and yelling. But what we didn't want to do was be out there any longer than we had to. Because I'm not risking my life in a street situation any more than is necessary for that action. If I thought the action was crazy, suicidal to begin with, I wouldn't even go out there, even though I thought politically it was a groovy action. 'Cause riots are getting out of hand. They're shooting people down in the streets. I'm still gonna do shit, they're gonna still know I'm around. But I do not suggest people go out and riot. If they like violence, they should form their own cells and go out and do something.

I still attend things, but shy away from some. Those last riots we had during the Cambodian incident were pretty bad. I was there, but I kind of stayed away afterwards. There was teargassing, beating heads, it was like martial law while all this stuff was going on. We didn't want to fuck with National Guardsmen. We figured we could talk to them, could radicalize them eventually. Because these people lived right in our community. I still think some of them can be saved and you want these people in the national guard not to shoot you but to put their arms around you and point their guns the other way. You be nice to them. A pig is a pig. But the National Guard is like guys do that to get out of the Army, so you know where some of their heads could be.

What would you like to see happen in America?

One of the things that I would like to do is some serious organizing among the labor people I've come in contact with. They are the most important. Say if people strike General Electric for political reasons — saying we don't want General Electric supporting the war — it can be incredible. You can stop the machine at home. Like I was reading Che, and he said,"You're right in the middle of the beast," and that is the most important struggle. If you can stop it here it can't go anywhere else and that means politicizing labor.

Basically I guess I'm some sort of communist. I would like to see some sort of socialist or communist type of revolution. I have definite anarchist leanings. But I must stress that I am not a Stalinist or anything. I don't think major universities will be open in five years. Black people are still going — really going — to get it in the head. All over. Students will possibly calm the riots and do some serious organizing among themselves and labor. This is what I would like to see and hopefully we'll know in a year if this will happen. I don't really expect this as I think a lot of people in the movement are jerks. They may think I'm a jerk for that, but I mean they don't see when the times are changing. All they want to do is organize hippies and stuff and keep the student revolution as the most important thing.

I used to have that egocentric view that we're the only people doing anything. But now I believe the whole population has to be moved. That of course doesn't mean everybody, but strategic militant segments of the The teamsters in Los Angeles for instance. When they went on strike everything stopped. About 200 of those cats didn't get their jobs back. I helped picket for them. They definitely were into militancy and into a rank and file wildcat strike.

This one cat I know in Santa Barbara is one of the teamsters who were really pissed off and militant. They had ripped off some mortars and set them up outside the building where they worked. They were very much contemplating shelling this fucking building, but they decided against it. They said they will wait until later.

What do you think is the value of the bombings?

Well, right now I'm not so sure. It's almost like a war was going on in this country and I guess there is. And I think the pace of the war will keep pace with the rising militancy of the people against government repression. If they continue the bombing at this pace they will force so much repression that there will be no movement. If they are going to bomb things I think they should at least avoid killing people at all costs. But the pig station is different. That is always going to be strategically and tactically correct. Because once you put that uniform on you are a pig. That's your job — you follow orders.

What about somebody like Rockefeller?

Oh, I wouldn't mind ripping him off. Of course any of their flunkies, any of their stong arms. They have to go. Now I would advocate something with real balls like picking off a particular general in Washington. It's just general violence and bombing that I question.

You were speaking of special organizing in the working class. Do you see violence as a way of organizing? How does it help?

Most workers would be afraid of us if they thought we were these crazy bombing people. They wouldn't understand that I want ultimately to get students and workers together. Like Berkeley kids were pretty successful at the Richmond Oil Strike. There were some contacts made in Santa Barbara. So I figure that students all over the country should just invite workers up to their houses for dinner. Talk to them. Bring their families. You know, we're not bad people. You're getting all this bullshit in the media and like you should just come in and see what's going on. And don't rhetoric them to death. Just let them know that, like, there is piggery going on in the country, and they're being screwed by it because they are workers.

What will you do in the future?

I have some ideas about organizing a cooperative-type venture. Hopefully I will acquire a skill before school closes. I may want to do something medical. That would be my specialty. A friend of mine will be making films. And we wanna get someone in who is an auto mechanic.

We would give free medical or dental care to people. And free auto and mechanic repairs. Another thing I advocate for all students is to help workers repair their houses. Some workers never get a chance to paint their houses. So help them paint it... you actually show them that you're concerned with them. They will ask you questions, like, "Why do you fix up my house when you burn a building on campus?" You can like explain that the ROTC office was involved in killing Vietnamese. And you should have a little more — because you really do a lot of hard work out there so I can go to school. You bust your ass. You should have little more. I feel solidarity with you. I feel we should be together instead of being split apart. That's why we do stuff like this. We don't do it because we're sneaky fuckers. We do it because we actually feel this way.

Do you have a scenario for a political apocalypse?

I see more of a civil war than a revolutionary struggle in the United States. In a civil war I believe our propaganda will be better than the pigs', and that eventually we will sway enough workers over to our side. Militarily, urban guerrilla tactics will give us a tremendous advantage over the pigs. So the civil war will be waged pretty much in guerrilla style. The whole country will become a kind of occupied territory, and there will be an underground and real guerrillas will walk down the streets looking just like the pig businessman. They will do their shit and go home and incredible things will happen at night.

There will be some armed insurrection in the cities. The Bay Area will liberate itself right off and I feel that a major part of New York will be liberated. New York is really heavy. I figure a lot of cities will be divided into liberated zones and pigs' zones. And when the pigs try and invade they will not get in so easily. And they are not going to shell them immediately because the liberals will still be screaming. And then there will be some repression for these screaming liberals and then — boom. Liberals are going to decide this is it. Hopefully. I figure that most people will get mobilized when their lives are truly affected. So far this government is not really into mass repression. They are just picking off leaders. And when repression picks up I figure they will pick off the liberal leaders first. Then the mass of liberals may actually do something. I hope. But even if they don't, most of the moderates will remain so passive, they could generally be swayed to our side.

And once resistance increases in the cities?

One of the most important things that I think will happen will be a breakdown in the national guard. In Chicago, for instance, a lot of the national guard just didn't want to be there. A similar, but not so broad, decomposition is taking place within the U.S. Army too. A lot of these cats are getting really militant. A lot of the black soldiers and the chicanos for sure, and a lot of white guys who are fucked over in the armed forces, can be counted on. There will be breakdowns and revolts in both the army and the national guard in cases of fighting guerrillas. They don't want to shoot their own people. I'm sure of that. Except maybe the sick ones, I figure a lot of them will come to our side.

Is there anyone in the movement you would like to see become President of the United States?

Well, none of the conspirators excite me. I don't really like Tom Hayden or Rennie Davis that much. I definitely like Huey Newton and Bobby Seale, and I guess I would like to see them in leadership of the country, but more I would like to see a balance of power between guys, if there was one group it could continue to create friction, like the blacks or any other took over.

Are you going to remain a student?

Yes, that's the way it looks. I want to build as many alliances in the university as I can. Maybe the universities will be able to stay open. And if we are really successful . . . but I don't really see that. That's like a dream, wow, like all this stuff is going to happen. I don't think like that. I think more on a hard line, that there is going to be more hard core things going on rather than big national movements.

What about money?

My parents are helping out while I'm going to school. And I've got a national student loan that I have no intention of paying back. I think it is very nice of them to send me here to school.

THE CRIME OF ROBBERY
IN THE U.S.

Arnold Sagalyn

THE CONFUSION OVER CLASSIFICATION

One of the basic problems involved in compiling and analyzing useful statistical data on robberies arises from the present system of classifying and reporting on the offense. The FBI Uniform Crime Reports (UCR) define robbery as: "Stealing or taking anything of value from the person by force or violence or by putting in fear, such as strong-arm robbery, stickups, armed robbery, assault to rob, and attempt to rob." [1] In its report on bank robberies in California, the Bureau of Criminal Statistics of the California Department of Justice observed: "Robbery has elements of both crimes against persons and crimes against property; the motive is monetary gain but it must be taken from or in the presence of another person." [2]

In the FBI Uniform Crime Reports, Part I Offenses are divided into two categories: (1) Crimes Against the Person (which comprise criminal homicide, forcible rape and assault), and (2) Crimes Against Property (robbery, burglary, larceny-theft, and auto theft). Although robbery is classified as a crime against property, for presentation purposes the FBI includes robbery with crimes against the person when it presents charts and statistics on Crimes of Violence. At the same time, it excludes robbery from its chart depicting Crimes Against Property. In charts showing the trend of "Crimes by Month" and "Crimes Cleared by Arrest," robbery is included in the category of "Crimes Against Property." [3]

Thus the UCR classifies robbery as a crime against property but treats it as a crime against the person as well as a crime of violence.

The Uniform Crime Reporting Handbook published for the guidance of law enforcement officials by the FBI states that where the element of force or threat of force are absent, as in pocket-picking and purse-snatching, the offense should be reported in the larceny-theft class. However, a purse-snatching is classified a strong-arm robbery if an unarmed thief uses force to overcome the resistance of the victim. [4]

This classification problem is further illustrated by the procedures a police department follows in determining the proper crime classification. If more than one offense is committed during the course of a crime, the sequential ranking of the Uniform Crime Reports is followed to select the proper classification. [5] Criminal homicide and forcible rape both precede robbery in the Uniform Crime Reporting System. Thus if in the course of a robbery, someone is killed, the crime reported is murder, not robbery. Or if a rape is committed in connection with the robbery, the classification process calls for the crime to be reported as a rape.

The dual nature of robbery and the ambivalent approach to classifying and reporting on it, which are reflected in the studies and data-gathering efforts that have been conducted into robbery, make it extremely difficult to identify and evaluate the critical factors which may determine the value and usefulness of measures and factors to control and prevent robberies. The Task Force on Individual Acts of Violence of the Eisenhower Commission on Violence devoted a chapter to the problem and needs of criminal statistics. It makes the following observations concerning the need for more refined classifications in the Uniform Crime Report practices and procedures:

"Offenses covering a wide range of seriousness are sometimes included in the same UCR category. This makes refined analysis of the crimes extremely difficult. To the extent that the public image of these crimes is couched in terms of the more serious (and generally more publicized) variations under the same crime category, the result may be a somewhat distorted conception of what the rate for the particular crime means.

"A prime example is robbery. There are many variations, ranging from an armed bank robbery, in which several people are shot and injured, to minor thefts, such as purse-snatching where force or threat of force is used. Dramatically profiling the lower end of the robbery spectrum was the report on the thefts in which one of the two 9-year-old boys twisted the arm of the other in the schoolyard in order to obtain 25¢ of the latter's lunch money. Because force was used, the police correctly recorded and counted the act as highway robbery.

"While these less serious events should be recorded, it does not seem reasonable to include them in the same category as the more serious offenses. At the very least, it would be desirable for analytical purposes to publish two index categories of robbery—perhaps armed robbery and unarmed robbery (strong-arm robbery, muggings, purse-snatching with force or threat of force, etc.)—in order to give a clearer picture of which kind of theft with force is recorded." [6]

As the Violence Commission report points out, the term and single category of robbery is used to cover a number of essentially different offenses with a wide variation in the degree of the violence threatened or used and in the economic loss to the victims. As noted previously, this makes it extremely difficult to analyze and assess robbery data, or to obtain an accurate picture of the nature of and critical factors involved in these offenses.

In this connection, more study and a reevaluation appears warranted with respect to the practice and wisdom of labelling all robberies as crimes of violence. For the studies reviewed tend to present a great deal of evidence that a wide variation exists between the perception and reality of the role of violence in robberies.

Contrary to the commonly held belief that a robbery usually involves the actual employment of violence and that a large proportion of the victims suffer injuries, a number of the studies reviewed disclose that the percentage and degree of violence used in actual practice by robbers proved to be relatively small.

Armed robberies in particular tend to result in little injury. In large measure, this appears to be attributable to the fact that the overwhelming nature of the threat of the weapons discourages and minimizes resistance. Most injuries that are suffered occur in strong-arm robberies where the victim is more likely to resist and where the offender tends to be youthful and more prone to readily employ physical force.

The Bronx, New York study, for example, found that less than 10% of robbery victims suffered any injury.[7] In his study of 722 cases of robberies in Philadelphia between 1960 and 1966, Normandeau found that 44% of all the robberies resulted in no injuries. Of the remaining 56% involving injuries, 26% were minor, 25% were discharged after treatment, and only 5% required hospitalization.[8] Normandeau reported that most of the injuries resulted from strong-arm robberies, which usually involved the employment of physical force by younger offenders.[9] Similarly, a survey of robbery cases in 17 cities conducted in 1967 for the Violence Commission Task Force on Individual Acts of Violence found that injuries occurred in only 14% of the armed robberies and in 28% of the strong-arm robberies. By way of comparison, injuries resulted in 21% of the rape cases and in 80% of the aggravated assault cases.[10]

Normandeau also raises some important questions about the intrinsically violent nature and behavior of persons who commit robberies. He disagrees with Wolfgang and Ferranti who, in the *Subculture of Violence*, argue that robbery arises out of the "subculture of violence." [11] Instead he sees robbers as a class to be relatively non-violent in their criminal activities.

"Robbers," Normandeau holds, "are not a special class, but are primarily thieves who occasionally, though rather rarely, use force to achieve their object. The display of violence in this context is on the whole an isolated episode. It is general persistence in crime, not a widespread specialization in crimes of violence, which is the main characteristic of robbers." Therefore, he states, the term "violent offender class" could not be applied to robbers without distorting the factual data to fit preconceived ideas. On the basis of his data, Normandeau concluded that robbery should be termed "a subculture of theft, rather than violence." Violence, he maintained, was used only as a tool by the robbery offender who kept it largely under control.[12]

This conclusion receives support from research studies undertaken in California. As a result of the work and recommendations of John P. Conrad, Chief of the Research Division of the California Department of Corrections in 1963, the California Department of Corrections undertook to classify all inmates according to an aggressive history profie (AHP).[13] Violent offenders were classified according to seven categories: culturally violent, criminally violent and pathologically violent, situationally violent, accidentaly violent, institutionally violent, and non-violent. All persons sentenced on charges of robbery were classified as "criminally violent." The definition for "criminally violent" was those who "will commit violence if necessary to gain some end, as in robbery." The criteria for such offenders was: (1) violence was used as a tool in carrying out some criminal act, typically robbery; (2) the offender carried a concealed weapon and is not classifiable as culturally, pathologically, or situationally violent.[14]

According to Conrad's theory, the criminally violent offender regards violence as a tool of his trade. He uses it not for personal satisfaction as does the culturally violent, but to gain other ends. Thus the robber, through planning and the judicious use of violence, hopes to gain a certain mastery over his circumstances and reap quick rewards. He does not use violence to inflict deliberate injury. If he can achieve his goal with only a threat of injury to his victim, so much the better.[15]

In a follow-up study of the criminal career occupational history and demographic characteristics of offenders classified in the AHP, Dr. Carol Spencer's findings corroborate Conrad's conclusions that the "criminally violent" type rarely uses actual violence. Spencer reported that 83% of those classified as criminally violent—which would cover the robbers—had no conviction for actual violence at any time in their criminal careers.[16]

"Rarely causing physical injury to their victims when committing their felonies, they were not much given to assaultive behavior at other times. They differ sharply from the other groups where approximately 90% had convictions for actual violence."[17] Spencer also found that fewer of the robbers he studied had a police record before the age of 18 than did other offenders; that juvenile violent offenses were relativly rare.

In a summary of findings on the Criminally Violent group, Dr. Spencer reported: "The relative lack of assaultive behavior, greater consistency of motivation, fewer conflicts with law enforcement and more cautious driving record all suggest better control. The criminally violent channel their aggressions into profitable avenues of robbery rather than into impulsive assaults."[18]

The above findings as to the high degree of control exercised by robbers over the violence at their employ and the very low record of any violence or injuries that result from robberies would seem to suggest that more attention needs to be given to this factor of violence and its reality in the crime of robbery. To the extent that a typical robber is not a violence-prone person and is unlikely to employ violence unless he is provoked or encounters resistance has important meaning and consequences for those who are victims of robberies, as well as for those responsible for preventing and controlling such offenses.

It is far from certain, however, that the relatively small number of injuries experienced in robberies which occurred in past years presents a reliable picture of what is currently happening. As in the drug problem, the non-violent nature of robberies and those who commit them may be changing.[19]

In his report on *A Contemporary History of American Crime*, Fred P. Graham quoted criminologist Marvin E. Wolfgang as follows: "Perhaps it is because the robbers tend to be younger and the young are more likely to use violence, but there has been a considerable increase in the level of violence in robberies." [20]

Another important consideration is the intolerable nature of the violence and danger inherent in a crime where serious bodily harm is threatened. This very point was made by J. Edgar Hoover in discussing bank robberies where the number of physical injuries suffered by victims has been relatively minimal. Referring to "the potential for violence and death inherent" in such robberies, Hoover pointed out that the threat to human life cannot be ignored.[21] Thus the public sense of personal as well as property security requires that the potential, horrendous threat of deadly force and serious bodily harm inherent in a robbery must be taken into full account in assessing the seriousness of the crime, even though the frequency or level of violence actually employed is relatively small.

NOTES

1. *FBI Uniform Crime Reports– 1968, op. cit.,* pg. 56.
2. *Bank Robbery in California,* Bureau of Criminal Statistics, Department of Justice, Sacramento, California, June 1967, p. 6.
3. *Uniform Crime Reports, op. cit.,* see charts Nos. 2, 3, and 12.
4. *Uniform Crime Reporting Handbook,* Federal Bureau of Investigation, U.S. Department of Justice, Washington, D.C., July 1966, pg. 20.
5. *Ibid.,* pg. 40.
6. Donald J. Mulvihill and Melvin Tumin, *Crimes of Violence,* Vols. 11, 12, and 13, National Commission on the Causes and Prevention of Violence, Staff Study Series (Washington, D.C.: U.S. Government Printing Office, 1970).
7. David Burnham, *New York Times, op. cit.*
8. Andre Normandeau, "Patterns in Robbery," *op. cit.,* pg. 4.
9. *Ibid.,* pg. 9.
10. *Crimes of Violence, Report of the Task Force on Individual Acts of Violence, op. cit.*
11. Andre Normandeau, "Patterns in Robbery," *op. cit.,* pg. 12.
12. *Ibid.*
13. Dr. Carol Spencer, *A Typology of Violent Offenders,* Research Report No. 23, California Department of Corrections, September 1966.
14. *Ibid.*
15. Abstracted from John T. Conrad, "The Nature and Treatment of the Violent Offender, *A Typology of Violent Offenders,* Appendix II, November 5, 1965.
16. Dr. Carol Spencer, *A Typology of Violent Offenders, op. cit.* pg. 13.
17. *Ibid.*
18. *Ibid.,* pg. 15.
19. See Chapter IV, *The Role of Alcohol, Narcotics and Dangerous Drugs.*
20. *A Contemporary History of American Crime, Violence in America,* Vol. II, A Report to the National Commission on the Causes and Prevention of Violence, June 1969, pg. 384.
21. John Edgar Hoover, "Violence and Bank Robbery," *The Tarhell Banker,* April 1968.

THE OFFENDER

On the basis of available studies to date, it is apparent that more up-to-date information and far greater research is required in order to obtain a fuller picture of who is responsible today for committing the various types of robbery and how he operates.

Such information as exists tends to be very fragmentary and sketchy, with insufficient detail and often obsolete.

More studies and related data have been conducted on bank robberies than on possibly any other type of robbery. Yet, after analyzing reports on 238 bank robberies which took place during a three-month period in 1964, the FBI concluded: "There is no such thing as a typical bank robber . . . There is no typical method of operation used by bank robbers." [1]

A training pamphlet on robbery published in 1966 by the International Association of Chiefs of Police describes a number of different types of robberies and tries to provide some guidance with respect to the commission of these crimes and the offenders. It notes that whereas bank robbery used to be committed by highly skilled professional criminals, in recent years a new type of bank robber has emerged who is essentially an amateur and "may strike at any time, sometimes almost compulsively." [2] Store and shop robberies are seen committed by "criminals ranging from the skilled and ruthless gunman to drug addicts." [3] Gasoline stations, particularly the all-night service station, located in outlying areas of a city or on the fringes of the metropolitan community are called "highly vulnerable" targets which attract robbers in the late evening and early morning hours. According to the IACP, the offender who robs residences usually possesses information as to the amount of valuables or currency he may obtain. This home invader is characterized as "one of the most vicious of all robbers," who frequently operates as a member of a gang. [4]

However, too little is known about whether or not a person who is robbing banks or residences is the same or different person who robs chain stores, gas stations, taxicabs, liquor and small retail stores or holds up pedestrians on the street. Nor do we know enough about the motivations or *modus operandi* of such robbers, including which type of offender is apt to be armed and with what kind of weapon or what measures and tactics to employ which will most effectively control and deter him.

Too little is known also about the economic factors involved. In two studies by the Pennsylvania Board of Parole of convicted robbers, it was found that 57% of those involved in the 1950 study and 74% in the 1965 study were unemployed at the time the robbery was committed. This led the Pennsylvania Parole Board to conclude that "a positive relationship exists between the crime of robbery and unemployment."[5] This would tend to corroborate other studies which have emphasized the essentially monetary gain motivation of the robber as the primary factor in this offense. Here again, however, there is inadequate information available on which to draw any useful conclusion and research efforts should be directed towards this need.

The Youthful Nature of the Robber

Studies of robberies by the FBI on a national basis disclosed that young offenders are responsible for a very large proportion of robberies that occur in the United States. The last available figures, covering the year 1968 for example, showed that 75% of all persons arrested for robbery were under the age of 25. Fifty-six percent were under 21 and 33% were juveniles. The FBI noted that youths tend to operate in groups, particularly in strong-arm robberies and most of the juveniles involved in robberies were arrested on charges of strong-arm robberies.[6]

The Chicago study of robberies in the Second District found that sixty-seven percent of robbery offenders were between 14 and 25 years of age. The strong-arm robbers tended to be youthful, 69% being 19 or under. Juveniles between the ages of 14 and 16 accounted for the highest number of strong-arm robberies. The Chicago study also disclosed that 92% of the strong-arm robberies took place on the street. No strong-arm robberies were found to have taken place in any business establishment.[7] A large number of victims were newsboys between the ages of 8 and 15 who were robbed by one, two or three unarmed boys a few years older than themselves. Where there was no resistance, there were usually no injuries.[8]

In a study of crimes of violence involving youth groups or gangs in 17 cities in 1967, the Task Force on Individual Acts of Violence found that youth groups and gangs were involved in a "significant percentage of all robberies . . ." An analysis of major crimes cleared by arrests showed that 9.5% of youth groups or gangs were involved in armed robbery and 6.8% in unarmed robbery. With respect to groups or gangs where the majority of offenders were juveniles, the percentage involved in armed robbery was 14.1% and in unarmed robberies, 18.6%. However, no youth group or gang was involved in 76% of the armed robberies or in 74% of the unarmed robberies.[9]

In view of the apparent contradictions between the above findings and those reported by the FBI Uniform Crime Reports and in other statistical analyses of robberies, more research is needed to clarify this aspect of robberies.

The Lone Offender

Unlike the study of bank robberies by the FBI, which found that the bank robber worked alone in 72% of the cases,[10] the Pennsylvania Board of Parole study showed that 32% of all robberies studied were committed by a lone robber. More than two-thirds had accomplices. This led the Board of Parole to conclude that another characteristic of robbers is that a large majority do not operate alone, but are assisted by accomplices.[11] (The Pennsylvania study was not limited to bank robberies, however.)

Dr. Donald Newman also found in his study of robbery offenders that the majority had partners in their crimes. These accomplices were not friends as much as someone with whom the robber could share responsibility and guilt for his offense. He also stated that there was little sense of guilt among the offenders studied. Rather, they tended to picture themselves more victimized than their victims. Dr. Newman also concluded that some of the robbers committed the crime deliberately in order to be returned to prison because of their need for a structured environment.[12]

A study conducted by Gerald Wolcott in March 1967 of 81 convicted robbers incarcerated at the California Conservation Center in Susanville found that 79% of all the robbers (none of whom appeared to have been bank robbers), had accomplices. The study also showed that 40% of all the robberies were committed against lone individuals; and that 65% of these were crimes of opportunity that were committed on the spur of the moment. Such situational spur-of-the-moment robberies were likely to be committed by lone robbers and involve a lone victim.[13]

In general, however, the data is too limited to try to make any deductions of significant assistance to law enforcement and criminal justice personnel.

NOTES

1. "Profile of a Bank Robber," *FBI Law Enforcement Bulletin,* November 1965.
2. Training Key No. 41, *Robbery,* published by the Professional Standards Division of the International Association of Chiefs of Police, 1966.
3.- *Ibid.*
4.- *Ibid.*

5. Pennsylvania Board of Probation and Parole, *Characteristics of Persons Arrested for Robbery* (Harrisburg: Board of Parole, March 19, 1965).

6. *Uniform Crime Reports—1968, op. cit.*

7. "Robbery in the Second District," *op. cit.*

8. *Ibid.*

9. Report of the Task Force on Individual Acts of Violence, *op. cit.*

10. "Profile of a Bank Robber." *op. cit.*

11. Pennsylvania Board of Probation and Parole, *op. cit.*

12. *Violence and the Role of the Gun, op. cit.*
    Newman's study was based on interviews with 31 youthful offenders, all of whom were between 19-22 years of age and were charged with violent crimes: murder, assault with a deadly weapon and armed robbery. Of the 31, more than 50% were armed robbers.

13. Gerald D. Wolcott, *A Typology of Armed Robbers,* Master of Arts Thesis, Sacramento State College, 1965.

THE FACTORS OF FIREARMS AND DRUGS

Role of Firearms

FBI Uniform Crime Reports show that, nationally, 60% of all robberies are committed with a weapon and that firearms are used in some 63% of these cases.[1] Bottoms' study of robberies in Chicago's Second District found that 57% of the robberies reported involved armed offenders, principally with a gun,[2] while Normandeau's data on Philadelphia robberies indicated the percentage of armed robberies to be around 50%.

In Kansas City, Missouri, an analysis of robberies during the first six months of 1969 indicated that guns were used in only 31% of the robberies studied, although this represented a 6% increase over the same period in 1968.[4] At the same time, a study limited to commercial robberies in Oakland, California, for a six-month period covering February 1, 1969, disclosed that guns were used in 73% of the robberies.[5]

As the above data indicates, firearms, principally hand guns, account for the great majority of all weapons employed in armed robberies. There is reason to believe that measures which could effectively limit the availability of firearms or otherwise deter persons from using a gun to commit a robbery would reduce significantly the number of armed robberies.

In a study on the role the gun plays in crime, prepared for the President's Commission on Violence, Dr. Donald Newman interviewed a number of convicted offenders charged with violent crimes. He reported that those who had engaged in robberies and had employed guns associated the gun with manliness. To them the gun represented the means to control others and to prove their manliness and worth by forcing others to do their will. For many of these, the most important element was not the actual acquisition of money, but the brief moment when the possession of the gun enabled them to force victims to follow their commands. It was this mastery over others, a desire to control, a sense of omnipotence—and not a desire to hurt—that appeared to characterize these persons. "For the most part the men involved in robbery were not very large and not very strong. Some were not very aggressive. The impression was that some of these men could not possibly carry out a robbery without a gun. In fact, the ready availability of the gun was the only reason there was a crime . . . the gun suggesting and encouraging the crime." [6]

The Role of Alcohol, Narcotics and Dangerous Drugs

The studies and data available on the role of alcohol, narcotics and dangerous drugs in the crime of robbery tend to be very inconclusive. Any attempt to delve more exhaustively into the problem is frustrated by the fact that in many of the studies into this aspect of the problem no distinction was made between the various drugs. Thus the opiates were not separated from the hallucinogens or other dangerous drugs— or even from alcohol.

In its study, the Violence Commission's Task Force on Individual Acts of Violence reported: "There is no direct causal connection between alcohol, drugs and narcotics and violence." [7] But, the report goes on to say, "while these substances can only modify behavior (they do not directly cause it), their involvement in acts of crime and violence— sometimes because of modifications of basic behavior patterns, sometimes for less direct reasons—cannot be overlooked." [8] With respect to the extent to which the chronic use of drugs and narcotics contribute to crime and violence, the Task Force noted that "the most important consideration is that an addict's need to support his habit often leads him to commit crime to secure funds for drugs." [9]

Hence, in cities with large concentrations of users, such as in New York City, significant numbers of crimes, particularly property crimes, were reported to be drug related. In this connection, a New York City study in 1967 revealed that "41% of those arrested for burglary were admitted users." Rates were similarly high for other property offenses.[10]

In his study, Dr. Newman reported that the vast majority of those interviewed "depended on drugs or alcohol prior to committing a crime, i.e., they could not rob, steal or involve themselves in gang fights without being under the influence of drugs and/or alcohol." [11] As to claims made that robberies were committed in order to support the addiction of the offender, Dr. Newman observed that his study indicated that the opposite was true, that the addiction appeared to support the crime. It was the character of the robbery itself and its psychological effect on the offender that made him turn to drugs. This observation seems to be contrary to the commonly held belief that addicts commit robbery to support their habit.

Another study of robbery offenders by Andre Normandeau found that alcohol was present either in the offender or victim or both, in less than 15% of the cases. Normandeau concluded that insofar as alcohol was concerned, it did not appear to be a triggering factor or to affect the "mean seriousness score" [12] (the amount of violence and related factors indicating the seriousness of the crime).

Wolcott, on the other hand, concluded that drugs and alcohol provided a stimulus or played a significant role in the case of 71% of offenders studied who committed spur-of-the-moment robberies. With respect to those who committed planned robberies, he found that 44% were under the influence of drugs or alcohol.[13]

A study of persons arrested and committed to the D.C. jail during the period of July-August 1969 disclosed that out of the 226 persons selected for the sample, 99 were found to be drug addicts, 15 of whom were being held on charges of robbery. (Fifty others had been arrested for property crimes other than robbery.) According to Nicholas Kozel, a Research Analyst at the D.C. Narcotic Treatment Agency, there is evidence that addicts are becoming increasingly involved in crimes against persons where there is financial gain, as in robbery. Kozel also noted that there was a great difference between the older and younger addicts in that the young addict was likely to be more aggressive and commit acts of violence.[14]

In an article describing the life and activities of lower-class heroin users in New York City, Edward Preble and John J. Casey, Jr., state: "One of the myths derived from the passivity stereotype of the heroin user is that the heroin user avoids crimes of violence, such as robbery, which involves personal confrontations. This no longer seems to be the case. A 1966 New York City Police Department study of the arrests of admitted narcotic (primarily heroin) addicts for selected felonies other than violations of the narcotic laws, showed that 15.1% of the arrests were for robbery. This compared with 12.9% robbery arrests of all arrests (addict and non-addict) during the same year . . . Among the addicts, 40.9% were burglary arrests, compared to 19.7% of all arrests; felonious assaults constituted 5.6% among the addicts, compared to 27.9% of all arrests.

"What these figures reveal is not that heroin users avoid crimes of violence as compared to non-addicts, but that they avoid crimes not involving financial gain . . . Where financial gain is involved, as in robbery, the risk of violence is taken by heroin users in a higher percentage of cases than with non-addicts. These statistics confirm the observations and opinions of street informants, both addict and non-addict."[15]

The above data and conclusions could be most significant and more research is needed to confirm the validity of these findings and to provide some reliable guidance as to the trend, dimensions and impact of this crime factor.

NOTES

1. *Uniform Crime Reports—1968, op. cit.*
2. "Robbery in the Second District," *op. cit.*
3. "Patterns in Robbery, *op. cit.*
4. Memorandum from Crime-Traffic Analysis Section, Kansas City (Missouri) Police Department, Six-Month Robbery Comparison, July 25, 1969.
5. Robert L. Marx, "A Preliminary Study of Commercial Robberies in Oakland, 1 February 1969-1 August 1969," Public Systems Incorporated, 30 October 1969.
6. *Violence and the Role of the Gun: Conversations with Protagonists,* by Dr. Donald E. Newman, Director, Psychiatric Services, Peninsula Hospital and Medical Center, Burlingame, California, a Draft Report prepared for the Commission on the Causes and Prevention of Violence.
7. With respect to the opiates, the Task Force report states: "While the public has all too frequently been shocked by general illicit drug use, the evidence to date demonstrates that opiate use does not lead to any compulsion to violence. When violence does occur in association with addiction, it must be viewed as related to personality, social and economic factors." *Crimes of Violence, op. cit.*
8. *Ibid.*
9. *Ibid.*
10. *Ibid.*
11. *Violence and the Role of the Gun, op. cit.*
12. "Patterns in Robbery," *op. cit.*
13. *A Typology of Armed Robbers, op. cit.*
14. Conversation with Nicholas Kozel, Research Analyst, District of Columbia Narcotics Treatment Agency and formerly with the D.C. Department of Corrections, May 1970.
15. Edward Preble and John J. Casey, Jr., "Taking Care of Business—The Heroin User's Life on the Street," *International Journal of the Addictions,* 4(1), pp. 1-14, March 1969.

THE MAFIA
AND THE WEB OF KINSHIP

Francis A. J. Ianni

One of the most extraordinary
sociological puzzles of the times is the contrasting conceptions about
the *Mafia* that have persisted for more than two decades, with seemingly no way of resolving almost diametrically divergent conclusions.
On the one hand there are criminologists such as Donald Cressey, a
consultant to a President's Task Force on Law Enforcement who
talk of "a nationwide alliance of at least 24 tightly knit *Mafia* 'families'
which control organized crime in the United States," the extent of
which is estimated "at $50 billion per year with $15 billion in profit."
On the other hand, there are writers, most recently Norval Morris
of the University of Chicago Law School and his colleague, a visiting
Australian criminologist, Gordon Hawkins who scoff at the evidence
and the figures and, while readily admitting the presence of Italian-
Americans in crime, are skeptical of the existence of a national crime
syndicate or cartel. Government officials over the years have talked
of the *Black Hand, The Unione Siciliana*, the *Mafia*, and, within the
last decade of *La Cosa Nostra*, though the latter name was never
used publicly before the disclosures of an Italian mobster, Joseph
Valachi.

William James once said that wherever there is a contradiction it is the result of the fact that the parties to the dispute have failed to make relevant distinctions. My own feeling is that the questions about the *Mafia* have been wrongly put. To look at the problem in terms of whether a "syndicate" or "corporate organization" exists is to miss the most salient cultural facts about Italian, particularly south Italian life, and thus to misperceive the nature of the ties which do exist among Italian gangsters and shape the modes of their activity. If organized crime here, as Daniel Bell once put it, is an "American Way of Life," then one must look at the *Mafia*, not as a specific kind of organization, but as an aspect of an "Italian Way of Life"—and then see if this perspective can illuminate the picture.

In 1967 Francesco Cerase of the Institute of Social Research in the University of Rome and I decided to do just that, and with financial support from the Russell Sage Foundation we began a comparative field study of criminal syndicates in the United States and Italy. Our interest was in looking at them as secret societies rather than merely criminal organizations, and in seeing if there is a common model—some system of order or code of rules—which describes social controls within all such groups. We saw our task as the formulation of the system of implicit rules shared by the members of Italo-American criminal syndicates by examining how those members apply these rules. The central question of our research was: What is the code of rules that makes a criminal syndicate a social system and how do its members play the game?

For the last three years we have been observing and recording patterns of behavior and social relationship in several organized crime "families" in New York and we have attempted to identify the cultural patterns—both Italian and American—which underlie and activate this ordering of behavior.

Government studies invariably point to some organizational link between the Sicilian *Mafia* and Italo-American crime syndicates. But anyone searching out the origins of Italo-American criminal syndicates in Sicily and its *Mafia* finds problems on both sides of the Atlantic. In the first place, by no means all of the reputed *Mafia* members are Sicilians. Many, like Vito Genovese came from in and around Naples; some like Frank Costello, are from Calabria. But, significantly, all *are* from the south of Italy. The second problem is that while the Sicilian *Mafia* is well-known to Americans, each of the other two southern provinces—Calabria and the Campagnia

(Naples and its environs)—also produced its own distinctive secret criminal society and there is no evidence of any organizational linkage among the three. These two facts, long known but largely ignored in studying the role of Italo-Americans in organized crime, are of fundamental importance when they are considered together and they are a basis for our answer to the question whether or not there is a *Mafia* in the United States.

The logic of our answer proceeds from field work in Italy which convinced us that *Mafia* is more than just a criminal organization; it is a generic form of social organization which developed in the south of Italy under particular social and cultural conditions. The *Mafia* is a social system in which power is distributed through a network of clan-like gangs which operate parallel to the law and which are held together by real and artificial kinship bonds. In order to deal with the problem of "the *Mafia*," one must turn first to southern Italy, and then consider whether or not the *Mafia*, or some variant of it, was transplanted in the United States.

II

There are, as almost everyone knows, two Italies—the urbane and economically-advanced north and the rural, still semi-feudal south. The northern Italian is a European; the spirit of capitalism and the acquisition of wealth motivate him as single-mindedly as they do the Swiss or the German. The southern Italian is a Mediterranean. The acquisition of material goods are secondary to him; the power to influence people—to command obedience and respect—are his primary concern. These differences are not superficial; they mold the behavior of the child; they shape all social relations. While beginning to change, these desires are still obvious in the three imperatives which shape southern Italian culture—the primacy of the family, the juxtaposition of church and state, and the ascendency of personal honor over statutory law. And these explain why the *Mafia* and other secret societies developed in the south.

Italy is a nation of families, not of individuals. In the south, especially, the family *is* the social structure and no social institution —not the state or even the church—has ever successfully challenged its supremacy. The family demands the southern Italian's first loyalty and within it he practices all of the virtues and self sacrifice which other men save for their church or state. The pattern of roles within the southern Italian family is recognizable from the model of the divine family in Catholicism. The authoritarian father is a patriarch who demands and commands immediate obedience. The true *pater-familius*, he represents the family's power and status in the community. The mother is subservient to the father and her humility, and willingness to bear all burdens enshrine the honor of the family and win the respect of her children. Daughters, like mothers, are humble, and their chastity is a matter of great moment to the family; in Italy wars have been waged over a daughter's honor. The son is obedient to his father and respects his mother. This pattern of relationship extends beyond the biological family by *comparaggio*—the practice of establishing fictive kinship with *compare* (godfathers) and *comare* (godmothers). Godparent-godchild relationships have far more potency in southern Italy than do the ceremonial godparent relationship we know in America.

Neither church nor state has ever been strong enough to challenge the family. The southern Italian treats government at any level with skepticism. He surrenders everything to the family but nothing to the state. And even those who are deeply religious do not really trust the church as an institution. In Italy, the church has always been an independent temporal power as well as a religious institution and this face of the church is distrusted just as much as any other government. It is this juxtaposition of church and state—a unified church to which all Italians belong and a weakly united state that few Italians serve—which has kept any strong political or religious authority structure from forming.

In southern Italy the rule of law is replaced by a familial social order which is regulated "invisibly." This social order is internalized in a code which exhorts each man, regardless of his age or rank, to protect the family's honor and to avenge any breech of that honor. The code is an integrative behavioral system which binds families to each other throughout each village and town in a ritualistic web difficult for the southern Italian to escape but just as difficult for the non-Italian to understand.

These major themes shape the culture of the south of Italy—a strong family, a weak political structure and a sense of honor which takes precedence over the law. Not only do they distinguish the southern Italian from his northern countrymen, they also explain how and why secret criminal societies formed in the south but not the north.

While the Sicilian *Mafia* is the best known of the Italian criminal societies (the Italians call them "delinquential" because not all of their activities are strictly criminal) the south of Italy has produced others as well. Throughout the south, the oppression by alien governments which preceded unification and the weakness of the central government which followed it, produced many bands of brigands whose aim ranged from profit-making to blood-revenge and even to reformist social justice. These social bandits—as Hobsbawm has described them—do not qualify as criminal secret societies in the *Mafia* sense because with few exceptions, they were *ad hoc* groups, with no past and a doubtful future. But they spring from the same cultural sources that produced the *Mafia* and other criminal secret societies, and in many ways they are ancestral to them.

In Calabria, the mountainous and remote province at the southernmost tip of mainland Italy, for example, an organization somewhere between social banditry and a criminal secret society seems to have existed almost unknown to the outside world (including the rest of Italy) for at least a century. Known colloquially as *'ndranghita* ("brotherhood" in Calabrian dialect), it is also called the *Onorata Società* (Honored Society). Although brigandage and smuggling were its primary functions, it became a powerful source of local, political and social control at the turn of the century. (The advent of fascism destroyed its political power.)

While the *Onorata Società* developed in the isolated mountain villages and then spread to the capital city of Reggio Calabria, another criminal secret society, the *Camorra*, was born in the city of Naples and then spread out to the villages and towns surrounding it. When the Camorra first became known in 1820 it was found only in the prisons of Naples where it had developed to the point that the control of the prisons was as much in the hands of *Camorristi* as it was of their Bourbon warders. Its influence spread outside the prisons, first into the city of Naples and eventually throughout the surrounding countryside. Discharged criminals formed the nuclei of the external *Camorra* gangs and for the next forty years, bands of *Camorristi* organized for robbery, blackmail, kidnapping and smuggling. Today, particularly in Naples, but elsewhere in the region as well, there are gangs and gangsters who smuggle cigarettes and gasoline (or, more frequently, expropriate them from NATO bases), extort money and operate the full range of familiar rackets. They are known to Italians as *Camorristi* or sometimes *"magliari"* (sledge hammers) but they retain little more than the aura of the old *Camorra*. The real *Camorra* required a weak government and social disorganization to flourish and, therefore, did not survive the first decade of fascism in Italy. If nothing else, Mussolini did bring strong, authoritarian government to Naples forcing the *Camorra* to go underground where it seems to have died.

The most famous of the secret societies in the south of Italy, the Sicilian *Mafia*, survived fascism. But what is alive and well are matters for conjecture. *Mafia* is a word which has at least two distinct meanings to Sicilians. When used as an adjective, it describes a state of mind and a style of behavior that Sicilians recognize immediately. It is bravura but not braggadocio. It bespeaks the man who is known and respected because of his contacts and ability to get things done. It suggests that he is unwilling to allow the merest hint of an insult or slight to go unanswered and it insinuates that he has means at his disposal to see that it doesn't. He is a "man of respect" who has "friends." In Palermo, even the style of dress, with the hat cocked to one side, the walk which we would call a self-assured strut, the manner of speech and the general air of self-reliance can mark a man as *mafioso* (the Sicilians actually say *mafiusu*). Such a man may or may not be a member of a formal organization in which he has a clearly defined role. Yet even in Sicily, the word *Mafia* also clearly denotes just such an organization when it is used as a noun.

Italians are trained from childhood to understand that things are not always what they seem. This use of double meaning has been a source of misunderstanding for years. The Italian scholar or journalist says "*mafia* is an attitude, not an organization." To the American this means that he is saying "there is no *Mafia*." He is saying nothing of the kind. He is suggesting that *mafia* as a pattern in Sicilian life exists regardless of the persistence of the *Mafia* as an organization, and that the organization would be impossible without the ethic. The distinction is subtle, but real. To the Sicilian it is impossible to separate the lower case state of *mafia* from the upper case powerful secret organization, *Mafia*. Both are part of the culture of Sicily which he learns from childhood.

The spirit of *mafia* derives from the fact that every man seeks protection for himself and his family. He cannot get this from the state, but only from a network of protection to which he finds himself bound. This network of friendship is a pattern of social obligation that has more permanence than religion and more legitimacy than law. Friendship becomes part of kinship. Each man and every family know what they owe to others and what is due from them. Favors become obligations and wrongs debts which demand redress; *"Si moru mi voricu; si campu t'allampu"* (If you kill me they will bury me; if I live, I will kill you). The spirit of *mafia* persists because it is born of this network and it is in turn the progenitor of the secret organization, *Mafia*.

In many ways, the term *organization* does not fit the Sicilian *Mafia*. European students of Mafia agree that there is no highly-centralized organization called the *Mafia* in Sicily (or anyplace else say the Italians); *Mafia* is a form of control over a particular community's life by a secret—or at least officially unrecognized, because everyone in the village knows who is involved—system of local groups. There is today an urban *Mafia* in Palermo that the Palermitani claim was brought back to Palermo by American gangsters who were deported to Sicily. But the true *Mafia* is overwhelmingly rural in origin and territory.

There is still a *Mafia* in western Sicily today but no one there calls it that. There, like its counterpart in Calabria, it has always been called the *Onorata Società*. It is also known by other names such as *la santa mamma* (the Holy Mother), or increasingly today, *gli uomini qualificati* (qualified men or specialists). Members do not call themselves *Mafiosi* and no one else calls them that. They are known simply as *gli amici*, the friends, or *gli amici degli amici*, the friends of friends.

Despite their secrecy we know enough about these societies to make a few generalizations about them as a form of social organization. First, *mafia* as a cultural model is not unique to Sicily although, like the southern Italian culture which produced it, it is most visible there. The Neopolitan *Camorra* and the Calabrian *Onorata Società*, though they differ from Sicilian *Mafia* in some features, are obviously of the same genus.

Mafia in the sense just described is more than a secret society. It is, as the Italians insist, a particular and peculiar state of mind. It is a basic form of social organization developed in the south of Italy to control or negotiate social conflict where there is a weak or absent state. The *Mafioso* operates as a middle man in a vacuum of political values, structures and organizations. He is a broker—although not always an honest one—who operates as a network builder and monitor between and among elements in an unstable system. To the *Mafioso* and his clients, this seems to be the natural order of things. Given the weakness of the state and the insecurity of the poor living under it, he offers protection but also a form of representation to the populace who have no other means of negotiating with the power structure. The base of *Mafia* power is the personal relationship, for the *Mafioso* reduces every social relationship to a personal level, a level in which he can feel and perform in a manner superior to other men. Because he has "friends"—he is more of a man than others. Where justice is powerless, says the *Mafioso*, there the injured must have recourse to his own strength and that of his friends. When the state does become strong or authoritarian—as in fascism—the *Mafia* begins to fall apart. After the Allied Occupation it reappeared in western Sicily.

Just as there are many local *mafie* in Sicily rather than a unified central *Mafia*, so they serve many functions. It is involved in criminal activities and oppression but it is also an integrative system. It does serve as a means of social control, a mechanism for the management of social conflict (admitting that it generates some of the conflict itself) and for the provision of services to a community that would otherwise remain unserved.

The old world *Mafia*, thus, is an outgrowth of a rudimentary ideology and system or organizing society institutionalized in the culture of the south of Italy and particularly in Sicily for the management of specific forms of social conflict. It seems fair to assume that anywhere and everywhere southern Italians are found in large enough numbers to sustain the culture, the strength of this ideology and the cultural imperatives that produced it would lead them to respond to similar social conflict and disorganization by importing or resurrecting the *Mafia*.

III

In the decade from 1900 to 1910, a total of 2,104,000 Italians emigrated to the United States. Eighty per cent of them came from southern Italy and Sicily; most of these settled in eastern cities in self-contained "Little Italies" where each tenement re-established the old village square. The Italians succeeded in bringing their villages with them and that village culture—not any new Italo-American or even any emergent pan-Italian culture—set the standards for their beliefs and behavior. All of the facets of that village culture—the primacy of ties to kinfolk, the spell of religion and superstition and the disdain for extra-familial foreign laws—came with them and settled in the same urban villages. One question, of course, is this: Did *mafia* also come with them and is it also a part of what they have retained?

It is deceptively simple to answer this question with a well-documented "no." The Sicilian *Mafia*—or, for that matter, the Neopolitan *Camorra* or Calabrian *Onorata Società*—could not and did not migrate as organizations to the United States. It took hundreds of years for *mafia* to develop within the cultural values of the south of Italy and just as long for the behavior associated with it to be operationalized in viable organizations. Despite strong cultural affinity, the Sicilian *Mafia*, for example, found the eastern end of Sicily inhospitable and so remained in the west. Why should it attempt to cross the ocean?

The conditions of the Italian migration to the United States also underwrite a negative answer to this question. It must be remembered that this was a proletarian emigration and was considered often a temporary move by most of the emigrants. At the time of the migration, *all* of the heads of the local *Mafie* in Sicily were men of some wealth, considerable power and prestige and hard-earned status. There was no reason for them to leave the island until Mussolini and his police prefect Cesare Mori began arresting and killing suspected *Mafiosi* in the 1920's. All of this is not to say that some few individual *Mafiosi* or *camorristi* did not come over as part of the emigration. Whole villages moved to America virtually *en masse* and minor *Mafiosi* and *Camorristi* probably were present among them, but they were few in number and almost certainly did not represent any potential leadership or they would have remained in Italy. What is more important is that they, like the vast majority of southern Italian immigrants, came as individuals and probably not to stay. The possibility that they were an advance party sent ahead to seek new territory and colonize is patently absurd to anyone who comprehends *Mafia*. The local *Mafie* were rooted in sentiment and power to the local community; neither was there any central organization or grand council that could make such a decision on a wider than local level.

Having set aside the contention that the *Mafia* or *Camorra* set up branch offices in the new world, it would be comforting as well as plausible to fall back on our distinction between *Mafia* and *mafia* and say that what the migrants did bring was some primaeval cultural sense of *mafia* with them which they used as a model for organizing crime. They did, and it has served them well, but that cultural model alone did not produce present-day Italo-American criminal syndicates. The emergence of Italo-Americans in a dominant role in organized crime is a post-1930 phenomenon. The strict diffusionist approach that sees only *Mafia* in Italo-American crime syndicates must therefore assume that the concept of *mafia* lay dormant among southern Italian immigrants for decades and then suddenly emerged as a model to organize Italo-American involvement in crime. Further, it must assume nothing was happening in the acculturative experience of Italo-Americans that allowed them to find better and already proven models in the native American setting. These assumptions do not bear up under analysis.

However potent the *mafia* model was in southern Italian culture, it had to be Americanized to be successful here. The social history of the Italo-Americans in the first thirty years of the century indicates the importance of southern Italian culture to the development of Italo-American criminal syndicates. However, social and economic conditions here were even more important.

IV

A number of social scientists have analyzed the relationships among ethnicity, organized crime and politics in American life. Daniel Bell describes the transfer in crime of one succession of European immigrants to another as the "queer ladder of social mobility;" in coming out of the slums, organized crime is one of the first few rungs. The Irish came first and early Irish gangsters started the climb up the ladder. As they came to control the political machinery of the large cities, the Irish won wealth, power and respectability through consequent control of construction, trucking, public utilities and the waterfront. The Irish were succeeded in organized crime by Jews and the names of Arnold Rothstein, Louis "Lepke" Buchalter and Jacob "Gurrah" Shapiro dominated gambling and labor rack-

eteering for a decade. The Italians came last and did not get a
commanding leg-up on the ladder until the late 1930's. They were
just beginning to find politics and business as routes out of crime
and the ghetto into wealth and respectability in the 1950's when
the Kefauver hearings took place. Since then, the assumption seems
to be that when they advance into business and politics, Italo-
Americans somehow take the *Mafia* with them. Unlike the Jews and
Irish before them, their movement into legitimate business and politics has not won them respectability. Instead, their presence indicates corruption and signals an attempt to "take over" control for
illicit purposes.

In the early days of the Italian ghettos the crimes reported in the
press were, in fact, *Italian* crimes. They were committed by Italians
against other Italians. They were the traditional crimes of the *Mafia*
and *Camorra*. And they were crimes which the Italians brought with
them—extortion through threats of death and bodily harm, vendettas
or blood feuds particularly between Neopolitans and Sicilians and
kidnapping of brides. Almost as soon as they arrived, the Italians
brought public notice to crime in the ghetto through the *Black Hand*
a series of threats, murders, maimings and bombings as a means of
extorting money from fellow immigrants. *Black Hand* activities,
however, were unorganized; they were the work of individual extor-
tionists or small gangs and there is no evidence which suggests that
there was any higher level or organization or any tie with the *Mafia*
in Sicily or *Camorra* in Naples. Without the protective network of
family and kindred, the immigrant was easy prey to anyone who
appreciated his vulnerability and individual entrepreneurs or small
gangs could operate freely in the police-less colonies. It is interesting
that in the dozens of *Black Hand* letters we have seen, never once is
there an explicit or implied threat that the *Mafia* or *Camorra* was in
any way involved. What seems clear from all of the evidence is that
the *Black Hand*, which lasted about 15 years (from the turn of the
century to the first World War) was a cultural but not an organizational offshoot of *Mafia* and was completely Italian in origin and
character.

It was the immigrants themselves who finally did away with the
Black Hand. As was true in the earlier frontiers of the westward
expansion, the lack of established patterns of social control and sanctioned codes of behavior provided an environment of "lawlessness"

where conflict and violence were always just below the surface. Within the ghettoes, protection against crimes was left almost entirely to the immigrants as a result of that characteristically American attitude toward minority group crime which stands aloof so long as they keep it among themselves. Faced with an absentee government, the immigrants did just as they had done in Italy and just what a previous generation of American frontiersmen had done for the west. A rough and ready system of internal policing developed along with a set of "courts" which arbitrated disputes and meted out justice to wrong-doers. In Italy the custom had been to go to a "man of respect"—a leader in the *Mafia* or *Camorra*—for redress of ills and protection from the vagaries of peasant life; in the Italian-American ghetto it was the same and the informal courts held continue in diminished power even today. As recently as 1967, Mayor Lindsay of New York City found it expedient to call on members of an Italo-American criminal syndicate to "cool off" intergroup hostility between Italo-American and black gangs in Brooklyn. And they did it.

While the immigrants policed the ghetto, their sons guarded its boundaries. Just as the Irish and the Jews had done before them, they formed into street-corner gangs to escape overcrowded homes and to seek compatible peer-group relationships. One important function of these gangs was to protect the turf within the colonies from marauding bands from outside. The bonds formed in these street gangs marked the first extra-familial socialization for Italian youngsters and they have persisted into adulthood.

There seems little question that all of the social conditions and the cultural imperatives that led to the formation of the *Mafia* and other secret criminal societies in the south of Italy did, in fact, exist in the American Little Italies by 1920. As we have seen, the immigrants brought the cultural imperatives through which fathers commanded and mothers were treated with respect. The social conflict produced by harsh and impoverished living conditions, exploitation by employers, lack of access to routes of social mobility, the remoteness of governmental authority, all of which had plagued them in Italy, were present in the ghettoes as well. Yet no Mafia-type organization developed prior to 1920 because two critical elements were missing. It had taken the *Mafia* and *Camorra* hundreds of years to develop in the friendly soil of southern Italian culture; twenty years was just not time enough for a new organization to take root in the United States.

Neither was there the established pattern of relationships—the social system of *mafia*—because the migrants had come as individuals and, despite the affinities of co-villagers in the tenements, new links, new patterns of authority and new sources for power and profit had to be established. These same cultural and linguistic difficulties made it impossible for any emergent Mafia to operate outside the colony in these early years. As the son of a Sicilian immigrant who was a well-known *Black Hander* in New York's Lower East Side Italian colony in the early 1900's explained to us:

> Can you imagine my father going up-town to commit a robbery or a mugging? He would have had to take an interpreter with him to read the street signs and say "stick 'em up" for him.

After 1920, however, two developments in this country and one in Italy changed all this. In the United States the immigrant's children were becoming Americans. Italo-Americans have managed to cling to their familialism more tenaciously than any other ethnic group, but culture contrast continues to loosen the grip for each succeeding generation. Educated in American schools where individualism, not family loyalty, was the basic lesson, they formed new friendships in the street gangs. These new alliances crossed the old village and provincial lines and in some cases even reached out into other ethnic groups. Then national Prohibition provided a new source for illicit profits and so a new and accelerated route to riches for both immigrant and second-generation Italo-American. This new market provided the source for power and profit which allowed an American Mafia to form in the ghettoes. Soon after Prohibition, small sweatshop stills were set up within the Italian colonies to distill the alcohol essential to producing liquor. Italians had traditionally produced their own wine and this "illegality" had been ignored by the American authorities before Prohibition. Converting home wineries to home stills was not difficult and the immigrant alcohol cooker could produce enough for himself and, if he was so inclined, enough to sell to friends and neighbors. Some of the home distilleries became large enough to make significant profits and the alcohol produced in these larger stills, combined with that collected from smaller stills, became an important source for the producers of illegal whiskey.

While the immigrants could produce and even organize collectives for illegal alcohol, they were unable to move out of the colonies to engage in the actual distribution process. Not so their sons who, through membership in street gangs, were being initiated into the world of the gangster. It is important to note that while the flamboyance of Al Capone has given an Italian characterization to the popular stereotype of Prohibition era gangster, Italo-Americans by no means dominated the rival bootleg gangs. The names of O'Bannion, Moran and O'Donnell, and of Buchalter, Kastel, Lansky, Siegal, Weiss, and Zwillman were far more important if less notorious than those of Aiello, Capone, or Torrio. Italo-Americans more often filled lower echelon, enforcer-type roles than leadership positions in gangs, although some individuals, like Capone, did rise to prominence. The role-model.ideal for these aspiring underlings was not the old-country oriented *Mafioso* or *Camorrista* who were contemptuously called "greenhorns," "greasers," "handlebars" or "Moustache Petes," but the more sophisticated Irish and Jewish mobsters who had mastered the secrets of business organization. While the profits from bootlegging afforded the second-generation growth in the demi-world of organized crime gangs, they also produced important developments among the immigrants in the ghettos. Since the immigrants could not handle large scale distribution themselves, an informal alliance developed between immigrant and second-generation Italians and between the second-generation and non-Italian gangsters, particularly the Jews. Then, after Mussolini's brief honeymoon with the Sicilian *Mafia* ended in the mid-1920's Sicilian *Mafiosi* found their kinsmen in the United States a safe haven and a number of them did come reinforcing the Sicilian culture base among the immigrant bootleggers. By the mid-1920's all of the ingredients necessary for the formation of a new Italo-American *Mafia* were available in the ghettos and it remained only to mix them in the proper proportion within these protective walls. Just such an organization does seem to have developed.

V

The name most frequently associated with this emergent Italo-American *Mafia* is the *Unione Siciliana*. While the *Unione* is often cited in government reports, the origin of the name and the structure of the organization are lost in the nether world of law enforcement informants. In our own field work we often hear reference to it. One of our respondents, for example, a Sicilian-American involved in boot-legging activities in Brooklyn throughout the Prohibition era, told us:

> . . . at that time (1928) all the old Sicilian "moustaches" used to get together in the backrooms of the club—it was a *fratellanza* (brother-hood) and they used to call it the *Unione*. They spent a lot of time talking about the old country, drinking wine and playing cards. But these were tough guys too, and they owned the alky cookers and pretty much ran things in the neighborhood. They had all of the businesses in Red Hook locked up and they got a piece of everything that was sold. If some guy didn't pay up they leaned on him. Everybody paid them respect and if some guy caused trouble in the neighborhood they called him into the club and straightened him out.

The *Unione Siciliana* was an informal confederation of local groups of Sicilian-Americans involved in extortion and protection in the Little Italies and in bootlegging activities particularly in organizing the cottage-industry home-distillers in the ghettos. By the late 1920's this organization had all of the cultural and organizational features of a new *Mafia* in the United States. Like the *Mafia* in Sicily, it served the Little Italies as a means of social control, a mechanism for the management of social conflict (and again like the Sicilian *Mafia*, generated some of the conflict itself) and as a source for illegal services to a public which would otherwise remain unserved. Its link with the outside world was through the American-born or American-raised second-generation. The colonies could offer a culturally sup-portive base for the new *Mafia* but not the production-supportive substructure necessary to nurture the new social system.

By the end of the 1920's, however, the stage had been set for the inevitable clash between the immigrants of the *fratellanza* or *Mafia*-model *Unione* and the aspiring and rising second-generation Italo-American gangsters who were now moving into leadership roles in gangland. Once again changes in the general society intervened and hurried organizational change in crime. First the Great Depression and then the inevitability of the repeal of Prohibition forecast the end of an era of prosperity where there was enough illicit profit for every-body. With the end of Prohibition it became necessary to find new areas for exploitation to continue the flow of dollars. Some areas such as gambling and labor racketeering were reprehensible to the now-old "Moustache Petes" who saw such activity as unworthy of a man of respect. Other, less noble conflicts of interest and influence were also involved as various groups struggled in the inevitable quest for power. It was this conflict between the old *Mafia*-oriented *Unione* and the new American gang-oriented Italo-American syndicates which seems to have brought the situation to a head and destroyed the *Unione*.

The drama began in 1930 when Giuseppe Masseria, a Neopolitan prominent in the gang world of New York, issued orders to exterminate a number of Sicilian "old Moustaches" whose association was with the Mafia-like *fratellanza* groups. There had been continuing speculation as to the reason. Some say it was a conflict over future areas for exploitation, others that he was simply hungry for greater power. The move touched off a war in New York that eventually spread throughout the country. With Masseria were those non-Sicilian, Italo-Americans such as Vito Genovese, Joe Adonis and Frank Costello whose alliances with non-Italian (principally Jewish) mobsters had been forged in the world of the gangs. Opposed to Masseria were the old-time Sicilian-American leaders who had risen to prominence in the *Unione* many of whom had come from or around the small town of Castellammare del Golfo on the Western coast of Sicily. The Castellammare, including Joseph Bonnano, and other Sicilians such as Joseph Profaci and Gaetano Gagliano gathered behind Salvatore Maranzano and each group launched attacks on the other.

The war raged throughout 1930 and the "old moustaches," particularly the Castellammare, were the most frequent victims. In one forty-eight hour period close to 40 of the old Sicilian leaders were killed in a purge that rivalled the "night of the long knives" in Nazi Germany. Despite his victories in these battles, Masseria lost the war and sued for peace, but Maranzano refused to come to terms. Masseria retreated to a heavily armed fortress in New York determined to hole up and hold out. His followers, however, seemed unwilling to go with him and five of his lieutenants—Genovese, Luciano, Livorsi, Straci and Terranova—surrendered to Maranzano and on April 20, 1930 the Castellammarese War came to an end as three of them executed Masseria in a Coney Island restaurant as they ate dinner together. Maranzano was assassinated by his own lieutenants on September 11, 1931.

Whatever else it was or did, the Castellammarese War brought the short melancholy life of the Italo-American *Mafia* to an end. The old "Moustache Petes," the custodians of the *mafia* tradition were either killed off or passed in obscurity. The younger immigrants and the second-and-succeeding-generations saw in the urban gangster, not the *Mafioso*, an American role-model filled with the excitement and promise their parents' nostalgic associations with social banditry of the *Mafia* and *Camorra* could no longer provide. They formed gangs of their own in the new form of urban criminal syndicates not the old rural brotherhoods. The new syndicates did not follow provincial lines, and working relationships with non-Italians, particularly Jews were established.

After 1930 the Italo-Americans succeeded the Jews as the major ethnic group in the ranks of organized crime. At about the same time that they reached prominence in organized crime, they also began to gain some political power in major cities particularly in the Middle Atlantic and northeast States which had been the settlement areas for a vast majority of southern Italian immigrants. Now, the new judges, the new lawyers and prosecutors, councilmen and even police had grown up in the Little Italies along with the new leadership in organized crime. They had lived together as children and strong bonds had been established; still they kept the associations through friendship and marriage. Alliances of power, friendships and kin relationship all merged and today this presents a difficult if not impossible job of sorting out those which are corrupt or corrupting from those which merely express the strength of kinship relations among southern Italians and their descendants. Yet there is no question that family structure forms the basic network which ties Italo-Americans together in organized crime and that kinship is the pivot for that integration. The Mafia-model *Unione* was a peculiarly southern Italian institution which could not and did not survive long in the new world. The acculturation process works in crime as elsewhere and the values which activated and informed the old *Mafia* model were no longer prized. But, for Italians at least, blood really is thicker than water and while the organizational form of *Mafia* disappeared, it has left a heritage of kinship which still integrates crime families and characterizes the involvement of Italo-Americans in organized crime.

VI

Since the hearings of the Kefauver Committee two decades ago, and increasingly since the report of the 1967 Task Force on Organized Crime of the President's Commission on Law Enforcement and Administration of Justice, government law enforcement agencies and their consultants have insisted that Italo-Americans in organized crime have, in fact, created a national organization.

La Cosa Nostra is the name government sources currently assign to this confederation of Italo-American criminals that they trace back through the *Unione* to the Sicilian *Mafia*. Whether the name is an invention by Joe Valachi or whether it is simply a term commonly used by members of Italo-American criminal syndicates to identify business activities of common interest it is not the name of a formal organization. The model which the Task Force report uses for the *Mafia* is a parody of the American corporate model. Leaving aside, for a moment, its international connections, *Cosa Nostra* seems not much different from the Bell Telephone System. Like Bell, it is described as a "nation-wide . . . cartel . . . dedicated to amassing millions of dollars' through the provision of services to the public. Unlike the Bell System, however, the services of *Cosa Nostra* are described as "illicit" and its ultimate aim is the corruption of "the basic economic and political traditions and institutions" of the country. Again like the Bell System, this national cartel is a confederation of local syndicates or "companies" which function with some independence at the local level but are subject to corporate policy decisions by a "national commission" which, structurally, at least, sounds like a board of directors. Just as "Ma" Bell rules over a family of local companies all of which provide the same service to their communities, so *Cosa Nostra* is made up of local units differentiated only by territoriality for each can "participate in the full range of activities (of) organized crime." Like any large corporation, this organization continues to function regardless of personnel changes because *Cosa Nostra's* local organizations are "rationally designed with an integrated set of positions geared to maximize profits." The descriptions of the local units or "families" continue the analogy in terms of positions, functions and authority structure. The position of *caporegima*, in the *Cosa Nostra,* for example, "is analogous to plant supervisor or sales manager" in a business organization and the *sottocapo* or "underboss" is "the vice-president" or "deputy." And like the Bell System, *Cosa Nostra* maintains contacts with its counterparts overseas. What this describes, of course, is the rational, deliberately designed *formal* organization constructed to achieve a set of specified goals. It sees "organization" as a chart describing positions, a hierarchy of jobs to be filled and carried out and as a blueprint which can be used to construct and reconstruct organizations everywhere.

Yet Italo-American crime "families" are *not* organizations in this sense at all. They are not rationally designed and consciously constructed; nor are they hierarchies of organizational positions which can be diagrammed or changed by merely redrawing the chart.

There is *no* formal organization or confederation of Italo-Americans in organized crime called *Mafia, Cosa Nostra* or anything else. There are numbers of Italo-Americans who are involved in organized crime, they do form highly organized local syndicates (or "families") and the families do cooperate with each other in licit and illicit activities. But they are not held together by a national membership organization with a ruling council or even some shared conspiracy in crime. They are joined by the looser form of obligations and protections of the south Italian system of family and kinship.

Italo-American criminal syndicates are rightly called "families" because the relationships established within them produce kinship-like ties among members, ties which are given greater power when they are legitimated through marriage or godparenthood. Every "family" member knows that every other member has some duties toward him and some claim on him. Whether the relationships are based on blood or marriage as they often are, or are fictive as in the intricate pattern of ritual alliances through godparenthood, it is also kinship which ties generations together and allies lineages and "families."

Membership in a "family" is not like membership in a gang or an organization. A member does not receive a salary. He is usually engaged in his own activities. Members of families may even be competitive with each other. Nor does a member of a family necessarily give a share of his earnings to the head of the family. The closest model is a feudal one wherein a member swears fealty, receives protection and provides his services to protect others when it is asked.

It is this feature which sets Italo-American crime "families" off from the gangs in organized crime of previous ethnic groups. Every government report, after the *de rigeur* disclaimer that "of course, the vast majority of Italians in this country are god-fearing and hard-working" goes on to marvel at how tightly knit Italo-American crime families are and how closely structured the network among "families." The most frequently used term is "clannishness." One report describes this clannishness as "the cement that helps to bind the Costello-Adonis-Lansky Syndicate;" another comments that among Italo-American crime families, "a certain clannishness contributed to the retention of the custom of clannishness." Once again, the term is apt because, if one sets aside the literal view that clans are descent groups from a real or imagined common ancestor and takes the common sense view that they are alliances of lineages, then Italo-American criminal "families" are very much like clans.

While they do not maintain a fiction of descent from a common ancestor, Italo-American crime "families" are actually a number of lineages linked together into a composite clan. Like clans everywhere, these crime "families" enter into exchange relations with each other and form alliances which, once formed, are perpetuated. Like clansmen everywhere, members treat each other as agnatic brothers and acknowledge mutual rights and obligations on a kinship pattern however remote they may be genealogically. Each clan has its own territory. Some clans grow too large to maintain the kinship-like bond and divide, sometimes splitting through internal dissention, sometimes sending off segments to new clan-territories. Some clans decline and die out or lose their territory in warfare. The clan, because of its kinship base and its territoriality, can establish and maintain its own rigid code of familial law and pass authority from one generation to another.

For over three years now, we have been looking at kinship relationships in Italo-American crime "families" in various parts of the country. The findings clearly indicate the role of kinship in integrating individual "families" and in creating alliances among them which perpetuate power. In the New York-based Italo-American "family" which we have most closely examined, every one of the 15 members in leadership positions is related by blood or marriage and frequently by godparenthood as well. Data we have gathered on "families" in other parts of the country show the same kinship-based organization. The chart below, for example, traces relationships among the 20 leading "syndicate" families in a major mid-western city. Not only are *all* 20 families intermarried, they have also formed alliances through marriage with crime families in Buffalo, New York City and New Orleans.

What the chart cannot show, however, is how intricately woven

MARRIAGE AND KINSHIP LINES AMONG 20 FAMILIES IN A MIDWESTERN CITY

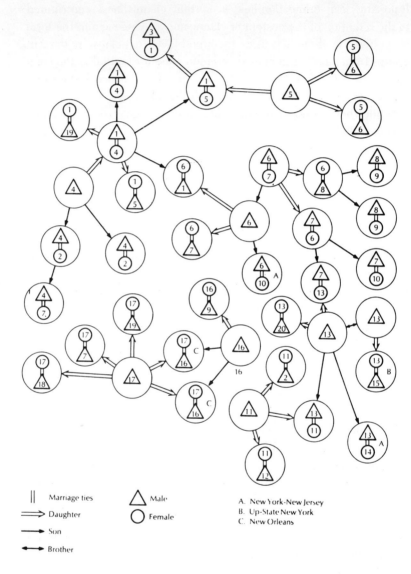

|| Marriage ties   △ Male   A. New York-New Jersey
⟹ Daughter   ◯ Female   B. Up-State New York
⟶ Son   C. New Orleans
◆⟶ Brother

1. Licavoli	6. Zerilli	11. Perrone	16. Matranga
2. Orlando	7. Tocco	12. Renda	17. Priziola
3. Abate	8. Corrado	13. Meli	18. Polizzi
4. Moceri	9. Vitale	14. Livorsi	19. Cammarata
5. Bommarito	10. Profaci	15. Butalino	20. Lucido

this web of kinship is and how it ties "families" in various parts of the country together. Consider just one alliance, that between the Tocco and Zerilli lineages. William Tocco married Rosalie Zerilli who is the sister of Joseph Zerilli. Joseph Zerilli's daughter Rosalie is married to Dominic Licavoli. Dominic Licavoli's brother Pete married Grace Bommarito. William Tocco and Rosalie Zerilli's son Anthony is married to Carmela Profaci, daughter of Joseph Profaci who was a "boss" of a "family" in New York City. Carmela Profaci's cousin is married to the son of Joseph Bonanno, a now-deposed former "boss" of another New York family. Profaci's other daughter Rosalie married the son of Joseph Zerilli. (Remember that Joseph Zerilli is the brother of Rosalie Zerilli who is married to William Tocco.) Willam and Rosalie Tocco's son Jack Tocco married Antoinette Meli who is the daughter of Angelo Meli. Antoinette's brother Salvatore Meli married Dolores Livorsi, the daughter of Frank Livorsi, who is a functionary in another New York area "family." Dolores' sister Rose is married to Tom Dio, a member of a New York family involved in labor racketeering. Jack Tocco's wife's (Antoinette Meli) cousin Marie is married to William Bufalino, a leading member of an up-state New York "family." Jack Tocco's wife's brother Vincent Meli married Pauline Perrone, daughter of Santo Perrone. Pauline's sister is married to Augostino Orlando; her other sister, Mary Perrone is married to Carl Renda. This network of alliances intersects with several others which reach into "families" all over the country and is strengthened by an equally complex pattern of godparent-godchild relationships.

This same basic pattern of kinship organization occurs in every major syndicate "family" we have looked at in this country. Not only are individuals within "families" related, there is widespread inter-marriage among "families" throughout the country. Of the more than 60 "Mafia bosses" identified as participants at the famous Apalachin meeting in November 1957, for example, almost half were related by blood or marriage, and even more if godparenthood is included as a kin relationship. At one point, three of the five "bosses" of New York's "families"—Carlo Gambino, Vito Genovese, and Thomas Lucchese—had children who were inter-married.

These relationships are actually a series of complex alliances binding together lineages in the same "families" together for systematic exchange of services. And in all relations with outsiders, a man acts not simply as an individual but as a representative of his clan.

This clan pattern of organization also provides a common system of roles, norms and values which not only regulate the behavior within the "family" but also structures relationships among families. It is the universality of this clan organization and the strength of its shared behavior system which makes Italo-American criminal syndicates seem so similar and suggests a national or even international organization. Southern Italians really do not accept any collective larger than the extended kin group and so are reluctant to recognize any moral or social force outside the family. When the extra-familial institutions are alien, as they are in this country, the reliance on family-centered moral systems is re-inforced.

It is this shared, kinship-based moral code, rather than fear or coercion which defines behavior within Italo-American crime "families." And it is a collective amorality toward extra-familial authority structures which binds the "families" to each other and to the Italo-American community. The "code of silence," for example, is hardly an exclusive feature of *Cosa Nostra* or even *Mafia*. In our research on secret societies, we have yet to find one where secrecy is not part of the basic code. What is *different* about Italo-Americans involved in organized crime is that their secrecy and silence in the face of official inquiry are not conditions of membership in some organization but are ingredients of culture passed on through the socialization process.

VII

The kinship model which ties Italo-American criminal "families" together is now disappearing. After three generations of acculturation, the Italo-American family is losing its insistence on father-obedience and mother respect and the authority structure in the crime "families" is changing too. Newer, utilitarian alliances with power establishments in the larger society are replacing the traditional generational authority structure. As American culture continues to errode the strength of family and kinship in Italo-American culture, the "families" must weaken and will give way to the next wave of aspiring ethnics, just as the Jews and the Irish did before them.

The evidence of this displacement is already apparent. In New York City, for example, blacks, Puerto Ricans and Cubans are now displacing Italo-Americans in the policy or numbers rackets. In some cases, particularly in East Harlem and in Brooklyn, this is a peaceful succession as the Italo-American "families" literally lease the rackets on a concession basis. The "family" supplies the money and the protection, the blacks or Puerto Ricans run the operation. In other cases we know of in central and west Harlem, however, the transition is not so peaceful and the Italian syndicate members are actually being pushed out. Current estimates are that upward to one-fourth of the control and operation of the policy racket in New York has already changed hands.

The outlook for the Italian crime "families" is not a promising one. Ethnic succession in organized crime will force them out, but their movement into legitimate business areas whether as "families" or as individuals is blocked because it comes at a time when interest in organized crime infiltration of business is at its height. They might, of course, go underground as the *Mafia* did in Sicily under Mussolini. But even if they do, there seems little chance they will re-emerge for Italo-American culture will not sustain them.

The "conspiracy" idea seems to be fading as well. Recently after a series of demonstrations and protests by Italo-Americans in the spring and summer of 1970, the Department of Justice dropped the terms *Mafia* and *Cosa Nostra* as generic for organized crime. Nixon administration spokesmen insisted that the decision was in no way related to the pressures of the demonstrations, which were, of course, attributed to the *Mafia* itself, but was the result of administration sensitivity to the argument that large segments of organized crime are obviously not Italian-dominated.

An era of Italian crime seems to be passing in large measure because of the changing nature of the Italian community and its inclusion in the society. To that extent, the pattern of Italian crime seems to be following that of previous ethnic groups described in Bell's essay "Crime as an American Way of Life." But what is distinctive about Italian crime is the "myth" that went with it, a myth that arose more out of the need of Americans, nourished in a populist politics, to believe in formidable conspiracies as a means of explaining reality. As I have tried to show, a *Mafia* did—and does exist; but its character is a compound of a cultural attitude and a web of kinships, which are attributes peculiar to the Italian scene, rather than the "big business" pattern, which is a projection of the American imagination.

THE POINT WHERE WAR
BECOMES MURDER

William Greider

It was a problem that Lincoln understood, though he never saw Vietnam or the stacks of bodies in Mylai hamlet.

"Men who take up arms against one another in public war," President Lincoln warned his soldiers, "do not cease to be moral beings, responsible to one another and to God."

In the midst of a bloody war, Lincoln tried to establish some rules. When the War Department issued General Order No. 100 in 1863, written by Dr. Francis Lieber, it was the first attempt to codify the humane limitations on how Americans fight their wars.

"Military necessity," the code declared, "does not admit of cruelty, that is, the infliction of suffering for the sake of suffering or for revenge, nor of maiming or wounding except in fight, nor of torture to extort confessions. It does not admit of the use of poison in any way, nor of the wanton devastation of a district."

All of these things have happened in Vietnam. Lincoln appreciated the difficulties in applying law-and-order to the battlefield. Despite the lofty expressions, his General Order No. 100 did not prohibit Gen. William Sherman's bloody march across Georgia or prevent the Army's periodic massacre of Indians later in the West.

Gen. Sherman was not tried as a "war criminal" (he was proposed for President). War has changed a lot since Lincoln; so have the rules.

Allen, Alvarez, Luczko, Licciardo, Ritter, Simpson, Garcia, Gervase, Zellers, Keenan — they sound like the all-American mix of names in an old war movie. But these men in uniform — and a lot of others like them — have returned home in shame, or worse, to prison. They were all accused of committing murder in the midst of war.

None was so shocking or so gross as the incident at Mylai hamlet, the mass homicide for which the Army is preparing to prosecute seven enlisted men and 10 officers on charges ranging from premeditated murder to dereliction of duty. The Mylai trials will raise many of the same issues of crime and punishment that other soldiers have already faced. Anyone who thinks Mylai was unique should study the court-martial files shipped home from Vietnam. Together, the Army and Marines have prosecuted more than 100 murder cases there in the last five years — most of them committed in a combat environment, not in a barroom or a brothel.

In mankind's long march toward civilization, perhaps these judicial proceedings will come to be regarded as an important milestone: a nation puts its own soldiers on trial as war criminals. Compared with Nuremberg, where the victors prosecuted the vanquished, it seems like a breath-taking departure, a bold new assertion of morality by warring nations.

If so, hardly anyone sees it that way at present. The citizens' letters that pour into the White House and the Pentagon and congressional offices express bewilderment and outrage (not at the alleged massacre — but at the prosecutions). George Wallace says he can't believe it about American boys. American Legion posts are raising money for a legal defense fund.

According to numerous public opinion samplings, a substantial majority of Americans prefer to believe that Mylai never happened. Or, if it did happen, it is explained away by Gen. Sherman's dictum that "war is hell." A Louis Harris poll found that 55 per cent of the people interviewed believe that the principal defendant, Lt. William L. Calley, accused of murdering 109 victims, "is being made a scapegoat by the government."

No one is toasting the prosecutors, not even those who are passionately against the war in Vietnam. To many left-liberal critics of the war, the criminal charges against field soldiers are an elaborate attempt to cover up greater atrocities — the military strategies that have produced so much death and destruction among Vietnamese civilians.

Mylai, in their view, represents a very small sliver of guilt compared with the overall conduct of the war. Indeed, they consider Mylai the natural product of the milieu of "free fire zones" and "search and destroy" missions and pattern bombing of primitive huts. If anyone should be standing in the dock, they insist, it is the war's architects, the generals and academicians and civilian officials who conceived America's first effort at modern counter-insurgency.

Everyone seems to recognize that the Mylai trials might become something more than proceedings to establish guilt and innocence for a few men. They will be used for larger purposes — to establish the Army's loyalty to the laws of warfare, to expose the war's basic strategies as the true crimes, to delineate the confused and cruel nature of this particular war and perhaps, the horror of all war. As the military recognizes, the trials may prove to be a more powerful testament than a dozen massive rallies staged by the peace movement or a thousand teach-in's on college campuses.

The common nagging question is posed in the letters of friends and loved ones whose men-in-uniform are among the accused.

"Why does the Army allow something like this to happen?" wrote the sister of Pvt. Kenneth E. Ritter, accused of an unpremeditated murder near the village of Kylien in August, 1968. "They are trained and sent to Vietnam to kill, so how does he deserve this?"

Pvt. Ritter, according to a witness, stood over an old man who was wounded while riding by on a bicycle, and asked: "Does it hurt?" Then Ritter raked the old man's body with automatic rifle fire. Age 19, a native of Galesburg, Ill., Ritter got 12 years from an Army court-martial.

Why put these young men in prison? Because it is against the law to murder people, even if it is done on the battlefield in the midst of wholesome killing. The military has been somewhat inhibited in explaining its answer to that question because any public statements by Army or Marine officers might provoke charges of prejudicial pretrial publicity in pending cases.

However, the legal definition of murder in warfare is amply documented for ground soldiers, starting with cases before Lincoln's time. Over the years, the distinctions have been refined further in the code of military justice, the "laws of land warfare" that govern U.S. troops; the Hague and Geneva international conventions that are also applicable; the German and Japanese war-crime tribunals that the United States helped operate, and the "rules of engagement" given to each U.S. combat unit in the field — rules that tell soldiers specifically when they can shoot and when they can't. All of these prohibit the intentional, unprovoked killing of noncombatants.

A month-and-a-half before Company C's fateful sweep through Mylai, the 11th Brigade issued new "rules of engagement" reminding its units:

> Every possible safeguard, short of endangering friendly lives, will be used t o avoid noncombatant casualties and indifference and indiscriminate destruction of private property when such action is being conducted in populated areas.
>
> Individuals that appear to be attempting to escape or evade may be frightened, innocent citizens. The commander on the site must exercise judgment as to whether to engage these individuals or not.

As this suggests, the definition of unlawful homicide depends primarily on the circumstances of the incident — not on the identity or political loyalties of the victim. If a North Vietnamese soldier is disarmed and in custody, his hands tied behind his back, killing him is murder. If a small boy reaches under his shirt and it appears that he may be going for a grenade, then shooting him may be justifiable.

"If children are sitting on the steps of a hut, and you take your rifle and shoot them, I say that's murder," Brig. Gen. Duane L. Faw, the Marine Corps judge advocate general explained. "If someone is firing at you from that hut and you return the fire, then you find dead women and children inside, I say that's the fortunes of war."

Committing a crime in combat depends on just such elements — the behavior of the victim, the circumstances of surrounding hostility, the rifleman's own judgment as to whether his life is threatened. But establishing the individual responsibility for a crime is vastly more complicated in warfare because soldiers are not free agents — they follow orders, sometimes orders to commit murder.

Theoretically, at least, that is not a defense. In the public's mind, the Nuremberg tribunal after World War II established, for all time, the principle that a soldier is responsible for his actions — and must disobey commands that are clearly criminal — such as exterminating Jews or lining up civilians beside a ditch and shooting them.

Actually that rule existed in U.S. military law long before Nuremberg, at least as a legal assumption, if not a practical one. Following an order is no defense for a soldier who commits murder, an Army review board ruled in a World War II case. The crime involved a white soldier who shot and killed a Negro battalion commander during a racial dispute at an airbase in Italy. The fact that he was following an order did not shield the triggerman from prosecution.

Even in the absence of a direct order, there are other informal pressures within a rifle company that the defendants have claimed make it difficult to resist illegal killing. One is the soldier's knowledge that he must keep living with these men; if he is a trouble maker, his life will be that much more unpleasant.

Pfc. Cipriano S. Garcia was one of four soldiers court-martialed and convicted after their reconnaissance patrol on Hill 192, Bongson Province. The Army charged that they kidnapped a 20-year-old woman, forced her to accompany the patrol, raped and murdered her. Garcia testified that he refused to rape the girl and emphasized he was sickened by his buddies' activities. Then why, the Army interrogator asked, did he take the slain girl's gold tooth?

"The reason I wanted the gold tooth," Garcia replied, "was just to make them believe, well, that I was like I was with them, you know. If they figured that I didn't have anything to do with it that I could tell on them and, actually, I didn't have nothing to do with it, you know."

These ambiguities of the battlefield were virtually all present in the court-martial and acquittal of Army Capt. John Kapranopoulos, accused of ordering his men to shoot two prisoners taken near the village of Pholuc. The captain conceded that he said something beforehand about getting a "body count," but he denied that he ordered any summary executions.

Two lieutenants in his company testified, to the contrary, that the captain had radioed instructions such as: "He is a gook, you know what to do with him." And: "Dammit, I don't care about prisoners, I want a body count."

But enlisted men in the unit solidly backed the captain in their testimony. They either didn't hear these remarks or they thought the captain's instructions were misconstrued by his accusers.

One unusual statement in defense of the captain came from Brig. Gen. Alexander R. Bolling Jr., commander of the 3rd Brigade of the 82nd Airborne, who referred the case for court-martial. Even while doing so, the general wrote, he felt compelled to explain mitigating circumstances in behalf of the captain — "one of the finest rifle company commanders in this brigade."

"The company involved," Gen. Bolling explained, "was attacked by an NVA sapper unit just a few days prior to the alleged incident. The company's entire mortar squad was wiped out and the unit accepted this action as a defeat although the attack failed. It is therefore natural that the entire unit would want to 'repay' the enemy and there existed throughout the unit a strong desire to eliminate all enemy elements contacted."

The general went on to explain something about the lieutenant who accused his commander: "The initial report was made by an officer who is a fine young man, but who did not enjoy the admiration and respect of his men. Although I have no reason to doubt the veracity of his statement, the fact that he reported the incident created great concern throughout the company."

In its investigative report on the Mylai homicides, the House Armed Services Committee offered the accused soldiers of Company C sympathy and a possible line of defense.

What happened at Mylai, the congressional report said, "was so wrong and so foreign to the normal character and actions of our military forces as to immediately raise a question as to the legal sanity at the time of those men involved."

Maybe so. But it appears that some of the defendants are spurning that advice, including the central figure, the platoon leader accused of 109 deaths. In fact, they are pursuing precisely the opposite argument — that what happened at Mylai was so normal and consistent with the character of the war that it was legal.

Mylai, they contend, was in harmony with U.S. war policy in Vietnam — not the written policy of the "Nine Rules" but the real policy of everyday action.

That policy, the defense lawyers assert, is to kill Vietnamese civilians loyal to the Vietcong in order to deprive enemy guerrillas of support, supplies and a place to hide.

George W. Latimer, a former judge of the U.S. Court of Military Appeals who is representing Lt. William Calley, had advanced this argument in his pretrial efforts to halt the prosecution. Several other lawyers, representing enlisted men from Company C, are taking similar stands.

In his brief, filed in U.S. District Court in Washington, Latimer asserts that the victims at Mylai were:

> A collection of persons who are adherents to a political ideology, which is abhorrent to the Constitution, laws and political philosophy of the United States of America, that the containment of that political ideology is and has been the mission of the United States forces in Vietnam, Korea and Southeast Asia . . . For that purpose, search for and destruction of groups adhering to such ideology, without regards to the means or method used in their destruction, and without regard to any consequences, except to block the spread of the ideology has been, since at least Aug. 10, 1964, the policies and pattern of military forces of the United States of America and its allies . . .
>
> That the underlying purpose of the charges and specifications in the criminal case . . . is to use the plaintiff (Calley) to shield others and to conceal for political ends the pattern and policy . . .
>
> That said pattern and policy leaves to the individual serviceman no moral choice consistent with his assignment and military duty, to determine their validity . . .

Behind the legal syntax, Latimer is implying that, if anyone must stand trial for the homicides at Mylai, it is the generals and politicians who dreamed up the "pattern and policy" of the war in Vietnam. Furthermore, he suggests, the prosecution of lowly combat officers and enlisted men is really an exercise in finding a scapegoat — a way of establishing that the high command honors the laws of warfare by punishing a few soldiers caught violating them.

This viewpoint coincides with what many of the left and liberal critics of the Vietnam war are saying about the Mylai prosecutions — that the defendants are scapegoats.

For instance Richard A. Falk, a Princeton University professor of international law, has been claiming for several years that basic elements of U.S. military policy in Vietnam constitute violations of the laws of warfare.

Among other things, he has cited free-fire zones, harassment and interdiction fire, Operation Phoenix, search and destroy missions, chemical defoliation, forcible transfer of civilians, pattern bombing by B-52's of undefended populated areas. Falk does not believe the Mylai defendants should be prosecuted.

"The circle of guilt is too small," he said. "Any prosecution leads to arbitrary and unjust results. It gives the illusion that one's maintaining morality whereas that's dealing with one percent of the issue and avoiding the larger crimes."

Obviously, that is a radical legal argument to advance in a military courtroom. In effect, it asks the majors and colonels who sit on court-martial panels to conclude that it is the generals who are guilty, not the privates and sergeants.

Moving the trial to a civilian courtroom does not eliminate this dilemma for the judge and jury. If the soldiers who pulled the triggers are not guilty, then who is? The President and the Congress who authorized the "policy and pattern"? Or the nation of people who accepted and generally supported what the government leaders were doing in their name?

As a legal defense, it has been tried before with mixed results, mostly unsuccessful. Numerous pleas by draft resisters have been based on the argument that they were being conscripted to commit "war crimes" and the principle of individual responsibility established at Nuremberg compelled them to resist. The courts generally have been unreceptive. Broad assertions about the nature of the war usually are not considered germane.

In the Vietnam murder prosecutions, the issue of policy was raised in a limited way to defend 1st Lt. James B. Duffy, a platoon leader charged with permitting a sergeant to shoot a prisoner, a farmer named Do Van Man. Duffy's lawyer argued that the Army's emphasis on "body count" was, in reality, a statement of policy, namely, that it was okay to shoot farmers.

Other infantry platoon leaders were called in as defense witnesses and said, in so many words, that they followed the same unwritten policy as Lt. Duffy.

"Our policy," 1st Lt. John Kruger testified, "was that once contact was made we continued firing until everything in the 'kill zone' was killed. We did not take prisoners."

Three psychiatrists examined Duffy and concluded — not that he was insane at the time — but that he thought he was doing his duty. One of the psychiatrists, Lt. Col. Franklin A. Moten, testified: "I consider Duffy's opinion at the time was that he was eliminating an enemy rather than thinking consciously, 'I am going to murder a detainee.'"

The eight-member court-martial panel convicted him, but reduced the charge from premeditated murder to involuntary manslaughter. He was given a six-month sentence, but he was not dismissed from the Army. The president of the court-martial, in announcing the verdict, said: "The court deliberated very long on the ramifications to the Army of this offense."

If the Mylai trials become the platform for a broader debate on the strategies of war, the defendants will find plenty of eyewitness or circumstantial testimonials charging U.S. violations of the Geneva convention. The war's critics have been collecting material for years.

The particular accusations range from wholesale and deliberate killing of noncombatants (B-52 pattern bombing, napalm, helicopter gunships that fire 5,000 rounds a minute) to unnecessary destruction of private property (burning huts) to officially sanctioned murder and torture (Operation Phoenix, counter-terrorist teams that allegedly assassinated Vietcong sympathizers among the civilian population).

Many of these issues were aired last winter at a two-day symposium sponsored by 10 antiwar congressmen, and the talks will be published soon as a book entitled, "War Crimes and The American Conscience."

Dr. Robert J. Lifton, a psychiatry professor at Yale, told the conference: "No GI I have talked to, and as far as I know, none of the 200 or so that a friend and colleague and historian has talked to in his investigations have ever been surprised by the news of Mylai. That is an interesting fact. The reason they have not been surprised is that they have either been part, witness to, or have heard at fairly close hand about hundreds or thousands of similar, if smaller, incidents."

The Citizens' Commission of Inquiry on U.S. War Crimes, an antiwar organization in New York City, has been collecting accounts from Vietnam veterans of what they saw in combat. The organization has offered its witness list of about 50 veterans to the Mylai defense lawyers. "What we're trying to do," said Jeremy Rifkin, "is shift the guilt away from the GIs and back to the policy."

To assert that U.S. policy called for wiping out civilians, war critics often turn to circumstantial evidence. They cite statistical estimates made by critics of what U.S. firepower has done to South Vietnam – 300,000 civilians killed; 5 million acres defoliated; 4 million to 7 million refugees driven to cities or temporary camps; more bombs dropped than in all of World War II.

Jonathan Schell, the journalist who described in The New Yorker magazine the air war aimed at Quangngai Province, the VC stronghold that included Mylai, concluded that the heavy bombing was intended to drive the rural villagers into refugee camps or to kill them – in order to deprive the Vietcong of safe harbor and support. Schell cited a propaganda pamphlet dropped on Quangngai entitled: "Marine Ultimatum to Vietnamese People."

The pamphlet showed two cartoons – one of Vietcong soldiers setting up inside a village; the second of the village and its people destroyed by bombs. "If the Vietcong do this . . . your village will look like this," the captain said. "The choice is yours. If you refuse to let the Vietcong use your villages and hamlets as their battlefield, your homes and lives will be saved." Schell reported that the Marines prepared a followup leaflet entitled, "Your village has been bombed."

No pilots have been prosecuted for murder although there have been numerous accounts of helicopter gunships aimlessly shooting at peasants below without the provocation of hostile fire. Some have been reprimanded for civilian deaths. Military legal experts point out that the problems of collecting evidence are much more difficult in air attacks and the helicopter pilot's judgment on whether an area is hostile depends on many more imponderables. If he intends to land men in a village, he wants to make sure they will not be killed before he gets them there.

In general, military men regard these broad accusations as slanders against men who served in Vietnam and the officers who commanded. Their perception of the ground war, as frequently expressed, is that it has been fought with remarkable restraint under the circumstances.

In answer to the veterans who tell stories alleging atrocities, they tell stories of soldiers who risked their lives by not firing at a suspicious hut or village — because the "rules of engagement" did not allow it. When soldiers are prosecuted, they point out, it is often because someone at the scene — sometimes even the defendant himself — knew the killing was wrong and reported it to a chaplain or a commanding officer. Likewise, the prosecutions were further testimony to the troops that murder would not be tolerated.

While some military men privately agree with the critics who say that too much bomb tonnage has been used indiscriminately, they do not agree that it constitutes a "war crime." The same uses of air war — including napalm — were used in World War II and Korea without any great outcries against them. Military strategists have usually looked at the last war to judge what is permitted in the next one.

The tactics of counterinsurgency are still being tested, of course, but the military view is that many approaches, originally designed to reduce civilian casualties, have been distorted by the critics and given the opposite intention. Free-fire zones, for example, were supposed to save lives by clearing an area of civilians before the shooting started. So were the propaganda pamphlets.

In the international articles governing humane warfare, the rules prohibit the destruction of private property, the unprovoked killing of civilians, the forced relocation of noncombatants, among other things. But the rules typically include an escape clause for military commanders — these actions are prohibited when "not justified by military necessity."

The definition of "military necessity" is elusive in a war that pits a world superpower against pajama-clad guerrillas. The pattern of enemy warfare, the military would say, has necessitated the pattern of U.S. response. To the critics, no military situation could justify the enormous weaponry that this nation has employed.

So the debate about "war crimes" and responsibility is really a debate about the true nature of the entire war and how it has been fought. These questions are not likely to be settled in any courtroom, even if the Mylai defense lawyers get a chance to lay out their case. There is no reliable forum to deal with them. Yet they are important questions because, if history is any guide, the wars of the future will be guided by what was acceptable in this one.

Like President Lincoln, Gen. Tomouki Yamashita understood the difficulties of imposing humane limits on men in war. If you have forgotten, Yamashita was the Japanese commander in the Philippines who presided over enemy troops during the last ragged, bloody months of World War II. Afterward, we hanged him.

The precedent of Yamashita is another troublesome item of history. If one rejects the "policy and pattern" war crimes alleged by the left-liberal critics (and the vast majority of Americans probably do), then the trial and execution of Yamashita still hovers over Vietnam.

The lawyer for one Mylai defendant, Sgt. Esequiel Torres, has used the Yamashita precedent to charge that Gen. William C. Westmoreland, now Army Chief of Staff, should stand trial for his role as the top commander in Vietnam at the time of Mylai.

The Army's "Law of Land Warfare" recognizes the Yamashita precedent by noting that, in some cases, a military commander may be held responsible for "war crimes" committed by men under his command — if the commander knew about them or should have known about them or failed to take "reasonable steps" to prevent them or punish violators.

The Yamashita case created a "Catch 22" for commanders. If he fails to prosecute on combat murders, he becomes responsible for them, too. But, when he does prosecute these crimes, he adds substance to the accusation that he should have prevented them.

Unlike most of the other war crime trials, Yamashita was not accused of deliberately plotting and ordering atrocities. He was accused of permitting them to happen. His written orders specifically prohibited the killing of unarmed civilians and he urged his troops to "handle the Filipinos carefully and to cooperate with them."

But Yamashita's troops were under attack from both the approaching U.S. forces and the hit-and-run ambushes of Filipino guerrillas (the same bolo men who cut up U.S. Marines 40 years earlier). Frustrated and near defeat, Japanese units staged a series of massacres — of men, women, and children — in rural villages suspected of aiding the guerrilla underground.

A. Frank Reel, who served as one of Yamashita's defense counsels, has asserted that "the Japanese soldiers' reaction was similar to the GIs' view of the Vietcong. The Japanese felt that practically the entire population of provincial areas had sprung to arms against them, that the placid Filipino 'civilians' who smiled at them by day were treacherously murdering them by night."

Yamashita, citing his official orders to the contrary, pleaded that he had no knowledge of these atrocities, and given the breakdown in communications, lacked the effective control over troops necessary to prevent them. The prosecution argued before a U.S. Military Tribunal that Yamashita "must have known" these things were happening, and by his failure to act, he implicitly endorsed them.

Yamashita's conviction was upheld by the U.S. Supreme Court, though a dissenting justice, Frank Murphy, noted: "He was not charged with personally participating in the acts of atrocities or with ordering or condoning their commission. Not even knowledge of these crimes was ever attributed to him."

A plea for clemency was rejected by President Truman; Gen. Douglas MacArthur ordered the execution, remarking that Yamashita "has failed utterly his soldiers' faith."

Twenty-five years later, it is easier to see how that could happen. The assignment of guilt for "war crimes" is a murky business, which will not necessarily be made any clearer by the ambiguities of fighting in Vietnam. Pointing a finger at military leaders may be a form of finding a scapegoat, too.

"Soldiers don't make wars, they die in them," Frank Kowalski, a retired Army colonel and former congressman, reminded the symposium on war crimes. "We are not in the senseless war in Vietnam because any mad-dog general or militarists decided to wage war there."

The basic decisions were made by civilians — with the implicit approval of the general public. Would it strengthen the nation's sense of morality to say that everyone, to some degree, shares the guilt for what happened at Mylai? Or does that destroy the rules by establishing that no one is individually responsible when he breaks them?

"I've come to the conclusion," said Richard Falk, the war critic, "that there are crimes, but no criminals. What we need is the basis for setting limits on what is permissible, rather than attempting to establish criminal responsibility." Maybe so, but that suggestion is absolutely no help to the commander on the battlefield who is responsible for maintaining the laws of warfare.

"If you don't prosecute a man," said one military judicial officer, "then that becomes your policy. If you don't prosecute them, then everybody can do it."

That is the moral dilemma posed for the nation when the young men of Company C go on trial.

During the Korean conflict, the same principle was applied to an airman accused of killing a Korean national at an Air Force trash dump. The Air Force court-martialed him — as well as the lieutenant who ordered the killing.

An individual soldier, the review board declared, "is not an automaton but a 'reasoning agent' who is under a duty to exercise judgment in obeying the orders of a superior officer to the extent that where such orders . . . are so palpably illegal on their face that a man of ordinary sense and understanding would know them to be illegal, then the fact of obedience to the order of a superior officer will not protect a soldier . . . "

Soldiers must resist an unlawful order. That is the general rule of law, but even so, the military courts recognize that the good soldier doesn't stop to examine his orders to decide if they are lawful — he instinctively obeys them. Therefore, he is permitted to plead in defense that his obedience to "superior orders" was a mitigating circumstance. The verdicts in Vietnam murder cases suggest that this is usually a powerful argument, one that may win acquittal or a light sentence even when the evidence indicates the murder was done in cold blood.

If the issues were confined to the neat legal premises, then the Army's case for prosecution of crime in combat would be compelling — a simple matter of upholding law-and-order. Unfortunately, the realities of the war make a shambles of the distinctions made in courtrooms.

An Army captain, charged with premeditated murder in Vietnam because men in his company allegedly shot two unarmed prisoners, explained to the investigating officers that he did not really give an order to kill prisoners.

"I would like to explain 'body count,' " the captain testified. "It is a phrase everyone in the company uses. Everyone on a combat assault or any other mission says, 'Let's get a body count.' I think I mentioned it as the men left the hill. I may have said, 'Let's get a body count.' Some of the men in the company even sent away for buttons that say, 'Wine, women and body count.' "

The captain was acquitted.

In another time, during a different war, a New York newspaper screamed: "These hideous acts of barbarity were committed under our flag by men wearing the uniform of the United States and commanded by American officers!"

The political shock wave touched off then by American atrocities only compounded the deep domestic division that already existed over the war. The pressures of public opinion led the highest military command in Washington to order a full investigation and the prosecution of soldiers, even high-ranking officers.

That was in 1902. The newspaper was the New York World, now defunct. The atrocities were committed in another Asian war, another unhappy chapter in U.S. history. The episode is virtually lost to the national memory — perhaps blotted out because of its ugliness. Its particulars foreshadow in a haunting manner current agonies.

If history texts mention the Philippine Insurrection at all, it is given a sentence or two, lumped with the Spanish-American war, though actually they were separate conflicts. After U.S. forces "liberated" Cuba and the Philippines from Spain, guerrilla leaders on the Pacific islands mistakenly assumed that the American victory meant independence for them.

Instead, President William McKinley heeded the religious, economic and patriotic impulses of the nation and declared, "There was nothing left for us to do but to take them all and to educate the Filipinos and uplift them and civilize and Christianize them, and by God's grace do the best we could by them, as our own fellowmen for whom Christ also died."

So Army and Marine units were sent to pacify the 11 major islands. For more than three years, they were resisted in treacherous guerrilla warfare. In scores of jungle villages, the Insurrectos of the Katipunan Society were friendly and cooperative by day — and bloody partisans by night. They massacred and mutilated when they could, decoyed and deceived the superior U.S. forces, then hid among the women and children as innocent peasants.

In that kind of war, the American troops learned quickly to distrust all natives, even those who worked for them as guides and laborers. The Filipinos were different racially and lived in thatched huts; the soldiers commonly called them "googoos" and "niggers," just as soldiers of today call Vietnamese "gooks" and "dinks."

The typical method of conquest on the most treacherous islands was a pre-napalm version of "search and destroy" — village huts were all burned, the people were rounded up and questioned, sometimes tortured, then forced to take oaths of allegiance to the new civil government that the Americans were establishing at Manila.

Inevitably, it seemed, the terrorism of the Insurrecto bolo men was matched by the army of occupation. Back home, while politicians argued over whether America should be involved at all, the public was shocked to learn that American soldiers were using the outlawed dumdum bullets, water torture and other techniques of deliberate cruelty.

The New York World's correspondent reported in one dispatch: "It is now the custom to avenge the death of an American soldier by burning to the ground all the houses, and killing right and left the natives who are only 'suspects.' "

Soldiers began writing letters home, telling war stories that found their way into public print as disclosures of atrocities. A report from the War Department to Congress said that 44 officers, soldiers and "camp followers" were tried for "cruelty, looting and like crimes" in a two-year period of the conflict.

In the search for precedents, nothing can be found from World War I or World War II or the Korean conflict that resembles the current Vietnam combat prosecutions so much as these forgotten cases from the dawn of imperialist democracy.

Certainly there is one striking parallel between the war in Vietnam and the Philippine conflict — the influence of racial differences. It was, undoubtedly, easier for American men to do some of these things against people who looked different, spoke a strange language, and lived in flimsy huts. In terms of public opinion back home, race may also have influenced the reaction to reported atrocities. The outrage might have been greater if the victims had been French or Italian or German women and children.

The most celebrated prosecution was aimed at a Marine battalion commander on the island of Samar — Maj. L.W.T. Waller — for ordering the summary execution of 11 Filipinos who had been working as guides and bearers for the Marine troops, but were suspected of guerrilla sympathies.

In the public uproar back home, Waller was labeled a "butcher" by editorial writers opposed to the Philippine venture. His court-martial was ordered directly by the Secretary of War, an instance of high-level "command influence" documented by Joseph L. Schott in his sympathetic account of the trial, "The Ordeal of Samar."

Waller did not deny that he ordered the executions, but he insisted they were legal, consistent with his orders from higher command and consistent with President Lincoln's rules of warfare, still in effect at that date. Waller's commander, Army Brig. Gen. Jacob H. Smith, had told the Marine major: "The interior of Samar must be made a howling wilderness." And the general informally gave this directive: "Kill and burn! Kill and burn! The more you kill and burn, the better you will please me. I want no prisoners, do you understand?"

Waller was acquitted, partly because he cited in his defense Article 82 of Lincoln's General Order No. 100. The article describes a special category of guerrilla participants in warfare — men who do not wear enemy uniforms, who raid and ambush occasionally, then return to their homes and assume "the semblance of peaceful pursuits, divesting themselves of the character or appearance of soldiers."

They were neither soldiers nor innocent noncombatants. These irregular warriors, the article said, "are not entitled to the privileges of prisoners of war, but shall be treated summarily as highway robbers or pirates." Waller contended successfully that he complied with the rules when he "treated summarily" the 11 Insurrecto suspects.

An American soldier who shoots a Vietnamese peasant suspected of Vietcong activities might plead the same defense; certainly the 1863 directive accurately describes the Vietcong. But, while guerrilla warriors still fall in a twilight category under the rules of warfare, the summary executions authorized in Lincoln's time are illegal. The irregulars are not entitled to the "due process" of a trial.

Waller continued his Marine career with honor and rose to major general. But Gen. Smith was court-martialed on a charge of "conduct to the prejudice of good order and military discipline," based on his flamboyant orders to kill and burn. He was convicted, reprimanded and retired from the Army, a lenient sentence because the court said the general clearly "did not mean everything that his unexplained language implied."

It is hard to say what lessons were learned from the ordeal. In his study, Schott concludes:

"Americans were shocked and sobered at the blunt first-hand accounts of the grim methods used by the Army to subdue the Filipinos. Even the most ardent imperialists began to realize that acquisition of new economic markets by means of warfare held sordid aspects that were impossible to justify to a squeamish electorate at home."

But it was all forgotten. Not just the scandals and court-martials, but the entire war was erased from the collective American memory. That is the most devastating commentary that history can render — to be forgotten because no one wants to remember.

Pfc. Michael Bernhardt, the soldier who refused to fire his rifle at the hapless civilians of Mylai hamlet, told an interviewer from The New York Times how combat in Vietnam had changed his notions about crime and criminals: "You know, when I think of somebody who would shoot up women and children, I think of a real nut, a real maniac, a real psycho, somebody who's just completely lost control and doesn't have any idea of what he's doing. That's what I figured. That's what I thought a nut was. Then I found out that an act like, you know, murder for no reason could be done by just about anybody."

Bernhardt's impression is more or less confirmed by Army and Marine court-martial records stored in Washington, the records of more than 100 murder cases involving Vietnamese as victims. An extensive sampling of these cases suggests that any soldier might become a defendant. Some of them could doubtless be described as unstable and weak-minded, probably crime-prone at home as well as in war. But others were regarded as "model youth" with no stain of violence in their past or personality.

Perhaps the one safe generalization about these young men is that many of them come from humble family backgrounds, and most of them have limited formal education, a high school diploma or less. But that describes the young men who typically get assigned to rifle companies — the "grunts" who endure the worst of ground combat.

In one sense, these other murder cases seem to vindicate the military on at least one point of criticism — the accusation that the Mylai prosecutions are unique and solely the result of domestic political pressure. The records testify that the Army and Marine Corps have been accusing soldiers of combat murder regularly since the Vietnam buildup of 1965, and that the number of prosecutions did not rise or fall in response to public opinion at home.

On another level, however, these cases add to a far darker portrait of the war and the manner in which it has been conducted. They make it doubly difficult to believe that the Mylai incident was an "aberration" or isolated occurrence. Compared with the other cases, Mylai seems unique only in its dimensions — and in the long delay before the Army took action on it.

From 1965 to July, 1970, the Army has held trials on 64 murder cases from Vietnam. Thirty-five men were convicted and 13 acquitted. Sixteen were acquitted of murder, but convicted of lesser charges such as negligent homicide or assault. From March, 1965, to mid-summer 1970, the Marine Corps has tried 41 men for murder and convicted 22 of them. Fifteen were acquitted; three were convicted of manslaughter and one of attempted murder. The Navy has had four murder trials with one acquittal.

It is impossible to categorize them precisely, but the cases fall roughly into three varieties of crime. A minor proportion — perhaps 25 or 30 per cent of the total — are no different from crimes that soldiers (or civilians) might commit on any Saturday night anywhere in the world — a shooting or stabbing in a barroom or brothel.

The remaining cases are related to the special fears and hostilities of the Vietnam war zone. The crimes occur in a combat environment, if not during an actual engagement, and appear to fall about evenly into two categories.

The first type involves homicides that appear totally aimless and unprovoked — even whimsical in some cases. Two soldiers "test fire" their rifles at peasants working in a field and kill a man. A private announces to his buddies that he is "going to shoot at some gooks in the fields . . . to see if I can scare them" — and hits a young girl in the head. Another, on guard duty at a trash dump, fires his .45-caliber submachine gun to scare away children playing there. A staff sergeant tosses grenades to keep Vietnamese civilians off the roadway where his men are repairing craters so truck traffic can resume.

The other type most resembles the Mylai incident — homicides committed in the course of completing a combat mission, frequently on the assumption that the victims were the enemy or at least that they collaborated with the Vietcong and therefore deserved what they were getting.

A "hunter-killer" patrol of Marines gets a body count of 16 in the village of Songthang — five women and 11 children. Two airborne troopers confront three peasants along a hedgerow near Landing Zone English, place them in a circle and shoot them. Six Marines, weary teams from six treacherous weeks in the battle of Hue, capture five suspected VC and a firing squad is appointed. The fifth victim is hanged, his throat cut. The bodies are dumped in a canal. A 1st lieutenant leading an infantry platoon permits a sergeant to execute a prisoner, a farmer named Do Van Man.

In numerous official circulars, the armed forces tell their men in Vietnam not to do that sort of thing. "The Enemy in Your Hands," an Army handbill, reminds soldiers that they must comply with the 1949 Geneva Convention on treatment of prisoners. "Mistreatment of any captive is a criminal offense," it warns. "Every soldier is personally responsible for the enemy in his hands."

At various points, soldiers and Marines are also told they must obey "lawful orders," which implies they do not have to obey unlawful ones. But no one pretends that enlisted men are instructed to examine each order for its legality and then decide whether to obey.

In some cases, someone on the scene saw what happened, felt it was wrong and told the chaplain or reported it to higher officers. In some others, bereaved families complained to the hamlet chief or to U.S. pacification officials who were trying to win "the hearts and minds" of the people.

Obviously, the pacification benefits of building schools and orphanages for rural hamlets would be negligible if a sweep by American troops produced murder. "We were extremely sensitive to our image," said Gen. Faw, who served with the 3d Marine Amphibious Force in the I Corps area. "The last thing we wanted was something of this sort to happen because it was counter-productive."

But, when the Army or Marine Corps enforced the rules, many of the cases revealed the contradictions that exist between the official policies found in the training manuals and the common reality familiar to GIs in the field. The lines of individual responsibility, essential to establishing criminal guilt, become blurred.

"One of the first things you learn," said one Vietnam veteran, "is to forget a lot of what they told you. In basic training, they told us over and over again not to throw away C ration cans because the Vietcong use them to make booby traps. Then you get over there and you see VC booby traps made with 500-pound bombs."

While the "Nine Rules" distributed to all military personnel in Vietnam emphasize politeness and respect, the common slang of officers and enlisted men labels all natives "gooks," "dinks" or "slopes." If an American soldier expects gratitude from the Vietnamese for risking his life and limb in their behalf, he soon discovers that many of them hate him. If the United States is building schools and orphanages, it is also burning down a lot of homes, not to mention bombing villages out of existence.

The "Nine Rules" command soldiers: "Always give the Vietnamese the right of way." But the operative vocabulary of the war centers on phrases such as "body count," "search and destroy," "free fire zone."

Like the Insurrecto guerrillas who fought American troops in the Philippines 70 years ago, the Vietcong and their noncombatant supporters are indistinguishable from the civilian population. Likewise, they are capable of treachery and cruelty outside the rules of war. Kids, too.

The young Marines who executed five peasants at Hue in May, 1968, had spent Easter Sunday recovering the mutilated bodies of Marine buddies whose fingers and genitals had been cut off. Six Marines went to prison. At another Marine encounter in the village of Thonhaicuu, Bravo Company radioed back that a baby had been killed. "Well, nothing we can do about it now," the company commander allegedly replied. "He probably would have grown up to be VC anyway."

In this milieu, the "Nine Rules" and the "Enemy in Your Hands" may seem wildly unreal to a young soldier, especially if he is under orders — or thinks he is — to shoot everything that moves.

"Put some more fire power out there," the platoon sergeant hollered. So Specialist 4th Class James C. Rodarte, who re-enlisted so his widowed mother in Tampa, Fla., would get the bonus money for Christmas, put a fresh magazine in his weapon. The two soldiers were firing at three men named Nguyen Dinh, Nguyen Kich, and Phan Tho, who were seated in a circle on the ground. Afterward, they detonated a grenade among the bodies to simulate an armed encounter.

At Rodarte's trial, a Roman Catholic chaplain who had heard the defendant's confession testified in his defense.

"His intention was not to commit an immoral act," said the Rev. Charles J. Davis. "I think . . . he was in a state of mind of confusion and fear . . . His fear was based on his relationship with his superior NCO, fear of retaliation, fear of going against a company policy which is 'always obey the orders.' "

Father David, whose testimony helped win an acquittal for Rodarte, recalled for the court his experience with a "character guidance" class in which he tried to explain that good soldiers must disobey unlawful orders. The priest described a hypothetical situation in which an officer tells his men to take no prisoners and kill everyone, even identifiable civilians.

"This is murder," the chaplain told the enlisted men.

"I was trying to make this distinction in the mind," Father Davis testified, "and to my surprise, a number of the class would say: 'No matter what — obey the command. Obey the order, no matter what.' "

Lance Cpl. Rudolph O. Diener followed the same rule in Thonhaicuu village. As the word filtered down to him, the company was under orders to kill everyone, but use your own discretion about children. Diener shot a woman in the back with his M-16 after leading her away from her hooch so her children wouldn't have to witness it.

"My job was to shoot her," he testified. Charged with murder, he was acquitted after the military judge instructed the jury panel to decide whether Diener thought he was following a legal order.

The judge declared: "Except in instances of palpable illegality, which must be of rare occurrence, the inferior should presume the order was lawful and authorized and obey it accordingly, and in obeying it, he can scarcely fail to be held justified by a military court."

The issue of guilt becomes even more clouded in cases where it is not clear from anyone's testimony whether a direct order to kill civilians was given. If the company commander says, "Let's get a body count," what does that mean to an 18-year-old rifleman, tired and scared and convinced that all Vietnamese are his mortal enemy?

III.

FACTORS CONTRIBUTING
TO CRIMINAL BEHAVIOR

George Jackson

Dear Greg,

      I probably didn't work hard enough on this but I'm pressed for time—all the time.

      I could play the criminal aspects of my life down some but then it wouldn't be me. That was the pertinent part, the thing at school and home I was constantly rejecting in process.

      All my life I pretended with my folks, it was the thing in the street that was real. I was certainly just pretending with the nuns and priests, I served mass so that I could be in a position to steal altar wine, sang in the choir because they made me. When we went on tour of the rich white catholic schools we were always treated very well—fed—rewarded with gifts. Old Father Brown hated me but always put me down front when we were on display. I can't say exactly why, I was the ugliest, skinniest little misfit in the group.

      Blackmen born in the U.S. and fortunate enough to live past the age of eighteen are conditioned to accept the inevitability of prison. For most of us, it simply looms as the next phase in a sequence of humiliations. Being born a slave in a captive society and never experiencing any objective basis for expectation had the effect of preparing me for the progressively traumatic misfortunes that lead so many blackmen to the prison gate. I was prepared for prison. It required only minor psychic adjustments.

It always starts with Mama, mine loved me. As testimony of her love, and her fear for the fate of the man-child all slave mothers hold, she attempted to press, hide, push, capture me in the womb. The conflicts and contradictions that will follow me to the tomb started right there in the womb. The feeling of being captured . . . this slave can never adjust to it, it's a thing that I just don't favor, then, now, never.

I've been asked to explain myself, "briefly," before the world has done with me. It is difficult because I don't recognize uniqueness, not as it's applied to individualism, because it is too tightly tied into decadent capitalist culture. Rather I've always strained to see the indivisible thing cutting across the artificial barricades which have been erected to an older section of our brains, back to the mind of the primitive commune that exists in all blacks. But then how can I explain the runaway slave in terms that do not imply uniqueness?

I was captured and brought to prison when I was 18 years old because I couldn't adjust. The record that the state has compiled on my activities reads like the record of ten men. It labels me brigand, thief, burglar, gambler, hobo, drug addict, gunman, escape artist, Communist revolutionary, and murderer.

I was born as the Great Depression was ending. It was ending because the second great war for colonial markets was beginning in the U.S. I pushed out of the womb against my mother's strength September 23, 1941—I felt free.

My mother was a country girl from Harrisburg, Illinois. My father was born in East St. Louis, Illinois. They met in Chicago, and were living on Lake Street near Racine when I was born. It was in one of the oldest sections of Chicago, part ghetto residential, part factory. The el train passed a few yards from our front windows (the only windows really). There were factories across the street and garage shops on the bottom level of our flat. I felt right in the middle of things.

Our first move up the social scale was around the corner to 211 North Racine Street, away from the el train. I remember every detail of preschool days. I have a sister 15 months older than myself, Delora, a beautiful child and now a beautiful woman. We were sometimes *allowed* to venture out into the world, which at the time meant no further than fenced-off roof area adjoining our little three-room apartment built over a tavern. We were allowed out there only after the city made its irregular garbage pickups. The roof area was behind the tavern and over an area where prople deposited their garbage. But, of course, I went out when I pleased.

Superman was several years old about then, I didn't really confuse myself with him but I did develop a deep suspicion that I might be Suppernigger (twenty-three years ahead of my time). I tied a tablecloth around my neck, climbed the roof's fence, and against my sister's tears would have leaped to my death, down among the garbage barrels, had she not grabbed me, tablecloth and all, and kicked my little ass.

Seeing the white boys up close in kindergarten was a traumatic event. I *must* have seen some before in magazines or books but never in the flesh. I approached one, felt his har, scratched at his cheek, he hit me in the head with a baseball bat. They found me crumpled in a heap just outside the school-yard fence.

After that, my mother sent me to St. Malachy catholic mission school. It was sitting right in the heart of the ghetto area, Washington and Oakley streets. All of the nuns were white; of the priests (there were five in the parish) I think one was near black, or near white whichever you prefer. The school ran from kindergarten to 12th grade. I attended for nine years (ten counting kindergarten). This small group of missionaries with their silly costumes and barbaric rituals offered the full range of Western propaganda to all ages and all comers. Sex was never mentioned except with whispers or grimaces to convey something nasty. You could get away with anything (they were anxious to make saints) but getting caught with your hand up a dress. Holy ghosts, confessions, and racism.

St. Malachy's was really two schools. There was another school across the street that was more private than ours. "We" played and fought on the corner sidewalks bordering the school. "They" had a large grass-and-tree-studded garden with an eight-foot wrought-iron fence bordering it (to keep us out, since it never seemed to keep any of them in when they chose to leave). "They" were all white. "They" were driven to and from school in large private buses or their parents' cars. "We" on the black side walked, or when we could afford it used the public buses or streetcars. The white students' yard was equipped with picnic tables for spring lunches, swings, slides, and other more sophisticated gadgets intended to please older children. For years we had only the very crowded sidewalks and alley behind the school. Years later a small gym was built but it just stood there, locked. It was only allowed to be used for an occasional basketball game between our school and one of the others like it from across the city's various ghetto areas.

Delora and I took the Lake Street streetcar to school each morning, and also on Sundays when we were forced to attend a religious function. I must have fallen from that thing a hundred times while it was in motion. Each time Delora would hang on to me, trying to save me, but I was just too determined and we would roll down Lake Street, books and all, miraculously avoiding the passing cars. The other black children who went to public school laughed at us. The girls had to wear a uniform, the boys wore white shirts. I imagined that the nuns and priests were laughing too every time they told one of those fantastic lies. I know now that the most damaging thing a people in a colonial situation can do is to allow their children to attend any educational facility organized by the dominant enemy culture.

Before the winter of my first-grade year, my father, Lester, prepared a fifty-gallon steel drum to store oil for our little stove. As I watched, he cleaned the inside with gasoline. When he retreated from his work temporarily for a cigarette he explained to me about the danger of the gas fumes. Later when he had completed work on the barrel, I sneaked back out to the roof with my sister Delora trailing me like a St. Bernard. I had matches and the idea of an explosion was irresistable. As soon as my sister realized what I was going to do, she turned her big sad eyes on me and started crying. I lit a match as I moved closer and closer to the barrel. The I lit the whole book of matches. By now Delora was convinced that death was imminent for us both. She made a last brave effort to stop me but I was too determined. I threw the matches across the last few feet. Delora shielded my eyes with her hand as the explosion went off. She still carries her burns from that day's experiences. I was injured around the lower face but carry no sign of it. Our clothes were burned and ripped away. I would probably be blind if not for this sister.

My parents had two more children while we were hanging on there at North Racine, Frances and Penelope. Six of us in the little walk-up. The only thing that I can think of that was even slightly pleasant about the place was the light. We had plenty of windows and nothing higher about us to block off the sun. In '49 we moved to a place in the rear on Warren near Western that was the end of the sun. We had no windows that opened directly on the street, even the one that faced the alley was blocked by a garage. It was a larger place but the neighborhood around the place was so vicious that my mother never, never *allowed* me to go out of the house or the small yard except to get something from one of the supermarkets or stores on Madison and return immediately. When I wanted to leave I would either go by a window, or throw my coat out the window and volunteer to take out the garbage. There was only one door. It was in the kitchen and always well guarded.

I spent most of the summers of those school years in southern Illinois with my grandmother and aunt, Irene and Juanita. My mother, Georgia, called it removing me from harm's way. This was where my mother grew up and she trusted her sister Juanita, whose care I came under, completely. I was the only man-child and I was the only one to get *special* protection from my mother. The trips to the country were good for me in spite of the motive. I learned how to shoot rifles, shotguns, pistols. I learned about fishing. I learned to identify some of the food plants that grow wild in most areas of the U.S. I could leave the house, the yard, the town, without having to sneak out of a window.

Almost everyone in the black sector of Harrisburg is a relative of mine. A loyal, righteous people; I could raise a small army from their numbers. I had use of any type of rifle or pistol on those trips downstate and everyone owned a weapon. My disposition toward guns and explosions is responsible for my first theft. Poverty made ammunition scarce and so ... I confess with some guilt that I liked to shoot small animals, birds rabbits, squirrels, anything that offered itself as a target. I was a little skinny guy; scourge of the woods, predatory man. After the summer I went back up north for school and snowball (sometimes ice-block) fights with the white kids across the street.

I don't remember exactly when I met Joe Adams, it was during the early years, but I do recall the circumstances. Three or four of the brothers were in the process of taking my lunch when Joe joined them. The bag was torn, and the contents spilled onto the sidewalk. Joe scrambled for the food and got all of it. But after the others left laughing, he returned and stuffed it all into my pockets. We were great friends from then on in that childish way. He was older by a couple of years (two or three years means a lot at that tender age), and could beat me doing everything. I watched him and listened with John and Kenny Fox, Junior, Sonny, and others sometimes. We almost put the block's businessmen into bankruptcy. My mother and father will never admit it now, I'm sure, but I was hungry and so were we all. Our activities went from stolen food to other things I wanted, gloves for my hands (which were always cold), which I was always wearing out, marbles for the slingshots, games and gadgets for outdoorsmen from the dime store. Downtown, we plundered at will. The city was helpless to defend against us. But I couldn't keep up with Joe. Jonathan, my older brother, was born about this time.

My grandfather, George "Papa" Davis, stands out of those early years more than any other figure in my total environment. He was separated from his wife by the system. Work for men was impossible to find in Harrisburg. He was living and working in Chicago—sending his wage back to the people downstate. He was an extremely aggressive man, and since aggression on the part of the slave means crime, he was in jail now and then. I loved him. He tried to direct my great energy into the proper form of protest. He invented long simple allegories that always pictured the white politicians as animals (jackasses, toads, goats, vermin in general). He scorned the police with special enmity. He and my mother went to great pains to impress on me that it was the worst form of niggerism to hook and jab, cut and stab at other blacks.

Papa took me to his little place on Lake and fed me, walked me through the wildest of the nation's jungles, pointing up the foibles of black response to crisis existence. I loved him. He died alone in southern Illinois the fifth year that I was in San Quentin, on a pension that after rent allowed for a diet of little more than sardines and crackers.

After Racine Street we moved into the Troop Street projects, which in 1958 were the scenes of the city's worst riots. (The cats in those projects fell out against the pig with heavy machine guns, 30s and 50s that were equipped with tracer ammunition.)

My troubles began when we were in the projects. I was caught once or twice for mugging but the pig never went much further than to pop me behind the ear with the "oak stick" several times and send for my mortified father to carry me home.

My family knew very little of my real life. In effect, I lived two lives, the one with my mama and sisters, and the thing on the street. Now and then I'd get caught at something, or with something that I wasn't supposed to have and my mama would fall all over me. I left home a thousand times, never to return. We hoboed up and down the state. I did what I wanted (all my life I've done just that). When it came time to explain, I lied.

I had a girl from Arkansas, finest at the mission, but the nuns had convinced her that love—touching fingertips, mouths, bellies, legs—was nasty. Most of my time and money went to the other very loose and lovely girls I met on the stairwells of the projects' 15-story buildings. That was our hangout, and most of the time that's where we acted out the ritual. Jonathan, my new comrade, just a baby then, was the only real reason that I would come home at all; a brother to help me plunder the white world, a father to be proud of the

deed—I was a fanciful little cat. But my brother was too young
of course. He's only seventeen now while I'm twenty-nine
this year. Any my father, he was always mortified. I stopped
attending school regularly, and started getting "picked up" by
the pigs more often. The pig station, a lecture, and oak-stick
therapeutics. These pickups were mainly for "suspicion of" or
because I was in the wrong part of town. Except for once or
twice I was never actually caught breaking any laws. There just
wasn't any possibility of a policeman beating me in a footrace.
A target that's really moving with evasive tactics is almost
impossible to hit with a short-barreled revolver. Through a
gangway with a gate that only a few can operate with speed
(it's dark even in the day) up a stairway through a door.
Across roofs with seven- to ten-foot jumps in between (the pig
is working mainly for money, bear in mind, I am running for
my life). There wasn't a pig in the city who could "follow the
leader" of even the most timid ghetto gang.

My father sensed a need to remove me from the Chicago
environment so in 1956 he transferred his post-office job to
the Los Angeles area. He bought an old '49 Hudson, threw me
into it, and the two of us cameWest with plans to send for the
rest of the family later that year. I knew nothing of cars. It
was the first car our family had ever owned. I watched my
father with great interest as he pushed the Hudson across the
two thousand miles from Chicago to Los Angeles in two days.
I was certain that I could handle the standard gearshift and
pedals. I asked him to let me try upon our arrival in Los
Angeles that first day. He dismissed me with an "Ah—crazy
nigger lay dead" look. We were to stay with his cousin Johnny
Jones in Watts until the rest of the family could be sent for.
He went off with Johnny to visit other relatives, I stayed
behind with the keys and the car. I made one corner, down
one street, waited for a traffic light, firmed my jaw,
dry-swallowed—took off around the next corner, and ended
the turn inside the plate-glass window and front door of the
neighborhood barbershop. Those cats in the shop (Watts) had
become so immune to excitement that no one hardly looked
up. I tried to apologize. The brother that owned the shop
allowed my father to do the repair work himself. No pigs were

called to settle this affair between brothers. One showed up by chance, however. I had to answer a court summons later that year. But the brother sensed that my father was poor, like himself, with a terribly mindless, displaced, irresponsible child on his hands, probably like his own, and didn't insist upon having the gun-slinging pig from the outside enemy culture arbitrate the problems we must handle ourselves.

My father fixed the brother's shop with his own hands, after buying the materials. No charges were brought against me for the damages. My father straightened out the motor bed, plugged the holes in the radiator, hammered out some of the dents and folds from the fender, bought a new light, and taped it into place on the fender. He drove that car to and from work, to the supermarkets with my mother, to church with my sisters, for four years! It was all he could afford and he wasn't the least bit ashamed of the fact. And he never said a word to me about it. I guess he was convinced by then that words wouldn't help me. I've been a fool—often.

Serious things started to happen after our settling in L.A. but this guy never abandoned me. He felt shame in having to bail me out of encounters with the law but he would always be there. I did several months in Paso Robles for allegedly breaking into a large department store (Gold's on Central) and attempting a hijack. I was 15, and full grown (I haven't grown an inch since then). A cop shot me six times point-blank on that job, as I was standing with my hands in the air. After the second shot, when I was certain that he was trying to murder me, I charged him. His gun was empty and he had only hit me twice by the time I had closed with him—"Oh, get this wild nigger off me." My mother fell away from the phone in a dead faint when they informed her that I had been shot by the police in a hijack attempt. I had two comrades with me on that job. They both got away because of the exchange between the pigs and me.

Since all black are thought of as rats, the third degree started before I was taken to the hospital. Medical treatment was offered as a reward for cooperation. At first they didn't know I had been hit, but as soon as they saw the blood running from my sleeve, the questions began. A bullet had

passed through my forearm, another had sliced my leg, I sat in
the back of the pig car and bled for two hours before they
were convinced that lockjaw must have set in already. They
took me to that little clinic at the Maxwell Street Station. A
black nurse or doctor attended. She was young, full of
sympathy and advice. She suggested, since I had strong-looking
legs, that instead of warring with the enemy culture I should
get interested in football or sports. I told her that if she could
manage to turn the pig in the hall for a second I could escape
and perhaps make a new start somewhere with a football. A
month before this thing happened a guy had sold me a
motorcycle and provided a pink slip that proved to be forged
or changed around in some way. The bike was hot and I was
caught with it. Taken together these two things were enough
to send me to what California calls Youth Authority Corrections. I went to Paso Robles.

The very first time, it was like dying. Just to exist at all in
the cage calls for some heavy psychic readjustments. Being
captured was the first of my fears. It may have been inborn. It
may have been an acquired characteristic built up over the
centuries of black bondage. It is the thing I've been running
from all my life. When it caught up to me in 1957 I was fifteen
years old and not very well-equipped to deal with sudden
changes. The Youth Authority joints are places that demand
complete capitulation; one must cease to resist altogether or
else . . .

The employees are the same general types found lounging
at all prison facilities. They need a job—any job; the state
needs goons. Chino was almost new at the time. The regular
housing units were arranged so that at all times one could see
the lockup unit. It think they called it "X". We existed from
day to day to avoid it. How much we ate was strictly
controlled, so was the amount of rest. After lights went out,
no one could move from his bed without a flash of the pigs'
handlight. During the day the bed couldn't be touched. There
were so many compulsories that very few of us could manage
to stay out of trouble even with our best efforts. Everything
was programmed right down to the precise spoonful. We were
made to march in military fashion everywhere we went—to the

gym, to the mess hall, to compulsory prayer meetings. And then we just marched. I pretended that I couldn't hear well or understand anything but the simplest directions so I was never given anything but the simplest work. I was lucky; always when my mind failed me I've had great luck to carry me through.

All my life I've done exactly what I wanted to do just when I wanted, no more, perhaps less sometimes, but never any more, which explains why I had to be jailed. "Man was born free. But everywhere he is in chains." I never adjusted. I haven't adjusted even yet, with half my life already spent in prison. I can't truthfully say prison is any less painful now than during that first experience.

In my early prison years I read all of Rafael Sabatini, particularly *The Lion's Skin*. "There once was a man who sold the lion's skin, while the beast still lived, and was killed while hunting him" This story fascinated me. It made me smile even under the lash. The hunter bested, the hunted stalking the hunter. The most predatory animal on earth turning on its oppressor and killing it. At the time, this ideal existed in me just above the conscious level. It helped me to define myself, but it would take me several more years to isolate my real enemy. I read Jack London's, "raw and naked, wild and free' military novels and dreamed of smashing my enemies entirely, overwhelming, vanquishing, crushing them completely, sinking my fangs into the hunter's neck and never, never letting go.

Capture, imprisonment, is the closest to being dead that one is likely to experience in this life. There were no beatings (for me at least) in this youth joint and the food wasn't too bad. I came through it. When told to do something I simply played the idiot, and spent my time reading. The absentminded bookworm, I was in full revolt by the time seven months were up.

I went to school in Paso Robles and covered the work required for 10th-year students in the California school system, and entered Manual Arts for the 11th year upon my release. After I got out I stopped in Bakersfield, where I planned to stay no more than a week or two. I met a woman who felt almost as unimpressed with life as I did. We sinned, I stayed. I was 16 then, just starting to get my heft, but this wonderful sister, so round and wild, firm and supple, mature . . . in one month she reduced my health so that I had to take to the bed permanently. I was ill for eleven days with fevers and chest pains (something in the lungs). When I pulled out of it I was broke. I'd collected a few friends by that time. Two of them would try anything. Mat and Obe. We talked, borrowed a car, and went off.

A few days later we were all three in county jail (Kern County) on suspicion of committing a number of robberies. Since the opposition cleans up the books when they find the right type of victim, they accused us of a number of robberies we knew nothing about. Since they had already identified me for one, I copped out to another and cleared Mat and Obe on that count. They "allowed" Obe to plead guilty to one robbery instead of the three others they threatened him with. They cleared Mat altogether. Two months after our arrest Mat left the county jail free of charges.

I was in the "time tank" instead of the felony tank because they had only two felony tanks (that was the old county jail) and they wanted to keep the three of us separated. After Mat left, a brother came into the time tank to serve 2 days. The morning he was scheduled to leave I went back to his cell with a couple of sheets and asked him if he would aid me in an escape attempt. He dismissed me with one of those looks and a wave of the hand. I started tearing the sheet in stripes, he watched. When I was finished he asked me, "What are you doin' with that sheet?" I replied, "I'm tearing it into these strips." "Why you doin' that?" "I'm making a rope." "What-chew gonna do with ah rope?" "Oh—I'm going to tie you up with it."

When they called him to be released that morning, I went out in his place. I've learned one very significant thing for our struggle here in the U.S.: all blacks do look alike to certain types of white people. White people tend to grossly underestimate all blacks, out of habit. Blacks have been overestimating whites in a conditioned reflex.

Later, when I was accused of robbing a gas station of seventy dollars, I accepted a deal—I agreed to confess and spare the county court costs in return for a light county jail sentence. I confessed but when time came for sentencing, they tossed me into the penitentiary with one to life. That was in 1960. I was 18 years old. I've been here ever since. I met Marx, Lenin, Trotsky, Engels, and Mao when I entered prison and they redeemed me. For the first four years I studied nothing but economics and military ideas. I met black guerrillas, George "Big Jake"Lewis, and James Carr, W.L. Nolen, Bill Christmas, Torry Gibson and many, many others. We attempted to transform the black criminal mentality into a black revolutionary mentality. As a result, each of us has been subjected to years of the most vicious reactionary violence by the state. Our mortality rate is almost what you would expect to find in a history of Dachau. Three of us were murdered several months ago by a pig shooting from 30 feet above their heads with a military rifle.

I am being tried in court right now with two other brothers, John Clutchette and Fleeta Drumgo, for the alleged slaying of a prison guard. This charge carries an automatic death penalty for me. I can't get life. I already have it.

When I returned to San Quentin Prison last week from a year in Soledad Prison where the crime I am charged with took place, a brother who had resisted the logic of proletarian-people's revolutionary socialism for the blackman in America sent me these lines in a note:

"Without the cold and desolation of winter there could not be the warmth and splendor of spring! Calamity has hardened my mind, and turned it to steel!! Power to the People"

George

POLICE VIOLENCE AND
ITS PUBLIC SUPPORT

William A. Gamson

James McEvoy

DURING the winter of 1970, a United Press International correspondent was taken into custody by police and held for twenty hours. He had been covering a student riot in Santa Barbara. During the period he was detained he was neither formally charged nor allowed to make a phone call. "War correspondents," California Governor Ronald Reagan explained with a grin, "have to realize that sometime they are going to get it. . . . He should be happy he was captured by the good guys." [1]

For many Americans, there is apparently a thin blue line between order and chaos. Breach it and untold furies lie beyond. The police require unconditional support when they are in combat; sins are understandable and forgivable when they occur in the stress of battle.

For others, of course, it is a quite different story. The police are a crude instrument of power, often failing to differentiate between criminals and bystanders and full of barely controlled aggressive impulses. Norman Mailer expresses this view eloquently in his description at the time of the 1968 Democratic Convention.

Every public figure with power, every city official, high politician, or prominent government worker knows in his unspoken sentiments that the police are an essentially criminal force restrained by their guilt, their covert awareness that they are imposters, and by a sprinkling of career men whose education, rectitude, athletic ability, and religious dedication make them work for a balance between justice and authority. [2]

This paper explores the sources of public support and opposition to police violence. The most highly publicized police violence of the last decade has taken place in a political context with the police confronting organized groups rather than isolated individuals. Since police frequently appear in such conflicts as protagonists, attitudes toward them are likely to be closely bound to support and opposition to the social movements that have occurred within American society during this period. Hence, we start with the more general issue of the nature of social movements before turning to the more specific phenomenon of attitudes toward the police.

SUPPORT FOR POLITICAL MOVEMENTS

Two broad orientations run through efforts to understand the sources of support for such movements as the radical right, student activism, black power, and the like. One orientation has roots in the theory of mass society and views the recruitment to such movements as primarily *reactive*. Potential supporters presumably become available to a movement because they are supposed victims of social strains or personal anxieties. In addition, certain social controls are thought to be absent for these individuals, making them especially promising targets for mobilization by the leaders of mass movements.

The second orientation has roots in class or conflict group analyses and views the recruitment to these movements as more *proactive*. Rather than being acted upon, the participants are seen as goal-directed actors pursuing social change through collective action. At the risk of overdrawing the differences, we will attempt to sketch these two orientations as competing models.

Reactive Model

The reactive model is characterized by weak social attachments and personal vulnerability.

In this model, there are two steps leading to participation in mass movements. The first of these is the formation of an aggregate of individuals who are psychologically ready for participation. Readiness to participate comes from the *absence* of those conditions that constrain others from involvement in essen-

tially irrational forms of political action. In this model, the mass movement participant presumably lacks the series of institutional affiliations and group loyalties that bind people into the political system and create loyalty to it. Those who are heavily embedded in such intermediate associations are less available for new loyalties. Those who are weakly attached and are peripheral to existing social networks are "loose" in the system. Being loose, there are few constraints preventing the development of support for proffered social movements.

Being unconstrained, however, is only part of the story. Mass movements must also promise to meet some important need to energize the unattached, potential recruit. Several different motivational bases have been suggested but, for our purposes, it is unnecessary to distinguish among them. We will use them here as examples of the same basic argument.

One might, for example, emphasize the personal anxiety that results from lack of strong social attachments. Participation in a mass movement provides the emotional satisfaction of being part of a group with strong solidarity—a satisfaction that the participant lacks prior to his participation. In this argument, participation in a movement fills an important psychological need of belongingness; Fromm and Hoffer write in this spirit.[3]

A structural example might emphasize status insecurity. Individuals occupying marginal social positions may experience common strains as social change occurs. Among these groups losing status in society, it will be especially those individuals with weak and conflicting group loyalties who will manifest these strains to the greatest degree. Those with inconsistent statuses, for example, may find that their claims based on their higher status characteristic are no longer socially validated; at the same time, they reject the lower status group into which they are moving and the psychological support that it might provide. Hence, their social marginality gives them a special kind of psychological vulnerability. There are other potential sources of status insecurity besides that of objectively inconsistent statuses but the argument is, in general, similar: By the symbolism and the meaning they give his social condition, by their myth of a better future, by the camaraderie and group support they provide, mass movements supply some important satisfactions for the unattached and vulnerable individual. Kornhauser and many of the authors in *The Radical Right* argue along these lines.[4]

Note that the participants in mass movements are primarily *reactive* in this model. A major part of the dynamic of mobilization is supposed to be provided by elites and, in some cases, demagogues who skillfully exploit the vulnerabilities of the masses for their own political ends. The primary empirical implication of this argument is that degree of social attachment will be negatively associated with support for social movements. In addition, degree of insecurity about one's social identity and degree of social marginality should be positively associated with movement support.

Proactive Model

The proactive model is characterized by conflict groups and group identification.

The mechanisms invoked in this second model are much more conventional. Participation in a social movement is assumed to involve much the same process as group participation in general. Those most available for participation will be those who are not handicapped by constraints such as cross-pressures or social isolation. Thus, the more socially imbedded one is in a group, the more likely he is to become involved in a social movement that involves the group's interest.

Note the underlying assumptions here about social movements. They are seen to embody challenges by relatively powerless groups. These challenging groups are the activist portion of some underlying solidary group. They represent a constituency on behalf of whom they are attempting to change the society. Much of their effort centers on the mobilization of this constituency and its conversion into an active political force. This political struggle takes the form of a mass movement because the groups involved initially lack the scale of organization, access, and appropriate response to operate effectively *inside* the existing political arena. If they ultimately acquire such access and resources, their organizational strategy will shift from that of a mass movement to the tactics of conventional politics.

This model assumes, then, that if groups were equal in their access to resources and were all well integrated into the political system, there would be little occasion for collective action outside of institutional channels. To a greater or lesser degree in different societies, however, political integration is not uniform among social groups. Groups with less access forge their own instruments of change and, in American society, this often takes the form of a mass movement. Tilly, Gamson, and Rogin write in this spirit.[5]

The activists in this political struggle are those members of the challenging group that most strongly identify and are most strongly embedded in the group. Those with the weakest group attachments will be less likely to be drawn into participation. In contrast with the previous model, this one is proactive; and the mass movement is viewed essentially as an instrumental form of organization by a group that lacks institutional power. The leaders are not "outsiders" who are using the movement for their own, separate purposes but "insiders" who embody the group's norms and values.

Thus, the empirical implications concerning group attachment contrast sharply with the first model. If a movement embodies a challenging group's interest, then the participants will tend to be those who are most strongly attached to the group. Those who are peripheral, who are socially isolated, cross-pressured, or otherwise marginal will be the least likely to participate in movement activities.

McCarthyism, Goldwater Support, and Student Activism

Both models may be helpful in explaining a given social movement, up to a point. Movements may change their character, appealing at one time to relative social isolates and at another to those with strong loyalties to a challenging group. Or, one wing of a complex movement may be best understood by one model while another part of it is handled by the other. Having conceded this, however, it is difficult for both to be generally correct, because they differ in their assumptions about the basic nature of the phenomenon being explained.

Take the case of McCarthyism in the early 1950's. Labeling McCarthy supporters as members of the "radical right" rather than as "conservative" invokes the first model. Bell, Hofstader, Lipset, and other students of Joe McCarthy's support emphasized status anxiety as the underlying cause of participation in the movement.[6] "Communists in government" provided

a psychologically rewarding (i.e., simplistic) conspiratorial explanation and scapegoat for the alleged insecurities and anxieties that the McCarthy followers were supposed to be experiencing.

Recently, however, Rogin has taken a fresh look at the McCarthy phenomenon and his analysis suggests that the proactive model is more appropriate. A close look at county voting records and at other evidence leads him to conclude that "McCarthy capitalized on popular concern over foreign policy, communism, and the Korean War, but the animus of McCarthyism had little to do with any less political or more developed *popular* anxieties. . . . McCarthy did not split apart an elite, the parts of which had been equally conservative before him. He rather capitalized on an existing liberal/conservative split within the existing Republican elite."[7] Polsby's analysis of poll data points in the same general direction. Party affiliation is the single best predictor of support for McCarthy—Democrats opposed him and Republicans supported him.[8] Rogin concludes from his own review, "In these polls, as in the data reported by Polsby, no other single division of the population (by religion, class, education, and so forth) even approached the party split."[9]

Rogin rejects the notion that McCarthy was sustained primarily by the vague discontents of frustrated groups. "McCarthy had powerful group and elite support. He did not mobilize the masses at the polls or break through existing group cleavages. . . . Communism and the Korean War played crucial roles."[10] Strange as it may seem, the issues on which McCarthy mobilized support were apparently real ones for his followers, not merely symbolic of private anxieties.

The first model is also a popular apparatus for explaining the support for

Senator Goldwater in 1964. It was frequently assumed that the early supporters of Goldwater were anomic, institutionally detached "cranks," neo-fascists, or "infiltrators" into the Republican Party. "Little old ladies in tennis shoes" became the popular phrase to capture the lunatic fringe imagery.

McEvoy has demonstrated that the evidence sharply contradicts this image of the Goldwater phenomenon.[11] Pre-convention supporters of Goldwater were compared on a number of variables with those who ultimately voted for him even though they had preferred another nominee prior to the convention. The early Goldwater supporters were very significantly higher on such variables as church attendance, income level, and education. They were more likely to be married. Furthermore, they were much higher in past participation in Republican Party politics. Finally, they exhibited average to low levels of objective status discrepancy. None of this evidence suggests lack of attachment; on the contrary, early Goldwater supporters seem to be strong conservatives with social support and respect from their friends and neighbors.[12]

The persistence of social science support for the reactive model in the absence of much data that support it suggests something about its ideological biases. It typically has a pejorative ring, suggesting that supporters of a political movement are irrationally seeking simple, illusory solutions for complex problems. Since social scientists who study right-wing movements are typically hostile to them, this model readily suggests itself and receives far less critical examination than it deserves.

When attention turns to movements of the left, there is much less tendency to invoke the reactive model. Although the McCone Commission Report on the Watts riot suggested that rioters were recent migrants with weak attachment to the community, social scientists were quick to test and demolish this hypothesis.[13] Similarly, this model has failed to gain a foothold as an explanation of student activists. While popular articles about student "rebels" may have postulated their personal maladjustment, serious studies put this myth to rest. Student activists, it turns out, are not the most marginal members of the student body but those most embedded in many aspects of life at the university. They are not academic failures, psychological wrecks, or social isolates, but those with better than average academic performance, with more liberal parents, with higher self-esteem, and with friends who have similar political views. They are, in short, well socialized and personally well-adjusted members of politically militant sub-groups in the university.[14] We do not mean to imply here that activists are "typical" students, but merely that they are actively and centrally involved in life at the university—in fact, more so than the typical student.

In all the above studies, the evidence seems more nearly to support the proactive model. We would not argue that this is necessarily true for all recruits to social movements. But at this point, we would be skeptical any time the reactive model is invoked to explain a movement when the person who invokes it is far removed from or unsympathetic to the movement or the issue in question.

MEASURING SUPPORT FOR POLICE VIOLENCE

The models discussed above apply rather generally to social movements. The issue of police violence, we argue, must be viewed in this more general context. Police may play two different roles in group conflict situations. They may take a relatively neutral posture, remaining on the sidelines as much as possible and operating to make sure that the means of carrying on conflict remain within certain limits. Or, they may be used as a partisan instrument or ally of one group in the conflict. The latter role is especially likely when the conflict is between the authorities and those challenging them.

Our underlying concern in this paper is with the presence or absence of constraint on the use of police as a partisan instrument against challenging groups. One aspect of this constraint is the climate of opinion that is reflected in public attitudes toward police violence. By understanding where the sources of public support and opposition to police violence are located, we can understand something about the nature and strength of this possible source of constraint on police behavior. The two models discussed above, as we will argue shortly, have direct implications for this issue. Before considering this, we turn to a description of our data and our measure of support and opposition for police violence.

The data we report were obtained from a national cross-section probability sample of adult Americans conducted for the National Commission on the Causes and Prevention of Violence, by Louis Harris Associates of New York in October, 1968.[15] The sample consists of 1176 completed interviews and is more fully described in Kirkham, Levy, and Crotty, and McEvoy.[16]

The interview schedule contained a section of 25 statements about violence in various contexts—personal, political, international, and so forth. Respondents were asked to express varying degrees of agreement or disagreement with each statement. A factor analysis of the entire set identified several distinct clusters, including one that we have labeled "police violence." This factor

showed high loadings on three items:

1. The police are wrong to beat up unarmed protestors, even when these people are rude and call them names. (Factor loading: .79)

2. The police frequently use more force than they need to when carrying out their duties. (Factor loading: .62)

3. Any man who insults a policeman has no complaint if he gets roughed-up in return. (reversed item, Factor loading: .61).

The overall distribution on these three items is included in Table 1. A score on support for police violence was computed for each individual by reversing the direction of the third item and summing it with scores on the other two items. These total scores were then reduced to a seven-point scale, with high scores representing greater favorableness toward police violence. The distribution of the sample on this index is reported in Table 2.

RESULTS

Our attempts to explain the variation in the index of support for police violence will be guided by two models derived from the more general models described in the first section of this paper.

Reactive Model

In this argument, we suggest that police violence raises a fundamental question for our respondents: Do they see police as embodying the law, or as subject to its constraints like other citizens? To appreciate this second view, one must embrace a complex normative principle. Those who have allegiance to it resemble those who are usually found to support principles of civil liberties. This means, especially, those who are well educated and have other characteristics associated with high normative

TABLE 1—Distribution of Responses to Items in Police Violence Index

	PERCENTAGES				
	STRONGLY AGREE	AGREE	DISAGREE	STRONGLY DISAGREE	DON'T KNOW
The police are wrong to beat up unarmed protestors, even when these people are rude and call them names.	12 ⎵ 49	37	36	9	6
The police frequently use more force than they need to when carrying out their duties.	9 ⎵ 28	19	46	18	7
Any man who insults a policeman has no complaint if he gets roughed-up in return.	13 ⎵ 57	44	32	7	4

$N = 1171$.

integration into the political system. During periods of sharp challenge to the distribution of power and privilege in a society, the police tend to be used as a partisan instrument in defense of privilege. When this happens, they usually become agents of established groups and opponents of challenging groups. Gamson defines trust in these terms: "Confidence in authorities means that they are perceived as the group's agents, that the group members identify with them. . . . Alienation from authorities means that . . . they are . . . the agents of groups with conflicting goals." [18]

The past decade has been a period of high conflict between challenging groups and authorities. Consequently, individuals will differ sharply in trust of the police, depending on whether they are part of groups attacking the established order or of groups defending it. Not only will group memberships determine attitudes toward the police, but the strength of group identifications and attachments will determine the degree of such support. [19]

More specifically, this model implies the following hypotheses: [17]

1) The higher the educational level, the more opposition to police violence.

2) Assuming that whites are higher in normative integration than blacks, whites will be more opposed to police violence than blacks.

3) Registered voters will be more opposed to police violence than those who are not registered.

4) People who identify with a major political party will be more opposed to police violence than those who lack such identification.

Proactive Model

In this argument, the police violence index primarily taps trust in the police.

More specifically, this model implies the following hypotheses:

1) Blacks will be more opposed to police violence than whites.

2) Young people will be more opposed to police violence than older people.

3) Poor people will be more opposed to police violence than rich people.

4) Financially dissatisfied people will be more opposed to police violence than financially satisfied people.

TABLE 2—DEGREE OF SUPPORT OF POLICE VIOLENCE

VIOLENCE INDEX	Oppose				Support			TOTAL
	0	1	2	3	4	5	6	
Number Interviewed	54	103	246	298	287	146	23	1157
Percentage	5	9	21	26	25	13	2	100
		35		26		40		

TABLE 3—RELATIONSHIP OF SELECTED VARIABLES TO ATTITUDES
TOWARD POLICE VIOLENCE

RESPONDENTS	OPPOSING POLICE VIOLENCE* *Percentage*	MIDDLE *Percentage*	SUPPORTING POLICE VIOLENCE* *Percentage*	NUMBER INTERVIEWED
Race				
White	27%	27%	46%	(929)
Black	69%	18%	13%	(215)
Education				
Not high school graduate	31%	28%	41%	(488)
High school graduate but not college graduate	36%	24%	40%	(542)
College graduate	45%	24%	30%	(125)
Age				
Under 30	45%	25%	30%	(276)
30–49	40%	23%	37%	(417)
50 or over	24%	28%	48%	(447)
Family Income				
Under $5000	36%	29%	36%	(222)
$5000–$9,999	36%	24%	40%	(361)
$10,000 and above	34%	26%	40%	(572)
Financial Satisfaction				
"Not satisfied at all"	42%	22%	37%	(257)
"More or less satisfied"	36%	27%	37%	(473)
"Pretty well satisfied"	29%	27%	44%	(425)
Party Identification				
Republican	25%	29%	46%	(288)
Democratic	38%	25%	38%	(576)
Independent, other, or none	39%	27%	35%	(238)
Voting Registration				
Registered	34%	26%	41%	(919)
Not registered	40%	26%	35%	(235)

* This column includes those in categories 0–2 in Table 2, the middle column contains category 3, and the third column combines categories 4–6.

Table 3 presents a series of bivariate relationships between the police violence index and the variables suggested by the hypotheses listed above. It should come as no great surprise to most readers that race sharply differentiates toward police violence: blacks are much more likely to be against police violence than are whites. Furthermore, there is some additional evidence that this difference is not merely a reflection of general distrust of authority, but is more specifically directed at the police. The interview schedule contained a rather extreme item expressing political distrust: "The government in Washington is the enemy, not the friend, of people like me." Only 8 percent of the whites in the sample agree with this statement; and the percentage for blacks is identical. Thus, the great difference between blacks and whites on the police violence index seems to reflect attitudes toward this specific object of trust or distrust.

Education shows a moderate effect. As education increases, so does opposition to police violence, from 31 percent for those with less than a high school diploma to 45 percent for college graduates. Family income shows no simple relationship to police violence, but age does: the younger group shows more opposition. However, those who are financially most dissatisfied are higher in their opposition to police violence (42 percent) than are those who are happiest with their financial position (29 percent).

As for our measures of political involvement, Republican Party identifiers show the least opposition to police violence (25 percent); Democrats and those without a major party identification are more opposed (38 percent). Finally, those who are registered to vote show slightly less opposition to police violence (34 percent) than those who are not participants in the electoral process (40 percent).

A multivariate analysis adds some additional information. Chart 1 presents the interaction between education and race. The figures in this chart represent the percentage of respondents in each category who fall at the anti-violence end of the index (categories 0–2). Education has no additional effect for blacks; those at all educational levels are opposed to police violence. For whites, education has some explanatory power; the percentage of whites opposed to police violence increases from 19 in the lowest group to 43 in the highest but remains considerably short of the overall black figure of 70.

Given the importance of race and of education for whites, Table 4 controls for these variables in exploring the relationship between the police violence index and several other relevant variables. Family income still shows no consistent relationship; at best, there is a slight suggestion that whites in the lowest income group are more opposed to police violence than their wealthier counterparts at each educational level. For blacks, the direction is reversed, and only 51 percent of those with income under $5,000 fall at the oppose-police-violence end of the index. Financial satisfaction shows a similar but more pronounced relationship for whites—the least satisfied are most opposed to police violence at each educational level; there is no clear direction on this variable for blacks. Age differences emerge more sharply, particularly for the college group. Of white college graduates under 30 years of age, 58 percent oppose police violence compared to one-third of those over age 50 with similar education.

The earlier results on party identification and voting registration emerge more clearly with race and education controlled. Those without a major party

POLICE VIOLENCE AND ITS PUBLIC SUPPORT

CHART 1

RACE AND EDUCATION BY POLICE
VIOLENCE INDEX

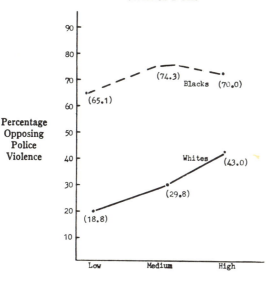

EDUCATIONAL LEVEL

identification have the greatest opposition to police violence, while Republican identifiers show the lowest opposition.[20] Furthermore, whites who are registered to vote are less likely to oppose police violence than those of the same educational level who are not registered voters. For blacks, this relationship is reversed.

INTERPRETATION

How well do our two models handle these results? The first model fares rather badly. It successfully predicts the positive relationship between education and opposition to police violence. However, it is not clear from this model why blacks, who most would argue are less normatively integrated, are so much higher on opposition to police violence. It seems reasonable to assume that registering to vote is a mark of integration

into the political system. If so, it is not clear from this model why those who are not registered to vote should be more opposed to police violence. The argument for the effects of major party identification is similar; but those who lack such identification are, if anything, more opposed to police violence.

The second model does considerably better. As predicted, blacks are more opposed to police violence than whites. Young college-educated whites are more opposed than other whites. The hypothesis concerning poor people receives equivocal support at best, with subjective satisfaction proving a better predictor than actual income. Perhaps the have/have-not dimension of conflict is less relevant at this time than the racial dimension.

By and large, then, the proactive

TABLE 4—Percentage of People Interviewed Opposing Police
Violence by Selected Variables Controlled for
Race and Education for Whites

	Blacks	Whites		
		Not HS Graduate	HS Graduate but Not College Graduate	College Graduate
Age				
Under 30	70% (64)	31% (35)	34% (141)	58% (36)
30–49	77% (82)	24% (93)	32% (193)	41% (49)
50 or over	56% (68)	15% (224)	22% (126)	28% (29)
Family Income				
Under $5000	51% (63)	22% (104)	35% (48)	71% (7)
$5000–$9999	75% (88)	17% (132)	30% (115)	35% (23)
$10,000 and above	71% (68)	19% (122)	29% (293)	46% (79)
Financial Satisfaction				
"Not at all"	63% (75)	27% (73)	32% (94)	57% (14)
"More or less"	74% (87)	20% (136)	29% (194)	46% (46)
"Pretty well"	69% (52)	13% (141)	30% (172)	35% (52)
Party Identification				
Republican	56% (18)	18% (88)	24% (135)	31% (42)
Democrat	69% (169)	18% (183)	28% (187)	47% (32)
Independent, other, none	88% (17)	18% (62)	38% (117)	51% (39)
Voting Registration				
Registered	72% (153)	17% (273)	27% (375)	42% (105)
Not registered	60% (60)	24% (79)	38% (81)	56% (9)

Percentages include those who fall at the anti-police-violence end of the index (categories 0–2); the number next to the percentage refers to the total number of respondents with the specified characteristic.

model makes good sense of our data. There is one exception to this success, and an important one: it fails to account for the effect of education. To the extent that education is solely a measure of privilege, increasing it should make one more supportive of police violence rather than less so. This hypothesis not only fails to be supported but, as Table 4 indicates, education has an effect on white attitudes even when income is controlled. This suggests that, as we might expect, there is something about education other than the privilege it brings that may be contributing to attitudes toward police violence. How,

then, can this model be enlarged to account for this additional result?

Each model treats education as an indicator of something else—of social integration (in the reactive model), or of privilege (in the proactive model). But perhaps it has an effect in its own right, through influencing the conceptual sophistication of the respondent. The more highly educated the respondent, the greater his cognitive differentiation between the police and the law. A highly educated respondent who is generally opposed to contemporary challenging groups may give his fealty to a more abstract conception of the law.

Transgressors should be treated harshly but with due process; the legal system, not the police, is the proper bulwark against extra-legal dissidence.

This conception leads to recognition that not only the control of dissidents but also the control of the police can become a problem. Mailer describes the reactions to police behavior in the streets of Chicago at the time of the 1968 Democratic convention:

What staggered the delegates who witnessed the [police] attack . . . on Michigan avenue was that it opened the specter of what it might mean for the police to take over society. They might comport themselves in such a case not as a force of law and order, not even as a force of repression upon civil disorder, but as a true criminal force, chaotic, improvisational, undisciplined, and finally—sufficiently aroused—uncontrollable.[21]

Education, we suggest, gives enough of a glimpse of this specter to sober the sympathetic attitudes toward the police that the sophisticated "law and order" supporter may have. We argued earlier that the police violence index taps trust in the police, and this trust is primarily a function of privilege. For respondents with low trust in the police—blacks, for example—the education factor is largely irrelevant, because differentiating between police and the law does not make them any more trusting toward the police. Respondents with high trust in the police but low education do not have their support for police violence inhibited by awareness of the police control issue. But as education increases for high trust respondents, this additional factor becomes more salient; their inclination to support police violence is retarded by their greater awareness of the problem of controlling the police.

CONCLUSION

Police comportment has an important effect on the degree of violence with which political conflicts are waged by challenging groups. As Stinchcombe argues,

Military control and liberty function together to stabilize political conflict. If the violent means of conflict are made much more expensive by effective enforcement by the police and army, while nonviolent means are made cheaper by the condition of liberty, then a rational organizational leader . . . will prefer less violent means. If the police and army are either ineffective, or enter into the conflict as full-fledged participants themselves by denying not only the right to riot but also the right to speak, then the comparative effectiveness of violent means in the competitive struggle increases, while the effectiveness of nonviolent means declines. Under these conditions, a rational organizational leader will choose a higher proportion of violent means.[22]

It is important to ask what constraints exist on the use of police as a partisan instrument or ally of one group in a conflict situation. Some of these constraints may be structural, including both aspects of internal police organization and linkages between the police and political, economic, and other organizations. This paper does not address these possible structural constraints but it does raise the question of normative constraints on police behavior. If police violence violates widely held norms in American society, then a public outcry against such behavior might serve to constrain it and to mobilize institutional pressure against it.

We find scant cause for optimism about any constraint from public opinion. Robinson describes what a sample of 1,005 respondents thought about police action at the Chicago convention in

1968.[23] Only 19 percent believed that the police had used too much force; 25 percent felt that they had not been forceful enough, and the rest were either satisfied with the amount of force used or had no opinion.

Our own data have the same thrust. With the possible exception of the effect of education, we have not found any support for the proposition that police violence seriously violates American political norms. Extra-legal police actions directed against unpopular targets are unlikely to draw censure or even disapproval from those substantial segments of the American public for whom the police are the "good guys." And for those who, like ourselves, see police participation in conflicts in a partisan role as an invitation to counter-violence on the part of challenging groups, we offer this warning: Nurture whatever organizational and structural constraints exist, for you will find few normative constraints in the present American political culture.

NOTES

1. Reported in the *San Francisco Chronicle*, Wednesday, March 4, 1970.

2. Norman Mailer, *Miami and the Siege of Chicago* (Cleveland: World Publishing Co., 1968), p. 175.

3. Erich Fromm, *Escape from Freedom* (New York: Rinehart and Co., 1941); Eric Hoffer, *The True Believer: Thoughts on the Nature of Mass Movements* (New York: Harper & Bros., 1951).

4. See especially Daniel Bell, Seymour Martin Lipset, and Richard Hofstadter in Daniel Bell, ed., *The Radical Right* (Garden City, N.Y.: Doubleday, 1964); and William Kornhauser, *The Politics of Mass Society* (New York: Free Press, 1959).

5. Charles Tilly, "From Mobilization to Political Conflict," multilith (Ann Arbor, Mich.: University of Michigan, 1970); William A. Gamson, *Power and Discontent* (Homewood, Ill.: Dorsey, 1968) and "Stable Unrepresentation in American Society," *American Behavioral Scientist* 12 (Nov.–Dec., 1968) 15–21; Michael Paul Rogin, *The Intellectuals and McCarthy: The Radical Specter* (Cambridge, Mass.: M.I.T. Press, 1967).

6. See Bell, op. cit.

7. Rogin, op. cit., pp. 216, 220.

8. Nelson W. Polsby, "Toward an Explanation of McCarthyism," *Political Studies* 8 (October, 1960), 250–271.

9. Rogin, op. cit., p. 234.

10. Ibid., p. 268.

11. James C. McEvoy, *Radicals or Conservatives? The Contemporary American Right* (Chicago: Rand McNally, 1970).

12. The weak attachment model might conceivably account for some "deviant" Goldwater supporters—that is, supporters from areas where ·few people were sympathetic.

13. See, for example, Nathan Caplan and Jeffery M. Paige, "A Study of Ghetto Rioters," *Scientific American* (August, 1968), 15–21, and Jeffery M. Paige, *Collective Violence and the Culture of Subordination* (Ph.D. diss., University of Michigan, 1968).

14. See the various articles in Edward E. Sampson, ed., *Stirrings Out of Apathy: Student Activism and the Decade of Protest*, special issue of the *Journal of Social Issues* 23 (July, 1967), for documentation of this point.

15. McEvoy served as special consultant to the Commission Task Force on Political Assassination.

16. James Kirkhan, Sheldon Levy, and William J. Crotty, *Assassination and Political Violence*, A Report to the National Commission on the Causes and Prevention of Violence (Washington, D.C.: U.S.G.P.O., 1969), and McEvoy, *Radicals or Conservatives?* op. cit.

17. It implies many others beyond those stated here. However, we confine ourselves to those hypotheses that our data enable us to test.

18. Gamson, op. cit., pp. 54, 56.

19. Unfortunately, we lack the data to test this part of the argument here.

20. There are no differences on this variable, however, for low education whites.

21. Mailer, op. cit., p. 175.

22. Arthur L. Stinchcombe, "Social Structure and Organizations," in James G. March, ed., *Handbook of Organizations* (Chicago: Rand McNally, 1965), p. 176.

23. John P. Robinson, "Public Reaction to Political Protest: Chicago 1968," *Public Opinion Quarterly* 34 (Spring 1970), 1–9.

IN THEIR OWN WORDS: ADDICTS' REASONS FOR INITIATING AND WITHDRAWING FROM HEROIN

Barry S. Brown

Susan K. Gauvey

Marilyn B. Meyers

Steven D. Stark

With the important exception of work by Chein et al. (1964), surprisingly little use has been made of the addicts' own ideas either about the reasons for their having gotten involved with narcotics initially or their reasons for trying to break themselves loose from the bonds of addiction. It is of value to learn the addicts' reasoning for their initial and continued drug use on two counts. Firstly, if effective treatment of addict-clients is to be undertaken, it is necessary to learn the forces the clients see as operating to pressure them both toward using drugs and toward giving up drugs. Secondly, if effective programs of prevention are to be organized, it is necessary to take cognizance of, and respond to, the pressures acting in the community both for and against addiction as those pressures are perceived by addicted members of that community.

In conducting this study, effort was made to compare the thinking of adult and juvenile addicts with a view toward exploring the changing role of narcotics in the lives of its users. Similarly, study was made of the role of heroin in the lives of male as compared to female addicts and clues derived for the development of programs specific to the needs of each.

Finally, effort was made to explore the extent to which the addict has placed himself outside the law before his first use of heroin. Studies by Finestone (1957), Chein et al. (1964) and O'Donnell (1966) indicated that addicts are increasingly likely to have been involved in criminal activity prior to their ever having become involved with narcotics. Other investigators have contended that most addicts do not become involved in criminal activity until after their becoming addicted (Garb and Crim, 1966). It was proposed therefore to ask questions of addicts designed to learn not only about initial use and withdrawal from heroin, but to learn also about the ages at which the street-visible addicts under study here first began using heroin and first became involved in criminal activity.

Method

Accidental samples of addict-clients were drawn from each of three treatment facilities of the Narcotics Treatment Administration of the District of Columbia. To obtain adult samples only those clients 21 or older were sampled; to obtain juvenile samples an upper age limit of 18 was established. The samples obtained were as follows:

(1) Male addict-clients 21 or older (N=105). The average age of this group was 28.6 years; the average education 10.3 years; 89% were black; 33% were married, 44% single and the remainder formerly married. Ten of these addicts had come to the treatment program through referral from the District of Columbia criminal justice system; all of the remainder were voluntary clients.

(2) Female addict-clients 21 or older (N=36). The average age of this group was 27.4 years; the average education 10.4 years; 95% were black; 22% married, 44% single and the remainder formerly married. All of these addicts were voluntary clients.

(3) Male addict-clients 18 and younger (N=77). The average age of this group was 17.2 years; the average education 9.58 years; 96% were black; 4% were married and 96% single. Seven of these addicts had come to the treatment program through the juvenile court system; all of the remainder were voluntary clients.

A sample of female addict-clients 18 and younger was not available.

Procedure

Subjects were given a structured questionnaire making use of the critical incident technique as described by Flanagan (1954). The questions relating to initial use of heroin and efforts to withdraw from heroin were as follows:

Think back to the very first time that you tried heroin. Describe the things that happened that led you to try heroin that first time. Tell me as much about it as you can remember.

Think back to the very first time you withdrew voluntarily. Describe the things that happened that led you to withdraw that first time. Tell me as much about it as you can remember.

Think back to the first time that you went back on drugs after voluntarily withdrawing. Describe the things that happened that led you to go back on drugs. Tell me as much about it as you can remember.

Think back to your decision to withdraw voluntarily *this* time. Describe the things that happened that led you to withdraw *this* time. Tell me as much about it as you can remember.

In addition, the addict-clients were asked to describe the events surrounding the commission of the first act that they knew to be illegal. Information was also obtained regarding age of first illegal act and age of first arrest and that data contrasted with age of first use of heroin.

Clients were interviewed individually and privately by research staff with assurance given them that their statements would be held in confidence. In all, 5% of those persons sampled were unwilling to cooperate in the study.

To analyze subjects' responses to the critical incident questions, categories were developed for the replies to each of the five open-ended questions. Three judges were then asked to group clients' responses in accord with these same categories. Over-all there was unanimous agreement among the three judges on 74% of the subjects' responses. A fourth judge rated those responses on which two of three judges were in agreement. A minimun of three of the four judges were in agreement on 89% of the subjects' responses and all of these were retained for study. Where all, or three of four, judges agreed that more than one response category was involved in one client's answer, both scorable responses were included as data.

Results

Initial Use of Heroin

Comparison was made between adult male, adult female and juvenile male addicts in terms of their descriptions of the critical incidents involved in their first heroin use. Here, as in the case of the comparisons described below, the percentages reported in the accompanying tables are based on the number of addict-clients in each group giving scorable responses. Percentages for any one question may total to more than 100% if clients gave more than one scorable response to that question.

When the categories influence of friends and influence of relatives were combined into a single influence of others category in order to permit statistical analysis, the three addict groups were found to differ significantly in terms of the reasons given for first use of heroin ($x^2 = 12.02$, $p < .05$). As compared with juveniles, adult males were far more likely to cite curiosity as a major reason for their first use of heroin, e.g. "I knew what a reefer made you feel like, I wondered if heroin was the same." Juveniles placed disproportionately large emphasis on the influence of friends, e.g. "The crowd I was in were all getting high; you can only say 'no' so many times" (see Table 1). For all groups, the influence of others and curiosity about the effects of heroin were the major reasons given for first heroin use.

Initial Withdrawal from Heroin

The two male groups resembled each other closely in their responses to question about initial effort at withdrawal (see Table 2). Both groups placed greatest stress on their intentions to change the overall patterns of their lives and functioning, e.g., "I got sick of being a worm in the ground, of not having anything or being anything." Secondarily both male groups cited a relationship between drugs and physical problems as well as the expense of drugs as major reasons for first withdrawal attempt. By comparison, nearly half the female clients gave drug-related physical problems as the reason for their decisions to make effort to withdraw from heroin.

For all groups it is noteworthy that neither the threat of punishment for illegal activities nor the influence of friends were important factors in the decision to attempt withdrawal. Punishment is apparently either not seen as a real consequence of heroin use or is not a sufficient reason to stop use. Friends in the community are a significant force for involvement with heroin, but are not seen as exerting an important influence on the decision to quit heroin.

Failure of First Withdrawal Effort

There is general agreement among addict-clients that the major reason for the failure of their first effort at withdrawal was that they had given up drugs only and that a psychological need remained, e.g. "It's like a mental problem; you keep thinking . . . I just want to get high today, only today" (see Table 3). Among juveniles the influence of friends was the next most frequently cited reason for returning to the use of heroin while for adult females the relief of personal problems was the second most frequently cited explanation. For adult males the easy availability of heroin and the use of heroin to relieve personal problems were of some consequence in resuming the use of heroin. Thus, many individuals found themselves contending not only with internal pressures to return to heroin use, but having to contend as well with external pressures to resume their addiction.

Current Withdrawal from Heroin

For all groups of addicts, a major reason cited for attempting withdrawal at the present time is once again the addicts' concern with changing their overall functioning and life patterns (see Table 4). For women, family problems come to be of particular significance in their decision to attempt withdrawal while physical problems associated with drug usage become of somewhat lesser consequence.

Once again, however, the threat of punishment and the influence of friends are of relatively small importance to the decisions of addicts to attempt withdrawal. So, too, the capacity of heroin to induce a high is rarely cited as having diminished. Consequently, it seems likely both the felt psychological need and external pressures to resume heroin use will again be present and must be dealt with in treatment.

Initial Illegal Act

A third of the female addicts who became involved in criminal acts cited the effort to obtain drugs as the reason for their first illegal act (see Table 5). By comparison, only 18% of the men and 14% of the juveniles first committed criminal acts in an effort to obtain drugs.

Similarly, 74% of the adult male addicts and 78% of the juvenile addicts committed illegal acts before their first use of heroin. However, only 40% of the females committed illegal acts prior to their first use of heroin. Moreover, 53% of the adult male addicts sampled, 55% of the juvenile males and 20% of the female addicts were arrested before they had ever used heroin.

Implications

The findings of this study would appear to have implications for two areas of program functioning. Although these two areas are in some measure related, each of them will be explored separately in this analysis.

1. Heroin Addiction and Crime

This study lends support to findings reported elsewhere suggesting that the addict — and particularly the male addict — is drawn from a culture or subculture already invested in illegal activity. This means that treatment programs must be organized to deal with the problems of the addict-criminal, i.e., the client whose addiction is superimposed on his criminal adjustment, rather than the problems of the criminal-addict, i.e., the client whose criminality is superimposed on his addiction. It should be noted that these findings relate to the functioning of an inner city addict population. Additional study is needed to learn whether these same findings would hold for a suburban addict population.

Nonetheless, any treatment program intended to serve effectively the inner city addict population must address itself to providing an alternative not only to the addict life style but to the criminal life style as well. The treatment program organized must therefore provide the client a range of new adjustive skills and behaviors that make it unnecessary, if not undesirable, for him to remain a part of the criminal subculture. Thus, the client will require the vocational and academic training and the counseling needed to permit him to change his role and functioning in the community. However, a second finding of this study, as will be explored below, suggests that the treatment program must be developed with the recognition that the treatment staff's only meaningful ally is likely to be the client himself and his desire to quit the hassle of the addict-criminal world.

2. Pressures For and Against Heroin Use

The addicts report that their friends in the community play a very significant role in their first heroin use. Moreover, teenage male addicts are considerably more likely to cite the encouragement of friends to initiate heroin usage than are older male addicts. This suggests that heroin is not only becoming increasingly available in the inner city, but that the use of heroin is also becoming more largely a part of social relationships formed in the inner city. Young people are encouraged to join the drug culture by their friends. For many, the use of heroin may then be one means of permitting the young inner city resident to adapt to the social situation in which he finds himself.

In that sense, there is the suggestion that heroin addiction — at least in the inner city — may be less a response designed to meet the pathology of the individual than a response designed to meet the social situation of the individual, i.e., the pathology of the community. Admittedly, this inference is based on data provided by the clients themselves and must, therefore, be treated as suggestive rather than as definitive. However, the differences between the responses of adult and juvenile addicts seem of sufficient consequence to justify that suggestion.

If the influence of other persons is credited by many addicts as an important factor in their first using heroin, friends and/or family are seen by only a very few male addicts as influencing their decisions to give up heroin. Male addicts, adult and juvenile, see pressures within the community leading to their use of heroin and see no countervailing community pressures to induce withdrawal.

If, then, the community as seen by the addict acts to produce and maintain addiction, it becomes necessary to organize treatment programs that make effort to place themselves more largely between the addict and his community. Two possibilities suggest themselves here. On the one hand, heroin replacement programs, e.g., those using methadone maintenance, can effectively capture the client and attempt to provide the assistance and support the client will need to redirect his behavior. The treatment source that becomes the client's "connection" stands in an obviously powerful position in its relationship to that client and is thereby better able to make real demands on his behavior and functioning. It is interesting to speculate whether the newer, more long lasting heroin-substitutes now being developed to replace methadone will be as effective in drawing the addict away from his community to relate to treatment staffs on the very frequent basis that methadone clients are now forced to do.

A second treatment alternative, by no means incompatible with the above, would consist of aggressive efforts by counseling staff to enter the addict world and to relate to the addict on a regular basis in the community in which he is located. In this way, the counselor could attempt to deal with the client's real problems in negotiating with the world in which he must live and at the same time provide a resource in that world giving the client the support in the community for his efforts to remain free of heroin that might otherwise be absent.

A third treatment form that also attempts to isolate the addict from his community involves the use of Synanon-like treatment organizations. Here, there is the creation of a new community to replace the addict's own neighborhood community. This, of course, is accomplished by treating clients in a hospital or prison program as well. However, unless the program is intended to provide the addict with a permanent alternative, it will still be necessary to structure mechanisms for permitting the addict to make a drug-free adjustment within the community he is destined to rejoin. This cannot be done unless treatment techniques are developed that permit the treatment staff to make impact on the client within his home community.

Summary

Samples were drawn from each of three narcotic addict client populations: adult male addicts (N=105), adult female addicts (N=36) and juvenile male addicts (N=77). Each person sampled was given a structured interview containing questions regarding his initial use of heroin, his efforts at withdrawal, his initial criminal act and selected items of demographic information. The findings indicated that addicts — particularly juvenile addicts — are encouraged to begin using heroin by friends in their communities, but the impetus to stop using heroin must come largely from within the self with little support available in the community. Moreover, the treatment program must expect to contend with the addict's own ambivalence about giving up drugs. On the one hand, he feels a very genuine dissatisfaction with the addict-criminal life style and, on the other hand, he feels a continuing psychological hunger for the drug.

It was also found that illegal activity by these male street-visible addicts — and indeed arrests of these same male addicts — typically precedes their first use of heroin. Among females, this is far less likely to be the case.

Consequently, in organizing treatment programs, effort must be made to provide the male addict with an alternative to the life style he has established as a criminal as well as providing him a means for giving up his use of heroin. In so doing, however, it will be necessary to create the support for abstinence from illicit drugs that will not be present in the community in which the addict must function. Means for providing this support have been discussed.

Table 1. ADDICTS' REASONS FOR FIRST
USE OF HEROIN

Responses	Adult Males (N=98)	Adult Females (N=35)	Juvenile Males (N=73)
Curiosity	44 (44.9%)	14 (40.0%)	21 (28.8%)
Influence of friends	43 (43.9%)	18 (51.4%)	48 (65.8%)
Influence of relatives	3 (3.1%)	5 (12.5%)	2 (2.7%)
Relief of personal disturbance	7 (7.1%)	7 (17.5%)	9 (12.3%)
Seeking a high	16 (16.3%)	2 (5.0%)	11 (15.1%)
Other	6 (6.1%)	0 (0.0%)	1 (1.4%)
Total	119 (121.4%)	46 (126.4%)	92 (126.1%)

Table 2. ADDICTS' REASONS FOR FIRST
WITHDRAWAL FROM HEROIN

Responses	Adult Males (N=62)	Adult Females (N=22	Juvenile Males (N=46)
Drug-related physical problems	12 (19.4%)	10 (45.5%)	10 (21.7%)
Drug-related family problems	8 (12.9%)	2 (9.1%)	6 (13.0%)
Concern about punishment for illegal acts	0 (0.0%)	0 (0.0%)	6 (13.0%)
Effort to change life patterns	24 (38.7%)	6 (27.3%)	16 (34.8%)
Heroin no longer producing a "high"	2 (3.2%)	1 (4.5%)	2 (4.3%)
Expense	11 (17.7%)	3 (13.6%)	8 (17.4%)
Influence of friends	2 (3.2%)	1 (4.5%)	6 (13.0%)
Other	3 (4.8%)	3 (13.6%)	1 (2.2%)
Total	62 (99.9%)	26 (118.1%)	55 (119.4%)

Table 3. ADDICTS' REASONS FOR FAILURE
OF FIRST ATTEMPTS AT WITHDRAWAL

Responses	Adult Males (N=57)	Adult Females (N=25)	Juvenile Males (N=45)
Easy availability of heroin	9 (15.8%)	1 (4.0%)	8 (17.8%)
Continued psychological need	22 (28.6%)	11 (44.0%)	17 (37.8%)
Relief of personal problems	8 (14.0%)	7 (28.0%)	9 (20.0%)
Relief of medical problems	2 (3.5%)	1 (4.0%)	0 (0.0%)
Influence of friends	5 (8.8%)	4 (16.0%)	12 (26.7%)
Dissatisfaction with treatment received	5 (8.8%)	0 (0.0%)	3 (6.7%)
Other	9 (15.8%)	2 (4.0%)	2 (4.4%)
Total	60 (105.3%)	26 (110.0%)	51 (113.4%)

Table 4. ADDICTS' REASONS FOR CURRENT
WITHDRAWAL FROM HEROIN

Responses	Adult Males (N=82)	Adult Females (N=31)	Juvenile Males (N=50)
Drug-related physical problems	7 (8.5%)	5 (16.1%)	6 (12.0%)
Drug-related family problems	10 (12.2%)	11 (35.5%)	9 (18.0%)
Concern about punishment for illegal acts	6 (7.3%)	5 (16.1%)	5 (10.0%)
Effort to change life pattern	36 (43.9%)	10 (32.3%)	25 (50.0%)
Drug no longer producing a "high"	1 (1.2%)	1 (3.2%)	1 (2.0%)
Expense	15 (18.3%)	4 (12.9%)	5 (10.0%)
Influence of friends	9 (11.0%)	3 (9.7%)	3 (6.0%)
Other	3 (3.7%)	2 (6.5%)	4 (8.0%)
Total	87 (106.1%)	41 (132.3%)	58 (113.0%)

Table 5. ADDICTS' REASONS FOR FIRST
ILLEGAL ACT

Responses	Adult Males (N=87)	Adult Females (N=21)	Juvenile Males (N=65)
Diversion or to occupy time	18 (20.7%)	0 (0.0%)	21 (32.3%
To obtain money or material benefit	28 (32.2%)	5 (23.8%)	19 (29.2%
To obtain drugs	16 (18.4%)	7 (33.3%)	9 (13.8%
To attack parents' system	5 (5.8%)	1 (4.8%)	5 (7.7%
To belong to a group	16 (18.4%)	4 (19.0%)	8 (12.3%
Other	7 (7.9%)	4 (19.0%)	5 (7.7%
Total	90 (103.4%)	21 (99.9%)	67 (103.0%
Not involved in illegal act	8 (8.4%)	12 (26.4%)	6 (8.5%

CHROMOSOMAL DEVIATION
AND CRIME

Menachem Amir

Yitzchak Berman

THE TENDENCY to search for the sources of both normal and deviant behavior in the biological endowment of man is very old, appealing, and, seemingly, simple. In the field of criminology, the question is as follows: Are there people who are condemned from birth to become criminals due to specific biological characteristics? And, if so, is the general tendency toward crime genetically inherited or is the specific crime itself inherited? One hundred years ago, the well-known criminologist Lombroso already spoke of "born criminals" as a result of degeneration, atavist regression, or other physiological defects.

Lombroso's theory was disputed by Goring[1] who proved that there are no definite biological or physiological differences between criminals and noncriminals, and that the physiological differences among noncriminals, are, at times, greater than between criminals and noncriminals. Furthermore, in Lombroso's time, no actual chromosome and genetic tests were known and no answer had been given to the questions, what is inherited, and how is it manifested in terms of behavior?

After Lombroso, alternate theories were purported in an attempt to find the relationship between heredity and crime. All these attempts only inferred genetic patterns from the presence or absence of bodily abnormalities. One school within the biological approach concerned itself, as it still does today, with the classification of character according to body type. This school was developed in Europe, for example Kretschmer[2] and received a more thorough formulation in the studies of Sheldon,[3] and, most recently, in the research of Eysneck. This approach is subject to criticism on account of its poor classification of crime and the failure to find a significant relationship between criminals and their body types.

A more valid test of the relationship between heredity and crime must necessarily examine the nature of the biologically inherited factor. The claim was put forth that by means of the chromosomes either a general or a specific predisposition to crime is transmitted.

Previous Biologically Oriented Research

On the basis of this assertion, three additional methods of investigation were developed which, so to speak, represent the history of the biological hereditary approach to the question of the cause of crime: studies in the genealogy of criminal families; twin studies; and, most recently, the study of the differences in the number and type of chromosomes of criminals and noncriminals. At the outset, we will review the first two types of studies, since the criticism leveled against them is essentially valid with respect to the third type of study as well.

Studies of criminal families or the history of crime in these families.—In essence, the claim is that specific negative hereditary factors are transmitted in these families. This type of study does not provide proof for the hypothesis that crime is genetically based, since it does not clarify what is inherited and how this negative inherited factor functions and is transmitted. Furthermore, the data collected on the biological and chromosomal characteristics of the members of the family and their offspring are incomplete and are not treated according to scientific methods. Many difficulties of validity and reliability of information are inherent in these and other biologically oriented studies such as, the lack of control through random sampling and experimental design for the possibility that observed relationships may be spurious, and that other factors may contribute to the behavior, but they are not differentiated.

Even when a background of psychic and social pathology is found in these families, as was found by Exner,[4] the frequency of such phenomena does not prove either the exclusiveness or the degree of importance of hereditary factors. The negative social, familial, and community influences to which the children of these families have been exposed cannot be overlooked, as they are important, even if not decisive, factors in their criminal behavior.

Furthermore, Dirksen found that the percentage of serious criminality among these families is actually extremely low: 0.3 percent in the famous Kallikak family, and only 6 percent in the Jukes family.[5]

Further research on criminal families was done by Healy[6] who studied 1,000 chronic criminals. In not a single instance was he able to establish proof of antisocial tendencies among the offspring of his subjects. On the other hand, Healy in the United States and Burt[7] in England, found, in the existence of negative mental and physical characteristics among criminals, sufficient proof of the indirect action of heredity. However, neither of them was able to establish what the hereditary factor is that thus indirectly influences the appearance of criminal behavior in its bearer.

Twin studies.—Twin studies were considered to provide firmer proof of the biological basis of crime. Identical twins (whose hereditary factors are identical) have been compared to fraternal twins (who are as similar as are siblings born at different times). The value of these studies is in the kind of methodology that can be employed in order to verify the biological hypothesis. By studying identical twins, the factor of heredity is held constant, so that any observed difference in behavior may be attributed to environmental factors. Conversely, if, despite environmental

differences, identical twins are found to have similar criminal behavior, it may be inferred that heredity is the important factor in the etiology of crime. Thus, identical twins enable us to control for heredity in a natural way.[8] Studies of identical twins revealed a high frequency of criminal behavior for one of the twins when his brother was a criminal; while, for fraternal twins, the frequency was much less.

There are several points of criticism to be raised with regard to twin studies, which are relevant as well to the chromosome studies.[9] First, there is the problem of getting reliable statistics. Even if a pair of identical twins is born in every 88 births, it is difficult to find a representative sample of twins where at least one of the twins is a criminal. The various samples studied are small, and do not allow the derivation of reliable conclusions or any kind of generalizations.

Verification is another problem; i.e., do studies of twins really measure what they intend to measure, viz, the influence of heredity or environment on criminal behavior? In light of our present knowledge, it is difficult to isolate the influence of these two factors, and the possibility or desirability of distinguishing between the two is questionable. If we agree that it is only the combination of heredity together with environment that determines a person's behavior, then it would certainly appear to be futile to try to differentiate between their individual influences.

In the majority of twin studies, the results are based on the method of "case study," i.e., an ex-post facto approach is used, so that the possibility exists of subjective bias on the part of the investigator.

Another problem in these studies is controlling for the variables, i.e., precisely differentiating between identical and fraternal twins. This is generally done on the basis of similarity in appearance, temperament, eye and hair color, rather than on the basis of blood type or chromosomes. In addition, control over the environmental factor also has not been complete, since, in general, only certain factors are taken into consideration, and not all possible ones. Geographic separation, which is generally considered, does not necessarily imply an environmental difference.

Again, if criminality or a criminal disposition is inherited, how can the large difference found between twins be explained when their environments are similar? Why are identical twins found where only one partner is a criminal?

It is possible that the high correlation of criminality in identical twins derives mainly or even solely from their having common life experiences. In order to resolve this problem, studies are needed of criminal identical twins who grew up separately; otherwise, how can it be determined whether the twins are criminals as a result of sharing a negative environment or as a result of having similar hereditary strains. Although, for the majority of identical twins studied, it is difficult to prove that they grew up in similar environments, the physical similarity between the twins, in fostering similar social attitudes toward them, certainly must, to some degree, ensure similarity of their psychological environments. For instance, if the twins grew up in the same social group, it is impossible to determine to what extent the environmental factor is more important than the hereditary factor.[10][11] Even given that two individuals having similar hereditary characteristics have the same defects, how much value has this fact in explaining what happens to people having different hereditary characteristics who are exposed to similar environments? Moreover, the criminal behavior which was investigated and found to be identical among the twins is inadequate for testing the biological theory. This is so because mainly arrests and imprisonments were investigated rather than criminality, and, further, no distinction was made between chronic and occasional criminals.

At what specific stage of development in the twins' life do the hereditary factors become apparent in behavior? This important question was raised by Rosanoff[12] who showed in his research that the delinquency of young delinquent identical twins is alike while that of adult delinquent identical twins not so. How, then, can it be explained that inherited characteristics—if they are really inherited—are in evidence at an early and not an older age?

Chromosomal deviation studies.—Up until this point, the criticism levelled against studies of twins is valid, also, with respect to the third type of study of the biological basis of crime, viz, chromosomal deviation studies. Studies of chromosome deviation seem, however, more promising since they may provide an answer to the basic question: What is the specific inherited biological factor that causes crime? There is also the possibility that identifying physical characteristics will be discovered that are related to chromosome deviation, and which are related to organic psychological and behavioral characteristics and, in turn, to deviant behavior in general and criminality in particular. However, unlike the cases of other sex chromosome deviations where there is an apparent lack of striking physiological and structural syndrome which underlines the chromosomal deviation, this is rare in the XYY phenomenon, and may explain its delayed and limited discovery. Only recently was it found that the fingerprints of XYY cases are noticeably

different than prints of the average person, a discovery which will enable easy sampling and selecting XYY deviates (this was reported at the recent meeting of the American Association for the Advancement of Science, at Boston.

The well-known criminal acts of Daniel Hogun in France, Hanel in Australia, and Richard Speck in the United States are but an illustration of these findings while they also serve to point out some important penological questions. Let us see what has been found in recent research. In the last 7 years there have been many genetic studies in which chromosomal deviations were found among mental patients, retarded persons, homosexuals, and criminals. These studies established that either a deficiency or an addition to the normal set of chromosomes, or a deviation in the gene itself, is expressed in an imbalance in the organism which induces negative psychological, morphological, and behavioral effects.

Studies of chromosomal deviation are based on the finding that there are males, and only males, having an extra male chromosome, called the Y gonosome; i.e., they are XYY, rather than the normal XY. In spite of the varied and conflicting results of the various studies, there are some suggestive consistencies of behavior and traits that appear to be evolved from the research. However, because of the skewed nature of the population tested no conclusive evidence is available. To present the detailed methodology and findings of all studies would go beyond the limits of the present discussion. Therefore, we shall limit ourselves to the general picture and results of work done in this field.[13]

1. The frequency of this chromosomal deviation varies in the different groups of criminals studied and ranges from 8.8 percent of XYY's in the sampling and 2 percent of the total institution population from which the sample was taken to 0.66 percent of XYY's and 0.66 percent respectively. The size of the groups studied has been generally small. In the main, institutionalized persons, mentally ill criminals, including hardened criminals, the criminally insane, and psychotics, have been studied.

2. It was found that among criminals, the chance of possessing an extra Y gonosome is up to 60 times greater than for the general population, and exceeds the theoretical expectation of 0.3 percent.

3. From the point of view of physique, those who possess an extra Y gonosome are taller and thinner when compared to control groups and their siblings. The average height of the bearer of an extra Y gonosome is over 6 feet tall.[14][15] No other specific somatic abnormalities were found for the XYY individuals. However, some have genital abnormalities such as, hypogenitalism,

hypospadias, and undescended testes. Abnormal EEG results and dermatological troubles were found.[16]

4. A higher frequency of aggressive and disturbed behavior (between 27 and 50 percent) was found among those having an extra Y gonosome.[17] In some studies, it was found that the personality structure of such men was defective, and that they possessed characteristics simulating the classical picture of psychopathy.[18] The question now arises as to what extent criminality is a result of such intermediary factors as retardation, aggressiveness, or various other behavioral disturbances which are known to be connected with having an extra Y gonosome.

5. No specific correlation was found between an extra Y gonosome and mental retardation. The I.Q. of extra Y gonosome bearers was found to fluctuate between mild retardation and an I.Q. of 118.

6. Higher rates of violent crime were found to be prevalent among men with an extra Y gonosome. However, the studies performed revealed, as well, substantial numbers of crimes against property, of arson, and various other types of criminal behavior.[19] It is important to note that in these studies no distinction was made between the chronic and occasional offender or whether the crime was internally motivated or had to do with environmental pressures or provocation.

7. It was found that criminals with an extra Y gonosome began their criminal activity at a relatively early age.[20] Criminal behavior was begun at an average of 13 years, starting for some at the age of 10 years; whereas, for groups of criminals lacking chromosomal deviation, the average age was 18 years. Further, those having chromosomal deviations were found to suffer from behavioral problems prior to committing their first crime.

8. Chromosomal deviations were found to be lacking among the siblings of extra Y gonosome bearers. The brother having the chromosomal deviation was found to stand out as the "black sheep" of the family.

9. Since most of the reports are about European populations there is no information about ethnic or racial composition in the sample. A study of Welch, et al.,[21] in America found only one Negro with the XYY phenomenon from among 35 males tested. More studies are needed to find ethnic and race differences for this phenomenon.

10. Treatment of criminals with an extra Y gonosome is problematic since they do not respond to the usual forms of treatment and, therefore, imprisonment is recommended for the majority of them.

It should be noted that in all but one study,[22]

no delinquency or other mental disturbances were found among the parents or brothers of extra Y gonosome bearers. This is in comparison to control groups of criminals where criminality was found among the parents and siblings of the criminals. It can be said, then, that what disposes the individual having an extra Y gonosome to criminality is no familial factor, but rather the factor of genetic mutation.

While some regularities of characteristic emerge from the research on the XYY phenomenon, no generalization can yet be made. This is because of the skewness of the sampled population, and the lack of accepted universal definitions of terms, such as "antisocial," "psychopathy," and "agressiveness." What evolves as a pattern from the various studies is that among institutionalized persons who are mentally ill, criminal and of subnormal intelligence, there is a much higher than expected (0.3 percent) incidence of XYY chromosomal deviation.

General Evaluation of Chromosomal Deviation Studies

What problems are raised by the above facts? In part, at least, they have already been referred to in our summary of studies of criminal families and twins.

The genetic findings need to be evaluated within the wider framework of the basic problem: the biological basis of crime; a part of the more inclusive question of the physiological basis of human behavior. Let us first analyze the general problem arising out of the biological assumption, and then move to the examination of the implications of the new genetic findings of the XYY phenomenon.

The biological theories of crime may be divided into the following main groups:

1. The first argues that the criminal act itself is biologically and hereditarily determined. From this premise, the following conclusions may be drawn: (a) A direct relationship exists between the biological structure and the behavior which is supposedly determined by it. (b) Human beings behave differently as a result of differing genetic characteristics. (c) From the methodological point of view, the physiological characteristics which differentiate criminals from noncriminals need first to be determined, and then personality differences and character types. On this basis, proof is to be sought that these differences are indeed the external manifestation of biological differences existing between criminals and noncriminals.[23] [24] (d) In light of the fact that crime is defined socioculturally and that the definition of crime varies and is relative in time and place, then, if the hypothesis is correct that a direct relationship exists between a biological source—which is constantly defective—and criminal be-

havior, this means that biological inheritance has enormous flexibility.

2. The second general hypothesis of the biological theories of crime is that what is genetically transmitted is a general tendency to maladjustment and that, given certain environmental pressures, this disposition leads to criminal behavior. Inherent in this hypothesis is that crime is just one of many possible outcomes of a defective physiological structure.

The conclusions that can be drawn from the above hypotheses are as follows:

First, if we accept that the factors determining criminal behavior already exist at birth, then it follows that the influence of environment is not very important. Here we are faced with a fatalistic approach of predestination and predetermination; i.e., that persons possessing defective biological makeups are bound to be either fools or criminals, etc., despite all the possible advantages or disadvantages life may hold in store for them. In addition, from a methodological point of view, in order to prove that crime is biologically determined, it must be assumed that persons with similar genetic deviations (e.g., as in identical twins) are subject to different environments. As long as this is not proved the claim has not been refuted that the criminal behavior of the identical twins results from common life experiences and not from identical genetic factors. If, on the other hand, it is proved that the genetic qualities of criminals are different, but environmental factors alike, the entire genetic theory has been refuted. Thirdly, if criminality is inherited, then noncriminality, or conforming behavior, must likewise be inherited. Thus, for example, if criminal behavior is frequently found among criminals lacking genetic defects, the genetic theory of crime becomes questionable. Conversely, if biological defects are found among a great number of noncriminals, again, the genetic theory of crime is subject to doubt.

If heredity creates a general tendency to difficulties in social adaptation which may lead to deviant behavior, then, in essence, a theory of constitutional defects is being asserted in which heredity is a very flexible factor in crime. This, again, is a refutation of the genetic theory of crime which stresses the specificity and exclusiveness of the heredity mechanism.[25] [26]

Methodological Evaluation of Chromosomal Deviation Studies

We shall now analyze some additional problems more specifically related to the subject of chromosomal deviation.

First, there is the problem of reliability. The populations studied were not only small, but very selective as well, consisting of hospital patients and prisoners. Hence, the high proportion of retardees in the samples. It is quite clear that these samples were biased. It is possible to argue, for instance, that persons having an extra Y gonosome are found in greater numbers in institutions because they are taller, and therefore appear to be more dangerous, and that psychiatrists and judges tend to recommend institutionalization for them in order to "protect society."

Theoretical Evaluation of Chromosomal Deviation Studies

Another problem is that even if we do accept the thesis that the extra Y gonosome causes crime, we still have not explained how this chromosome exerts its influence, or, in other words, what is the mechanism by which the extra Y gonosome is activated.

Various explanations are proposed for the causality and relationship between the XYY deviation and the various aspects of the syndrome apparent in such deviation. Cerebral dysrythimis or damage in the nervous tissues hormonal changes which lead to embryopathy, premature birth predisposing brain damage.[27] However, it is social factors which may determine the choice of aggression or an outlet for the frustrations encountered by mentally subnormal youngsters who happen to be tall. The existence of extremely retarded persons having an extra Y gonosome suggests a possible answer to the question of the relationship between chromosomal deviation and deviant behavior; viz, that an indirect relationship exists wherein the extra gonosome causes a general tendency to commit criminal acts, given conducive conditions, or that the relationship exists through various intervening factors such as when emotional instability, retardation, agressiveness, etc., accompanied the XYY deviation. Therefore, all possible intervening factors must be taken into account; for example, subnormal IQ, adverse environmental conditions. It should be remembered that criminal behavior cannot, in itself, constitute an indicator of the underlying process involved, and that the causal chain, even if it does have a genetic basis, is always in great part related to external social and environmental factors as was shown in studies of aggression. For example, it was found, in one study of a random population sample, that the percentage of aggressors having antisocial behavior was greater than that of criminals having an extra Y gonosome. To a large extent, aggression is an inherited reactive trait which is related to male role characteristics, and, therefore, constitutes a desirable trait in the social classes from which most criminals emanate.

The questions arise as to what stage in the development of the individual does the extra gonosome begin to exert its influence on behavior and whether or not this influence is the same in all human beings. The answers to these questions might help to explain, at least in part, the existence of chromosomal deviations among criminals as well as noncriminals.

Research in the field of genetics shows that genetic factors are specific. The proof of the relationship of genetic factors and behavior is explicit: The genes of an individual unequivocally determine the color of his eyes, hair, and other various specific physiological characteristics. On the other hand, criminality, since it is nonspecific, cannot be inherited, according to genetic theory. Criminal behavior is a social fact or situation, which is defined by society as such. The types of crimes and the possible kinds of behavior they cover are practically innumerable; yet, if we assume that crime is inherited, then the genetic factor for crime must necessarily be a specific one. This means that there must be a genetic factor which determines that an individual be a pickpocket, rather than an embezzler or car thief or forger, etc. Yet, this is clearly not so. All of us know that the types of crime are defined by specific kinds of behavior and that these definitions change independently of the hereditary characteristics of law breakers. In other words, in contrast to biological definitions, which are again specific, the criminal cannot be considered a specific biological type.

It is possible to claim, as we saw above, that while the individual does not inherit a specific genetic factor for a specific crime, he does inherit a general tendency to commit a specific crime, for example, a tendency to commit forgery. If genetic factors determine in which type of crime criminals will specialize, then it follows that they must also determine the specialization of noncriminals. In other words, it is as much predetermined that a person be a university lecturer as it is that the color of his eyes be blue. If, on the other hand, the claim is that individuals inherit a general tendency for breaking the law, independent of which law, then this conflicts with the Mendelian genetic theory which is founded on the inheritance of specific genetic factors.

Furthermore, criminological research shows that most criminals obey most of the laws most of the time and that many criminals commit a variety of crimes. The variability of offenses committed by a certain offender cannot be explained by the theory of specific genetic inheritance with all that it implies. Also, the meaning of aberrant behavior, as was pointed out, is a relative matter which varies in contrast with the stability of genetic heredity. Even if it is

assumed that a genetic factor causes a predisposition to aggression, or rebellion, etc., yet do not all of us know people who behave aggressively without breaking the law? Criminality is a status, conferred by society, and not all people who break the law are defined as criminals. Whether a person is a "criminal" is highly dependent on the mechanisms of the law and law enforcement, and this mechanism cannot be explained by means of biological theory.

It is, of course, possible to argue that the biologist deals with "true" criminals and not with criminals, as defined by the law. However, the difficulty then arises in that the biologist himself has no choice but to use legal criteria in selecting his cases. He has no other way of differentiating between the criminal and the noncriminal other than the use of police or court files, since, from the biological point of view, both conforming and criminal behavior are, organically speaking, "normal." Aggression by itself is not yet considered a crime, and only social definitions and reactions connected with the physiological differences stemming from the genetic factor can explain the process of becoming a "social" criminal, although from the physiological standpoint, the "social" criminal may be considered a sick or exceptional person.

Attempt at Reconciliation

The extreme point of view which we have taken—against the biological theory of crime and against the attempt to see in the discovery of chromosomal deviations support for a biological theory of crime—is well known in criminological theory. As has already been noted, the problem with which we are dealing today is another example of the general problem: heredity or environment? It would be unfair, however, to leave the subject in complete rejection of the new genetic findings as they relate to criminology. A few words of compromise and concession are in order.

Even if we do not know the way in which the extra Y gonosome influences criminal behavior, the possibility of such an influence cannot be discounted; perhaps, intermediary factors are involved. Secondly, it can be assumed that as with other biological factors, the extra Y gonosome exerts its influence on personality, and to the extent that criminal behavior is a resultant of personality development or immediate situations encouraging specific types of behavior, a relationship, although as yet unclear, can be assumed to exist between the specific genetic load of the extra Y gonosome and other specific biological factors on the one hand, and on the other hand, behavior which is defined as criminal.

Although it is not yet possible to measure the

influence of the extra Y gonosome on personality, it may well be that it bears an important role in the manner in which an individual reacts to social experiences. The hereditary genetic mechanism determines physiological and psychological characteristics, e.g., aggression, which, in turn, determine to what degree environmental pressure and negative conditions can be withstood until deviant and unacceptable behavior—defined (by society) as criminal—erupts. In other words, heredity determines and sets for the individual the specific structural and physiological limits of his ability to withstand environmental pressures. From here it follows that while the genetic potential may be similar in individuals, yet behavior may vary greatly. It is difficult to isolate the respective effects of the genetic and environmental factors on behavior since their influence is interwoven. It is clear to us that the environment determines if and how a man will react in accord with the functional ability with which he is endowed by heredity. His reaction, if it deviates from the norm, may be defined as "criminal." Thus, the question needs to be asked: To what extent is behavior mainly organic in its source or mainly psychogenetic?—not the question: Is behavior organic or is it psychogenetic?

It is still premature to negate the benefit of any additional genetic research in the field of crime. However, the drive to find a biological cause is so strong and the technological developments in the efforts to find a relationship between physiological determinants and criminal behavior are so promising, that it seems likely that there will be fresh developments in the study of the relationship between biology and crime.

The Significance for Penology

Long before the mechanisms of XYY syndromes are well understood, and their frequency well documented for larger populations, the XYY deviation has entered the courtroom; thus, in conclusion, some remarks on the repercussions of the new genetic findings for penology, or mainly the question of criminal responsibility.

In court, defendants found to have chromosomal deviations are either charged guilty of their crimes and punished accordingly, or are dealt with mildly on the claim of diminished responsibility. It is possible that the difference in handling such cases is a result of differences in the approaches of various courts to the problem of criminal responsibility. But the basic question remains: Are these individuals responsible, and to what degree, for their deeds? To a large extent this depends on research into the proportion of XYY males in the general population and the proportion of nondelinquents among them.

But until more research will substantiate a high correlation between the XYY phenomenon and criminal behavior, the problems of criminal responsibility will most probably be determined by the court considerations supported by psychiatrists and geneticists about individual cases. Their aims and their tendency will be to prove mitigation of criminal responsibility as a defense, to rebut contention of premeditation or police aforethought. A re-education process of the law and court is expected, with more and better knowledge about genetics like the long, not yet successful, education the law has with psychiatric terminology and theory.

Another problem is that if chromosomal deviation is accepted as a reason for diminished responsibility, then it is possible to assert that other factors over which the individual has no control must be similarly considered as affecting diminishing responsibility. The individual with an extra Y chromosome did not choose to have it, nor did the ordinary criminal choose to be brought up in a detrimental environment.

And finally, on a more general level—if we accept the biological theory, chromosomal or otherwise—we have to ignore not only criminal responsibility but also general human responsibility, i.e., not only "achievements" in crime but also in other positive human endeavor. Thus, excellence in intellectual, social, and athletic abilities are no more deemed as a result of personal achievement due to will, sweat, and effort but due to genetic endowment only. We are no more what we are because of what we make of ourselves, but because we are endowed with certain inherited factors.

Now, it can be argued that the concept of punishment as a means of revenge has not yet been eradicated from the theory of punishment, and for many judges it is frequently difficult to be more progressive than the population whom they serve. It may be that it is these very cases of chromosomal deviation, however, that will enable society to achieve a more progressive approach to the treatment of criminals since, if the courts will accept the argument of diminished responsibility on the basis of chromosomal deviation, this will open the door to use of this argument with regard to other types of criminals and other causes of diminishing responsibility.

It is clear, nevertheless, that if we accept the fact that chromosomal deviation leads to crime, then we cannot consider the offender having this defect to be a deliberate criminal. He requires hospitalization for the protection of society, and not incarceration with the ordinary offender. This is as long as we have not found a way of correcting or overcoming this defect. The great danger in this fatalistic approach of biological determinism is that the public will start to see the criminal as someone who cannot be reformed, but rather is to be eliminated or subjected to some type of eugenic measure. This must be prevented at any cost.

A LINK between the XYY syndrome—an inborn, male chromosome abnormality—and criminal behavior is not clearly demonstrated at the present time, according to the findings of a conference in June 1969 sponsored by the National Institute of Mental Health Center for Studies of Crime and Delinquency. A group of experts from the fields of genetics, psychiatry, psychology, sociology, and law discussed research, ethical, and social policy issues related to the XYY syndrome. A consensus was reached that, at the present time, no definite conclusions can be drawn about the relationship between the presence of the XYY chromosome and deviant, criminal, and violent behavior.—FEDERAL PROBATION, *September 1969.*

NOTES

1. C. Goring, *The English Convict.* London: Darling & Sons, 1913
2. E. Kretschmer, *Physique and Character.* New York: Harcourt, Brace and Co., 1925.
3. W.H. Sheldon, *Varieties of Delinquent Youth: An Introduction to Constitutional Psychiatry.* New York: Harper, 1949.
4. F. Exner, *Kriminologie.* Berlin: Springler-Verlag, 1949, pp. 123-4.
5. W.C. Reckless, *The Crime Problem* (3rd ed). New York: Appleton-Century-Crofts, 1961, p. 271.
6. W. Healy, *The Individual Delinquent.* Boston: Little, Brown, 1915, p. 154.
7. D. Burt, *The Young Delinquent* (3rd ed.). London: University of London Press, 1938, p. 605.
8. H.H. Newman, *Multiple Human Birth.* New York: Doubleday, 1940, p. 124.
9. L.R. Kupperstein, "The Twin Method of Exploring the Effects of Heredity and Environment on Criminal Twin," University of Puerto Rico, 1967.
10. A. Montague, *Human Heredity.* New York: The New American Library, 1960, pp. 132-134.
11. S. Yoshimasu, "The Criminological Significance of the Family in the Light of the Study of Criminal Twins," *Acta Criminologiae et Medicinae, Legalie Japanica,* 27, 1961, pp. 117-41.
12. A.J. Rosanoff, et al., "Criminality and Delinquency in Twins," *Journal of Criminal Law, Criminology and Police Science,* 24, 1934, pp. 923-34.
13. For a summary see L. Moor, "Aberrations Chromosomogues Portant sur les Gonosomes et Comportement Anti-social," *International Annals of Criminology,* 6, 1967, pp. 459-79.

14. M.D. Casey, et al., "YY Chromosome and Anti-Social Behavior," *Lancet,* 2, 1966, p. 859.

15. W.H. Price, et al., "Criminal Patients With XYZ Sex Chromosome Complement," *Lancet,* 1, 1966, p. 565.
16. M.A. Telfer, D. Baker, and L. Longtin, "YY Syndrome Is an American Negro," *Concept,* 95, 1968.
17. W.H. Price, et al., *op. cit.*
18. W.H. Price and P.B. Whatmore, "Behavior Disorders and Patterns of Crime Among XYY Males Identified at a Maximum Security Hospital," *British Medical Journal,* 1, 1967, pp. 533-37.
19. W.H. Price and P.B. Whatmore, *op. cit.*

20. J. Cowie and J. Kohn, "XYY Constitution in Prepubertal Child," *British Medical Journal,* 1968, pp. 748-749.
21. J.P. Welch, et al., "Psychopathy, Mental Deficiency, Aggressiveness, and the XYY Syndrome," *Nature,* 214, 1967, pp. 500-501.
22. W.H. Price and P.B. Whatmore, *op. cit.*
23. A.N. Foxe, "Heredity and Crime," *Journal of Criminal Law, Criminology and Police Science,* 36, 1945, pp. 11-16.
24. D.H. Stott, "Evidence for a Congenital Factor in Maladjustment and Delinquency," *The American Journal of Psychiatry,* 118, 1940, pp. 427-37.
25. D.H. Stott, *Ibid.*
26. S.J. Fox, "Delinquency and Biology," *University of Miami Law Review,* 16, 1961, pp. 65-91.
27. J. Cowie and J. Kohn, *op. cit.*

A PSYCHO-ANALYTIC PEEK
AT CONSPIRACY

Al Katz

There is . . . in the American temper, a feeling that "somewhere," "somebody" is pulling all the complicated strings to which this jumbled world dances. In politics the labor image is "Wall Street" or "Big Business"; while the business stereotype was the "New Dealers."

D. Bell, The End of Ideology
140-41 (rev. ed. 1962)

I.

In these few pages I will attempt a theory of why people seem to have a tendency to "explain" events in terms of "a conspiracy." The theory is based on Freudian psychoanalysis, so it must be presented here with some foreword. Though I feel psychoanalytic insights are often useful outside of or beyond an individual therapeutic regime, one must heed Freud's warning that

> it behooves us to be very careful, not to forget that after all we are dealing only with analogies, and that it is dangerous, not only with men but also with concepts, to drag them out of the region where they originated and have matured.[1]

I have tried to remain conscious of the analogous quality of this enterprise throughout. If both parties to this communication are at least partly successful in this way perhaps the theory presented will prove useful.

II.

The circumstances of the Kennedy assassination caused many people to believe that this act of murder was the result of an insidious and elaborate plan, a belief not altogether dissipated by the Report of the Warren Commission. More recently a series of suggestive circumstances and ambiguous symbols grew into widespread conviction that Paul McCartney of "The Beatles" died several years ago and the remaining members of the group constructed an elaborate plan to conceal the fact. The United States Government chose to prosecute Dr. Spock and four others for conspiracy even though an indictment for aiding and abetting draft evasion was more likely to result in conviction. Apparently everybody loves a conspiracy as much as a parade. This is not to say that conspiracies are imaginary things, but one does wonder at their appeal in the face of often substantial contradictory evidence.

It is perhaps understandable for people to look for indications of a conspiracy because all experience is relatively ambiguous. There may be a simple apparent explanation for an event as well as a complex opaque one. How does one know which is real? How can one know what is really happening or what has actually happened? So saying, some degree of suspicion is probably justified, but there is a point where one begins to feel that the search for conspiracies is motivated by something deeper than the essential ambiguity of ordinary experience. I would like to suggest a possible explanation: the disposition to find conspiratorial enemies is a manifestation of the anxiety produced by an unconscious primal scene fantasy. (Conspiracy derives from *conspirare;* to breathe together.) Freud found that many of his patients claimed to have witnessed their parents having intercourse.[2] Whether these were reports of historical events or fantasies he did not regard as a crucial question.[3] In any event, "the scene . . . is likely to produce a 'traumatic state' by flooding the organism with an inappropriate excitation."[4] It is the anxiety produced by this witnessing of a secret event that I believe accounts in part for our fascination with and fear of conspiracies.

Those who are reluctant to accept apparent explanations of an event will often defend their scepticism by saying something like, "There is more to this than meets the eye." The cliché is highly suggestive, for it applies wherever reality appears as a mask for a very different sort of reality. For the child the apparent reality of an asexual intraparental relationship takes on this quality of a mask for the sexuality of the bedroom.[5] In some quite literal sense, from the child's point of view, there is indeed more to this (mother—father relationship) than meets the eye.

As one might expect the phrase is over-determined. "More to it than meets the eye" implies a hidden quality about the unrevealed reality. Parental sexuality may take place behind a closed door or in darkness. Furthermore, the "eye" is generally the medium through which the child imagines that he witnesses the event. It is this sort of "spying" activity which, while necessary to get at the truth, produces guilt to the extent one has "intruded" into an event that was meant to be private and obscured.

Not long ago Justice Harlan stated that "every conspiracy is by its very nature secret."[6] This dictum has great appeal for reasons not entirely practical. To the extent "there is more to this than meets the eye" identifies the suspicion of a conspiracy; one that is obvious can hardly be imagined. Justice Harlan identifies the conventional mental imagery stimulated by the term conspiracy: a clandestine, secret meeting under cover of darkness. If I pass a group of men huddled together in a dark alley whispering quietly to each other the immediate reponse may be that they are "up to no good." In my youth the neighborhood kids would have said something like "those guys are gonna fuck somebody," or "somebody (the victim) is going to get it in the ass" or "take it in the shorts." These phrases are suggestive, particularly the latter two. Freud reported that the coitus always appears to have been performed *a tergo*[7] or *more ferarum*.[8] There is, therefore, a connection between the ambivalence of the primal scene fantasy and our ambivalent adult response to a suggestion of conspiracy. That is, there is clearly a mixture of fear and excitement or fascination at the thought that a conspiracy "may be behind it all." "Thus such an experience (the primal scene) is likely to connect the ideas of sexual excitation and danger."[9] I think this connection can also be seen in the dissents from the findings of the Warren Commission. There is an uneasy excitement in having discovered a conspiracy to kill Kennedy which is not present if the act was planned by a single individual.

One of the more familiar types of conspiracy is the vice ring; the so called spy ring is perhaps equally familiar, and both entities are often headed by someone called a ring leader. These terms identify not only the purposes of the enterprise, but—if they are properly used—the structure of the combination as well. "There may be one person . . . round whom the rest revolve. The metaphor is the metaphor of the center of a circle and the circumference. There may be a conspiracy of another kind, where the metaphor would be rather that of a chain; A communicates with B, B with C, C with D. and so on to the end of the list of conspirators."[10]

Because the ring or circle type structure facilitates the division of labor and control, combinations of any size tend to be of this type. The following observation by Fenichel makes this structural fact quite significant.

> In psychoanalytic practice, we have the habit of stating, when sensations of this kind [equilibrium and space] come up, such as rotating objects, rhythmically approaching and receding objects, sensations of crescendo and decrescendo, that 'primal scene material is approaching.' But of course, sensations of this kind are not specific for 'becoming aware of sexual scenes in the surroundings.' They are, rather, specific for being overwhelmed by excitation.[11]

There is one further suggestive phrase worth mentioning here. We often speak of people who are admitted to an existing conspiracy (let in on) as having been admitted to the "inner sanctum." This is even true of presidential cabinets where, although one knows the membership, one does not know what transpires "within." The phrase "inner sanctum" is particularly good at generating that excitement of the dark and mysterious which accompanies the fear of discovering what lies within. If my memory serves me, "inner sanctum" was the title of a radio mystery program with particular appeal to children. Though it is undoubtedly overdetermined, "inner sanctum" certainly suggests an image of that bedroom wherein the primal scene is re-enacted in fantasy.

The anxiety generated by conspiracy is reflected in specific legal prohibitions which are justified by the particular potential force which conspiracies may release. In other words, next to the potential power of conspiracies individual criminality is relatively impotent. I think the latent meaning here is a fantasied comparison between the tremendous sexual power of the parents and the almost complete sexual impotence of the child. But discovery allows the individual to manage the anxiety in at least two ways. Simply by "knowing" the discoverer can maintain a degree of psychic control over the event, and what he knows can be imaginatively recreated in fantasy and repeated in play; in either case knowledge is a precondition to control. Furthermore, knowledge facilitates ego satisfaction. The phrase "they tried to put one over on us" is instructive here. Where a conspiracy succeeds one has been "had" (overcome by genital power), but when it "comes to light" it has been "foiled" (overcome by genital power). The power potential of the conspiracy or the sexual power of the primal scene are to some extent neutralized by knowledge. In a somewhat different sense, attributing a conspiracy to an event amounts to an assertion that events do not occur without an act of conscious, more or less rational, human will. Anxiety producing events simply do not happen but are the product of (perhaps evil) human will. It may be that this suggests a regression to that developmental stage where children tend to regard their parents as omnipotent with respect to the world. If something happens the parents must have had a hand in it or at least be able to do something about it.[12]

In a recent paper John McDermott developed the thesis that technology as an ideology has the effect of widening the cultural and social gap between social classes. The arcane quality of the learning, the skills and the language of technology works to exclude the lower classes from the system and the forces that affect their lives. The management of technological society is entrusted to the highly trained (upper) classes.[13] McDermott relates a story which he uses as a parable to describe the effect of this development. The story and his application of it have direct relevance to my concern here.

> According to GI reports which the soldiers
> had heard and believed, the Viet Cong had long

ago hollowed out most of the [Black Lady] mountain in order to install a very big cannon there. The size of the cannon was left somewhat vague—'huge fucking . . .'—but clearly the GI's imagined that it was in the battleship class. In any event, this huge cannon had formerly taken a heavy toll of American aircraft and had been made impervious to American counterattacks by the presence of two—'huge, fucking'—sliding steel doors, behind which it retreated whenever the Americans attacked. Had they seen this battleship cannon, and did it ever fire on the camp, which was easily within its range? No, they answered, for a brave flyer, recognizing the effectiveness of the cannon against his fellow pilots, had deliberately crashed his jet into those doors one day, jamming them, and permitting the Americans to move into the area unhindered.[14]

The imagery in this story is striking: a huge fucking cannon inside Black Lady Mountain which is impervious to attack or observation because protected by two huge doors. But the GI's are safe now because a "brother" flyer crashed into the doors, though this invasion cost him his life. The manifest content of this story barely disguises the primal scene fantasy. The power or energy contained behind the doors is an immediate threat which can only be *permanently* contained at the cost of one's "life." But even though the "flyer" loses his life, his "brothers" are free to move into the area. The brother-flyer split allows both Oedipal desire and castration fear to be represented.

McDermott explains this story by noting that the GI is never let in on the facts regarding the actual circumstances or position of his group. Rather, he is given specific instructions which he is expected to follow with "blind" obedience. "Under such circumstances, reality becomes elusive. Because the soldiers are not permitted to deal with facts in their own ways, facts cease to discipline their opinion. Fantasy and wild tales are the natural outcome."[15]

McDermott seems to be on the right track; he seems to be saying that when men are in the position of children they begin to regress, to behave like children. Consequently they fill in the gaps in their knowledge with fantasy. But for the purpose of understanding our fascination with conspiracy the use to which McDermott puts this story is even more interesting. He argues that "the effect on those who are excluded from self-management" by a technological society is similar to the effect of ignorance on GI's.[16] "Soldiers in Vietnam are not alone in believing huge, secret guns threaten them from various points; that same feeling is a national malady in the U. S."[17]

The essential and general point is that relative powerlessness in terms of knowledge and understanding of what is going on at the centers of decision-making tends to produce a disposition toward a "conspiracy" response. I think this point can be made particularly clear in the Spock case. It is still a matter of some speculation as to why the government chose to prosecute the "Boston Five" for conspiracy rather than for simple aiding and abetting. The case for the latter was strong but quite weak for the former. But if the purpose, or at least one purpose, of the prosecution was widespread publicity about the trial the conspiracy theory is much more useful. What I am suggesting is that in an almost instinctual way the government realized that everybody does indeed "love" a conspiracy, at least enough to pay some attention to it, and that they are much more afraid of what is "behind" a conspiracy than they are of the harmfulness of aiding and abetting criminal activity. The instinctual appeal of conspiracy means that if people are given any suggestion that a conspiracy exists their psychological matrix of expectations shifts the burden of proof to the extent of creating in their own minds a presumption in favor of the reality of such a conspiracy. In other words, people seem more ready to believe an allegation of conspiracy ("there is more to this than meets the eye") than they are to accept apparent explanations.

Quite apart from the effect of this presumption on the outcome of actual litigation, it has significant political and social consequences. By employing the rhetoric of plot or conspiracy, any group (and I am not necessarily claiming this as a conscious tactic) can generate substantial apprehension, and use the anxiety thus generated to support policy decisions which might otherwise not stand up against rational argument.

In this respect I would call attention to two alleged conspiracies which had tremendous social and political consequences. As a basis for passing the Communist Control Act of 1954 into law, Congress had to find the existence of an "international communist conspiracy" directed from the Soviet Union. This finding identified American communists as "foreign agents" and conspirators, rather than people potentially dangerous because of their adherence to a hostile ideology. Finding a heretofore "hidden" conspiracy ("behind the iron curtain") intensified the danger in the popular imagination and diminished potential conflicts with the first amendment and traditional notions of criminal responsibility.[18] Furthermore, the finding of conspiracy shifted the burden of proof not only in a psychological sense but, in at least one respect, in a legal sense as well.[19]

No one needs to be reminded of the tremendous utility the allegation of a Jewish conspiracy had to the Third Reich. This is certainly an extreme instance and I would hesitate to apply the thesis of this essay to it as an essential explanation either of the genesis of the claim or the force of its appeal. But the general point retains clear significance: as a device to direct social consciousness, pointing to the power of a hidden, insidious conspiracy has tremendous utility for the reasons I have described.

I should hasten to point out that the government has no monopoly on appeals to primal scene fantasy. Anti-establishment ideology increases its appeal in direct proportion to its use of conspiracy rhetoric. "Ruling Class," "Power Elite," "Military-Industrial Complex," "Intellectual Mandarins," and "Crisis Managers" are all phrases that imply subtle "connections" with the power to overcome the impotent masses (lower class, workers, students, are all substitute terms for psychosocial purposes). Note, for example, that the law does not prohibit all steel manufacturers from charging the same prices for their products. It only prohibits them from *agreeing* to do so. The radical attack on modern capitalism mirrors the establishment's attack on dissent by charging that the companies do in fact agree to set prices but do so in subtle, fundamental ways: the power of the corporate giants derives from the conspiracy of self-interest in maintaining its own supremacy.

McDermott hypothesized that an increasingly technological society means a widening cultural gap between social classes, between the managers and the managed. Those below the managerial elite would come to understand less and less about the decision making process and consequently have less control over it.[20] The implications of McDermott's hypothesis for some future species of "red-hunting" and a broader use of the rhetoric of conspiracy in political discourse are frightening to say the least.

III.

It has been suggested to me in discussion that the Conspiracy-as-Primal Scene theory set forth above fails to distinguish conspiracy from other types of deception such as fraud, counterfeiting and so forth, and also fails to explain why conspiracy proneness is not better accounted for by a theory having its roots in repressed homosexuality. I will attempt to remedy these defects in turn.

These are several clear legal distinctions between conspiracy and other forms of deception. First off, conspiracy requires at least two parties; other forms of illegal deception may or may not be engaged in by more than a single actor. In addition, the crucial operative legal factor in conspiracy is the agreement; in other forms of illegal deception it is the illegal action which is the crucial factor. Certainly in these other cases if there is joint action conspiracy could also be charged, but this is a matter of prosecutorial choice. In any event, in law it is the agreement between two or more persons which is the focus of concern.

These legal distinctions provide a clue to the psychological difference between one's responses to and perception of conspiracy and other forms of deception. The possibility that one may be deceived by any other individual is, of course, always present. In general, it seems that people feel competent to cope with this possibility, which is the possibility "of being had." I would suggest that excessive concern with "being had," being deceived, is indeed rooted in repressed homosexuality, but is quite different from the anxiety generated by the possibility that "there is more to this than meets the eye."

I think the confusion lies in the failure to make the following types of distinctions. In its aggravated form, concern with deception becomes a persecution delusion of the sort Freud dealt with in Schreber's case.[21] In its aggravated form, concern with conspiracy takes the form of an anxiety neurosis of the sort Freud dealt with in the "Wolf Man" case.[22] The two are quite different.

The tendency to suspect that conspiracies are behind events cannot be explained as a consequence of repressed homosexuality to the extent this theory relies on Freud's examination of Schreber's case. There are several reasons for this. First of all, the word conspiracy appears only in a single sentence in the account, and even here it is Schreber who uses it, not Freud: "In this way a conspiracy against me was brought to a head."[23] From the context I think it certain that Schreber is using the word only very loosely, so that he is not in fact referring to his perception of a concerted agreement to do something to him. Schreber is expressing his fear that while he is under Dr. Flechsig's care in an institution he will be *"handed over to a certain person . . .* with a view to sexual abuse."[24] While this certainly implies that more than one person will do the handing over, it is also clear that these individuals are mere hirelings. The abusive operation will be done by Flechsig; there is no other named or otherwise identified primary figure in the scheme.[25]

There is, however, a more important distinction between this case and the conspiracy situations to which I have been referring in this paper. It is crucial to notice that in Schreber's case not only is the source of the threat, in the main, a single individual, but the threat in a particular and immediate form is addressed directly and almost exclusively at Schreber personally. This is true even though both the source of the threat and its object "decompose" at a later point in the history of Schreber's illness. In other words, Schreber himself, and only he, is being persecuted. If one compares this to the anxiety neurosis discussed in the "Wolf Man" case, one can see clearly the distinction. In the former we are dealing with an immediate personal fear stemming from a perception of persecution; in the latter we are dealing with a sense of acute anxiety stimulated by representational figures—such as pictures of a wolf.

Apart from these significant differences in symptom formation there are real differences in the genesis of the disorder. In Schreber's case Freud notes that the persecutor is almost certainly a figure representing someone who was formerly loved.[26] In the "Wolf Man" case the disturbance has something to do with the management of ambivalent feelings toward a loved individual, but are traced in particular to real or fantasied events which overwhelm the disturbed individual.[27] This difference is parallel to one aspect of the distinction between conspiracy and other forms of deception I have been urging here. The notion of conspiracy is useful in "explaining" the anxiety one feels toward otherwise ambiguous events (*e.g.*, the Kennedy assassination and campus disruptions) which are unlikely, however, to cause one to *fear* for one's *personal* safety or security. The notion of persecution, on the other hand, is only useful in "explaining" the fear one feels for one's personal safety and security. In the former instance, the "explanation" goes to the genesis, cause or force behind the event; in the latter instance the "explanation" goes to the object or purpose of another individual's behavior (*e.g.*, fraud). The occasions for these two "explanations" and the form they assume are quite distinct.

I cannot here attempt a detailed defense of the conspiracy-as-primal scene thesis on the basis of these two single papers by Freud other than to suggest, again, that the thesis is stated in terms of an analogy, and that a detailed comparison of the "Wolf Man" case with Schreber's case shows that the two are quite different. The tendency to "explain" events by attributing them to a conspiracy is better understood in terms of the primal scene fantasy rather than repressed homosexuality.

IV.

I would like to make one further observation which points in a somewhat different direction. In a recent paper I suggested that the legislative choice respecting the kinds of behavior which should be discouraged by the criminal law ought to be guided by the different responses people have to actions which are feared and those actions which simply generate anxiety: only actions which provoke fear should be proscribed by the criminal law.[28] I argued there that this difference had a great deal to do with the proximity of the threat in time and space, and in turn the objective—as opposed to conceptual—quality of the threat.[29]

In dealing with conspiracies as threats to collective security, I conceded that conspiracies are properly proscribed because they are feared; conspiracies do not simply generate anxiety.[30] Insofar as this would appear to be inconsistent with the thesis of this paper I want to point out that such is not the case. It is true that real or

supposed *persecutions* are feared because they are specifically directed at the individual and the threat is perceived as proximate.
It is also true that ambiguous events in the world whether or not
"explained" by a conspiracy theory, tend to generate anxiety for
the reasons I have attempted to identify here. The point is, however, that as conspiracies take on a more objective quality in the
mind of the perceiver, as the relation between the conspiracy and
the perceiver becomes more proximate, anxiety is readily displaced
by fear. Thus, in the earlier paper, I was able to defend making
certain conspiracies criminal only on the condition that the "clear
and present danger" test is retained.[31] In sum, I believe the discussion of conspiracy in my former paper is consistent with the conspiracy-as-primal scene thesis presented here.

NOTES

1. S. Freud, Civilization and Its Discontents 141 (The Int'l Psycho-Analytical Lib. No. 17, 1930).

2. 3 S. Freud, *From the History of an Infantile Neurosis*, in Collected Papers 473, 509 n.1 (The Int'l Psycho-Analytical Lib. No. 9, E. Jones ed. 1959) [hereinafter cited as *Infantile Neurosis*].

3. *Id.* at 534.

4. O. Fenichel, The Psychoanalytic Theory of Neurosis 214 (1945).

5. *Infantile Neurosis* 555.

6. Grunewald v. United States, 353 U.S. 391, 402 (1957).

7. *Infantile Neurosis* 534.

8. S. Freud, *The Paths to Symptom Formation*, in The Complete Introductory Lec-tures on Psychoanalysis 369 (J. Strachey tranl. 1966).

9. O. Fenichel, *supra* note 4, at 214.

10. Rex v. Meyerick, [1929] 21 Crim. App. 94, 102 (Eng. C.C.A.).

11. O. Fenichel, *supra* note 4, at 215.

12. *See* J. Piaget, The Moral Judgment of the Child 61, 62, 63 (1965).

13. McDermott, *Technology: The Opiate of the Intellectuals*, The New York Review of Books, July 31, 1969, at 25.

14. *Id.* at 29-30.

15. *Id.* at 30.

16. *Id.* at 32.

17. *Id.*

18. Communist Party v. Subversive Activities Control Board, 367 U.S. 1 (1961).

19. *See id.*

20. McDermott, *supra* note 13, at 25, 31-32.

21. 3 S. Freud, *Psycho-Analytic Notes Upon An Autobiological Account of a Case of Paranoia (Dementia Paranoides)*, in Collected Papers 387 (The Int'l Psycho-Analytical Lib. No. 9, E. Jones ed. 1959) [hereinafter cited as *Psycho-Analytical Notes*].

22. *Infantile Neurosis* 473.

23. *Psycho-Analytical Notes* 427.

24. *Id.* (Freud's emphasis).

25. *Id.*

26. *Id.* at 424.

27. *Infantile Neurosis* 480-521.

28. Katz, *Dangerousness: A Theoretical Reconstruction of The Criminal Law,* 19 BUFFALO L. REV. 1 *passim* (1969).

29. *Id.* at 24-25.

30. *Id.*

31. *Id.* at 25-26.

IV.

DETERRING
CRIMINAL BEHAVIOR

DETERRENCE
AND SPECIFIC OFFENSES

Deterrence should not be treated as a monolithic problem. General propositions accepting or rejecting deterrence ought to belong to the past. The question is not whether punishment has deterrent effects, but rather under what conditions and to what extent the deterrent purpose is effected.

It is important initially to distinguish between the deterrent effect of the threat of punishment (general deterrence) and the deterrent effect of the imposition of punishment (special deterrence).[1] Professor Chambliss has suggested that the distinction between general and special deterrence, perhaps useful in the abstract, is difficult to maintain in empirical research and may in fact obscure more than it clarifies.[2] His own discussion, however, demonstrates that failure to make the distinction may lead to mistaken conclusions. Chambliss concludes, on the basis of research showing high rates of recidivism among drug addicts, that drug addiction, like murder, is relatively unaffected by either the threat or imposition of punishment.[3] This statement may be correct if restricted to those users who have already become addicts, since the great physiological need for drugs may vitiate the deterrent effect of punishment. But it is not correct to presuppose, as does Chambliss, that the limited success in the treatment of drug addicts necessarily suggests a similar failure to deter non-addicts and drug dealers. In fact, statistics concerning recidivism among drug addicts reveal nothing about the deterrent effect of drug laws on non-addicts and drug dealers. Howard Becker's study of the marijuana user may be instructive.[4] Becker identifies three stages in the career of a marijuana user: beginner, occasional user, and regular user. The beginner is faced with two major obstacles created at least in part by the drug laws. First, he must overcome his fears of criminal penalties and social disapproval. Second, even if he overcomes these fears, he must locate a supplier. Since sale of the drug is subject to severe criminal penalties, its distribution is confined to illicit, not readily available sources.[5] Thus, even though special deterrence with regard to the convicted drug addict may fail, general deterrence may operate effectively to prevent potential users from becoming addicts.

In discussing deterrence it is also necessary to distinguish among offenses. Common sense tells us that the threat of punishment does not play the same role in offenses as different as murder, rape, tax evasion, shoplifting and illegal parking. The different offenses vary greatly as to both motivation and extralegal restraints upon commission of the crime. Chambliss agrees that deterrent effects differ according to the type of offense, but makes a general distinction between expressive and instrumental acts. An act such as drug use or murder is expressive in that it "is committed because it is pleasurable in and of itself and not because it is a route to some other goal."[6] Acts such as parking violations and shoplifting are, on the other hand, instrumental. According to Chambliss, the available research suggests that expressive acts are resistant to punishment as a deterrent, whereas instrumental acts are more likely to be influenced by the threat or imposition of punishment.

The analytical value of Chambliss' distinction is doubtful. It does not seem self-evident that expressive acts are less influenced by social sanctions than are instrumental acts. Experience from social intercourse shows that the fear of even mild social sanctions often leads to the suppression of expressive acts (for example, yawning, picking one's nose, or crying out angrily).

Moreover, the distinction does not seem very clear. For instance, Chambliss considers the use of narcotics a typically expressive act. It may seem pedantic to object that taking the drug is instrumental in bringing about the ultimate effects of the drug. But certainly the purchase or possession of the drug is instrumental in relation to the later use. Criminal acts to obtain the drug or to obtain money to buy it are even more clearly instrumental. Yet experience seems to show that the desperate addict is deterred no more from committing these instrumental acts than he is from committing the expressive act—use of the drug. Thus, what leads to a lack of deterrent effect is not the expressive character of drug use, but rather the overwhelming motivating power of the addiction. That carefully planned acts are more easily deterred than those that result from a sudden, emotional impulse is an old proposition. The latter acts are probably more commonly labeled expressive. Apart from this distinction, however, referring to the act as expressive or instrumental does not seem to give a significant clue to the problem. A much more detailed analysis is needed.

I have previously discussed the general deterrent effect of punishment in relation to six broadly defined categories of offenses: violations of police regulations; violations of economic legislation; crimes against property; moral offenses; murder; and political crimes.[7] In this article I shall consider three more specific offenses: infanticide, criminal abortion and drunken driving. The discussion is limited to general deterrence, using the term "deterrence" broadly to include the possible moral or habit forming effects of criminal laws.

I. INFANTICIDE

Infanticide, typically an unmarried woman's murder of her newborn child, was one of the great problems of the criminal law in the eighteenth century. Erik Anners, a Swedish legal historian, has provided useful information on the crime in his study of criminal law reforms during the Age of Enlightenment.[8] Although rare until the end of the sixteenth century, infanticide became more common during the seventeenth and eighteenth centuries and came to be regarded as a major social evil. The increased frequency of infanticide seems to have been attributable primarily to the development of stronger religious and legal proscriptions of extra-marital relationships. These pressures created a strong temptation to hide the pregnancy and kill the child after its birth.

When the infanticide rate increased, due partly to the law itself, the threat of severe punishment was considered to be the only remedy. Therefore, partly for deterrent reasons and partly because of the religious view that a life must be paid for with a life, infanticide became a capital crime. Between 1759 and 1778, 217 of the 617 executions in Sweden were for infanticide. Those executed were usually from the poorer classes, and more often than not were countryside housemaids. The situation in other European countries was basically the same.

In the late eighteenth century, King Gustav III[9] of Sweden attempted to reduce the punishment for infanticide. He argued, perhaps to disarm his opponents, that capital punishment was an inadequate deterrent. He urged that a woman convicted of infanticide be first flogged and then imprisoned, perhaps for life. On the anniversary of the crime she was to be flogged before the common people. The King thought that this would create disgust for the crime and fear of the punishment. Opposition from conservative jurists and theologians, however, prevented enactment of these reforms. Not until 1861 was capital punishment for infanticide abolished, although granting of pardons had ended executions for the offense a generation earlier.[10]

It is difficult to ascertain the frequency of infanticide in eighteenth century Sweden. In 1773 the Swedish Supreme Court stated that infanticide and abortion are "yearly committed in such numbers over the whole country that the country loses considerably in population due both to the crime itself and to the ensuing penalty." Crime statistics and execution records, however, do not support so strong a statement. The Supreme Court must therefore have presumed that infanticide was committed much more frequently than the statistics indicated, and some evidence suggests that this assumption was correct.[11] It is also possible that the punishment itself, severe even to people of that era, contributed to the feeling that infanticide was a great problem.

Veli Verkko, a Finnish statistician, has investigated the frequency of infanticide in Finland and Sweden during the eighteenth century, when the two countries were united and ruled by the same law.[12] His investigations, based on an evaluation of death statistics, reveal that the frequency of illegitimate births was greater in Sweden, but that the frequency of infanticide was greater in Finland. In Finland, the infanticide rate was highest in those counties in which the frequency of illegitimate births was lowest. His fairly plausible explanation is that strong sexual mores and social bias against the unwed mother resulted in fewer pregnancies among unmarried women, but also caused many of those who did have an illegitimate child to commit infanticide. He concludes that: "[w]e have here an example of the peculiar phenomenon under which a rigid morality can have a criminogenic-crime-producing effect."[13]

Infanticide was still prominent in the crime statistics of the nineteenth century.[14] In the 1860's there were annually between ten and twenty convictions for infanticide in Norway; and in Sweden, with approximately double Norway's population, there were between thirty and forty. In the twentieth century, infanticide has gradually become less frequent and the penalty has consistently become less severe. In Norway, between 1957 and 1966, seven persons were found guilty of infanticide. In five of these cases prosecution was waived, and in the two that were brought to court the defendants received a suspended sentence of imprisonment for the minimum term of one year.[15] In Sweden, during the same period, eight defendants were convicted, but the sentences are not specified in the statistics.

What explains this decline in the frequency of infanticide? It is unlikely that increased knowledge of contraceptives is a major cause of the decline. The number of children born out of wedlock has not, in a long term perspective, dramatically decreased. In Norway, in 1866, 4,310 children, or about eight per cent of the total live births, were illegitimate. A hundred years later the number was 3,285, about five per cent of all live births. Thus, increased knowledge of contraceptives appears largely to have been neutralized by relaxation of sexual mores during this century. Furthermore, there is reason to believe that knowledge of contraceptives has been slow in reaching the levels of society in which infanticide was most prevalent.

Two further hypotheses seem more plausible as explanations for the decline in the infanticide rate. First, the more liberal attitude of society towards extra-marital relationships coupled with better care of illegitimate children serve to mitigate the stigma which formerly attached to an unwed mother. Second, the solution to an unwanted pregnancy, previously provided by infanticide, is now abortion. Both of these factors probably have had an effect, although a detailed discussion of them is outside the scope of this article.

In view of the decline in the infanticide rate during the last century, can one conclude that the severe eighteenth century penalties for infanticide were useless brutality without deterrent effect? Anners seems to come to this conclusion,[16] but he may be too bold. One cannot reject out of hand the possibility that more unhappy women might have resorted to infanticide had the penalty been less severe. But neither can such a hypothesis be proven. What one can safely conclude, however, is that a social problem, previously thought to require drastic criminal penalties, has been solved in other ways. It is also likely that most people today would find it easier to accept an increased infanticide rate than to impose the severe penalties once thought to be required by religion and deterrence. History reveals that strong beliefs in deterrence, particularly when combined with the moral or religious belief that sin should be punished, can produce results which later generations will consider unnecessarily brutal.

II. ABORTION

The abortion situation in most western countries is characterized by strict laws, weak enforcement and a high rate of criminal abortions. The number of illegal abortions is astronomic compared to the number of prosecutions or convictions for the crime. It is often said that the criminal law in this area is ineffective in that it does not have an appreciable effect on the abortion rate. This notion is reflected in a recent paper by B.J. George:

> Will even the most wildly liberal abortion statute make much difference in the incidence of abortion? I doubt it. The gross rate of abortions probably remains unaffected by efforts at legal regulation of the practice: the chief question is how many of the abortions actually performed will be done openly in hospitals or clinics.[17]

Sanford Kadish states that:

> [As a] hard fact [the] abortion laws do not work to stop abortion, except for those too poor and ignorant to avail themselves of black-market alternatives, and . . . the consequences of their retention is probably to sacrifice more lives of mothers than the total number of foetuses saved by the abortion laws.[18]

These statements illustrate how even excellent scholars can be guilty of sloppy thinking, probably due in this case to the widespread skepticism among criminologists with regard to the efficacy of the criminal law.

It is undoubtedly true that many women who desire to terminate a pregnancy but who cannot do so legally successfully procure an illegal abortion. But it seems obvious that this is not true of all women who would have an abortion if available on request. Some women may be too helpless, too passive, or too poor to find and use the alternatives open to the more active and resourceful. In other cases, a woman who would have an abortion if available on request may hesitate to make the rounds from one doctor to another begging for help or to permit a "quack" to perform the abortion.

These conclusions seem obvious and are supported by statistical evidence. Follow-up studies of women whose requests for abortion were denied show that although a great number of them subsequently obtain a criminal abortion, this is by no means true for all. A Danish study revealed that eighty-one per cent of the 3,700 women whose requests for abortion were denied or withdrawn in 1958 and 1959 completed their pregnancies.[19] The percentage among housewives was considerably higher than among office workers: eighty-eight per cent and seventy per cent respectively. Swedish inquiries showed similar results.[20] A Norwegian study made before the abortion law was liberalized showed that only thirty-six per cent of the women whose applications for abortion were denied completed pregnancy.[21] Married women were more likely to bear the child than unmarried women: thirty-nine per cent and twenty-eight per cent respectively. A study under the present law showed that sixty-eight per cent of the women whose applications were denied completed pregnancy: eighty-one per cent of the married applicants and fifty-four per cent of the single applicants.[22] It thus seems clear that the percentage of women who complete unwanted pregnancies depends on such factors as marital and occupational status and on the more or less easy availability of criminal abortions. The stronger the motivation for abortion and the easier the access to criminal abortion, the higher the percentage of women who will solve their problem in this way.

Another possible method of assessing the effect of abortion legislation is to compare the change in legal abortions following a liberalization of the law with the trend in the birth rate. In places, such as the Scandinavian countries, where more liberal laws changed the accepted grounds for abortion only moderately, the number of legal abortions is too small to have a noticeable effect on the birth rate.[23] In contrast, the number of legal abortions has increased dramatically in those Eastern European countries where post-war legislation legalized abortion at the mother's request.[24] Concurrent with the increase in legal abortions was a sharp decline in the birth rate. In Hungary, the number of legal abortions in 1964 exceeded the number of live births by almost forty per cent.[25] On the other hand, in East Germany and Albania, the two Eastern European countries that had not legalized abortion, there was a modest increase in the birth rate.

While the relationship between the birth rate and liberalized abortion law is not simple, an open-minded study of the statistics seems to support Professor Tietze, who, after a thorough study of the available information, concluded that the legalization of abortion has had a depressant effect on the birth rate in most Eastern European countries.[26] The most striking example is Romania where abortion on demand was legalized in 1957 but again prohibited in 1966. The birth rate had declined from 24.2 per thousand in 1956 to 14.3 per thousand in 1966. It is estimated that the number of abortions in 1966 was four times the number of live births. The reasons for the repeal of the 1957 law were stated in the preamble to the 1966 law: "[there has been] great prejudice to the birth rate and the rate of natural increase."[27] The effects of the new law were dramatic. The birth rate jumped from 14.3 per thousand in 1966 to 27.3 per thousand in 1967, 26.7 per thousand in 1968 and 23 per thousand in 1969.[28] It should be noted that in conjunction with the reversed abortion policy, the government increased family allowances and ceased official importation of contraceptives. In Bulgaria, a tightening of abortion legislation in December, 1967, led to an increase (albeit not as great as in Romania) in the birth rates in 1968 and 1969. One can confidently conclude that the increased number of legal abortions in some of the East European countries includes some cases where previously a criminal abortion would have been performed and others in which the woman would have completed her pregnancy.[29]

Paradoxical as it may seem in view of the high rate of illegal abortions, there are probably few areas where so little enforcement has so much effect as in the field of abortion. This is due primarily not to the effect of the criminal law on the motivation of women who want to terminate pregnancy, but rather to the effect on the medical profession. Since safe abortion requires a doctor, preferably in a hospital, and since the medical profession on the whole is quite susceptible to the threat of law and the censure of society, the legal prohibition may prevent the mother from obtaining abortion without respect to her own attitude. Moreover, abortion is an area of the law in which the law may itself have a moral impact. If abortion were legalized, women would find it easier to overcome the feeling of guilt that now often accompanies the act. It is probably of no great significance whether the mother is herself subject to punishment. It is enough that abortion is criminal. Legalization of abortion may also result in carelessness in the use of contraceptives, producing more unwanted pregnancies and increased demand for abortions. The effect of abortion laws is obviously dependent on a variety of factors including religious beliefs, attitudes of the medical profession, knowledge and availability of contraceptive techniques, and social and economic conditions.

Abortion and infanticide are both the result of pregnancy which is viewed as a threat to the future life or happiness of the mother. But infanticide is, in contrast to abortion, a simple, primitive crime which does not require expert assistance. Moreover, the moral inhibitions against infanticide are much greater than those against abortion. For these reasons the effect of criminalization on the two types of conduct differs markedly.

To avoid misunderstanding, it should be pointed out that the deterrent effect of making abortion criminal is not a decisive argument against the liberalization of abortions. It can be argued that the mother ought to have the right to decide for herself whether to complete a pregnancy. Assuming that an unwanted child is a greater evil than a terminated pregnancy, it seems logical to conclude from the usual rise in the abortion rate after liberalization that there is a legitimate need for abortion which is not met under present law. But the indications of a deterrent effect are not without impact on the argument over liberalization: the policy problem would be different and easier to solve if there were no deterrent effect, that is, if it could be shown that the effect of liberalization would be only to legalize abortions which would be performed anyway.

III. DRUNKEN DRIVING

For many years the Scandinavian states have had strict legislation against drunken driving, coupled with strict enforcement policies. In Norway, for example, the law prohibits driving when the blood alcohol level exceeds .05 per cent. Any person suspected of drunken driving must submit to a blood test. Upon conviction, the driver's license is automatically revoked for one year and, in addition, the consistent policy of the courts has been to impose a prison sentence. This strict policy seems to have had a considerable effect on driver attitudes with regard to driving under the influence of alcohol, and drunken driving now causes a very small percentage of highway accidents.[30] However, this legislation has been in force since a time when there were far fewer automobiles and accidents than today. It is therefore impossible to demonstrate statistically the impact of the legislation.

The situation is different in Great Britain, which recently adopted a new highway safety act.[31] The new legislation retained existing provisions which led to conviction only in cases involving a high degree of intoxication but added a new offense: driving with an undue proportion of alcohol in the blood. The prescribed limit is eighty milligrams of alcohol in one hundred milliliters of blood (.08 per cent). If the police have reasonable cause to believe that a driver has been drinking or has committed a moving traffic offense, they may ask the driver to take a breath test. The police may always request a breath test if the driver has been involved in an accident.[32] If the test indicates that the driver's blood alcohol content is probably above the legal limit, he may be arrested and taken to the police station. There the driver is requested either to submit to a blood test or, if he refuses, to furnish two urine specimens for analysis. Failure to cooperate with these requests renders the driver liable to the same penalties that attach to driving with the proscribed blood alcohol content. Upon conviction for the new offense, the driver's license is automatically revoked for one year, except in extraordinary circumstances, and the driver is also subject to a fine of up to £100, four months imprisonment, or both.

An intensive publicity campaign, beginning two weeks prior to the effective date of the Act (October 9, 1967) and continuing for four months, accompanied passage of the new law. The campaign, estimated to have cost nearly £350,000, was particularly intense in the beginning and during the December holiday season. News coverage and comments in the press, radio and television provided additional publicity for the new law. As a result, there was great public awareness of the new law, and unusual interest in highway safety in general.

Highway accident statistics were carefully compiled to gauge the effect of the new legislation. This is one of the few instances in which an effort has been made to learn the precise effects of a new policy. According to official figures, highway accidents decreased substantially after the Act took effect.[33] The following table is compiled from those figures.

PERCENTAGE DECREASE IN HIGHWAY CASUALTIES IN GREAT BRITAIN, OCTOBER TO DECEMBER, 1967, COMPARED WITH SAME PERIOD IN 1966

	Oct.*	Nov.	Dec.	Oct.-Dec.	Christmas
Fatalities	17	20	33	23	36
Seriously injured	15	15	22	17	30
Slightly injured	11	13	20	15	

* Figures for October represent the period after the Act took effect.

In the first nine months of 1967 there was no consistent trend in the incidence of highway accidents; there was an increase over the previous year during some months and a decrease in others. Overall, there was a two per cent decrease in casualties as compared with 1966. Total traffic was estimated to have increased from 1966 by five per cent in October, two per cent in November, and to have decreased one per cent in December. Neither the figures for 1966 nor those for the first nine months of 1967 reflect any remarkable change in comparison with previous years. In the 1950's and 1960's there had been a slow but steady upward trend in highway casualties. The annual number of fatalities had increased from about 5,000 in the early 1950's to approximately 8,000 during the period from 1964 to 1966.

After the passage of the Highway Safety Act of 1967, there was a larger decrease in serious accidents than in minor accidents. This result is in harmony with the findings of previous highway accident research showing that accidents involving drivers with blood alcohol levels over .08 per cent tend to be more serious than the average accident.[34] Different drinking and driving habits during the holidays may explain the great reduction during the Christmas season. While changes in weather conditions may influence the figures for each month, the consistency of the figures is remarkable.

A striking pattern emerges if the accidents are correlated to the periods of the day in which they occurred. During working hours (8 a.m. to 6 p.m.) the decrease is slight: two per cent of fatal and serious accidents in October and November; seven per cent in December. Between 8 p.m. and 4 a.m. the figures were thirty-six per cent in October, thirty-eight per cent in November and forty-one per cent in December. For the early morning hours considered alone they were even higher. The inevitable conclusion is that, in this socially important area, new legislation has had a considerable impact on people's behavior, at least temporarily.[35]

A study of about half of the fatal accidents in Great Britain in December, 1964, and January, 1965, showed that thirty per cent of the fatally injured drivers had more than .05 per cent blood alcohol content. Twenty-three per cent of the fatally injured drivers had more than .08 per cent blood alcohol content and twelve per cent had more than .15 per cent. Seventy-five per cent of the drivers killed between 10 p.m. and 2 a.m. had at least .05 per cent blood alcohol content compared with ten per cent of the drivers killed between 6 a.m. and noon.[36]

These figures do not mean, of course, that drinking was the cause of the accident in all cases, but the implications are obvious.

Several alternative hypotheses which might be thought to explain the decrease in highway accidents in Great Britain deserve discussion. It may be argued that increased awareness of the dangers of drunken driving rather than the threat of punishment led to the reduction in the number of accidents. This theory credits the publicity campaign rather than the law itself for causing the decrease. This argument, however, does not appear to be supported by the facts. There had been long-standing public discussion of the problem of drunken driving, and the publicity campaign began two weeks before the new law took effect. Yet, in the first eight days of October, 1967, there was a reduction in highway casualties (compared with the same period in 1966) of only two per cent—the same reduction obtained in the first nine months of 1967. In that portion of October after the Act took effect, the reduction was twelve per cent. The decrease in fatalities was one per cent in the eight days of October before the Act took effect and seventeen per cent for the remainder of the month. Moreover, surveys conducted among drivers in September, 1967, and January, 1968, showed that drivers' toleration of drinking and driving and their opinion of the amount they could drink without affecting their driving remained substantially unchanged.[87] It seems clear that the dramatic reduction in highway accidents is directly attributable to the new legislation. The report of the surveys concluded that the publicity campaign had been valuable only in the sense that it made drivers aware of the new law.

Even if this conclusion is accepted, it does not necessarily follow that the explanation for the decrease in highway accidents is the effect of the new law on alcohol consumption before driving. An alternative hypothesis is that drivers, expecting increased police surveillance during the period immediately following the effective date of the new Act, exercised greater caution in driving quite apart from the Act's effect on alcohol consumption. It may well be that some part of the reduction of accidents is due to this factor. However, the distribution of the decrease in accidents according to time of day indicates that the most important factor was change in drinking and driving habits.

An important question is whether the effects of the new law are permanent. Other cases exist where an initial reduction in the commission of the proscribed offense, resulting from a new law accompanied by intensive publicity, has been followed by an eventual return to the previous level.[38] There is some indication of a similar development in Great Britain. In the last three months of the first year in which the Act was in effect, fatalities were nine per cent less than in the previous year, seriously injured seven per cent and slightly injured seven per cent.[39] While these decreases are less impressive than those for the months immediately following the effective date of the Act, the development is somewhat ambiguous. As stated above, December is probably the month in which the most social drinking occurs. In December, 1967, the decrease from the 1966 level was thirty-three per cent and in December, 1968, the decrease was thirty-two per cent. The figures for seriously injured were twenty-two and nineteen per cent and for slightly injured, twenty and eighteen per cent. Thus, the reduction in the level of casualties for this month was practically the same as in the first year of the law's operation. It is possible that other safety measures introduced by the Ministry of Transport during the year influenced these figures. Nevertheless, the Ministry's conclusion "that a fair proportion of the reductions are being maintained, although it is clearly too early to assess the long term effects,"[40] seems well founded. Post mortem examinations of fatally injured drivers revealed that the percentage of such drivers with blood alcohol content of over .08 per cent fell from a previous average of twenty-eight per cent to fifteen per cent in the first year after the effective date of the Act.[41]

For the first twelve months after the effective date of the Act the total reduction in casualties compared to the previous year was ten per cent. This represents 1,152 fewer fatalities, 11,177 fewer seriously injured and 28,130 fewer slightly injured. Opinion polls indicate that a majority of the population favors the new Act. But when fifteen per cent of drivers who are fatally injured in highway accidents have blood alcohol content of over .08 per cent and eleven per cent have over .15 per cent, a serious drunken driving problem still exists. It would be interesting to have comparable information from the Scandinavian countries, where drunken driving legislation is older and stricter.

A decrease in the deterrent effectiveness of the new law with the passage of time can be interpreted in three ways:

(1) The publicity in connection with the Act created an exaggerated fear of detection for drunken driving. Later, drivers began to make a more realistic assessment of the risk of detection, and consequently the deterrent effect was weakened. The law had been "oversold." In addition, many loopholes in the law gradually became public knowledge, thus reducing the deterrent effect.

(2) The motivating force of a risk is dependent not only on the intellectual knowledge of the risk, but also on the degree of awareness. If, for example, one witnesses a traffic accident, his awareness of the risks of driving is greatly increased. In the same way, it can be assumed that the risk created by a new law is fresh in the minds of drivers, especially if enactment is accompanied by intense publicity. This high degree of risk awareness is gradually weakened, even when no reassessment of the risk is made. It is impossible to maintain the same level of publicity after the initial period of the Act's operation, and even if this were attempted, public sensitivity would probably be reduced when the publicity lost its news interest. Thus, a certain decrease in the "shock effect" of new legislation must be expected as a normal development.

(3) To the extent that the immediate reduction of highway casualties is due not to a changed pattern of alcohol consumption, but to the general driver expectation of more intense traffic control, the effect of the new law will necessarily be temporary.

These considerations could have been evaluated more effectively had surveys of drivers been made periodically. This would have been an important supplement to the accident statistics and would have revealed more about the psychological effects which led to the decreases. The survey research that has been done failed to cover such questions as how drivers assess the risk of detection.

The foregoing discussion has been concerned primarily with the awareness of the risk of punishment. However, I do not intend to imply that the effects of the new legislation are a result only of fear. Although survey research does not indicate a change in attitudes toward drinking and driving per se,[42] the desire to obey the law may well have played a considerable role in the change in behavior. Therefore, it cannot be assumed that similar legislation, even when enforced in the same manner as in Great Britain, will have the same effects in a country whose citizens view obedience to the law differently. My personal view, however, is that the major factor in the success of the British legislation is mere deterrence. Creation of similar awareness of risk in a different society would have similar results if the drinking patterns and the social characteristics of the drivers were approximately the same.

Statistical evidence of the general preventive effects of punishment is scarce. What broader conclusions can be drawn from the British experience? Why do the British statistics yield the unequivocal results which are usually so difficult to obtain? Two points should be mentioned.

First, driving under the influence of alcohol differs from traditional crimes in that conduct not previously criminal has been made criminal, and it is therefore possible to measure the total impact of the new law. Crimes such as murder, robbery, rape and burglary remain substantially the same from one generation to the next. Changes relevant to the deterrent effect of the law usually concern the level of penalties or the level of enforcement. With such crimes, instead of measuring the total impact of the criminal provisions, there is the more difficult task of measuring the marginal effect of a change in the penalty or the degree of enforcement.

Second, in this case statistics of highway accidents provide an independent measure of the effects of the law. It is thus possible to avoid many of the difficulties of measuring the extent of violations. When the scope of a penal law is extended or contracted, it is theoretically possible to measure the total impact of the extension or contraction of the law. But "before" and "after" tests in these situations are especially difficult because criminal statistics do not provide a "before" measure for conduct that is now criminal or an "after" measure for conduct that has ceased to be a crime.

It should be noted that the number of highway accidents resulting from drinking may not be presumed to vary directly with the number of violations of the drunken driving laws. The effect of the law often may be that the driver reduces his consumption in order to decrease the risk of detection, even though his blood alcohol content remains higher than the maximum legal limit. Because the risk of an accident increases as the amount of alcohol increases, such reductions in consumption may be very important in relation to the goals of the law. If the legal limit is low, a high proportion of fringe violators may be of minor importance for highway safety. Since the aim of the law is to promote highway safety, the influence of the law on the number of accidents is a better measure of its efficacy than would be "before" and "after" statistics on the number of drivers whose blood alcohol content exceeds the limit.

Since the change in accident statistics shows the total impact of the new legislation, it is a poor basis for forecasting the effects of changes in the level of penalties or in the stringency of enforcement. Norwegians generally accept the proposition that non-suspension of prison sentences imposed for drunken driving has been very important in promoting the deterrent effect of the law. In Great Britain, the sentence usually consists of a fine and temporary loss of the driver's license. This contrast gives reason for questioning the importance of prison sentences. Perhaps fines and license revocation can achieve almost the same results as prison sentences; but further discussion on this point would require a much more thorough study.

For several reasons, a stronger deterrent effect may be expected from drunken driving laws than from laws against many other types of offenses. Driving under the influence of alcohol is not restricted to a criminal sub-culture, and it is not subject to severe moral condemnation. Nor is it behavior triggered by strong emotions. The decision whether or not to drink is usually made deliberately, as a rational choice; and the motivation to commit the offense is not strong. The law interferes only slightly with personal liberty. It asks the citizen neither to stop drinking nor to stop driving. It merely prohibits combining the two activities. Thus, the drunken driving situation is one in which common sense tells us that the risk of punishment can be expected to have more effect than in the case of many other offenses. This point should not, however, be overstated. There is no standard of the normal or average crime to which drunken driving is an exception. Every offense must be considered separately. Indeed, the motivational situation in many socially important types of offenses may be more similar to drunken driving than, for example, to murder or rape.

As enforcement of a law becomes more effective and penalties for its violation become stricter, the class of lawbreakers becomes more abnormal. It is no doubt correct that drunken driving was common throughout the population before the passage of strict criminal sanctions. Distribution of the violators is not so widespread after the passage of the new legislation. The composition of the class of drunken drivers will be altered. Instead of a fairly random sample of drivers, the drunken drivers will be primarily the problem drinkers and those with previous records for drunken driving—people less amenable to being deterred. This fact must be taken into account in forecasting the effect of any increase in the level of enforcement or punishment of an offense which is already strictly enforced and punished. He who invests in increased severity, has to expect diminishing returns.

NOTES

1 On the question of terminology see Andenaes, *The General Preventive Effects of Punishment,* 114 U. PA. L. REV. 949 (1966), and Hawkins, *Punishment and Deterrence: The Educative, Moralizing, and Habituative Effects,* 1969 WIS. L. REV. 550.

2 Chambliss, *Types of Behavior and the Effectiveness of Legal Sanctions*, 1967 WIS. L. REV. 703, 704 n.3.

3 *Id.* at 708.

4 H. BECKER, OUTSIDERS ch. 4 (1963).

5 Hauge gives a similar description from Oslo. The use of marijuana and hashish is relatively widespread in some circles in Oslo, but even if one could identify these circles, it would be a long time before they would trust him enough to sell the drugs to him. If the individual were conspicuously different from those in the drug-using circles, they would probably never sell drugs to him. Hauge, *Narkotikamisbruk som Gruppefenomen* (The Use of Narcotics as a Group Phenomenon), PRISMET 161, 163-64 (1969).

6 Chambliss, *supra* note 2, at 708, 712.

7 Andenaes, *General Prevention—Illusion or Reality?* 43 J. CRIM. L.C. & P.S. 176, 181-90 (1952).

8 E. ANNERS, HUMANITET OCH RATIONALISM (Humanitarianism and Rationalism) (1965).

9 King of Sweden, 1771-1792.

10 K. OLIVECRONA, OM DÖDSSTRAFFET (On Capital Punishment) 53-54 (1891).

11 *See* E. ANNERS, *supra* note 8, at 142, 207-08.

12 Verkko, *Barnamorden och Sexualmoralen i Sverige-Finland pa 1700-Talet*, NORDISK TIDSSKRIFT FOR STRAFFERET 35 (1946).

13 *Id.* at 45.

14 The development can be illustrated partly by the crime statistics and partly by the death statistics. Between these two sources there are, at least in Norway, discrepancies which are difficult to explain. Unfortunately, because of several rearrangements of the statistics, I have not been able to present them in a coherent graph of the development.

15 Information on the sanctions is provided by the Prison Department of the Ministry of Justice.

16 E. ANNERS, *supra* note 8, at 154.

17 B. George, The Law Governing Abortion, April 28, 1968, p. 12 (unpublished paper delivered at The University of Chicago Conference on Abortion).

18 Kadish, *The Crisis of Overcriminalization*, 374 ANNALS 157, 163 (1967).

19 Beretning om Mödrehjælpsinstitutionernes Virksomhed 45 (1963).

20 Ekblad, *Induced Abortion on Psychiatric Grounds*, ACTA PSYCHIATRICA ET NEUROLOGICA SCANDINAVICA, supp. 99, ch. VIII (1955).

21 INNSTILLING FRA STRAFFELOVRAADET OM ADGANGEN TIL A AVBRYTE SVANGERSKAP (Report from the Penal Code Commission on Abortion) (1956).

22 Strom, *Svangerskapsavbrot i Visse Höve*, TIDSSKRIFT FOR DEN NORSKE LAE GEFORENING 761, 769 (1969).

23 In the Scandinavian countries the total number of legal abortions is 5-10% of the number of live births.

24 The Soviet Union does not publish statistics on abortions and is not included in the discussion of Eastern European countries.

25 Tietze, *Abortion in Europe*, 57 AM. J. PUB. HEALTH 1923, 1930 (1967).

26 Tietze, *The Demographic Significance of Legal Abortion in Eastern Europe*, 1 DEMOGRAPHY 124 (1964). Professor Tietze also comments that in Hungary in 1952 and 1953, before the liberalized abortion legislation, concerted efforts were made to enforce the existing abortion laws. "These efforts led to an increase in births in 1953 and 1954." *Id.*

27 Tietze, *supra* note 25, at 1931.

28 H. David, Family Planning and Abortion in the Socialist Countries of Central and Eastern Europe, 1970, at 21, 127 (mimeo.). In Table 14 the changes in the birth rate after the 1966 law was passed can be followed from month to month. *Id.* at 131.

29 In Japan the great increase in the number of legal abortions performed after passage of liberal post-War legislation has been accompanied by a marked decline in birth rates. Tietze, *Some Facts About Legal Abortion*, in HUMAN FERTILITY AND POPULATION PROBLEMS 223, 228-29 (R. Greep ed. 1963).

30 *See* Andenaes, *supra* note 1, at 968-69.

31 Road Safety Act 1967, c. 30 (effective Oct. 9, 1967).

82 The proposal in MINISTRY OF TRANSPORT, ROAD SAFETY LEGISLATION, 1965-66, CMND. No. 2859, at 11 (1965), to give the police the power to make random tests did not receive the approval of Parliament. "The system of random checks, however unpalatable, is evidently the only way in which the new law can be enforced for it is usually only at levels in excess of 150 mg./100 ml. that a motorist's conduct exhibits obvious signs of unfitness." 1966 CRIM. L. REV. (Eng.) 65, 67. In the light of later experience, this seems to be too pessimistic a view.

83 Ministry of Transport Press Notices, No. 892 (Dec. 19, 1967), No. 78 (Feb. 8, 1968), and No. 157 (Mar. 21, 1968).

34 *See, e.g.*, R. BORKENSTEIN, R. CROWTHER, R. SHAMATE, W. ZIEL & R. ZYLMAN, THE ROLE OF THE DRINKING DRIVER IN TRAFFIC ACCIDENTS 176-77 (1964) [hereinafter cited as BORKENSTEIN].

35 A paper issued by the ministries involved before the law came into effect said that it had been calculated that in the absence of driving after drinking, the number of drivers involved in accidents would be reduced 6%. Drinking and Driving—Background Information (issued on behalf of Ministry of Transport, Home Office, Scottish Development Department, Welch Office). That figure, which was considerably exceeded since the Act took effect, was apparently based on a computation by the Road Research Laboratory from the findings of the Michigan "Grand Rapids Survey." BORKENSTEIN, *supra* note 34. The survey was based on comparisons between drivers involved in accidents and a random sample of drivers. The report from the Ministry of Transport, *supra*, summarizes research findings of the Road Research Laboratory concerning the frequency of drinking among people involved in highway accidents. The Laboratory's report gives 12.6% as the reduction in total accidents which would have occurred if drivers with blood alcohol content of .08% or more had been prevented from driving. *Id.* at 167-69. The method of computation of the Road Research Laboratory is explained in Alsop, *Drinking Drivers*, 170 NEW SOC'Y 12 (1965), and in Alsop, *Alcohol and Road Accidents*, Road Research Laboratory Report No. 6 (1966).

36 Older & Sims, *Blood Alcohol Levels in Road Accident Fatalities Occurring in Great Britain During December 1964 and January 1965*, Road Research Laboratory Report No. 32 (1966). In the United States, blood tests performed on fatally injured drivers have revealed extremely high proportions of drunken drivers. A study of single vehicle accidents in Westchester County, New York, showed that 49% of the drivers had blood alcohol content of .15% or more, and that an additional 20% had blood alcohol content between .05% and 1.5%. Haddon & Bradess, *Alcohol in the Single Vehicle Fatal Accident, Experience of Westchester County, New York*, in ACCIDENT RESEARCH 208, 211 (1964). *See also* McCarroll & Haddon, *A Controlled Study of Fatal Automobile Accidents in New York City*, in ACCIDENT RESEARCH 172 (1964).

87 Sheppard, *The 1967 Drink and Driving Campaign: A Survey Among Drivers*, Road Research Laboratory Report LR 230 (1968).

38 *See, e.g.*, Middendorff, *Desirable Developments in the Administration of Justice*, II COLLECTED STUDIES IN CRIMINOLOGICAL RESEARCH 45, 59 (1966). Judge Middendorff discusses the German Second Road Traffic Act which became effective January 2, 1965.

89 The figures are taken from a communication to the Norwegian Committee on Traffic Research from the Road Research Laboratory, Ministry of Transport, and are for the months of July, August, and September, 1968.

40 Ministry of Transport, The Road Safety Act 1967 and its Effect on Road Accidents in the United Kingdom (undated mimeo.).

41 Road Research Laboratory Report No. 32, *supra* note 36, at 3-4 & Table IV (referring to a Road Research Laboratory Report by R.F. Newbay in course of preparation).

42 Road Research Laboratory Report LR 230, *supra* note 37. This sort of change may come at a later stage, when the initial success of the law in reducing the accident rate has become known among drivers.

SEVERITY OF FORMAL SANCTIONS
AS A DETERRENT
TO DEVIANT BEHAVIOR

Richard G. Salem

William J. Bowers

The imposition of penalities for violation of criminal laws has been traditionally justified for such reasons as social justice and retribution. Today, perhaps the main justification for imposing severe penalties on those who violate the law is that such punishments serve as a specific deterrent to future violations by the offender and as a general deterrent to violations by others who might be tempted to follow his lead.

The extent of this deterrent force and the way in which it operates are, however, largely a matter of conjecture. One explanation relies on a rationalistic conception of human behavior. The individual is seen primarily as one who optimizes resources in the pursuit of his goals. The more costly a particular form of behavior becomes for him, the less likely he is to engage in it (Homans, 1961). Imposing severe sanctions for deviant behavior, it is anticipated, will make the potential offender realize that "crime does not pay." In Bentham's words, "The value of the punishment must not be less in any case than what is sufficient to outweigh that of the profit of the offense" (Pincoffs, 1966: 78).[1]

Yet, this perspective leaves out a significant dimension—the importance of sanctions for normative stability. Durkheim formulated this argument clearly by stressing that the deterrent effect of formal sanctions occurs, not so much by means of the direct impact they may have on potential offenders, but more through their indirect effect in strengthening and buttressing social norms. Thus he asserts (1964: 108) that punishment:

does not serve, or else serves quite secondarily, in correcting the culpable or in intimidating possible followers. From this point of view, its efficacy is justly doubtful, and, in any case, mediocre. Its true function is to maintain social cohesion intact, while maintaining all its vitality in the common conscience.

Hence formal punishment acts to affirm the rule which has been transgressed and to restore the unanimity of the collective sentiment. For Durkheim, then, the effect of formal sanctions in deterring deviant behavior occurs only secondarily by way of the individual's "calculus of utilities." The sanctions' primary effect is through their capacity to strengthen the normative climate of the community—to reinforce and mobilize informal social disapproval (Coser, 1967; Toby, 1964).

Durkheim's contention that the imposition of sanctions validates the conformist's behavior and reclarifies the norm for the general community is reflected in Cohen's (1966: 4-5) observation that "the most destructive impact of deviance on organization is probably through its impact on trust, on confidence that others will, by and large, play by the rules." Here again deviance must be pointed up and defined as inappropriate in order to assure the community that the "old rules" are still in effect. We see, then, that formal reaction to deviance can be conceived of as acting directly as a deterrent, or as acting indirectly in the reaffirmation of rules.

While it is generally assumed, as in both the above arguments, that formal sanctions have some kind of deterrent effect on deviant behavior, there is little systematic evidence on the nature or extent of such an effect. We know from small-group studies that an individual's attitudes and especially his behavior can be modified by the prospect of informal social sanctions (positive as well as negative). However formal sanctions as part of the legal structure of the society or community are another matter. They are more remote and often irrelevant to the large bulk of the population. Seldom do they figure in the activity of most people.

Moreover, available research—largely studies of capital punishment—seriously questions the deterrent effect of formal sanctions. Thus Sellin (1966), in examining the effect of the death penalty on homicide rates, presents data which show, for example, that during 1917-1918, when the death penalty was abolished in Arizona, the number of people convicted of murder was no different from previous and subsequent periods when the death penalty was in effect.[2] Schuessler (1969), in comparing contiguous abolition and death penalty states over a period of approximately thirty years, demonstrates the similarity of homicide rates. In fact the rates for abolition states are sometimes lower than those for death penalty states, and certainty of execution does not lower the homicide rates among the 41 death penalty states. He concludes that "statistical findings and case studies converge to disprove the claim that the death penalty has any special deterrent value" (Schuessler, 1969: 388).

This research, however, is limited to a rare crime of passion and perhaps the most severe punishment of all. But what about less serious crimes and less extreme punishments? Gibbs (1968) has recently tried to assess the effects of durations of imprisonment, rather than the death penalty, on homicide rates. He concludes (1968: 525) that

> even though the relation between severity and the criminal homicide rate is obviously not a close one by any standard, the evidence of an additive effect [with certainty of sanctions] cautions against entirely rejecting the possibility in some way operates as a deterrent.

A reexamination of his data, however, shows that Gibbs' claim that there is an independent relationship between severity of sanctions and homicide rate appears unfounded (see Bowers 1970).

In a more comprehensive attempt to isolate the separate effects of severity and certainty of formal sanctions, Tittle (1969: 417) examines rates of homicide, robbery, burglary, larceny, assault, auto theft, and sex offenses. He concludes that the

> examination of the relationship between severity and offense rate at constant levels of certainty reveals that severity of punishment has little consistent independent or additive effect.

Tittle's findings on the deterrent effects of certainty of penal sanctions have been challenged, but there is no indication that his findings on severity of sanctions—that it "has little consistent independent or additive effect"—must be qualified (see Chiricos and Waldo, 1970).

Chambliss (1969) cites evidence that certain less serious forms of deviance are definitely responsive to formal sanctions. In particular he cites parking meter violations and shoplifting (by nonprofessional thieves) as examples of behaviors which are reduced by increasing the severity of formal sanctions. The research he cites, however, unlike that of Gibbs and Tittle, makes no effort to separate the effects of severity and certainty of sanctions. On the basis of this limited evidence, then, it would seem that deviant behavior is relatively unresponsive to direct formal sanctions, and that when such effects do occur, they are highly contingent upon the type of behavior considered, the conditions under which it occurs, and the nature of the individuals involved (Ball, 1955: 348-351).

Perhaps the main reason for the limited amount of research on the deterrent effects of formal sanctions lies in the methodological difficulties of isolating such effects. In particular it is difficult to find a sample of societies, communities, or institutions sufficiently alike in other respects that differences in their rates of deviant behavior can be attributed to differences in formal sanctions and not to other factors.

For the purposes of this work, college communities will be examined to determine whether: (1) formal sanctions have a *direct* deterrent effect on deviant behavior, and (2) they have an *indirect* deterrent effect through their ability to stimulate and reinforce informal social norms. To evaluate the influence of these formal and informal mechanisms we will be using data on: (1) the rates of specific forms of deviant behavior; (2) the extent to which these actions are disapproved; and (3) the usual legal or institutional sanctions imposed for these forms of misbehavior in a number of different social contexts. These data have been obtained by Bowers (1964) in a nationwide study of academic dishonesty among college students.

The Data

Information on formal sanctions: During the school year 1961-1962 a survey was made of deans and student body presidents from all regionally accredited, four-year, degree-granting colleges and universities, asking for information on the usual reactions of their institution to various forms of student misconduct. Deans and student body presidents from 838 colleges and universities responded.

Information on deviant behavior and normative climate: During the 1962-1963 academic year 100 of these institutions were selected for more intensive study. At each of these schools, questionnaires were sent to a sample of 75 to 100 students who were drawn randomly from institutional directories or records of the registrars. Sixty percent of the sample returned completed questionnaires; 91 schools were represented by at least 40 students. One school had to be dropped because of difficulties in reaching the students, leaving a total sample of 5,422 students from 99 colleges and universities. (For further details of the sampling procedure see Bowers, 1964: app. c.)

The students in this survey were asked to indicate their attitudes toward and involvement in various forms of campus behavior. Five of the actions about which students report their attitudes and behavior in the 1962 survey correspond quite closely to offenses for which deans and student body presidents indicated the usual formal sanctions at their institutions a year earlier. Thus the merging of data from these two surveys permits us to examine the interrelationships among formal sanctions, normative climate and rate of violation for each of the five forms of behavior at 99 colleges and universities. (See Bowers and Salem, 1970, for a discussion, based on the same data, of variations in rates of misconduct and institutional sanctioning policies by type of institution.)

Formal Sanctions and Deviant Behavior

In this section we shall examine the extent to which formal sanctions for a given offense affect its prevalence; the next section will investigate how this effect occurs—whether, as Bentham would argue, by making the action more costly to engage in or, as Durkheim holds, by strengthening the force of informal normative constraints.

If formal sanctions have a deterrent effect on behavior, we must find that the rates of the various offenses decline as the penalties for them become increasingly severe. Table 1 shows the relationship between formal sanctions and rates of involvement in five different forms of deviant behavior. For purposes of comparison, the column to the right shows the percentage difference per interval as a rough index of the effect of formal sanctions on behavior.[3]

TABLE 1

MEAN PERCENTAGE ENGAGING IN FIVE DEVIANT ACTIONS BY FORMAL SANCTION[a]

Offense	Sanctions Imposed for Drinking and Library Offenses						Percentage Difference per Interval
	Dismissal		Suspension		Restriction of Privileges		
	%	(n)	%	(n)	%	(n)	
Violating alcohol-use rules	19	(15)	35	(35)	39	(35)	-7.6
Getting drunk[b]	25	(17)	35	(44)	41	(30)	-7.4
Stealing library books	15	(13)	13	(39)	21	(31)	-5.0
Marking up library books	—	(0)	28	(7)	24	(70)	+4.0

	Sanctions Imposed for Cheating[c]						Percentage Difference per Interval
	Suspend or Expel		Fail Course		Fail Specific Piece of Work or Less		
Cheating index[d]	38	(19)	52	(43)	56	(30)	-7.9

a. The mean percentage in each cell is computed by averaging the rates for all schools in that cell. The numbers in parentheses represent schools rather than students. The number of respondents for any cell will be approximately 55 times the number of schools in that cell. The danger here is not that the number of respondents will be too small to yield reliable percentages, but rather that the number of schools from which they come will be too few to adequately represent institutions with a particular sanctioning policy. Where the dean and student body president disagreed about the sanction usually imposed at their school, the report of the dean was used. When both responded, the dean and student body president usually agreed.

b. Penalty imposed, according to dean's reports, is for "being drunk and disorderly"; offense reported by students is simply "getting drunk."

c. Items referring to cheating on a midterm exam, a final exam, and plagiarism on a term paper were combined to produce a cheating sanctions index which is used to represent this form of behavior.

d. Students are classified as cheaters by this index if they have "used crib notes during an exam," "copied from another student during an exam," "plagiarized on a term paper," or "turned in work done entirely or in part by another student." (See Bowers, 1964: ch. 3 for further details.)

Generally speaking, this table shows that deviance decreases as the sanctions become stronger. There is, however, substantial variation in the *extent* of the deterrent effects of formal sanctions by type of offense. A relatively strong effect is to be found among the offenses involving the use of alcohol. These two items show a seven- to eight-point percentage difference per interval. A weaker effect occurs among the items referring to property offenses in the library. In the case of marking up library books there is actually a slight reversal; misconduct is a little more prevalent where the punishments are more severe. (It should be noted, however, that formal sanctions for this offense are not very severe at most schools. The effect we do find is dependent upon a small minority of only seven schools which may depart in other relevant ways from the rest.) Finally, cheating is affected to about the same degree as the alcohol-related offenses (although, of course, the sanctioning categories differ).

There is also variation in the *pattern* of effects of formal sanctions by type of misconduct. Hence for the two drinking violations the most pronounced deterrent effect occurs only when the maximum formal sanction—dismissal from school—is usually imposed. For stealing books from the library, however, dismissal and suspension show approximately the same ability to deter the deviance. Similarly, in the case of cheating, the difference in rates of misconduct comes largely between dismissal and suspension on the one hand and the lesser sanctions on the other.

Clearly, then, the effects of formal sanctions are uniform neither in extent nor pattern. They are, however, evident at least to some degree in four of the five cases at hand, suggesting that formal sanctions have a modest deterrent effect on the incidence of deviant behavior. Next, the normative climate will be examined as a mechanism through which formal sanctions may have their effect.

The Role of the Normative Context

In a recent study using these data, Bowers (1968) has shown a strong negative relationship between the climate of disapproval of a given action at a college and the incidence of that action. The study indicates that the climate of disapproval has a deterrent effect on behavior in two distinct ways: through "the effect of the individual's own sense of disapproval, and the effect of the normative feelings of others in his social context" (Bowers, 1968: 383). The measure of the normative context we are using for this analysis thus combines both of these effects.

Following Durkheim, we would expect to find a relationship between formal sanctions and the strength of normative sentiments toward a particular form of behavior. Table 2 shows this relationship for the five offenses under consideration. As in Table 1, strong effects are found for drinking-related behavior. In fact, formal sanctions show an even stronger relationship with disapproval (Table 2) than with behavior (Table 1). For library offenses, the relationship between formal sanctions and disapproval is again relatively weak. In the case of marking up library books, there is no relationship whatsoever. (Consequently the slight negative effect of formal sanctions in Table 1 cannot be attributed to differences in normative climate. This suggests that severe formal sanctions for this action provoke a slightly greater incidence of it.)

Perhaps the greatest surprise in Table 2 occurs with the cheating offenses. Whereas Table 1 showed a modest deterrent effect of formal sanctions, Table 2 shows essentially no association between formal sanctions and disapproval. Apparently students' attitudes are relatively insensitive to the formal sanctions imposed for cheating, although their behavior is not. Obviously the normative climate, at least as represented by students' reported feelings of disapproval, does not account for the apparent deterrent effect of formal sanctions in the case of cheating behavior.

With the exception of cheating, the *pattern* of effects in Table 2 is also very similar to that in Table 1. For the two alcohol-related offenses, the largest effects come between dismissal and all other sanctions; and for stealing library

TABLE 2

MEAN PERCENTAGE STRONGLY DISAPPROVING[a] OF FIVE DEVIANT ACTIONS BY FORMAL SANCTION

	Sanctions Imposed for Drinking and Library Offenses					
	Dismissal		Suspension		Restriction of Privileges	Percentage Difference
Offense	%	(n)	%	(n)	%	(n)	per Interval
Violating alcohol-use rules	62	(15)	41	(35)	35	(35)	+10.5
Getting drunk	62	(17)	48	(44)	39	(30)	+10.8
Stealing library books	64	(13)	67	(39)	58	(31)	+ 5.5
Marking up library books	—	(0)	56	(7)	56	(70)	0.0

	Sanctions Imposed for Cheating					
	Suspend or Expel		Fail Course		Fail Specific Piece of Work or Less	Percentage Difference
							per Interval
Cheating index	38	(19)	35	(43)	39	(30)	1.3

a. Single items were used to measure personal disapproval for the drinking and library offenses. In the case of cheating, students were classified on the basis of their strong agreement with four items: under no circumstances is cheating justified; students are morally obligated not to cheat; the individual's personal integrity and self-respect should be the basis for the decision not to cheat; and cheating directly contradicts the goals of education. (See Bowers, 1964: ch. 5, for further details.)

books, the effect appears primarily between dismissal and suspension on the one hand and lesser penalties on the other.

Thus we find that both the extent and the pattern of variations in disapproval (Table 2) are quite comparable to their variation in behavior (Table 1) for most of these actions. And, since there is a strong negative association between the normative climate and the incidence of deviant behavior (Bowers, 1968), the deterrent effects of formal sanctions in Table 1 may occur largely through their association with the normative climate.

Formal Sanctions, the Normative Context, and Deviant Behavior

Table 3 shows the relationship between formal sanctions and misconduct, controlling for the normative context. Beginning with the drinking-related items, we find that the control for normative context removes virtually all of the effect of formal sanctions on behavior. For both getting drunk and violating alcohol-use rules, the per interval effects within the five disapproval contexts are very small; overall or average effect is less than one percent per interval in both cases.[4]

For stealing books from the library, the results are similar. The relationship between formal sanctions and behavior is reduced except in the lowest disapproval context. And only a few schools are responsible for the deterrent effect in this category. (In fact, it would take a modest increase in the rate of library theft at only one of these schools to virtually eliminate the deterrent effect.) For marking up library books, the positive effect shown in Table 1 reappears—again based on a very small minority of the colleges under investigation.

In the case of cheating, the results are quite unlike those for the other four offenses. Although the overall deterrent effect of formal sanctions is reduced slightly from -7.9 to -6.7% per interval, this remaining effect is considerably greater than that shown for any of the other violations. Apparently academic dishonesty, unlike the other behaviors, is directly responsive to the imposition of formal sanctions. Perhaps this is because cheating is the most instrumental and rationally motivated form of deviance under consideration. Chambliss (1969: 368-372) argues that instrumental deviance is significantly more susceptible to the impact of sanctions than deviance of a more expressive nature, e.g., violations involving the use of alcohol.

Yet the effect of formal sanctions on cheating behavior varies by college context. There is generally an increase in their deterrent effect as the context of disapproval becomes stronger. Apparently the weight of severe sanctions is more clearly brought home to potential offenders where informal disapproval is more intense. We know from previous research (Bowers, 1964: ch. 10) that disapproval levels are generally higher at schools that employ the academic honor system. It could be that in these more disapproving contexts the honor system, which often requires students to report their peers for cheating, makes more salient the formal sanctions which may remain relatively remote under other systems of control.

TABLE 3

MEAN PERCENTAGE ENGAGING IN FIVE DEVIANT ACTIONS BY FORMAL SANCTIONS AND NORMATIVE CLIMATE OF COLLEGE

Type of Deviant Action	Percentage on Campus Strongly Disapproving	Sanctions Imposed for Drinking and Library Offenses						Percentage Difference per Interval
		Dismissal		Suspension		Lesser Penalty		
		%	(n)	%	(n)	%	(n)	
Violating	1-20	—	(0)	56	(7)	57	(12)	- 1.0
alcohol-use	21-40	45	(2)	43	(9)	42	(9)	+ 1.2
rules	41-60	24	(6)	29	(13)	28	(11)	- 1.1
	61-80	9	(4)	15	(5)	8	(1)	- 3.4
	81-100	6	(3)	5	(1)	2	(2)	+ 1.8
				Average Percentage Difference				- 0.5
Getting drunk	1-20	—	(0)	65	(7)	64	(7)	+ 1.0
	21-40	61	(2)	49	(7)	47	(8)	+ 4.0
	41-60	32	(6)	30	(18)	33	(11)	- 1.2
	61-80	14	(7)	17	(10)	19	(2)	- 2.8
	81-100	5	(2)	7	(2)	7	(2)	- 1.0
				Average Percentage Difference				- 0.1
Stealing library	21-40	23	(1)	—	(0)	40	(3)	- 8.5
books	41-60	18	(5)	22	(11)	27	(14)	- 4.7
	61-80	12	(6)	10	(23)	12	(14)	- 0.8
	81-100	11	(1)	7	(5)	—	(0)	+ 4.0
				Average Percentage Difference				- 3.1
Marking up	21-40	—	(0)	43	(1)	48	(5)	- 5.0
library books	41-60	—	(0)	29	(3)	26	(41)	+ 3.0
	61-80	—	(0)	21	(3)	16	(24)	+ 5.0
				Average Percentage Difference				+ 3.1

		Sanctions Imposed for Cheating						Percentage Difference per Interval
		Suspend or Expel		Fail Course		Fail Specific Piece of Work or Less		
Cheating index	1-20	—	(0)	71	(3)	62	(3)	+ 9.0
	21-40	46	(13)	56	(26)	59	(17)	- 6.0
	41-60	25	(5)	40	(13)	50	(8)	-11.9
	61-80	11	(1)	49	(1)	39	(2)	- 6.0
				Average Percentage Difference				- 6.7

The Academic Honor System and Peer Disapproval

Information is available on whether the schools in our sample operate under the honor system, thus permitting us to determine if the effectiveness of formal

TABLE 4

MEAN PERCENTAGE CHEATING BY FORMAL SANCTIONS, NORMATIVE CLIMATE, AND CONTROL SYSTEM OF COLLEGE

		Honor System						
	Percentage Strongly Disapproving	Suspend or Expel %	(n)	Fail Course %	(n)	Fail Specific Piece of Work or Less %	(n)	Percentage Difference per Interval
Cheating index	21-40	34	(5)	28	(3)	47	(5)	- 6.6
	41-60	24	(4)	33	(7)	52	(1)	-11.0
	61-80	11	(1)	—	(0)	39	(2)	-14.0
		Average Percentage Difference						- 9.0
		No Honor System						
Cheating index	1-20	—	(0)	71	(3)	62	(3)	+ 9.0
	21-40	53	(8)	60	(23)	65	(12)	- 5.8
	41-60	27	(1)	49	(6)	49	(7)	- 2.8
	61-80	—	(0)	49	(1)	—	(0)	—
		Average Percentage Difference						- 3.6

sanctions for cheating is somehow enhanced by this system of social control. Table 4 shows the relationship between formal sanctions and cheating, controlling for normative context and whether or not the college has an honor system.

Several things are evident from the table. First, as we noted above, the level of personal disapproval of cheating is generally higher at the honor system schools. Second, the honor system schools more regularly administer severe sanctions for academic dishonesty. Third, rates of cheating are generally lower at the honor system schools even when their counterparts without honor systems are comparable in normative climate and severity of sanctions.

More important for the purposes of this analysis is the fact that the direct deterrent effect of formal sanctions seems to be concentrated at the honor system schools. The average per interval effect of formal sanctions at the honor system schools is higher than the value for all schools (shown in Table 3), while at the schools without honor systems this effect is considerably reduced. Apparently the honor system does make formal sanctions more relevant to the potential offender. Clearly, personal disapproval does not absorb the effects of formal sanctions as it does for other forms of misconduct.

Peer attitudes of disapproval may be of greater importance than personal sentiments in the honor system context. Under most honor systems the individual is responsible not only for his own behavior but also for the conduct of his peers. Thus the peer group is a prominent source of informal social sanctions under this system.

TABLE 5

LEVEL OF PERSONAL AND PEER DISAPPROVAL BY CONTROL SYSTEM OF THE COLLEGE

	Honor System	Other System
Mean percentage expressing strong personal disapproval	43%	33%
Mean percentage perceiving strong peer disapproval[a]	51%	28%
Number of schools	(28)	(64)

a. The measure of perceived peer disapproval is constructed from two items which ask the respondent how strongly "a close friend" and "the students you go around with" would disapprove if they learned that you had cheated. (See Bowers, 1964: ch. 8 for further details.)

Fortunately the data include the respondent's perceptions of the disapproval of his peers. Table 5 allows us to compare levels of personal and peer disapproval at schools with and without honor systems.

Both types of disapproval are, of course, stronger at the honor system schools. Their relative strength is reversed, however, in the two contexts. At the large majority of institutions, those without honor systems, strong personal disapproval is more often reported than is strong peer disapproval. At the honor system schools, on the other hand, more students perceive strong disapproval among their peers then say they personally feel a strong sense of disapproval of cheating.

In effect, at the honor system schools the perceived climate of peer disapproval is quite strong relative to the level of personal disapproval that prevails. Personal attitudes seem to have become *social reality* under the honor system so that students are aware of and sensitive to the disapproval of their peers. It seems quite plausible, then, that this heightened sense of peer disapproval is what conveys the deterrent forces of formal sanctions under the honor system.

Table 6 shows the relationship between formal sanctions and cheating, controlling for the climate of peer disapproval and the system of control at the college. As in Table 4, the direct deterrent effects of formal sanctions continue to be clearly evident at honor system schools, contrary to our expectation that peer disapproval might account for this effect. On the other hand, peer disapproval produces a reduction in the deterrent effects of formal sanctions.

TABLE 6

MEAN PERCENTAGE CHEATING BY FORMAL SANCTIONS, PEER DISAPPROVAL, AND CONTROL SYSTEM OF COLLEGE

| | Percentage Strongly Disapproving | Honor System | | | | | | Percentage Difference per Interval |
| | | Suspend or Expel | | Fail Course | | Fail Specific Piece of Work or Less | | |
		%	(n)	%	(n)	%	(n)	
Cheating index	1-20	48	(1)	—	(0)	—	(0)	—
	21-40	34	(2)	36	(2)	44	(2)	- 5.0
	41-60	29	(3)	33	(5)	47	(5)	-10.3
	61-80	19	(4)	25	(3)	40	(1)	- 7.8
				Average Percentage Difference				- 8.3
		No Honor System						
Cheating index	1-20	63	(3)	66	(13)	71	(7)	- 4.4
	21-40	57	(3)	58	(15)	57	(11)	+ 0.6
	41-60	31	(3)	40	(3)	44	(3)	- 6.5
	61-80	—	(0)	46	(2)	47	(1)	- 1.0
				Average Percentage Difference				- 2.5

The average per interval effects for both honor system and others are slightly lower in Table 6 than they were in Table 4.

Thus peer disapproval is generally more effective than personal disapproval in accounting for the relationship between formal sanctions and cheating behavior,[5] yet neither peer disapproval nor personal disapproval accounts for the deterrent effects of formal sanctions against cheating at the honor system schools as well as they do at schools without the honor system, or as well as personal disapproval does for drinking and library offenses at all schools.

Our assumption that peer disapproval would account for the deterrent effects of formal sanctions at honor system schools was clearly mistaken. If we examine our argument and the data more closely we may find out why. We argued that under the honor system, the student's peers become an important source of disapproval—that formal sanctions may activate peer disapproval which, in turn, discourages cheating. (To be sure, the slight reduction in deterrent effects in Table 6, as compared to Table 4, may very well reflect this fact.) Yet under the honor system, responsibility for the behavior of one's peers usually involves more than simply expressing disapproval informally to an offender. Most systems have a "reporting clause" that requires a student who has witnessed a cheating incident to report the offender to appropriate authorities, or to ask the offender to report himself and then to report him if he fails to do so. The honor system is thus designed to increase the likelihood that formal sanctions will be brought to bear. The student's peers are directly responsible for activating the formal sanctioning machinery. As a result, formal sanctions, which are often imposed by a student court, are far less remote from the would-be offender. And indeed we might expect them to be more salient to him as the proportion of his peers who are strongly committed to the system increases.

Table 6, in fact, supports this interpretation. Not only does it show a generally greater deterrent effect of formal sanctions at honor system schools for a given level of peer disapproval, but it also shows an interaction effect between peer disapproval and formal sanctions at these schools. Thus the stronger the climate of peer disapproval, the greater the reduction in cheating behavior resulting from a given increase in formal sanctions.[6] Although this pattern is based on a limited number of schools, it holds without exception. It strongly suggests that the reason for the direct deterrent effects of formal sanctions at honor system schools lies in the ability of these systems to bring formal sanctions into play, or at least to make students think they will come into play.[7]

Preselection versus Conversion Effects of Formal Sanctions

There is little support in our data for the rationalistic view that potential offenders are directly inhibited by the prospect of severe formal sanctions, as Bentham and the general utilitarian viewpoint would contend. Except for a minority of schools which seem to have a unique capacity for making formal sanctions relevant through the academic honor system, no direct deterrent effects vis-à-vis drinking, library, and cheating offenses remain after we control for the normative climate of the school. This is not to say that formal sanctions have no effect on behavior, but simply that by and large the effects they do have seem to occur largely through informal normative processes.

What, then, is the connection between formal sanctioning policy and the normative processes of the school? Perhaps the most straightforward assumption is that formal sanctions influence the attitudes of students *after* they reach the campus. It is quite possible, however, that the sanctioning policy of an institution affects the *kinds of students it attracts*. Thus since the use of alcohol is central to much of campus social life, and since potential students are attracted to colleges at least in part on the basis of the schools' social reputations, it is quite plausible that a punitive sanctioning policy in this area will attract students who diapprove and repel those who do not. Rules of conduct and sanctions imposed for library offenses, on the other hand, would seem to be less relevant as criteria in deciding what college to attend. And indeed, Table 2 showed that there is a stronger relationship between severity of sanctions and feelings of disapproval for the drinking-related items than for the library offenses. Do these relationships come about as a result of a selection process in which students gravitate toward schools where the sanctioning policies are compatible with their own predispositions? Or are they a result of a conversion process in which a change in attitude occurs after the students have made the decision to attend a particular school?

The answer is contained in Table 7. It shows how students with a particular level of drinking or cheating behavior in high school[8] are distributed among colleges with varying sanctioning policies.

There is no evidence to speak of in Table 7 that students who are predisposed toward drinking or cheating choose to attend schools with more lenient policies in these areas. Sanctioning policy of the college attended is virtually unrelated to the previous behavior of students. The relationship between formal sanctioning policies and personal feelings of disapproval with regard to drinking offenses therefore appears to be a function of normative changes which take place after students reach college, not of a selection process that occurs either before or during college.[9]

Yet the case of cheating casts doubt on the power of formal sanctions to produce a change in normative sentiments. The fact that formal sanctions in this area show no association either with students' predispositions before coming to college (Table 7) or with their attitudes in college (Table 2) seriously questions the possiblity of any pervasive or consistent connection between formal sanctions and the normative climate that emerges. The suggestion is that some broader, more fundamental aspect of the insitution determines the normative climate, and perhaps in some cases the formal sanctions as well. Indeed, the institution's sponsorship or type of control, or the particular forms of disciplinary administration in effect may strongly influence the normative climate. Obviously further research will be required to establish the links between formal sanctions and the normative climate, which seem to exist with respect to some offenses and not others.

Discussion and Conclusion

In view of our findings that the severity of formal sanctions has no direct deterrent effect on deviant behavior except under the special conditions of an academic honor system, it is time to seriously consider why this should be the case. There is little doubt that man is in part a rational animal who seeks to minimize his losses or potential losses in terms of power, prestige, popularity, and self-esteem (compare with Homans, 1961). How is it that sanctions which are essentially designed to deprive him of these things seem not to affect his behavior?

Certainly the foremost answer, one we have suggested above, is that formal sanctions are extremely remote to most people. There is evidence that most people, notably those who have had little contact with the law, are not aware of the prescribed legal sanctions for various criminal offenses (California State Legislature, 1968: 12 ff.). Formal sanctions for drinking, library, and cheating offenses are probably remote from most students at most colleges. Only a tiny fraction of those who violate in these areas ever come to the attention of

TABLE 7

**FORMAL SANCTIONS OF COLLEGE ATTENDED BY HIGH SCHOOL
DRINKING[a] AND CHEATING BEHAVIOR**

		Level of Behavior in High School		
Formal Sanctions For:		% Non-drinker	% Moderate Drinker	% Heavy Drinker
Violating	dismissal	19	19	16
alcohol-use	suspension	42	49	42
rules	restriction of privileges	39	32	42
	total	100	100	100
	number of students	(2284)	(320)	(1901)
Getting	dismissal	18	17	16
drunk	suspension	50	49	50
	restriction of privileges	32	34	34
	total	100	100	100
	number of students	(2425)	(346)	(2128)
		% Noncheater		% Cheater
Cheating	suspend or expel	24		21
index	fail course	45		49
	fail specific piece of work or less	31		30
	total	100		100
	number of students	(2263)		(2554)

a. Here the drinking of beer and/or liquor is considered. A moderate drinker has used one or the other at least once, while a heavy drinker has used both at least once in high school.

authorities (Bowers, 1964: ch. 1). Even if students are aware of the appropriate sanctions in these areas, knowing many others who have violated without consequences will certainly contribute to the impressions that there is little risk of formal sanctions.

Studies which purport to demonstrate the deterrent effects of formal sanctions generally focus on offenses of relatively high certainty and low severity of formal sanctions, such as parking violations (Chambliss, 1966), speeding violations (Ross and Campbell, 1968), and violations of the income tax laws (Schwartz and Orleans, 1967; Schwartz, 1969). In these cases, detection is routine, and the sanction is a monetary one. The potential offender can assess the risk of detection from his own past experiences and the experience of others; he can evaluate the sanction in terms of financial loss. People will talk in calculative terms about the chances of getting caught and whether they can afford it.

There is no specific evidence in these studies, however, that *severity* of sanctions plays an important part. No attempt is made to examine the effects of severity *independently* of certainty. Moreover, those studies which do attempt to separate the effects of severity and certainty (Tittle, 1969; Gibbs, 1968), whatever their methodological shortcomings, indicate that certainty rather than severity of legal sanctions is the primary deterrent factor. In fact, in Tittle's data, severity showed no consistent relationship to offense rates even under conditions of relatively high certainty. This latter point calls the simple, rationalistic formulation still further into question since, according to this logic, increasing certainty should add to the weight given severity of sanctions in the decision to act.

Perhaps there are "negative feedback processes" at work which tend to offset the expected deterrent effect of formal sanctions. Schwartz (1969) has recently provided evidence that the threat of formal sanctions generates what he calls "resistant side effects." While most people increased their compliance with income tax laws under threat of sanctions, a minority responded with substantially increased claims for deductions, as if they had been provoked to "beat the system."

More generally, severe formal sanctions or punitive threats may produce a certain degree of alienation, hostility, and rebelliousness, particularly when they do not reflect informal sentiments.[10] Under these circumstances, violation can become a symbolic act, one predicated on a commitment to social justice or personal pride. When those who feel these reactions also share other social attributes, especially common group membership, noncompliance may even become a subcultural response. Thus the willingness to risk severe sanctions will be a sign of commitment to the subgroup and will elicit the respect of the other members—noncompliance, then, will be socially motivated and reinforced, at least within the subgroup. Thus, for example, Erikson (1966: esp. 114-126) writes of the Quakers of Puritan Massachusetts argues that, with increasing severity of punishment for their offenses, increasing numbers of violators appeared as if to invite legal sanctions.

There may be another closely related source of resistance to severe formal sanctions—the insulating effect of peers. We know from previous research on cheating (Bowers, 1964: 141) that students are much more willing to express their disapproval informally to an offender than to report a fellow student to the authorities for that offense. Moreover there is evidence that when the offender is a close friend, students will actually take steps to protect him from the authorities (see also Stouffer, 1949; Stouffer and Toby, 1951; Turner, 1959). This protective tendency among particularistic or primary group relations may grow even stronger as formal sanctions become more severe. While the motivation in this case may be the loyalty of personal friendship rather than the injustice of alien sanctions, the effect is the same—to neutralize or counteract severe formal sanctions.

In effect, the academic honor system is designed to remove or to offset these sources of resistance by making peers themselves the agents of formal control. Formal sanctions are imposed not by an outsider to insure conformity with his norms, but by insiders to enforce norms to which the members of the group subscribe. Under these conditions, formal sanctions may actually take on the meaning and functions that informal social sanctions possess in most groups.

Perhaps honor systems have been less effective in controlling excessive drinking, disorderly social conduct, and other more expressive forms of misconduct because such behavior is more closely tied in with the collegiate subculture. It will be difficult to extract a commitment within the peer group to report those who break the rules when the behavior is a group enterprise supported by subcultural values.

Chambliss (1969) has argued that instrumental actions which the offender adopts as a specific means to an end (e.g., cheating) are more subject to control through formal sanctions than are expressive actions in which an offender engages as part of a broader style of life to which he is committed (e.g., drinking violations). The data in Table 3 do tend to confirm this proposition; formal sanctions against cheating continue to show a deterrent effect after we control for the normative climate, whereas this effect totally vanishes in the case of drinking-related offenses. More specifically, the data suggest that the deterrent effects remain in the case of cheating because, and to the extent that, peers become the agents of formal control. Thus the deterrent effect is concentrated at honor system schools, particularly where a large proportion of peers are perceived to strongly disapprove of cheating. Presumably objective and subjective certainty of formal sanctions are the greatest under these circumstances.

In conclusion, then, we find little evidence of a direct deterrent effect of severe formal sanctions. More substantial is their role in anchoring and buttressing the normative climate. For most of the offenses under investigation, the level of formal sanctions appears to influence students' attitudes and thus to affect the normative climate that develops at a college. This "conversion effect" is not, however, uniform in pattern or extent. For drinking-related offenses it is strong and clear; for cheating offenses it is altogether absent.

Since we find only modest and irregular deterrent effects, either direct or indirect, it might be appropriate at this point to consider briefly some effects of severe sanctions apart from deterrence. The fact that the commonly assumed direct deterrent effects are largely a myth should focus our attention on those for whom the myth may serve some function. One possibility is that severe sanctions have important implications for those who impose them. As long as everyone believes in their deterrent effects, severe sanctions represent a powerful tool for authorities in meeting their responsiblities, and a sign to the broader community that they are taking those responsibilities seriously. Thus, when authorities are having difficulty catching offenders, they can impose more severe sanctions "to insure that violations will be curbed." Or when the rate of violations is increasing and pressure is mounting for more effective control, authorities can "crack down" with more severe sanctions. In both these cases, the imposition of severe sanctions is a visible sign of action in response to failure in the system of social control.[11]

Research on the deterrent effects of formal sanctions is still at a relatively primitive stage. Different methods are being employed, including ecological analysis, natural and controlled experimentation, and survey research. Yet most of the studies to date have not uncovered processes through which formal sanctions may be having effects. In fact, the balance of evidence thus far collected weighs against a deterrent effect directly attributable to the severity of formal sanctions. Only under exceptional conditions do they directly deter deviant behavior. The evidence concerning the deterrent effects of certainty of formal sanctions is only slightly more convincing. Needless to say, further work in separating and evaluating the relative effects of severity and certainty of formal sanctions is required. In view of the largely negative findings in the area of deterrence, at least in the research to this point, it would also seem advisable in future research to examine other possible functions of formal sanctions. These might include their role in stimulating and reinforcing the normative climate of the community—what we have here described as indirect deterrent effects—and their role as resources and signs of performance for those who impose them.

Notes

1. Of course Bentham is only one of a group of legal philosophers and criminologists who developed theories of deviant behavior and social control upon the assumption that individuals who engage in deviant acts rationally respond to the administration of formal penalties. In summarizing the contribution of classical theory, Vold (1958: 23) indicates: "Puzzling questions about the reasons for or 'causes' of behavior, the uncertainties of motive and intent, the unequal consequences of an arbitrary rule, these were all deliberately ignored for the sake of administrative uniformity."

2. This assumes that the potential murderers of Arizona were aware of the changed situation in 1917-1918. Although the prospect of death as the punishment for their crimes did not seem to faze them, it could be argued that this two-year interlude was not long enough to produce a weakening in the normative climate and hence was not an adequate test of the indirect effects of formal sanctions.

3. The percentage difference per interval is a weighted average computed as follows:

$$\frac{(a\text{-}b)na \cdot nb + (b\text{-}c)nb \cdot nc}{na \cdot nb + nb \cdot nc} = \frac{(a\text{-}b)na + (b\text{-}c)nc}{na + nc}$$

where a, b, and c are the rates of a given form of deviant behavior under the most severe, the intermediate, and the most lenient sanctioning categories respectively, and where na, nb, and nc are the number of schools contributing to a, b, and c respectively. Where nb=o, we let $b = \frac{a+c}{2}$.

4. In addition to percentage difference per interval for each context of disapproval, the table also shows the average percentage difference for the several normative contexts of a given offense, as a rough index of the overall deterrent effect of formal sanctions after the effects of the normative context have been removed. The average percentage difference is computed as follows:

$$\frac{\Sigma_i \left[(a_i - b_i)na_i + (b_i - c_i)nc_i \right]}{\Sigma_i (na_i + nc_i)}$$

where the i's represent control categories $1, 2, 3, \ldots , n$, on the independent variable. (For preliminary considerations, see note 3.)

5. It is, of course, quite possible that peer disapproval would have accounted for the deterrent effects of formal sanctions against drinking and library offenses; however measures of perceived peer disapproval were not available for these other forms of behavior.

6. This pattern is not reflected in the index of percentage difference per interval because the differences are weighted by the number of schools on which they are based. If we were to disregard the number of schools in our per interval measure, the differences would read: 5.0, 9.0, and 10.5 respectively for the 21-40, 41-60, and 61-80 disapproval contexts, showing that deterrent effects increase with increasing peer disapproval.

7. Further research reveals that students at honor system schools believe that fewer students cheat and that more of them get caught than do their counterparts at schools without such systems. Moreover, students under the honor system are more likely to know of existing incidents that have come to the attention of authorities, but less likely to know the students involved on a personal basis than are students under other systems. In effect, students' knowledge and perceptions seem to reflect a sense of more effective control under the honor system.

8. Ideally we would have wanted high school attitudes measured *prior* to college. We know, however, that there is a relatively close association between behavior and attitudes in these areas. (There is a strong negative relationship between attitudes and behavior in college and between high school behavior and college attitudes.) Therefore this recall information on high school behavior should serve as a rough index of predisposition in these areas.

9. Had we found a relationship between sanctioning policy and high school behavior, it would not have been possible to determine whether (or to what degree) selective recruitment as against selective attrition was at work without information on dropouts. Since the two variables are unrelated, however, the data in Table 7 discount both processes.

10. This reaction may also occur when severe formal sanctions are imposed selectively in an effort to control the behavior of some subgroup in the population or when they are used to curb some other associated form of behavior.

11. If severity of sanctions imposed were largely a response to variations in the rate of misconduct, there would actually be a *positive* association between these two variables. The fact that we find no relationship suggests the possiblity of two countervailing effects: a deterrent effect of formal sanctions on misconduct; and a crackdown effect in which variations in misconduct produce corresponding variations in formal sanctions. In effect, the two could be linked in a negative feedback circuit which is in turn influenced by the normative climate of the college or the expectations of institutional authorities. (For a model of this kind of functional process, see Stinchcombe, 1968: 87 ff., esp. Figure 3.7.)

REFERENCES

BALL, J. C. (1970) "Crime, punishment, and deterrence: a reexamination." Unpublished.

——— (1955) "The deterrence concept in criminology and law." J. of Criminal Law, Criminology and Police Sci. 46 (September/October): 347-354.

BOWERS, W. J. (1968) "Normative constraints on deviant behavior in the college context." Sociometry 31 (Winter): 370-385.

——— (1964) Student Dishonesty and Its Control in College. New York: Bureau of Applied Social Research, Columbia University.

——— and R. G. SALEM (1970) "Student disciplinary administration." pp. 7/36-7/63 in A. S. Knowles (ed.) Handbook of College and University Administration. New York: McGraw Hill.

California State Legislature (1968) Deterrent Effects of Criminal Sanctions. Progress report of the Assembly Committee on Criminal Procedure.

CHAMBLISS, W. J. (1969) Crime and the Legal Process. New York: McGraw-Hill.

——— (1966) "The deterrent influence of punishment." Crime and Delinquency 12 (January): 70-75.

CHIRICOS, T. G. and G. P. WALDO (1970) "Punishment and crime: empirical evidence?" Presented at the meetings of the American Sociological Association, Washington, D.C.

COHEN, A. K. (1966) Deviance and Control. New York: Prentice-Hall.

COSER, L. A. (1967) Continuities in the Study of Social Conflict. New York: Free Press.

——— (1962) "Some functions of normative flexibility." Amer. J. of Sociology 68 (September): 172-182.

DURKHEIM, E. (1964) The Division of Labor in Society. New York: Free Press.

ERIKSON, K. T. (1966) The Wayward Puritans. New York: John Wiley.

GIBBS, J. P. (1968) "Crime, punishment, and deterrence." Southwestern Social Sci. Q. 48 (March): 515-530.

HOMANS, G. C. (1961) Social Behavior: Its Elementary Forms. New York: Harcourt, Brace & World.

PINCOFFS, E. L. (1966) The Rationale of Legal Punishment. New York: Humanities Press.

ROSS, H. L. and D. T. CAMPBELL (1968) "The Connecticut speed crackdown," pp. 30-35 in H. Lawrence Ross (ed.) Perspectives on the Social Order. New York: McGraw-Hill.

SCHUESSLER, K. F. (1969) "The deterrent influence of the death penalty," pp. 378-388 in W. J. Chambliss (ed.) Crime and the Legal Process. New York: McGraw-Hill.

SCHWARTZ, R. D. (1969) "Sanctions and compliance." Presented at the American Sociological Association meetings, San Francisco.

——— and S. ORLEANS (1967) "On legal sanctions." Univ. of Chicago Law Rev. 34 (Winter): 274-300.

SELLIN, T. (1966) "Effect of repeal and reintroduction of the death penalty on homocide rates," pp. 339-351 in H. A. Bedau (ed.) The Death Penalty in America. Chicago: Aldine.

STINCHCOMBE, A. L. (1968) Constructing Social Theories. New York: Harcourt, Brace & World.

STOUFFER, S. A. (1949) "An analysis of conflicting social norms." Amer. Soc. Rev. 14 (December): 707-717.

——— and J. TOBY (1951) "Role conflict and personality," pp. 481-496 in T. Parsons and E. A. Shils (eds.) Toward a General Theory of Action. Cambridge: Harvard Univ. Press.

TITTLE, C. R. (1969) "Crime rates and legal sanctions." Social Problems 16 (Spring): 409-423.

TOBY, J. (1964) "Is punishment necessary?" J. of Criminal Law, Criminology and Police Sci. 55, 3: 332-337.

TURNER, R. H. (1959) "An experiment in the modification of role conception." Year Book of the Amer. Phil. Society: 329-333.

VOLD, G. B. (1958) Theoretical Criminology. New York: Oxford Univ. Press.

IS PUNISHMENT DEAD?

Walter Bromberg

FOR ALL its effect on the generation occupying the older side of 30, punishment,
like God, is considered to be dead. It is as
effective as holy water against a ten-ton
megaton bomb. Felons, misdemeanants,
those who break the rules of school or university, and those who oppose their parents'
fiats or flout good taste and decency are
equally unaffected by the threat of punishment. The militant who captures the dean's
office and hustles him out the side door and
the student who howls down as irrelevant an
English professor's analysis of Blake's
poetry unite in making punishment an
anachronism, a senile maneuver at best,
totally inadequate in today's scene.

We do not have to examine the draft card
burner for signs of youthful intransigence;
we need only listen to a 12-year-old school
boy who, when faced with the punishment
of being kept after school for misbehavior,
said as he walked out of the classroom, "It's
either detention or Little League practice....
I choose baseball." What has happened to
the deterrent effect of punishment, to its
moral force?

Punishment for wrongdoing has always
stood upon solid legal grounds. No one
questioned its pertinence in law; no one

gainsaid its position as a right of parents on
the family hearth. Punishment was an automatic corollary of the Ten Commandments,
and although not explicitly included as a
consequence of "Thou shalt not....," was as
self-evident as the sequence of day and
night. From the lopping off of a hand decreed in the Code of Hammurabi for the
crime of adultery in ancient Babylon to execution or life imprisonment for first degree
murder in our day, punishment and crime
were and are linked in an indissoluble bond.

If it were necessary to provide a rationale
for punishment, theorists readily supplied it;
punishment deterred others from crime; it
allowed retribution by an outraged society;
or it opened the way for penitence and rehabilitation (read counseling for penitence
and psychotherapy for rehabilitation). Finally, the aim of punishment was reprobation. Reprobation as an aim of punishment
strikes at the heart of the matter, for it simply means unconditional disapproval for a
criminal act. Originally the word reprobation meant "rejected by God, beyond the
hope of salvation." The philosopher Kant
wrote in 1785, "juridical punishment...must
in all cases be imposed only because the individual...has committed a Crime. The Pe-

nal Law is a Categorical Imperative"(1)!

For all the latter-day explanations covering the essence of punishment, it stands starkly as social disapproval. Reprobation embodies the whiplash of condemnation, whether the punishment is a reprimand for "boosting" an article off a department store counter, a prison sentence for assault, or a death sentence for murder. Reprobation carries the warhead, the moral force of punishment, the charge that sets off the detonation of guilt.

The Ineffectiveness of Punishment

Yet it is increasingly apparent that during the last three years punishment has lost its sting. As a deterrent to crime it is completely ineffective. For the under-30 half of our populace, reprobation is a soft hand on the shoulder or a clumsy maneuver to be dealt with when necessary with the simple command, "Flake off." There was a time in the history of English law when a judge could thunder down from his exalted stratosphere on the bench, "You are a miserable soul.... I condemn you to hang until dead...." while the public openly reflected on his righteousness.

Modern judges do not permit themselves the luxury of expressing society's feelings in statements from the bench; reprobation has lost status. Insensibly, during the past 50 years or more, crime has ceased being an evil and hence lost some of its function as whipping boy for the spirit of reprobation. Crime has become misbehavior; this semantic change has wrought a tremendous influence on the unconscious feelings behind punishment and softened the moral thunderbolt hidden in it so that it appears as flat as last night's champagne instead of as strong as today's bitter medicine. The pain of punishment is discounted: punishment has lost its sting as our changing society rolls on. The under-30 people have unerringly put their finger on one large defect in the establishment's ethical code: its basic presupposition that punishment follows crime.

Besides this perception by the oncoming generation that punishment has lost its usefulness (militants, for example, will not take discipline or submit to punishment, and erring juveniles laugh at school suspensions) there are signs that society itself has reduced its reprobative "instinct." For one thing, the outcry against capital punishment has resulted in a steady attrition of the death penalty; for another, the sentence of life imprisonment now means only 13 years, if that. But more importantly, the civil rights movement has made crime less an evil and more an experience, less an injury than an assertion of rights. And the mature public—those older than 30—have found themselves swept along in the downgrading of wrongdoing and the minimizing of punishment by the mechanism of finding reason behind legal disobedience.

Like the outpost sentinels who, facing each other as enemies across no man's land in World War I, found themselves drawn closer psychologically by virtue of their spatial relationship, the establishment finds itself wondering about the validity of the feelings of the young, examining their complaints and really listening to what they are saying about the hypocrisies of our culture. We are undergoing what psychologists call a process of unconscious identification: it might also be called the alchemy of association. Whatever it is called, this new attitude that questions the heaven-sent authority of punishment is softening the rigid division of the criminals and the law-abiding into separate and distinct species. And more significantly, this attitude is opening the way for the attenuation of punishment as an eternal good.

This changed attitude can be glimpsed at work in a secondary way in the semantics of penology and sociology. Juvenile offenders, once called "incorrigible children," now are classified as "wayward minors" or "beyond parental control"; chronic offenders are called "maladjusted"; jail birds are called "recidivists"; "enemies of society" and "born criminals" are diagnosed as "chronic character neuroses." Just as political prisoners in Europe held a special position of honor among fellow inmates—thieves, murderers, and rapists—so now "misbehavers" carry their new designations as a badge of honor instead of the mark of Cain. This is especially true for those whose aggression is in the service of pacifism, militant overthrow of the educational establishment, or direct action aimed to "overcome...." The truth of the business is that aggression in criminal areas has been democratized and hallowed: no longer is there a criminal class from the ranks of the lowborn, the illiterate, the other-side-of-the-track citizens. Criminal aggression has infiltrated all ranks among those under 30.

The New Role of Aggression

Like sex, aggression has passed through certain phases of liberation during the past half-century in its democratization. These two "instinctual" drives run a parallel course. The sexual revolution, stimulated by psychoanalysis, which unearthed perverse sexuality in the dreams and sublimations of normal persons, swept aside taboos and prohibitions, permitting the young to enjoy sexual experience. Similarly, the present revolution, through analyses of child behavior disturbances and inhibited adults, sees aggression as a normal component of the human soul. Sex was discovered to be a natural right, not a duty designed only for procreation; similarly, aggression was discovered to be a human right. Just as the sexual impulse was acknowledged to be normal, hostility was welcomed: death wishes became the legitimate and proud possessions of emancipated persons. Esoteric knowledge about the human condition filtered down to the mid-educated and the educationally deprived: the vast black cloud of inhibitions and prohibitions thinned out. Aggression, like sexuality, became a knowable and approved human quality that, if used to enhance what one considered one's right, could no longer be jammed into a steel casing called criminal. Add to these considerations the flood of nationalistic uprisings during the past 15 years where the use of aggression was in the service of "truth" and political deliverance, and it becomes evident that the mantle of evil has slipped from the shoulders of assault, theft, murder, mayhem —in short, from aggressive crime.

Proof of the reorientation of the youth of this country toward criminal sanctions can be seen in the attitudes of juvenile and adult offenders in custody. From New York to California, the house of detention to which juvenile miscreants are sent awaiting court hearing is affectionately known as "Juvy" or the "House of D." To have been in Juvy at one time or another in one's high school career has become a source of quiet pride rather than a badge of sin. Juveniles encountered in court clinics or in their own habitats out of the hearing of adults indicate their elevation in the hierarchy of adolescence by a spell in Juvy. One 18-year-old school dropout said with a touch of swagger

that she "graduated" at Juvy. Similarly, older prisoners speak of the penitentiary or prison in familiar terms, calling them the "Joint" or the "House," thus betraying a kind of unconscious dependence on an impersonal protector. The inmate in today's prison who studies law, art, political science, and even creative writing in prison has been known to refer to the institution as his alma mater after his release.

Members of militant organizations do not fear arrest and incarceration; draft card burners welcome imprisonment as a measure of recognition of their righteous actions; drug users and pushers take no umbrage at enforced treatment in institutions. It is viewed as a misuse of time, a temporary encumbrance, a stupid method of expressing the senile, impotent wrath of the establishment. Irritation, anger, and sullen defiance can be read in the attitudes of prisoners before the bar, but the moral weight of a judicial sentence is missing from the consciousness of today's offender against many of our laws.

The result of this subtle reorientation toward lawful imprisonment is that punishment has lost its fearsome poignancy. This is not to say that prisoners who have served time are not often embittered by their experience. But the psychological fact is that lawful punishment is no longer a searing, coruscating experience to contemplate. In short the deterrent effect of punishment is close to zero.

If these indications are granted, and contact with wrongdoers of all ages and psychic complexions proves their truth daily, then is it not time to abolish punishment as an outmoded representative of society's need to reprobate? Public officials, sincerely dedicated to the need to eradicate or reduce crime, call for funds to increase police protection to destroy organized criminal cartels. Actually, however, the majority of crimes today are not caused by organized mobs but by individuals, chance offenders, unstable personalities, angry young and old men, and those impelled by a sense of the rightness of their actions.

Here is the dilemma: law enforcement agents are essential to our national life, but if punishment has lost its bite, is not this painstaking labor of apprehending offenders and sentencing them a lost cause, a miscarriage of honest, well-meant effort?

A Possible Solution

While the machinery of justice must grind on, the cure for crime in the upcoming generation can only be the distant one of emotional education. This does not mean hortatory lectures, moralizations, pleadings, or the example of virtue and such time honored methods of inculcating ethical standards that the youth of today deride as products of a hypocritical establishment. The education espoused here is, to put it bluntly, a campaign of perpetual brainwashing through television.

It must be conceded that this idea comes up hard against the inbred urge toward reprobation. That crime leads to punishment is a presupposition as unassailable and irreducible as the statement that cause leads to effect. To deny these equations is to court accusations of insanity.

But new suppositions can be offered without vitiating the old. Thus today's students are upsetting the tradition expressed in the formula, "I teach, you learn." They want to participate in selecting teachers, methods, subject matter, and educational directions.

Brainwashing has the misfortune to have had a bad press; actually it is merely the planting of ideas, attitudes, and standards through a process of conditioning. Television is ideally suited to such a process of painless mass education. Every day we are brainwashed to improve our sanitation (Two deodorants, not one!); eat correctly (Breakfast on - - - and you'll look better); eradicate dandruff (...he got the raise); banish bad breath (...and get lover's breath); save your lungs; preserve your hair; take Command; hoodwink greying hair, buy sex appeal; reduce your girth; to the point where try as we might, we cannot erase these conditioned standards from our automatic nervous mechanisms. If we can brainwash the public to buy consumer goods, why not brainwash them against criminal impulses? Why can't universal television imprint the simple fact upon our brains that in an overpopulated world, in order to live at all we must preserve the obvious tools of life—a usable body and the necessary material to feed, clothe, and recreate ourselves?

What the techniques will be to instill rational consideration of the prime facts of life is a matter for television technicians: the writers, directors, actors, and producers. The basic principle is to educate the public the same way that theatrical drama reaches so effectively into the brain cells where emotion influences the intellect. Although the message is rational, the means for imprinting it may be irrational—that is, beyond the control of a judging mind. If the medium is the message it can carry a message also: the medium of television can dip its electronic fingers into our midbrains to fixate automatic behavior that will eventually govern our judgments and decisions.

Brainwashing, propaganda, and education are in our culture the ultimate weapons for control of action. Why not use them in the war that has never been won, the protective war against crime? Here, as in other modern wars, reduction of activity on the front can be the only true victory. For although crime is not remediable it is at least controllable. That control should function prior to crime and thus in place of punishment. It is chiefly applicable among the young from whose ranks the next generation of wrongdoers will emerge.

REFERENCE

1. Kant, I, cited in The science of right, in Great Books of the Western World, vol 11. Chicago, Encyclopedia Briticannica, 1952, p 489

V.

PLANNING FOR JUSTICE

THE URBAN CRISIS AND CRIME

Sheldon Krantz

William D. Kramer

I. Introduction

Recently, many large-city mayors have stated that problems in our nation's major cities are virtually beyond solution. Crime is prominent among these problems. Annually, the Uniform Crime Reports, prepared by the Federal Bureau of Investigation, inform the public that crimes in most index categories are increasing at a disturbing rate, while clearance rates (the rates indicating the percent of crimes that have been "solved" by an arrest of the alleged offender) remain low for most types of offenses.[1] Most of these crimes occur in urban areas.[2] Further, many studies have shown that the average citizen's perception and fear of crime in the inner city is dramatically affecting the life style of a high percentage of major-city residents.[3] There are even signs that many residents of ghetto areas who formerly were bitter about alleged police brutality or harassment are now less concerned about such police action and more concerned about obtaining better police protection against crime.[4] It is not surprising, therefore, that in a national Gallup Poll released on May 14, 1970, crime was considered to be the domestic problem that should be given the highest priority by government during 1970 and 1971.[5]

Without question, most crime problems appear to the public to be beyond the capabilities of government to control. It is easy to understand why this attitude prevails. There is a tendency on the part of the public, the news media, and even law enforcement agencies to view crime as a single, massive phenomenon. Considered in this way, the frightening statistics of criminal conduct nationally, within one state, or even within a single city make the problems of crime seem overwhelming and uncontrollable. But it is not rational to view crime as a monolithic problem. The nature of various types of criminal conduct differs widely. This means that the response to different crimes, potential offenders, and offenders must differ widely as well.[6]

Organized crime; violent crimes against the person (such as rape, assault, or armed robbery); crimes against property (such as burglary and larceny); juvenile offenses (such as truancy, shop-lifting, or vandalism); and crimes related to civil disorders or dissent (such as looting or trespassing), for example, are categories of crimes that have little relationship to one another and require quite different responses by government.[7] This is rarely recognized in public debates about crime.

Typically, public debates about reducing crime seem to center on two approaches, which are poles apart ideologically, but which fail to an equal extent to recognize the diversity and complexity of the crime problem. The first of these approaches is the view that effective crime reduction requires simply expanding the capabilities of the police to deal with crime (including reversing United States Supreme Court opinions that "unduly restrict the police in the performing of their critical tasks").[8] The second is the view that it is impossible to successfully contend with crime directly, since it is only a symptom of deeper societal-problems. It is argued that efforts must instead be aimed at the underlying causes of crime (*e.g.*, poverty, unemployment, hunger, inadequate housing and education).[9]

Although the latter approach is undoubtedly a more accurate reflection than the former of what must ultimately be done to reduce crime, neither approach accurately assesses what can and must be done to contend with crime and delinquency this year or even five to ten years from now. With reference to the approach of expanding police power through reversing the United States Supreme Court holdings in such cases as *Miranda*,[10] *Escobedo*,[11] and *Wade*,[12] several studies have shown that these opinions, in fact, have had little impact on conviction rates or on the problem of crime generally.[13] On the other hand, although the underlying causes of criminal behavior must be given immediate and high priority, cities cannot afford to ignore shorter term solutions specifically related to their present crime problems.[14]

In view of the increasing pressure on mayors and other governmental officials to do something about crime now, there is a danger that the frustration with mounting crime and the perception of crime as a monolithic problem may create an environment conducive to the pursuit of a more repressive approach toward crime. This danger will continue as long as government and the public view crime as simply a law enforcement problem. Aside from the obvious concern that should arise from concentrating crime control efforts primarily on strengthening law enforcement, it should also be recognized that pursuing a law enforcement strategy alone will not reduce crime. Professor James Q. Wilson noted:

> The police can do relatively little about preventing most common crimes. . . . A community concerned about lowering its crime rates would be well advised to devote its attention and resources to those parts of the criminal justice system, especially the courts and correctional agencies, which, unlike the police, spend most of their time processing—often in the most perfunctory and ineffective manner—persons who repeatedly perpetrate these crimes.[15]

What is needed now is concentrated effort directed toward identifying how major cities, which have the most serious crime problems,[16] can develop comprehensive strategies of crime prevention and control that are both directly relevant to their crime problems and are capable of providing some fairly immediate solutions to them. This Article will attempt to identify some specific weaknesses in existing approaches, to describe some of the ways in which effective strategies may be developed, and to provide examples of early priorities that may be selected.

II. PRESENT EFFORTS

A look at weaknesses in present approaches to urban crime can contribute to an understanding of approaches providing greater promise. These weaknesses vary in character. Some relate to the present condition of criminal justice agencies and programs; others relate to the tasks they are asked to perform; still others relate to the perspective and attitudes of major-city policy-makers (mayors and city managers); some reflect the absence of needed structures and techniques; and others result from a failure to address certain critical problem areas—a failure to see that needed programs and services are provided.

The condition of the criminal justice system—the primary crime control instrument available to policy-makers—clearly contributes in an important way to the ineffectiveness of present efforts. The weaknesses of the existing system have been frequently identified and extensively documented, although not widely recognized and understood. Traditionally, the criminal justice system has had low status and has been given low priority. As a result, it is now grossly underresourced. The system is understaffed with undercompensated, inadequately trained and inadequately educated personnel. Needed specialized expertise is lacking. Equipment and facilities are inadequate. Advanced technology and management methods have rarely been applied.[17]

Beyond this failure to commit needed resources, the efforts of policy-makers and agency personnel are inhibited by the fact that the criminal justice system is asked to perform many functions that it is not well-equipped to perform, such as dealing with the alcoholic and the drug-dependent person.[18] Further, responsibility and authority for functions appropriately performed by the criminal justice system are widely dispersed among various jurisdictions and levels of government. Finally, the system is not effective because it is inbred and to a significant extent inflexibly bound to traditional approaches and unaccustomed and unreceptive to innovation.[19]

While the condition of the criminal justice system presents serious obstacles to effective action to prevent and control crime, the perspective typical of major-city decision-makers presents equally significant obstacles. In the areas of crime and delinquency, quick and easy solutions are constantly pursued—solutions that little disrupt the status quo—solutions not involving radical change. The enormous complexity of effective responses is not perceived. The critical need for extensive planning prior to action is not recognized. A mayor who would not think of attempting to grapple with the problems of pollution or urban renewal, mental health or education without thorough planning is prepared to act to combat crime without any systematic examination of alternative approaches. As a result, the action he takes generally involves a perpetuation or intensification of traditional approaches, which never have been particularly effective and many of which are no longer relevant or adequate.

As noted earlier, oversimplification of the crime problem often takes the form of viewing the problem as solely or primarily a police problem. This narrowness of perspective is not limited to vociferous advocates of law and order. It is common, as well, among policy-makers who are generally sensitive to the urgency and complexity of social problems and to the responsibility of government to act in response to human needs.[20]

The tendency of major-city decision-makers to think of crime as a police problem is not surprising. Most people think of crime in just this way. Moreover, action that promises immediate solutions has political appeal. There are many additional explanations as well. The emphasis upon the police reflects the existing allocation of responsibility and authority among jurisdictions. The primary criminal justice function presently performed by local government is the police function. It is natural for a city administrator to think first in terms of his city agencies. The police department generally represents a substantial portion of the total responsibility, manpower, and budget of major city governments.[21] In addition, police departments typically are not without political power. They are able to act to see that their needs and priorities are recognized. The extreme financial difficulties faced by most major cities and the police in particular also create an understandable pressure toward using crime prevention and control resources first and primarily for building up the city's police capabilities.

Although for all of these reasons it is understandable that major-city crime is thought of and dealt with essentially as a police problem, this narrowness of perspective cannot be afforded. Perception of crime as a police problem results in a failure to act to improve other components of the criminal justice system, such as the courts, prosecution and defense; correctional and youth service agencies and programs; other agencies that can and should become involved in working with potential offenders and offenders; and the community itself. In addition, this perception results in a failure to understand the system as a single process, composed of necessarily interdependent, although not effectively interrelated elements—a process that flows from the community—where the causes of criminal behavior, criminal events, and the resources needed to respond to crime lie—through the police, the courts and correctional agencies, back once again to the community with the return of the offender.

The need to intervene at points of weakness throughout the process is not understood. Nor is there understanding of the critical importance of integrating into the entire process the expertise and the resources of related governmental programs and of the community, e.g., mental health, education and vocational rehabilitation programs; Model Cities; private social service agencies; the skills of the academic community and private enterprise; and the efforts of paraprofessional and professional volunteers.

Among the most critical consequences of the tendency to view crime as simply a law enforcement problem has been the failure of most major cities to act in other areas essential to an effective response to crime. Crime can be expected to continue as a serious problem unless the major cities sharply increase their commitments in such areas as the provision of community-based prevention and rehabilitation programs and services to juveniles; institutional and community-based rehabilitation and reintegration programs for adult offenders; comprehensive efforts to provide security to high-crime areas and to prevent and control specific crimes; and rehabilitation and treatment programs for alcoholics and drug dependent persons. Although cities alone cannot afford and are not well-equipped to assume many of these responsibilities, it is clear that they have failed to do what they can. They have failed to commit available resources to these purposes; they have failed to actively seek such a commitment from others; and they have failed to effectively utilize existing programs of these kinds.

The failure of cities to act in these areas does not reflect a deliberate decision to assign them a low priority. It reflects instead the absence of any systematic city response to crime. For the most part, major cities have not developed any rational strategies for crime prevention and control. Crime is dealt with instead on a crisis-oriented, ad hoc basis. To a significant extent, this results from the absence of a criminal justice capability within most city governments: cities have police capabilities, and often perform other specific criminal justice functions, such as youth service programs and prosecution, but they do not have criminal justice capabilities. Cities have no resource or mechanism capable of giving policy-makers a comprehensive view of the city's criminal justice problems and needs; of evaluating the performance of criminal justice agencies and programs; of setting objectives and priorities, and allocating resources; and of performing a broad range of other needed functions. In short, cities lack the capability to develop and implement comprehensive strategies for crime prevention and control—strategies effectively involving criminal justice agencies from various jurisdictions, strategies effectively involving the full range of agencies and programs related to the criminal justice system, and strategies effectively involving the community.

III. WHAT CITIES CAN DO

If cities are to meet the challenge of crime, attitudes and perspectives must change; the criminal justice system must be provided with new skills and resources and its responsibilities must be better defined; cities must act in areas in which they have failed to act; and finally, they must have the capability to develop and undertake comprehensive strategies designed to achieve all of these objectives.

A critical first step is the creation within each major-city government of a criminal justice planning and action capability with a high quality inter-disciplinary staff.[22] Such a capability exists in only a few cities today.[23] The central aspect of such an effort would be planning—identifying crime prevention and control objectives, and developing strategies for the achievement of those objectives. Simply stated, its role would be to provide the basis for informed and rational decisions by city policy-makers regarding the crime problem—the basis for deciding, for example, whether to invest in a new police command and control system or in intensive probation services for juveniles; or whether to focus on upgrading the investigative capability of the police or on improving the performance of the lower courts.

Performance of this central function will require a range of related activities, including research (for example, in-depth analysis of the nature and incidence of specific crimes), evaluation of programs (both operational and experimental innovations), and resource allocation analysis (among functions, agencies, and programs).

To be effective, the capability must go beyond planning. It must act as a catalyst, stimulating innovation within and among the criminal justice and related agencies serving the city. It must act to see that strategies are implemented and priority needs met. Action of many types will be needed. Funds and other resources will have to be sought. Needed legislative changes (local, state and federal) will have to be identified, legislation will have to be developed and its enactment sought. Demonstration programs will have to be conducted to test the value of new approaches.

The development of performance standards may be required. The agency may find the provision of technical assistance (in such areas as planning, evaluation, systems analysis, and grantsmanship) an important tool for stimulating change and improvement. Clearly, an important responsibility will be inter-agency and inter-jurisdictional coordination and programming. Efforts to increase the degree to which the criminal justice system is effectively integrated with and supported by related agencies and the community will also be a significant concern.

Finally, the new capability should play a significant role with respect to the Omnibus Crime Control Act and other federal programs, not only in such areas as planning and program evaluation, but also in such areas as the implementation of demonstration programs and the administration of federal funds. The Crime Control Act program is discussed below. It should be noted at this point, however, that if that program is to succeed, it must succeed in major urban centers; and it cannot do so without the kind of creative planning and action at the city level that requires a criminal justice capability of the kind described here.

If cities are to meet the challenge of crime, they must try new approaches, and they must act in areas in which they have previously failed to act. One area of particular importance is that of community-based prevention and rehabilitation programs for juveniles. In most cities existing programs of these kinds—e.g., youth resources bureaus, intensive and specialized probation programs, and residential centers—are completely inadequate. Young people with serious problems are not identified early enough, few services are available to them, and adequate treatment planning and follow-up mechanisms do not exist. Equally serious deficiencies exist in community-based programs for adult offenders, alcoholics and the drug dependent. An effective response to crime requires imaginative new efforts on a large scale in each of these areas.

The need for creative action is not limited to programs directed toward the offender. Effective law enforcement requires new approaches as well. Two promising possibilities are comprehensive programs aimed at specific crimes (e.g., burglary or auto theft) and intensive programs directed at specific geographical areas where the incidence of serious crimes is con-centrated. In each case, careful analysis and planning must precede action, evaluation must accompany action, and a full range of approaches and resources must be utilized, including in particular extensive and active involvement of the community. An effective response to major city burglary, for example, may require the following range of actions: in-depth analysis of the pattern of incidence and character of the criminal events, changes in police patrol patterns and techniques, enactment of ordinances requiring that security measures be taken (*e.g.* installation of adequate locks), provision of information and assistance to the public regarding preventive measures, and the development of new investigative techniques.[24]

Innovative, comprehensive programs of these kinds require the development within city government of capabilities of the kind described above. The optimal form for such capabilities will vary and can only be identified through experimentation. Certain features would appear to be essential, however. First, the capability ought to be directly responsible to the city's chief executive—the mayor or city manager. This is a prerequisite to the independence and balanced perspective required for effective performance of many of its functions (*e.g.*, program performance evaluation and resource allocation).

In addition to a significant degree of independence, such a capability must have strong and extensive ties to existing criminal justice and related agencies (through such techniques as policy and advisory boards, joint programming, provision of services, staff interaction and staff exchange), because it is essential that the new capability become an integral part of a comprehensive effort to respond to crime. For the same reason, strong links to the community are important as well. The capability should not have authority over any part of the city's existing criminal justice system. The diversity of purpose and dispersion of initiative that presently exist among system components should be preserved, and the new capability should not have direct operational responsibility for crime prevention and control programs. As a final point, it should be noted that adequate funding and a diversified, high-quality staff are essential to a successful undertaking of this kind.

Approaches to crime of the kind described here are expensive, controversial, and time-consuming. It is, however, an effort of this kind that is required. If cities are willing to commit the resources that are needed and to explore new approaches, the challenge of crime can be met.

IV. The Federal Government and Urban Crime

Many mayors undoubtedly are willing to try new approaches to control crime (or to contend more effectively with other urban problems). But undertaking new approaches or even maintaining present efforts at operational (or crisis) levels appears to be beyond the financial capability of most cities. This was recently noted by Mayor John V. Lindsay in his book, *The City*:[25]

The ultimate problem is money—or, rather, the problem of not enough money. Whatever else a city can do, it cannot provide the services its people want if it does not have the money to pay for them. And our cities don't have the money. There is no other business I can think of where the proprietor knows absolutely that he will face bankruptcy every year. Yet my own city's expenses—with no increase at all in programs—go up each year three times as fast as revenues. That does not make for tranquillity. It does make for citizens who must wonder every year whether their local library will cut back its hours, whether their children will be forced to attend split sessions in the schools, whether their hospital can be modernized to meet inevitably higher demands.

Although, parts of the criminal justice systems serving major cities are supported by other levels of government,[26] these agencies (e.g., prosecution, probation, and parole) are also typically underfinanced. In addition, their goals and programs may not be compatible, or may be directly inconsistent with a city's criminal justice goals.[27]

In its report in 1967, the President's Crime Commission recognized that new approaches to crime were beyond the financial capabilities of the cities.[28]

[M]ost local communities today are hardpressed just to improve their agencies of justice and other facilities at a rate that will meet increases in population and in crime. They cannot spare funds for experimental or innovative programs or plan beyond the emergencies of the day. Federal collaboration can give State and local agencies an opportunity to gain on crime rather than barely stay abreast of it, by making funds, research, and technical assistance available and thereby encouraging changes that in time may make criminal administration more effective and more fair.

Based on the Commission's work, President Lyndon B. Johnson introduced the Safe Streets and Crime Control Act of 1967.[29] Essentially, the legislation authorized the Department of Justice to provide criminal justice planning and program grants to state and local governments and to establish a national criminal justice research program. Although there had been a small law enforcement grant program in existence since 1965,[30] the President's proposal represented the first significant federal commitment proposed to assist state and local governments in testing new approaches to the crime problem.

When the bill was enacted in 1968 complete with the compromises necessary to accommodate various congressional points of view on crime control,[31] federal financial support to state and local governments for criminal justice planning and programs began and has since increased significantly. The total appropriation to the Law Enforcement Assistance Administration, the administering agency within the United States

Department of Justice, for fiscal year 1969 was sixty-three million dollars; for 1970, two hundred sixty-eight million dollars; and as of this writing, it appears that for 1971 the figure will be four hundred-eighty million dollars.[32] Most of those funds go to the states in block grants for action programs included in their comprehensive criminal justice plans. Given the tenor of the times, it is likely that the appropriations for this program will reach one billion dollars within the next year or two.

Thus, substantial federal financial support is now becoming available to assist cities in their crime control efforts.[33] Collateral support is no longer limited to federal funds, either. On July 23, 1970, the Ford Foundation announced the creation of a thirty million dollar Police Development Fund to assist experiments and pilot programs by police departments seeking to make basic changes in their operation and to upgrade their performance. Thus, financial support, which will undoubtedly amount to several millions of dollars annually to large cities quite soon, could, if the cities plan wisely, be used to undertake and evaluate new approaches to their most serious crime problems (in terms of both financial and human costs). Moreover, crime control funds, if thoughtful strategies for their use are developed, can stimulate other programs to shift their direction or emphasis to coincide with a city's crime control priorities. Existing resources with this potential include federal programs (e.g., Model Cities); state programs (such as correctional, mental and public health efforts); and private programs (such as delinquency prevention efforts).

It is clear, however, that the funds available from LEAA are not being used for these purposes in many cities. First, as noted earlier, the cities, with rare exceptions, have no mechanism for developing comprehensive crime control strategies, for selecting program and project priorities and for measuring program success or failure. As a result, city action programs often simply reflect what seems topical or political at the moment (e.g., drug education programs), are not tied to any longer-range strategy, and do not provide adequately for evaluation.

Secondly, since most cities have difficulty in meeting even day-to-day operational needs, such as police equipment, there is a strong temptation to use federal funds to supplant city expenditures. For example, rather than increasing city allocations to a police department to meet pressing equipment needs, federal grant support would be utilized for that purpose.

Although it is understandable that a city would use federal funds in this way, such use can be expected to have little short or long-range impact on crime. The changes that must be made within the criminal justice system are radical and will not be accomplished by the acquisition of automobiles, walki-talki's, computers, or more probation officers. The changes that ultimately must be made will require: (1) altering the goals and functions of criminal justice agencies and the relationships of these agencies to each other; (2) utilizing new types of personnel throughout the criminal justice system and obtaining new types of support from citizens and other agencies in the prevention of crime, apprehension of criminal suspects and the rehabilitation of offenders; and (3) overhauling the definitions of what constitutes criminal or delinquent behavior and what the responses to this behavior should be.

In other words, federal funds should not now be used to reinforce the current way in which the criminal justice system operates. Rather, they should be used to assist in analyzing the current defects of the criminal justice system, in setting new directions for the system, in developing and implementing new approaches to crime problems, and in testing the success or failure of such approaches.

There is great danger, however, in having the federal government support a large-scale criminal justice demonstration program without strong leadership within the Department of Justice. At the present time, the states and the cities are engaged in designing and undertaking demonstration efforts without knowing what has occurred or is occurring elsewhere and what has succeeded or failed. This has already caused enormous waste. Serious concern about many different jurisdictions "rediscovering the wheel" is justified. Thus, LEAA must assume the critically important responsibility of continually keeping informed about criminal justice research and demonstration programs and disseminating information about these programs quickly so that successful efforts rather than mistakes are duplicated.

If one billion dollars annually are spent in this way and if each major city develops strategies for allocating federal funds to its most critical problems (as described earlier and with recognition of demonstration efforts elsewhere), then there is hope that the crime control program will find some of the needed ways to confront the more troublesome aspects of urban crime.

Assuming that new and successful approaches to crime will be identified by utilizing crime control funds in this way,[34] it is obvious that the ultimate cost of implementing these new approaches nationally (*e.g.*, new programs for recasting the functions and personnel of police agencies, and for creating community-based prevention and rehabilitation services) will be enormous —well beyond the capabilities of state and local government. This being so, while the federal government should not use its resources to reinforce a system that is now failing, it should also not stimulate desperately needed experimentation if it is not willing to support implementation of experiments that prove to be successful. Most federal demonstration programs in the past have failed because the responsibility for implementation was left to underfinanced local governments.

Therefore, as effective approaches are identified, the federal government should begin to provide subsidies (possibly gradually increasing to five to ten billion dollars annually) to assist state and local governments in implementing successful criminal justice programs meeting specific standards on a continuing basis. These subsidies could be provided in many ways: as part of a general federal revenue-sharing system; through expansion of the LEAA criminal justice block grant program to provide specifically for subsidies; or through categorical grant programs in such areas as delinquency prevention, drug treatment, corrections, and police improvements. Under any system, though, the cities or other possible grant recipients should be required to establish that selection of programs for implementation has followed from comprehensive planning and the testing of alternative strategies.

Support to cities for improving their crime reduction efforts should not be limited to federal efforts. State governments should provide assistance as well. Although the states, like local governments, are finding it increasingly difficult to support needed services, their potential sources of revenue are normally much broader than those available to cities. Further, there is precedent for states providing financial and technical assistance to help city governments contend with a wide range of local problems. In fact, it is unusual that state governments have done so little to date in the field of criminal justice beyond supporting certain state-level efforts, particularly with respect to law enforcement and correction. This was noted by the Governor's Committee on Law Enforcement and the Administration of Criminal Justice in Massachusetts in a report issued in 1969:[35]

> The difficulty lies not only in the fact that local government is already bearing a disproportionate share of the load, but also in the fact that what is needed is an expanded commitment of the kind that local government cannot now and will not in the future be able to make. The local property tax has already exceeded its limits as an effective and equitable source of revenue. In the area of law enforcement and criminal justice, unlike such areas as education and welfare, the Commonwealth has not stepped in to support local efforts to meet growing needs. The Commonwealth must exhibit the same type of leadership and support for crime reduction that it now provides to education through the State Department of Education. But this support, like the new federal crime control commitment, must be in the form of increased funds and services to local communities and not in the supplanting of local responsibility.

States could provide assistance in any of the following ways: by providing crime control grant-in-aid programs of their own (or in the alternative, by assisting cities in meeting federal matching requirements); by providing technical assistance in areas where expertise is limited; and by assuming the responsibility for certain services that can best be provided on a statewide basis (*e.g.*, crime laboratory services, criminal justice research, specialized criminal justice training programs).

The combination of these two federal efforts—supporting innovation and subsidizing the implementation of new approaches to law enforcement and criminal justice—and assistance from state governments should begin to effect a significant reduction in crime in priority-crime areas if joined by a willingness on behalf of state and local officials to, in the words of the President's Crime Commission:[36]

> . . . stop operating, as all too many do, by tradition or by rote. They must re-examine what they do. They must be honest about the system's shortcomings with the public and with themselves. They must be willing to take risks in order to make advances. They must be bold.

This willingness to change, however, must be shared by mayors and legislators and by employee groups such as police unions as well. Criminal justice agencies cannot be bold, for example, unless legislators rewrite archaic criminal codes and eliminate the deadly constraints of civil service laws, which protect mediocrity and discourage high quality personnel from entering into careers in criminal justice.

Further, if necessary change is to take place within the criminal justice system, it will require a commitment on behalf of the academic community. The system will never have the research capability of the universities nor their ability to design and evaluate new programs. If professors and students were available to assist cities in researching, designing, and testing crime control strategies in "live" laboratory settings, not only would the cities derive benefits, but the quality and pertinency of certain aspects of higher education could be improved as well.

With all this being said, there is serious doubt that the present, more limited crime control program will go much beyond allowing police departments to buy some needed equipment and other criminal justice agencies to shore up some woefully inadequate criminal justice programs. This concern is confirmed to a large extent by the allocations made in many states of the first year's action funds under the crime control program. It is believed, however, that there is increasing interest nationally in more effectively utilizing these funds. But there is question whether this will be acceptable to Congress.

The basis for this concern can best be illustrated by referring to a recent debate in the House of Representatives on whether to increase the present appropriation to the National Institute of Law Enforcement and Criminal Justice, the research arm of the Law Enforcement Assistance Administration. The administration, in requesting that the appropriation for LEAA be increased from two hundred sixty-eight million dollars to four hundred eighty million dollars for fiscal year 1971, asked that within this total increase the National Institute appropriation be increased from seven and one half million dollars to nineteen million dollars. On May 12, 1970, the House voted to appropriate four hundred-eighty million to LEAA for fiscal year 1971 but to limit the National Institute to its current budget. Some of the debate that occurred prior to this vote follows:[37]

Mr. Scheuer. Is it not true that the administration requested $19 million for the National Institute of Law Enforcement and Criminal Justice in effect to apply science and technology to improve our criminal justice system? Is it not also true that in the committee report [House Committee on Appropriations] it was mandated that additional funds requested for research and development should be used for increases in the action grant programs, which in effect denies these funds to the National Institute of Criminal Justice?

Mr. Rooney of New York—The committee felt that the action grant programs are far more important.

We need policemen to keep law and order—and not professors writing books and creating expensive nonproductive studies—I have a list of them here if the gentleman wants to discuss them later on.

. . . .

Mr. McClory. However, the Federal Government should encourage the best talents to devote time and study to the solution of problems connected with criminal justice and then disseminate the results of the studies among State and local law enforcement officials. Also, we must recognize that law enforcement and criminal justice are, in the words of the Attorney General, an uncharted field. If we did not have the great research facilities we have with regard to health, science and defense, we would not have the capability that we have in those fields. Yet in the field of criminal justice we are operating, for the most part, in the dark. If we want to act responsibly and meet our responsibilities as the national lawmaking body, we should devote our principal emphasis to the support of the National Institute.

. . . .

Mr. Gross. Mr. Chairman, will the gentleman yield?

Mr. McClory. Surely, I yield to the gentleman from Iowa.

Mr. Gross. I thought one of the best contributions to law and order which has been made in a good many days was made the other day by the construction workers in New York.

. . . .

Mr. Rooney. We have a study of the mentally abnormal offenders. Where? In Sweden. We have an attempt to enhance the accuracy of classification of sex offenders through measuring pupillary and other autonomically mediated responses; augmentation of moral judgment in the adolescent juvenile delinquent, and so on and so on ad infinitum, page after page of these studies made at the expense of the taxpayers.

So your committee felt that instead of using money for this sort of thing, we should use the money to help law enforcement by furnishing equipment to the police officers in the various states of the Union.

The outcome of this recent congressional debate does not augur well for the urban crisis and crime. There are many other indications as well that most of the cities and states are not ready to respond in the way that they must to intelligently grapple with crime problems or nearly any other serious urban problem. Since, unlike most other "urban crises," there are resources immediately available to allow for some boldness and critical self-evaluation in the criminal justice field, it will be a tragedy if attitudes like those reflected above continue to prevail.

NOTES

1 See, e.g., Federal Bureau of Investigation, U.S. Dep't of Justice, Crime in the United States, Uniform Crime Reports—1968 (1969). By the time this Article appears in print, the UCR for the year 1969 will have been released. Early indications are that the trend of increases for nearly all index crimes will have continued.

2 The President's Commission on Law Enforcement reports that the rise in the incidence of crime has been greater than the rise in the population and is worst in the urban areas. President's Comm. on Law Enforcement and the Administration of Justice, The Challenge of Crime in a Free Society 30, 35-36 (1967) [hereinafter cited as Challenge of Crime]. See also the Report of the National Advisory Commission on Civil Disorders 133-36 (1968).

3 The extent to which the fear of crime has affected the lives of Baltimore residents is described in Rosenthal, The Cage of Fear in Cities Beset by Crime, Life, July 11, 1969, at 18-21. See also the results of surveys conducted for the President's Crime Commission by National Opinion Research Center of the University of Chicago and the Bureau of Social Science Research of Washington, D.C., on the personal fear of crime and its impact on city life. Challenge of Crime 50-53 (1967).

4 Byrn, Urban Law Enforcement: A Plea from the Ghetto, 5 Crim. L. Bull. 125 (1969); Rosenthal, The Cities: Police Role Shifting, N.Y. Times, May 18, 1970, at 1, col. 4.

5 See Gallup Poll, Public Puts Crime Atop Priority List, Boston Globe, May 14, 1970, at 14, col. 3.

6 Richardson, A Strategy for Change: A Comprehensive Program for Crime Control, 53 Mass. L.Q. 299, 301 (1968), notes the variety of crime and the complexities of the criminal justice system in calling for a comprehensive approach to the problems of crime.

7 See Challenge of Crime 3.

8 Cf. Lombard, Some Consequences of the Criminal Justice Revolution, 56 Geo. L.J. 695 (1968); McDonald, Law Enforcement—Have We Gone Too Far in Protecting the Accused?, 39 N.Y.S.B.J. 408 (1967); O'Brien, Dilemma of Criminal Justice in a Democratic Society, 3 U.S.F.L. Rev. 1 (1968).

9 Cf. Ford Foundation, A More Effective Arm (July 23, 1970). See also Byrn, supra note 4, at 128.

10 Miranda v. Arizona, 384 U.S. 436 (1966).

11 Escobedo v. Illinois, 378 U.S. 876 (1964).

12 United States v. Wade, 388 U.S. 218 (1968).

13 See, e.g., Note, Interrogations in New Haven: The Impact of Miranda, 76 Yale L.J. 1519 (1967). This and other studies are analyzed in the ALI Model Code of Pre-Arraignment Procedure 101-69 (Study Draft No. 1, 1968).

14 See Byrn, supra note 4, at 128. See also Ford Foundation, A More Effective Arm 5 (July 23, 1970), where it states:

All of these prestigious reports [The Challenge of Crime in a Free Society, the Report of the Commission on the Causes and Prevention of Violence, the Report of the Commission on Civil Disorders] emphasize that the causes of crime are inextricably bound to the conditions of life in our society. They point out that fundamental attack upon crime will require a national effort to lessen poverty, slum housing, ill health, and illiteracy. But they also make clear that the country must deal quite specifically and speedily with the component parts of the criminal justice system—police, prosecutor, and defense systems, courts, and prisons. The need to remedy shortcomings of the system cannot wait for action on the full range of our social ills.

15 J. Wilson, Varieties of Police Behavior 295 (1968).

16 See note 2 supra and accompanying text.

17 Conditions in the courts are a good example. The President's Commission found conditions in the lower courts to be shocking, especially in the urban high-crime areas. Facilities were found to be inadequate and personnel untrained or undertrained. Challenge of Crime 128-29.

18 See H. Packer, The Limits of the Criminal Sanction (1968); President's Comm. on Law Enforcement and Administration of Justice, Task Force Report: Narcotics and Drug Abuse (1967) and Task Force Report: Drunkenness (1967).

19 See Challenge of Crime 14.

20 Although Mayor John V. Lindsay takes a fairly enlightened approach to crime problems in his recent book about the urban crisis, even he primarily discusses crime as a police matter. See J. Lindsay, The City 164-88 (1969).

21 For example, in the budget submitted for the city of Boston for fiscal year 1970, close to $30 million out of the total budget of approximately $176 million was for police services. See City of Boston & County of Suffolk Budget Recommendations for the Fiscal Year 1970, at 4-5 (as submitted to the Boston City Council by Kevin H. White, Mayor).

22 In 1967, the National Crime Commission recommended the creation of city and state criminal justice planning capabilities: "A State or local government that undertakes to improve its criminal administration should begin by constructing, if it has not already done so, formal machinery for planning. . . . The Commission's point is not the elementary one that each individual action against crime should be planned, but that all of a State's or a city's actions against crime should be planned together, by a single body. The police, the courts, the correctional system and the noncriminal agencies of the community must plan their actions against crime jointly if they are to make real headway." Challenge of Crime 279-80. In 1969, the Violence Commission also recommended the creation of criminal justice coordinating councils within city governments. National Comm. on the Causes and Prevention of Violence, Law and Order Reconsidered: Report of the Task Force on Law and Law Enforcement 275-78 (1969). In August 1970, the National Urban Coalition restated these recommendations: "A vital and necessary prerequisite to reform of the criminal justice system is the development of comprehensive city-wide or metropolitan-wide programs. The cities must take the initiative to create offices of criminal justice . . . ." National Urban Coalition, Law and Disorder II: State Planning and Programming under Title I of the Omnibus Crime Control and Safe Streets Act of 1968, at 17 (1970).

23 Among the few cities that have begun the process of establishing such capabilities are New York, Boston, Cleveland and Hartford. Henry Ruth, former Director of the National Institute of Law Enforcement and Criminal Justice was recently appointed Director of the New York City Criminal Justice Coordinating Council and is presently assembling a full-time professional staff for the council. Boston established a Coordinating Committee for the Administration of Justice in 1969. For an excellent example of an initial major city comprehensive plan see Mayor's Coordinating Comm. for the Administration of Justice, Challenging Crime: The Boston 1970 Comprehensive Justice Plan (Apr. 17, 1970).

It is fair to ask where funds are to be found to support the creation of such capabilities. The Omnibus Crime Control and Safe Streets Act of 1968, 82 Stat. 197, requires State planning agencies to make at least 40% of planning funds allocated to the State under the Act "available to units of general local government or combinations of such units to enable such units and combinations of such units to participate in the formulation of the comprehensive State plan." Tit. I, § 203(c). This provision makes available substantial funding that could be used to support city criminal justice planning and action capabilities of the kind proposed. The guidelines under the Act provide that: "Priorities in funding local planning should be given to the State's major urban and metropolitan areas, to other areas of high crime incidence and potential, and to efforts involving combinations of local units." U.S. Dep't of Justice, Law Enforcement Assistance Administration, Office of Law Enforcement Programs, Guide for Comprehensive Law Enforcement Planning and Action Grants: Fiscal Year 1970, at 7 (1970). It should be noted that through December 31, 1969, states awarded 70% of the local share of Crime Control Act planning funds to regional entities, rather than city governments. Advisory Comm. on Intergovernmental Relations, Information Bull. No. 70-5: Making the Safe Streets Act Work, app. at 19 (1970). An additional source of funds is the 1970 Law Enforcement Assistance Administration discretionary grant program under tit. I, § 306, of the Act, which provides support for "special city-wide coordinating or planning councils or commissions" in eligible large cities. A third possibility has been suggested by Professor Daniel J. Freed of Yale Law School, who has proposed enactment of federal legislation to provide direct financial aid to cities submitting suitable plans for a resource of this kind. National Comm. on the Causes and Prevention of Violence, Law and Order Reconsidered: Report of the Task Force on Law and Law Enforcement 278 (1969). Probably in response to this proposal, a bill to amend the Omnibus Crime Control Act now before the Congress specifically encourages "the establishment of a Criminal Justice Coordinating Council for any unit of general local government to assure improved coordination of all law enforcement activities, such as those of the police, the criminal courts, and the correctional system." H.R. 17,825, 91st Cong., 2d Sess. (1970). For further discussion of federal support for crime control programs see pp. 352-56 infra.

Foundations and other private sources may also provide support. In Cleveland, Ohio, the Administration of Justice Advisory Committee, established as the result of private efforts in October, 1968, has received more than $450,000 in private funding from the Cleveland Foundation, the Greater Cleveland Associated Foundation, and the Ford Foundation. Efforts are presently underway to interest a consortium of colleges and universities, including Case Western Reserve University Law School and the Center for Urban Affairs at Cleveland State University, in providing for continuation of the Advisory Committee. Administration of Justice Advisory Committee, Staff Paper, 1970, at 2 (on file at the Mass. Governor's Committee on Law Enforcement and the Administration of Criminal Justice). In Hartford, Conn., the Criminal and Social Justice Coordinating Committee, established in the fall of 1969, is funded by the Hartford Foundation for Public Giving and the Ford Foundation. The Committee is presently seeking funds from the business community. Criminal and Social Justice Coordinating Committee, Staff Paper, 1970, at 1, 6 (on file at the Mass. Governor's Committee on Law Enforcement and the Administration of Criminal Justice).

24 For a more detailed discussion of comprehensive programs directed toward specific crimes and toward high crime areas see Mass. Governor's Committee on Law Enforcement and Administration of Criminal Justice, 1970 Comprehensive Criminal Justice Plan 25-44 (Apr. 15, 1970).

25 J. Lindsay, supra note 20, at 15.

26 State and county governments normally pay for much of the prosecutorial, defense, court, and correctional services, for example.

27 One of the significant values of a city having a criminal justice planning capability is that it can work with agencies in other governmental jurisdictions to insure that criminal justice programs serving the city are integrated to the fullest extent possible and that programs are not operating at cross-purposes.

28 Challenge of Crime 284.

29 H.R. 5037, 90th Cong., 1st Sess. (1967), introduced on February 8.

30 Law Enforcement Assistance Act of 1965, Pub. L. No. 89-197, §§ 1-11, 79 Stat. 828.

31 Before this proposal was enacted on June 19, 1968, as the Omnibus Crime Control and Safe Streets Act of 1968, 82 Stat. 197 (partially codified in scattered sections of 5, 18, 42, 47 U.S.C.), acrimonious debates occurred both on the roles of respective levels of government in administering the program and on other types of tools that were needed

to fight crime. The fight on jurisdictional control related to whether the states should administer the program under a comprehensive state plan or whether the Department of Justice should be able to bypass the states and deal directly with individual cities. The principle of working through the states ultimately prevailed. For the arguments on this issue see House Comm. on the Judiciary, The Law Enforcement and Criminal Justice Assistance Act of 1967, H.R. Rep. No. 488, 90th Cong., 1st Sess. (1967); 101 Cong. Rec. 9908-10 (1967); Senate Comm. on the Judiciary, Omnibus Crime Control and Safe Streets Act of 1967, S. Rep. No. 1097, 90th Cong., 2d Sess. (1968). At the time of the writing of this Article, amendments altering the present "block grant" approach were being considered in the House. H. 14,341, 91st Cong., 2d Sess. (1970). Thus, the debate over control of this program is still very much alive.

With reference to the ideological differences in Congress on how to fight crime, the proponents for fighting crime by expanding police power were successful in adding, among other items, the following to the final version of Title I of the Safe Streets Act. 82 Stat. 197: (1) priority funding for riot control training and equipment (§§ 301(b)(6), 520); (2) broadened rules of evidence for admissibility of confessions and evidence of eyewitness testimony in federal cases—attempts to alter holdings in Miranda and Wade (§ 701); and (3) permissive wiretapping and electronic surveillance (§ 801).

[32] On May 15, 1970, the United States House of Representatives approved an appropriation of $480 million for the Law Enforcement Assistance Administration.

[33] Two specific federally funded programs of particular importance to the development of effective responses to urban crime should be noted. A program sponsored by the National League of Cities and the U.S. Conference of Mayors is receiving $240,575 in federal support from LEAA. The program is designed to assist the 29 largest cities in the United States to improve their criminal justice systems. Each participating city is contributing $5,000 toward the program, so that total funding of $405,575 will be available. The program will evaluate existing criminal justice activities in major cities, and will propose methods to improve system coordination and performance. In addition, the program will explore ways to more effectively relate major-city crime control efforts to the LEAA program. A second program of particular significance is the LEAA Pilot Cities and Counties program, which will be funded through the National Institute of Law Enforcement and Criminal Justice. To date, grants totalling $1,008,981 have been approved to support the development of model criminal justice systems in the cities of San Jose, Santa Clara County, California, and Dayton, Montgomery County, Ohio. The San Jose project, which has received $312,481, will involve the Institute for the Study of Crime and Delinquency in Sacramento. The Dayton project, which has received $696,500, will involve Community Research, Inc. of Dayton. Institute of Judicial Administration, Criminal Justice Coordinating Councils Make Slow Progress, Crim. Justice News Letter, Pilot Issue, No. 2, Aug. 1970, at 2.

[34] There have been many cases in the past of new approaches that have proved successful in demonstration (for example in the field of corrections), but which have never been broadly implemented. See the discussion of the Highfield Project and other projects in Challenge of Crime 171.

[35] Mass. Governor's Comm. on Law Enforcement and Administration of Criminal Justice, The Office of Criminal Justice Services: A Proposal for State Assistance to Local Communities for Crime Control 3 (Jan. 16, 1969) (on file at the Mass. Governor's Committee on Law Enforcement and Administration of Criminal Justice).

[36] Challenge of Crime 15.

[37] 116 Cong. Rec. 4378, 4384, 4389 (daily ed. May 14, 1970).

REHABILITATION:
RHETORIC AND REALITY

Norval Morris

Gordon Hawkins

THE AMERICAN correctional system handles about 1.3 million offenders on an average day; it has 2.5 million admissions in the course of a year; its annual budget is over a billion dollars, of which well over half goes to feed, clothe, and guard adult criminals in prisons and jails. The facilities, programs, and personnel of the correctional systems are badly overtaxed. Moreover, assuming that present trends in courts and convictions continue, the system will in the future, unless policies are radically changed, have to face even more extreme pressures.

Imprisonment remains the core of the system, and, as Hans Mattick pointed out, "the genius of American penology lies in the fact that we have demonstrated that eighteenth and nineteenth century methods can be forced to work in the middle of the twentieth century."

There are 25 prisons in the United States over a hundred years old. Sixty-one prisons opened before 1900 are still in use. Inside these fortress structures only a small fraction of those confined are exposed to any kind of correctional service other than restraint. As for the local jails which handle those awaiting trial and misdemeanants, these were described by a task force of the President's Crime Commission as "generally the most inadequate in every way . . . . Not only are the great majority of these facilities old but many do not even meet the minimum standards in sanitation, living space, and segregation of different ages and types of offenders that have obtained generally in the rest of corrections for several decades."

Our program thus addresses an antique, overloaded, neglected, expensive, cruel, and inefficient "correctional" system. Hence, our edicts:

1. The money bail system shall be abolished. All but the small number of offenders who present high risk of flight or criminal acts prior to trial shall be granted pretrial release upon such conditions and restrictions as the court may think necessary and with stringent penalties for failure to appear.
2. Unless cause to the contrary can be shown, the treatment of offenders shall be community-based.
3. For a felony no term of imprisonment of less than 1 year shall be imposed by the courts.
4. All correctional authorities shall develop community treatment programs for offenders, providing special intensive treatment as an alternative to institutionalization.
5. All correctional authorities shall make an immediate start on prison plans designed to reduce the size of penal institutions, develop modern industrial programs, and expand work release, graduated release, and furloughs for prisoners.
6. All state and federal laws restricting the sale of prison-made products shall be repealed.
7. All local jails and other correctional facilities including probation and parole services shall be integrated within unitary state correctional systems.
8. All correctional authorities shall recruit additional probation and parole officers as needed for an average ratio of 35 offenders per officer.
9. Parole and probation services shall be made available in all jurisdictions for felons, juveniles, and such adult misdemeanants as need or can profit from them.
10. Every release from a penal institution for felons and for such categories of misdemeanants as the correctional authorities see fit shall be on parole for a fixed period of between 1 and 5 years.

The Custodial Function: Bail

A primary function of the jail remains, as it has always been, the custody of persons pending trial; so that the bulk of the jail population is made up of unconvicted defendants. A large proportion of these, from 40 to 60 percent, will later be released without being convicted. In addition to those found not guilty and released, there are large numbers who on conviction are given shorter terms than they have already served while awaiting trial or are placed on probation rather than imprisoned. The majority of the persons thus detained are there because they cannot pay bail.

Justice and economy demand that there should be a substantial increase in the proportion of accused persons released pending trial. Quite apart from the costs in terms of human suffering and the wastage of human resources involved in needless pretrial detention, the cost in terms of money is enormous. We must reduce pretrial detention to the minimum by abolishing money bail and releasing all defendants save the few for whom detention is essential in the interests of the community.

It has been argued against our plan for the abolition of money bail that it would be improper to empower magistrates and judges to jail only defendants they believe to be dangerous on the ground that reliable methods for predicting dangerousness have not been developed. But judges at present commonly set high money bail as a means of keeping in jail persons they fear will commit crimes if released before trial, although the only recognized constitutional purpose of the bail system is ensuring appearance at trial. Further, judges are no better qualified to predict nonappearance than to predict dangerousness, although the whole bail system postulates their ability to do so. Research which has already begun on identifying the factors relevant to the risk of flight before trial should be continued and intensified, and further research is certainly necessary to discover the factors bearing on the likelihood of persons' committing various offenses while released pending trial. This does not mean, however, that we can afford to preserve the present largely ineffective, highly inequitable, and almost criminally wasteful bail and detention system until those researches have been completed.

The Correctional Function

There is a marked tendency for some of the experts in the field of corrections to declare flatly that imprisonment has failed. Others have been more cautiously agnostic and have said merely that we know nothing about the effectiveness of imprisonment. It is necessary therefore, first of all, to say something about this prevailing pessimism or skepticism, to consider how far it is rationally justified or to what extent it may be due to the demise of exaggerated hopes and the frustration of ideals. One source of disaffection is easy to identify. The President's Commission Task Force Report on Corrections states: "The ultimate goal of corrections under any theory is to make the community safer by reducing the incidence of crime." But at a time when the incidence of crime does not appear to have been reduced—rather the reverse—and the community certainly doesn't feel safer, this "ultimate goal" seems to be receding rather than coming closer. So, not surprisingly, some persons have assumed that all our correctional programs have failed.

About this two things need to be said. In the first place the incidence of crime is not simply a function of penal practice. There is no evidence that the volume or rate of crime is so related to penal policy that it is dependent upon and varies with changes in correctional programs and practices. But there is considerable evidence that the amount and rates of crime are related to such factors as the density and size of the population; the age, sex, and race composition of the population; the strength and efficiency of the police force; and many other factors outside and beyond the control of penal administration. To attribute an increase in crime to penal policy is therefore like holding an umbrella responsible for the rainfall. Nevertheless the principal function of the prison is the treatment of convicted offenders, the declared purpose of that treatment being to prevent the offender from offending again. And this means that in one respect, at least, it is possible to talk meaningfully about the effectiveness of imprisonment. For the effectiveness of the prison system as a crime control agency in relation to the offenders who have been processed through it is, to a degree, measurable.

Here, too, it is frequently and quite confidently asserted that we have failed. "Between 60 percent and 70 percent of the men who leave prison come back for new crimes," says John Bartlow Martin. Where what Daniel Glaser in *The Effectiveness of a Prison and Parole System* (1964) calls "the legend that two-thirds return to prison" originated is not known. Possibly it started in this methodologically confused way. Most prison populations include about two-thirds who have been in prison before. It is easy but wrong to conclude that prisons therefore have a 60- to 70-percent failure rate. The prison is a sample grossly skewed by recidivists. Much lower failure rates can produce a prison population where two-thirds are ex-prisoners; prison is in large part a collection of its own failures.

The kind of rigorous studies necessary to determine the extent to which released prisoners in the United States return to prison have not been done. Those studies which have attempted to follow releasees suggest on the contrary that about two-thirds do *not* return. One of the principal conclusions of Glaser's study is that "in the first two to five years after their release, only about a third of all the men released from an entire prison system are returned to prison." In view of the fact that many studies have shown that a 3-year followup accounts for about 90 percent of the probable future returns to prison, Glaser's findings suggest that it is unwise to dismiss prisons as complete failures.

On the other hand, neither can one say that their effectiveness has been demonstrated. The two-thirds "success" rate, a figure which incidentally also holds for the English prison system, no doubt masks a great deal of "spontaneous remission" in cases where the experience of imprisonment was irrelevant to later lawful behavior and conceivably more rigorous followup studies would uncover a good deal more postrelease criminality than the rather crude methods so far employed.

However that may be, it leads us to consider a deeper source of disquiet and cynicism—the fact that there is some evidence to support what Nigel Walker calls "the hypothesis of the interchangeability of penal measures." This is the hypothesis that of the offenders who do not repeat their offenses after a given type of sentence all but a very few would have refrained similarly after most other kinds of sentence—in other words, that for most offenders penal measures are interchangeable. There is no reason, however, why these findings should be regarded as depressing or should give rise to cynicism.

The similarity between the reconviction rates of offenders despite differences in their sentences is not really very surprising. "Treatment" in penal institutions generally consists of little more than variations in the conditions of custody, and probation rarely involves more than cursory supervision. It would be surprising if either proved a significant influence on conduct.

It is, of course, understandable that anyone committed to belief in the superiority of a particular penal method should feel some chagrin. But for an objective observer there are positive inferences to be drawn for social policy which, to a large extent, counterbalances any negative implications. For the interchangeability hypothesis indicates that one of the major penological problems of our time—overcrowding, shortages of adequate staff and equipment, and all the social and economic costs of maintaining penal institutions—can be drastically reduced without any increase in reconviction rates simply by sentencing fewer offenders to imprisonment.

Community Treatment

In the light of our phenomenal ignorance, what rational strategy is possible? The first point to note is that our ignorance is not total. Three propositions advanced by Leslie Wilkins in a survey he did in 1967 for the Council of Europe entitled "The Effectiveness of Punishment and Other Measures of Treatment" are directly relevant to policy making in this field:

1. Humanitarian systems of treatment (e.g., probation) are no less effective in reducing the probability of recidivism than severe forms of punishment.
2. Money (if not souls) can be saved by revised treatment systems. The cheaper systems are more often than not also more humanitarian.
3. Much money is wasted in many countries by the provision of unnecessary security precautions.

One of the most striking pieces of evidence which would support those propositions is an impressive attempt at controlled experimentation in the correctional field: the California Youth Authority's Community Treatment Project, now in its eighth year. The saving in public money is certainly substantial. The cost of the California Community Treatment Project per youth is less than half the average cost of institutionalizing an offender. Moreover, the program is now handling a group larger than the population of one of the new juvenile institutions that the California Youth Authority is building. An investment of some $6- to $8-million is thus obviated. At the same time the program offers not merely "equal protection to the public" but also, at less than half the price, much more effective protection than the traditional methods.

It is true that there are always likely to be offenders who because of the nature of their offenses (e.g., gross cruelty, violence, or sexual molestation) will have to be imprisoned if only because the community would not accept their release. And in some cases involving multiple offenses or serious, persistent recidivism institutionalization may offer the only effective protection for society. But, as the President's Crime Commission reported, "for the large bulk of offenders . . . institutional commitments can cause more problems than they solve.

Our edict dealing with the development of community treatment programs also reflects our judgment that, in regard to the general deterrence question, it is better in the present state of knowledge for the penal system to concentrate on the task of making the community safer by preventing the actual offender's return to crime upon his release than to pursue the problematic preclusion of offenses by others. This does not mean that the general preventive aspect of penal policy is to be disregarded. But over a wide area it is likely that the shame, hardship, and stigma involved in arrest, public trial, and conviction are the principal elements in both individual and general deterrence rather than the nature of the sentence or the disposition of offenders. We must not habitually and thoughtlessly override the immediate object of preventing the offender from repeating his offense by assumptions of the efficacy of punishments on deterring potential imitators.

Institutional Treatment

We have argued that one of the principal practical implications of our discussion is that the enormously expensive and clumsy machinery of imprisonment is today relied on excessively and that its use could be drastically curtailed with great advantage in terms of financial, social, and human costs. This is not a revolutionary theory. Indeed today it would be widely accepted as a truism of sound sentencing practice that a prison sentence should be imposed only when no alternative punishment is reasonably appropriate. This approach to sentencing has received a most interesting formulation in the sentencing provisions of the American Law Institute's Model Penal Code. The code specifically directs the court not to impose a sentence of imprisonment unless it is of the view that such a sentence is necessary for the protection of the public. The code further provides that for a felony no term of imprisonment of less than 1 year shall be imposed by the court. This is, of course, not a technique for increasing the duration of prison sentences, though it may in occasional cases have that effect; the theory is that if a court does not think the crime or the criminal merit or require a prison sentence of at least a year's duration then punishment other than imprisonment should be imposed. In England —and the story is substantially the same in most countries—only about 1 in every 30 of those convicted by the criminal courts is sentenced to prison; if only indictable offenses are considered, less than 1 in every 5 so convicted is imprisoned. As the excellent sentencing handbook prepared by the Home Office for the use of the courts puts it: "Imprisonment is thus increasingly coming to be regarded as the sentence to be imposed only where other methods of treatment have failed or are considered inappropriate."

Nevertheless the fact remains that although the prison or penitentiary as we know it will almost certainly have followed the death penalty, banishment, and transportation into desuetude before the end of the century, institutional confinement in some form will remain necessary for some offenders. The kinds of diversification and modification in the prison system which will develop cannot be planned in detail or predicted with certainty. In a dynamic situation it is unwise to attempt to impose final lines of development, but

some forms of innovation and variation are already in evidence. Moreover, change is essential. Worldwide experience with all "total institutions," prisons and mental hospitals alike, reveals their adverse effects on the later behavior of their inmates. For some time, therefore, experimental development has been taking place, tending toward the eventual elimination of prison in the form we now know it.

That form is, in outline: a walled institution where adult criminals in large numbers are held for protracted periods, with economically meaningless and insufficient employment, with vocational training or education for a few, with rare contacts with the outside world, in cellular conditions varying from the decent to those which a zoo would not tolerate, the purposes being to lead the prisoners to eschew crime in the future and to deter others of like mind from running the risk of sharing their incarceration. It is confidently predicted that before the end of this century prison in that form will become extinct, though the word may live on to cover quite different social organizations.

This is not, of course, advocacy of a general "gaol delivery." Prison, the basic sanction of criminal justice, must be preserved until its alternatives and its modifications are demonstrably of greater social utility. In our present ignorance of the effectiveness of our armory of punishments against criminals and of their educative and deterrent effects on the community, experimentation cannot be precipitate, and penal reforms within the walls remain an important aim. What is suggested is that the variations and modifications of prison are already at a stage where their recognition as such is necessary. We deal here with a few aspects of that experimentation which merit further development.

The open institution plays an increasingly important part in the prison systems of the world, for long-term and short-term prisoners, for the unconvicted and the convicted, for the duration of confinement, and as a release measure. Its role must be expanded. Likewise, though it would be unwise to turn our prisons into mental hospitals, there is a proportion of prisoners for whom effective treatment can be given only in an institution which in its routine, purposes, and techniques is closer to a mental hospital than to a prison. Hence institutions like Patuxent in Maryland, Grendon Underwood in England, and Herstedvester in Denmark are the shape of the future for, say, 10 percent of prisoners now in our security institutions.

One aspect of the work in the Danish institution, Herstedvester, leads helpfully to a further variation or mutation on prison. The period that criminals actually spend in Herstedvester has been steadily reduced over the years until now the norm is less than 2 years. At a rough estimate, the norm of "time in" for similar criminals in England and Australia would be 4 years, and in America 7 years. The period and intensity of supervision is, however, much greater after the prisoner leaves Herstedvester than is the after-care supervision following imprisonment in most other countries, and there is a much higher like-lihood of the criminal's return to Herstedvester for misbehavior or difficulty in social adaption short of crime. If necessary, those paroled from Herstedvester are helped and supported in the community, supervised and controlled, for many years; the period in the institution is merely a part of the overall correctional effort, institutional and in the community, and in duration it is often the lesser part.

A similar idea is to be seen also in the reorgani-zation of the Swedish correctional system,* with the administrative consolidation of probation, prison, and aftercare services, regionalization, flexibility of release and transfer procedures, and a deliberate plan to make the prison term merely a part of the correctional plan and to reduce the period of imprisonment. Such plans are creating, in effect, a new short-term imprisonment, with surveillance and support in the community there-after, instead of the former protracted prison sentences.

No matter how modified, prison remains ex-pulsion from the group. It is a banishment. And it is a strange and inefficient banishment since there is normally a return; a new and meaningful life is not possible in the place to which the criminal is banished, and life there tends to sever his cultural roots and to cripple him socially and sometimes psychologically for his return.

Other modifications of the prison are also taking place, however, and these have as their purpose the reduction of the degree and duration of banish-ment, the diminution of the social isolation of prison, and the preservation of the familial and social ties which are so important to a law-abiding life. Some of these modifications are home leave, working out, day leave, furloughs to find employ-ment, unrestricted correspondence, frequent visits by family and approved friends, and halfway hostels as release procedures.

There is a conflict inherent in our prison pur-poses. As a deterrent punishment we impose social isolation and at the same time we aspire to influ-ence the prisoner to reformation; yet experience, and such evidence as we have, leads inexorably to the view that in the preservation and strengthen-ing of the prisoner's familial ties, and the preser-vation and creation of other social links with the community, lies our best hope for his avoiding crime on release. We must, in our own interests,

* See "Lessons from the Adult Correctional System of Sweden," FEDERAL PROBATION, December 1966.

preserve and nourish his family and community relationships.

Letters to and from family and friends have been treated as rare privileges; the advanced cor-rectional administrators of the world now regard letters as necessities of rehabilitation, and pathetic arguments about the administrative problems of censoring so many letters are quickly met. Like-wise, visits are moving from rare privileges to essential and reasonably frequent therapeutic opportunities.

Some countries develop systems of home leave, allowing all but a few prisoners regular home leave after part of their sentence has been served. Such systems start as a release procedure but work their way back into the prison regime; they start as a privilege allowed to the younger pris-oners and develop into a wise rehabilitative pro-cess applicable to most prisoners. Home leave must be used in our penal system, not for reasons of sentimentality but because it better protects the community and maximizes the chances of reform by preserving the prisoner's familial and desirable community relationships. When allied with some indefiniteness in the duration of the sentence, the regular testing of fitness for release by a home-leave program is obviously sound community pro-tection.

Similar pressures lie behind "day leave" in the Scandinavian systems and behind "working out" as it develops in several regions of the world. Part-time imprisonment thus stands both as an alternative to prison and as a modification of prison.

Yet even when reduction of the social isolation is achieved there are a number of features of the prison system which demand urgent attention; the problem of providing effective prison indus-tries is one of them. In the vast majority of cor-rectional institutions penal work programs are small and inefficient and involve repetitious drudg-ery with outdated equipment. The President's Crime Commission found that idleness was the "prevailing characteristic of most American pri-sons and jails." A number of state and federal laws restricting the sale of prison-made products have helped to ensure the continuance of this situation.

Such legislation represents a pernicious per-version of public policy. It is based on the un-acceptable premise that when a person is convicted of a crime and sent to prison he ceases to be a citizen. The threat to organized labor or business interests in the community by prison industry is minuscule. The extent of the demoralization en-tailed in keeping prisoners in a state of workless, infantile dependency is incalculable. The develop-ment of prison industries can provide not only for the habilitation of inmates to constructive and rewarding employment but also provides opportunities for training in vocational skills. That effective prison industries can be developed has been demonstrated by the success of Federal Prison Industries, Inc. A better model for state systems possibly, because of the scale of operations, might be the Swedish work program where the penal administration slogan is: "First build a factory, then add a prison to it." Soon in this country we must experiment with the full wages prison, since the logic behind it is compelling.

Another respect in which American prisons are deficient and indeed represent dangerous anachronisms is in their size. Forty years ago the American Prison Association warned that no prison should contain more than 1,200 inmates. Today not only do some 45 American penal institutions contain more than that number but there are also a number of prisons such as the State Prison of Southern Michigan at Jackson, San Quentin in California, and the Ohio Penitentiary at Columbus which hold more than three times that number. Yet even 1,200 inmates would be regarded as far too many by most penologists today. The British Howard League for Penal Reform has stated that 150 is the optimum size and the energetic and imaginative Swedish director-general of prisons, Torsten Eriksson, regards 60 inmates as the maximum desirable population for a penal institution! Be that as it may, our institutions are grossly too large. There is little point in arguing the merits of this; few will disagree. It is the question of ignorance and tradition masquerading as political and social priorities. With small institutions, much else that we all seek to achieve in our correctional work is possible; with the mega-institution, little is possible. Discussing the number of staff and prisoners with a warden of a small jail, one of the authors asked, "What is your inmate-staff ratio?" and received the comforting reply, "Some like it, some don't."

Parole and Probation

Although, as we have said, four-fifths of the correctional budget is spent and nine-tenths of correctional employees work in penal institutions, only one-third of all offenders are confined in them; the remaining two-thirds are under supervision in the community. We have already indicated that, for the great majority of those confined, special community programs must be developed as alternatives to instutionalization. It remains to deal with the two-thirds of offenders already being supervised outside the walls on parole or probation.

More than 60 percent of adult felons in the Nation as a whole are released on parole before the expiration of the maximum terms of their sentences. But there are sharp variations in the extent of parole use in different states, from one in which only 9 percent of prisoners are paroled to some where virtually all are. Most juveniles are released on parole but supervision is commonly inadequate. Most misdemeanants are not paroled. Nearly two-thirds of the local jails have no parole procedures and those that do, release only 8 percent of inmates in this way. Slightly more than half of all offenders sentenced to correctional treatment are placed on probation. Yet there are still many jurisdictions which lack any probation facilities for misdemeanant offenders. Of 250 counties studied by the President's Crime Commission Survey of Corrections one-third provided no probation service at all. Many small juvenile courts rely almost entirely on suspended sentences in lieu of probation supervision.

Various studies have attempted to measure the success of parole and probation. As far as parole is concerned, authoritative estimates indicate that among adult offenders 55 to 65 percent of those released are not subsequently returned to prison. And only about one-third of those that are returned have been convicted of new felonies; the remainder are returned for other parole violations. Success rates for probation are generally considerably higher than for parole.

Yet these successes in both parole and probation have been achieved by services for the most part grossly understaffed, almost always underpaid, and too often undertrained. The best estimate available from current research indicates that an average of 35 cases per officer is about the highest ratio likely to permit effective supervision and assistance in either service. Of course, no caseload standard can be applied to all types of offender. The optimum overall caseload of 35 is based on a determination of what an average caseload would be when different types of offenders were given the appropriate kinds and degrees of supervision. Up to 20 persons in a caseload of 35 could receive close intensive supervision; if none required such supervision, the caseload could be larger.

Current average caseloads vastly exceed the optimum level. Over 76 percent of all misdemeanants and 67 percent of all felons on probation are in caseloads of 100 or more. Less than 4 percent of the probation officers in the Nation carry caseloads of 40 or fewer. Adults released on parole are supervised in caseloads averaging 68; and over 22 percent of adult parolees are being supervised in caseloads of more than 80. The average caseload for juveniles is about 64.

It is clear that there is considerable need for additional probation and parole officers. It must be remembered that offenders are kept under such supervision at much less cost than in institutions. The national survey of corrections done for the President's Crime Commission found, for example, that to keep a juvenile offender on probation costs only one-tenth of the amount required to keep him in a state training school. Similar 1-to-10 cost ratios prevail in regard to both felons and misdemeanants. It is true that this difference arises in part because expenditures for probation and parole are currently inadequate but, as the President's Crime Commission points out, probation and parole expenditures "can clearly be increased several fold and still remain less expensive than institutional programs." When one takes into account also capital costs (up to and beyond $20,000 per bed in a correctional institution), the cost of welfare assistance for prisoners' families, and the loss in production and taxable income involved in imprisonment, the 1-to-10 ratio is clearly a considerable underestimate of the real cost differential. In these circumstances the failure to provide adequate probation and parole facilities for misdemeanants, who make up more than two-thirds of the nearly 2 million commitments to all correctional facilities and programs in a year, is extremely costly as well as unsound penal practice.

Integrated and Regional State Correctional Systems

One of the currently contentious issues in the organization of corrections in the federal system is whether the federal probation and parole services should be joined with the Federal Bureau of Prisons and the Federal Parole Board in a single department administratively responsible to the Department of Justice. Unification and regionalization at the federal level, and in a country the size of the United States, raise problems of great complexity, with political and jurisprudential penumbrae which at present we would prefer to avoid; let us therefore suggest only some of the advantages of a unified and regionalized structure for a state as distinct from a federal correctional system.

Such an integrated, regional correctional system is, of course, not unknown in this country. The Wisconsin system is so organized. The advantage of unifying institutional and extra institutional processes into some coherent single administrative structure of probation, prison, and parole, flows essentially from the fact that the connection between institutional and noninstitutional correctional processes is growing closer and requires overall planning. The prison is now rarely thought to provide an independent, self-contained correctional process. All who hope to rehabilitate offenders see the process as involving a gradual release procedure and an effective aftercare program linked in a single plan. And effective probation is coming to be seen as requiring some institutional support in an appreciable proportion

of cases. The probation hostel may be necessary for some cases; institutional control of leisure in community treatment centers may be needed for others.

And so prison, probation, and parole grow closer together and structurally intertwine. The prison may be required as a base from which the prisoner goes out to work; a halfway house may be used as a release procedure; and aftercare will always be closely linked with the prison program and should provide the last stage in the execution of the prisoner's rehabilitative plan. It is hard to provide such continuous institutional and postinstitutional correctional processes, and such institutional and contemporaneously noninstitutional processes (halfway house, working out, community treatment center, probation hostel) unless there is the closest of ties between those responsible for the various services.

Continuity of treatment plan and execution is necessary to the release procedure; it also proves necessary when we apply more effective control mechanisms in our aftercare processes, for this reason: At present when a prisoner on parole breaks a condition of his release, the choice facing the correctional authorities is too limited. He can be warned, or he can be taken back into custody. Just as we are developing "halfway-out" houses as release procedures so should we develop "halfway-in" houses to provide for those released prisoners who require a period of closer control than can be given when they are relatively free on parole but who do not need to be sent back to prison. This group may not be large, but it is appreciable, and again there is a happy confluence between better rehabilitative processes and less cost.

Another advantage of unification of correctional service should be mentioned. It has long seemed to us that the prison warden, to be entirely effective in his job, should not only be informed concerning probation and parole work but also should have had a period of active involvement in casework in the community. Likewise, the senior probation or parole officer should have had institutional experience if he is to be most effective. Within the correctional system, no one should reach a high position without a variety of work experiences both inside and outside the walls. Thus the theme of continuity of treatment would be maintained by the very structure of the services involved.

So much for the value of unification in a state system. Regionalization needs little justification. It carries forward the theme of avoiding enterprises too large for any single man to have reasonably close and detailed acquaintance with their workings. And there is also the advantage of linking the correctional system, in each of the regions, close to the needs, opportunities, and social attitudes of the particular social group in which the offender lived and will live; regional differences require appropriate differences in correctional systems. Finally and obviously, regionalization greatly facilitates maintaining closer ties between the prisoner and his family, by visits and furloughs, than is possible where correctional administration is not regionalized.

Sentencing

To Blackstone the judicial function of sentencing the convicted criminal presented no trace of intellectual challenge, the judge acting merely as a channel through which the law expressed its predetermined and impartial decision. We expect more from our criminal sanctions than we did in Blackstone's day, but we have neither developed techniques nor fashioned principles to meet our expectations. Over 20 years ago Mr. Justice Frankfurter said that "the inadequacy of our traditional methods for determining the appropriate treatment for offenders, once wrongdoing is established, can no longer be disregarded." But in the intervening years there has been little change, although about half the states are now undertaking projects to revise their penal laws and sentencing codes.

Insofar as the work of the correctional system is largely determined by the court's sentence, it is necessary to say something about sentencing policies and procedures. In this we are broadly in agreement with the approach taken by the American Law Institute in its Model Penal Code; and this agreement is reflected in several of the edicts in this chapter.

We are not here concerned to deal with the precise number of punishment categories required or the penalities to be attached to each category. The important points are that there should be what Herbert Wechsler calls "discipline in legislative use of penal sanctions."

The code embodies statutory criteria and separate sentencing provisions to discriminate between offenders requiring lengthy imprisonment and others. Thus courts are allowed to impose extended terms of imprisonment—beyond the ordinary maximum—in cases where the defendant is a persistent offender, a professional criminal, a dangerous, mentally abnormal person, or a multiple offender whose criminality is particularly extensive. The provision of statutory criteria of this kind to guide courts in the exercise of their discretion is an important move in the direction of rational sentencing policy.

No less important are the code's provisions regarding statutory standards governing the granting of probation. In almost every jurisdiction of America legislatures have restricted the power of the courts to grant probation. These arbitrary denials of discretion to the courts, like mandatory prison sentences, are met with evasion in many cases but they represent an improper obstruction to the course of justice. At the same time, the statutory provisions authorizing the use of probation are commonly couched in such vague and general terms that, as the President's Crime Commission puts it, "each judge is left virtually unrestrained in applying his own theories of probation to individual cases."

The Model Penal Code directs the court to suspend sentences or grant probation unless it finds that imprisonment is necessary for the protection of the public because (a) there is undue risk that during the period of a suspended sentence or probation the defendant will commit another crime; or (b) the defendant is in need of correctional treatment that can be provided most effectively by his commitment to an institution; or (c) a lesser sentence will depreciate the seriousness of the defendant's crime. These standards too are general but they clearly accord a priority to dispositions which avoid institutionalization. And at the same time, the code provides a lengthy list of grounds which "shall be accorded weight in favor of withholding sentence of imprisonment."

We are also in agreement with the provision of the Model Penal Code regarding parole. Our edict to the effect that every release be upon parole for a fixed period of between 1 and 5 years is derived from the code. It is based on the theory that parole should be seen as an essential part of every institutional sentence and not as an act of benign clemency on the part of the authorities. The parole period is a period of supervised conditional release required for community protection which starts when parole release occurs. At present the period of parole is measured by the length of the unexpired portion of the prison sentence, which is dangerously irrational. It means that those who are the worst risks and therefore are held longest in institutions have the shortest period under supervision, whereas the best risks, released early, have the longest terms under supervision.

Another respect in which sentencing practices are deficient at present relates to the imposition of fines. An inordinate number of offenders are imprisoned for failure to pay fines. For some states as many as 60 percent of jail inmates have been imprisoned for default in payment of fines. Sentences which offer the choice of paying a fine or going to prison are discriminatory in that those unable to pay are punished more severely. A substantial reduction in needless imprisonment can be achieved by allowing time to pay fines and by the use of civil attachment and execution for the collection of unpaid fines. In England the number of committals in default of payment of fines was reduced from 85,000 in 1910 to less than 3,000 in 1947 by these methods; and today less than 1 percent of fines lead to imprisonment for default.

Conclusion

The program outlined here will provide both cheaper and more effective social protection. At the same time it will in the main be less afflictive and involve less disruption of family life and less suffering on the part of innocent dependents. No doubt those who still subscribe to the curious notion that by hurting, humiliating, and harassing offenders we can somehow morally improve them will see this as a defect in our approach. But until some evidence is adduced in support of this idea we are not disposed to take it seriously.

BET TAKING, COSA NOSTRA,
AND NEGOTIATED SOCIAL ORDER

Donald R. Cressey

ABOUT A YEAR AGO PRESIDENT NIXON told the American people that the economic base of *Cosa Nostra*, our dominant organized crime cartel, is "primarily derived from its virtual monopoly of illegal gambling, the numbers rackets, and the importation of narcotics."[1] In this special message on organized crime, the President was trying to "educate the public," just as President Kennedy and President Johnson earlier tried to educate us. But Mr. Nixon's statement hardly revealed new and shocking facts. It has long been known that the *Cosa Nostra* organization controls all but a tiny part of the illegal bet taking in the United States, and that the income from this business is the syndicate's greatest source of income.

However, the public has yet to understand or take seriously the fact that anyone making an illegal bet on a horse race or a football game, or who buys a number in an illegal lottery, is contributing to a culture of fraud, corruption, violence, and murder. This was the real import of the President's special message. The millions of innocent looking bets made daily with innocent looking bet takers are, collectively, so profitable that the bosses of the bet takers are able to buy anything they need including officials of the legislative, executive, and judicial branches of local, state, and federal government. My recent book was an attempt to add my voice to the small but persistent chorus of voices that for at least a decade has been telling us that we are in trouble.[2] *Cosa Nostra* is gradually but inexorably undermining our basic economic and political institutions. The nation must invent new, vigorous, and effective methods for stopping this trend.

At stake is what old liberals call "democracy" and young radicals call "participatory democracy." *Cosa Nostra* bosses have indicated by their economic and political activities, and by their own form of illicit governmental organization, that they favor a political and economic system in which the strong increasingly come to agreements with the strong, powerfully increasing the ability of the strong to exact tribute from the weak. If they are allowed to achieve a monopoly on democratic processes, or even to approach such a monopoly, there will no longer be a steady movement toward continuous, total, and strategic commitment to the construction of a democratic world. Instead, we will regard as inevitable or even as "democratic" a world of ghettos, inequality, and discriminatory practices.

Most proposals for "doing something" to halt *Cosa Nostra's* march toward monopoly are based on the assumption that organized crime is merely a law-enforcement problem. There have been many calls for more effective police work in this area. These have ranged from demands for less corruption to pleas for better law-enforcement tools, such as wire-tapping and electronic bugging, and to plans for computerized information-sharing systems and regional, cooperative police "strike forces."[3]

But *Cosa Nostra* also has been seen as a bureaucracy which owes its existence to a moral, economic, and political order with which law-enforcement agencies cannot effectively deal. Reform proposals based on this view have in common the fact that they would attack *Cosa Nostra* as an *organization*, rather than as a motley collection of individual criminals whom law-enforcement officers should try to arrest one by one. Robert F. Kennedy, when he was Attorney General, frequently suggested, for example, that the *Cosa Nostra* organization itself would be damaged if the public could be persuaded to stop purchasing the illegal goods and services it has for sale. Attorney General John Mitchell and Senator John L. McClellan have both proposed, alternatively, that the economic base of the organization be attacked by new laws, similar to antitrust laws, which would divest *Cosa Nostra* members of their profits.[4] Similarly, it is frequently proposed that the organization would suffer if additional forms of gambling were legalized, thus putting gambling money into the public treasury rather than into the pockets of organized criminals.[5] This last proposal must be given careful consideration by legislators and citizens alike.

There is room for pessimism about the effectiveness of traditional law-enforcement methods as tools for dealing with Cosa Nostra. After all, since the days of Prohibition we have been trying to seek out and destroy organized criminals one by one, and organized crime has steadily increased its strength. Police departments, like the criminal law itself, are not equipped to deal with organizations. But Cosa Nostra is an efficient bureaucracy, and in an efficient bureaucracy no man is indispensable. In the 1930's Benito Mussolini, Fascist Premier of Italy, used dictatorial police methods to eradicate most members of the Sicilian Mafia, but the organization was not destroyed. New members were recruited, and the apparatus was thriving again within a decade. In the United States, the killing of Jesse ended the James gang, but the deportation of Charles Luciano merely resulted in the passing of Cosa Nostra leadership to Frank Costello. The incarceration of a Cosa Nostra boss, Vito Genovese, in 1958 had no discernible effect on the amount of crime committed by his organized crime machine.

The lesson taught by these and other experiences seems clear enough. The Cosa Nostra organization, not merely its membership, must be attacked. It also is clear that this attack will require modification of either our practices or our policies with reference to gambling. It is these practices and policies that give the syndicate a large share of its immense wealth. If public patronage of illegal bet selling agencies were curtailed, the organization's principal source of income would dry up. And, alternatively, if more forms of gambling were legalized, legitimate businessmen or the government itself could reap much of the $6 billion to $7 billion annual income now serving as the economic foundation of the illicit organization.

Perhaps the late Senator Kennedy's insistent call for less patronage of Cosa Nostra's illicit businesses will eventually be heard by our "new generation," who will see and denounce the hypocrisy of a society that outlaws street gambling yet insists on the right to participate in it. To date, however, no one has been able to convince gamblers that they must stop supporting Cosa Nostra's gambling enterprises. Accordingly, we must again give serious consideration to the proposal that we go into competition with Cosa Nostra by legalizing more forms of gambling. This suggestion has recently become a burning issue in New Jersey; last November the voters approved a constitutional amendment authorizing the state to go into the lottery business. The supporters of the amendment argued that a legal lottery would drive out Cosa Nostra's illegal lotteries and, at the same time, would produce great revenue for the state, thus serving to prevent tax increases. Earlier, supporters of the New Hampshire and New York lotteries used the same argument. It also has been used with reference to the legalization of on-track horse-race betting and, more recently, with reference to off-track betting in New York.

Four fundamental facts must be kept in mind as we consider suggestions for "legalized gambling" which would put us in competition with *Cosa Nostra's* formidable illegal bureaucracy. First, there are three principal kinds of commercialized gambling—bet taking, lotteries, and casinos—and the systems of legally operating each of them need not be identical. Second, an ideal "gambling operation," involving any of the three types, is a business in which the operators do not gamble. The maker of the bet gambles, but the taker of the bet simply takes a percentage of the amount gambled. Third, *Cosa Nostra* has tremendous amounts of working capital, highly trained specialists in the business of gaming, powerful political connections, and a willingness to maim and murder in order to make money and collect debts. Fourth, the phrase "legalized gambling" does not itself indicate whether the proposed operation is to be run by a government, by private enterprise, or by some combination of the two. Neither does it suggest a proper relationship in the gambling field between local, state, and federal governments.

In lotteries and in casino gambling it is obvious that the operator does not gamble. He merely deducts a proportion of the amount gambled. But bookmakers—who are engaged in the business of taking bets on the outcome of horse races and athletic contests—must have a rather elaborate apparatus for minimizing risks. They need expert information on the probable outcome of the contest (a "line" or a "wire service") and a reinsurance system ("lay-off," "edge"). These two devices were invented to take the gambling out of bet taking. Both have been provided by *Cosa Nostra*. Of the two, the lay-off is more insidious. This is an operation which enables bet takers all over the country to reinsure their bets, much as a small casualty insurance company might reinsure itself with a large company capable of handling a big insurance transaction.

The details of the lay-off business, well known to every bookmaker and to many gamblers, are not reported here. Basically, the arrangement is one which enables the bookmaker to place with a bookmakers' bookmaker ("lay-off man" or "edge man"), a bet equal to the amount of money needed to pay off winners minus the amount bet on losers, after the bookmaker has deducted a percentage for himself. Legitimate race-track operators, who provide gambling opportunities for persons wealthy enough to spend an afternoon at the track, do not gamble. They take the money bet on losers, deduct from 15 to 20 percent (depending on the laws of their state), and then divide the remaining funds among the persons betting on winners. In illegal bet taking, the ideal lay-off operation works in such a way that bookmakers can do precisely the same thing. A hierarchy of lay-off men services cities, regions, and the nation. For a percentage of the profits, each level of the hierarchy reinsures the bets of the level below it. When all the illegal bets sold on a single race or contest are pooled in this way, no bet taker can lose. One national-level lay-off man takes in about $20 million a year, and his annual profit is about 4 percent of the gross, or $800,000.

Most American lay-off men are members of *Cosa Nostra* or are controlled by someone who is. The geographical and hierarchical organization of the lay-off system is almost a carbon copy of the organization of *Cosa Nostra*. If significant proportions of the public continue to gamble and the lay-off operation is not eliminated or modified, *Cosa Nostra* members will continue to accumulate the fortunes which are enabling them to steal the nation. But if a legal lay-off system could be invented and controlled, all three of the joys claimed for legalized gambling—competition with *Cosa Nostra*, revenue for the state without exploitation of the poor, and convenient places for sports to spend their money—could be rather painlessly accomplished.

In *Theft of the Nation* I suggested that if a state were to legalize gambling, "perhaps a partnership between free enterprise and government could be arranged, with free-enterprise merchants providing the setting for gambling while civil servants conducted the lay-off operation from the state capitol. The resources of a state, thus, would provide the backing for 'mom and pop' bet takers across the state, and the state would reap the profits now reserved mostly for persons high in the hierarchy of *Cosa Nostra*."[4]

I still like the ring of these words. Basically, the suggestion is that we put bet taking into the class of enterprise supervised and assisted by the Small Business Administration. No special license would be needed. Anyone could set up a bet taking shop, just as anyone can now open a gasoline station or a grocery store. But every merchant would be required, under penalties of the criminal law, to call his lay-off bets to an agent of the state. It also would be a crime to accept a lay-off bet. The plan calls for free enterprise in an old-fashioned sense, with the riches going to the operators who sell the most bets and take the greatest risks. (The fewer bets one lays off, the greater his profits and, also, the greater the probability that he will go broke.) The poor could be bookmakers rather than gamblers.

But this plan has two basic flaws. First, it does not squarely face up to the fact that *Cosa Nostra* is an organization with deathly monopolistic tendencies. While the syndicate would lose its lay-off apparatus to the government, it could still monopolize the retail operation by intimidation or even by more legitimate methods made possible by its great wealth. Second, the plan for governmental monopoly of lay-off betting naively assumes that *Cosa Nostra* will obey the law without receiving a reward for doing so. It will not. If the plan were to go into operation, *Cosa Nostra* undoubtedly would use its political influence to set up a parallel lay-off system, thus continuing to reap most of the great profits it now enjoys.

It was with these flaws in mind that I proposed, at the end of my book, that we work out a compromise with *Cosa Nostra*. Unfortunately, I used the word "negotiate" rather than "compromise."[7] Some reviewers got an image of Attorney General Mitchell, Assistant Attorney General Wilson, and FBI Director Hoover sitting down around a large negotiating table with *Cosa Nostra* bosses Bruno, Colombo, Gambino, Maggaddino, Sciacca, Zerilli, and others. I did not foresee a peace treaty pounded out in this way. What I had in mind was some arrangement whereby *Cosa Nostra* could, legally and without corruption, keep some of the profit, after payment of taxes, on bet taking. In exchange, the syndicate would withdraw from its political involvements and its illegal operation of legitimate businesses, which in combination threaten to undermine the whole nation. This state of affairs could be achieved by legalizing free-enterprise bet taking shops while giving *Cosa Nostra*, not the government, a monopoly on the lay-off system needed by the owners of these shops.

This is a radical proposal. But the situation is so desperate that radical proposals are needed. As President Nixon said in his special message last spring, "The threat of organized crime cannot be ignored or tolerated any longer." Moreover, the proposal is not as wild as it seems at first glance. To understand it, one need look at the system local policemen now use, haphazardly and often corruptly, to deal with gambling in their communities.

In the United States we have arranged our program for the combat of organized crime so that we may in fact maintain it. Law enforcement is decentralized to local levels, and such decentralization puts an impossible burden on policemen and other local officials. They must ignore bet taking and other crimes because they serve on the front line of diplomacy between citizens who want anti-gambling laws enforced and citizens who do not. On the one hand, there are community interests in morality, efficiency, and law enforcement. But on the other hand there are community interests in immorality, soft political jobs, favors, domestic tranquility, and evasion of the law. When these interests are both powerful—when there is community support for illegal gambling as well as community support for its suppression—the police and their bosses must decide what constitutes an "appropriate level" of law enforcement. Yet if they openly and honestly try to regulate the demanded sale of bets they almost certainly are viewed as corruptees rather than as the diplomats they are. My proposal asks that the diplomacy be brought out into the open.

While our cities have more than their share of corruption, some police and local politicans appear to be corrupt when they in fact are not on the payroll of any criminal or criminal organization. Some honest policemen overlook illegal gambling because they are saddled with nonenforcement policies formulated by corrupt officials above them in rank and power. Others are stuck with nonenforcement policies —usually called "tolerance policies"—formulated by elected officials who themselves have quite honestly negotiated a compromise between citizens who want anti-gambling ordinances enforced and those who do not. It is difficult for either gamblers or elected politicans to agree wholeheartedly that off-track betting is immoral while betting at the track is not.

The compromised and negotiated character of tolerance policies can be observed in economic as well as political terms. Thus, some communities seem to be openly and almost unanimously opposed to the activities of bet takers, but not enough to pay for arresting, prosecuting, and incarcerating them. Perhaps that is why we keep talking about alternative approaches, such as more extensive legalization of gambling.

One outcome of conflicting community demands, with consequent assignment of diplomatic rather than law-enforcement functions to the police, is a negotiated social order. A balance is struck. An "understanding" is put into operation. Peace reigns. But in times of crisis, usually arising from insistent complaints about corruption or from some incident of violence connected with illegal bet taking, the negotiated order is upset. The police lose their unofficial roles as diplomats and must function as law-enforcement officers, thereby shaking up the whole community. There are shifts in spheres of influence, power plays, bluffs, and gun battles, just like those occurring when the negotiated order of international relations gets upset by an event such as seizure by North Korea of the Pueblo intelligence ship. A new round of negotiations is then moderated by police and local officials.

The negotiated character of contemporary community order shows that communities are "corrupt," in the sense that they tolerate activities previously declared to be illegal. Yet we do not consider the United States to be corrupt when we work out "sphere of influence" arrangements with the Soviet Union, in violation of treaties and understandings with weaker nations. Neither do we consider ourselves corrupt when we deal and bargain with North Korea over return of the Pueblo.

Whether it be called "corruption" or not, the negotiated character of community order makes it appear that the tolerated level of law violation is a harmless little game. This is an illusion. Just as rum-running and bootlegging were not parts of a harmless little game in the 1920's, the current order resulting from the diplomatic efforts of local officials is by no means harmless. As indicated, the game shunts billions of dollars into the hands of *Cosa Nostra* members, where currently it is exempt from control by any significant regulatory agency.

For those who would legalize gambling, then, the real problem is that of modifying the community order resulting from unofficial tolerance of illegal gambling. Our suggestion is that the order be modified by shifting the level of diplomacy upward, to the level of federal government. The new, and legitimate, negotiated order would be one in which small free-enterprise merchants provide the setting for bet taking and gambling, as in the plan whereby the state government would handle all lay-off bets. The difference is this: *Cosa Nostra* would be given the lay-off business in exchange for its agreement to pay its taxes and to withdraw from political involvements and from illegal operation of legitimate business. The "agreement" would not, of course, be in the form of a written document. It would come about through reasonable governmental regulation and auditing of *Cosa Nostra's* lay-off business and other legitimate businesses. And implicit in the agreement would be prohibition of chain-store type ownership and operation of the retail bet-taking establishments.

Except for the fact that *Cosa Nostra* is involved, the proposal is not radically different from current bet-taking arrangements in Great Britain. In that country, the most important lay-off bank is William Hill, Ltd. This perfectly respectable company has more than two million credit betting clients, but it also handles, through its Trade Department, lay-offs for owners of betting shops in every section of England, Scotland, and Wales. Other companies are also engaged in the lay-off business. William Hill, Ltd. handled about three-quarters of a million dollars a week in lay-off bets during 1962-1963, and it probably handles much more than that now.*

British betting shops are patronized by the poor. London boroughs that are overwhelmingly working class have as many as 5 or 6 betting shops per 10,000 population, while boroughs that are predominantly middle- and upper-class have only 1 or 2 per 10,000. American patrons of illegal bookmakers also tend to be poor. Any proposal for legalized gambling in the United States must recognize that currently, the direct victims of *Cosa*

Nostra are the urban poor. This means, especially, poor blacks. Numbers lotteries and the bookmaking business thrive on the quarters and dollars of unskilled Negroes, not on bets by the rich, the well-educated, the well-housed, and the well-employed. Congressman Joseph M. McDade of Pennsylvania recently announced, "We are losing ground in the war on poverty because organized crime takes from the urban poor far more money than the government puts in."[9] The Reverend Martin Luther King, Jr. said, similarly, "Permissive crime is the name for the organized crime that flourishes in the ghetto—designed, directed, and cultivated by the white national crime syndicates operating numbers, narcotics, and prostitution rackets freely in the protected sanctuaries of the ghettos."[10]

Our proposed plan to reduce *Cosa Nostra's* profits and sinister corruptive influences by handing it the nation's lay-off business would not eradicate the injustice inherent in all legalized systems of off-track betting, namely that they reduce the taxes of the rich by taking money from the poor. The principal patrons of the proposed legal bookmaking shops are likely to be the persons now patronizing illegal bookmakers, and these are the persons who can least afford to finance local, state, or federal projects such as education, welfare, space exploration, and war. But there is one saving grace: the dispersion of the ownership of betting shops on a free-enterprise basis would permit ownership by persons who are now poor. The poor would pay, but the poor also would benefit. Moreover, *Cosa Nostra*, operating the lay-off system in much the manner a public utility company runs electricity plants, would pay in taxes the monies now going to corruption rather than to the welfare and education of the poor. The new negotiated social order would be legal, and it would be more beneficial than the current, unofficial, negotiated order. *"Cosa Nostra"* might even become a respectable household word.

Notes

[1] 115 CONG. REC. H2949 (1969) (address of President Nixon on organized crime).

[2] D. CRESSEY, THEFT OF THE NATION: THE STRUCTURE AND OPERATIONS OF ORGANIZED CRIME IN AMERICA (1969).

[3] For a list of many of these proposals, *see* PRESIDENT'S COMMISSION ON LAW ENFORCEMENT AND ADMINISTRATION OF JUSTICE, TASK FORCE REPORT: ORGANIZED CRIME, 16-24 (1967).

[4] Address by Attorney General John N. Mitchell, Antitrust Section of the American Bar Association, March 27, 1969, at 11; 115 CONG. REC. S279-81 (1969) (remarks by Senator John L. McClellan on the Corrupt Organizations Act of 1969). *See also* ORGANIZED CRIME CONTROL ACT OF 1969, COMMITTEE ON THE JUDICIARY, S. REP. No. 91-617, 91st Cong., 1st Sess., at 80 (1969).

[5]*See* Schelling, *Economic Analysis and Organized Crime*, in PRESIDENT'S COMMISSION ON LAW ENFORCEMENT AND ADMINISTRATION OF JUSTICE, TASK FORCE REPORT: ORGANIZED CRIME (Appendix D), 114-26 (1967). *See also*, R. SALERNO & J. TOMPKINS, THE CRIME CONFEDERATION, 354-62 (1969).

[6]D. CRESSEY, THEFT OF THE NATION: THE STRUCTURE AND OPERATIONS OF ORGANIZED CRIME IN AMERICA 296 (1969).

[7]D. CRESSEY, THEFT OF THE NATION: THE STRUCTURE AND OPERATIONS OF ORGANIZED CRIME IN AMERICA 323 (1969). The statement is as follows: "In the organized-crime field, appeasement, accomodation, resistance, and punishment are now more readily available to the criminals than to the noncriminals, principally because the 'respectables' have found no acknowledged organizational officials with whom to negotiate. At present, local officials do negotiate with local members of *Cosa Nostra*, often in a haphazard and corrupt fashion, and with little or no knowledge of the organizational implications of their transactions. But no state or federal agency has ever come to an understanding with *Cosa Nostra's* Commission in the way the Department of State has come to an understanding with the Kremlin. It is highly unlikely, but not inconceivable, that *Cosa Nostra* would agree to give up its political involvements and its illegal operation of legitimate businesses, which in combination threatens to undermine the whole nation, if it could be assured that it will be permitted to keep the profits, after payment of taxes, on bet taking."

[8]Paley & Glendinning, *Pattern for New York? A Report on Off-Track Betting in England*, in NEW YORK STATE ASSEMBLY WAYS & MEANS COMMITTEE (1963).

[9]Address by Congressman McDade on Organized Crime and the Urban Poor, before the National Civil Liberties Clearing House, Oct. 12, 1967.

[10]King, *Beyond the Los Angeles Riots: Next Stop: The North*, SATURDAY REVIEW, November 13, 1965, at 34.

PSYCHOANALYSIS, CRIMINAL JUSTICE PLANNING AND REFORM, AND THE LAW

C. G. Schoenfeld

The Omnibus Crime Control and Safe Streets Act of 1968 (Public Law 90-351) offers to persons interested in criminal justice planning and reform an opportunity to play a decisive role in helping to reduce the huge incidence of crime in the United States —crime that (in the words of Title I of the Act) "threatens the peace, security, and general welfare of the nation and its citizens." The Act provides, for example, for the creation of a new federal agency—the Law Enforcement Assistance Administration of the United States Department of Justice—and grants to this agency the power to dispense considerable sums of money each year to state law enforcement planning agencies that submit to it for approval yearly state-wide plans for crime control.[1]

Before the creation of the Law Enforcement Assistance Administration, only a handful of states had criminal justice planning agencies or state-wide crime control reform programs. But in response to the Omnibus Crime Control and Safe Streets Act of 1968, crime control planning agencies were set up within a year in all fifty states of the Union; and these planning agencies have been submitting state-wide criminal justice improvement plans to the Law Enforcement Assistance Administration and have already received very large sums of money from it to implement the reforms embodied in these plans.

The basic objective of this paper is to provide legislators, judges, lawyers, and other members of the public interested in criminal justice planning and reform (including members of both the Law Enforcement Assistance Administration and the various state crime control planning agencies) with some basis for judging, from a psychoanalytic point of view, the psychological soundness of plans for criminal justice reform. By no means is this to suggest that psychoanalytic psychology is the only system of psychology that can be employed to evaluate the psychological soundness of plans for crime control—or, indeed, to help to formulate these plans.[2] It is to say, however, that implicit in psychoanalytic psychology are a number of insights regarding crime, criminals, and the criminal law that, plainly, are of value to persons concerned with criminal justice planning and reform; and it is also to remind these persons that (in the words of Edward S. Robinson) "men who resolve to think about human affairs without recourse to psychology never actually succeed in avoiding psychology; they simply make up a crude, uncritical psychology of their own."[3]

Basic, perhaps, to any meaningful psychoanalytic discussion of criminal justice planning and reform is the psychoanalytic discovery that "we are all of us born criminals in the sense that we are extensively endowed with impulses which, if unchecked, lead to anti-social conduct."[4]

[S]ide by side with loving attitudes and peaceful contentment, there are always to be found [in infants and young children] mental processes reminiscent of the most primitive aspects of savage life of an intensity that is only faintly mirrored later on by the distressing aspects of our international relations, including even the tortures and other atrocities. Violent and ruthless impulses of destruction (i.e., murder in adult language) follow on the inevitable minor privations of this period. The jealousies, hatreds, and murderous impulses of which signs may be detected in childhood are, in fact, the weakened derivatives of a very sinister inheritance we bring to the world and which somehow has to be worked through and chastened in the painful conflicts and emotions of infancy.[5]

Not only do psychoanalysts stress the primitive and savage urges that frequently beset infants and young children (urges that would be regarded as "criminal" if acted upon by adults), but psychoanalysts also postulate the existence of a fundamental and powerful aggressive drive or instinct (which they believe greatly affects man during his entire life). In Freud's words:

> [M]en are not gentle, friendly creatures wishing for love, who simply defend themselves if they are attacked, but . . . a powerful measure of desire for aggression has to be reckoned as part of their instinctual endowment. The result is that their neighbour is to them not only a possible helper or sexual object, but also a temptation to them to gratify their aggressiveness on him, to exploit his capacity to work without recompense, to seize his possessions, to humiliate him, to cause him pain, to torture and to kill him. *Homo homini lupus;* who has the courage to dispute it in the face of all the evidence in his own life and in history?[6]

If men are the very aggressive creatures—indeed, the "born criminals"—described above by psychoanalysts, then one can hardly accept the theory that crime is simply learned behavior (a theory that, in less simplistic terms, was espoused by the noted sociologist George Sutherland[7]); nor can one accept the notion that crime is simply the product of unfortunate social and economic conditions (a notion which, in a sense, is implicit in the Marxist doctrine that law will "wither away" in a classless Communist society,[8] and which is closely identified with such Marxist sociologists as William Bonger[9]). From a psychoanalytic point of view, then, criminal justice planning and reform that ignores man's aggressive nature and, instead, is based only upon the concept that crime is learned or only upon the more popular concept today that crime is the spawn of bad social and economic conditions is blatantly simplistic and incomplete; and as such, is hardly likely to prove adequate or effective. In fact, even if it were true (as many sociologists believe) that crime is more a product of social and cultural conditions than of instincts, drives, needs, and the like[10]; it would still be irresponsible (to say the least) for criminal justice planning and reform to fail to take into account in some way man's innate aggressiveness and anti-social urges.

Though psychoanalytic psychology stresses man's considerable aggressiveness as well as his primitive and savage psychic inheritance, it also emphasizes the controlling effect upon him of his conscience or moral faculty—of what, in psychoanalytic terminology, is referred to as his "superego." [11] Psychoanalysts have learned, for example, that it is man's conscience or superego that ordinarily prevents his aggressive, primitive, and violent wishes from finding expression in acts that society regards as abhorrent, labels "criminal," and punishes as such. Psychoanalysts have also learned, however, that the superego, *by itself,* is often unable to prevent these anti-social wishes from expressing themselves in criminal conduct; and that to help curb these wishes, the superego or conscience may need the support at times of such agencies as religion, custom, morality—and the law. [12]

The superego's need for the law's support in helping to control man's anti-social urges may well find expression in demands that certain types of conduct be prohibited and punished by the law. For instance, as is stressed in Ranyard West's psychoanalytically-oriented study, *Conscience And Society,* when a man demands that there be stringent penal laws curbing certain forms of aggression, he may be governed not so much by a fear of the aggression of others as by an inner fear that his superego will prove unable to control his own aggression. [13] And in like manner, when a man insists that the criminal law punish certain sexual practices, he may be motivated more by an inner need to help his superego to control his *own* desire to engage in these practices, than by a deep-rooted concern regarding the behavior of others. [14] As J. C. Flugel has put it, law may serve at times "as a social institution the purpose of which is to reinforce our individual consciences." [15]

To know that demands for the prohibition of certain types of conduct by the criminal law may reflect at times not so much objective evaluations of this conduct as the inner needs of certain members of the public to reinforce their conscience or superego in its efforts to defend against the temptation to engage in this very conduct is, perhaps, to begin to understand why the public and its representatives in legislatures may be so reluctant at times to reform the criminal law in certain seemingly obvious ways. For example, there seems to be little doubt that attempts by the criminal law to curb gambling, drinking, prostitution, and other so-called "victimless" offenses have, to date, proven largely unsuccessful—and may, in fact, have had the paradoxical effect at times of making these offenses more attractive than they might have otherwise been.[16] It surely seems self-defeating, for instance, for the criminal law to declare homosexuality between consenting adults to be a crime and then to punish those found guilty of this offense by sending them to monosexual jails where (as criminologists have repeatedly observed) homosexuality is rampant—and where, indeed, persons who might otherwise have tried to abstain from homosexuality are likely to be forced against their will to participate in homosexual acts.[17] Yet when members of the public and their representatives in legislatures appear to be unmoved by these and related facts regarding homosexuality and other "victimless" offenses and refuse to effect changes in the criminal law that would begin to take such facts into account, these persons may be acting not irrationally, irresponsibly, or with indefensible stubbornness, but rather in accordance with *an inner need to retain the criminal law's prohibitions against homosexuality, gambling, drinking, and the like as a means of reinforcing their moral faculty or superego in its attempts to curb the temptation within themselves to engage in these very acts.* And if so, then he who is interested in criminal justice planning and reform can hardly expect his proposals to gain prompt legislative approval if they ignore the way in which the criminal law may help to reinforce the superego; and, instead, are based solely upon such a seemingly unobjectionable criterion as whether the criminal law has, on some statistical or measurable basis, succeeded in curbing certain anti-social behavior. Rather, for a person concerned with criminal justice planning and reform to proceed realistically—and certainly if he hopes to induce the public and its legislative representatives to effect meaningful changes in the criminal law—he must take into account not only such clearly pertinent matters as whether the criminal law appears to have failed, objectively, to reduce the incidence of certain anti-social conduct, but also whether the criminal law helps the superego of the law-abiding members of the public (and of their representatives in legislatures) to control the urge within themselves to engage in just such objectionable behavior.

Not only the prohibition of certain anti-social behavior by the criminal law, but—in addition—the demand for the punishment as well as the actual punishment of those persons who violate the criminal law by engaging in this forbidden conduct may, as psychoanalytic studies reveal, help to reinforce the superego of the law-abiding members of the public (and serve some of their other inner needs as well).[18] To understand how and why the demand for the punishment as well as the actual punishment of criminals may succeed in having such an effect, it might prove of help to recall here that (as was pointed out at the beginning of this paper) all of us are "born criminals" in the sense that we bring with us into the world a violent and savage inheritance which, unless checked, is likely to lead to what society regards as criminal behavior. Further, as psychoanalysts have learned, many of the primitive and savage urges constituting this anti-social or criminalistic inheritance do not simply disappear during infancy and early childhood; but, instead, are relegated to an unconscious level, where (cut off from access to consciousness and from ready access to motor expression) they exist unaltered by time[19] and are kept more or less in check by the superego. Indeed, possibly because these anti-social desires (which presumably find expression in the behavior of criminals) exist to some extent in "the unconscious" of even the most law-abiding of persons; there is, as psychoanalysts have discovered, a tendency on the part of many law-abiding persons to identify themselves on an unconscious level with criminals.[20] And as a result of, this unconscious identification[21] of the law-abiding with criminals, the anti-social wishes and feelings in the unconscious of the law-abiding tend to become aroused and to seek access to consciousness and motility—a process that frequently causes the superego of the law-abiding to engender intolerable guilt as it tries to regain control over and to calm down these anti-social wishes and feelings. In fact, some psychoanalysts believe that the antipathy felt by many law-abiding persons toward the criminal and the tendency of these persons to shun and avoid the criminal may reflect in part an unconscious fear of identification with the criminal (and of the consequences of this identification: the stirring up of unconscious anti-social urges in the law-abiding and the resultant engendering of guilt by their superego).[22] Be this as it may, there can be little doubt that the law-abiding tend, in the main, to isolate, to reject, and to avoid the criminal:. to try, in effect, to build a wall around him—to try, "above all, to keep the criminal at a distance."[23] And if so, then persons who are interested in criminal justice planning and reform ought to be aware that this marked aversion experience by the law-abiding in regard to criminals and the related desire of the law-abiding to isolate and to avoid criminals—especially if these reactions are based upon a strong unconscious fear of identification with criminals—are hardly likely to lend support to practices designed to increase, rather than to decrease, the contacts of the law-abiding with criminals. On the contrary, persons desirous of advancing the cause of criminal justice planning and reform ought to know that when they suggest mechanisms that help to maximize the likelihood of contacts between the law-abiding and criminals (when, for example. they advocate an increase in the use of probation, or of parole, or of prison work-release programs—or even when they champion programs designed to facilitate the rehabilitation and absorption into society of ex-convicts), they may—because of the antipathy of the law-abiding toward criminals and the concomitant tendency of the law-abiding to shun and avoid criminals—be advocating practices that many law-abiding members of the public find extremely difficult (and sometimes impossible) to accept; and as a result, these practices or mechanisms may—unless thought through completely and designed with the greatest of care—prove to be at times (as, unfortunately, experience has demonstrated) little more than exercises in futility.[24]

Whether or not programs that seek to increase the contacts between criminals and the law-abiding members of the public are unduly contrary to the inner needs of the public, there can be little doubt that, as was suggested earlier, *the demand for the punishment as well as the actual punishment of criminals may serve the inner needs of the law-abiding*—especially if (as a result of the self-identification of the law-abiding with criminals—or, indeed, for some other reason) anti-social urges in the unconscious of the law-abiding have been stirred up and seek to gain access to consciousness and motility. For example, when a law-abiding person demands that criminals be punished, he is often able thereby to curb to some extent the anti-social urges that have been stirred up within him—and in so doing, to help his superego to control these urges more easily and completely. This is accomplished, in the view of Franz Alexander and Hugo Staub, because "the demand that the law-breaker be punished is [in effect] . . . a demonstration against one's own inner drives, a demonstration which tends to keep these drives amenable to control. . . . [P]unishment [serves] as an intimidating example . . . against one's own primitive . . . repressed instinctual drives."[25] In fact, not only does the demand for the punishment of criminals help to satisfy the inner need of the law-abiding to reduce the pressure exerted by unconscious anti-social ideas and feelings (and thus unable the superego to control them more effectively), but this demand also helps to alleviate the guilt engendered by the superego because of the presence of these activated anti-social ideas and feelings. In the words of David Abrahamsen: "When law-abiding citizens react mercilessly toward a criminal and his deed, it is not only because they want to see the law obeyed or because they want retribution, but also because the offender acts out anti-social impulses which so many people would like to act out but do not dare to because of fear of the consequences. Unconsciously they identify with the criminal because of their own latent anti-social tendencies and somehow vicariously demand and accept the punishment to relieve their own guilt feelings."[26] But if the demand for the punishment as well as the actual punishment of criminals serve the psychic needs of the law-abiding (by calming down their criminalistic wishes and tendencies and by helping to alleviate the guilt engendered by their superego), then persons concerned with criminal justice planning and reform who seek to ameliorate and to reduce the punishments inflicted upon criminals—and to substitute for these punishments, rehabilitation and treatment—may be advocating a course of action contrary to the inner needs of the law-abiding. Indeed, persons interested in criminal justice planning and reform who urge that the punishment of criminals be rejected in favor of rehabilitation and treatment[27] (and who, in so doing, may well fail to take into account the role played by the punishment of criminals in helping the law-abiding to keep their own criminalistic urges under control) may make it much more difficult than before for the law-abiding to prevent themselves from engaging in criminal conduct—a result that can hardly be considered desirable.

Not only may the demand for the punishment as well as the actual punishment of criminals help the law-abiding to control their own criminalistic tendencies; but in addition, the punishment of criminals may also provide the law-abiding with a method of satisfying what appears to be *an imperious inner need to find outlets for and ways of expressing strong aggressive wishes and feelings in a morally and socially-acceptable manner.*[28] Though sports, politics, and war would certainly seem to help to fulfill this need at times, there is nothing that appears to satisfy it so well and so completely as the punishment of criminals. In fact, Ruth S. Eissler has contended that: "for society in general there remains only one justifiable outlet for aggression, which can be rationalized on the basis of morality and which can provide the desired relief. . . . This is the persecution of the wicked, the criminals."[29] Whether or not this is so, there can be little doubt that (as was indicated earlier) man is, fundamentally, a very aggressive—and frequently cruel—creature; and some of the punishments that the law once imposed upon criminals—flaying, disemboweling, tearing with red hot pincers, breaking on the wheel, and so on *ad nauseam*[30]—would certainly seem to have reflected man's aggressive and cruel urges. Today, fines, imprisonment, and occasional "painless" executions (in gas chambers and in electric chairs, for instance) have largely replaced the older and more openly aggressive and cruel punishments sanctioned by the penal law. And as a result, it may sometimes seem as if the punishments set forth by the criminal law no longer serve man's aggressive and hostile urgencies to any great extent. As penologists have repeatedly pointed out, however, imprisonment (today's most usual punishment for serious crime) frequently proves to be extremely destructive to those who undergo it: the endless monotony, absence of privacy, incredibly minute regimentation, and abnormal deprivations (especially sexual deprivations) even in the best of prisons all too often turn men into depraved and perverted wrecks.[31] These facts concerning the deleterious effects of prison life are, of course, well known—so well known that psychoanalysts sometimes wonder whether what happens to men in jail is not what society actually wants to happen. Indeed, some psychoanalysts have suggested that society seduces men into a life of crime so that they may serve (both in and out of prison) as targets for society's aggressive urgencies.[32] This appears to be the view of Karl Menninger, who contended in 1968 in his now-famous book on the punishment of criminals—*The Crime Of Punishment*—that "society secretly *wants* crime, *needs* crime, and gains definite satisfactions from the present mishandling of it!"[33] But if so, then persons interested in criminal justice planning and reform who design programs that seek to minimize crime and to reduce the number of criminals may well be acting (at least to some extent) contrary to the wishes and needs of society. In fact, herein may be found one of the basic reasons why apparently sound programs suggested by persons who seek to advance the cause of criminal justice planning and reform may gain so little societal support —and may, indeed, arouse considerable opposition.

Closely related to man's basic psychological need to find outlets for aggression that are morally and socially acceptable is what psychoanalysts have described as man's instinctive need or desire to wreak vengeance upon criminals and others who threaten his existence in society. According to Franz Alexander and Hugo Staub, the punishment of criminals reflects "an instinctive demand which is active in every living being and is independent of social agencies. . . . Every animal strikes back with hate at the one who attacks it."[34] Or, to employ the terminology of David Abrahamsen, the punishment of criminals expresses "the self-preservation instinct within the group."[35] Be this as it may, legal historians are convinced that *one of the main ways in which the law has traditionally succeeded in keeping the peace has been to substitute vengeance by society against criminals* (often in the form of cruel penal sanctions) *for private vengeance against them.*[36] To quote from *The Common Law* by Oliver Wendell Holmes, Jr.: "The first requirement of a sound body of law is, that it should correspond with the actual feelings and demands of the community, whether right or wrong. If people would gratify the passion of revenge outside of the law, if the law did not help them, the law has no choice but to satisfy the craving itself, and thus avoid the greater evil of private retribution."[37] But if this viewpoint is sound, then persons concerned with criminal justice planning and reform must take into account the possibility that if they design programs that will reduce the vengefulness of the criminal law, they may well be courting private vengeance—and with it, social disorder. Admittedly, there are many persons who believe that retributive and vengeful punishments are unworthy of man—that, in the words of Ramsey Clark: "The day . . . when vengeance could have any moral justification passed centuries ago."[38] Yet, as Robert Waelder has observed, such statements do not really prove the absence in man of strong retributive urges.

> Many people have taken a stand against the principle of retribution altogether and have denounced it as a relic of barbarian times. This fact may suggest that the request for punishment of the offender is not a universal need of the human mind. But it turns out upon closer examination that the opponents of retribution are actually not what they claim to be; they are not free of the wish that "evil" men should be punished but have merely changed the object of their retributive strivings. While they do not feel that the criminal is guilty and should be punished, they are yet in a fully retributive mood towards "society," "the ruling class," the judges, etc. They are no exceptions from the rule that punishment appears to us as a postulate of justice; they have merely turned the tables and substituted the "respectable" citizen for the lawbreaker in their penitentiary.[39]

In short, persons interested in criminal justice planning and reform must understand that if the programs that they devise succeed in eliminating vengeance from the criminal law—and as a result, the criminal law fails to serve man's retributive and other inner needs (for example, the basic psychological needs stressed in this paper of obtaining acceptable outlets for aggression, finding ways of reinforcing the superego, and alleviating the guilt engendered by the superego)—men may no longer use the law to obtain justice against criminals, but may resort instead to private vengeance, a state of affairs that no viable modern industrial state could possibly tolerate for long. As Morris R. Cohen has put it: "The sentiment that injuries should be avenged . . . cannot be ignored within the life of any community. . . . If the natural desire for vengeance is not met and satisfied by the orderly procedure of the criminal law we shall revert to the more bloody private vengeance of the feud and of the vendetta."[40]

Like so many of the other conclusions suggested in the preceding pages that were based upon psychoanalytic insights, the conclusion suggested above that the vengefulness now inherent in the criminal law may prove of value in helping to keep men from taking the law into their own hands would appear, at least at first sight, to lend credence to the charge frequently made by sociologists that applying psychoanalytic psychology to the problem of crime leads (in the terminology of Richard Cloward) to a "conservative definition" of crime—to a way of approaching crime that seeks "no kind of institutional change or realignment," but "only individual acceptance of and conformity to the way things are."[41] To someone familiar with the history and development of psychoanalytic psychology, however—who knows, for instance, that (certainly prior to World War I) Freud was regarded by many of his "respectable" contemporaries as a dangerous psychopath whose theories posed a grave threat to civilization[42]—the charge that psychoanalytic psychology, in effect, urges men "to preserve the *status quo*"[43] is very difficult to accept. For one thing, psychoanalysts are very much aware that "mere conformity or 'adjustment' to a given culture does not constitute normality";[44] and as a result, most psychoanalysts would probably agree with Erich Fromm that the proper aim of psychoanalytic therapy "is not primarily adjustment but optimal development of a person's potentialities and the realization of his individuality."[45] Further, psychoanalytic psychology is by no means consistent with the basic values of all societies (for example, the values of self-realization, independence, freedom, and truth implicit in psychoanalytic theory and method[46] appear to be contrary to the major values implicit in the more immediate actions and goals of the leaders of the Soviet Union; and on this basis, it may be possible to understand why psychoanalysis has, in effect, been outlawed in the Soviet Union[47]). Even more to the point, however, there are certain psychoanalytic insights regarding the motivation of criminals that would surely appear to require changes in the way in which society now deals with these criminals. For instance, psychoanalysts have discovered that certain persons commit crimes with the unconscious intent of being caught and punished. These "criminals from a sense of guilt" (to use Freud's apt phrase) are beset by considerable unconscious guilt; and to help assuage this guilt, these persons commit crimes in such a way as to virtually ensure apprehension and punishment.[48] (On this basis, it is possible to understand why, for example, certain criminals return to the scene of their crimes—and into the waiting arms of the police; or why other criminals in effect autograph their crimes by using a self-identifying *modus operandi*—and thus ensure apprehension and punishment.) But if certain persons commit crimes with the unconscious aim of being caught and punished, then *by punishing such persons* (as is society's present practice), *the law may actually encourage—rather than discourage—the commission of crimes by them.* Hence some change would certainly seem to be required in society's reaction to these offenders, if law enforcement agencies are to avoid becoming (at least in regard to these "criminals from a sense of guilt") what Helen Silving has described as "unwitting tools of the offender."[49]

It may well be that offering some appropriate form of psychoanalytic therapy to "criminals from a sense of guilt"—and, indeed, to other offenders as well—would be a more desirable societal reaction to their conduct than punishment. Unfortunately, however (and contrary to the hopeful views of many psychoanalytically-oriented case workers), there are a number of reasons having to do with the requisites and characteristics of the psychoanalytic process why psychoanalytic therapy is unlikely (except, perhaps, in atypical cases or under unusual circumstances) to prove effective in regard to criminals. For one thing, psychoanalysis requires of the analysand that he be sufficiently articulate and have sufficient intelligence and self-control to be able to talk out (rather than having to act out) the anti-social urgencies that beset him—characteristics that, to say the least, hardly typify the average juvenile delinquent or criminal. Also, psychoanalysis is an extraordinarily laborious and time-consuming procedure; and as a result, the cost of offering psychoanalytic therapy to criminals (unless, perhaps, some form of group therapy were used[50]) would clearly be prohibitive—especially since there is a paucity of psychoanalysts at the present time and literally tens of thousands of additional psychoanalysts would have to be trained. Further, even with the most skilled of psychoanalysts and the most tractable of patients, the success of psychoanalytic therapy must always be considered problematical—which is, of course, anything but a hopeful omen for the psychoanalyst faced with the extraordinarily difficult task of treating criminals who are likely to be highly suspicious, almost surely resentful, and probably as uncooperative as they dare to be.[51]

By no means is all this to say that psychoanalytic psychology is of little or no value in dealing with criminals or crime. What it is to say, however, is that psychoanalytic *therapy* ought not to be regarded by persons concerned with criminal justice planning and reform as *the* psychoanalytic solution to the problem of crime (psychoanalytically-oriented case workers to the contrary notwithstanding). In fact, if any psychoanalytic "solution" to the problem of crime does exist (which, certainly at this time, seems doubtful), it would probably have to do with the light that psychoanalytic psychology is able to shed upon child rearing: upon methods of bringing up children that would enable their superegos (without engendering undue guilt) to control successfully the criminalistic urges that inevitably seek access to consciousness and motility.[52] In any event, however, there can be little doubt that, as this paper has attempted to reveal, some of the major implications in psychoanalytic psychology for criminal justice planning and reform pertain to the unconscious and urgent psychic needs of the law-abiding that the criminal law and the treatment of criminals help to fulfill. Indeed, if there is any lesson regarding crime and criminals implicit in psychoanalytic psychology for persons interested in criminal justice planning and reform, it is that before proposing reforms in the criminal law and in the administration of criminal justice, considerable thought should be given to the possible effect of these reforms *upon the law-abiding*. To fail to do this (and thereby to fail, perhaps, to pay sufficient attention to the psychic needs of the law-abiding) is to run the risk that the reforms proposed are likely to prove unacceptable or unenforceable—or even if accepted and enforced, to prove more harmful than the conditions they were intended to remedy.

NOTES

[1] The ambit of the Omnibus Crime Control and Safe Streets Act of 1968 is discussed in detail in brochures published by the Law Enforcement Assistance Administration. See, *e.g.*, the brochure entitled "A Program For A Safer, More Just America" (1970).

[2] An outline of a number of psychological systems that may conceivably prove relevant to criminal justice planning and reform is to be found in Hall & Lindzey, Theories of Personality (2d ed. 1970). Factor or trait theory, for instance (outlined in chapter ten of this book) has already been applied in a most interesting fashion to the problem of preventing recidivism among criminals. See the Preliminary Report of the Governor's Special Committee On Criminal Offenders 286-316, which was submitted to Governor Rockefeller of New York on June 24, 1968.

[3] Robinson, Law And The Lawyers 111 (1935).

[4] Flugel, Man, Morals, And Society 190 (Compass Books ed. 1961).

[5] Jones, Hamlet And Oedipus 85 (Doubleday Anchor ed. 1955).

[6] Freud, Civilization And Its Discontents 85 (1930).

[7] A short but incisive summary of the views of George Sutherland regarding crime as learned behavior is to be found in Cressey, *The Development of a Theory: Differential Association*, in Wolfgang & Savitz & Johnston, The Sociology Of Crime And Delinquency 81-90 (1962).

[8] For a brief critique of this Marxist dogma, see Patterson, Jurisprudence: Men and Ideas of the Law 436-38 (1953).

[9] For a concise and fascinating account of the theories and influence upon criminology of William Bonger, see Radzinowicz, Ideology And Crime 42-46 (1966).

[10] Typically, sociologists tend to de-emphasize the effect upon man of instincts, drives, needs, and so on, and to emphasize instead the influence upon him of social and cultural conditions. See, *e.g.*, Faris, *The Discipline Of Sociology*, in Handbook Of Modern Sociology 1, 6 (1964).

[11] The superego includes what is meant by the term "conscience," but is in large measure unconscious. For a description of the moral functions exercised by the superego, see Brenner, An Elementary Textbook of Psychoanalysis 125 (Doubleday Anchor ed. 1957).

[12] See Jones, *The Genesis Of The Super-Ego*, in Papers on Psycho-Analysis 145-52 (5th ed. 1950), for a short but authoritative summary of modern psychoanalytic theory concerning the superego. For a study in depth of the way in which the superego functions, see Flugel, *op. cit. supra* note 4.

[13] See West, Conscience And Society 165-69 (1945).

[14] Relevant here is Weihofen, The Urge to Punish 28 (1956).

[15] Flugel, *op. cit. supra* note 4, at 133.

[16] See, *e.g.*, Kadish, *The Crisis of Overcriminalization*, 374, The Annals of The American Academy of Political and Social Science 157-70 (1967).

[17] See, *e.g.*, Barnes & Teeters, New Horizons In Criminology 372-78 (3d ed. 1959).

[18] See Alexander & Staub, The Criminal, The Judge, And The Public 209-23 (Rev. ed. 1956), for an excellent summary of psychoanalytic discoveries concerning the punishment of criminals.

[19] Ideas and urges relegated to an unconscious level ordinarily fail to "grow up" or change with the passage of time: if originally infantile, they tend to remain so throughout life. See Freud, Beyond The Pleasure Principle 33 (1950).

[20] See, *e.g.*, Abrahamsen, The Psychology Of Crime 3 (First Science ed. 1964).

[21] As used in this context by psychoanalysts, the term "identification" is intended to refer to the largely unconscious mechanism or process by which "we appropriate and absorb in our own personality certain values and characteristics associated with others. Through a sort of coalescence of our personalities with persons or objects in the outside world their purposes or qualities are felt to be our own." Noyes, Modern Clinical Psychiatry 29 (3d ed. 1948).

[22] See the excellent psychoanalytic discussion of the antipathy of the law-abiding for criminals in Reiwald, Society And Its Criminals 66-98 (1949). See also Reik, The Compulsion to Confess 167-68 (First Evergreen ed. 1961).

[23] Reiwald, *op. cit. supra* note 22, at 66.

[24] For what is surely a more hopeful view of probation, parole, and other practices designed to minimize the isolation of criminals, see Sutherland, Principles of Criminology 421-42, 544-88 (5th ed. 1955).

[25] Alexander & Staub, *op. cit. supra* note 18, at 215.

[26] Abrahamsen, *op. cit. supra* note 20, at 3.

[27] See, *e.g.*, Clark, Crime in America 219-20 (1970).

[28] See, Reiwald, *op. cit. supra* note 22, at 246-82; Wittels, Freud And His Time 378-83 (1931).

[29] R. Eissler, *Scapegoats Of Society,* in K.R. Eissler, Searchlights On Delinquency 288, 295 (1949).

[30] A description of these and many other horrible punishments once inflicted upon criminals is to be found in Laurence, A History Of Capital Punishment (1960).

[31] For particularly horrifying summations of the effect of imprisonment, see Menninger, The Crime Of Punishment 71-81 (1968); Clark, *op. cit. supra* note 27, at 212-38.

[32] See, *e.g.*, R. Eissler, *op. cit. supra* note 29, at 295, 304-05.

[33] Menninger, *op. cit. supra* note 31, at 153.

[34] Alexander & Staub, *op. cit. supra* note 18, at 218.

[35] Abrahamsen, *op. cit. supra* note 20, at 3.

[36] See *e.g.*, Pound, *The End of Law as Developed in Legal Rules and Doctrines,* 27 Harv. L. Rev. 195, 200 (1914); Harding, *Individual Responsibility In Anglo-American Law,* in Responsibility In Law And In Morals 41-79 (1960).

[37] Holmes, The Common Law 41 (1881).

[38] Clark, *op. cit. supra* note 27, at 218.

[39] Waelder, *Psychiatry And The Problem Of Criminal Responsibility,* 101 U. Pa. L. Rev. 378, 386-87 (1952).

[40] Cohen, Reason and Law 54 (Collier Books ed. 1961).

[41] Martin & Fitzpatric, Delinquent Behavior 106 (1964).

[42] Jones, 2 The Life and Work of Sigmund Freud 108-09 (1955).

[43] Martin & Fitzpatric, *op. cit. supra* note 41.

[44] Roche, The Criminal Mind 22 (1st Evergreen ed. 1959).

[45] Fromm, Psychoanalysis and Religion 74 (1950).

[46] See, *e.g.*, Schoenfeld, *Psychoanalytic Guideposts For The Good Society,* 55 Psychoanalytic Review 91 (1968).

[47] See, *e.g.*, Fedorov, *The Soviet View of Psychoanalysis,* 9 Monthly Review, No. 8 (1957).

[48] Freud, *Some Character-Types Met With In Psycho-Analytic Work,* 4 Collected Papers 342-44 (1956).

[49] Silving, *Psychoanalysis And The Criminal Law,* 51 J. Crim. L., C. & P.S. 19, 23 (1960).

[50] Group psychotherapy may be the one great hope of successfully employing psychoanalytic therapy in the treatment of a meaningful number of juvenile delinquents and criminals. See, *e.g.*, Aichhorn, Wayward Youth 111-43 (Meridian Books ed., 1955).

[51] For a detailed—and a more sanguine—view of the psychoanalytic treatment of

juvenile delinquents and criminals, see the relevant sections of Glover, *The Roots Of Crime* (1960); Friedlander, *The Psycho-Analytical Approach To Juvenile Delinquency* (1947).

[52] See, *e.g.,* Schoenfeld, *A Psychoanalytic Theory Of Juvenile Delinquency* (to appear in 1971 in *Crime And Delinquency*).

VI.

DIVERSION FROM THE CRIMINAL JUSTICE SYSTEM

INNER-CITY YOUTH, THE POLICE, THE JUVENILE COURT AND JUSTICE

Theodore N. Ferdinand

Elmer G. Luchterhand

The fact that black adolescents receive harsher treatment than whites at the hands of the police and courts has been well documented in the criminological literature. A large number of studies show essentially that black youths are more likely to be questioned on the street (Piliavin and Briar, 1964: 212); if questioned, they are more likely to be arrested (Piliavin and Briar, 1964:212); if arrested, they are more likely to be sent to court (Goldman, 1963:35-47); and if sent to court, they are more likely to receive a severe disposition than whites (Axelrod, 1952:569-574). In the face of this evidence many observers have concluded that the legal institutions of our society discriminate systematically and broadly against blacks.

But this judgment may be somewhat premature, for other factors besides racial discrimination may be contrib- uting to this singular pattern. Female delinquents, for example, are also dealt with more harshly by the police and courts; and the reason seems to be that female offenders as a class present more serious behavioral disorders and greater disturbances in the family than male delinquents (Hathaway and Monachesi, 1953; Toby, 1957). Thus, as far as girls are concerned, the police and courts intervene more frequently and more actively, for simply to return them to their usual environment would probably be more detrimental to the girl than utilizing other avenues of "treatment."

It is conceivable that somewhat the same situation may prevail with black adolescents. The police and the courts may be influenced in their treatment of black youths by assumptions regarding the anti-social nature of their attitudes and by disorganization in their homes and neighborhoods (Werthman and Piliavin, 1967: 72-74).

The validity of this hypothesis has not yet been examined directly because the young people in question were generally unavailable to researchers interested in this issue. But the present study does permit an evaluation of the problem, since in addition to official police and court records, we have obtained extensive information regarding the personal values and attitudes and the social backgrounds of a large sample of adolescents, representative of a middle-sized city.

METHOD

A random sample of 1,525 teenagers in six inner-city neighborhoods was selected in 1964, and their attitudes and behavior in a large number of areas were assessed by means of both interviews and questionnaires.[1] A complete listing of the teenagers in our sample was compared with the files of the Youth Division of the Easton Police, the Easton Juvenile Court, and the Central Arrest Bureau in Capital City; and from these sources a record of each adolescent in our sample who had come to the attention of the police or the courts in the state was obtained.[2] Altogether some information on 408 adolescents, or 27 percent of our sample, was obtained in this fashion. Inevitably, however, there were gaps in the records of some, with the result that complete information was available on 324 teenagers, or 21 percent of the total sample.

The analysis was guided by three basic questions: First, what is the treatment accorded black and white teenagers by the police and juvenile court of Easton? Second, are there any differences in the values, attitudes, or social backgrounds of black and white delinquents that might account for the treatment accorded them by the court and police? And, finally, are these differences unique to our delinquent sample, or are they paralleled by differences in the broader, non-delinquent sample as well?

RESULTS

Whether the police treat white and black teenagers in the same way can be answered by examining Table 1, in which the dispositions of first offenders by the Easton police are given. It is clear from this table that, indeed, black teenagers are labeled as delinquent by the police and refererd to the juvenile court disproportionately more often than their white counterparts.

However, differences in Table 1 need not reflect racial discrimination on the part of the police. It could be that black delinquents are committing more serious crimes, or that they include more females who typically require court intervention more frequently, or that they are older and therefore more likely to have been involved with the police. Examination of Tables 2, 3, 4, and 5 reveals that none of these hypotheses is valid.

In Table 2, the police dispositions are analyzed in terms of the type of crime involved; and for all three types, blacks were classified as pre-delinquent disproportionately *less* often than whites. The difference is greatest for Other Offenses, which includes juvenile crimes, sex offenses, and violations of public ordinances, and least for Crimes Against the Person; but it is consistently there.

Moreover, when Tables 3 and 4 are

TABLE 1

POLICE DISPOSITION OF FIRST OFFENDERS BY RACE[1]

| Race | Police Disposition[2] | | | |
	Pre-delinquent[3]	Delinquent[4]	Total	
	%	%	%	N
White	37	63	100	110
Black	24	76	100	178
Total	29	71	100	288

[1] The χ^2 for this table is 5.65, d.f. = 1, p < .02.

[2] There were several dispositions available to the police which were not easily assessed by the researchers (informal warning, and referred to Circuit Court) or which had little bearing upon the questions under research (referred to Juvenile Court by the Circuit Court). The two categories presented here, however, do give an indication of the arresting policies of the Easton police regarding black and white teenagers.

[3] Pre-delinquent refers to a probation-like disposition in which the police agree not to pursue the youth's case further if he does not get into any further trouble.

[4] Delinquent is the disposition that youths routinely get who are referred to Juvenile Court.

TABLE 2

POLICE DISPOSITION BY TYPE OF OFFENSE AND RACE[1]

Nature of Offense	Pre-delinquent	Delinquent	Total	
	%	%	%	N
Against Person[2]				
White	50	50	100	16
Black	35	65	100	54
Against Property[3]				
White	35	65	100	65
Black	20	80	100	98
Other[4]				
White	34	66	100	29
Black	15	85	100	26

[1] The sample includes all first offenders, i.e., boys and girls.

[2] Includes all forms of violent, abusive behavior directed at the individual.

[3] Includes all forms of theft, burglary, vandalism, and fraud.

[4] Includes juvenile crimes, i.e., truancy, runaway and incorrigibility, sex offenses, and offenses against public ordinances, e.g., motor vehicle, liquor and firearms violations, and a miscellaneous category.

examined it can be seen that the difference in disposition by race does not result from a preponderance of girls among black offenders. Indeed, among males only it can be seen that racial differences in police dispositions remain strong (Table 3) whereas among females the difference in disposition seems to disappear (Table 4). Although black males are treated more harshly by the police, black females are not.

In Table 5, the age distribution of first offenders is examined in terms of race; and the absence of any substantial difference in age between the

TABLE 3
POLICE DISPOSITION BY OFFENSE AND RACE FOR MALE FIRST OFFENDERS

Nature of Offense	Pre-delinquent	Delinquent	Total	
	%	%	%	N
Against Person[1]				
White	53	47	100	15
Black	39	61	100	36
Against Property[2]				
White	36	64	100	59
Black	19	81	100	86
Other[3]				
White	41	59	100	22
Black	9	91	100	11
Total[4]				
White	39	61	100	98
Black	23	77	100	133

[1] The χ^2 for this portion of the table with 1 degree of freedom is not significant.
[2] The χ^2 for this portion of the table is 4.67, d.f. $= 1$, p $< .05$.
[3] The χ^2 with Yates correction for this portion of the table with 1 degree of freedom is not significant.
[4] The χ^2 for this portion of the table is 6.39, d.f. $= 1$, p $< .02$.

races suggests that this factor cannot be responsible for the differences cited in Table 1.

It is clear, then, that the harsher dispositions received by blacks, as described in Table 1, cannot be explained as a result of the types of offenses blacks commit, nor as a result of imbalances in the age or sex distribution of black offenders.

Social Attitudes and Police Disposition

It may be, however, that black offenders exhibit more seriously anti-social values and attitudes or present more deeply disturbed social backgrounds. The police generally take both of these factors into account (Goldman, 1963:120-124) when deciding the fate of a youngster; and if black males make poorer impressions on either count, it could explain why they are given more severe dispositions. To examine this possibility, white and black offenders were compared on a series of measures that assessed behavior patterns, values and attitudes, and the quality of home life. Although the results were not entirely consistent, they do suggest overall that black offenders are *less* anti-social and *less* aggressive than white offenders in the inner-city neighborhoods.

To begin, let us examine the behavior patterns of these two groups of offenders. Fifty-six items were included in our testing instruments that assessed the behavior patterns of adolescents, among which factor analysis revealed ten distinct factors.[3] Table 6 provides a comparison of white and black male offenders on each factor.

The most interesting finding in this table is the fact that there were few differences between the two groups on those factors that were clearly assessing delinquent or delinquent-like behavior. The factors measuring General Delinquency, School Misconduct, and Row-

TABLE 4

POLICE DISPOSITION BY OFFENSE AND RACE FOR FEMALE FIRST OFFENDERS

Nature of Offense	Pre-delinquent	Delinquent	Total	
	%	%	%	N
Against Person				
White	0	100	100	1
Black	28	72	100	18
Against Property				
White	50	50	100	4
Black	33	67	100	12
Other				
White	14	86	100	7
Black	20	80	100	15
Total[1]				
White	25	75	100	12
Black	27	73	100	45

[1] The χ^2 for this portion of the table is not significant.

TABLE 5

DISTRIBUTION OF MALE OFFENDERS BY AGE AND RACE[1]

	Age at First Offense				
	7-12	13-14	15+	Total	
	%	%	%	%	N
Race					
White	43	28	29	100	114
Black	40	37	23	100	149
Total	41	33	26	100	263

[1] The χ^2 for this table is not significant.

diness all failed to distinguish white and black offenders. Similarly, that factor measuring the antithesis of delinquent behavior, Principled Individualism, failed to distinguish the two groups of offenders. Only Defiance of Parental Authority, Minor Delinquency, and Gregarious Mischief differentiated the two groups; and of these, black offenders scored higher on only one, Gregarious Mischief. White offenders were significantly higher on Defiance of Parental Authority and Minor Delinquency, both of which are probably more serious in terms of deviant behavior than Gregarious Mis-

chief. These results suggest, therefore, that any major differences in anti-social inclinations that exist between white and black offenders in our inner-city sample favor the latter. Black offenders seem less anti-social and defiant of conventional normative patterns than white offenders.

These same differences between whites and blacks are also repeated in the larger, non-delinquent sample, which may mean that they are largely irrelevant to the dispositions meted out to offenders by the police. But it is clear that if the offenders' anti-social tendencies were basically responsible

TABLE 6

TEN FACTORS ASSESSING BEHAVIOR ACCORDING TO RACE[1]

Factor[2]	Mean Score of White Offenders	Mean Score of Black Offenders	t-ratio of difference
General Delinquency	0.51	0.72	1.08
School Misconduct	—0.23	—0.26	0.19
Rowdiness	0.26	0.02	1.59
Principled Individualism	—0.10	—0.14	0.29
Defiance of Parental Authority	0.18	—0.29	3.62**
Minor Delinquency	0.48	—0.04	2.58**
Gregarious Mischief	—0.61	—0.40	1.74*
Adventurous Dating	0.30	—0.06	2.08*
Participation in Community Recreation	0.02	—0.40	3.24**
Helping in the Home	—0.71	—0.06	4.82**

[1] This table is based on 106 whites and 157 blacks.
[2] A high score indicates a high degree of the factor.
 * Significant at the five percent level.
** Significant at the one percent level.

TABLE 7

AGGRESSION AND RACE[1]

Item[2]	Mean Score of White Offenders	Mean Score of Black Offenders	t-ratio of difference
"If anyone should stand in Ann's way, she would. . ."	5.24	4.80	.99
"When something gets me real mad I. . ."	3.26	2.38	2.21*
"If somebody tries to push me around, I usually. . ."	2.26	3.12	4.00**
"If somebody tries to push me around, I should. . ."	2.72	3.40	3.20**

[1] This table is based upon 111 white and 149 black males.
[2] The first two items were coded such that a large mean score indicates greater physical aggressiveness. The last two were coded such that a small mean score indicates greater physical aggressiveness.
 * Significant at the five percent level.
** Significant at the one percent level.

for the relatively harsh dispositions given blacks, the results would not have shown this pattern.

The remaining factors, i.e., Adventurous Dating, Participation in Community Recreation, and Helping in the Home, all distinguish white offenders from black offenders, but in every case the nature of the difference paralleled precisely the differences between blacks and whites in our larger sample. Thus, these differences are probably more relevant to the differences between white and black youngsters generally than between white and black offenders.

When we look at the aggressive tendencies of the two offender groups, again it can be seen that white offenders

TABLE 8
EIGHT ATTITUDINAL FACTORS BY RACE[1]

Factor	Mean Score of White Offenders	Mean Score of Black Offenders	t-ratio of difference
Trouble Expectation	0.02	0.03	0.41
School Appreciation	—0.13	—0.10	0.99
Anxiety	0.06	0.10	1.59
Familism	—0.06	—0.08	0.66
Unprincipled Expediency	0.02	—0.02	3.46**
Authority Rejection[2]	—0.03	—0.07	1.77*
Apathetic Disorientation[2]	0.05	0.10	2.17*
Opportunity Pessimism	—0.01	—0.09	4.18**

[1] This table is based on 139 white and 180 black males.
[2] A low score indicates a high degree of the factor.
* Significant at five percent level.
** Significant at the one percent level.

are more anti-social than the blacks. The adolescents' reactions to four open-ended sentences that assessed aggressive tendencies are given in Table 7. The white offenders in each case are more physically aggressive than the blacks, indicati..g perhaps greater anti-social tendencies in the former. These results parallel the findings for the total group, i.e., white teenagers in general are more physically aggressive than black teenagers; consequently our finding for the two groups of offenders may represent the influence of general social patterns more than anything else. But if the aggressiveness of the young offender was influencing his disposition by the police, we might have expected black *offenders* to show more physical aggressiveness than white *offenders;* instead we find the reverse. Turning now to the offenders' broader values and attitudes, it is apparent from Table 8 that most of those attitudes and values indicative of anti-social tendencies either fail to distinguish white and black offenders or show blacks to be less anti-social than whites.[4] Those factors most closely

associated with delinquent behavior, .i.e., Trouble Expectation and School Appreciation, fail to distinguish between the two groups; and the same is true for those factors indicating personal stress and feelings toward family, i.e., Anxiety and Familism. Black offenders, it is true, do exhibit a greater degree of Authority Rejection than whites, but on the remaining factors, i.e., Unprincipled Expediency, Apathetic Disorientation, and Opportunity Pessimism, white offenders score higher.

The most interesting finding in these results is the fact that Authority Rejection alone among the eight attitudinal factors shows black offenders to be more anti-social than the white offenders. Black offenders were either indistinguishable from or exhibited a more conventional response than their white counterparts on all the other factors. Since Authority Rejection is an attitude that is likely to be quite obvious to an arresting officer, it may well be that the Easton police take this factor into account when about to make a disposition (cf. Piliavin and Briar,

TABLE 9
MEAN REJECTION OF AUTHORITY BY RACE, OFFENSE AND DISPOSITION[1]

Race of Offenders	Police Disposition				Referred to Juvenile Ct. from Circuit Ct.[7]	
	Pre-delinquents		Delinquents			
	$\bar{x}$	n	$\bar{x}$	n	$\bar{x}$	n
Offenders Against Person						
White	−0.02[2]	8	−0.15[3]	7	0.13[2, 3]	5
Black	−0.04	14	−0.07	21	—	—
Offenders Against Property						
White	−0.04	25	−0.04	37	−0.10	6
Black	0.01[4, 5]	17	−0.10[4]	69	−0.06[5]	11
Other Offenders						
White	−0.07[6]	9	−0.02	12	0.15[6]	5
Black	−0.09	4	−0.11	11	0.01	1

[1] A low mean score indicates a high degree of Authority Rejection.

[2, 3, 4, 5, 6] The means with corresponding superscripts are significantly different at the five percent level or better by a t-test.

[7] Referred to Juvenile Court from Circuit Court, strictly speaking, is not a disposition made by the police, but rather a disposition initiated by the Circuit Court. But the youths in question were first referred to the Circuit Court by the police, probably because they were over 16 and had committed a relatively serious offense.

1964:212; Werthman and Piliavin, 1967:74; Goldman, 1963:106).

To evaluate this possibility, we examined the mean level of Authority Rejection, holding race and offense constant (Table 9). It can be seen that white offenders are *not* given a disposition according to the level of Authority Rejection they exhibit.

There are no significant differences on this factor among those whites who are classified as pre-delinquent or delinquent. For black offenders against property, on the other hand, the attitude toward authority does seem to make some difference. They are given more severe dispositions if their attitude toward authority is particularly defiant.

Going one step further, a hint of a similar pattern can be found in the other two types of black offenders as well. Although the differences are not large enough to be significant, black offenders against the person as well as blacks who commit other offenses are given more severe dispositions if their attitudes toward authority are negative. However, this same pattern does not appear consistently among white offenders. White offenders against the person show a tendency to receive more severe dispositions if their attitudes toward authority are rejecting, but white offenders against property and white teen-agers who commit other offenses are clearly not given dispositions in terms of their attitudes toward authority.

From these findings it would appear that black youngsters who come to the attention of the police are given dispositions largely in terms of their superficial attitudes and demeanor toward the police, whereas white offenders are judged by different and probably more basic criteria.

There are two interpretations that might be made of this finding, both of which are probably valid. It may be that because the police are often from the same neighborhoods and quite familiar with many of the white adolescents they ultimately must arrest, they are in a reasonably good position to assess the youth's overall prospects in the community and to adjust their decisions accordingly. But since the Easton police are almost entirely white, they cannot have the same kind of broad familiarity with black delinquents and cannot bring the same informed understanding of *their* situation to their cases. Hence, as far as black delinquents are concerned, the police are forced to make dispositions on the basis of more superficial criteria.

At the same time, it may be that many of the policemen harbor racial prejudice toward blacks in general and use different criteria in evaluating their situation, primarily to punish them with more severe dispositions. These data do not allow an assessment of either of these explanations, although both appear on the surface quite plausible to close observers.

It might also be argued that the direction of causation is just the reverse of that assumed here. It may be that a teenager's attitude toward authority depends basically upon the nature of his experience with the police. Those teenager's who receive more severe dispositions from the police quite naturally are going to resent authority more than those who do not. The fact that in Table 9 those young people who are returned to the Juvenile Court by the Circuit Court often have more positive attitudes toward

authority lends substance to this suggestion. But if this were, indeed, the direction of causation, we would also expect it to hold for those white youths who receive more severe dispositions. As can be seen from Table 9, however, those white teenagers who are classified as "delinquent" by the police do not systematically show more defiant attitudes toward authority than those white teenagers who are classified as "pre-delinquent." It would appear, therefore, that the level of a black youngster's Authority Rejection is an important factor determining his disposition by the police, not the other way around.

It is rather curious that black offenders tend to score high on Authority Rejection but low on Defiance of Parental Authority. It might be expected that these factors would be closely related, but Table 6 shows that black offenders have significantly lower scores on Defiance of Parental Authority than white offenders. This lack of agreement may indicate that Authority Rejection measures the teenagers attitudes toward public authority, while Defiance of Parental Authority tends to assess the attitudes toward his own parents. The lack of consistency between these two factors probably indicates that black youngsters tend to expect the worst from public (i.e., white) authority figures but that they have more positive attitudes toward those authority figures closer to home. As has been indicated, since their attitudes toward public figures condition the actions such figures take toward black youngsters, these attitudes can constitute a self-fulfilling prophecy.

*Family Background and
Police Disposition*

Finally, let us examine the family relationships of the offenders. We were able to assess not only the formal structure of their families but also the quality of relationships they experienced there; and the results suggest that although white offenders came from complete families[5] more often, their relationships in the home were typically more discordant than those experienced by black offenders. Table 10 indicates the responses of offenders to the question "Do you live with . . . ?". The results show that less than half of our sample of black offenders were from complete families. At the same time Table 11 clearly in-dicates that there is less discord in the families of black offenders than in white offenders' families.[6]

In view of the picture presented here, it seems likely that the police are taking into account the offender's family structure when making a disposition of his case and that some of the difference in dispositions handed out to whites and blacks can be explained in terms of this practice by the police (See Goldman, 1963:131 for a similar conclusion). At the same time it is also quite clear that they are not attending to the less obvious qualities of family life in making their disposition; for if

TABLE 10
FAMILY STRUCTURE OF WHITE AND BLACK OFFENDERS[1]

| Race | Family Structure | | | | | | | |
	Mother and Father	Mother Only	Mother and Other Relative	Father Only	Father and Other Relative	Other	Total	
	%	%	%	%	%	%	%	N
Blacks	46	2	17	0	2	33	100	247
Whites	68	2	5	2	1	22	100	161

[1] This table is based on the total sample of offenders including those for whom information on official misconduct is incomplete.

TABLE 11
FAMILY RELATIONSHIPS OF WHITE AND BLACK OFFENDERS[1]

Factor	Mean Factor Score of White Offenders	Mean Factor Score of Black Offenders	t-ratio of difference
Estrangement from Family[2]	−0.46	−0.48	0.19
Parental Permissiveness[3]	0.25	0.36	0.80
Seeking Parental Advice[4]	0.01	0.01	0.02
Family Discord	0.00	0.26	1.92*

[1] This table is based upon 146 black and 89 white males. There was some attrition of cases making these groups somewhat smaller than in other tables.
[2] The higher the score, the *lower* the estrangement from family.
[3] The higher the score, the *greater* the parental permissiveness.
[4] The higher the score, the *greater* the seeking of parental advice.
[5] The higher the score, the *lower* the family discord.
* Significant at the five percent level.

they were, blacks would not be given more severe dispositions than whites. Thus, a broken home may have quite different implications in the two racial groups.

In sum then, we have examined the behavioral characteristics, the aggression patterns, the attitudes and values, and the family relationships of the two groups of offenders. In general, the results indicate that black offenders are less anti-social and less aggressive than white offenders but that they are also more rejecting of public authority and more likely to come from incomplete families. In spite of the rather promising picture black offenders generally present, however, the factors that seem to weigh most heavily upon the police in making their dispositions of black youths are their level of Authority Rejection and the structure of their families. In view of this it would seem that greater sensitivity on the part of the police to the nature of black experience would result in a more equitable handling of their cases.

Nature of Offense and Police Disposition

The importance of race, however, tends to diminish as more dramatic factors enter the picture (See Goldman, 1963:127). In Table 12, in which dispositions of *third* offenders are presented, it is apparent that white and black offenders are given more comparable dispositions for the same offense.

Along these same lines, when Table 4 is examined, where dispositions handed out to female first offenders are presented, it can be seen that there is little difference between the two racial groups. Female offenders as a rule present a more serious anti-social pattern than male offenders, and the same is true of third offenders in comparison with the first offenders. Furthermore, if Table 2 is re-examined it is apparent that the percent of black offenders classified as pre-delinquent tends to approach the percent of white offenders similarly classified as the of-

TABLE 12

POLICE DISPOSITION BY OFFENSE AND RACE FOR MALE THIRD OFFENDERS

Nature of Offense	Police Disposition					
	Pre-delinquent	Delinquent	Reinvestigation Referral	Sent to Circuit Court	Total	
	%	%	%	%	%	N
Against Person						
White	25	75	—	—	100	4
Black	10	50	30	10	100	10
Against Property						
White	11	78	—	11	100	18
Black	3	89	5	3	100	35
Other						
White	—	67	—	33	100	3
Black	8	58	8	25	99	12
Total[1]						
White	12	76	—	12	100	25
Black	5	75	11	9	100	57

[1] The χ^2 for this portion of the table was not significant.

fense becomes more serious, i.e., as we move from Other Offenses, to Offenses Against Property, to Offenses Against the Person. In terms of this pattern, then, it would seem that when a youth's delinquency is rather pronounced, his disposition is made primarily in terms of factors immediately relevant to his case; but when delinquency is relatively mild, racial membership is a factor in his disposition.

A third factor that also seems to influence an offender's disposition is the policy of the Juvenile Court toward his particular offense. Table 13 reports the dispositions handed out to offenders in terms of their offenses; and it appears, though only weakly, that the police give *less* harsh dispositions to those youngsters who commit offenses against the person than those who commit offenses against property. On the surface this finding is puzzling, since crimes against the person are generally regarded by both the police and the courts as more serious than crimes against property. It might be anticipated, therefore, that both the police and courts would treat crimes against the person more harshly. The answer, however, is contained in Table 14 where the dispositions meted out by the Juvenile Court for different types of crimes is presented. There it seems that the Juvenile Court does

tend to make more severe dispositions for crimes against the person than crimes against property. The fact that the police are reluctant to send a boy to the Juvenile Court may mean that they are giving the youngster the full benefit of the doubt, especially when he is likely to receive a severe disposition in the Juvenile Court. Hence, those teenagers who are dealt with most severely by the court seem to be handled most cautiously by the police, (See also Goldman, 1963:101; Wheeler, et al., 1965:48-50).

The Juvenile Court and Race

Another interesting pattern in Table 14 is the apparent lack of discrimination in dispositions by the Juvenile Court. There is some variability in the dispositions given black and white delinquents, but black delinquents do not consistently receive appreciably harsher dispositions from the court than white offenders. As with the police, as the seriousness of the offense increases, the discrepancy between the dispositions given white and black youths seems to decrease. But in this case the discrepancy is so small that it probably reflects in the main the court's interest in intervening when the youth's home situation seems to require it. Black delinquents, as has been shown, come from incom-

TABLE 13

POLICE DISPOSITION BY OFFENSE FOR MALE FIRST OFFENDERS[1]

Nature of Offense	Police Disposition			
	Pre-delinquent	Delinquent	Total	
	%	%	%	N
Against Person	43	57	100	51
Against Property	25	75	100	147
Other	30	70	100	33
Total	30	70	100	231

[1] The χ^2 for this table is 5.89, d.f. = 2, p < .07.

TABLE 14

JUVENILE COURT DISPOSITION BY OFFENSE AND RACE
FOR MALE FIRST OFFENDERS

Nature of Offense	Nolle	Warning	Court Disposition			Total	
			Unoff. or Official Probation	Fine or Agency Referral	Confinement		
	%	%	%	%	%	%	N
Against Person							
White	—	60	20	20	—	100	5
Black	—	61	8	23	8	100	13
Against Property							
White	—	90	5	2	2	99	42
Black	—	86	3	5	6	100	66
Other							
White	5	89	4	2	—	100	45
Black	—	83	10	5	2	100	41
Total[1]							
White	2	88	5	3	1	100	92
Black	—	82	6	7	5	100	120

[1] The χ^2 for this portion of the table is not significant.

plete family situations more often than whites. The court's more active intervention in the lives of blacks may reflect its concern with this fact rather than discrimination.

This interpretation is supported in Table 15 where the family situation of white and black delinquents is presented. Although the number of youngsters who receive dispositions other than "Warning" for first offenses is too few to allow firm conclusions, it does seem, at least for offenses against property, that a youth from an incomplete family runs a slightly greater risk of receiving a disposition other than "Warning" than one from a complete family.

At the same time, however, it also appears that the court is not unreasonably influenced by the teenager's family situation when deciding his disposition. Black youth from incomplete families are not uniformly given more severe dispositions, and whites are seemingly given dispositions regardless of their family situation. Thus, the court responds to the much greater proportion of incomplete families among black offenders by intervening in their situation only slightly more often.

CONCLUSION AND SUMMARY

In this report we have examined the behavioral patterns, values, and attitudes of white and black teenagers in relation to their treatment at the hands of the police and the Juvenile Court. It has been shown that in general there is very little difference between the two groups on those factors that assess delinquent or delinquent-like attitudes. This finding is entirely reasonable since, after all, the police are focusing their attention upon teenagers who have broken the law; and those who have broken the law might be ex-

TABLE 15
JUVENILE COURT DISPOSITION OF FIRST OFFENDERS BY RACE,
OFFENSE, AND FAMILY SITUATION[1]

	Family Situation[2]			
	Complete		Incomplete	
Court Disposition For:	White	Black	White	Black
	%	%	%	%
Offenders Against the Person				
Warning	89	83	100	92
Other	11	17	—	8
	100 (9)	100 (6)	100 (2)	100 (12)
Offenders Against Property				
Warning	96	95	93	88
Other	4	5	7	12
	100 (24)	100 (38)	100 (14)	100 (33)
Other Offenses				
Warning	92	100	100	100
Other	8	—	—	—
	100 (12)	100 (2)	100 (3)	100 (3)
Total[3]				
Warning	93	93	95	90
Other	7	7	5	10
	100 (45)	100 (46)	100 (19)	100 (48)

[1] The figures in parentheses are the totals upon which the percentages are based.
[2] A complete family situation is one in which both biological parents are present.
[3] The χ^2 for this portion of the table is not significant.

pected to score uniformly high on those factors that assess delinquent or delinquent-like attitudes and behavior.

The differences that do arise between whites and blacks appear most consistently in those attitudes and values that are not directly related to law violations. And almost without exception black offenders present a better adjusted picture than the whites. For example, white delinquents were significantly higher on those factors measuring Defiance of Parental Authority, Minor Delinquency, and Adventurous Dating. They were more aggressive physically than black delinquents, and they showed more Unprincipled Expediency, Apathetic Disorientation, Opportunity Pessimism, and Family Discord than blacks. Black teenagers, on the other hand, scored higher on the factors measuring Gregarious Mischief and Authority Rejection, and they were from incomplete home situations more often than white offenders. Finally, when dealing with blacks, the police seem much more likely to take into account the youth's manifestations of attitudes toward authority and his family situation in making their dispositions; although when dealing with white teenagers, the police apparently pay little heed to such factors, focusing more upon the nature of the offense and the offender's overall promise in the community.

These results might suggest that the police are practicing racial discrimination to some extent by applying more rigerous standards to blacks. On the other hand, it could be that the police, who are nearly all white, are more familiar with many of the white teenagers they encounter and consequently can bring a broader range of information to bear in deciding what to do in their cases (Goldman, 1963:129; Wilson, 1968:21-23).

The solution to this problem depends upon its cause. If the problem is essentially the result of a lack of familiarity and understanding between the police and black adolescents, the solution is rather straight-foward. The police should attempt to recruit proportionately as many black officers as blacks appear among delinquents. When parity has been achieved, we can probably anticipate that black police officers will have the same kind of relationship with black teenagers as white officers now do with white teenagers. Under these conditions, it might be anticipated that those black youth who show considerable promise in the community would be dealt with informally in the family and neighborhood rather than formally by the Juvenile Court. Thus, a chronic pattern of injustice would be avoided; the great gap between the police and the black community would to some extent be closed.

APPENDIX A

Definitions of ten behavioral factors in Table 6. Only the four most heavily weighted items in each factor are listed.

I. General Delinquency

		Factor Loadings
1.	"Beat up" on kids who hadn't done anything to you	.68
2.	Broken into a place	.67
3.	Hurt or inflicted pain on someone else just to see him squirm	.65
4.	Forced kids to give you money	.64

II. Principled Individualism

1.	Stood up for something you believed in, even when everybody else seemed to disagree	.67
2.	Stood up for a friend who was unpopular	.65
3.	Admitted doing wrong when you could have said nothing	.56
4.	Gone without something so that a member of your family could have something that he wanted	.56

III. Adventurous Dating

1.	Gone on double dates	.77
2.	Necked	.69
3.	Gone to dances	.59
4.	Gone on blind dates	.57

IV. Participation in Community Recreation

1.	Stayed after school to help teacher with something	.68
2.	Played ping-pong or tennis	.68
3.	Played checkers or chess	.60
4.	Played a musical instrument	.56

V. Helping in the Home

1.	Surprised your mother by doing the dishes or cleaning the house	.75
2.	Done housework	.70
3.	Surprised your parents by doing some special jobs	.42
4.	Kept a diary	.39

VI. Defiance of Authority

1.	Disobeyed your parents	.67
2.	Defied your parents' authority to their faces	.52

3. Taken little things (less than $2.00) that did not belong to you   .49
4. Purposely destroyed or damaged property   .47

VII. Gregarious Mischief

1. Played baseball or football   .60
2. Had a fist fight   .58
3. Hung around on street corners   .49
4. Annoyed teachers on purpose   .45

VIII. Minor Delinquency

1. Been arrested for something other than a traffic violation   .60
2. Cheated on tests in school   .51
3. Broken windows on purpose in a building or a car   .49

4. Hurt or inflicted pain on squirm   .39

IX. School Misconduct

1. Been placed on school probation or expelled from school   .54
2. "Run away" from home   .52
3. Skipped school without a legitimate excuse   .46
4. Done your homework   —.52

X. Rowdiness

1. Driven a car without a license   .45
2. Driven a car too fast   .41
3. Purposely damaged property   .41
4. Hurt or inflicted pain on someone to see him squirm   .39

Appendix B

Definition of eight attitudinal factors in Table 8. Where there were more than four items in a factor, only the four most heavily weighted items are listed.

I. Trouble Expectation   Factor Loadings

1. I've been told that I am headed for trouble with the law   .64
2. My teacher thinks I am headed for trouble with the law   .56
3. My mother (or stepmother) thinks I am headed for trouble with the law   .55
4. I will probably have to go to jail sometime   .49

II. School Appreciation

1. Sometimes I wish I could quit school   —.58
2. I never cared much for school   —.62

III. Anxiety

1. I often wonder what the meaning of life really is   .57
2. It gets harder and harder to be sure of anything   .54

3. Most of the time I feel alone   .45
4. Nobody seems to understand me or how I feel   .38

IV. Familism

1. I enjoy letting my parents in on my big moments   .64
2. I enjoy talking over my plans with my parents   .60
3. A person owes his greatest obligation to his family   .46

V. Unprincipled Expediency

1. It's better to stick by what you have than to try new things you're not sure about   .56
2. People should keep promises only when it is to their benefit   .54
3. It makes no difference whether you work or go on relief, just so you get along   .52
4. The only reason for staying in school is to get a better job when you get out   .46

VI. Authority Rejection

   1. Policemen and other officials will tell you one think and do another   .50

   2. Most teachers play favorites   .45

   3. The school counselors don't understand our problems   .44

   4. Police stick their noses into a lot of things that are none of their business   .44

VII. Apathetic Disorientation

   1. I trust the judgment of my friends more often than I do my own judgment   .50

   2. I can't seem to keep my mind on anything   46

   3. I can stick to my work until I have finished it   —.38

   4. I have a great deal of confidence in myself   —.49

VIII. Opportunity Pessimism

   1. I'll never have enough money to go to college   .51

   2. I probably won't be able to do the kind of work I want to do because I won't have enough education   .46

   3. My family can't give me the opportunities that most persons have   .37

   4. A person like me has a pretty good chance of going to college   —.63

APPENDIX C

Definitions of four family factors in Table 11. Only the four most heavily weighted items on each factor are listed.

                                Factor

I. Estrangement from Family   Loadings

   1. My mother or stepmother thinks I am headed for trouble with the law   .65

   2. I say to myself, "What my parents don't know won't hurt them"   .56

   3. No one understands me   .54

   4. A person should not worry what his family thinks of his doings   .53

II. Parental Permissiveness

   1. How much freedom do your parents give you on when to get home at night?   .66

   2. How much freedom do your parents give you on whom to date?   .61

   3. How much freedom do your parents give you on how to dress?   .61

   4. How much freedom do your parents give you on spending your money?   .53

III. Seeking Parental Advice

   1. Who would you go to for advice if you were thinking of quitting school?   .61

   2. Who would you go to if you were having trouble with your school work?   .60

   3. Who would you go to if you were having trouble with your teacher?   .58

   4. Who would you go to for advice about work in the future?   .54

IV. Family Discord

   1. How much disagreement is there at home between children and parents?   —.65

   2. How much disagreement is there at home between mother and father (or stepparents)?   —.63

   3. How much disagreement is there at home between brothers and sisters?   —.58

   4. How often do your mother and father disagree in telling you what to do?   —.41

Notes

[1] A complete description of the method of sampling, the nature of the sample, or the kind of factor analysis used in this study can be obtained by writing to the second author, who directed the series of inner-city studies of which the present paper is but one report.

[2] Easton is a fictitious name we have used to refer to the site of the study. The city was founded in the 17th Century. Around the middle of the 19th Century, new industries began to develop and to attract large numbers of Italian, Irish, and black migrants. Today Easton's population of approximately 150,000 is 30 percent black.

[3] See Appendix A for items which define these ten factors.

[4] For items which define these several factors, see Appendix B.

[5] An incomplete home in this context is one that does not include both biological parents.

[6] See Appendix C for items which define these several factors.

REFERENCES

Axelrod, Sidney
  1952 "Negro and white institutionalized delinquents." American Journal of Sociology 57(May): 569-574.

Goldman, Nathan
  1963 The Differential Selection of Juvenile Offenders for Court Appearence. New York: National Council on Crime and Delinquency.

Hathaway, Stark, and Elio Monachesi
  1953 Analyzing and Predicting Juvenile Delinquency. Minneapolis: University of Minnesota Press.

Piliavin, Irving, and Scott Briar
  1964 "Police encounters with juveniles." American Journal of Sociology 70 (September): 206-214.

Toby, Jackson
  1957 "The differential impact of family disorganization." American Sociological Review 22(October: 505-512.

Wheeler, Stanton et al.
  1968 "Agents of delinquency control." Pp. 31-60 in Stanton Wheeler (ed.), Controlling Delinquents. New York: John Wiley & Sons, Inc.

Wilson, James Q.
  1968 "The police and the delinquent in two cities." Pp. 9-30 in Stanton Wheeler (ed.), Controlling Delinquents. New York: John Wiley & Sons, Inc.

Werthman, Carl and Irving Piliavin
  1967 "Gang members and the police." Pp. 50-98 in David J. Bordua (ed.), The Police. New York: John Wiley & Sons, Inc.

ST. LOUIS DIAGNOSTIC AND DETOXIFICATION CENTER: AN EXPERIMENT IN NON-CRIMINAL PROCESSING OF PUBLIC INTOXICANTS

Raymond T. Nimmer

I. BACKGROUND

The task of handling the public drunk is faced by every police department in this country. As indicated by a national total of over 2,000,000 arrests for public drunkenness (almost 40% of the total nontraffic arrests), this task consumes a large portion of total police time and produces a significant. burden upon the functioning of other criminal justice agencies.[1] That dealing with the public intoxicant remains largely the exclusive concern of the criminal justice system is more a result of tradition, resort to expedient methods and indifference on the part of other agencies, than of any notion that the intoxicated man is a criminal deserving punishment.[2] Despite this, many drunkenness arrests result in conviction and criminal penalty.

The drunkenness laws are seldom enforced uniformly. The police prefer to handle middle and upper class intoxicants through informal means such as transporting them to their home. On the other hand, arrest and criminal prosecution are commonplace in lower class, and especially, Skid Row sections of a city.[3] In non-Skid Row areas, handling the publicly intoxicated resident is regarded as a sidelight, an insignificant and bothersome protective task. In Skid Row areas, enforcement of the drunkenness laws is frequently the primary job of a specialized squad of officers, and represents the most visible and extensive system of providing social services and controlling the men. One study of police operations on Skid Row characterized these laws as virtually the only law that the Skid Row man knows.[4]

This differential enforcement has been explained as resulting from the fact that there is no way other than an arrest to protect the Skid Row drunk.[5] Although the explanation is certainly more complex, this statement does emphasize one important factor about the enforcement of the drunkenness laws. The purpose behind the enforcement of these laws is not found in the common criminal law rhetoric of deterrence, punishment, of even rehabilitation.

Thus, what is commonly referred to as the "public drunkenness problem" is best understood in its Skid Row context.[6] Although the policies followed and the level of enforcement vary, several concerns reoccur among the jurisdictions. Arrests of non-disorderly, but usually intoxicated, derelict men allegedly provide the men with a brief respite from the extended drinking which can be one facet of a Skid Row way of life. In some cities, enforcement practices establish the jail as a substitute for non-existent municipal shelter facilities providing the men with free housing for one night.[7] Additionally, they deal with medical problems of the men and serve the law enforcement concern of protecting them from the possibility of violent assault and robbery. Often the arrests are employed primarily to service a perceived community concern to remove the unsightly derelict men from the sight of the "normal" populace, and these pressures can lead to an extremely high arrest rate.[8]

Intra-system pressures are important in shaping enforcement policy. Each criminal justice agency must allocate scarce resources according to its own priorities. There is substantial feedback among the agencies—the arrest process is influenced by court procedures and the facilities available at the jail.[9] Also an element of irrationality is injected in that policies and procedures often reflect traditional approaches in the jurisdiction, rather than continuing re-assessment of fact.

Despite some arguably laudible motives, the criminal process provides no more than minimal, temporary assistance. Arrests are processed on a mass basis, frequently as a result of the operations of a specially designated "bum squad". The arrestees are herded into cells with inadequate size and almost no facilities to treat the medical and other problems that arise. Long before the men are led into the courtroom, the cells become filthy and permeated with the stench of dried blood, sweat and vomit. The court procedure is also based on a mass production model. Aided by a large number of guilty pleas, it is not uncommon for over 100 men to be processed in less than one hour. Little attention is paid to the niceties of due process requirements.[10]

At its best, the procedure is a stop gap measure, filling the void left by a failure of other social help agencies to meet the needs of the men. Recidivism rates demonstrate that no more than short-term help is provided. Nevertheless, the cost of processing these arrests is immense. In Chicago the annual cost of processing over 50,000 derelict-drunk arrests is estimated at over $750,000.[11] Further, the social cost of the burden placed upon the police and the lower criminal courts, and the impact upon respect for criminal justice resulting from the perverted, mass production accommodation to the arrest and re-arrest process is inestimable.

In recent years, the propriety of delegating this task to the criminal justice system has been much discussed.[12] The commentators invariably suggest that the criminal label be discarded. Although there is some disagreement,[13] most commentators go from this position to suggest that alternative programs be developed to replace the criminal process. The clear trend, embodied in the recommendations of a Presidential Commission and an AMA-ABA Committee, is toward the notion that the criminal process should be replaced by "civil detoxification systems." This article discusses the results of an American Bar Foundation study of the oldest and the most widely publicized detoxification program, the St. Louis Detoxification and Diagnostic Center for Intoxicated Men.[14]

The results of this study are significant on two levels. First, and most obvious, the study provides a means to evaluate the impact of the St. Louis program. Second, the problems and achievements of the St. Louis program provide a base from which to speculate concerning the concept of replacing criminal laws with civil detoxification systems.

II.   DETOXIFICATION CONCEPTUALIZED

The detoxification concept involves the creation of a medically-oriented facility to which public intoxicants are taken.[15] The facility resembles a hospital in terms of the medical services available, except that serious ailments are referred to other hospital facilities. The detoxification center focuses upon the diagnostic process and care for minor ailments. Although the detoxification center may accept walk-in patients, the system is designed primarily to service men who are brought in either by the police or by a special civilian squad. The patient is held at the center for only a few days and, in addition to medical care, may receive vocational or therapeutic counseling and referral to long-term treatment or residential facilities.

It is possible to identify five objectives of the new system. First, by removing the criminal label and inserting a civil procedure, the new system seeks to avoid the stigmatizing effect that the criminal law allegedly has and which supposedly serves as a block to rehabilitation. Although this aspect is frequently emphasized, there is evidence that the criminal system has little stigmatizing impact upon Skid Row offenders.[16] Extensive research concerning the attitudes of the men involved is needed to assess the extent to which the relabeling represents a social gain, but such an effort was beyond the scope and the resources of our research.

Second, the new facility provides "more appropriate, humane and sanitary" shelter for the men than is typically found in the "drunk tank" of the jail. Under the criminal process the conditions of the drunk tank frequently are deplorable, but in comparison to many of the other shelter services available to the man or to the prospect of spending a hazardous night on the street, the jail often appears to the arresting officer as the preferable alternative.[17] By providing a more aesthetically pleasing environment the choice of the officer is more clear cut.

Third, the new facility makes expert medical help available to the men. Physical deterioration, latent medical illness and emergency medical needs are characteristic of the Skid Row men who become involved in the arrest process. Often the obvious medical debilitation of the man is the primary motive for arrest. Nevertheless, no medical care is available at the local jail and many deaths occur and serious illnesses go undetected.[18]

Fourth, the system reduces the burden on the criminal agencies resulting from processing the large number of drunk arrests. The need to divert resourses to processing these essentially non-criminals allegedly hinders effective handling of more violent crimes and criminals. Also, the new system is expected to reduce the overall drain upon the public treasury.

Fifth, the system introduces the potentiality of rehabilitative therapy or referral.[19] Rehabilitation here is loosely defined to include vocational, residential, drinking and psychiatric improvement. This is the only one of the objectives which is not one of the justifications advanced for the arrest of the men under a criminal charge. It is a clear departure from the essentially short-term concerns of the criminal agencies, and it represents, to a limited extent, the notion that the ultimate goal of any system relating to the derelict men is to achieve their rehabilitation. There are variations among the programs concerning the extent of emphasis upon rehabilitation therapy which show up in the number of days that the man is held at the Center, and the extent to which referral or in-house care is the primary rehabilitative tool. None of the operating detoxification programs challenges the assumption that rehabilitation is a proper goal.[20]

There is a significant divergence of opinion concerning the preferable method of bringing the men into the program. All of the programs recognize the necessity of seeking the men out on the street. Although a few detoxification programs utilize "civilian rescue teams" to pick up the men, most of the programs retain the police as the primary intake agency.[21] When the patient's contact with the program is initiated by civilian rescue teams the entire process is voluntary. When patrolmen are used the voluntary nature of the system is uncertain and a critical question of state power is presented which has seldom been subjected to debate.[22]

III. THE STRUCTURE OF THE ST. LOUIS PROGRAM

A. *Physical Characteristics.*

With these comments as background, we turn our attention specifically to the St. Louis detoxification program. The St. Louis program was the first operative detoxification system in the United States. It was initiated in late 1966 with the help of a demonstration grant from the U.S. Office of Law Enforcement Assistance. The idea for the center came through the combined efforts of several local experts in the field of alcoholism treatment and members of the St. Louis Metropolitan Police Department. The program budget is in excess of $200,000 per year, and it is designed to handle a maximum of 1,600 cases per year.[23]

The St. Louis version of the detoxification system involves a seven day stay at the treatment center. Intoxicants are picked up from the street during the normal patrols of the St. Louis police. Only men brought in by the police are accepted for the program. The procedure requires the officer to inquire whether the arrested person wishes to be taken to the detoxification center.[24] This choice has been labeled "voluntary or else."

During the first year of operation of the detoxification system, the center was located in the St. Mary's Infirmary. This facility was centrally situated with respect to the areas of the highest incidence of drunkenness arrests, and it proved to be a convenient location for the police officers. However, after the Justice Department grant expired, the facility was faced with a monetary crisis.[25] Eventually, funding was obtained from a state agency, on the condition that the center would be moved out of the infirmary and into a state operated facility. This new location was far removed from the locale of the most drunkenness arrests, and this move had some severe effects upon the functioning of the system which are discussed later.

Although billed as a "sobering-up station," the St. Louis center is tied quite closely to an effort to rehabilitate the Skid Row men.[26] A basic premise for establishing the new system was that "the St. Louis Metropolitan Police Department believes that the chronic police case inebriate is salvageable. . . . it proposes to establish a sobering-up station for rehabilitation of some of the offenders."

> [T]he St. Louis police department plans to utilize the detoxification center in order that chronic inebriates may be detoxified, built up physically, and exposed to an alcoholism treatment mileau at the center. Furthermore, they will receive counseling concerning their employment potential with a referral to the appropriate community agency as well as a followup. Those individuals who may need retraining will be counseled and referred appropriately for the necessary rehabilitation. It is believed that this exposure through the multidisciplinary team and the mileau at the center will have an effect upon each patient. . . . This technique should have an impact upon his chronicity, and serve as an impediment to the "revolving door" process of arrest, jail, release, intoxication, re-arrest, and jail again.[27]

Thus, the system attempts to meet rehabilitative objectives both by providing therapy during the patient's stay at the center and by providing appropriate referrals to aftercare agencies.

B.   Target Population.

It is not possible to attempt to evaluate, or even to discuss, the performance of the St. Louis program in the absence of a more precise definition of what the program seeks to accomplish. There are three possibilities. First, to provide medical, shelter and rehabilitation services to *all Skid Row* types who are in need of these services. Second, to provide these services to *all public intoxicants* in St. Louis who need them. Third, to improve the services that are provided to public intoxicants who would otherwise be processed through the criminal system.

There is no evidence in either the literature or the statements of the project personnel to indicate that the center was designed to deal with the first of these.[28] To do so would have converted the detoxification center into a multi-purpose Skid Row service agency. While there are strong arguments which indicate that this is the only rational course to follow, the purpose of this article is to discuss the St. Louis performance in terms of its own goals.

The evidence is that the St. Louis program adopts the third formulation stated above. Under a sub-heading entitled "Target Groups or Organizations Affected," the application for a demonstration grant states the "primary goal" of the program as involving "the treatment of individuals arrested by the police for being 'drunk-on-street.'" Similarly, under the heading of "need to be met" the application states:

> It has been clearly shown that repeated jailing does not act as a deterrent to the public police case inebriate. . . . It is evident that there is a need to provide medical treatment and rehabilitative services for the chronic public intoxicant and thereby remove him from the "revolving door" of arrest, detention, and incarceration. If this need is met, it will relieve the burden upon the St. Louis Metropolitan Police Department and all other local police agencies confronted with similar problems.[29]

It is clear that this language does not result from the assumption that the pre-existing arrest process identified all or even a large portion of the public intoxicants in the city. The application for a grant specifically recognizes the fact that the rate in St. Louis has traditionally been one of the lowest per capita rates in the country. For example, the St. Louis arrest rate for 1964 and 1965 did not exceed 4,000, while the annual arrest rate in Washington, D.C., a city of similar size, exceeded 40,000.[30]

That this difference did not result solely from a lower number of incidents of public drunkenness in St. Louis is shown by the fact that in St. Louis in 1963 the arrest rate rose to 7,847. This sharp increase was due to two procedural changes within the police department. First, an efficient method of processing the drunkenness arrestees was instituted whereby the arresting officer could call for a specialized van to take the men through the processing stage. Second, departmental orders were issued during 1963 directing patrolmen to increase their diligence in arresting drunken men. It should be noted that although these changes were in effect for only a few months, the impact was enough to more than double the annual arrest rate.[31]

The two changes noted above were coupled with the introduction of an innovative procedure to deal with the medical ailments of publicly intoxicated men. Labeled Code 26, this process requires that drunkenness arrestees be taken to a hospital for examination prior to taking them to a police lock-up. By adopting this procedure and simultaneously directing an increased level of enforcement, the department demonstrated its perception that not only are the medical needs of the public intoxicants significant, but that the low arrest rate fails to reach all of those who need medical help.

Nevertheless, the police were retained, along with their preexisting law enforcement policies, as an intake mechanism, and the new facility was designed in terms of number of beds and length of stay to accommodate no more than the caseload under the criminal system. The new program relied on the police practices to determine both the extent of the "problem" and the people who would be reached by the treatment process. The assumption had to be that the arrestee population was selected on the basis of some criteria bearing a rational relationship to the immediate care and long term rehabilitation objectives of the new system.

The comments of program personnel are obscure as to exactly in what situations the public drunkenness law was being invoked. As the 1963 incidents verify, under the law enforcement policy of St. Louis, neither public intoxication, nor public intoxication accompanied by apparent medical needs describe the arrest criteria. Perhaps the most perceptive comments on this issue were made by David Pittman, a leading figure in the movement to establish the St. Louis detoxification program. He notes that the police, due to processing requirements discussed later in this article, preferred not to arrest any public intoxicants, but preferred to send them home or to their family or friends for care.[32] The implication is that arrests selected out destitute (Skid Row) intoxicants who had neither family or friends nor resources to obtain shelter.

Although accurate, this analysis fails to go far enough. Not all destitute intoxicants were arrested and processed through the formal system. Pittman fails to take full account of the effect of intradepartmental pressures to avoid drunkenness arrests. As we suggest in the next section, these pressures result in arrests initiated only when immediate pressures do not allow the patrolman to ignore the intoxicant, and there is no convenient way of removing the man without arrest. The result is that many intoxicants needing the help of the center are left on the street, and those who are picked up may suffer less from the afflictions of intoxication than from the malady of being in the wrong place at the wrong time.

It might be argued that the program is less concerned with arrest patterns prior to instituting the new system, than with the police activities after the program began operation. Such an argument is based upon the probability that police arrest practices are affected by changes in the type of disposition the arrestee receives. The suggestion is that the police will come to see the new program as desirable for the intoxicants and will structure their arrest criteria so as to make full use of the services available. A comment by a command level officer is relevant there,

> The detoxification center will change the attitude of the police. They know now there is some place to take the drunks for help and to get them out of their hair.[33]

In order to encourage this effect, Dr. Kendis, the co-director of the center, gives a series of lectures on alcoholism and public intoxication to each new class at the policy academy. However, as indicated in the following pages, our research indicates that, rather than recognizing the program as a positive step, St. Louis patrolmen generally are dissatisfied with the new center.[34]

IV. THE IMPACT OF THE NEW PROGRAM ON ST. LOUIS POLICE PRACTICES

A.   Policies Prior to the Detoxification Program.

Appraisal of the impact of the detoxification program requires an understanding of police practices before it was started. The traditionally low St. Louis arrest rate does not result from police perception of the problems of the public drunks as small or infrequently encountered. Instead, it is a function of the influence of tradition and internal department pressures and priorities.

The influence of tradition is found primarily in the atypical reaction of the department to public pressures for clean streets. One factor which seems unique to the St. Louis department is that the formulation of official departmental policy has been substantially unrelated to any public desire to "clean up" the streets by removing the eyesore, derelict drunks. In all other cities visited during our research this was an important determinant of police policy. Part of the explanation for its relative nonimportance in St. Louis is that the derelict men are scattered throughout the city and tend to settle in poor, out-of-the-way areas where the desire for clean streets is not important.

We do not suggest that our research found businessmen, political leaders and others commonly interested in clean streets to be uninterested in having the drunks removed in St. Louis. Most certainly they are not uninterested. Several businessmen interviewed during the summer expressed extreme displeasure about the lack of police interest in removing the drunks. An influential businessman's group is presently considering hiring a special, private force to deal with the public drunk. The political spectrum, apparently also is sensitive about the public presence of these men. During the summer, there were persistent rumors that pressure was being exerted on the police to implement a campaign to remove derelict-drunks from the area surrounding the government buildings. This pressure resulted in 13 arrests for loitering in one day, but was eventually ignored by the police.

The key point here seems to be that complaints to the department are seldom made because, when such demands are entered, the police response, if any, is limited. In other cities studied, the police devote substantial effort to respond to such pressures. Reasons for the apparent independence in St. Louis are that other activities have created substantial good will with the influential citizenry and that the police are regulated financially by the state, not the city government. Equally important now is a strong tradition of independence which has developed, at least in this area.

The absence of effective external pressure to concentrate on problems of the public drunk permits the department to establish a very low priority for drunkenness arrests, reflecting the belief that the task of a police department should be to focus upon serious or violent crimes.[35] This is implemented through an informally communicated, but nonetheless official, policy of limiting the number of "non-quality arrests" (i.e. drunkenness, vagrancy, loitering) that are made by the officers of the department. There are indications that such arrests produce negative intra-departmental evaluations of the officers' work if they become too frequent. Also, several officers suggest that fellow patrolmen look down upon those who make frequent non-quality arrests.

An additional factor which limits these arrests concerns the Code 26 procedure, mentioned above. As initially enacted, this procedure provided a very efficient way of handling the drunk arrest. Although the specialized police vans were later withdrawn, the requirement of taking the arrestee to a hospital was retained. The result was that the processing of a drunkenness arrest took a large amount of time. Police estimates indicate that over 3 hours were required for processing the average arrest.[36] When combined with the departmental characterization of the drunkenness arrest as non-desirable and unimportant, this was a strong deterrent for the use of a formal arrest as a method of dealing with the public drunk.

This does not mean that the St. Louis police invariably ignored the public intoxicant. It indicates only that the formal drunkenness arrest was avoided. Informal methods of handling the drunk were available and frequently used. These procedures included taking the drunken man to his home, putting him in a cab, driving him off of the patrolman's beat, pushing him into an inconspicuous corner, and dumping him at the riverfront. However, since the police keep no statistics on these activities, there is no way to estimate their frequency.

An additional method of handling the public drunk is through a protective custody arrest. The department maintains no statistics concerning these arrests, but several sources indicate that the protective custody arrest was once used at a three-to-one ration with the drunk arrest.[37] However, it is used much less today, primarily because this, also, requires taking the arrestee to a hospital, under the Code 26 procedure.

As a result of these various factors, the patrolmen were ambiguous about their role with respect to the public intoxicant. Paternalistic or protective attitudes were not general throughout the department. At best, these attitudes were found in only a minority of the officers. The typical posture with respect to the drunk arrest was to view it as an unnecessary diversion, to be used only where other means could not be employed to dispose of the man and the circumstances indicate that he could not be ignored. Even in those cases in which paternalistic or protective concerns motivated the arrest, the officers apparently tended to think in terms of short-term goals and were rather skeptical concerning rehabilitation of the men.

 B.   Police Operations Under the New System.

With the insertion of the detoxification center the orientation of one agency in the system became rehabilitation and treatment, but the ambiguity on the part of the individual patrolmen remained. In spite of official press releases which indicated that departmental policy was to further the treatment objectives of the detoxification center, internal departmental pressures remained on the patrolmen. There are indications that individual patrolmen interpreted this publicity as not reflecting the actual position of the department.

Dr. Kendis' lectures seem to have not reached the younger patrolmen, and the effort that has been made to re-instruct veteran patrolmen concerning their role under the new treatment system has not been successful. In view of the scattered nature of the intoxicant population and the consequent involvement of many patrolmen, it is doubtful that efforts to establish a uniform policy could be effective. In general, officers interviewed reflected a lack of enthusiasm for the program and were influenced by the pressures existing before detoxification, coupled with a new skepticism concerning the success of treatment.

The problems which might be expected from the differing orientation of the center and the police did not appear during the early history of the detoxification center. A number of factors contributed to keeping the attitudes of the patrolmen below the surface. Perhaps the most important was that the original location of the center, at St. Mary's infirmary, was convenient for officers in the highest arrest district. Regardless of any desire to help the intoxicated men, patrolmen were inclined to take intoxicants to the center when circumstances required their removal, rather than to handle them informally or to invoke formal arrest procedures in a loitering or a vagrancy arrest. The location of the center reduced dramatically the processing time required for an arrest for drunkenness. Also, the atmosphere at St. Mary's was confortable for the patrolmen. Personnel at the facility made significant efforts to integrate the officers into their paternalistic attitude.

When the center was moved to the outskirts of the city, however, the conflict which had always existed came to light in two specific ways. The first of these was revealed in a series of articles appearing in one of the daily newspapers concerning brutal handling of the Skid Row men.[38] The St. Louis Post-Dispatch printed several articles describing testimony indicating that derelict men were frequently dumped on the riverfront and often beaten by officers.

Brutal handling of destitute intoxicants occurs in every jurisdiction visited by the ABF during the course of this study. However, control of officers responsible for such acts in St. Louis is more difficult because the Skid Row population is scattered throughout the city, meaning that many officers become involved with the men, and because informal handling of the intoxicants is frequent.

Officers whom we interviewed reported that they did occasionally take men to the riverfront. (We did not run across any specific evidence relating to possible brutality.)[39] This practice apparently had a long history in the St. Louis department before the detoxification system was enacted. As suggested above, this was only one end result of a general attitude favoring the informal handling of Skid Row arrestees. The riverfront is an ideal location at which to dump the men because it puts them out of sight of the "normal" citizenry.

The new location requires a 30 minute ride each way from the area of most drunkenness arrests. Probably the fact that the officially acceptable disposition of the men is now inconvenient played a role in increasing the incidence of this practice after the center moved. Also, in addition to patrolmen whose attitude towards the derelicts could be described as punitive, officers whose attitudes were more neutral might become engaged in this practice. Many officers express frustration with the new system, a frustration which has three causes. First, is the fact that officers willing to take the necessary time were frequently told that there was no room left at the center for the intoxicant they had picked up. Second, is the observation that many of the men taken repeatedly to the center would reappear drunken on the streets. The officers feel that these men were abusing a beneficent program and that the program has failed to live up to its promises of rehabilitation. Third, the continued quality arrest emphasis contributes to an uncertainty concerning high level support for the program.[40]

A second manifestation of the conflict between police and the center was the falling off of the admissions rate. The early period of operation of the center showed gradual increase in police contacts, but this soon leveled off at a rate only slightly higher than under the criminal process. During the summer however, admissions dropped to an average of between 70 and 80 per month, a 20% reduction from earlier operating levels. During one two-day period in the summer no men were brought to the center.

The extent to which the police avoided use of the center during this time was indicated during the one-day cleanup effort in response to the political pressures which we mentioned earlier. The police produced 13 arrests on this one day, but these were made under the loitering statute.

Even when there was pressure to arrest the derelicts the detoxification alternative was voided.

The need to obtain greater police use of the center was foremost on the minds of the consultants for the program and many of the staff members. The project codirector, Dr. Kendis, was forced on several occasions to direct requests to various police districts that more men be brought to the center.[41] One such communique asked that three or four men be brought to the center during the evening. Apparently, similar pressures succeeded in temporarily increasing the admissions rate during December of 1969.[42]

There are a number of causes for the lack of interest in taking men to the center. The unusual situation exists in which the police department officially supports the center, but internal evaluation, namely the non-quality arrest policy, tend to de-emphasize the use of the center. It is the opinion of the past chairman of the police board of commissioners that this results from lack of interest of the head officials in the department.[43] He supports our observation that this apparent ambivalence is perceived by the patrolmen.

Several of the officers whom we interviewed indicated that they had taken men to the St. Mary's location, but would not take men out to the state hospital. Transportation time out to the new location involves a 30-minute ride in each direction. This additional processing time is a persuasive argument against the officer taking the man to the center, particularly in the context of a pickup which is not looked upon favorably within the department.

Perhaps of equal weight is the fact that the new location seems out of place to the officers as a place for derelict men.[44] The hospital itself is a large sprawling complex, located in a middle class residential area, and many of the officers feel uncomfortable there. Additionally, as noted above, many officers reported that drunken men were refused admission on several occasions. This anomaly of empty beds with a refusal to take new patients apparently resulted from the disinterest of several of the evening staff members.

V.   Measure of Success in Achieving Program Goals

A.   General Comments.

As we have seen, the St. Louis detoxification program defines its goals in terms of a very limited problem population, and under existing enforcement practices, the treatment program never comes into contact with a large percentage of the public intoxicant population and many of the Skid Row intoxicants. Under prevailing police practices, the men who are taken to the center are selected on what appears, with respect to treatment objectives, to be an irrational or a random basis. Given these limitations we turn to the issue of how well the program achieves its goals with respect to the men it does receive.

The goal of providing a more humane shelter for the arrestees is difficult to quantify in order to objectively measure the impact of the new system. The determination of a scale of humane handling procedures is clearly subjective. On this point, it is possible to note, however, that some improvement over the city jail has occurred.

Much has been said to the literature concerning the need for immediate medical treatment and for diagnosis of latent injuries and illnesses of the public drunkenness arrestees. The medical services provided by the detoxification center would be a marked improvement over that available in most jurisdictions. However, in St. Louis, the detoxification program must be measured against the pre-existing Code 26 procedure which provided the emergency medical care and diagnosis that is lacking in other cities. Thus, the medical benefit, gained in the detoxification program in St. Louis cannot involve this aspect.

The gain, if any, lies in the effects that holding the man at the center for seven days and giving him continuing treatment and food has upon his general physical well-being. A study of the detoxification center by James Weber, which we discuss in greater detail below, recognized the difficulties in constructing an objective index of this variable.[45] Weber's study, based on observations of untrained interviewers, merely reports that a general improvement was noted in many of the men interviewed.

B. Rehabilitation

Weber suggests that the success of the program in rehabilitation is crucial to establishing the desirability of the detoxification effort. "Not only must his kind of treatment program be shown to be economically feasible, but . . . the individuals treated must accrue some positive therapeutic effects." If these effects are not proven, Weber suggests that the objection may be raised that the new system is nothing more than a revised version of the "revolving door" of arrest-incarceration-release-rearrest.[46]

Weber recognizes that rehabilitation in this context has a multiple meaning. His study attempts to deal with the evaluation of rehabilitation by several indexes. These include residential factors, employment, income, drinking characteristics, and the number of police arrests. Weber's method was to interview 200 patients processed through the detoxification center, and then to follow up with further interviews no earlier than 90 days after the men had been released. Based upon his study, Weber suggests that 50% of his sample of 200 patients experienced some overall improvement.[47]

Unfortunately, the methodology of the study is such as to render the results unreliable. First, Weber excluded from his sample those persons who left the treatment program prior to the termination of the seven day period and those persons who had not been residents of the St. Louis area for at least three months prior to the day they were taken to the center. These two exclusions accounted for 30% of the patient intake at the center. Second, practical restrictions forced Weber to limit his efforts to a 90 day follow up. This compares to the one-year follow up period which Weber recognizes as an optimal balancing of cost and scientific validity. Third, the data for the follow up study was developed through open-ended interviews in which the derelict men made their own assessment of their condition in the last three months. While this interview technique is highly successful as a means of gathering information concerning alcoholism patients if there is strong rapport between the interviewer and his subject, the interview team used in Weber's St. Louis study was composed of two St. Louis police officers dressed in civilian clothes. It seems doubtful that the necessary rapport existed. Fourth, in studying residence patterns of the subjects Weber because of his short follow up period, was unable to adjust for the fact that his efforts were disclosing only the length of time that a patient remains at a facility to which he has been first referred. Fifth, the study did not utilize a control group, and we are unable, therefore, to judge what portion of the group would have remained abstinent or improved their living style on their own, in the absence of the detoxification process.

Since Weber's results are inconclusive, it is necessary to turn to other indications of how effective the program has been in achieving its long-term rehabilitation objectives. The center's reports contain an analysis of after-care referrals with respect to employment and housing. This referral process was designed as a primary method of improving the life pattern of the men. However, the data indicates that only a small percentage of patients accept referrals in these two areas.[48] For example, during the period of April 1, 1969 through June 30, 1968 there were 338 admissions; 142 (42%) of these were judged to need assistance in the employment area, and 28% of these accepted the aid that was offered. This represents approximately 12% of the total number of patients admitted. With regard to housing, during the summer months referred to above, aid was accepted in the form of a housing referral by approximately 12% of the total patient load.

While we are not prepared to say that the detoxification center is merely a relabeled version of the "revolving door," the apparent failure to establish success in terms of rehabilitation variables is important. The program spends approximately $42.00 per patient per day. A large percentage of this is devoted to the referral and therapy efforts. Also, the desire to rehabilitate has caused the system to be designed in terms of a seven day stay per patient. This, of course, precludes the program from handling a larger caseload. It seems reasonable to suggest that a more substantial proof be required that the efforts towards rehabilitation are successful to such a degree as to justify the expenditure and the restrictions placed upon this system.[49]

C.   *Reduction in Public Costs.*

The Weber study attempted an analysis of the cost of treatment in the program compared to the cost of the old system of processing the arrestees through the criminal process. This involved a "simple cost accounting" methodology. As might be expected, cost reductions are found in the prosecutor's office, courts and the jail system. There was a 40% decrease in the number of informations issued against drunkenness offenders in 1966 as compared to 1964. Also, there was a 38% decrease in the number of persons committed to the city workhouse on the charge of "drunk-on-the-street" during the same period.[50]

An important consideration in evaluating these comparisons is that, even prior to the detoxification system, the burden upon the criminal justice agencies in St. Louis was not severe. The extremely low arrest rate meant that few drunkenness cases were ever processed by the prosecutor, courts or jails. As far as the St. Louis system is concerned the primary burden on the criminal system is found in connection with police time devoted to handling drunkenness offenders.

Weber's study reports that there occurred a 57% reduction in the processing time that the officers were required to devote to an average drunk-on-the-street pickup: However, the 57% reduction must be taken, not as indicating the timesaving to the police which can be expected in a traditional criminal system, but as measuring the benefits of providing a central location for diagnosis and treatment at which the officer can leave the patient. Prior to the creation of the detoxification center, the Code 26 procedure required the police to take drunkenness offenders to various city hospitals, and to wait for their arrestees to be examined. Under the new system, the officers no longer were forced to wait for the examination to be completed. It should also be noted that the 57% reduction refers to the operations of the center while at the St. Mary's facility. Its present location substantially increases the processing time for most of the drunkenness pickups, because of the longer riding time from the site of most pickups to the detoxification center. Adjusting the statistics to reflect this increased riding time indicates that the time reduction is about 33%.

Another aspect of relative costs concerns whether or not these decreases reflect a savings to the entire public structure. While it is clear that the agencies in the criminal justice system are saving some money, these savings may be more than compensated for by the increased expenditures necessary to construct and to implement the detoxification system. Its budget of over $200,000 exceeds what might reasonably be estimated to be the cost to the city of processing the drunk as a criminal case, and compares to a "saving," not including the project budget, of $64,000 projected in 1967.[51]

VI. OBSERVATIONS

The St. Louis detoxification program is a social experiment which, at least, has not completely failed. Certainly, however, the growing tendency to view the detoxification concept as a panecea for the ills of the criminal system in processing the public intoxicant is not warranted in light of the St. Louis experience.[52] The data concerning rehabilitation are inconclusive, and there is indication that the rate of success is not high. This should not be surprising, however, since any person knowledgeable in the problems of Skid Row men would not expect resounding success in any treatment program, especially where the treatment calls for no more than a seven-day in-house experience. The inconclusive results, however, are important when contrasted with the cost of the program.[53]

The difficulties experienced with the police are signficant. Even if rehabilitation is not often achieved, the new approach is justified on the basis of providing a centralized locale at which proper medical attention is available. The medical care only reaches those persons who are brought in by the police, and the extent to which the police fail to bring in destitute intoxicants in need of these services limits the success of the new program.

Much of the difficulties experienced with the police result from a failure to "package the detoxification product" in such a way as to make this alternative attractive to the individual patrolmen, thereby increasing their use of the program. The concept of better packaging involves many variables, and the necessary steps would vary in each jurisdiction according to prevailing tradition and pressures. Several specific comments concerning St. Louis illustrate the approach. First, the tradition of the department relating to non-quality arrests and the evaluative structure which maintains this tradition should be altered. The emphasis within the department, not merely in official communiques but also in attitudes of command personnel, should be to encourage the patrolmen to use the new program. Second, steps should be taken which minimize the processing time required for the arresting officer who wishes to take his man to the detoxification center. Third, informal handling of destitute intoxicants should be discouraged. Fourth, officers should be instructed that the detoxificaion alternative is beneficial to the men. Fifth, the capacity of the center should be such as to ensure that when an intoxicant is picked up, there will be room for him at the center. If the internal modifications produce an increased arrest rate, the size of the center should be increased to meet the growing need, or the length of each patient's stay should be reduced.

The St. Louis experience gives good cause to consider whether the intake operation should be handled through the police or by civilian teams. Typical arguments for retaining the police relate to availability (they are already organized and trained), experience (they have handled this problem for many years), cost (it would be expensive to train a civilian force to cover the entire city) and the potentiality of violence (they are trained to handle the occasional recalcitrant or disorderly man). On the other hand, the civilian procedure is advocated because it most often is conceived of as a voluntary process (avoiding controversial state power issues and giving a more co-operative treatment population) and because the attitudes of specially trained functionaries are likely to be more understanding of the men (police officers may brutalize the drunk).

The difficulties in St. Louis suggest that an additional, practical consideration is the extent to which the treatment facility is able to control its intake process. The police labor under the influence of traditional ways of handling the men, a general attitude that the police task is to handle violent crime and skepticism concerning the validity of treatment as an effective method of handling the drunk. These attitudes are especially difficult to alter without the full and continuing co-operation of the command structure in the department.

At the heart of this choice is, of course, a determination of what problem population the new program is designed to reach. Too often the complexity of this issue is ignored on the assumption that in some ill-defined way, the drunkenness arrestee population represents a unique grouping, both in terms of immediate needs and rehabilitative potential. However, the composition of this unique group is determined by police arrest criteria, and these criteria often are most responsive to departmental tradition, intra-system pressures and external pressures, than to the needs of the intoxicated men. The extent to which the unique characteristics of this group have meaning for the treatment program is determined by the relation of the selection criteria to the treatment objectives.

An illustration demonstrates the disparity which might arise. Our research in New York's Bowery reveal that various pressures restrict police arrest practices to a minimum. The drunkenness pickups that are made are designed primarily to develop statistics to demonstrate that the police are "doing something about" the Skid Row men. However, the New York police never arrest the most debilitated public intoxicants because they must process their defendant through a day long procedure, and therefore desire a man who is ambulatory. If a detoxification program were attached to this police enforcement technique, the relevance of its emphasis on medical care would be questionable in light of its failure to reach those Bowery men who are most in need of immediate help. Significantly, efforts to remove drunkenness from the criminal sphere in New York employ civilian, not uniformed police, rescue squads to remove the derelicts from the street.[54]

If we look beyond the arrestee population in search for a target grouping, at least two possibilities emerge. These are: the entire destitute public intoxicant population and the Skid Row derelict population. The choice involves a difficult policy determination. This first category makes some sense in that there are common characteristics which relate to the treatment and service objectives. These men are presumably all intoxicated and, by being in a public place, may present a situation in which intervention is indicated to protect them.

The relevance of the second grouping is indicated by the traditional focus of the criminal law enforcement of these laws. Public intoxicants with homes or resources have commonly been handled by the police on an informal basis, and the practicality and preferability of this disposition seems seldom to be questioned. Rather, these laws are frequently used to deal with the needs of the Skid Row men whose physical condition places them in danger from the elements or other men or whose resources are insufficient to obtain aid. It is instructive that many of the men arrested on Skid Row are not drunk and that the fact of the person's intoxication is seldom the primary cause for arrest.[55]

In either of these two contexts the St. Louis program appears as only a one-half program. It cannot possibly deal with either of these two groups, both of which are larger than the arrestee population. The police could not, even if they desired to, increase the pickup rate to reach more men because of the bed limitations of the program. The center cannot expand its contacts merely by increasing the number of beds because traditional police policies and internal pressures interfere with an increased pickup rate.

Also, there is a structural consideration which is seldom discussed. By emphasizing rehabilitation of all of the patients, the St. Louis program must devote intensive efforts upon each and this necessitates high cost per patient and a longer patient in-house term. This latter result prevents the new program from handling a large caseload with the same number of beds as is done in Washington where the average stay per patient is around two days and the per day cost is approximately $16.00. The Washington model is better able to deal with the protective concerns and it relegates the rehabilitation concern to be applied only to those patients who wish to be transferred to a longer term care facility. The loss, if any, in terms of number of successful efforts at rehabilitation has not been measured.

The upshot of these observations is not that the detoxification model should be abandoned, but that its use and structure should be subjected to more incisive scrutiny. The difficult policy questions involved in choosing intake source, treatment emphasis and problem population identification cannot be answered on a generalized basis. The needs of each jurisdiction may vary and the program should be modified to meet these needs, after the policy questions have been discussed and resolved.

Notes

1. Six recent editions of the F.B.I. Crime Reports list the following figures:

1961: 1,504,671 arrests
1962: 1,593,076 arrests
1963: 1,514,680 arrests
1964: 1,458,821 arrests
1965: 1,535,040 arrests
1966: 1,485,562 arrests

Adjusted to reflect data from non-reporting jurisdictions, the 2,000,000 figure is a reasonable estimate. *See* PRESIDENT'S COMMISSION OF LAW ENFORCEMENT AND THE ADMINISTRATION OF JUSTICE, TASK FORCE REPORT: DRUNKENNESS (1967) [hereinafter cited as DRUNKENNESS REPORT].

2. The typical drunkenness statute contains two elements: the fact of the actor's intoxication and the intoxicant's presence in a public place. *See, e.g.,* ARK. STAT. ANN. § 48-943 (1947); IND. ANN. STAT. § 12-611 (Burns 1956). The numerous variations on this theme include requirements of "loud and boisterous" or "disorderly" conduct accompanying the intoxication. CODE OF ALA. tit. 14, § 120 (1959); GA. CODE ANN. § 58-608 (1965). Occasionally, public intoxication is defined as disorderly conduct. CHICAGO CITY COUNCIL. J. 2562 (1969).

3. This differential enforcement may have been the original intention in enacting the drunkenness statutes. In any event, the "public place" requirement produces a de facto focus on lower class drinkers who are less able and less inclined by cultural norms to confine their drinking to private places. ALCOHOLISM AND DRUG ADDICTION RESEARCH FOUNDATION OF TORONTO, REVOLVING DOOR: A FUNCTIONAL INTERPRETATION 1 (1966). With respect to enforcement patterns, see W. LAFAVE, ARREST 109 & n.29 (1965); LAW ENFORCEMENT IN THE METROPOLIS (D. McIntyre ed. 1967).

4. Note, *The Law on Skid Row,* 38 CHI.-KENT L. REV. 22 (1961). Concerning the relationship between the drunkenness laws and other vagrancy-type crimes, *see* Foote, *Vagrancy-type Law and Its Administration,* 104 U. PA. L. REV. 603 (1956).

5. W. LA FAVE, ARREST 109 (1965).

6. There have been a number of published articles discussing the enforcement of these laws. *See, e.g.,* SOUTH CAROLINA DEPARTMENT OF PUBLIC HEALTH, PUBLIC DRUNKENNESS IN SOUTH CAROLINA (1968); Hutt, *The Changing Legal Approach to Public Intoxication,* 31 FED. PROB. 40 (1967); Hutt, *Modern Trends in Handling the Chronic Court Offender: The Challenge of the Courts,* 19 S.C.L. REV. 305 (1967); Miller, *Arrests for Public Intoxication in Cleveland,* 3 Q.J. OF STUDIES ON ALCOHOL 38 (1942); Nimmer, *Public Drunkenness: Criminal Law Reform,* 4 VAL. U.L. REV. 1 (1969); Stern, *Public Drunkenness: Crime or Health Problem?,* 374 ANNALS 147 (1967).

7. *See* Note, *The Law on Skid Row,* 38 CHI-KENT L. REV. 22 (1961); R. Nimmer Enforcement of Vagrancy-type Laws in Chicago (unpublished manuscript 1969).

8. This situation obtained in Washington, D.C., prior to a disruptive Appellate Court ruling. PRESIDENT'S COMMISSION ON CRIME IN THE DISTRICT OF COLUMBIA, TASK FORCE REPORT: DRUNKENNESS (1967).

9. *See* Murtagh, *Status Offenses and the Law,* 36 FORD. L. REV. 51 (1967); Murtagh, *Arrests for Public Intoxication,* 35 FORD. L. REV. 1 (1966).

10. Although there are few acquittals, there are indications that many of the arrested men are not intoxicated at the time of their arrest.

On the basis of the Breathalyzer Test, only 73% were actually legally intoxicated. . . . Others were apparently picked up because of their gait which was unsteady due to other reasons, such as severe malnutrition. . . . Still others may have been captured accidentally.

PHILADELPHIA DIAGNOSTIC & RELOCATION SERVICE CORPORATION, ALTERNATIVES TO ARREST 15 (1967). *See also* REPORT OF THE ALCOHOL PROJECT OF THE EMORY UNIVERSITY DEPARTMENT OF PSYCHIATRY 10 (1963).

11. The annual cost of processing over 40,000 arrests in Washington, D.C., was estimated at over $3 million. PRESIDENT'S COMMISSION ON CRIME IN THE DISTRICT OF COLUMBIA, TASK FORCE REPORT: DRUNKENNESS 485 n. 57 (1966).

12. In addition to the previously cited articles, *see* F. ALLEN, THE BORDERLAND OF CRIMINAL JUSTICE 7-9 (1964); E. LISANSKY, THE CHRONIC DRUNKENNESS OFFENDER IN CONNECTICUT (1967); MINNESOTA COMMISSION ON LAW ENFORCEMENT, MISDEMEANANT OFFENDERS (1968); UNITED STATES DEPARTMENT OF HEALTH, EDUCATION AND WELFARE, THE COURT AND THE CHRONIC INEBRIATE (1965); Hutt, *Recent Forensic Developments in the Field of Alcoholism*, 8 WM. & MARY L. REV. 343 (1967); H. Mattick & R. Chused, The Misdemeanant Offender (unpublished, University of Chicago Center for Studies in Criminal Justice, 1967).

13. H. PACKER, THE LIMITS OF THE CRIMINAL SANCTION 345 (1968).

14. Although this study was supported by the A.B.F. with funds from the Ford Foundation, the conclusions stated herein are those of the author and do not represent the official position of the Bar Foundation or of Ford. Much of the following discussion is based upon observation of police practices during the summer of 1969 and confidential interviews with various participants in the system.

15. DISTRICT OF COLUMBIA DEPARTMENT OF PUBLIC HEALTH, DETOXIFICATION CENTER OPERATING PROCEDURES (1968); DRUNKENNESS REPORT 4-5, 50-58.

16. *See* Amir, *Sociological Study of the House of Correction*, 28 AM. J. CORR. 20 (March-April 1966); Rubington, *Failure as a Heavy Drinker: The Case of the Chronic Drunkenness Offender*, SOCIETY, CULTURE AND DRINKING PROBLEMS 146 (D. Pittman & C. Synder eds. 1962).

17. Observations of a research team from Toronto suggest that the repeated incarceration serves to enhance, noticeably, the physical condition of the men. J. OLIN, THE CHRONIC DRUNKENNESS OFFENDER: PHYSICAL HEALTH 62 (1968).

18. PRESIDENT'S COMMISSION ON CRIME IN THE DISTRICT OF COLUMBIA, TASK FORCE REPORT: DRUNKENNESS 475-78 (1967) 16 deaths in 1964-65 in Washington, D.C.).

19. H. Mattick & R. Chused, The Misdemeanant Offender 37 (unpublished, University of Chicago Center for Studies in Criminal Justice, 1967).

20. *But see* Morris & Hawkins, *The Over-reach of the Criminal Law*, 9 MIDWAY 1, 9 (1969).

21. *See* DRUNKENNESS REPORT 58-65 (description of the Vera Justice Foundation's Bowery Project).

22. Although it is beyond the scope of this article to explore fully the doctrinal problems involved in the police-initiated systems, a few comments are appropriate. Where the system is structured to compel the man to enter and remain at a treatment facility it appears as a variant of civil commitment for mental illness, but it is based solely upon a police pick-up without intervening court adjudication. The questions of establishing sufficient criteria and of the ability of a patrolman to apply those criteria are crucial.

There are, apparently, two current theories of action. The first is to justify the pick-up under a public health law, severely limiting the number of days that the man is held at a detoxification center. *See* D.C. Alcoholic Rehabilitation Act of 1967, D.C. CODE ANN. § 90-452 (Supp. 1968). The second is followed in St. Louis, and involves defining the pickup and detention as "voluntary," giving the intoxicated man an "on-the-street" choice between criminal charges and transportation to the detoxification center. During the stay at the center, the criminal charges are held in suspension with the threat, seldom enforced, that they will be re-instituted if the man leaves the program prior to completing the prescribed term. If a seven-day confinement would be invalid without the voluntary label, this arguably represents an illustration of the state using threats to accomplish indirectly what it cannot do directly. Also, it is questionable that the intoxicant can make a reasoned decision while drunk, and it is likely that the wishes of the authority figure (patrolman) would be a strong influence.

A final observation is that the justification for any pick-up operation varies according to the goals of the system. Where the goals are short-range, the pick-up function performs an emergency care role. There are arguments that this can be justified under common law grounds. However, where rehabilitation is the primary purpose of the program, the pick-up process serves to encourage "unmotivated" derelict men to enter a treatment program. The encouragement can often become indirect coercion which must be justified on grounds similar to those established for civil commitment for mental illness. In most programs, both goals are present and the justification for pick-up is a combination.

23. ALCOHOL, ALCOHOLISM AND LAW ENFORCEMENT 35-45 (D. Gillespie ed. 1969); St. Louis Metropolitan Police Department, Application for Grant 5 (1966) [hereinafter cited as Application].

24. A police officer, upon observing an intoxicated individual who by reason of his condition may prove to be a danger either to himself or others, will detain the individual and convey him to the Detoxification Center . . . when:

1. There are no other criminal charges against the individual;
2. No signs of injury . . . ;
3. No complainant wishes to pursue the incident as a prosecuting witness, or
4. The intoxicant does not indicate a wish for a trial or legal representation.

Upon arrival at the Center the officer will prepare a City Court summons on the charge of "Public Drunkenness." At this point the officer will release the individual to the custody of a member of the Center's staff. After the subject is admitted his stay is purely voluntary.

. . .

If the intoxicant leaves the Center prior to medical release by the physician, the summons will be processed.

Letter from G. Gaertner, Associate City Counselor to Chief of Police Broston, July 11, 1966.

25. These problems and the eventual solution are discussed in newspaper articles reprinted as supplements to the Quarterly Reports of the Project.

26. *Compare* St. Louis Globe-Democrat, May 24, 1966, at 1, col. 4, *with* V. STRECHER, LAW ENFORCEMENT POLICY DEVELOPMENT SOURCE BOOK A-27 (1968) ("places them in a medical, social and psychological treatment environment.").

27. Application at 10.

28. This is not to say that there was no recognition by the planners that most of the arrestees are Skid-Row types. Jacobs, *Medical Approach to Handling Drunks*, St. Louis Post-Dispatch, June 26, 1966, at 1, col. 3 ("They are the men who populate Skid Row."). *See generally* D. PITTMAN & W. GORDON, REVOLVING DOOR (1958).

29. Application at 7.

30. *See also* DRUNKENNESS REPORT 2.

31. The arrest rates for the following years were: 3761 (1964), 2445 (1965). Arrest data furnished by the St. Louis Metropolitan Police Department.

32. S. AUERBACH, HOSPITAL REPLACES THE DRUNK TANK IN ST. LOUIS ALCOHOLISM PROGRAM 3 (1966).

33. *Id.*

34. The response of the program to allegations that the police operations are selecting out public intoxicants on a different basis than before is founded in demographic statistics of the patients which indicate that they are similar to public drunkenness arrestees in other cities. This, of course, merely verifies that police pick-ups continue to be made from out of the same general category, and says nothing concerning the condition of the men when arrested which is the significant variable for the purposes of the immediate care concerns. *See* ST. LOUIS DETOXIFICATION CENTER, FIFTH QUARTERLY REPORT 16 (1968); V. STRECHER, LAW ENFORCEMENT POLICY DEVELOPMENT SOURCE BOOK A-28 (1967); J. WEBER, FINAL EVALUATION

Report, St. Louis Detoxification and Diagnostic Center (1969) [hereinafter cited as Weber].

35. Weber 16. Comparing the "tolerant" attitude of St. Louis to other cities, Weber makes the following observation:

For the year 1965, St. Louis reports a total number of arrests of 44,701 while Washington, D.C. and Atlanta, Georgia, report 86,464 and 92,965 arrests respectively. Now, by deducting all drunkenness, disorderly conduct, and vagrancy arrests . . . one finds St. Louis has a total of 36,262 "quality arrests" as compared to 20,334 in Washington and 21,751 in Atlanta . . . . What is demonstrated here is not a leniency or tolerance for law violations but rather a different set of professional standards as to what constitutes good enforcement.

Weber 16.

36. Under the efficient processing model, arresting officer time involved an average of 30 minutes. Letter from Lt. James Chapman to G.W. Fahlgren, A.B.F. staff, August 19, 1966.

37. St. Louis Police Department Intra-departmental Report, Analysis of the Pilot Program "Drunk on the Street," March 28, 1963.

38. St. Louis Post-Dispatch, Nov. 6, 1969, § A, at 1, Col. 3; Leeming, *City Police Dumping Alcoholics Near Floodwall Despite Protests,* St. Louis Post-Dispatch, Nov. 5, 1969, § A, at 1, col. 1.

39. The St. Louis police department conducted an investigation of the brutality charges which produced inconclusive results. Officially, the study found that it could neither confirm nor refute the allegations. Several weeks later the local branch of A.C.L.U. then criticized what it described as one more example of a departmental "whitewash" investigation. See Leeming, *ACLU Rebukes Police on Inquiry on Drunks,* St. Louis-Dispatch, Jan. 16, 1970, § A, at 1, col. 1.

40. E.L. Dowd, former president of the Police Board of Commissioners, charged that command officers have failed to support the center in recent months.

Dowd said it was unfortunate that a young officer should be disciplined for dumping drunks on the riverfront when the officer was simply conforming to the attitudes and policies established by his superiors.

Leeming, *Dowd Censures Dump-Drunk Activity,* St. Louis Post-Dispatch. Jan. 18, 1970, § A, at 14, col. 2.

41. Leeming, *More Use of Drunk Center Sought,* St. Louis Post-Dispatch, Jan. 15, 1970, § A, at 3, col. 6 ("Kendis . . . said that he had on occasion urged the police department to bring patients to the center because of the high number of empty beds.").

42. Several months after our study was completed, in response to a controversy created by several St. Louis Post-Dispatch articles, one of the personnel at the center cited the fact that admissions had increased. He noted that the admission rate was very high (111 patients) in December. The implication that was intended from this argument is two-fold. First, there was the suggestion that the difficulties which had developed were cured. Second, the indication was that there were no difficulties, but that police are generally tighter in winter in that the low admissions rate in summer was a result of this.

With respect to the first implication, the discontent and dissatisfaction that we found with the center was too deep to be removed without an extensive effort. Many of the patrolmen had reached the point where they thought the center was of no benefit to the men. This attitude, and all of the other difficulties, are well ingrained in the minds of the arresting officers.

The second factor does not hold true in other cities. Also, a check of police statistics for years prior to the detoxification center indicates that winter and summer arrests are fairly constant. To the extent that there is a trend, the arrest rates are slightly higher in summer months. Arrest data furnished by the department indicates that, in 1965, April, May and June had the three highest monthly rates.

The conclusion to be drawn is that the increase in admissions, assuming that the statistics that were cited are accurate, is artificial, and is created by pressures such as those that Dr. Kendis exerted during the summer. If the higher rate is artificially imposed by pressures originating from the detoxification center personnel, the greater cooperation is likely to be temporary.

43. This is intangible, of course, and impossible to measure objectively. The comment of former Board President Dowd is relevant:

> Every effort should be made to return the center to its old location. . . . The atmosphere of a state mental hospital is not really conducive to the kind of thing our department . . . envisioned.

Leeming, *Dowd Censures Dump-Drunk Activity*, St. Louis Post-Dispatch, Jan. 18, 1970, § A, at 14, col. 2.

44. *Id.*

45. WEBER at B 10.

46. WEBER at B 1.

47. ALCOHOL, ALCOHOLISM AND LAW ENFORCEMENT 41 (D. Gillespie ed. 1969); WEBER at B 21-23.

48. ST. LOUIS DETOXIFICATION CENTER, SEVENTH QUARTERLY REPORT, APPENDIX (1968).

49. See Morris & Hawkins, *The Overreach of the Criminal Law*, 9 MIDWAY 1, 9 (1969) (wherein a program not involving substantial rehabilitation efforts is proposed as being economically feasible).

50. ST. LOUIS DETOXIFICATION CENTER, FIFTH QUARTERLY REPORT (1968).

51. Projected savings for 1967 were:

POLICE:	
Manhours	$12,500
Holdovers	2,500
Administrative	7,500
	$22,500
CITY AGENCIES:	
Hospital	$22,000
Court	3,500
Workhouse	16,000
	$41,500
	$64,000

V. STRECHER, LAW ENFORCEMENT POLICY DEVELOPMENT SOURCE BOOK 31 (1968).

52. *See* H. Mattick & R. Chused, The Misdemeanant Offender 37 (unpublished, University of Chicago Center for Studies in Criminal Justice, 1967).

53. The notion that a treatment cure is appropriate for these arrestees stems from the influence of alcoholism theory upon the problem. A relatively new concept, the illness characterization of alcoholism has been central to several appellate rulings relating to public drunkenness. *See, e.g.*, Powell v. Texas, 392 U.S. 514 (1968); Driver v. Hinnant, 356 F.2d 761 (4th Cir. 1966). A problem is that it over-emphasizes drink-related difficulties to the exclusion of welfare, residential and medical problems of the men. One expert suggests that alcoholism theory is irrelevant to Skid Row drinking. Wallace, *The Road to Skid Row*, 16 SOC. PROB. 92, 93 (1968).

54. DRUNKENNESS REPORT 58.

55. PHILADELPHIA DIAGNOSTIC & RELOCATION SERVICE CORPORATION, ALTERNATIVES TO ARREST 15 (1967).

A STUDY OF SOME FAILURES
IN METHADONE TREATMENT

Marvin E. Perkins

Harriet I. Bloch

I N A PREVIOUS paper (1), we reported the results of a survey of heroin addicts who had applied to the methadone maintenance program of Beth Israel Medical Center and of patients admitted to the treatment services of Morris J. Bernstein Institute (MJBI). A subgroup of 73 of the 512 patients who were admitted, namely those who had been discharged during the three-year period of the study, was identified and compared with the patients who were still active in the program. The study to be presented here, conducted in the summer of 1969, is concerned with the group of discharged patients who failed to be stabilized or maintained within the structure offered by the MJBI services.

This subgroup of 73 constituted the whole number of patients who, for whatever reason, had been unable to continue in the program. On review of all 73 clinical records, however, one case was found to have been erroneously classified as discharged; this patient had actually advanced in the program to phase three, the highest level of the rehabilitative process. In addition, six of these 73 were those who had died while in the program; they were technically classified as discharged. For follow-up purposes, then, this reduced the number discharged for various administrative considerations to 66. Our purpose in this study was to ascertain whether a diligent follow-up effort would result in the location of the majority of this group of unsuccessful former patients and whether the discharged patients who were located would cooperate in an assessment by interview of their current situation and adjustment.

Extended waiting time for admission to the methadone maintenance program had forced the administration to seek ways to maximize the utilization of existing resources. Patients were systematically evaluated and those whose progress was unsatisfactory were discharged. Patients who continued to abuse drugs and/or alcohol were administratively discharged. Several patients were voluntarily discharged.

The prevailing opinion was that the group, being a mobile one, might offer insuperable obstacles to location. Moreover, having fallen out with the methadone program, these patients, even if located, might choose not to participate in the study. Of the 66 patients, 60 (91 percent) were located; six had died since leaving the program; only one, who was located in a state mental institution, refused to be interviewed (see table 1).

TABLE 1

Effectiveness of Follow-Up of 66 Discharged Patients

CATEGORY	NUMBER	PERCENT
Located and interviewed	53	80
Located but not interviewed (unwilling)	1	2
Located—deceased since discharge	6	9
Not located	6	9

Method

A systematic precoded questionnaire was designed to obtain four categories of information: operational data, background characteristics, objective follow-up, and subjective follow-up. Operational data included length of treatment, the interval between discharge and follow-up, the reason for discharge, the location of the interview, and follow-up status. The initial intake history, obtained at time of application to the program, had produced nonuniform results. A test survey indicated these data were frequently incomplete and inaccurate. Hence, preadmission background characteristics were to be verified and an accuracy check was to be performed. Objective follow-up items were intended to describe the respondents' present levels of social and physical functioning, as well as their drug and alcohol use. In the subjective follow-up items, respondents were to compare various aspects of their lives from discharge to present, rating these as better, the same, or worse.

First the necessary identification characteristics were obtained from records available in MJBI, including name, date of birth, last known address, the methadone program control number, and the individual unit number. Then letters were sent to the respondent at his last known address, explaining our interest and seeking his cooperation. Forty-five of these letters were returned stamped "addressee unknown" or otherwise marked undeliverable.

With the mobility of this population group disconcertingly validated, we resorted to other locating procedures. We wrote to people who were noted in our records to be significantly related to the patients, or we telephoned them. The Drug Addiction Service at MJBI was queried each day to learn whether these patients had been admitted for detoxification. Lists of the patients being sought

were posted in methadone outpatient clinics throughout the city, and letters were sent to various drug addiction rehabilitation agencies throughout the city and state. To better engage the informal network among addict patients, we employed a methadone maintenance patient on the research team to help locate former patients.

Our original approach was designed not to make any offer, explicit or implied, for readmission to the program, admission for detoxification, referral service, or other personal assistance. However, in recognition of the serious situations most of the respondents were in, we were led to modify this almost at once. Most wished to return to the methadone program; some wanted (and needed) hospitalization. We were able to offer immediate hospitalization for those needing and desiring it. Ten took advantage of the offer and were hospitalized for detoxification. Two more, scheduled for admission, were incarcerated before arrangements were completed. Fifteen were given a modest monetary allowance out of petty cash. We have reason to believe that knowledge of our ability to provide some personal assistance persuaded a few, who might not have cooperated otherwise, to contribute to the study. The results of the interviews with the 53 former patients who were located and interviewed are presented below.

Operational Data

A note on the interval between discharge and the follow-up interview is in order. The interval between discharge and the follow-up interview ranged from 18 months to over four years (50 months); the mean was two and a half years.

Reason for Discharge

The major reason for discharge among these 53 was uncooperative behavior: 16 were discharged for this reason. Nine were discharged for drug abuse, seven had psychiatric problems, six abused alcohol, five had been arrested, and two had medical problems not related to drugs or mental health.

Location of Interview

Twenty-five patients were interviewed at MJBI. Fourteen were interviewed in hospitals or penal institutions. In several instances, when the respondent was institutionalized upstate or out of the state, a staff member of that institution conducted the interview and returned it to us by mail. The remaining respondents were interviewed in the street, in their homes, and in hotels, bars, restaurants, and places of employment. One respondent was interviewed in California by long-distance telephone.

Length of Treatment

The length of time in treatment ranged from less than one month to 31 months. Fifty-three percent of those discharged were discharged during the first six months; 75 percent of the total were discharged during the first year. Twenty-one percent were discharged during their second year. The mean length of treatment for all 53 respondents was approximately eight months.

Background Characteristics

In our previous report we indicated that there was no significant difference between the failures in the program and those who continued according to background characteristics denoting ascribed status. On the other hand, the risk of failure or administrative discharge was found to be greater for those who were unemployed and those who were unmarried (variables of achieved status).

Ascribed Status

Forty-six of those we interviewed were men and seven were women; 33 were white and 20 were black or brown. At the time of the follow-up interview, the mean age of the men was 34 and of the women, 37. The age ranges for the two sexes were comparable: men, 33–46; women 31–46. When asked in what religion they had been raised, 29 professed a Catholic background, 14 Protestant, six Jewish, two claimed no religion and two, other. The grandparents of 18 were from various parts of Europe, those of ten were from Puerto Rico, and those of 13 were born in the United States. Other ethnic and national origins were claimed by smaller numbers.

Achieved Status

At intake 27 stated they had never married; on follow-up the number never married was 19. Only seven were married at intake, while 12 were married at the time of follow-up. Nine were divorced and seven were separated at follow-up. At the time of intake,

only nine were working, 20 were doing nothing about employment, and 19 were engaged in illegal activities. At follow-up, 15 were employed, at least part-time (an increase of six), one was in school, and 13 were doing nothing (a decrease from 20). However ten were in jail and 14 were engaged in illegal pursuits. At intake 25, nearly half of the number, had claimed to have had some high school education; 18 were high school graduates, three had had some college, and one was a college graduate. Unlike the marital and occupational variables, the level of educational achievement had not been found to be different between those successfully retained in the program and those who failed and were discharged. Since discharge from the program, none of the respondents had continued his education.

Follow-Up Data on Adjustment

Problem Presented

At follow-up, 31 (59 percent) considered their most serious problem to be drugs; others selected work, the law, health, family, or other matters. Twenty-six (49 percent) believed their problems had worsened since discharge. If the 13 with no change in problem are added to the 26 who believed their problems to be worse, then 73 percent of the group were the same or worse. Five more indicated new problems had started during the interval. Only nine reported their problems were better at follow-up than they had been at intake. In summary then, for 88 percent of the respondents, problems had stayed the same or become worse, or new ones had developed.

Criminal-Legal Involvement

Since discharge from the program, the criminal-legal involvement of the group was extensive. Forty respondents (75 percent) had been arrested; only 13 had not. Thirty-four respondents each reported one to five convictions during the interval. In total, the group accounted for more than 110 arrests and 63 convictions. Thirty-eight of the respondents had been incarcerated since discharge; they accounted for 78 incarcerations.

At the time of the follow-up interview, 32 respondents denied any current involvement with the law. Of the other 21, 13 had recently been convicted, two were on probation, one was on parole, four had court cases pending,

TABLE 2
Use of Drugs or Alcohol at Time of Follow-Up (N = 53)

CATEGORY	NUMBER	PERCENT
Currently using		
Heroin	29	55
Other opiates	10	19
Barbiturates	4	8
Amphetamines	7	13
Tranquilizers	4	8
Psychedelics	3	6
Alcohol	21	40
Denied current drug use	19	36
No information	1	2
Amount of current heroin use ˙ ˙		
1 - 2 bags	0	
3 - 4 bags	5	9
5 - 6 bags	9	17
7 - 8 bags	1	2
9 - 10 bags	7	13
11 or more bags	7	13

Responses in this section are not additive, the question provided
for multiple choice of drugs
Expressed in $5 00 bags

and one had just been arrested.

Health Status

Hospitalization since discharge was denied by 19 (36 percent); of the other 34, 22 claimed hospitalization for physical disease, 25 for detoxification, and four for mental disorder. Asked their opinion as to their health, the majority felt their physical and mental health had become somewhat worse.

Drug and Alcohol Use

Thirty-six of the 38 respondents who were not in institutions were currently using some drug or alcohol. As to the substances used, the largest number—29—admitted using heroin. Twenty-one respondents used alcohol, but only four admitted a problem with it (see table 2). Thirty-one of the respondents were under the influence of some substance during the follow-up interview. Only two respondents were considered to be clean (one for 46 and another for 16 months); both of these had been successful in abstinence programs.[1]

During the period since discharge, the number of periods of voluntary abstinences ranged from none to eight or more, with 19 admitting no voluntary abstinence and 17, only one. The modal length of voluntary abstinence for ten patients was less than a month, but others claimed abstinence for

[1] Nearly a year after conducting our interviews, we learned that the respondent who had been clean for 46 months had died of a physical illness.

longer periods, ranging from a month to over three years.

Attempts at rehabilitation, including detoxification, had been made one or more times by 31 (58 percent) of the group. The largest number of these—14—had secured care at MJBI. The balance were distributed among some fourteen agencies.

Subjective Perceptions of Quality of Life

The majority of patients felt that both their physical and mental health had declined from the time of the intake interview to the time of follow-up (see table 3). Thirty-five (65 percent) rated their mental health as excellent or good at time of intake; at follow-up, only 55 percent thought it was excellent or good—a decline of ten percent.

A slightly larger decline was reported in their perception of their physical health. At intake, nearly three-fourths rated it as excellent or good; at follow-up only 62 percent so rated their physical health.

Despite this decline in perceived quality of physical and mental health, the decline in our respondents' perception of life in general was negligible. The overwhelming majority (approximately 80 percent) rated their life as fair to poor at both intake and follow-up. No one rated his life as excellent at intake, and only one respondent did so at follow-up.

Summary

Four and a half years after the first methadone patients were admitted to MJBI, a follow-up effort resulted in the location of over 90 percent of those discharged live during the first three years of operation. Of those located, six (or one in ten) had died since being discharged from the methadone program. Of 53 former patients located and interviewed, nearly 60 percent considered their most serious problem to be related to drugs. Nearly 90 percent thought that since discharge their problems had stayed the same or worsened, or that new ones had developed.

Although 25 percent had not been arrested, 28 percent had not been jailed, and 36 percent had not been convicted since discharge from the program, the others accounted for more than 110 arrests, 78 incarcerations, and 63 convictions.

Except among the 15 in the institutionalized group, where abstinence was en-

TABLE 3
Comparison of Judgments of the Quality of Life at Intake and at Follow-Up (N = 53)

CATEGORY	EXCELLENT		GOOD		FAIR		POOR	
	NUMBER	PERCENT	NUMBER	PERCENT	NUMBER	PERCENT	NUMBER	PERCENT
Mental health								
Intake	5	9	30	57	9	17	9	17
Follow-up*	1	2	28	53	11	21	12	23
Physical health								
Intake	10	19	29	55	11	21	3	6
Follow-up	9	17	24	45	13	25	7	13
Life in general								
Intake	0		11	21	19	36	23	43
Follow-up	1	2	9	17	20	38	23	43

* One patient did not respond to this question

forced, use of heroin continued to be a dominant activity. Only two were in methadone programs and only two had been abstinent for any length of time at the follow-up interview.

Thirty-four, the majority group, had been hospitalized since discharge for physical and mental conditions or for detoxification.

The postdischarge course of the 60 located heroin addicts who failed to continue in the methadone program appears to be in striking contrast to those who are reported as successfully maintained. Death, criminal-legal involvement, incarcerations and hospitalizations, and continued drug abuse patterns appear to be great risks for this group of failed patients. We believe this evidence suggests that intensified efforts to retain addicts may be needed in methadone pro-grams. An alternative might be to redesign a new program for those who "fail." Perhaps both approaches should be undertaken.

We believe that measures that would make current programs more stringently regulated might have the effect of extruding more patients from the present system of care, and hence might consign more addicts to the street with a very poor prognosis for rehabilitation. On the other hand, because of the enormous social problems these people present, we doubt that the administration of methadone without the adjunct services is a style of treatment suited to this group of patients.

REFERENCE

1. Perkins ME, Bloch HI: Survey of a methadone maintenance program. Amer J Psychiat 126:1389-1396, 1970

VII.

THE OPERATION OF THE CRIMINAL JUSTICE SYSTEM

THE POLICE

COURTS AND JUDGES

CORRECTIONS

PRODUCTION OF CRIME RATES

Donald J. Black

SOCIOLOGICAL approaches to official crime rates generally fail to make problematic the production of the rates themselves. Theory has not directed inquiry to the principles and mechanisms by which some technically illegal acts are recorded in the official ledger of crime while others are not. Instead crime rates ordinarily are put to use as data in the service of broader investigations of deviance and control. Yet at the same time it has long been taken for granted that official statistics are not an accurate measure of all legally defined crime in the community (e.g., de Beaumont and de Tocqueville, 1964; Morrison, 1897; Sellin, 1931).

The major uses of official crime statistics have taken two forms (see Biderman and Reiss, 1967); each involves a different social epistemology, a different way of structuring knowledge about crime. One employs official statistics as an index of the "actual" or "real" volume and morphology of criminal deviance in the population. Those who follow this approach typically consider the lack of fit between official and actual rates of crime to be a methodological misfortune. Historically, measurement of crime has been the

dominant function of crime rates in social science. A second major use of official statistics abandons the search for "actual" deviance. This is managed either by defining deviance with the official reactions themselves—a labeling approach—or by incorporating the official rates not as an index of deviant behavior but as an index of social control operations (e.g., Kitsuse and Cicourel, 1963; Erikson, 1966; Wilson, 1968). In effect this second range of work investigates "actual" social control rather than "actual" deviance. Hence it encounters methodological problems of its own, since, without question, social control agencies do not record all of their official attempts to counteract or contain what they and others regard as deviant conduct.[1] A striking feature of police work, for instance, is the degree to which officers operate with informal tactics, such as harassment and manipulative human-relations techniques, when they confront law-violative behavior (e.g., Skolnick, 1966; La-Fave, 1965; Bittner, 1967; Black, 1968; Black and Reiss, 1970). In sum, when official statistics are used as a *means* of measurement and analysis, they usually function imperfectly. This is not to deny that such methods can be highly rewarding in some contexts.

This paper follows an alternative strategy that arises from an alternative conceptual starting point. It makes official records of crime an end rather than a means of study (see Wheeler, 1967; Cicourel, 1968:26–28). It treats the crime rate as itself a social fact, an empirical phenomenon with its own existential integrity. A crime rate is not an epiphenomenon. It is part of the natural world. From this standpoint crime statistics are not evaluated as inaccurate or unreliable. They are an aspect of social organization and cannot, sociologically, be wrong. From the present perspective it nevertheless remains interesting that social control systems process more than they report in official statistics and that there is a good deal more rule-violative behavior than that which is processed. These patterns are themselves analytically relevant aspects of crime rates.

An official crime rate may be understood as a rate of *socially recognized* [2] deviant behavior; deviance rates in this sense are produced by all control systems that respond on a case-by-case basis to sanctionable conduct. This does not say that deviant behavior as a general category is synonymous with socially recognized deviant behavior. As a general category deviance may be defined as any behavior in a *class* for which there is a *probability* of negative sanction subsequent to its detection (Black and Reiss, 1970). Thus, whether or not an agent of control detects or sanctions a particular instance of rule-violative behavior is immaterial to the issue of whether or not it is deviant. Deviance is behavior that is *vulnerable* to social control. This approach generates three empirical types of deviance: (1) undetected deviance, (2) detected, unsanctioned deviance, and (3) sanctioned deviance. It should be apparent that, while every control system may produce a rate of socially recognized deviance, much unrecognized deviance surely resides in every social system.[3] By definition undetected deviance cannot be recognized by a control system, but, as will become apparent in this presentation, even detected deviance may not be recognized as such. The notion of sanctioned deviance, by contrast, presumes that a social

recognition process has taken place. The concept of social recognition of deviance is nothing more than a short-hand, more abstract way of stating what we mean by concrete expressions such as invocation of the law, hue and cry, bringing a suit, blowing the whistle, and so forth.

The concept of deviance should be applied with reference to specific systems of social control. For example, deviance that is undetected from the standpoint of a formal, legal control system, such as the police, may be detected or even sanctioned in an informal control context, such as a business organization, neighborhood or friendship group, or family. Crime rates then are rates of deviance socially recognized by official agencies of criminal-law enforcement. They are official rates of *detection* ("crimes known to the police") and of *sanctioning* (arrest rates and conviction rates).[4] Enforcement agencies handle many technically illegal acts that they omit from their official records. This paper explores some of the conditions under which the police produce official rates of crime detection in field encounters with citizens.

SOCIAL ORGANIZATION OF CRIME DETECTION

Detection of deviance involves (1) the discovery of deviant *acts* or behavior and (2) the linking of *persons* or groups to those acts. Types of deviance vary widely according to the extent to which either or both of these aspects of detection are probable. Some deviant acts are unlikely to be discovered, although discovery generally is equivalent to the detection of the deviant person as well. Examples are homosexual conduct and various other forms of consensual sexual deviance. Acts of burglary and auto theft, by contrast, are readily detected, but the offending persons often are not apprehended. These differential detection probabilities stem in part from the empirical patterns by which various forms of violative behavior occur in time and social space. In part they stem as well from the uneven climate of social control.

The organization of police control lodges the primary responsibility for crime detection in the citizenry rather than in the police. The uniformed patrol division, the major line unit of modern police departments, is geared to respond to citizen calls for help via a centralized radio-communications system. Apart from traffic violations, patrol officers detect comparatively little crime through their own initiative. This is all the more true of legally serious crime. Thus crime detection may be understood as a largely *reactive* process from the standpoint of the police as a control system. Far less is it a *proactive* process. Proactive operations aimed at the discovery of criminal behavior predominate in the smaller specialized units of the large police department, particularly in the vice or morals division, including the narcotics squad, and in the traffic division. Most crimes, unlike vice offenses, are not susceptible to detection by means of undercover work or the enlistment of quasi-employed informers (see Skolnick, 1966). Unlike traffic offenses, furthermore, most crimes cannot be discovered through the surveillance of public places. Since the typical criminal act occurs at a specifically unpredictable time and place, the police must rely upon citizens to involve them in the average case. The law of privacy is another factor that presses the police toward a reactive detection system (Stinchcombe, 1963). Even without legal limitations on police detective work, however, the unpredictability of crime itself would usually render the police ignorant in the absence of citizens. Most often the citizen who calls the police is a victim of a crime who seeks justice in the role of *complainant*.

Vice control and traffic enforcement generally operate without the assistance of complainants. It appears that most proactive police work arises when there is community pressure for police action but where, routinely, there are no complainants involved as victims in the situations of violative behavior in question. In the average case proactive detection involves a simultaneous detection of the violative act and of the violative person. Proactively produced crime rates, therefore, are nearly always rates of arrest rather than rates of known criminal acts. In effect the proactive clearance rate is 100%. Crime rates that are produced in proactive police operations, such as rates of arrest for prostitution, gambling, homosexual behavior, and narcotics violation, directly correlate with police manpower allocation. Until a point of total detection is reached and holding all else constant, these vice rates increase as the number of policemen assigned to vice control is increased. On the other hand, the more important variable in rates of "crimes known to the police," is the volume of complaints from citizens.

Nevertheless, rates of known crimes do not perfectly reflect the volume of citizen complaints. A complaint must be given official status in a formal written report before it can enter police statistics, and the report by no means automatically follows receipt of the complaint by the police. In the present investigation patrol officers wrote official reports in only 64% of the 554 crime situations where a complainant, but no suspect, was present in the field setting. The decision to give official status to a crime ordinarily is an outcome of face-to-face interaction between the police and the complainant rather than a programmed police response to a bureaucratic or legal formula. The content and contours of this interaction differentially condition the probability that an official report will be written, much as they condition, in situations where a suspect is present, the probability that an arrest will be made (Black, 1968; Black and Reiss, 1970).

Whether or not an official report is written affects not only the profile of official crime rates; it also determines whether subsequent police investigation of the crime will be undertaken at a later date. Subsequent investigation can occur only when an official report is forwarded to the detective division for further processing, which includes the possibility of an arrest of the suspect. Hence the rate of detection and sanctioning of deviant *persons* is in part contingent upon whether the detection of deviant *acts* is made official. In this respect justice demands formality in the processing of crimes. This paper considers the following conditions as they relate to the probability of an official crime report in police-complainant encounters: the legal seriousness of the alleged crime, the preference of the complainant, the relational distance between the complainant and the absentee suspect, the degree of deference the complainant extends to the police, and the race and social-class status of the complainant.

FIELD METHOD

Systematic observation of police-citizen transactions was conducted in Boston, Chicago, and Washington, D.C., during the summer of 1966. Thirty-six observers—persons with law, social science, and police administration backgrounds—recorded observations of routine encounters between uniformed patrolmen and citizens. Observers accompanied patrolmen on all work-shifts on all days of the week for seven weeks in each city. However, the times when police activity is comparatively high (evening shifts, particularly weekend evenings) were given added weight in the sample.

Police precincts were chosen as observation sites in each city. The precincts were selected so as to maximize observation in lower socioeconomic, high crime rate, racially homogeneous residential areas. This was accomplished through the selection of two precincts in Boston and Chicago and four precincts in Washington, D.C.

The data were recorded in "incident booklets," forms structurally similar to interview schedules. One booklet was used for each incident that the police were requested to handle or that they themselves noticed while on patrol. These booklets were not filled out in the presence of policemen. In fact the officers were told that our research was not concerned with police behavior but only with citizen behavior toward the police and the kinds of problems citizens make for the police. Thus the study partially utilized systematic deception.

A total of 5,713 incidents were observed and recorded. In what follows, however, the statistical base is only 554 cases, roughly one-in-ten of the total sample. These cases comprise nearly all of the police encounters with complainants in crime situations where no suspect was present in the field situation. They are drawn from the cases that originated with a citizen telephone call to the police, 76% of the total. Excluded are, first, encounters initiated by policemen on their own initiative (13%). Police-initiated encounters almost always involve a suspect or offender rather than a complainant; complainants usually must take the initiative to make themselves known to the police. Also excluded are encounters initiated by citizens

who walk into a police to ask for help (6%) or who personally flag down the police on the street (5%). Both of these kinds of police work have peculiar situational features and should be treated separately. The great majority of citizen calls by telephone are likewise inappropriate for the present sample. In almost one-third of the cases no citizen is present when the police arrive to handle the complaint. When a citizen is present, furthermore, the incident at issue pertains to a noncriminal matter in well over one half of the cases. Even when there is a criminal matter a suspect not infrequently is present. When a suspect is present the major official outcome possible is arrest rather than a crime report. Finally, the sample excludes cases in which two or more complainants of mixed race or social-class composition participated. It may appear that, in all, much has been eliminated. Still, perhaps surprisingly, what remains is the *majority of crime situations* that the police handle in response to citizen telephone calls for service. There is no suspect available in 77% of the felonies and in 51% of the misdemeanors that the police handle on account of a complaint by telephone. There is only a complainant. These proportions alone justify a study of police encounters with complainants. In routine police work the handling of crime is in large part the handling of complainants. Policemen see more victims than criminals.

LEGAL SERIOUSNESS OF THE CRIME

Police encounters with complainants where no suspect is present involve a disproportionately large number of felonies, the legally serious category of crime. This was true of 53% of the cases in the sample of 554. When a suspect is present, with or without a citizen complainant, the great majority of police encounters pertain only to misdemeanors (Black, 1968). In other words, the police arrive at the scene too late to apprehend a suspect more often in serious crime situations than in those of a relatively minor nature.[5] In police language, felonies more often are "cold." A moment's reflection upon the empirical patterns by which various crimes are committed reveals why this is so. Some of the more common felonies, such as burglary and auto theft, generally involve stealth and occur when the victim is absent; by the time the crime is discovered, the offender has departed. Other felonies such as robbery and rape have a hit-and-run character, such that the police rarely can be notified in time to make an arrest at the crime setting. Misdemeanors, by contrast, more often involve some form of "disturbance of the peace," such as disorderly conduct and drunkenness, crimes that are readily audible or visible to potential complainants and that proceed in time with comparative continuity. In short, properties of the social organization of crime make detection of felony offenders relatively difficult and detection of misdemeanor offenders relatively simple, given detection of the act.[6]

When the offender has left the scene in either felony or misdemeanor situations, however, detection and sanctioning of the offender is precluded unless an official report is written by the police. Not surprisingly, the police are more likely to write these reports in felony than in misdemeanor situations.[7] Reports were written in 72% of the 312 felonies, but in only 53% of the 242 misdemeanors. It is clear that official recognition of crimes becomes more likely as the legally defined seriousness of the crime increases. Even so, it remains noteworthy that the police officially disregard one-fourth of the felonies they handle in encounters with complainants. These are not referred to the detective division for investigation; offenders in these cases thus unknowingly receive a pardon of sorts.

Now the reader might protest an analysis that treats as crimes some incidents that the police themselves do not handle as crimes. How can we call an event a law violation when a legal official ignores that very event? This is a definitional problem that plagues a sociology of law as well as a sociology of deviance and social control. How is a violation of the "law on the books" properly classified if "in practice" it is not labeled as such? It is easy enough to argue that either of these criteria, the written law or the law-in-action, should alone define the violative behavior in question. No answer to this dilemma is true or false. It is of course all a matter of the usefulness of one defini-tion or another. Here a major aim is to learn something about the process by which the police select for official attention certain technically illegal acts while they bypass others. If we classify as crimes only those acts the police officially recognize as 'crimes, then what shall we call the remainder? Surely that remainder should be conceptually distinguished from acts that are technically legal and which carry no sanctions. For that reason, the present analysis operates with two working categories, crimes and officially recognized crimes, along with an implicit residual category of non-crimes. Crime differs from other behavior by dint of a probability, the probability that it will be sanctioned in a particular administrative system if it is detected. The written law usually—though not always—is a good index of whether that probability exists. "Dead letter" illegal acts, i.e., those virtually never sanctioned, are not classified as crimes in this analysis. Crime as a *general category* consists in a probability of sanction; official recognition in the form of a crime report is one factor that escalates that probability for a *specific instance* of crime. It is worthwhile to have a vocabulary that distinguishes *between crimes* on the basis of how the police relate to them. Without a vocabulary of this kind police invocation of the law in the face of a law violation cannot be treated as empirically or theoretically problematic. Rather, invocation of the law would *define* a law violation and would thereby deprive sociology of an intriguing problem for analysis. Indeed, if we define a law violation *with* invocation of the law, we are left with the peculiar analytical premise that enforcement of the law is total or universal. We would definitionally destroy the possibility of police leniency or even of police discretion in law enforcement.

THE COMPLAINANT'S PREFERENCE

Upon arriving at a field setting, the police typically have very little information about what they are going to find. At best they have the crude label assigned to the incident by a dispatcher at the communications center. Over the police radio they hear such descriptions as "a B and E" (breaking and/or entering), "family trouble," "somebody screaming," "a theft report," "a man down" (person lying in a public place, cause unknown), "outside ringer" (burglar-alarm ringing), "the boys" (trouble with juveniles), and suchlike. Not infrequently these labels prove to be inaccurate. In any case policemen find themselves highly dependent upon citizens to assist them in structuring situational reality. Complainants, biased though they may be, serve the police as primary agents of situational intelligence.

What is more, complainants not infrequently go beyond the role of providing information by seeking to influence the direction of police action. When a suspect is present the complainant may pressure the police to make an arrest or to be lenient. When there is no available suspect, it becomes a matter of whether the complainant prefers that the crime be handled as an official matter or whether he wants it handled informally. Of course many complainants are quite passive and remain behaviorally neutral. During the observation period the complainant's preference was unclear in 40% of the encounters involving a "cold" felony or misdemeanor. There were 184 felony situations in which the complainant expressed a clear preference; 78% lobbied for official action. Of the 145 misdemeanor situations where the complainant expressed a clear preference, the proportion favoring official action was 75%, roughly the same proportion as that in felony situations. It seems that complainants are, behaviorally, insensitive to the legal seriousness of crimes when they seek to direct police action.

Police action displays a striking pattern of conformity with the preferences of complainants. Indeed, in not one case did the police write an official crime report when the complainant manifested a preference for informal action. This pattern seen in legal perspective is particularly interesting given that felony complainants prefer informal action nearly as frequently as misdemeanor complainants. Police conformity with those complainants who do prefer official action, however, is not so symmetrical. In felony situations the police comply by writing an official report in 84% of the cases, whereas when the complaint involves a misdemeanor their rate of compliance drops to 64%. Thus the police follow the wishes of officially-oriented complainants in the majority of encounters, but the majority is somewhat heavier when the occasion is a legally more serious matter. In the field setting proper the citizen complainant has much to say about the official recognition of crimes, though the law seemingly screens his influence.[8]

Recall that the raw inputs for the official detection rate are generated by the citizenry who call the police. At two levels, then, the operational influence of citizens gives crime rates a peculiarly democratic character. Here the servant role of the police predominates; the guardian role recedes. Since an official report is a prerequisite for further police investigation of the crime, this pattern also implies that complainants are operationally endowed with an adjudicatory power. Their observable preferences can ultimately affect probabilities of arrest and conviction. While the structure of the process is democratic in this sense, it most certainly is not universalistic. The moral standards of complainants vary to some extent across the citizen population, thereby injecting particularism into the production of outcomes. There appears a trade-off between democratic process and universalistic enforcement in police work. This is an organizational dilemma not only of the police but of the legal system at large. When the citizenry has the power to direct the invocation of law, it has the power to discriminate among law-violators. Moral diversity in the citizen population by itself assures that some discrimination of this kind will occur. This is true regardless of the intentions of individual citizens. When a legal system organizes to follow the demands of the citizenry, it must sacrifice uniformity, since the system responds only to those who call upon it while it ignores illegality that citizens choose to ignore. A legal system that strives for universalistic application of the law, by contrast, must refuse to follow the diverse whims of its atomized citizenry. Only a society of citizens homogeneous in their legal behavior could avoid this dilemma.

RELATIONAL DISTANCE

Like any other kind of behavior, criminal

behavior is located within networks of social organization. One aspect of that social organization consists in the relationship existing between the criminal offender and the complainant prior to a criminal event. They may be related by blood, marriage, friendship, neighborhood, membership in the same community, or whatever. In other words, the adversarial relation that is created by a crime may itself be viewed as it is structured within a wider social frame. The findings in this section permit the conclusion that the probability of official recognition of a crime varies with the relational network in which the crime occurs.[9] The greater the relational distance between citizen adversaries, the greater is the likelihood of official recognition.

Citizen adversaries may be classified according to three levels of relational distance: (1). fellow family members, (2) friends, neighbors, or acquaintances, and (3) strangers. The vast majority of the cases fall into the "stranger" category, though some of these probably would be reclassified into one of the other relational categories if the criminal offender were detected. The complainant's first speculation generally is that a stranger committed the offense in question.

Table 1 shows that when a complainant expresses a preference for official action the police comply most readily when the adversaries are strangers to one another. They are less likely to comply by writing an official crime report when the adversaries are friends, neighbors, or acquaintances, and they are least likely to give official recognition to the crime when the complainant and suspect are members of the same family. The small number of cases in the "fellow family members" category prohibits comparison between felony and misdemeanor situations. In the other relational categories this comparison reveals that the police follow the same pattern in the handling of both felonies and misdemeanors. With the relational distance between the adversaries held constant, however, the probability of an official report is higher for felony than for misdemeanor situations. The highest probability of an official response occurs when the crime is a felony and the adversaries are strangers to one another (91%); the lowest calculable probability is that for

misdemeanors when the adversaries are related by friendship, neighborhood, or acquaintanceship (42%). On the other hand, it appears that relational distance can override the legal seriousness of crimes in conditioning police action, since the police are more likely to give official recognition to a misdemeanor involving strangers as adversaries (74%) than to a felony involving friends, neighbors, or acquaintances (62%). Here again, therefore, the law screens but does not direct the impact of an extra-legal element in the production of crime rates.

Beyond the importance of relational distance for an understanding of crime rates as such is another implication of these findings. Because a follow-up investigation of the crime report by the detective division may result in apprehension of the criminal offender, it is apparent that the probability of an official sanction for the offender lessens as the degree of social intimacy with his adversary—usually his victim—increases. When an offender victimizes a social intimate the police are most apt to let the event remain a private matter, regardless of the complainant's preference. A more general consequence of this pattern of police behavior is that the criminal law gives priority to the protection of strangers from strangers while it leaves vulnerable intimates to intimates. Indeed, victimizations of strangers by strangers may be comparatively more damaging to social order and hence, from a functional standpoint, require more attention from the forces of control. A victimization between intimates is capsulated by intimacy itself. Furthermore, as social networks are more intimate, it surely is more likely that informal systems of social control operate. Other forms of legal control also may become available in the more intimate social relationships. In contrast there is hardly anyone but the police to oversee relations among strangers. Seemingly the criminal law is most likely to be invoked where it is the only operable control system. The same may be said of legal control in general (see Pound, 1942; Schwartz, 1954; Nader and Metzger, 1963). Legal control melds with other aspects of social organization.

THE COMPLAINANT'S DEFERENCE

Evidence accumulates from studies of

TABLE 1. PERCENT OF POLICE ENCOUNTERS WITH COMPLAINANTS ACCORDING TO TYPE OF CRIME AND RELATIONAL TIE BETWEEN CITIZEN ADVERSARIES, BY SITUATIONAL OUTCOME: COMPLAINANT PREFERS OFFICIAL ACTION

| | Type of Crime and Relational Tie between Citizen Adversaries | | | | | | | | |
| | Felony | | | Misdemeanor | | | All Crimes | | |
Situational Outcome	Family Members	Friends, Neighbors, Acquaintances	Strangers	Family Members	Friends, Neighbors, Acquaintances	Strangers	Family Members	Friends, Neighbors, Acquaintances	Strangers
Official Report	(4)	62	91	(3)	43	74	41	51	84
No Official Report	(5)	38	9	(5)	57	26	59	49	16
Total Percent	...	100	100	...	100	100	100	100	100
Total Number	(9)	(16)	(92)	(8)	(23)	(62)	(17)	(39)	(154)

police sanctioning that the fate of suspects sometimes hangs upon the degree of deference or respect they extend to policemen in field encounters (Westley, 1953; Piliavin and Briar, 1964; Black, 1968; Black and Reiss, 1970). As a rule, the police are especially likely to sanction suspects who fail to defer to police authority whether legal grounds exist or not. Situational etiquette can weigh heavily on broader processes of social life (see Goffman, 1956 and 1963). This section offers findings showing that the complainant's deference toward the police conditions the official recognition of crime complaints.

The deference of complainants toward the police can be classified into three categories: (1) very deferential or very respectful, (2) civil, and (3) antagonistic or disrespectful. As might be expected, complainants are not often antagonistic toward policemen; it is the suspect who is more likely to be disrespectful (Black and Reiss, 1967:63–65). The number of cases of police encounters with antagonistic complainants is too few for separate analysis of felony and misdemeanor situations. When felonies and misdemeanors are combined into one statistical base, however, it becomes clear that by a large margin the probability of an official crime report is lowest when the complainant is antagonistic in the face-to-face encounter. (See Table 2.) Less than one-third of the disrespectful complainants who prefer official action see their wishes actualized in a crime report. Because of the small number of cases this finding nevertheless should be taken as tentative. The comparison between the very deferential and the civil complainants, which is more firmly grounded, is equally striking. The police are somewhat more likely to comply with very deferential complainants than with those who are merely civil. In sum, then, the less deferential the complainant, the less likely are the police to comply with his manifest preference for official action in the form of an official crime report.[10]

Table 2 also shows that the complainant's degree of deference conditions crime-reporting in both felony and misdemeanor situations. In fact, it seems that the complainant's deference can predict official

recognition as well, or even slightly better than the legal seriousness of the crime. The probability of a crime report in misdemeanor situations where the complainant is very deferential (85%) is as high as it is in felony situations where he is only civil toward the police (80%). Still, when we hold constant the complainant's deference, the legal seriousness of the incident looms to importance. In felony situations where the complainant is very respectful, the police satisfy his preference for official action in no less than 100% of the cases.

The findings in this section reveal that the level of citizen respect for the police in field encounters has consequences beyond those known to operate in the sanctioning of suspects. Here we see that the fate of citizens who are nominally served, as well as those who are controlled by the police, rides in part upon their etiquette. The official response to an avowed victimization in part depends upon the situational *style* in which the citizen presents his complaint to the control system. Official crime rates and the justice done through police detection of criminal offenders, therefore, reflect the politeness of victims. That sanctions are sometimes more severe for alleged offenders who are disrespectful toward the police can be understood in many ways as a possible contribution to the control function. Perhaps, for example, disrespectful offenders pose a greater threat to society, since they refuse to extend legitimacy to its legal system. Perhaps deterrence is undermined by leniency toward disrespectful suspects. Perhaps not. The point is that rationales are available for understanding this pattern as it relates to the police control function. It should be apparent that such rationales do not apply as readily to the tendency of the police to underreport the victimizations of disrespectful complainants. Surely this pattern could have only the remotest connection to deterrence of illegal behavior. Etiquette, it would seem, can belittle the criminal law.

THE COMPLAINANT'S STATUS

The literature on police work abounds in speculation but provides little observational evidence concerning the relation of social

TABLE 2. PERCENT OF POLICE ENCOUNTERS WITH COMPLAINANTS ACCORDING TO TYPE OF CRIME AND COMPLAINANT'S DEGREE OF DEFERENCE, BY SITUATIONAL OUTCOME: COMPLAINANT PREFERS OFFICIAL ACTION

	Type of Crime and Complainant's Degree of Deference								
	Felony			Misdemeanor			All Crimes		
Situational Outcome	Very Deferential	Civil	Antagonistic	Very Deferential	Civil	Antagonistic	Very Deferential	Civil	Antagonistic
Official Report	100	80	(2)	85	65	(1)	91	73	30
No Official Report	..	20	(1)	15	35	(6)	9	26	70
Total Percent	100	100	..	100	100	..	100	99	100
Total Number	(15)	(127)	(3)	(20)	(79)	(7)	(35)	(206)	(10)

status to police outcomes. The routine policing of Negroes differs somewhat from that of whites, and the policing of blue-collar citizens differs quite massively from that of white-collar citizens. Nevertheless, there is a dearth of evidence that these differences arise from discriminatory behavior by policemen. It appears that more consequential in determining these outcomes are aggregative differences between the races and classes in the kinds of incidents the police handle along with situational factors such as those the present analysis examines (e.g., Skolnick, 1966; Black, 1968; Black and Reiss, 1970). Nevertheless, the research literature remains far too scanty to permit confident generalization on these questions.

Studies in the discretionary aspects of police work focus almost solely upon police encounters with suspects. The present sample provides an opportunity to investigate the relation between a complainant's race and social-class status and the probability that the police will give official recognition to his complaint. The tabulation limits the cases to those where the complainant expresses a preference for official action and to those where he is civil toward the police. This section concludes that the race of complainants does not independently relate to the production of official crime rates, but there is some evidence that the police give preferential treatment to white-collar complainants in felony situations.

For all crimes and social-class statuses taken together, the difference between Negroes and whites in the probability of an official crime report is slight and negligible (see Table 3); it is a bit higher for whites. Table 3 also shows that this probability is the same for blue-collar Negroes and blue-collar whites in felony situations, though it is comparatively higher for blue-collar Negroes in misdemeanor situations. Evidence of racial discrimination thus appears weak and inconsistent. It should nonetheless be noted that if there were consistent evidence of a race differential it is not readily clear to whom a disadvantage could be attributed. Considered from the complainant's standpoint, a higher frequency of police failure to comply with complainants of one race could be viewed as discrimination *against*

that race. But police failure to write a crime report also lowers the likelihood that the offender will be subjected to the criminal process. Since we may assume that complainants more commonly are victims of offenses committed by members of their own race than by members of another race (Reiss, 1967), then disproportionate police failure to comply with complainants could be viewed as discrimination *in favor* of that race, considered from the offender's standpoint. Race differentials in arrest rates for crimes where there is an identifiable victim necessarily pose a similar dilemma of interpretation. Definitionally, there always is a conflict of legal interests between offenders and victims. Offender-victim relationships tend to be racially homogeneous. The social organization of crime therefore complicates questions of racial discrimination in law enforcement.[11]

Along social-class lines there is some evidence of discrimination against complainants and offenders. Table 3 shows that in felony situations the police are somewhat more likely to comply with white-collar complainants than with those of blue-collar status. In fact an official crime report resulted from every encounter between the police and a white-collar felony complainant of either race. The probability of official recognition drops to about three-fourths for blue-collar felony complainants. There does not appear to be a clear social-class differential in misdemeanor situations, however.

Only in felony situations, then, does an inference of discrimination offer itself. In these encounters the police seem to discriminate against blue-collar complainants. Moreover, when both white-collar and blue-collar complainants report felonious offenses, we should be able to assume that the offenders characteristically are of blue-collar status. There is every reason to believe, after all, that white-collar citizens rarely commit the common felonies such as burglary, robbery, and aggravated assault. A possible exception is auto theft, a crime in which youths from white-collar families occasionally indulge. Since this study was conducted in predominantly blue-collar residential areas the assumption should be all the more warranted. It would follow that the police dis-

TABLE 3. PERCENT OF POLICE ENCOUNTERS WITH COMPLAINANTS ACCORDING TO TYPE OF CRIME AND COMPLAINANT'S SOCIAL-CLASS STATUS AND RACE, BY SITUATIONAL OUTCOME: COMPLAINANT PREFERS OFFICIAL ACTION AND IS CIVIL TOWARD POLICE

	Type of Crime and Complainant's Social-Class Status and Race												All Crimes and Classes	
	Felony						Misdemeanor							
	Blue-Collar		White-Collar		Class Unknown		Blue-Collar		White-Collar		Class Unknown			
Situational Outcome	Negro	White	Negro	White	Negro	White	Negro	White	Negro	White	Negro	White	Negro	White
Official Report	77	77	(5)	100	(3)	90	69	55	(2)	64	(2)	80	72	76
No Official Report	23	23	...	...	(5)	10	31	45	...	36	(3)	20	28	24
Total Percent	100	100	...	100	...	100	100	100	...	100	...	100	100	100
Total Number	(64)	(22)	(5)	(18)	(8)	(10)	(26)	(22)	(2)	(14)	(5)	(10)	(110)	(96)

criminate against blue-collar citizens who feloniously offend white-collar citizens by being comparatively lenient in the investigation of felonies committed by one blue-collar citizen against another. In this instance the legal system listens more attentively to the claims of higher status citizens. The pattern is recorded in the crime rate.

OVERVIEW

The foregoing analysis yields a number of empirical generalizations about the production of crime rates. For the sake of convenience they may be listed as follows:

I. The police officially recognize proportionately more legally serious crimes than legally minor crimes.
II. The complainant's manifest preference for police action has a significant effect upon official crime-reporting.
III. The greater the relational distance between the complainant and the suspect, the greater is the likelihood of official recognition.
IV. The more deferential the complainant toward the police, the greater is the likelihood of official recognition of the complaint.
V. There is no evidence of racial discrimination in crime-reporting.
VI. There is some evidence that the police discriminate in favor of white-collar complainants, but this is true only in the official recognition of legally serious crime situations.

On the surface these findings have direct methodological relevance for those who would put official statistics to use as empirical data, whether to index actual crime in the population or to index actual police practices. Crime rates, as data, systematically underrepresent much crime and much police work. To learn some of the patterns by which this selection process occurs is to acquire a means of improving the utility of crime rates as data.

It should again be emphasized that these patterns of police behavior have consequences not only for official rates of detection as such; they also result in differential investigation of crimes and hence differential probabilities of arrest and conviction of criminal offenders. Thus the life chances of a criminal violator may depend upon who his victim is and how his victim presents his claim to the police. The complainant's role is appreciable in the criminal process. Surely the complainant has a central place in other legal and nonlegal control contexts as well, though there is as yet little research on the topic. Complainants are the consumers of justice. They are the prime movers of every known legal system, the human mechanisms by which legal services are routed into situations where there is a felt need for law. Complainants are the most invisible and they may be the most important social force binding the law to other aspects of social organization.

Notes

[1] An approach that operationally defines criminal deviance as that which the police record as criminal—and nothing else—is immune to these problems. This would be the most radical "labeling" approach. It would exclude from the category of crime, for example, a murder carried out so skillfully that it goes undetected. It would necessarily exclude most "police brutality," since crimes committed by policemen are seldom detected and officially recorded as such.

[2] In his definition of law, Hoebel (1954:28) notes that enforcement of law is a "socially recognized" privilege. In the same vein a crime rate may be understood as a socially recognized product of law enforcement work. Malinowski (1962:79–80) stresses the importance of social recognition of deviant acts for the community as well as for the deviant person.

[3] The moral and physical organization of social life into public and private places guarantees contemporary society some volume of secret deviance (Schwartz, 1968; Lofland, 1969:62–68). As far as criminal deviance is concerned, other well-known factors are the failure of citizens to report victimizations to the police and the failure of the police to report what is reported to them.

Evidence from victimization surveys suggests that underreporting of crime in official statistics is more a consequence of police discretion than of the failure of citizens to notify the police. Citizens claim that they report far more crimes to the police than the police ultimately report; this margin of unreported crime exceeds that which citizens admit they withhold from the police (Biderman, 1967).

[4] The "clearance rate" is a hybrid form of crime rate produced in American police systems. This is

the proportion of "crimes known to the police" that have been solved, whether through arrest or some other means (see Skolnick, 1966:164–181).

[5] It is interesting to note that in ancient Roman law the offender caught in the act of theft was subject to a more serious punishment than the offender apprehended some time after detection of his theft. In the *Laws of the Twelve Tables* these were called "manifest" and "non-manifest" thefts. The same legal principle is found in the early Anglo-Saxon and other Germanic codes (Maine, 1963:366–367). It could well be that a similar pattern is found in present-day law-in-action. What is formal in one legal system may be informal in another.

[6] The heavier penalties that the law provides for felonies may compensate for a loss in deterrence that could result from the relatively low rate at which felons are apprehended. Likewise, the law of arrest seemingly compensates for the social organization of crime that gives felons a head start on the police. In most jurisdictions the police need less evidence in felony than in misdemeanor situations to make a legal arrest without warrant. By a second technique, then, the legal system increases the jeopardy of felony offenders. The power of substantive law increases as procedural restrictions on legal officials are weakened. By both penalty and procedure, the law pursues the felon with a special vengeance.

[7] Crime situations were classified as felonies or misdemeanors according to legal criteria. These criteria were applied to the version of the crime that prevailed in the police-citizen transaction. The observation reports required the observer to classify the incident in a detailed list of categories as well as to write a long-hand description of the incident. The felony-misdemeanor breakdown was made during the coding stage of the investigation. The major shortcoming of this strategy is that the tabulation allows no gradations of legal seriousness within the felony and misdemeanor categories. This shortcoming was accepted in order to facilitate more elaborate statistical analysis with a minimum of attrition in the number of cases.

It should also be noted that the tabulations do not provide information pertaining to the kind of official report the police wrote for a given kind of crime situation. Occasionally, the police officially characterize the crime with a category that seems incorrect to a legally sophisticated observer. Most commonly this involves reducing the legal seriousness of the crime. However, there are cases where the officer, sometimes through sheer ignorance of the law or inattention, increases the legal seriousness of the crime. In one case, for example, a woman complained about two young men in an automobile who had made obscene remarks to her as she walked along the street near her residence. She claimed she was prepared to press charges. After leaving the scene the officer filled out an official report, classifying the incident as an "aggravated assault," the felonious level of assault. Before doing so he asked the observer for his opinion as to the proper category. The observer

feigned ignorance.

[8] Here two general remarks about analytical strategy seem appropriate. One is that the present approach abdicates the problematics of psychological analysis. The observational study does not provide data on the motives or cognitions of the police or the citizens whose behavior is described. Still, findings on patterns of behavior make prediction of police behavior possible. They also offer opportunities for drawing inferences about the impact or implications of police work for social organization. Much can be learned about man's behavior in a social matrix without knowing how he experiences his behavior. The consequences of behavior, moreover, are indifferent to their mental origins.

Secondly, the strategy pursued in this analysis is not sensitive, except in the broadest terms, to the temporal dimension of police-citizen transactions. Thus, simply because the complainant's preference is treated prior to other variables does not mean that it is temporally prior to other aspects of police-citizen interaction. Like the other variables treated in this investigation, the complainant's preference is prior in time only to the final police response to the encounter.

[9] Hall (1952:318) suggests that the relational distance between the victim and offender may influence the probability of *prosecution*. The present investigation, following Hall, seeks to predict social control responses from variations in relational distance. A different strategy is to predict community organization from the relationships between adversaries who enter the legal system, under the assumption that legal disputes bespeak a relative absence of informal control in the relational contexts where they arise (see Náder, 1964).

[10] The findings in this section present a problem of interpretation, since no information about the police officer's behavior toward the citizen is provided apart from whether or not he wrote an official report. Therefore, nothing is known from the tabulation about whether the officer behaved in such a way as to *provoke* the citizen into one or another degree of deference. Nothing is known about the subtle exchange of cues that takes place in any instance of face-to-face interaction. Other studies of the role of deference in police work are subject to the same criticism. Here, again, no inquiry is made into the motivational dimensions of the pattern. It nevertheless should be emphasized that whatever the motivation of the complainant behavior, the motivation was not the failure of the police to write an official report. In the cities studied the complainant ordinarily did not even know whether or not an official report was written, since the police ordinarily wrote the report in the police car or at the police station after leaving the encounter with the complainant. During the encounter they recorded the relevant facts about the incident in a notebook, whether or not they intended to write an official report. As some officers say, they do this "for show" in order to lead the complainant to believe they are "doing

something." Thus, in the average case, it can be assumed that the complainant's deference is not a consequence of the situational outcome. Furthermore, the observers were instructed to record only the level of citizen deference that appeared prior to the situational outcome. A separate item was provided in the observation booklet for recording the citizen's manifest level of satisfaction at the close of the encounter. It therefore remains reasonable to hold that the complainant's deference can aid in calculating the probability of an official crime report.

[11] It may seem that in criminal matters the costs are slight for the complainant when the police fail to comply with his preference for official action. However, it should be remembered that crimes frequently involve an economic loss for the victim, a loss that can sometimes be recouped if and when the offender is discovered. In other cases, discovery and punishment of the offender may net the victim nothing more than a sense of revenge or security or a sense that justice has been done—concerns that have received little attention in social science. For that matter, social scientists generally examine questions of discriminatory law enforcement *only* from the offender's standpoint. Ordinary citizens in high crime rate areas probably are more interested in questions of discrimination in police allocation of manpower for community protection.

REFERENCES

Biderman, Albert D.
1967 "Surveys of population samples for estimating crime incidence." The Annals of the American Academy of Political and Social Science 374 (1967):16–33.
Biderman, Albert D. and Albert J. Reiss, Jr.
1967 "On exploring the 'dark figure' of crime." The Annals of the American Academy of Political and Social Science 374 (1967):1–15.
Bittner, Egon
1967 "The police on skid-row: A study of peace-keeping." American Sociological Review 32 (1967):699–715.
Black, Donald J.
1968 Police Encounters and Social Organization: An Observation Study. Unpublished Ph.D. Dissertation, Department of Sociology, University of Michigan.
Black, Donald J. and Albert J. Reiss, Jr.
1967 "Patterns of behavior in police and citizen transactions." Pp. 1–139 in President's Commission on Law Enforcement and Administration of Justice, Studies in Crime and Law Enforcement in Major Metropolitan Areas, Field Surveys III, Volume 2. Washington, D. C.: U.S. Government Printing Office.
1970 "Police control of juveniles." American Sociological Review 35 (February):63–77.
Cicourel, Aaron V.
1968 The Social Organization of Juvenile Justice. New York: John Wiley and Sons, Inc.

de Beaumont, Gustave and Alexis de Tocqueville
1964 On the Penitentiary System in the United States and Its Application in France. Carbondale, Ill.: Southern University Press. (orig. pub. 1833)
Erikson, Kai T.
1966 Wayward Puritans: A Study in the Sociology of Deviance. New York: John Wiley and Sons.
Goffman, Erving
1956 "The nature of deference and demeanor." American Anthropologist 58 (1956):473–502.
1963 Behavior in Public Places: Notes on the Social Organization of Gatherings. New York: The Free Press.
Hall, Jerome
1952 Theft, Law and Society. Indianapolis, Ind.: The Bobbs-Merrill Company. (2nd Ed.)
Hoebel, E. Adamson
1954 The Law of Primitive Man: A Study in Comparative Legal Dynamics. Cambridge: Harvard University Press.
Kitsuse, John I. and Aaron Cicourel
1963 "A note on the uses of official statistics." Social Problems 11 (1963):131–139.
LaFave, Wayne R.
1965 Arrest: The Decision to Take a Suspect into Custody. Boston: Little, Brown and Company.
Lofland, John
1969 Deviance and Identity. Englewood Cliffs, N. J.: Prentice-Hall.
Maine, Henry Sumner
1963 Ancient Law: Its Connection with the Early History of Society and Its Relation to Modern Ideas. Boston: Beacon Press. (orig. pub. 1861)
Malinowski, Bronislaw
1962 Crime and Custom in Savage Society. Paterson, N. J.: Littlefield, Adams and Co. (orig. pub. 1926)
Morrison, William Douglas
1897 "The interpretation of criminal statistics." Journal of the Royal Statistical Society 60 (1897):1–24.
Nader, Laura
1964 "An analysis of Zapotec Law cases." Ethnology 3 (1964):404–419.
Nader, Laura and Duane Metzger
1963 "Conflict resolution in two Mexican communities." American Anthropologist 65 (1963):584–592.
Piliavin, Irving and Scott Briar
1964 "Police encounters with juveniles." American Journal of Sociology 70 (1964):206–214.
Pound, Roscoe
1942 Social Control Through Law. New Haven: Yale University Press.
Reiss, Albert J., Jr.
1967 "Measurement of the nature and amount of crime." Pp. 1–183 in President's Commission on Law Enforcement and Adminis-

tration of Justice, Studies in Crime and Law Enforcement in Major Metropolitan Areas, Field Surveys III, Volume 1. Washington, D.C.: U.S. Government Printing Office.

Schwartz, Barry
1968 "The social psychology of privacy." American Journal of Sociology 73 (1968):741–752.
Schwartz, Richard D.
1954 "Social factors in the development of legal control: A case study of two Israeli settlements." Yale Law Journal 63 (1954):471–491.
Sellin, Thorsten
1931 "Crime." Pp. 563–569 in Edwin R. A. Seligman (ed.), Encyclopaedia of the Social Sciences, Volume 4. New York: The Macmillan Company.

Skolnick, Jerome H.
1966 Justice Without Trial: Law Enforcement in Democratic Society. New York: John Wiley and Sons.
Stinchcombe, Arthur L.
1963 "Institutions of privacy in the determination of police administrative practice." American Journal of Sociology 69(1963): 150–160.
Westley, William A.
1953 "Violence and the police." American Journal of Sociology 59 (1955):34–41.
Wheeler, Stanton
1967 "Criminal statistics: A reformulation of the problem." Journal of Criminal Law, Criminology and Police Science 58 (1967):317–324.
Wilson, James Q.
1968 Varieties of Police Behavior: The Management of Law and Order in Eight Communities. Cambridge, Mass.: Harvard University Press.

POLICE EAVESDROPPING: LAW-ENFORCEMENT REVOLUTION

Fred P. Graham

Any one of a number of incidents might legitimately be singled out as the one that did most to trigger the remarkable change that took place in the law of electronic eavesdropping in the final years of the Warren Court. But in retrospect, it appears that Al Kee moved the pebble that loosed the avalanche when he shoved Edward Levinson's desk from its accustomed spot in the Fremont Hotel and gambling casino on Saturday morning, April 27, 1963.

The official story that has since been told in court proceedings and to the press is that it all happened by accident, that it was just an unlucky day for the Federal Bureau of Investigation. According to the official version, Al Kee, an employee of the Central Telephone Company of Las Vegas who knew all about the workings of telephones, happened to be moonlighting that day to pick up some extra cash and as a personal favor to Levinson. Levinson was president and major stockholder of the Fremont Hotel, and the story has it that his office there was beginning to bore him. He called in his friend Kee to do some rearranging, to move the furniture around and jazz things up. To move the desk, Kee had to adjust the telephone cord, which revealed a puzzling thing: inside the cord were four wires, not the usual three. Kee traced the fourth wire up into the telephone base. There, tucked into a nook inside the telephone's works, he found a tiny microphone.

By tracing the mysterious fourth wire back to the hotel's telephone room and then by referring to the telephone company's cable diagram, it was learned that the little microphone hidden in the telephone on Ed Levinson's desk had been connected to a line leased by the telephone company to the Henderson Novelty Company. It did not take Levinson long to discover that no such company existed in Las Vegas, and that the leased line led to the Las Vegas office of the Federal Bureau of Investigation.

The unofficial version of the discovery, the one that is believed by many people in top law-enforcement circles in Washington, is less colorful but more credible. It is that Levinson and his Washington attorney, Edward Bennett Williams, were the beneficiaries of a rare "leak" from within the F.B.I.—that they had been told that the "bug" was there and that the remodeling was staged to let Kee find it. In any event, word of his discovery flashed immediately along the green felt grapevine of Las Vegas' gambling casinos, where searches uncovered more "bugs"—first in the Sands Hotel (where the device may have picked up some famous voices, since Frank Sinatra and Dean Martin were shareholders), then in the Dunes, the Stardust, the Desert Inn and, finally, in the home of one casino operator.

To the men who found the tiny devices in their offices, sitting rooms and bedrooms, the meaning was unmistakable. With the election of John F. Kennedy as President in 1960 and the appointment of his brother Robert as Attorney General, the Federal government had developed a strong prosecutorial interest in the activities of the nationwide crime syndicate known as the Mafia, or as it was then coming to be called, "La Cosa Nostra." It was no secret that the F.B.I. believed that the key to the Mafia's secrets might be found in Las Vegas, where some casinos were said to represent the most visible enterprises of La Cosa Nostra.

In the years of litigation that followed, it came to light that the F.B.I. had leased twenty-five lines in Las Vegas, and that a number of them were used to maintain around-the-clock surveillance of certain gambling casinos. Similar eavesdropping was being employed in Kansas City, Chicago, Miami, New York, Providence and perhaps a dozen other cities where the crime syndicate had flourished. As the successive disclosures of governmental eavesdropping were publicized and as the inevitable court challenges worked their way through the courts, the Supreme Court and Congress were forced to come to grips with the reality that police surveillance was widespread and was out of legal control. It had long been apparent that the law of electronic eavesdropping was in a hopeless muddle, but the Government had given the impression that very little of it was going on. The discovery that it was in wide use, and that it was so effective that pressures for its further use would inevitably increase, preceded one of the odd phenomena of the Warren Court. At a time when the Court tended to take a critical view of many police investigative techniques and was actively expanding the constitutional protections of individuals to speak boldly without fear of reprisal, the Warren Court enlarged the legal power of the Government to spy on its citizens by means of the new electronic technology.

The story of how this electronic anomaly came into being affords a revealing insight into how factors other than briefs, arguments and precedents go into making of law in the Supreme Court. For in retrospect it appears that two separate developments outside the Court and one within it converged in the mid-1960s to change the Supreme Court's course. One was the F.B.I.'s intensive use of electronic bugging, which produced proof of the scope of organized crime and the capacity of electronic surveillance to penetrate it, as well as a public flap over the disclosures. Another was the efforts of a small but stategically placed group of lawyers on the staff of the National Crime Commission and in other law-enforcement positions, who became alarmed about organized crime and began to advocate electronic eavesdropping as a weapon to use against it. The third was a movement within the Court, begun by Justice William J. Brennan, Jr., to re-examine an eavesdrop doctrine which he considered dangerously inadequate to the task of regulating the sophisticated new electronic devices.

When the microphone and the telephone were invented in the late 1800s, the law was unprepared to deal with the new threats to privacy, and it has been scrambling to catch up ever since. People had barely ceased to marvel over Alexander Graham Bell's first public demonstration of telephones in 1876 before the police department in New York began to tap them. In no time the

police established a cozy working relationship with the New York Telephone Company to permit ease in tapping phones. By 1895, New York's finest had been caught for the first time using wiretaps. In time, earphones became such a mainstay of law and order that New York wrote into its Constitution as well as its statute books the authority of the police to tap wires with court consent.

Only the fact that the police in most communities were under-educated, unimaginative and ill-equipped prevented a parade of eavesdrop scandals, and in the few large cities where the police were in better shape, scandals abounded. Many states passed laws against wiretapping, but the police rarely felt that the laws applied to them. The lawmakers at the Federal level—Congress and the Supreme Court—proved their ineptitude in this area early and often, so that for the most part police eavesdropping was limited primarily by law-enforcement officials' lack of imagination, sense of propriety or fear of public outrage.

This condition of laissez-faire was threatened in 1928 when the Supreme Court finally considered the constitutionality of wiretapping by Federal agents. Law and order usually meant parched palates in those days of Prohibition, and the issue predictably came before the Court in the form of the convictions of a group of bootleggers. Wiretaps on the home and office telephones of the ringleaders of a Canada-to-Seattle bootleg operation had proved so productive that eighty-one individuals in the liquor trade in and around Seattle were indicted, and many went to jail. In an effort to avoid this, the boss of the operation, Roy Olmstead, and a handful of his lieutenants, brought a landmark appeal to the Supreme Court. They argued that wiretapping was unconstitutional because it violated the Fifth Amendment's privilege against compulsory self-incrimination, and that it invaded a zone of privacy that is protected by the Fourth Amendment's prohibition against unreasonable search and seizures.

The Fifth Amendment argument struck the Court as farfetched, since they voluntarily conducted their illicit business over the telephone. But the Fourth Amendment has been designed to insulate private premises from unreasonable government intrusion, and four of the nine Justices concluded that the wiretap evidence was illegally obtained. The majority, however, took the Fourth Amendment at its face value. There had been no "search" because the Prohibition agents had carefully avoided entering private premises, and there had been no "seizures" because words are not things with handles that police may grasp. There had, indeed, been a state statute that made wiretapping a crime, but the Supreme Court felt that U.S. courts could not vary their rules of evidence according to each state's law. The decision was an occasion for one of Brandeis' eloquent dissents, protesting that the Fourth Amendment applied to "any unjustifiable intrusion by the Government upon the privacy of the individual." Holmes added his unforgettable remark that illegal police wiretapping is "dirty business."

However logical it was to conclude that the Founding Fathers did not intend to strike at a then-unimagined form of electrical surveillance when they drafted the Fourth Amendment, the *Olmstead* decision had the eventual effect of creating a labyrinthian maze of laws governing electronic eavesdropping. By 1963, when Al Kee found the bug in Ed Levinson's telephone, a few of the legal possibilities were these:

If the device picked up both ends of conversations over the bugged telephone, then it would have been a wiretap forbidden by

Federal law but occasionally authorized by the Attorney General in national security investigations. No information or leads gained by a wiretap would have been admissible in Federal court if the tap had been the work of Federal or state agents, but evidence from a wiretap installed without a trespass by state or local police would have been admissible under Federal law in state but not Federal courts.

If the device was a "bug"—a microphone that picked up conversations in the room but not both ends of calls over the telephone—then there would have been no Federal law specifically forbidding its use. But since it was placed in private premises by stealth, no information obtained by it could have been admitted in court, and under the law of Nevada, whoever planted it committed a crime.

All of which was of scant consolation to the gambler-businessmen who had been bugged, because they knew that however the legalities sorted out, such elaborate surveillance would not have been carried out unless it was distinctly to their disadvantage. The fact that they had been victimized by pervasive F.B.I. eavesdropping attested to the legal deterioration that was in an advanced stage by the early 1960s. Some of the devices had been in operation for more than two years; the F.B.I. had become so blasé that its agents planted a final bug in another casino several weeks after F.B.I. eavesdroppers heard Al Kee find the Levinson bug. Almost a quarter-century had passed since *Olmstead v. United States,* and police eavesdropping was virtually outside the law.

It all began with the unstated assumption by the Justices in the *Olmstead* case that if police wiretapping were covered by the Fourth Amendment, then all wiretapping must necessarily be forbidden.

To make this assumption virtually decided the case, for police eavesdropping seemed too valuable a law-enforcement tool to be strangled in its cradle by the Supreme Court. Yet, in 1928, it was quite logical to assume that if police wiretapping were controlled by the Fourth Amendment then it would have to be prohibited as an inherently unreasonable form of search and seizure. The Court found itself paying a price for its own zeal in shrinking the area of legal searches. As a practical matter, it had lost the option to bring wiretapping within the Fourth Amendment, because the rules for warrants were so strict that they seemed to preclude a valid warrant to wiretap.

In the first place, the Fourth Amendment requires that all warrants state the particular things to be seized. But a wiretap is inherently indiscriminate, seizing all the words that flow on the tapped lines. Inevitably, a warrant to overhear certain conversations would pick up others as well, amounting to a warrant to conduct a "general search." Another stumbling block was the "mere evidence" rule which forbade the seizure of items other than the fruits or instrumentalities of crime. Words could never be anything but evidence, so under the Supreme Court's rules, they could not legally be taken by the police for use in court. Finally, a valid search always requires notice to the subject of the search. Prior notice of a wiretap would be like asking permission to administer a hotfoot.

So, torn between absolute prohibition and complete toleration of police eavesdropping, the law wobbled, contorted, stretched. In 1934, Congress passed the Federal Communications Act, which carried over from the earlier act a prohibition against the interception of any communication and the divulgence or use of such communication. The Supreme Court, apparently relieved to have a statutory basis for approaching the problem without freezing its solutions into the Constitution, ruled that this made wiretapping a crime, even when done by the police. Nothing had been said in the statute about excluding evidence by wiretap, but the Supreme Court nevertheless tagged an exclusionary rule onto the law, making it the first act of Congress to be thus reinforced by the Court.

An awkward double standard quickly developed, because the Supreme Court, having dealt imaginatively with the statute to ban wiretapping by Federal officers, concluded that it would be unseemly to encroach on states' rights by applying the exclusionary rule to state and local police. The Court did say that these police would commit a crime whenever they testified in court about their interceptions. But because the Justice Department was quietly fudging on the antiwiretap law itself, it was in no position to prosecute local police for the same failing, and no local officer was ever prosecuted. Eventually, the laws of five states came to authorize police wiretapping with court approval—yet each time a policeman testified in court as to what he overheard with a state judge's approval, he committed a Federal crime.

While the law was foundering over wiretapping, it was also being outflanked by technological developments in the science that came to be known as "bugging." The invention of transistors made possible the construction of tiny microphones and radio transmitters—"bugs"—that could do their work at unlikely times and places. The bugged olive in the martini that captured the public's imagination was probably never used (it was suggested by a Senate investigating committee to illustrate the possibilities), but other equally ingenious devices were. The Russians bugged the Great Seal of the United States that hung in the Ambassador's study at the American Embassy in Moscow. An inventor in New York devised a bug that can be placed in a telephone and activated from anywhere in the world. The eavesdropper simply dials the number of the bugged telephone and quickly blows a harmonica tone into his own telephone. This silently activates the bug in the other telephone, which monitors all conversations in the room until the eavesdropper hangs up or the bugged telephone is lifted from its cradle.

Other instruments even removed the necessity for illegal entry to plant bugs. A device called a "detectaphone" looks and operates much like a physician's stethoscope. When pressed against the outside wall of a room it overhears the conversations within. The sill mike is designed to rest on the floor outside a closed door, where it can overhear conversations inside without a physical intrusion into the room.

For outside surveillance, the type of directional microphones used by television sports announcers to pick up sounds on the playing field can also overhear private discussions in parks and streets. To further complicate the trespass question, eavesdroppers can bug a victim without his knowledge, turning him into a walking eavesdropping device to enter private premises for the eavesdropper. An intriguing illustration of the potentialities of this technique surfaced in Washington several years ago when rumors spread that the Central Intelligence Agency had bribed a local cobbler to plant bugs in the heels of foreign diplomats' shoes.

Although these techniques posed a greater threat to privacy than wiretaps because they tended to operate when speakers were least on their guard, as late as 1963 they were largely outside the reach of the law. There was no Federal statute against bugging (although theoretically, Federal agents might have been punished under a statute that forbade them to conduct illegal searches), and since the *Olmstead* case had held that the Fourth Amendment did not apply to seizures of words, evidence obtained by police bugging was admissible in court unless the police committed a physical trespass to plant the bug. This led to legal results that verged on the ridiculous. In a leading case, *Goldman v. United States,* the Supreme Court demonstrated how capricious its rules could be in practice. Federal agents had entered a suspect's office at night to plant a microphone, which failed to work. So they pressed a detectaphone against the outside wall and overheard conversations, including those of a suspect within speaking into a telephone. Because the device planted by trespass wasn't used, and because only one end of the telephone conversations were overheard, no legal rule was violated, and the conviction was upheld. Yet in a subsequent case, when a police "spike mike" penetrated the common wall between a room being used by eavesdropping police officers and an adjoining suspect's room, the Supreme Court found a physical trespass and excluded all that the eavesdroppers had overheard. The Court reached the ultimate refinement of this theory in 1964 when it reversed a conviction because the police used a listening device that penetrated the outside wall the depth of a thumb tack

—exposing the Court to the jibe that under its doctrines a thumb-tack's length could separate an individual from the protection of the Bill of Rights.

These legal quirks inevitably shaped the Government's eaves-drop policy. Because wiretapping was a Federal crime, most of the official attention centered on it, while bugging was developing into a greater threat to privacy. Even after the Supreme Court ruled that the 1934 law applied to law-enforcement officers, the Justice Department insisted that it could still tap wires without violating the law, so long as it did not divulge the wiretap infor-mation outside of the Government. This resulted in enough wire-tapping to produce an unseemly succession of public disclosures of Governmental snooping, and in March of 1940, Attorney Gen-eral Robert H. Jackson announced that the Justice Department had "completely abandoned the practice" of wiretapping. This self-denial quickly gave in to an important exception. The im-pending war brought a threat of espionage and sabotage and Pres-ident Roosevelt decided that the Government should use wire-tapping in self-defense.

Roosevelt took great care, in these instructions to Jackson, to create only a narrow exception to the general ban on Governmental wiretapping. The President began by expressing his agreement with the Supreme Court's restrictions on wiretapping by the police. "The Court is undoubtedly sound in regard to the use of evidence secured over tapped wires in the prosecution of citizens in criminal cases," he said, "and is also right in its opinion that under ordinary and normal circumstances wiretapping by Government agents should not be carried on for the excellent reason that it is almost bound to lead to abuse of civil rights." But he felt that the Court did not intend to preclude wiretapping regarding "grave matters involving the defense of the nation," so he authorized Jackson to use it, limited "to a minimum," and "insofar as possible, to aliens."

About a year after Roosevelt's death, a future member of the Warren Court played a key role in prying open this narrow excep-tion to permit wiretapping beyond cases involving foreign intrigue.

Tom C. Clark, the new Attorney General, wrote a letter to President Harry S Truman on July 17, 1946, quotong one passage of Roosevelt's wiretap instructions, but leaving out Roosevelt's statement that wiretapping in criminal cases would threaten civil liberties and his orders to confine it as much as possible to investigations of foreign-born spy suspects. Clark observed that "the country is threatened by a very substantial increase in crime," and that while he was reluctant to use such measures in domestic cases, "it seems imperative to use them in cases vitally affecting the domestic security, or where human life is in jeopardy." His letter left no doubt that he was requesting an expansion of the Roosevelt policy, but it downplayed the significance of the change.

Truman granted the new authority to use wiretapping in domestic cases. Clark lost no time in using it. He encouraged J. Edgar Hoover to crank up the F.B.I.'s "Top Hood" gangbusting program and he is said personally to have approved the wiretapping of such rackets figures as Mafia playgirl Virginia Hill, and Ralph Capone, brother of the notorious Al.

A measure of the shifts in legal thinking that occurred within the Warren Court came twenty years later, when Justice Tom Clark wrote the Supreme Court's opinion in *Berger v. New York*. He declared unconstitutional New York's permissive police eavesdropping law, with the warning that "few threats to liberty exist which are greater than that posed by the use of eavesdropping devices."

As fascinating as the national leaders' contortions over wiretapping proved to be, they obscured the true conditions of police violations of privacy, rather than illuminating it. For the word "wiretapping" came to be equated in the public mind with electronic eavesdropping in the broad sense. If high public officials eschewed all wiretapping, or reeled off careful statistics to show how little wiretapping was going on, then people assumed that their private words were fairly safe from Government ears. This was totally misleading, for the strictures on wiretapping had encouraged other types of governmental eavesdropping that were far more destructive of privacy than the tapping of telephone lines.

One of the rituals of public deception was the annual appearance of J. Edgar Hoover before the House Appropriations Committee. Until the lid blew off the F.B.I.'s surveillance activities in the late 1960s, Hoover unfailingly gave careful statistics as to the limited amount of wiretapping that was going on and omitted any public reference to the mushrooming use of bugging by the F.B.I. Several weeks before Al Kee found the F.B.I. bug in Las Vegas, Hoover appeared before an appropriations subcommittee and explained that as of that day the F.B.I. had a total of ninety-five wiretaps in operation, all in "security cases." "In accordance with the policy of many years standing," he added, "telephone taps are utilized only in cases where the internal security of the country is involved, or where kidnapping and extortion may bring about the jeopardy of human life. The F.B.I. does not have authority to authorize a wiretap. Each one must be authorized in advance and in writing by the Attorney General."

This was, of course, only an artful half-truth. While the F.B.I. was keeping a careful public tally of its national security wiretaps, it was planting bugs across the country in domestic criminal cases as well as in security investigations. That was why the devices hidden in the telephones in Las Vegas were wired so that they would not intercept calls on the bugged phones, although apparently they could easily have been installed so that they would have done so. By picking up only words spoken in the room where the bugged telephone sat, they did not qualify as "wiretaps," and thus could be omitted from Hoover's report.

The F.B.I.'s wiretap total eventually took on such psychological importance that the Bureau went to extreme exertions to keep the figure below 100. One ex-agent has told of an instance when the number of taps was pushing 100 and an instruction came down to disconnect a wiretap in order to free a tap for a more important case. He did so. Then, under orders, he picked the lock of the home where the tapped telephone had been and planted a bug in its place. By 1965, when acting Attorney General Nicholas deB. Katzenbach insisted on seeing a list of the F.B.I.'s anti-Mafia bugs, he was stunned to find 98 then in use—meaning that the Bureau's eavesdropping was roughly double what the public had been led to believe.

Officially, the impression was given that F.B.I. electronic surveillance was being kept under the watchful eye of the Attorney General and was limited to internal security investigations. Even many sophisticated journalists missed the distinction between wiretapping and bugging. This led them to ask the wrong questions of public officials, and allowed the officials to perpetuate the false impression of limited governmental eavesdropping. Three years after the Las Vegas disclosures, when Robert Kennedy and Hoover were feuding over who was ultimately to blame for the violations of privacy, a reporter on a television interview show asked Senator Kennedy: "Did you authorize the F.B.I. wiretaps of gamblers telephones in Las Vegas in '62 and '63?"

"No, I did not," Kennedy solmenly replied, knowing that the devices had been bugs—not taps. He then vowed that he had never authorized wiretaps except in national security cases. Later, Hoover released documents that left little doubt that Kennedy had given the F.B.I. a virtual blank check to bug suspected Mafia chieftains.

It also came to light toward the end of the Warren era that the Government's concept of "national security" wiretapping was far more elastic than the public generally realized. Because the Government had inherited its wiretap policy from Roosevelt's 1940 directive, most people assumed that wiretapping was being used basically to thwart espionage and sabotage efforts by foreign powers. But when a series of court challenges by defendants who had been overheard exposed the nature of some of the F.B.I.'s national security wiretapping, it became clear that the Government considered it in the interest of national security to keep taps on home-grown radicals as well.

Two subjects of sustained wiretap surveillance were revealed to have been Dr. Martin Luther King, Jr., civil rights leader and Nobel Prize winner, and Elijah Muhammad, leader of the Black

Muslims. In Dr. King's case, the surveillance had been started well before he became an international celebrity, and it had its benevolent aspects. President Kennedy had become closely identified with Dr. King as early as 1960, when a telephone call from candidate Kennedy to the then imprisoned civil rights leader's wife assured Kennedy the lion's share of the Negro vote. Later, when Attorney General Robert Kennedy came to believe that Dr. King was in some danger of becoming a cat's-paw for Communists, he felt that it was a good idea for both President Kennedy and Dr. King if the Government were to keep the civil rights leader under protective surveillance. In Elijah Muhammad's case, also, the wiretapping was said to have been partially prompted by reasons other than keeping tabs on black militants. But whatever the reasons, this use of constant electronic surveillance to keep the Government informed of the activities of dissident elements was reminiscent enough of George Orwell's *1984* to bring a sense of urgency to legislative and judicial efforts to bring governmental surveillance within legal bounds.

In the Supreme Court, the first public move came in May of 1963—before the news of the F.B.I.'s anti-Mafia bugging had spread beyond Las Vegas—in the form of a dissenting opinion issued by William J. Brennan, Jr. One mark of an influential Justice is the capacity to single out deficiencies in the law and to articulate persuasive reasons why the law should be changed. That is why Holmes, Brandeis and Black have been so widely admired for their numerous dissents that later became majority rulings. Justice Brennan wrote such a dissent when he took stock of the eavesdrop situation and proposed a fundamental constitutional change.

The case, *Lopez v. United States,* was an unfortunate one for this purpose, because it involved a hybrid form of electronic listening that could logically be said not to constitute eavesdropping at all. It grew out of a situation in which a government agent who had been offered a bribe had tucked a transmitter into his clothing and had gone to talk money with the briber, with other agents listening in. The Court had already held, in a 1952 case, that there is nothing improper about this surreptitious use of electronics. The Justices reasoned that the person who speaks under these circumstances is not betrayed by the hidden transmitter but by his decision to converse with a second person, who could testify to the conversation in court, even without the electronically provided corroborations.

Brennan argued that a person engaged in private conversation should at least be assured that third persons could not throw the words back at him in court. Brennan's point was that this use of electronics need not be precluded, but only controlled, if brought within the Fourth Amendment. He felt that the Supreme Court had shied away from overturning *Olmstead*, even though it had been eroded by subsequent events, because the Justices had assumed that no wiretap warrant could be drawn that would satisfy the standards of the Fourth Amendment. The difficulties, he felt, had been exaggerated by the analogy with search warrants. Wiretapping is a distinct form of searching, so he argued that the Fourth Amendment might well tolerate differences between wiretap warrants and search warrants. Brennan attempted to make the point that it was an open question as to whether bringing eavesdropping within the Fourth Amendment would curtail its usefulness to the police, but his invitation to the more conservative Justices to reopen the question smacked of the spider speaking to the fly; as the Fourth Amendment precedents stood, it seemed unlikely that they would permit much eavesdropping. His dissent was joined by only Douglas and Goldberg—two Justices who rarely saw things the police's way. In any event, Brennan warned that an attempt should be made to bring electronic surveillance within constitutional controls, before surveillance became so widespread that the people's rights of political anonymity and free speech were undermined.

From this equivocal initiative in 1963, the constitutional atmosphere surrounding eavesdropping changed so rapidly that by 1969 police wiretapping was being authorized by Federal judges and the fruits were being used as evidence in United States courts. Moreover, this did not come in spite of the Supreme Court; it was encouraged by it. Within three years after *Lopez*, the Supreme Court majority began to take steps that in retrospect can be seen as preparation for a reversal of the *Olmstead* decision, without automatically eliminating police eavesdropping. In 1968 the Court pointedly nudged Congress toward enactment of a permissive eavesdrop law.

For the Supreme Court, this was blinding speed—and there were developments on the outside that helped account for it. The Las Vegas disclosures and the others that followed soured many people on lawless police snooping, and defense lawyers were learning to ferret it out where formerly it would have gone unnoticed. The prospect was that years of tiresome litigation would be required to determine which convictions had been tainted and which had not. Unless some way were found to legitimate reasonable police eavesdropping and eliminate the rest, this would become a chronic judicial headache.

However, the litigation of this type that did take place proved very educational to the Federal judiciary and to the American public. The first logs of F.B.I. surveillances were revealed secretly to a few Federal judges in 1966 in the course of routine criminal trials. This began to happen with increasing frequency as defense lawyers, realizing that their clients may have been overheard by F.B.I. bugs in Las Vegas or elsewhere, began to demand that trial judges require the F.B.I. to produce the transcripts and logs of all surveillances that arguably could have related to the charges against the defendants. The Justice Department cooperated by systematically reviewing the transcripts of surveillance to determine if anyone being prosecuted by the Government had ever been a victim of illegal eavesdropping.

In order to satisfy themselves that none of this illegally obtained information contributed in any way to the Government's case, trial judges found it necessary to comb through huge volumes of transcripts and digests of the unguarded conversations of crime syndicate bosses. Later, a few such logs became public in the course of litigation, disclosing that the F.B.I. learned almost daily of extortion, blackmail, narcotics smuggling and other crimes, and that the agents even prevented some murders and learned of others through these conversations. It may have been that when word of the scope of the F.B.I.'s eavesdropping and the value of its findings became known within the Federal judiciary, that the Justices became impressed with the urgency of curbing the practice without eliminating it.

In any event, it new seems clear that by 1966 a majority of the Court had been won over to Brennan's view that something had to be done about eavesdropping, although there probably was not then a consensus of the Court as to what it should be. The situation raised a novel problem of Supreme Court methodology. For all of the activism of the Warren Court, it had operated within the traditional appellate framework, resolving points brought for decision by opposing advocates. Here, Brennan was asking the Court to change its course, when change was not being vigorously urged upon the Court by either side in the police wiretap controversy. Both sides were essentially satisfied with the status quo on wiretapping, since both stood to lose if changes were made. Law enforcement had been denied the authority in most situations to use electronic eavesdropping to gather evidence for courtroom use, but the Las Vegas disclosures demonstrated that eavesdropping was still well worth the Government's trouble in terms of providing criminal intelligence (plus, many defense lawyers suspected, some well-disguised leads to evidence). In view of the Warren Court's tendency to rule on defendants' behalf, the police could not be enthusiastic over the prospect of closer judicial attention to police wiretapping. Civil libertarians, on the other hand, realized that under the prevailing law-and-order mood in the country, any ferment would probably bring changes that they would not like.

The result was that neither side was pressing the Supreme Court to do what it was suddenly prepared to consider—sweeping electronic surveillance within the ambit of the Fourth Amendment, while relaxing the rules so that some form of eavesdropping could be employed with proper court approval. Even if the Justice Department had wished to test the idea, there was no convenient way to do so; Federal statutes did not provide for court-approved wiretapping. Then in 1966 a unique chain of circumstances combined to bring before the Supreme Court an unprecedented instance of eavesdropping that had been approved by a Federal court.

It had begun two years before, when a prominent Tennessee lawyer set out to use bribery to hang a jury in the prosecution of Teamster President James R. Hoffa. Two factors were responsible for the extraordinary steps that had been taken by the Justice Department in investigating this very special bribery case: Z. T. "Tommy" Osborn was one of Nashville's most popular lawyers, and Jimmy Hoffa was one of the country's most consistently successful defendants. Until the bribery scandal broke in 1963, Osborn was the Cinderella lawyer of the Nashville legal community; the poor boy from across the tracks who had gone to night law school, had become a crack trial lawyer, had argued for the city voters before the Supreme Court in the historic reapportionment case, *Baker v. Carr,* and who was slated to be the next president of the city bar association. Hoffa had been prosecuted so often that he claimed more courtroom experience than some of his lawyers. Yet the Justice Department had never been able to convict him; his legal tactics were known to be wily, to say the least. So when Robert Vick, a Nashville policeman with a cloudy reputation, brought a story of attempted bribery to the Federal prosecutors who were preparing to try Hoffa in Nashville for tampering with a jury in an earlier case, the Government lawyers were understandably wary.

Vick's story was that Osborn had hired him to help run background investigations on prospective jurors, but that when the lawyer learned that one of the veniremen on the panel was Vick's cousin, Osborn suggested that Vick offer the cousin $10,000 to vote for acquittal and hang the jury. The routine procedure in such cases would have called for U.S. agents to confirm the bribery charge by equipping Vick with a hidden recorder for his future conversations with Osborn. But the Government's lawyers suspected that the incident might have been a Hoffa ruse to mouse-trap the prosecution into eavesdropping on Osborn. This could give the Teamster chief grounds to accuse the Justice Department of violating the confidentiality of his attorney-client relationship. The prosecutors were also painfully aware that the Federal Government was then in bad odor with many citizens of that Southern city and that Federal electronic surveillance of one of its leading lawyers would be a major scandal unless it were clearly justified.

With matters in such a delicate state, the Government lawyers had Vick put his report in the form of a sworn affidavit, which they presented in chambers to the court's two Federal District judges. The judges authorized the use of the hidden recording device by Vick, thus setting up the first known instance of court-approved eavesdropping by Federal judges, done for a narrowly limited purpose that the Supreme Court could later warmly approve. Wired for sound, Vick returned to Osborn's office and obtained a vivid recording of the lawyer's offer to pay the juror $10,000 to hang the case, plus Osborn's further promise that the bribed juror could be assured that "there will be at least two others with him."

When the Supreme Court accepted Osborn's appeal of his jury-tampering conviction, close observers anticipated that the Justices were preparing to make an important statement about eavesdropping. Osborn's situation was almost identical to the surveillance that the Court had approved in the *Lopez* case, except for the prior judicial approval of the Osborn surveillance. Thus it seemed that the petition for certiorari had most likely been granted to give the Justices an occasion to applaud this approach to law-enforcement eavesdropping. This proved to be the case. The opinion by Potter Stewart pointed out that even without the two District judges' approval, the use of the recorder was permissible under the *Lopez* rationale. Nevertheless, the Court approved the surreptitious recording of Osborn's words on the broader ground that the procedure that had been used complied with the warrant requirements of the Fourth Amendment. Quoting Justice Brennan's assertion in his *Lopez* dissent that "the procedure of antecedent justification before a magistrate that is central to the Fourth Amendment" is "a precondition of lawful electronic surveillance," the Stewart opinion dwelt at length on the benefits that the prosecution had gained in terms of credibility and legitimacy because of the compliance with the Fourth Amendment standards. Without actually reversing *Olmstead,* the Court had applied Fourth Amendment standards to an eavesdropping situation, and had given a sign that some electronic surveillance could still survive.

Only Douglas dissented in the *Osborn* case. He felt that the use of the recorder was a "search" for "mere evidence," and he reminded the majority that the lawbooks were sprinkled with decisions that said such evidence was barred by the Fourth Amendment. But that obstacle to a warrant system of eavesdropping was about to be swept away, too. A few months later the Supreme Court jettisoned the mere evidence rule in the landmark *Warden v. Hayden* decision. The opinion by Justice Brennan did reserve judgment as to whether "there are items of evidential value whose very nature precludes them from being the object of a reasonable search and seizure." Technically, this preserved a rationale for a subsequent invalidation of eavesdropping. But psychologically, it eliminated an old (and therefore, to lawyers, a substantial) barrier against legitimation of eavesdropping.

Two weeks later sweet reason suffered a jolt in the form of the parting shot of retiring Justice Tom C. Clark. Supreme Court decisions are frequently a mixed product of reason, indignation, egotism and horse-trading, yet it is a process that permits a surprising flow of continuity in the law. Each Justice constantly feels the tug of his own past record and the realization that tomorrow's decision must be squared with the positions taken today. For Tom Clark in June of 1967, though, the usual forces of equilibrium had gone awry. He had decided to retire from the bench to clear the way for his son, Ramsey, who had been appointed Attorney General by Clark's old friend and fellow Texan, Lyndon Johnson. The elder Clark had agreed to step down because it was felt that his son's position as the Government's chief legal officer might give an appearance of legal logrolling from son to father. Justice Clark's final decision showed that those fears were well founded.

As Acting Attorney General, Ramsey Clark had become strongly identified as a partisan on one public issue; he abhorred police eavesdropping. Clark considered it unconstitutional, distasteful, and not an efficient law-enforcement tool. On the final day of the Supreme Court term, Justice Clark, who as Attorney General had once used fancy footwork to maneuver Harry Truman into expanding the Justice Department's wiretap authority, and who had often chastised the Court's liberals for dealing too sternly with the police, delivered an opinion that seemed to all but preclude constitutional eavesdropping by the police. At issue in *Berger v. New York* was the conviction of an enterprising entrepreneur who had arranged to obtain a liquor license for a new Playboy bunny club in Manhattan by bribing officials of the State Liquor Authority. The District Attorney's office got wind of the plot and obtained court orders authorizing the bugging of the offices of two men believed to be serving as middlemen for the payoff. The bug picked up and recorded conversations that later proved persuasive to a jury, which found Berger guilty on two counts of conspiracy to bribe. When the case reached the Supreme Court it presented a mixed bag of constitutional issues, but the four-man liberal core of the Warren Court—Chief Justice Warren, and Justices Brennan, Douglas and Fortas—with Justice Clark unexpectedly on their side, seized the opportunity to declare New York's eavesdrop law unconstitutional under the Fourth Amendment.

On the face of it, *Berger v. New York* should have been a turning point in the law, but Clark's opinion of the circumstances surrounding it were so enigmatic that the legal profession did not know quite what to make of it. Berger's conviction could have been painlessly overturned without a pronouncement one way or the other on the constitutionality of the eavesdrop statute (the bugging warrant was apparently defective), but the Supreme Court seemed determined to render what amounted to an advisory opinion. Yet the advice was mostly negative; it seemed to imply that no eavesdrop law could be drafted with enough built-in safeguards to square with the Fourth Amendment.

The Clark opinion held the New York law invalid on its face, primarily on the ground that the court-approved surveillance technique permitted "general searches," in which conversations other than the one being sought by the police were also likely to be overheard. It also found fault with the fact that the "bug" was not to be removed as soon as the desired conversations were obtained. In a final, devastatingly understated observation, the Clark opinion noted that the law didn't require prior notice to the suspect of the intended eavesdropping—or proof of exigent circumstances to justify waiving the notice. As an additional hint that the outcome of the decision was to preclude and not to control police eavesdropping, Justice Clark included an argument—reminiscent of the sentiments of Ramsey Clark—that police bugging is an inefficient way to combat crime anyway, and that "techniques and practices may well be developed that will operate just as speedily and certainly."

After the decision, almost nothing changed except that Clark left the Court, thus dissolving the five-member majority that had issued the ruling. New York's highest court upheld subsequent convictions obtained under the same bugging statute, simply by reinterpreting the law in a way that the state court said cured the deficiencies cited in the *Berger* decision. New York's prosecutors let it be known that they were continuing to wiretap under a companion statute to the supposedly defunct bugging law. On the national political scene, Richard Nixon and the House Republicans competed with Democratic Senator John L. McClellan in pushing for a Federal wiretapping and bugging law.

This effort encountered slow going in the muddy constitutional terrain surrounding eavesdropping, until the Supreme Court firmed things up six months later in *Katz v. United States*. There, Government agents had convicted a bookie by attaching a microphone to the outside of the telephone booth where he habitually conducted his business. Under all of the classic tests, the Government had steered clear of the Bill of Rights and the wiretap law with this surveillance; the job had been done without a physical intrusion into private premises; no interception of telephone calls had occurred; and the agents had even disconnected the microphone when the suspect wasn't using the telephone booth. But the court declared the lack of physical intrusion into the booth irrelevant, and held that "the Fourth Amendment protects people, not places." Since the gambler had every reason to believe that his conversations were confidential, then even in his favorite telephone booth, the Fourth Amendment protected him from unreasonable eavesdropping by the Government. The Court declared that after almost forty years, *Olmstead v. United States* had become so eroded by qualifying decisions that it no longer would be followed. Only Justice Black dissented.

Having brandished the stick of the Fourth Amendment, the Court offered the carrot of the wiretap warrant. If the officers had obtained a warrant to bug the telephone booth, Potter Stewart wrote for the Court, then the eavesdropping would have been constitutional, even though it was a clear-cut example of electronic spying by the Government on an unsuspecting person. He said that the precautions taken to limit the intrusion into private affairs were careful enough to meet the Fourth Amendment's standards of particularity, and thus a judicial order "could have accomplished 'the legitimate needs of law enforcement' by authorizing the carefully limited use of electronic surveillance." As for the heavy hint in Tom Clark's *Berger* opinion that eavesdropping could never be done constitutionally because the Fourth Amendment requires prior notice of the search and seizure, Stewart noted that if officers can constitutionally finesse formalities and kick a door down to prevent the destruction of evidence, they could eavesdrop without prior notice.

Six months later, Congress passed the Omnibus Crime Control and Safe Streets Act of 1968, which contained in Title III the first Federal statute authorizing the police to use court-approved wiretapping and bugging to gather evidence. This unaccustomed harmony between Congress and the Supreme Court on criminal law had many roots, but some of the most interesting involved a young law professor who played a role similar to that of James Vorenberg on confessions, only with considerably more success. G. Robert Blakey had been one of Robert F. Kennedy's young hotshots in the organized crime section of the Justice Department in the days when hardly anyone outside that intense circle knew what La Cosa Nostra meant. He became convinced that organized crime was a cancer, and that it was lunacy not to let the police use electronic surveillance to combat it. Blakey saw electronic eavesdropping as no different from any other police tool; it would be abused if not controlled, but that to him was no reason to bar its use entirely. He moved to the law faculty at Notre Dame, where he developed a complex, detailed model law designed to permit police eavesdropping with court approval, all supposedly within the Byzantine constitutional rules that were then being laid out by the Supreme Court.

Often, the major obstacle to new legislation is getting people to agree on details, not goals. This did not happen when it came time to consider a law to authorize police wiretapping, because the subject was so complicated that the various interested Congressmen and legal groups did not undertake to draft their own bills. Instead, the American Bar Association's Project on Minimum Standards for Criminal Justice, the President's National Crime Commission, and leaders in both Houses of Congress decided to call in outside help. In each case, the call went to G. Robert Blakey. Not surprisingly, the various groups' proposals were remarkably alike. The result was Title III, which went through Congress with little quibbling among wiretap proponents as to detail, so they were easily able to subdue those who opposed police eavesdropping on principle. A major step had been taken toward finally bringing governmental eavesdropping within legal control. But it remained to be seen if the Supreme Court, having chosen to ride the tiger of electronic surveillance, might yet end up inside, locked into a permissive position that would encourage police eavesdropping without effectively controlling it.

For having invited the enactment of an eavesdrop statute, the Supreme Court had limited its own freedom to thereafter strike it down. It could still tighten up the law by giving some provisions narrowing interpretations. It could also knock out particularly obnoxious sections. But it appeared barely conceivable under the political conditions of the 1970's that the Supreme Court would attempt to make it impossible for the Government to tap lines and bug premises with court approval and to use the fruits in court. To do so would provoke political reprisals that the Court would be in no position to withstand. Attorney General John N. Mitchell, a staunch advocate of the new eavesdrop law, took care to use it sparingly, so that he could boast that his Justice Department was still doing less eavesdropping than his Democratic predecessors did before eavesdropping was legalized. Now that the Government was in a position to publicize its use of legalized snoopery to bring criminals to book, while still concealing its surreptitious "dirty business," the courts were likely to find it difficult to cut back on eavesdropping.

Yet doubts have arisen already as to the bargain the Court struck when it traded legitimacy for controls. Nobody imagined that Congress would spread police eavesdropping around as generously as Title III eventually did. Under it, Federal agents can get warrants to eavesdrop in investigations of offenses ranging from planting marijuana in the south forty, to running off homemade greenbacks, to crossing state lines to instigate campus riots. The Federal Government has not used it so widely, but the law authorizes states to do even more if they pass laws similar to Title III. If they do, then with only the approval of the local District Attorney and a friendly judge, local police could, if their statute allowed, eavesdrop on any felony involving a threat to life, limb or property—which in some states could include such relatively innocuous pursuits as chicken stealing, snake handling and wife beating.

There have been other second thoughts about potential abuses of court-approved eavesdropping under Title III, but the most explosive question to be raised about the new eavesdrop law came from the Office of Attorney General John Mitchell, and had nothing to do with judges and warrants. The public understanding behind Title III was the legitmation of governmental eavesdropping in exchange for control over that same surveillance. The most corrosive aspect of the earlier regime had been fear. So long as the Government was forced to eavesdrop in the shadows outside the law, then nobody knew the extent of that surveillance and anyone could suspect that it had happened to him. The advantage of Title III, as generous as it was, was that court approval had to be obtained, statistics of eavesdropping had to be published each year, and the subjects of governmental eavesdropping had to be told (after each device was disconnected) what had been done. Officialdom had been given a reluctant green light, but at least the public would finally feel that the law had a grasp on the Government's Big Ear.

Then on June 13, 1969, Attorney General Mitchell let it be known that the Government intended to have its cake and eat it too. On that day the Justice Department filed papers in the Federal District Court in Chicago in connection with the Government's prosecution of eight of the activists who had led the peace demonstrations during the Democratic National Convention in 1968. The defendants had demanded to be shown transcripts of any conversations involving them that had been picked up by illegal government listening devices, so that they could be satisfied that no unconstitutionally obtained evidence was being used against them. Mitchell's answer: no disclosure of any such surveillance needed to be made, because they were not "illegal"; the President had the constitutional authority to order electronic surveillance of their activities and those of any other domestic groups "which seek to attack and subvert the government by unlawful means."

With this claim, Mitchell revealed fully for the first time how little the Government intended to concede in the deal to legitimate

eavesdropping. Title III of the Crime Control Act, for all its protective procedures and reporting requirements, had expressly left
open the question of the legality of eavesdropping aimed at gathering "foreign intelligence information or preventing the overthrow
of the Government by force or other unlawful means," or "any
other clear and present danger to the structure or existence of
the Government." Now the Government was saying that surveillance of radical domestic groups was within that zone of unfettered
discretion that the executive branch occupied in matters concerning national security—thus this brand of eavesdropping was unaffected by all of the nice procedures written into the 1968 law.
As the Government's position paper filed in the Chicago case put
it, the country had experienced urban riots and violence stirred
up by dissident groups, and "the question whether it is appropriate
to utilize electronic surveillance to gather intelligence information
concerning the activities and plans of such organizations in order
to protect the nation against the possible danger which they present
is one that properly comes within the competence of the executive
and not the judicial branch."

This claim of a blank check to wiretap was based upon a facet
of eavesdropping that had been dimly understood outside of select
Government circles. That is, for law-enforcement purposes, the
use of electronic listening devices to keep tabs on suspect groups
is quite distinct from its use to gather evidence of crimes. The
procedures set out in Title III work nicely when the police have
probable cause to suspect that a specific crime is being committed
but lack the evidence to convict the guilty parties. The police can
listen until they hear what they want, stop listening, arrest the
offenders and bring them to trial.

But electronic surveillance has another use which is a product
of its peculiarly insinuating nature. It is an incomparable technique for gathering intelligence of subversive or criminal elements.
Electronic surveillance has taught Government officials some surprising truths about human communications—that even revolu-
tionaries and professional criminals feel compelled to talk to each

other about their common interests, and that they will do so despite well-founded suspicions that their telephones are tapped. Justice Department officials can recount astounding admissions by shrewd men over suspect telephones, admissions so damaging that the officials can only partially explain why they occur. Often it is inconvenient for the eavesdrop victims to communicate in more secure ways, or they assume that the Government knows the information anyway, or they simply succumb to wishful thinking that nobody is listening.

Moreover, protracted surveillance has shown that by monitoring the conversations of a few forceful leaders, the Government can keep itself informed of the doings of the activist elements of a nation of 200 million people. By eavesdropping on Dr. Martin Luther King, Jr., Elijah Muhammad, and perhaps a dozen other black leaders with whom all dissident blacks were likely to touch base at some time, the Government could be fairly certain that it was not ignorant of any major movement among this large and frequently disgruntled segment of the population. According to persistent rumors in Washington, the same type of surveillance has been directed at leaders of the Ku Klux Klan, the American Nazis, and other right-wing extremist groups. Title III's procedures do not hold the answer to this brand of snoopery; even if the judges who approved such interesting surveillances could be trusted to keep them secret, the Government might find it difficult to show probable cause to listen for years to the sitting room conversations of Nobel Prize winners and religious leaders.

Yet the men who run the Government are supposed to know what is going on in this vast country, and John Mitchell's legal stand in Chicago showed how important unfettered eavesdropping is to them. The problem is that it brings the eavesdrop question full cycle from 1963, minus the ground that was lost in terms of privacy by the warrant technique of Title III. For if the men in the Government can decide in the secrecy of their own councils who may be placed under surveillance as posing a threat to the existing form of government, then despite the best efforts of the custodians of the law, governmental eavesdropping is open-ended. When it comes to taking the measure of an alleged national threat, the past performances of men in high office are not always reassuring. In 1965, when an organization of young Marxists called the DuBois Club (pronounced du-boys, after the Negro civil rights leader, W. E. B. DuBois) became briefly notorious and some patriots mistakenly pilloried the Boys Club of America, Richard Nixon, then a national director of the Boys Clubs, issued a public statement denouncing the name similarities as an example of a deliberate and duplicitous Communist effort to smear the Boys Club. On another occasion, when the F.B.I. was found to have bugged a gangster hangout in Kansas City known as Red's Taco House, an F.B.I. spokesman justified the surveillance on the ground that the Mafia was a threat to the national security.

Such episodes have moved some lawyers to suggest that judges might be better equipped than elected public officials or bureaucrats to decide when domestic groups should be bugged. This is what is at stake in Attorney General Mitchell's demand for a free hand in such matters, and the Government has demonstrated that it can be stubborn when its autonomy in this area is questioned by the courts.

Solicitor General Erwin N. Griswold, a former Harvard law dean who revered the Supreme Court as one who for years was mentioned as a possible nominee, once reacted so heatedly to a Supreme Court incursion into this field that he handed the Court what amounted to a veiled threat in urging it to change its position. It happened in 1969, after the Court ruled that the Government must let criminal defendants, in all cases, including "national security" cases, see all records of illegal governmental eavesdropping concerning them. Mr. Griswold filed a rare Justice Department petition for a rehearing arguing that this would permit defendants to romp through files of the most sensitive nature—including, he implied, wiretaps on foreign embassies in Washington. Unless the Court saw things the Government's way, Mr. Griswold said, the Justice Department might be forced to deviate from its long tradition of candor with the courts and to stop telling the Justices of the existence of wiretap transcripts that the Government considered none of the judiciary's business. The Court quickly backed away, with Potter Stewart writing an opinion to assure the Government that the Court had not yet decided whether eavesdropping in foreign intelligence investigations is covered by the Fourth Amendment and is thus "illegal." Stewart chided Griswold for becoming prematurely excited about the prospect of disclosure, which will never materialize if the Court eventually holds that national security surveillance is entirely within the President's discretion.

The Potter Stewart-Erwin Griswold spat had enlivened the issue enough to obscure the fact that it had only been pushed into the background. Then Attorney General Mitchell's move in Chicago quickly reminded the Court that it must soon decide if it must go to the mat with the President over who shall supervise and control electronic surveillance of the nation's radical groups. When the Court finally confronts this question, the Justices may have to sacrifice, in the interest of national security, much of William Brennan's vision of tight judicial control of surveillance. If they conclude that the sacrifice is too great, then the Court may find itself again in conflict with the other branches of the Government, as it has been whenever it has sought to impose tight controls on investigative activities by the police.

COMPARATIVE ANALYSIS
OF PATTERNS OF COMPLIANCE WITH
SUPREME COURT DECISIONS

"Miranda" and the Police

in Four Communities

Neal Milner

Political scientists until recently have ignored the study of the process involved in complying with Supreme Court decisions. As Richard M. Johnson (1967: 4) has stated, to neglect such studies "is to neglect an indispensable segment of the total judicial process." Despite the increasing awareness of the importance of this aspect to the judicial process, there are still almost no studies which attempt a comparative analysis of patterns of compliance with or resistance to Supreme Court decisions.

Many of the compliance studies have been concerned with response to Supreme Court decisions involving religious activities in schools (Johnson, 1967; Patric, 1957; Birkby, 1966; Sorauf, 1959; Muir, 1968). This concentration on a single policy area would be more worthwhile if these studies could be easily compared with one another. Unfortunately, they provide neither the conceptualizations nor the methods which would facilitate such comparisons. The foci of the studies vary greatly. For example, some of them attempt to give a detailed account of the reaction to Court decisions in one small geographic area (Johnson, 1967; Muir, 1968). Others are less systematic in discussing patterns of compliance, but discuss the impact of Court decisions on a much more general scale (Sorauf, 1959; Patric, 1957). Not only is it difficult to generalize from these studies, but also one finds very little agreement over the meaning of such concepts as "impact" or "compliance."

The present study compares four Wisconsin police departments (see Table 1) in their process of complying with the Supreme Court's Miranda v. Arizona (1966) decision. Primarily, it relates this process to the degree of professionalization

TABLE 1

POPULATION AND SIZE OF POLICE DEPARTMENTS—FOUR WISCONSIN CITIES (population from 1960 Census unless otherwise indicated)

	City			
	Green Bay	Kenosha	Racine	Madison
Population	76,888[a]	62,899	89,144	160,000[b]
Size of department	120	120	158	202

a. Includes 1963 annexation of about 14,000.
b. Special census, 1964.

found within each department. In the majority opinion of the Miranda case, Chief Justice Warren established certain procedures that the police must follow before and during the interrogation of a suspect. Prior to interrogation, the police must advise a suspect of his right to remain silent. The suspect must also be told at this stage that anything he says may be held against him. The police officer must further inform the suspect that, even if the suspect decides to talk, he may discontinue talking at any time. The suspect must also be told that he has a right to have an attorney present during the interrogation, and that, if he is indigent, a lawyer will be provided at government expense. Confessions or other self-incriminating statements made during the interrogation are inadmissible in court unless the suspect was informed of these rights and, prior to making these statements, intelligently waived such rights.

Compliance and deviance are both regularized and routine patterns of behavior on the part of all classes in organized society. One cannot divide society into two groups—individual compliants (or conformists) and deviants. Because of the regularity with which both compliance and deviance occur, and because both manifest a complex combination of behavior and attitudes, one must study the *conditions and distribution* of compliance (Krislov, 1963: 5). Only certain aspects of these conditions and distribution of compliance will be considered in this study.

Aspects of Compliance

This study investigates the *degree* of compliance with a Supreme Court decision. Degree of compliance depends upon perceptions and attitudes held by those who evaluate whether a decision-making body is complying with the Court decision. For example, a civil rights organization might have far more stringent criteria for evaluating school board compliance than does the school board itself. Both the school board members and members of the civil rights group might agree on what the school board's behavior was, but might violently disagree about whether such behavior should be considered compliance. In the present study the goals that the Supreme Court justices posited in the Miranda majority opinion will be used as the criteria. Other important actors in the communications process may have different standards and goals, and other sources may be more important and more frequently used than is the opinion of the Court. Nonetheless, the opinion sets the initial standards and can be used as an indicator of the goals which the majority of the justices desired to communicate about police interrogation.[1] One cannot assume, however, that these goals and standards are automatically communicated from the Court to the decision .makers who are expected to implement the Court's decision. Thus the communications process must also be studied.

There are several reasons why I compare police organizations according to the degree of their professionalization. Police response to legal change is often discussed in terms of police professionalization. In fact, FBI officials, prosecuting attorneys, and other influential members of professional organizations discussed the Miranda decision in these terms (Milner, 1968: 180-200). In their discussion of police reform, advocates of such reform often use criteria of professionalization which are similar to criteria usually used to measure the extent of professionalization in other occupational organizations (compare President's Commission on Law Enforcement [1967: 43-61, 120-143] with Carr-Saunders [1966: 3-9]). Furthermore, it is possible to obtain indicators of professionalization which can be used to compare organizations.

A profession is defined as an ideal type which serves as the model for an occupational group. Professionalization is thus considered to be the *process* involved in developing toward this ideal type (Vollmer and Mills, 1966: vii-viii). Organizations can be compared according to the stages they have reached in this process (Hall, 1968). Writers concerned with the concept of professionalization generally agree that, to some degree, specialization and expertise are criteria for professionalization (Greenwood, 1966).[2] The extent of professionalization can thus be established by criteria which measure the degree of expertise and specialization, and by criteria which indicate the nature of incentives that exist to sanction the development of expertise and specialization.

Using these criteria, I ranked the departments according to an index of professionalization. The following items were used as indicators of the degree of professionalization in each of the four departments:

(1) patrolman's monthly salary;

(2) detective's monthly salary;

(3) the percentage of full-time civilian employees in the department;

(4) the percentage of criminal investigators in the department;

(5) the percentage of officers with at least a high school diploma;

(6) the percentage of officers with at least some college;

(7) weeks of required police recruit training;

(8) annual in-service training hours per officer.

In order to rank the departments and compare them according to their degree of professionalization, I computed the sum total of each of these eight variables and then established the fraction of this total that each department composed. For example, the Green Bay department required 10 weeks of recruit training, Kenosha required 8 and Racine and Madison required 12 and 14, respectively. The sum of the required hours equals 44. Thus, for that item Green Bay received a score of .23, that is, $\frac{10}{44}$, while Kenosha's score was .18, Racine's .27, and Madison's was .31. For all of these items, a higher score was equated with a greater degree of professionalization. Both Green Bay's and Kenosha's mean score was .22. Racine's was .26 and the Madison department's mean score was .30. The Green Bay and Kenosha departments are the least professionalized, followed in order by Racine and Madison (see Appendix).

The data for this study were gathered between June 1966, and April 1967. Data came from literature published by local police departments (especially their annual reports), from questionnaires submitted to all police officers in the four cities, and from nonstructured interviews with informants in these cities.[3] Additional information about behavior during interrogation was obtained in each community through direct observation of the interrogation process and through field work with detectives.

FINDINGS

SOURCES OF POLICY INFORMATION

The process of disseminating law enforcement information from state to local authorities involved neither a hierarchical nor a centralized communications structure. Consequently, the four Wisconsin police departments had a great deal of discretion in choosing from which sources, if any, they would obtain information about the Miranda decision. The state attorney general made a special effort to disseminate such information, but he had no formal powers to require departments to accept his information, much less his viewpoint (Milner, 1968: 220-268). Advocates of increased police professionalization contend that professionalized police departments are more interested in receiving information about changes in law enforcement policy (President's Commission on Law Enforcement, 1967: 32-35). On the surface, the data support this contention. The officers in Green Bay, one of the least professionalized departments, received information from an average of 4.95 sources, while the averages for all the other departments were higher; Kenosha (5.20), Racine (5.24), and Madison (5.82).

Conferences which were organized at the behest of their respective departments and in-service training sessions were the sources of information most frequently mentioned by the officers in each department. Table 2 further compares the departments' communication processes. Table 2 shows that the degree to which officers remembered being exposed to conferences or training sessions varied almost directly with the degree of professionalization of the departments. Ninety-two percent of the Madison officers remembered learning about the Miranda decision at such sessions, while only 69% of the Racine officers, 67% of the Kenosha officers, and 61% of the Green Bay officers learned about Miranda from these sources.

While not varying directly with professionalization, the other variables in Table 2 nevertheless help elucidate the differences between Madison and the other cities. The two least professionalized departments fall between Madison and Racine in their likelihood to consider training sessions as the best source of information. Of all four departments, the officers in the Madison department were *most* likely to rate the training sessions that were organized by their departments as the best source of information about the Miranda decision, and they were *least* likely to rate local officials (judges, prosecutors, and other local attorneys) as the best source. Officers in Racine, the second most professionalized department, reacted in completely the opposite manner. That is, of the officers in the four departments, those in Racine were *least* likely to perceive the training session as the best source but *most* likely to choose local officials as the best source of information. These conclusions might surprise certain advocates of police professionalization who frequently suggest that the most professionalized police departments are most amenable to information from sources other than those from the law enforcement occupation (President's Commission on Law Enforcement, 1967: 32-35). Local judges and lawyers could conceivably have participated in the Madison in-service training program, and thus the officers might not have listed local officials as a separate source of information,

TABLE 2

OFFICERS' SOURCES OF INFORMATION IN THE *MIRANDA* COMMUNICATIONS PROCESS (by department)

Source	Department			
	Green Bay (n=70)	Kenosha (n=64)	Racine' (n=58)	Madison (n=78)
Percentage Responding:				
Learned about decision at conference training session.	61	67	69	92
Conferences, training sessions rated *best* source of *Miranda* information.	37	34	24	45
Local officials rated the *best* source of *Miranda* information.	7	13	17	4

but in fact this was not the case. Neither the local judiciary, the local prosecutor, nor local lawyers were asked to participate in these programs. Moreover, all departments used other law enforcement personnel, namely the FBI, in their training sessions, although, as we shall see, the degree of the use of this organization varied.

Other studies of professionalization help to shed light on the reasons for this reversal of the pattern expected by advocates of police professionalization. As an occupation becomes more specialized, and as it begins to develop a systematic body of abstract principles governing the behavior of the occupation, its members begin to feel that they have a monopoly of expertise about the nature and proceeding of that occupation (Greenwood, 1966). One should then expect that, as a police department undergoes professionalization, its members would have more confidence in their ability to determine the proper rules of occupational behavior. This confidence was particularly apparent among the high-ranking policy-making officers in the Madison department. In the words of the most knowledgeable of these officers:

> FBI agents are the best teachers of the police . . . . Attorneys don't know how to talk to the police. This includes the district attorney. He is not a law enforcement official; he's an attorney, and his perspective differs . . . . He [the district attorney] contributed very little [to the process of disseminating information about Miranda]. In fact, I invited his staff to sit in on the FBI lectures.

This official not only refused to recognize the expertise of a local official who was in constant contact with the police, but in fact specifically listed a member of the law enforcement profession, albeit from a different agency, as the best source of police information. Although all departments used the FBI as a source of information, this sentiment about the value of the FBI was most clearly expressed in Madison. In Racine, the second most professionalized department, the district attorney was a more important source of information than his counterparts were to any of the other departments.[4]

In all four communities, information furnished by the FBI was based on lectures prepared by that bureau's expert on police education. This information was presented in a more thorough manner in Madison than it was in any of the other cities. Although these lectures stressed that police must be aware of the ramifications of Miranda, the information was generally presented in a manner which suggested that the FBI was especially concerned with allying the anxieties of law enforcement officers. Although cautioning against resistance to Miranda, these lectures definitely emphasized ways of maintaining pre-Miranda procedures.[5]

The Madison department was thus most exposed to this source of information which quite explicitly tried to minimize the degree to which Miranda changed the status quo. The most professionalized department, then, made greatest use of information offered by an organization that attempted to express views that were congruent with the values and attitudes of the law enforcement profession.

THE DEGREE AND PATTERN OF COMPLIANCE

The goals of the Miranda v. Arizona (1966) majority can be summarized as follows:

(1) to discourage whenever possible the use of confessions, *all* of which are obtained under circumstances which *inherently* lead to coercion of the suspect (444-445, 467-476);

(2) to make certain that all suspects are informed of their right to remain silent and their right to have an attorney present to protect this right, even if the suspect could not afford to hire his own lawyer (480-481);

(3) to improve the quality of police officers so that the officers would be able to perform their jobs effectively while still operating under the norms of due process (447, 452, 460); and

(4) to allay police anxieties by specifically stating that, despite these new constraints created by the Court, interrogation can still at times continue to be a legitimate and effective weapon (477-478).

Both the Court and the FBI sought to ease the anxieties of the police, but the FBI more greatly emphasized that the police could continue to use interrogation techniques of the type which in fact the majority of the Court in Miranda seemed to disapprove (compare Dalbey, 1967 with Miranda). Both the Court in Miranda and the FBI agreed that under certain circumstances police questioning was still possible without being preceded by a Miranda warning. The difference was one of emphasis; clearly the Miranda majority was more anxious to discourage the use of confessions.

Police perceptions of the meaning of the decision were obtained from responses to the following question: "Recently the Supreme Court decided the case *Miranda v. Arizona.* This case resulted in a rule about interrogation procedures. Describe this rule as best as you can by putting an 'x' next to *all* of the following statements which you think apply to the rule." On all but two items there was little difference between the departments' ability to identify the stipulations of the rule. Table 3 presents a comparison of these two items. The pattern of these perceptions, as shown in Table 3, did not vary directly with the degree of professionalization. The Green Bay department's relatively great response (forty percent) to the first item can be partially attributed to a Wisconsin Supreme Court case which explicitly sanctioned such behavior on the part of that department (State v. Miller, 1967). Still, the officers in Madison were most likely to perceive correctly stipulations consistent with the Court's

TABLE 3

OFFICERS' "CORRECT" PERCEPTIONS OF STIPULATIONS OF THE *MIRANDA* RULE (by department)[6]

Stipulation	Department			
	Green Bay (n=70)	Kenosha (n=64)	Racine (n=58)	Madison (n=78)
Percentage Giving "Correct" Response:				
Can still ask person to come voluntarily to the police station.	40	38	35	63
May still talk to person without advising him of his rights.	21	34	33	54

goals of allaying police anxieties because these stipulations (Table 3) *limit the constraints* placed on police departments by the procedures stated in the Miranda opinion. Admittedly these findings are ambiguous, but it is interesting to note that the perceptions of the officers in the most professionalized departments were most congruent with both the Court's and the FBI's goals stressing limitations of Miranda's scope.

The degree of approval of the decision also varied directly with the degree of professionalization. Eleven percent of the Green Bay officers, 11% of the Kenosha officers, 17% of the Racine officers, and 36% of the Madison officers approved of the decision. Advocates of police professionalization would probably expect such findings. They contend that the more professionalized police departments are, the more amenable are these organizations to accepting the views of those advocating police reform. In order further to investigate the relationship between professionalization, attitudes toward the decision, and perceptions of its impact, we must investigate the ideology of these organizations, that is, the degree of their "professionalism" (Vollmer and Mills, 1966: vii-viii).[7]

The degree of the departments' professionalization should be related to the nature of the departments' professional ideology in regard to the *Miranda* decision. The nature of this ideology was investigated on the basis of the officers' responses to the following question: "If you so desire, please make any other comments about the *Miranda* rule. Why, for example, do you think the Supreme Court decided the *Miranda* case the way it did?" Sixty percent of the respondents answered this question, and all departments were represented in virtually the same proportion as they were in the larger number of respondents. The more professionalized the department was, the more likely were its members to discuss this question in terms of what police professionalization advocates would probably call an ideology of professionalism. That is, the officers in the two most professionalized departments more frequently either approved of Miranda on the grounds that the decision's stipulations would help improve the police profession *or* discussed the decision in a manner similar to the discussions by advocates of police professionalization.[8] Of the respondents to this question, 14% of the Green Bay officers, 23% of the Kenosha officers, 28% of the Racine police, and 33% of their Madison counterparts responded in terms of professionalism. This relationship between professionalization, attitudes, and perceptions cannot simply be explained in terms of amenability to non-law enforcement sources of information because earlier evidence indicated that Madison did not consider most outside, non-law enforcement sources of information to be very important in the Miranda information process. Factors other than professionalization must be considered.

The Green Bay organization was one of the least professionalized, yet it was also the department least likely to encounter the situations where interrogations were necessary. This community had by far the lowest crime rate of the four communities, and interrogation occurred quite infrequently. This lack of need to use the Miranda stipulation seems to be an important reason why only 24% of the Green Bay officers thought their jobs changed greatly because of Miranda. The Kenosha, Racine, and Madison departments all operated in a milieu in which interrogation situations frequently arose. Sixty-three percent of the Kenosha department, 45% of the Racine department, and only 32% of the Madison department thought their jobs had been greatly changed by the Miranda decision. Of these three departments, the extent of perceived job change varied *inversely* with the degree of professionalization. Thus Kenosha, a relatively unprofessionalized department which operated in an environment where interrogations were often deemed necessary, was most likely to see a great change as a result of Miranda.[9] The more professionalized departments facing roughly the same situation were less affected.

Each officer was also asked to list the two greatest effects Miranda had on his own job. Changes in methods of obtaining evidence and changes in the education process were the most frequently mentioned in all four organizations. Table 4 compares the departments according to the frequency of these responses.

The responses to the two items in Table 4 follow the same pattern as the responses concerning the extent of job change. Officers in the departments toward the extremes of the professionalization ranking—Madison and Green Bay—least frequently mentioned changes in the methods of obtaining evidence or in education programs. Certainly the fact that the Green Bay department received fewer sources of information about Miranda and had a relatively less-pervasive intradepartmental training system is significant in explaining these responses. In addition, the nature of the Green Bay department's tasks did not require that Miranda be made more salient. The need for change was less visible both because of the communications process and because the lack of need for crime investigation lessened the perceived need for change. For the same reasons, Kenosha police were more likely to perceive great change. The Kenosha officers

TABLE 4

OFFICERS' PERCEPTIONS OF EFFECTS *MIRANDA* HAD ON THEIR OWN JOBS (by department)

Effects	Department			
	Green Bay (n=70)	Kenosha (n=64)	Racine (n=58)	Madison (n=78)
Percentage Responding:				
New methods of obtaining evidence now must be used	47	70	64	49
Education and training has increased.	41	72	53	50

were far more likely than their Green Bay counterparts to see such specific changes resulting from Miranda.

Perhaps among the other departments, where interrogations were more frequent and visible, the more professional organizations, prior to Miranda, had adjusted their education and interrogation procedures in anticipation of such a decision. Madison officers, however, were similar to Green Bay and Kenosha in their failure to anticipate the Miranda decision. Twelve percent of the Green Bay officers, 14% of Kenosha, 22% of Racine, and only 13% of the Madison police anticipated that decision. This finding is particularly surprising because of the relationship between approval and anticipation. In the complete sample, 32% of the officers who anticipated the decision approved of Miranda, while only 16% of those not anticipating the decision approved. As stated previously, Madison had the greatest percentage of approving officers, but, *despite* the differences both in the communications process and degree of approval, the Madison department was no more likely to anticipate the decision than were the two least professionalized departments.

The Racine communications process might be an important factor in explaining the greater degree of anticipation in the Racine department. Of the four departments, Racine officers were least likely to consider conferences and training sessions as the best source of Miranda information and most likely to look toward local groups for such information. This also seemed to be the case prior to Miranda. These non-law enforcement groups might have emphasized anticipation of future decisions more than the in-service training programs featuring FBI officials. There were, of course, important differences between Madison and the two least professionalized departments in regard to their in-service training programs, and these differences also existed prior to Miranda. The FBI training, which did not emphasize anticipation, was exceptionally important in Madison and may have decreased anticipation of future court decisions even though after Miranda the Madison department was more likely to approve of that decision. This explanation is tenuous, and it may well be that the differences in professionalization were not related to this difference in anticipation.

There is another possible explanation for the lack of perceived change in more professionalized departments. Perhaps, contrary to the assumptions of police reformers, more professionalized departments like Madison were simply less willing to change their procedures. Officers in the two most professionalized departments with high interrogation visibility were least likely to perceive change in interrogation methods. Admittedly, the more approving attitudes of the more professionalized departments and the greater congruence between their perceptions of some of the Court's goals and the actual goals suggest that such departments are more likely to react to the Miranda decision in ways which disseminators of information about the Court's decision would call compliance. There was no apparent difference, however, between the degree of a department's professionalization and the interrogation behavior of its detectives. The Miranda stipulations were quite regularly given in all departments, but this procedure was to a great extent *pro forma*. The detectives informed the person of his rights but then required this person to make an *immediate* decision about whether he wished to waive these rights. Usually waiver was obtained, and the suspect was then immediately questioned. Psychological ploys, which, according to Chief Justice Warren's majority opinion in Miranda, made confessions inherently coercive, continued to be used. Thus the officers' behavior may be considered congruent with the Court's goal of stressing the advisement of right, but interrogation behavior was not congruent with the Court's goal of encouraging alternatives to confessions as sources of evidence. In fact, in all departments the general procedure was to attempt at least initially to obtain incriminating statements. Also contrary to the Court's goals was the fact that lawyers played almost no active part in actually supervising the interrogation process. As previously mentioned, most suspects waived their rights to an attorney. If an attorney was called into the case, he usually told his client to say nothing.[10] Consequently there occurred either interrogations using pre-Miranda techniques or no interrogations at all.[11]

The evidence suggests that despite a more sympathetic attitude toward the decision, professionalized departments did not change interrogating behavior any more than did less-professionalized departments. Changes were minimal perhaps because upper-level police administrators were unable to supervise such isolated and often decentralized police activity (Wilson, 1968: 57-83). Furthermore, officers in more professionalized departments who might be more concerned with bringing formal action against a suspect and thus pressure for a confession would consequently be greater in these departments (compare Wilson, 1968). Two limitations in the methods of gathering the interrogation behavior data must be noted. First, no attempt was made to observe the interrogation behavior differences between officers who approved of Miranda and those who did not, and no such comparison was made between officers who viewed Miranda in a manner more characteristic of professionalism and those who did not. Second, the time obstacles faced by a single observer who investigated interrogation behavior over a relatively short period of time (from 45-60 hours in each community) perhaps limit the reliability of my conclusions. These findings, however, were consistent with those of other recent studies of post-Miranda interrogation behavior (Reiss, 1968; Yale Law J. [Note], 1967).[12]

CONCLUSION

The concept of professionalization was helpful in explaining the differences between the sources of Miranda information which were visible in the four departments. The more professionalized departments received information from more sources and the most professionalized department was most likely to isolate itself from non-law enforcement sources. This isolation seemed consistent with characteristics attributed to relatively highly professionalized organizations. Among the four departments, however, the degree of isolation did not vary directly with the degree of professionalization.

To a lesser extent, the data showed a relationship between the professionalization of a police department and the perceptions and attitudes its members had about the Miranda decision. Attitudes toward the decision and the likelihood of perceiving it in terms of professionalism varied rather directly with professionalization, but the likelihood of anticipating Miranda did not. In Green Bay, one of the least professionalized departments, great change was not perceived, probably because the low crime rate made interrogation relatively infrequent. In the other departments, where the interrogation process was more visible, the degree of perceived change varied inversely with the degree of professionalization.

Despite these organizational and task differences, interrogation behavior was similar in all departments. Both our limited knowledge of interrogation behavior and our limited knowledge of the methods of compliance, however, prevent us from completely accepting as yet such a sweeping conclusion. Thus, along with refining independent variables for comparative analysis, we must also refine one important dependent variable; the degrees of behavioral compliance with Court decisions. We know that it is inaccurate to distinguish simply between deviance and compliance becuase there are degrees of each, yet we still know little about what these degrees are.[13] Because only four departments in one state were studied, the reliability of the conclusions are limited. I did not choose to study these four cities because of the difference in departmental professionalization. I investigated professionalization only after I chose the cities. Thus, it may be that these four departments, when compared to a larger sample, are relatively homogeneous in their professionalization, and the present study may underestimate the differences between professionalized departments.[14] But a good portion of the data used as the basis of the index of professionalization is relatively easy to obtain, especially from public organizations. We have, then, the clear opportunity for further exploration of the hypotheses with which some work has been done in this study. A comparison of a large number of organizations should allow some firmer statements than were possible here with regard to the relationship between professionalism in police departments, and a tendency to comply with Supreme Court requirements.

NOTES

1. Judicial opinions may not be accurate reflections of a judge's motives, goals, or policy preferences, but, regardless of the accuracy of the opinions' reflections, others must use them to determine what the legal rules are supposed to be. Martin Shapiro (1968: 36, 38-39) calls this communications function "the most vital function of an appellate [court] opinion [because these opinions] provide the constraining directions to the public and private decision-makers."

2. For a critical view of the use of such criteria alone, see Skolnick (1966: 235-239).

3. Questionnaires were distributed to each department, and in the two departments where each officer had his own mailbox (Madison and Green Bay), a questionnaire was placed in each mailbox. Otherwise, superior officers distributed them at roll calls. The questionnaires were sent back in postpaid envelopes. The response rate was as follows:

Green Bay	58%
Kenosha	54%
Racine	37%
Madison	39%
Total	45%

There is, of course, no sure way to check for sampling error in such a sample. Generally, detectives were overrepresented especially in the larger departments (see' Milner, 1968: 524-528).

4. The anticipated relationship between professionalization and the perceived importance of local officials held for Racine, Kenosha, and Green Bay. Thus, it is perhaps somewhere between the stages of professionalization in Madison and Racine that the great emphasis on specialized knowledge and on the occupation's monopoly of expertise occurs.

5. Inspector Dwight Dalbey is the FBI specialist spoken of here (see Dalbey, 1967.)

6. The following are the stipulations presented to the officers: "Recently the U.S. Supreme Court decided the case Miranda v. Arizona. This case resulted in a rule about police interrogation procedures. Describe this rule as best you can by putting an 'x' next to *all* of the following statements which you think apply to the rule. (1) A person in custody must be advised of his right to remain silent. (2) A person in custody must have an attorney whether he wants one or not. (3) Confessions may no longer be used as evidence. (4) A person in custody must be advised that anything he says may be held against him in court. (5) A policeman may no longer talk to a person about a crime without first informing the person of his right to remain silent. (6) Wiretapping will no longer be tolerated. (7) Any person in custody has the right to an attorney if he wants one. (8) A person in custody who cannot afford to hire his own attorney has the right to have one appointed at county

expense. (9) Voluntary confessions are no longer legal sources of information. (10) A police officer can still ask a person to come voluntarily to the police station without first advising him of his constitutional rights." Items 1, 4, 7, 8, and 10 are considered to be stipulations consistent with the Miranda rule. Thus an officer responded correctly to each of items 1, 4, 7, 8, and 10 if he marked these items and responded correctly to each of items 2, 3, 5, 6, and 9 if he did not.

7. For a discussion of the importance of ideology in the professionalization process, see Skolnick (1966: 238-239) and Wilson (1966: 184-193).

8. The following criteria were used as a measure of professionalism. An officer was considered to view Miranda in terms of professionalism if: (1) the reasons that he gave for the Court's decision were generally consistent with those given by those advocates of police professionalization whose views of the Court's Miranda goals are consistent with the Court's view; or (2) he approved of the Miranda decision on the grounds that it would improve the police profession. Choosing item 1 does not necessarily mean that the officer approved of the decision.

9. The particularly great emphasis on change in Kenosha can partially be explained by the fact that a suspect in an especially brutal murder, which was quite important in the community and in the department could not be interrogated by the police because his attorney would not allow it. The detectives insisted that this suspect was the killer, and attributed to the Miranda rule their inability to question him.

10. Interrogation behavior could conceivably have been influenced by the presence of an outside observer. Such observer bias in this study is limited for two reasons. First, the data showed that despite the presence of an observer, detectives did not always behave in a manner which seemed consistent with the goals of Miranda. Second, to check on such influence, I listened to some interrogations unbeknownst to the investigators.

11. For a criticism of the Court's refusal to consider the differences between its goals and the goals of organizations involved in the local criminal process, see Blumberg (1968: 169-184).

12. All such studies could be improved if more sophisticated methods of observing behavior in nonexperimental settings were available. See Deutscher (1966). A similar point is made from a different perspective in Froman (1968: 43-44).

13. Muir (1968) offers some insight about this in his discussion of how the subjects of his study avoided dissonance created by certain school prayer decisions.

14. For a study comparing two police departments which vary greatly in professionalization, see Wilson (1968). He finds distinct differences in the ways these departments handle juveniles. Also, departments may be more similar in the way they carry out such law enforcement as opposed to order maintenance behavior. Compare Wilson (1968).

APPENDIX: Testing and Construction of Index of Professionalization

I used an analysis of variance to test the null hypothesis that all the data used to construct the index were drawn from the same sample. The formula is as follows:

$$F = \frac{m\Sigma \, (\bar{x}i - \bar{\bar{x}})^2 \, /n-1}{\Sigma \, (x_{ij} - \bar{x}_j)^2 \, /n(m-1)}$$

where

x_{ij} = individual deviation for i^{th} row, j^{th} column

$\bar{x}_j$ = column mean of column j

$\bar{\bar{x}}$ = mean of all observations

m = number of rows

n = number of columns

F = 6.13473, which means that the null hypothesis is rejected; the statistic is significant at the .01 level. The table below presents the data which were used to construct the index of professionalization discussed in the text. It also presents an alternative method of constructing the index. The rank order of each department on each variable is presented, with the absolute number for each variable presented in parentheses. Because this alternative index does not take into consideration the extent of departmental differences in any single variable, I chose not to use it, and employed instead the index explained in the text. Note, however, that according to the alternative index Kenosha is more professionalized than Green Bay.

ALTERNATIVE COMPARATIVE PROFESSIONALIZATION INDEX: FOUR CITIES

Item:	Green Bay Rank	Green Bay Amount	Kenosha Rank	Kenosha Amount	Racine Rank	Racine Amount	Madison Rank	Madison Amount
Patrolman's Monthly Salary[a]	4	($530)	3	($586)	1	($588)	2	($575)
Detective's Monthly Salary[a]	4	($610)	3	($648)	1	($655)	2	($651)
% Full-time Civilian Employees[b]	3.5	(9.6%)	2	(10.7%)	3.5	(9.6%)	1	(23.8%)
% Investigators in Department[c]	3.5	(13.5%)	2	(15.4%)	3.5	(13.6%)	1	(18.3%)
% Officers with at least High School Diploma	3	(89.0%)	1	(94.3%)	4	(83.0%)	2	(89.7%)
% Officers with some college	3	(26.5%)	4	(17.1%)	2	(34.5%)	1	(37.2%)
Weeks of Required Recruit Training	3	(10 wks.)	4	(8 wks.)	2	(12 wks.)	1	(14 wks.)
Annual In-Service Training Hours per Officer	4	(55 hrs.)	3	(61 hrs.)	1	(100 hrs.)	2	(90 hrs.)
Total Rank Score	28		22		18		12	
Average Rank	3.50		2.75		2.25		1.50	

a. Average based on annual salary ranges.

b. Includes stenographers, janitors, police cadets, radio operators, dog pound, and meter officials.

c. Includes detectives, juvenile investigators, and special non-traffic investigators.

CASES

MIRANDA v. ARIZONA (1966) 384 U.S. 436.

STATE v. MILLER (1967) 35 Wis. 2d 454; 151 N.W. 2d 157.

REFERENCES

BIRKBY, R. H. (1966) "The Supreme Court and the Bible Belt: Tennessee reaction to the *Schempp* decision." Midwest J. of Pol. Sci. 10 (August): 304-319.

BLUMBERG, A. (1967) Criminal Justice. Chicago: Quadrangle.

CARR-SAUNDERS, A. M. (1966) "Professionalization in historical perspective," pp. 3-9 in H. M. Vollmer and D. E. Mills (eds.) Professionalization. Englewood Cliffs: Prentice-Hall.

DALBEY, D. (1967) Police Interrogation and the Miranda Rule. Washington: FBI National Academy.

DEUTSCHER, I. (1966) "Words and deeds: social science and social policy." Social Problems 13 (Winter): 235-254.

FROMAN, L. A. (1968) "The categorization of policy content," pp. 41-54 in A. Ranney (ed.) Political Science and Public Policy. Chicago: Markham.

GREENWOOD, E. (1966) "The elements of professionalization," pp. 10-19 in H. M. Vollmer and D. G. Mills (eds.) Professionalization. Englewood Cliffs: Prentice-Hall.

HALL, R. H. (1968) "Professionalization and bureaucratization." Amer. Soc. Rev. 33 (February): 92-104.

JOHNSON, R. M. (1967) The Dynamics of Compliance. Evanston: Northwestern Univ. Press.

KRISLOV, S. (1963) "The perimeters of power: patterns of compliance and opposition to Supreme Court decisions." Presented to the American Political Science Association, New York.

MILNER, N. A. (1968) "The impact of the *Miranda* decision on four Wisconsin communities." Ph.D. dissertation. University of Wisconsin.

MUIR, W. (1968) Prayer in the Public Schools. Chicago: Univ. of Chicago Press.

PATRIC, G. (1957) "The impact of a court decision: the aftermath of the McCollum case." J. of Public Law 6 (Fall): 455-463.

President's Commission on Law Enforcement and the Administration of Justice Task Force (1967) Report: The Police. Washington: Government Printing Office.

REISS, A. J., Jr. [ed.] (1968) President's Commission on Law Enforcement and the Administration of Justice, Studies in Crime and Law Enforcement in Major Metropolitan Areas. Washington: Government Printing Office.

SHAPIRO, M. (1968) The Supreme Court and Administrative Agencies. New York: Free Press.

SKOLNICK, J. (1966) Justice without Trial. New York: John Wiley.

SORAUF, F. J. (1959) "*Zorach v. Clausen*: the impact of a Supreme Court decision." Amer. Pol. Sci. Rev. 53 (September): 777-791.

VOLLMER, H. M. and D. G. MILLS (1966) Professionalization. Englewood Cliffs: Prentice-Hall.

WILSON, J. (1968) Varieties of Police Behavior. Cambridge: Harvard Univ. Press.

——— (1966) "The police and the delinquent in two cities," pp. 184-193 in D. Bordua (ed.) The Police: Six Sociological Essays. New York: John Wiley.

Yale Law J. [Note] (1967) "Interrogations in New Haven: the impact of Miranda." 6 (July): 1519-1648.

POLICE-COMMUNITY RELATIONS:
A NEED IN SEARCH
OF POLICE SUPPORT

Robert A. Mendelsohn

As the society responds to changes in technology, increased educational levels, redistribution of population centers, admission to civil society of previously excluded groups, and a host of other structural phenomena, so does the role and method of operation of the police. One major consequence of these trends for the police has been to place them under considerably more restraint than was true even a short time ago (Bordua, 1968; President's Commission on Law Enforcement and Administration of Justice, 1967b). Thus, it would be reasonable to assume that instances of "police brutality" are less frequent than in the past, and that police officers are less able to administer "street justice." Though officers may complain about the role of Supreme Court decisions and the activities of civil liberties groups in these changes, their real source lies in the far-ranging developments listed above. A second major result of these broad social changes has been an increasing demand, among the black· citizenry, for improved police services combined with an increasing impatience and anger at police for real and imagined mistreatment of citizens. A third major consequence has been the impetus for increasing police professionalization. This in effect is an attempt to transfer the motivating forces on officers from control by a given subcommunity to internalized standards of conduct. These standards are presumably derived from the canons of effective and responsible police work.

POLICE-COMMUNITY NEGATIVISM

All these changes increase the stress on the police by disrupting traditional methods of operation or by requiring an increased degree of contact with, and understanding of, negatively viewed groups.

Yet it is reasonably clear that, unless a disastrous and panicky repression sets in, these are the trends of the future, if for no other reason than they are consistent with trends in the larger society.[1] In fact, moreover, the potential for improving police work that resides in these trends is quite substantial. It is a truism that effective police work requires the support of the community. As the President's Commission (1967b: 144) puts it:

> Even if fairer treatment of minority groups were the sole consideration, police departments would have an obligation to attempt to achieve and maintain good police-community relations. In fact, however, much more is at stake. Police-community relationships have a direct bearing on the character of life in our cities, and on the community's ability to maintain stability and to solve its problems. At the same time, the police department's capacity to deal with crime depends to a large extent upon its relationship with the citizenry. Indeed, no lasting improvement in law enforcement is likely in this country unless police-community relations are substantially improved. . . . A dissatisfied public will not support the police enthusiastically . . . when the police and public are at odds, the police tend to become isolated from the public and become less capable of understanding and adapting to the community and its changing needs. . . . Poor police-community relations adversely affect the ability of the police to prevent crime and apprehend criminals.

While no one would be naive enough to believe that improved police-community relations will in themselves, given the multiple causes of crime and riots, eliminate these disruptive events, it is difficult to see how much can be done without a change in police attitudes toward the black community.

The truism, unfortunately, may be a truism for only a minority of officers. Within the department in Detroit, there was, following the riot, a most striking absence of concern with the importance of police-community relations as a riot deterrent.[2] There was also a lack of appreciation of the role police play in contributing to riot etiology. Strikingly illustrative of this disinterest are the responses to the question, "What needs to be done to prevent future riots?"[3] although responses to other questions would perhaps do as well. As can be seen, until the inspector and above rank (labelled "inspectors")[4] is attained, there is no support whatever among white officers for improved police-community relations; indeed, far and away the most popular response calls for a better trained, better equipped, and larger force, and "stricter" law enforcement.[5] Certainly, there is little in this to suggest that there is any comprehension of, much less support for, the idea, which I will advocate, that the role of the police should include close ties with persons in the community, considerable openness to public scrutiny, increased community service, and a major advocacy role for the disadvantaged and oppressed.

The irony of this reaction is that the police, despite a self-conception that their role is one of apprehending law-breakers and keeping blacks in

TABLE 1

WHAT NEEDS TO BE DONE TO PREVENT FUTURE RIOTS?
(in percentages)

Race[a]	White					Black
Rank[b]	Insp. (n=93)	Lt. (n=41)	Sgt. (n=52)	Det. (n=60)	Ptr. (n=113)	All Ranks (n=54)
Program						
Law and/or more efficient police	21.5	43.9	55.8	66.7	65.5	18.5
Social action (e.g., education, better race relations)	37.7	31.7	25.0	20.0	25.6	46.3
Improve police-community relations	19.4	4.9	3.8	3.3	0.0	13.0
Other	21.5	19.5	15.4	10.0	8.8	22.2
TOTAL	100.1	100.0	100.0	100.0	99.9	100.0

a. Although the views of black officers are not the main focus of this paper, it is instructive to examine the difference in views of white and black officers. Accordingly, the views of black officers are included in this and the other tables.

b. The data in the table record the first two reasons mentioned by the respondents. Accordingly it is a table of responses rather than subjects. Those officers who responded with "don't know" or not applicable answers are not included. This was the case for four inspectors, five lieutenants, six sergeants, seven detectives, nineteen patrolmen, and two black officers.

their place (Edwards, 1968), in fact, probably provide more essential services to lower-class residents than most other governmental service organizations. Intervention in family quarrels, running an "ambulance service" working with troubled youth, and a large variety of other responsibilities consume more police time than the apprehension of criminals. As can be seen even by this superficial recitation, many of these are among the most difficult or most undesirable to be found in large cities. Yet it is the police who perform these services, not the professionals who flee the city after daylight hours. Furthermore, even though many police officers think of themselves as functioning to control the black population, it is probably easier, as Bordua (1968) has pointed out, for a ghetto resident to obtain a needed service from the police than from a teacher, a social worker, a housing inspector, a psychiatrist, or a sanitation man. More specifically, then, the irony is that the police are already providing many of the services that potentially form the basis for an effective police-community interaction but cannot grasp its implications for improving their effectiveness in the area of crime control—the very area in which their conception of police work requires them to be effective.

The failure to make the connection between police-community relations and the perceived role of the police in crime prevention and control may be attributed to two main factors. First, the average officer is undereducated and the ability to perceive what is, after all, a complex connection requires analytical abilities that are distinctively functions of education. As Skolnick (1969) has pointed out, the average officer joining the force is less educated than his civilian peers, and the educational level of officers has actually been declining since the Depression.[6] It is this, rather than the assumed authoritarian character structure of the officer, that matters. In fact, while studies of police officers' personalities are rare, the available evidence (Niederhoffer, 1967)[7] would indicate that officers, on joining the force, are not particularly authoritarian. They are, however, certainly conventional and become authoritarian and cynical as they continue with the force.

The second main factor blocking improved police-community relations is the police attitude toward the people with whom they would have to frankly and intimately interact if they are to develop an effective program. Numerous studies presented or reviewed in Skolnick (1966, 1969) have clearly shown that many, indeed most, police officers manifest considerable anti-black feeling and find it difficult to avoid viewing themselves, literally, as front line troops against the rebellious and uncivilized blacks. To be sure, white police officers are not particularly different from working-class whites in general in this anti-black feeling; rather perhaps, the average officer is more direct in his verbal utterances than the equivocating, but just as hostile, civilian.

The study in Detroit provides some of the dimensions of this dislike. The typical white officer, lieutenant and below, interprets the motives for the riot in predominantly negative terms. He clearly does not see it as a meaningless event but, rather, as a reflection of the undisciplined, hostile or morally corrupt nature of the black community. This is shown in Table 2. This interpretation is consistent with his general view of the black community. As Table 3 shows, he sees the black community as a privileged minority which, rather than rebelling against white authority, obviously ought to be grateful to that authority. Furthermore, he sees the lower-class black community as manifesting relatively little respect for law and order. This comparison takes on more significance when it is compared to his view of the white community. These data are presented in Table 4.[8]

TABLE 2
WHAT DO YOU THINK WAS THE LONG TERM CAUSE OF THE RIOT?
(in percentages)

Race	White					Black
Rank[a]	Insp. (n=94)	Lt. (n=40)	Sgt. (n=43)	Det. (n=49)	Ptr. (n=104)	All Ranks (n=53)
Cause						
Persons (e.g., agitators, militants)	18.1	22.5	14.0	14.3	26.9	9.4
Undisciplined self-interest (e.g., something for nothing)	6.4	10.0	32.6	26.5	17.3	11.3
Protest (e.g., frustration, jobs, mistreatment)	43.6	17.5	20.9	20.4	22.1	54.7
Temper of the times (e.g., violence elsewhere, no respect for authority)	27.6	50.0	27.9	34.7	31.7	24.5
Other	4.2	0.0	4.6	4.1	1.9	0.0
TOTAL	99.9	100.0	100.0	100.0	99.9	99.9

a. The data in the table record the first two reasons mentioned by the respondents. Accordingly, it is a table of responses rather than subjects. Those officers who responded with "don't know" or not applicable answers are not included. This was the case for five inspectors, nine sergeants, three detectives, fifteen patrolmen, and five black officers.

Finally, the officer's view of citizen hostility toward him as an officer shows a clear differentiation between white and black. He is not unsympathetic toward white hostility, as Table 5 shows, but he interprets black hostility (Table 6) in highly negative terms with relatively little insight into its likely causes or the police contribution. This interpretation is, of course, consistent with a warfare view of his relations with the black community and with his other views which have been presented above.

TABLE 3

HERE IS A LIST OF AREAS IN WHICH SOME PEOPLE SAY NEGROES ARE NOT TREATED FAIRLY. DO YOU THINK THEY ARE TREATED VERY UNFAIRLY, SLIGHTLY UNFAIRLY, THE SAME AS WHITES, OR THAT THINGS ARE ACTUALLY IN THEIR FAVOR?

(in percentages)

Race	White					Black
Rank	Insp. (n=59)	Lt. (n=33)	Sgt. (n=36)	Det. (n=36)	Ptr. (n=86)	All Ranks (n=36)
Area						
Housing						
VU	24	12	22	6	12	67
U	34	39	39	28	29	25
S	30	33	25	56	37	3
F	10	12	14	11	19	3
DK, NA	2	3	0	0	3	3
Schools						
VU	3	0	0	0	0	47
U	7	6	3	3	0	33
S	44	45	31	33	40	14
F	41	48	67	64	59	3
DK, NA	5	0	0	0	1	3
Jobs						
VU	15	3	11	6	5	56
U	25	18	14	22	17	33
S	30	36	44	56	43	8
F	29	42	31	17	31	0
DK, NA	0	0	0	0	3	3
Welfare Agencies						
VU	0	0	0	0	0	8
U	2	0	0	0	0	19
S	25	15	14	11	10	39
F	64	79	83	86	86	28
DK, NA	8	6	3	3	3	6
Stores						
VU	12	3	8	0	1	22
U	5	9	8	8	13	33
S	71	76	72	86	70	36
F	5	9	8	6	13	3
DK, NA	7	3	3	0	3	6
Law Enforcement Agencies						
VU	2	0	6	0	0	56
U	14	15	14	3	7	31
S	68	55	53	72	57	6
F	14	30	28	25	34	3
DK, NA	3	0	0	0	2	6

TABLE 4

MEAN PERCEIVED SCORES ON RESPECT FOR LAW AND ORDER
(at the present time) IN MIDDLE-CLASS AND
SLUM COMMUNITIES BY RACE

Race	White					Black
Rank	Insp.	Lt.	Sgt.	Det.	Ptr.	All Ranks
Group						
Black middle class	6.8	6.5	6.3	6.4	6.0	7.0
White middle class	8.0	7.6	7.6	7.8	7.6	7.4
Black slum	4.1	2.6	2.4	2.6	2.0	3.0
White slum	4.7	3.7	3.6	4.3	3.3	4.1

TABLE 5

MANY PEOPLE HAVE NOTED THAT THE AVERAGE WHITE
CITIZEN OFTEN HAS NEGATIVE FEELINGS TOWARD THE
POLICE. WHY DO YOU THINK THEY FEEL THAT WAY?
(in percentages)

Race	White				Black
Rank[a]	Lt. (n=33)	Sgt. (n=36)	Det. (n=36)	Ptr. (n=86)	All Ranks (n=36)
Reason					
Antisocial nature of white community	12.1	2.8	5.6	8.1	11.1
Unpleasant experiences; everyone hates authority a little bit	57.6	69.4	52.8	48.8	41.7
Statement not true	15.2	8.3	11.1	18.6	11.1
Other	15.2	11.1	16.7	18.6	22.2
DK, NA	0.0	8.3	13.9	5.8	13.9
TOTAL	100.1	99.9	100.1	99.9	100.0

a. Unfortunately, inspectors and above ranks were not asked this question.

Summing up, the typical white officer (below the rank of inspector[9]) views the black community as a privileged minority, unsatisfied with its already privileged position and prepared to use violence[10] to attain still further advantage over the white community. The community is perceived, further, as susceptible to the influence of agitators capable of galvanizing into action a people without real grievances. Finally, the black community is viewed as deficient in respect for law and order. Implicit in this view is a conception of the black community as primitive, emotional, and easily

TABLE 6

**A RECENT SURVEY IN THE *FREE PRESS* FOUND THAT
A MAJORITY OF NEGROES IN THE RIOT AREAS
FELT THAT POLICE BEHAVIOR TOWARD NEGROES
WAS A MAJOR CAUSE OF THE RIOT.
WHY DO YOU THINK THEY FEEL THAT WAY?**

(in percentages)

Race	White					Black
Rank	Insp. (n=59)	Lt. (n=33)	Sgt. (n=36)	Det. (n=36)	Ptr. (n=86)	All Ranks (n=36)
Reason						
Police behavior or perception of police behavior by Negroes[a] (e.g., Negroes treated unfairly)	54.2[b]	27.3	19.4	19.4	19.8	69.4
Antisocial nature of black community (e.g., no respect for law and order; more Negroes are criminals)	0.0	33.3	55.6	50.0	39.5	5.6
Statement is not true	15.2	6.1	11.1	11.1	11.6	5.6
Other	23.7	18.2	8.3	8.3	19.8	19.4
DK, NA	6.8	15.2	5.6	11.1	9.3	0.0
TOTAL	99.9	100.1	100.0	99.9	100.0	100.0

a. Very few white officers believe that police *in fact* discriminate against blacks with the exception of inspectors (see note b). Most of the officers responding within this category are saying that Negroes *feel* police discriminate. Black officers reverse the explanation. The majority responding in this category believe police *in fact* do discriminate.

b. Half the inspectors responding in this category state blacks feel the way they do because the police represent the power structure. Only inspectors give this reason.

aroused to antisocial action, and with an ultimate goal of domination over whites rather than a goal of equality.[11]

This is, of course, not to say that he acts on this conception in all his interactions while on duty. Quite the contrary—most of the time, as Skolnick (1966) has pointed out in his discussion of the warrant policeman, practical considerations play a major role. Further, the professional standards to which most officers strive to adhere are of great influence. But obviously an officer carrying around such a view of the black community is going to act on it at some points. For example, a view of blacks as hostile toward him predisposes an officer to use unnecessary force when he interprets the situation as threatening. In turn, what he decides to be threatening is a function, in part, of his generalized belief system about the black community. If he is wrong, or at times even when he is right, the resulting police-community tensions can have far-reaching and explosive consequences. In terms of the concern of this paper, however, even if he is able to behave judiciously despite these views, they hardly would incline him toward concern with improving police-community relations, and that is, as I have been arguing, a critical need.

These beliefs, then, make such far-reaching programs for police-community relations, as proposed by the President's Commission (1967b) and Bordua (1968), most difficult, perhaps impossible, to attain. The following considerations complicate adequate solution still further: (1) the increasing crime rate[12] with its demands for more vigorous police control despite the likely failure of such tactics to affect the crime rate in the long run (Menninger, 1968); (2) the pervasive feeling among officers that theirs is a disrespected profession[13] (Wilson, 1963; President's Commission, 1967b) with its concomitant and resulting reinforcement of in-group loyalties and alienation from the larger society; and (3) the reluctance of the police to add still another "disrespected" group to the list of police responsibilities. It thus becomes apparent that implementation of an effective and revolutionary program in police-community relations is highly problematical. Still, given the strategic importance of the police, an effort must be made.

Such an effort must begin where there are positive potentials at work. These may be identified as follows. First, from the black side, there is an increasing demand for better police services. Studies reported by the President's Commission (1967b) clearly indicate that a majority of blacks would support, indeed desperately want, a fair and effective police presence. This is hardly surprising since it is predominantly blacks who are the victims of crime.

Second, there is, among many—particularly higher echelon—officers, some recognition of the need for effective police-community relations and a corresponding realization that the police contribute, at least in some measure, to the problems in the community. For example, sixty-six percent of officers of the rank of inspector agree with the statement that "the behavior of the police in the past has contributed to the tense situation that exists in the Negro areas of the city." Sixty-nine percent of inspectors favor increased police involvement with the community. Furthermore, these officers have a positive view of the purpose of police-community relations work. Twenty-nine percent of inspectors hope such programs will produce closer contact between police and community or open lines of communication, seventeen percent feel it would let people present their problems and complaints to the police, forty-nine percent believe it would promote better understanding of *each other's problems* and improve police relations with the black community, and seventeen percent think it would help in the pursuit of solutions to police and community problems that are mutually acceptable. By contrast, very few inspectors cite using such contacts as an intelligence source, to promote a positive police "image," or to get citizens to respect law and order. Finally, fully eighty-one percent of these executive officers thought the police should do more in the way of police-community relations.[14] Fifty-four percent of those who believed more should be done felt it should take the form of increased involvement in community affairs, many advocating more meetings with citizens' groups.[15]

Among lower-echelon officers, there is considerably less support but, even here, a majority of officers state that they favor a human relations approach toward the black community. It is doubtful that this support goes very deep but it may be something on which to build. In addition, there is some evidence from Niederhoffer that many officers begin their police careers with some idealism and desire to help others. While his data clearly show that most of this idealism is lost, it may be possible to recapture it. Suggestions for how this might be done are presented below.

RECAPTURING THE IDEALISM

Considering the balance of positive and negative forces, presented here, affecting the development of an effective police-community relations program, the conclusion must be that to date the negative forces predominate. If this situation is to change, a number of steps are required.

First, there must be an explicit redefinition of the police role, reinforced by strongly supported professional norms. This redefinition would conform with what police in fact do in providing public service. Explicit recognition must be given to the police responsibility for assisting citizens who lack resources or sufficient power to obtain such resources. Equally important, the redefinition of the police role must provide a rationale for the importance of this work from both a general humanitarian and a practical point of view. This is to say, the officer needs to learn the connection between good community relations and greater effectiveness in crime control. Given the attitudes of most officers, it is difficult to see how this redefinition can be accomplished without strong professional norms supporting such activity. Professional norms would also shield the police, to some extent, from those groups in the community that reflect antipathy toward black Americans. Another way to put this last point is that so long as the police permit themselves to be used to carry out the mandate of large segments of the white population, they will always be cast in the role of victimizers and victimized. They will carry out the mandate of the white citizenry but unlike the citizenry cannot avoid that policy's implications. They thus become the visible representatives of the white power structure, a point not lost on a number of police administrators.[16]

There is good reason to believe that those professional norms which implicitly require officers to disengage themselves from a firmly held set of attitudes before they take action will not be easily inculcated. As Wilson has pointed out, police officers' conception of their roles is often at variance with idealized professional norms. For example, many officers regard violence as a way of instilling "respect" for police, a belief that most professionally oriented officers would reject. In addition, there are some professional norms that fly in the face of the hostility many officers feel toward blacks. Both impediments to the adoption of professional norms do not seem to be functions of specific police experience with black citizens.[17] Rather they come from attitudes learned from their primary reference groups in the process of growing up in a society that discriminates against black Americans and from generalized police tradition and attitudes. Since police agencies have no control over the early socialization experiences of the men who become officers, it is they who must take primary responsibility for the education of their officers.

This discussion leads to the second and third recommendations. There must be increased university training for police officers and more effective in-service training programs. Such programs will provide the intellectual background for understanding the centrality of police-community relations. As indicated earlier, the need for increased education has been recognized by the Detroit Police Department. Third, it is absolutely essential that command and executive officers reward, through promotion and other positive reinforcements, officers who exemplify good relations with the community and who innovate new techniques for improved relations. Of all the steps that can be taken, none may be more potent than reward by superiors of officers who exemplify commitment to positive community attitudes.

A fourth recommendation is that a program of research must be vigorously undertaken to evaluate the effect of new (and old) programs pertaining to police-community relations. Nothing succeeds like demonstrated success. Research may provide that evidence of success. This means that close ties between the police and the academic community must be vigorously established.

Finally, innovation and willingness to try new ideas in the area of police-community relations must be strongly rewarded. Included must be a recognition that old solutions are not adequate. The following are several programs suggested by Bordua and briefly noted here. They really deserve complete discussion but are presented mainly to provide an idea as to what innovation might involve. Police must be willing to talk with all groups in the community, including militants. As the most visible representatives of law and order, they must make that role more than a euphemism for repression by adopting an advocacy role in regard to the poor and disadvantaged. Police must expand and professionalize their Youth Bureaus. To earn the confidence of the community, they must develop a citizen observer program (with observers recruited from all political groups). They must know community mores and through careful program and operations analysis determine which police practices offend such mores without commensurate pay-off in crime reduction or decrease in police-community tensions.

The police are inevitably and inextricably involved in the black community. The sole question is how they will relate to that community. While obviously substantially improved police-community relations will be just one factor in reducing both urban crime and the likelihood of further riots, it is a certainty that the way the police handle their relations with the black community will play a major role in the direction that American cities take.

NOTES

1. Bordua argues that there has been a relative shift from coercion as a method of social control. He cites human relations approaches to industrial management, child rearing techniques, and other evidence. He goes on to argue that social control is becoming more and more "distributive" in nature. Included in this latter category are economic sanctions, persuasion, and a vast array of welfare state programs.

2. Although it may be argued that these responses occurred two years ago and in response to a cataclysmic event, it is the author's belief that the beliefs expressed in these responses are stable and have not changed markedly in two years. Probably some shifts in belief have occurred in this time span but whatever shifts have occurred are hardly commensurate with the need.

3. This question and all other data from Detroit referred to in this paper come from a survey on police attitudes, particularly about the riot of 1967, carried out from November 1967 through March 1968. A random sample, stratified by rank and race, were exhaustively questioned on riot interpretation, police response to the riot, police work in general, attitudes toward both blacks and whites, morale, and police-community relations. In addition, the usual demographic material was obtained along with a variety of responses to the officers' status and hopes. The white officers interviewed were fifty-seven inspectors and executives, thirty-three

lieutenants, thirty-six sergeants, thirty-six detectives, and eighty-six patrolmen. The black officers interviewed included thirty-eight officers. In the tables, the thirty-six black officers of rank of lieutenant and below are not differentiated by rank. The number of black officers in each rank is too small for such a breakdown. The two black inspectors are included with the inspectors. For further details, see Mendelsohn (1969).

4. Inspectors include officers from the highest professional rank, the superintendant, to various executives and to those with the rank of "inspector." This group as a whole generally exercises command and executive functions. For example, an inspector will ordinarily be in command of a precinct. Lieutenants are superior to sergeants who, in turn, are superior to patrolmen, the lowest rank. If assigned to a precinct, a lieutenant may command a platoon. Detectives may be of various ranks but in the sample of this study, they do not carry additional rank such as detective sergeant. Those with ranks of detective sergeant or detective lieutenant were coded as sergeant and lieutenant respectively. This is the correct procedure for two reasons: (1) they are superior in rank to that of detective; (2) they were obtained, respectively, from the sergeant and lieutenant rosters provided by the Police Department. With a few exceptions, these ranks constitute all the ranks within the department.

5. Obviously, there is not that much support at the inspector level either. Evidence to be presented later, however, indicates that a need for improved police-community relations is recognized by a substantially larger group than shown in response to this question. How deep and insightful this support is will be discussed later.

6. This deficiency has been recognized by the Police Department in Detroit and is also a central point in the reforms suggested by Locke (1969), a former administrative assistant to the commissioner, in his recent book on the Detroit riot. Officers are encouraged to pursue college studies and are rewarded for this by reducing the time spans required to take promotional exams and by other rewards as well.

7. Niederhoffer (1967) notes that recruits to the New York Police Department score about average on the California F Scale. They seem reasonably idealistic about police work but rapidly change in the direction of the substantial cynicism that characterizes the veteran officer. Interestingly, this increase in cynicism occurs while they are still in the Academy and before they have any real street experience. Later in this paper, I will discuss the effects of street experience on police attitudes.

8. Most striking, of course, is the fact that the officers' chief differentiation is along class lines, even though all officers (including black ones) always rate whites as higher in respect for law and order than blacks. This class differentiation made by white officers is potentially of great value to an effective police-community relations program. It hardly needs to be said, however, that to most officers, a black is lower class unless the citizen proves otherwise. Then there may be a change in attitude toward him. By then, however, it is often too late. The seriousness of the officers' dislike of the lower-class black is compounded by the fact that, despite the increased entry of blacks into the middle class, proportionally larger numbers of blacks are lower class than are whites.

It should also be pointed out that black officers make the same differentiations as do white officers. They rate the middle class as higher than the slum group and, within class, evaluate white citizens as having more respect for law and order than black citizens. Black officers, however, assign higher respect for law and order, among blacks, than all white officers (except inspectors). Most significantly, they do not assume that anger at the police by black citizens is a function of the antisocial nature of the black community but is rather due to real or perceived police mistreatment of black citizens.

9. Of all white officers, the inspectors present the most understanding and sympathetic view of the black community as can be seen from the tables. This likely comes about from their increased sophistication, their contact with leaders and concerned citizens of the black community, and their removal from the confrontations of the street. It may also be a function of the kind of persons who become inspectors. The issue is discussed in Mendelsohn (1969).

10. The majority of white officers below the rank of inspector responded "yes" to the question "Do you believe the more that Negroes get the more they want and the more they will rely on force to get it?"

11. Except for the emphasis on law and order and a disinclination among officers of ranks of detective and above to see the riot as planned, there is nothing especially distinctive about white officers' interpretation of the riot or their views of the black community. The same may be said for black officers. White officers mirror the views of the white citizenry, particularly the working-class citizenry, and black officers mirror the views of the black community. Further, although persons in the community sample of the Detroit study were not asked about whether blacks suffer from discrimination, past and recent polls (Pettigrew, 1964; Newsweek, 1969b) show that police attitudes in this matter are quite similar to those of whites in general. It is clear that most of the variance in riot interpretation and view of the black community is a function of race and class. This suggests that there is little variance remaining to be influenced by the effects of experience as a police officer qua officer in these matters. This indeed turns out to be the state of affairs. Patrolmen who have served only in all white precincts are not differentiable in attitudes from those whose sole experience has been in all black precincts. Nor are officers (of ranks from lieutenant to patrolmen) whose major experience has been in white areas differentiable from officers whose major experience has been in black areas. Certainly the claim that officers' attitudes are understandable in the face of the dangers they face and the experiences they have with blacks is challenged by such data.

Since, as innumerable surveys (Herbers, 1968; Hedegard, 1969; Newsweek, 1969a) have shown, the goal of the overwhelming majority of black citizens is equality rather than domination, integration rather than separation, the potential for misunderstanding and conflict between white officers and black citizens is ominous.

12. The best evidence would suggest that, even accounting for more efficient methods of reporting crime, the rate has been rising (President's Commission, 1967a). Whether, however, it is in fact higher than in previous eras of our nation's history is open to question.

13. This is an incorrect belief particularly as it applies to the white community. The President's Commission (1967b) reviews the evidence of public reaction to the police, and, by and large, the police are positively viewed by whites.

14. Response to this question may be an over-estimate of the commitment of the inspectors to police-community relations. The question specified should police do more *if time and money were available*. Thus the question avoids the issue of priorities on police time and money.

15. Though these responses are correctly cited as positive potentials, it must be pointed out that there remains a large group of police executives who are not convinced of the importance of even these minimal programs. Perhaps more significant is the fact that only a handful of officers see improved police-community relations as functionally related to reducing crime. Finally, police executives more

strongly support programs for crime reduction and riot avoidance which place the responsibility on other social forces or agencies. For example, the two most popular responses given by these officers on ways to prevent future riots is improvement in the socioeconomic and educational status of blacks and the imposition of stiffer penalties by the courts. Both kinds of social change are well beyond the power of the police to effect. It is undoubtedly true that improvement in the status and skills of the black community is a critical step to make in eliminating riots and reducing crime. It is also true that this police response attests to some sophistication and sympathy and is a realistic one. The danger, however, is that, given this view, the police will be inclined to do less than they could. Of course, quite aside from the inspectors' views, there remains the problem of getting the cooperation and support of lower-echelon officers.

16. As Table 5 shows, twenty-seven percent of inspectors believe the reason blacks blame police for the riot is that police represent the white power structure. With second mentions included, this rises to thirty percent. This explanation is totally absent among officers below this echelon.

17. As indicated earlier, the specific assignment of officers (with the exception of those at the inspector level) does not seem related to attitudes. This suggests that police attitudes toward blacks (and indeed work norms) is a function of police tradition and attitudes, and primary reference group attitudes. These provide the "filtering system" through which experience is channeled. Thus, it is the filtering system that matters and which must be changed if officers are going to accept the changes being advocated.

REFERENCES

BORDUA, D. J. (1968) "Comments on police-community relations." Unpublished paper.

EDWARDS, G. (1968) The Police on the Urban Frontier: A Guide to Community Understanding. New York: Institute of Human Relations Press.

HEDEGARD, J. M. (1969) "Detroit community attitudes on race and urban rioting." Detroit Riot Study, unpublished paper.

HERBERS, J. (1968) "Study says Negro justifies rioting as social protest." New York Times 118 (July 28): 1 ff.

LOCKE, H. G. (1969) The Detroit Riot of 1967. Detroit: Wayne State Univ. Press.

MENDELSOHN, R.A. (1969) "The police interpretation of the Detroit riot of 1967: an examination of the dimensions and determinants of the interpretation." Detroit Riot Study, unpublished paper.

MENNINGER, K. (1968) The Crime of Punishment. New York: Viking Press.

Newsweek Editors (1969a) "Report from black America." Newsweek 73 (June 30): 17-35.

––– (1969b) "The troubled American: a special report on the white majority." Newsweek 74 (October 6): 28-68.

NIEDERHOFFER, A. (1967) Behind the Shield. New York: Doubleday.

PETTIGREW, T. F. (1964) A Profile of the Negro American. Princeton: D. Von Nostrand.

President's Commission on Law Enforcement and Administration of Justice (1967a)

The Challenge of Crime in a Free Society. Washington, D.C.: U.S. Government Printing Office.

––– (1967b) Task Force Report: The Police. Washington, D.C.: U.S. Government Printing Office.

SKOLNICK, J. H. (1969) The Politics of Protest. New York: Ballantine Books.

––– (1966) Justice Without Trial. New York: John Wiley.

WILSON, J. Q. (1963) "The police and their problems: a theory." Public Policy 12: 189-216.

A PROPOSAL FOR REFORM OF THE
PLEA BARGAINING PROCESS

Welsh S. White

Prosecutorial efforts to induce guilty pleas play a central role in the administration of criminal justice. In most jurisdictions prosecutors grant special concessions—usually dismissals of certain charges or reduced sentence recommendations [1]—to defendants who enter guilty pleas and thus waive their constitutional right to a trial before a judge or jury.[2] This "plea bargaining" practice disposes of a remarkably high percentage of cases.[3]

Despite commentators' arguments in favor of abolishing plea bargaining,[4] the Supreme Court recently acknowledged its validity in *Brady v. United States*.[5] The defendant in *Brady* was charged with kidnapping and faced a possible maximum penalty of death upon conviction by a jury.[6] By pleading guilty he reduced the maximum possible sentence to life imprisonment.[7] In a subsequent action he sought to invalidate his plea on the grounds that it was induced both by his fear of the death penalty and by the prosecutor's representations concerning reduction of sentence and clemency. With regard to the latter claim, the Court noted:

> We decline to hold . . . that a guilty plea is compelled and invalid under the Fifth Amendment whenever motivated by

the defendant's desire to accept the certainty or probability of a lesser penalty rather than face a wider range of possibilities extending from acquittal to conviction and a higher penalty authorized by law for the crime charged.

. . . .

. . . [W]e cannot hold that it is unconstitutional for the State to extend a benefit to a defendant who in turn extends a substantial benefit to the State and who demonstrates by his plea that he is ready and willing to admit his crime and to enter the correctional system in a frame of mind which affords hope for success in rehabilitation over a shorter period of time than might otherwise be necessary.[8]

The Court also recognized that plea bargaining is essential to effective utilization of "scarce judicial and prosecutorial resources."[9] Prosecutors in large cities are confronted with an increasing backlog of cases. The available judges, trial assistants, and courtrooms are barely adequate to handle the workload generated by a system in which only a small minority of cases are actually litigated.[10] Although some defendants may plead guilty solely for reasons of conscience, a large number undoubtedly enter their pleas primarily in expectation of prosecutorial concessions.[11] Removal of the incentive to plead guilty would place an intolerable strain on the system.[12]

The advisability of attempting to provide sufficient resources to eliminate the need for guilty pleas is doubtful. As Professor Enker has pointed out:

Even if the money were readily available, it would still not be clear that we could call upon sufficient numbers of competent personnel. A lowering of standards in order to man the store adequately may well result in poorer justice. It may also divert both funds and personnel from other segments of the criminal process, such as corrections work, where they are arguably more needed.[13]

Reducing the number of guilty pleas would also additionally burden both witnesses and jurors.[14]

Accepting the premise that prosecutorial encouragement of guilty pleas is a necessary feature of our present system of justice, it is important to formulate guidelines which retain the advantages yet minimize the undesirable consequences of plea bargaining. This Article will describe some of the practices presently utilized to induce guilty pleas, point out the salient problems with these practices, and offer suggestions for improvement.

I. Plea Bargaining in Philadelphia and New York

Several studies have described the general characteristics of plea bargaining, identifying the differing approaches of prosecutors and the types of bargains made.[15]   To provide a slightly new perspective, I will discuss various aspects of plea bargaining as it is conducted in the Philadelphia and New York district attorneys' offices.   Because these offices are reputedly among the finest in the country, their plea bargaining practices should reflect a high level of prosecutorial efficiency and responsibility.   The discussion of the Philadelphia prosecutor's office is based on personal observations made while serving as an assistant prosecutor in that office from 1966 to 1968, and on interviews conducted in March and April 1970 with members of the office and with Philadelphia defense attorneys.   The discussion of New York plea bargaining practices is based entirely on interviews conducted in April and May 1970 with William F. Keenan, Chief of the New York Homicide Division, and with several New York defense attorneys.

A. *Philadelphia*

In Philadelphia, guilty pleas dispose of approximately thirty-five percent of all felony and misdemeanor cases.   This figure is somewhat misleading because many cases recorded as "waivers" (trials before a judge without a jury) can be more accurately characterized as "slow pleas of guilty."   That is, the defendant's counsel facilitates the presentation of evidence and implicitly or explicitly admits that the defendant is guilty of some offense, but does not enter a formal plea. Were all of these cases classified as guilty pleas, the figure would probably rise to above fifty percent.

1. Office Policy

Like most prosecutors, the Philadelphia district attorney has not established any formal rules or procedures governing plea bargaining.[16] He and his top assistants have developed general policies, however, which are communicated to other assistant prosecutors in office meetings and intra-office memos, and through a general process of osmosis. For example, absent exceptional circumstances,[17] office policy forbids sentence concessions to induce pleas in certain "very serious" cases where society's interest in obtaining an appropriate sentence is deemed paramount. No systematic attempt is made to designate which cases belong in this category but, according to District Attorney Arlen Specter, the cases most likely to be considered "very serious" are those in which the crime indicates that the defendant presents a serious and continuing threat of violence.[18]   Thus, sentence concessions are forbidden in cases involving the brutal rape of a stranger or an armed robbery in which the victim is injured.   On the other hand, plea bargaining is condoned in dealing with crimes of passion. The theory is that such crimes are unlikely to be repeated and thus society's interest may be adequately served by the imposition of a substantially shorter sentence than the defendant would probably receive following a trial and conviction.[19]

Philadelphia office policy also opposes granting concessions merely because a case might result in an acquittal.   According to First Assistant District Attorney Richard Sprague, the primary purpose of plea bargaining is to save time and clear the dockets. If the trial prosecutor has a weak case which may be tried without delay, no major concessions should be offered.[20]

Within this basic framework, each trial prosecutor has broad discretion regarding the concessions to be made to induce a plea. The trial prosecutor is in the best position to assess the nature of his case and to form an opinion on the defendant's probable future danger to the community, and thus his determination of an appropriate plea bargain is usually final. He is expected to consult with a superior before agreeing to a plea only in the more serious cases,[21] and then his opinion is given great weight. The manner in which the trial prosecutor disposes of his cases generally receives rather cursory review.[22] When a guilty plea is entered, his sentence recommendation may be scrutinized, but seldom is the evidence available to him at the time of the plea independently examined. When no guilty plea is entered, top assistants do not evaluate the trial prosecutor's efforts to induce a plea.

2. Actual Practice

Because Pennsylvania judges generally have a great deal of flexibility in sentencing,[23] prosecutorial concessions usually involve sentence recommendations rather than dismissal or reduction of charges.[24]   To induce a guilty plea, the assistant prosecutor may promise to make a specific sentence recommendation or, in some cases, to make no sentence recommendation or not to oppose probation.   The judge is generally not a party to this arrangement.   In rare cases, however, the defendant will refuse to enter a plea unless he receives assurance that the judge will not impose a sentence exceeding the assistant prosecutor's recommendation.   While the assistant prosecutor's sentence recommendation is not binding, Philadelphia judges generally adhere to it.   The concessions offered by Philadelphia prosecutors, therefore, have the effect of limiting the maximum sentence which the defendant will receive.

The assistant prosecutor's bargaining power and the tactics he employs to induce a guilty plea depend largely on whether the case has been designated "major" or "non-major" and, if "non-major," on whether the defendant is out on bail or in jail.

Nearly all cases, except those involving major felonies or excessive violence, are designated "non-major" and listed for trial in a "bail room" if the defendant is free on bail or in a "jail room" if he has been unable to make bail.   On any given day, an assistant prosecutor will have approximately ten cases listed for trial in his court room.   This volume of cases in the "list room" generally prevents the prosecutor from initiating plea bargaining before the trial date, and an absent witness, missing piece of evidence, or dilatory defense counsel frequently hampers the immediate disposal of a case on the day of trial.   The prosecutor will thus generally be willing to offer substantial concessions to induce a guilty plea and thereby dispose of the case at that time.[25] But if a case is ready for trial, the prosecutor is less likely to offer concessions either to save time or to discount the possibility of acquittal because list room trials are brief and generally result in guilty verdicts.

Several factors enhance the prosecutor's bargaining position when the defendant is in custody.   If the prosecutor believes that the defendant has already been incarcerated for a sufficient period of time and is willing to recommend a "time-in" sentence, the defendant will invariably agree to plead guilty to obtain immediate freedom.[26]   Even if the prosecutor does not agree to a "time-in" sentence, an incarcerated defendant, frightened and demoralized by the prospect of an indefinite period of confinement, may be willing to enter a plea and accept a fixed period of imprisonment.   Finally, in a "jail room" case, the prosecutor deals almost exclusively with an assistant voluntary defender.   Because the defender will probably work with the prosecutor again and will be interested in maintaining a good relationship, he may often be highly receptive to guilty plea negotiations.[27]

The prosecutor's bargaining position is weaker if the defendant is free on bail and he must make substantially greater concessions to induce a guilty plea. Bailed defendants will naturally be reluctant to enter a plea which will result in loss of freedom. Unlike the defendant in prison, the bailed defendant can only profit by postponement of his case. Over time, evidence may disappear, memories may fade, and the defendant may be able to build a record of good behavior to help him at sentencing. Furthermore, a bailed defendant is likely to be represented by a private attorney who deals infrequently with the prosecutor. The private attorney will thus have little incentive to develop a good working relationship with the assistant prosecutor and can concentrate on obtaining the best possible result for his client.

"Major cases" include the four main felonies (homicide, rape, robbery, and arson), other serious cases such as extortion by a public official or extremely aggravated assault and battery, and cases requiring special attention because of complex legal or factual issues. Because a major trial prosecutor is expected to prepare each case carefully, he is assigned his relatively few cases at an early stage of the proceedings. In theory, then, he has an opportunity to negotiate a guilty plea well before the trial date. But in practice, major trial prosecutors generally do not conduct serious plea negotiations in one case while trying another. As a result, plea negotiations are often deferred until the day the case is listed for trial.[28]

The major trial prosecutor's willingness to offer concessions often depends largely on factors unrelated to the seriousness of the case or its probable trial time. For example, his pending work load may be quite important. If he has several cases listed for trial at approximately the same time, he will be anxious to obtain pleas in some of them in order to ease his schedule and improve the condition of the dockets.

Contrary to office policy, likelihood of conviction is generally very important in determining what concessions will be offered to induce a plea. While some trial prosecutors enjoy the challenge of a difficult case, most will offer substantial concessions rather than risk losing a jury trial. Moreover, as one member of the office candidly stated, each prosecutor's attitude towards the trial of a weak case depends on "his position in the office at the time of the trial."[29] Assistant prosecutors in the major trial division feel that they are evaluated more on their ability to win jury trials than to dispose of cases efficiently. An assistant prosecutor who has just been assigned to the major trial division or who has recently lost one jury trial may offer substantial concessions in a case which he believes would be difficult to win before a jury rather than jeopardize his position in this prestigious division by a jury trial loss.

Some major trial prosecutors admit that their interest in a case influences the type of concessions they will offer to induce a plea. As one assistant prosecutor stated, "When I get a case that looks interesting and I think I can win it, I don't want to encourage a guilty plea. I joined the district attorney's office so that I could try that kind of case to a jury." [30]

The same assistant also noted that he would be more willing to offer concessions to induce a plea if he considered the defendant's counsel personally objectionable.[31] Other prosecutors suggested that they would be more likely to offer substantial concessions to attorneys they found consistently honest and cooperative.[32] In addition, many admitted that they are willing to increase the concessions offered to induce a plea when the defense attorney's skill decreases the chances of conviction.[33]

Of course, major trial prosecutors assign considerable importance to the nature of their case in determining sentence concessions. But in assessing the seriousness of a case, most prosecutors do not rely solely on such objective factors as the type of crime committed and the defendant's age and prior criminal record. More than two thirds of the Philadelphia major trial prosecutors stated that their personal evaluation of the defendant is an important determinant of sentence recommendations.[34] This subjective evaluation naturally introduces into the plea bargaining process an additional element of uncertainty and further opportunity for arbitrariness.

B. *New York*

The New York Supreme Court Bureau [35] disposes of an extremely high percentage of felony cases by guilty pleas. Of the 1,404 cases prosecuted from January 1, 1970 to April 29, 1970, 45 were disposed of by jury trial, 8 by trial before a judge, and 1,351 (96.2 percent) by guilty pleas.[36]

1. Office Policy

The need to induce guilty pleas is much greater in New York than in Philadelphia. According to Homicide Chief William Keenan, the New York Supreme Court Bureau must dispose of approximately 5,000 felony cases annually.[37] Due to limited courtroom and other administrative resources, only 150 to 175 of these cases can be tried to a jury. Defense attorneys do not readily agree to nonjury trials,[38] and thus a very large number of defendants must be persuaded to plead guilty.

Concessions are offered to induce pleas in most cases but, according to Chief Keenan, the extent of these concessions depends primarily upon the defendant's age, his prior criminal record, the type of crime he is charged with, and the strength of the state's case.[39] The nature of the crime committed is most important. Top prosecutors strongly support the view that their limited resources should be conserved for the trial of cases involving particularly serious offenses. As in Philadelphia, the seriousness of a case depends on various factors, particularly the defendant's probable future danger to the community.

After preliminary arraignment, each case is assigned to an assistant prosecutor for trial,[40] who must dispose of his cases with reasonable speed to retain his position as a major trial prosecutor.[41] Prosecutors with substantial trial experience have complete discretion to strike whatever guilty plea bargains they deem appropriate, and top assistants review their decisions only briefly.[42] Despite the freedom given individual prosecutors, office policy favors uniform plea bargaining practices. Chief Keenan asserts that this goal is substantially achieved because, by sharing experiences with other assistant prosecutors, judges, and defense counsel, each assistant develops a common understanding of the appropriate concessions to offer in each case.[43]

2. Actual Practice

Plea bargaining practices in New York differ from those in Philadelphia in two important respects. First, as noted earlier, because more guilty pleas must be entered in New York, the concessions offered to defendants are concomitantly increased.[44] Second, the New York trial judge plays a far more important role in the bargaining process than does his Philadelphia counterpart. According to Martin Erdman of the New York Legal Aid Society, most New York defense attorneys will not enter a plea unless they are certain what the judge will do. In some cases the assistant prosecutor and defense counsel may seek judicial approval of a tentative plea arrangement.[45] The judge generally agrees to accept the plea and either to impose the sentence requested [46] or to permit withdrawal of the plea if he finds a more severe sentence warranted. In other cases New York judges actively participate in negotiations and often suggest appropriate plea bargains.

For the most part, however, New York plea bargaining practices parallel the Philadelphia practices rather closely. Despite the office policy in favor of uniformity, New York defense counsel have noticed a marked disparity in concessions offered by individual prosecutors.[47] As in Philadelphia, the type of bargain defense counsel can strike depends in part on his relationship with the assistant prosecutor and on whether his client is in jail.[48] Finally, in deciding upon appropriate prosecutorial concessions, the strength of the state's case is far more important in practice than it is in theory.[49] According to Martin Erdman, "Prosecutors in this city hate to have a defeat on their record. When they think they have a weak case, they'll go to great lengths to avoid a trial." [50]

II. PROBLEMS WITH THE PRESENT PRACTICES

The trial prosecutor's unchecked discretion is perhaps the most undesirable feature of the plea bargaining process, and the major part of this section will be given over to a catalogue of the potential harm to society in general as well as to the prosecutor's office resulting from this lack of restraint.[51] Then the role of the judge in the bargaining process will be briefly assessed.

A. *The Trial Prosecutor's Unchecked Discretion*

Professor Davis has discussed the problems likely to arise when an administrative agency's powers are not properly defined and controlled.[52] In the present situation, these problems are magnified because each individual trial prosecutor is free to apply plea bargaining policies he considers appropriate and to change these policies from case to case:[53] the potential for arbitrariness and inequality of treatment is indeed great.[54] Furthermore, if a defendant perceives that his ability to strike a favorable plea bargain depends on his counsel's effective manipulation of the system or on a particular trial prosecutor's attitude, his natural reaction will be cynicism and disrespect for the law.[55]

The low visibility of the present plea bargaining system also creates problems for the prosecutor's office. Plea bargaining should be employed in a manner calculated to maximize the efficient use of available trial resources. The absence of enforceable bargaining standards, however, enables individual prosecutors to reject or accept guilty plea arrangements for reasons unrelated to considerations of office efficiency. The prosecutor's personal desire to try a case may preclude entry of a guilty plea in an otherwise appropriate situation. Conversely, the prosecutor's need to protect his litigation record may lead to unwise acceptance of pleas.

The prosecutor's unrestrained discretion may also reinforce his tendency to take advantage of the relatively ineffective bargaining position of defendants unable to make bail. This practice plays a significant part in perpetuating inequality between the rich and the poor in the criminal process. The jailed defendant, because he is often unable to prepare his defense adequately, may plead guilty in exchange for minor prosecutorial concessions.[56] In addition, as Professor Foote has observed: "It is plausible, at least, that denial of pretrial liberty provides a psychological inducement to plead guilty which would be absent if the defendant were at liberty pending trial."[57] Our commitment to the principle of equal treatment for poor criminal defendants, expressed in *Griffin v. Illinois*,[58] is subverted when prosecutors take advantage of the jailed defendant's vulnerable position in conducting plea negotiations.[59]

Vesting trial prosecutors with complete responsibility for plea bargaining also creates administrative burdens and may frustrate possibilities for rehabilitation of defendants. Because trial prosecutors, especially major trial prosecutors, tend to devote full attention to the case currently on trial or the next case on the docket, they usually postpone any attempt to negotiate a guilty plea until the day of trial. The delay in the entry of the plea results in inefficiency because witnesses must make unnecessary trips to court and because it is difficult to estimate the number of trial courtrooms needed at any given time. But more important, it is generally agreed that punishment or treatment of criminals has maximum deterrent and rehabilitative effect if imposed on the offender as soon as possible after commission of the crime.[60] When the prosecutor's failure to negotiate a guilty plea results in a delay in the imposition of sentence, the beneficial effect of the sentence is reduced.

Prosecutorial inducement of guilty pleas in weak cases also poses potentially serious problems. When a New York or Philadelphia assistant prosecutor has a case which he believes is weak, he will frequently offer large concessions to induce a guilty plea. For example, a Philadelphia major trial prosecutor related that in one case he reduced his guilty plea sentence recommendation by two thirds in order to induce a defendant who had a forty percent chance of acquittal to forego trial.[61] According to Martin Erdman, New York prosecutors often reduce their sentence recommendations by at least fifty percent if they believe that there is a fifty percent chance of a hung jury, and by a great deal more if they believe that there is a fifty percent chance of acquittal.[62] If the chances of acquittal are greater, the practice in both offices is to offer at least proportionately higher concessions.

Granting disproportionate sentence concessions in weak cases may mean that an inordinate number of strong cases go to trial.[63] An effective allocation of limited prosecutorial resources would probably send only uncertain—neither ascertainably weak nor strong—cases to trial. Moreover, society may not receive adequate protection when defendants are given disproportionate sentence concessions in exchange for pleas of guilty. Finally, as many commentators have noted, this prosecutorial practice may compel innocent defendants to plead guilty.[64]

Prosecutors argue that appropriate precautions are taken to guard against the possibility that an innocent defendant will plead guilty. Chief Keenan asserts that all New York assistant prosecutors understand that they must dismiss the charges against a defendant if they are not morally certain of his guilt.[65] Martin Erdman, however, states that in certain cases, particularly those in which the prosecutor is relying primarily on identification evidence, an innocent defendant may well plead guilty in exchange for a reduced charge or sentence concession.[66] Mr. Erdman further states that in these cases defense counsel may be obliged to acquiesce in a plea bargain even though he is not convinced of his client's guilt.[67] The defense counsel's duty is to obtain the optimal disposition of his case, not to determine his client's innocence or guilt. Even if his client is innocent, counsel may urge acceptance of a plea to a reduced charge carrying a short sentence rather than risk a trial in which the defendant may receive a much longer prison term.[68]

B. *The Judge's Role in Plea Bargaining*

For the most part, judges have not contributed to the smooth functioning of the plea negotiation process. The Philadelphia office's experience with judicial participation in plea bargaining suggests that its value to the prosecutor is doubtful. Prior to 1969, assistant prosecutors and defense counsel would occasionally meet with judges to explore the possibility of a guilty plea.[69] In these pretrial conferences the judge would encourage [70] the parties to explore areas of agreement. According to First Assistant District Attorney Sprague, the meetings were not very fruitful because neither the assistant prosecutor nor the defense counsel was willing to "talk turkey." The judge's presence actually inhibited meaningful negotiation and decreased the chances of reaching a plea bargain.[71]

In New York, active judicial participation has facilitated the negotiation of plea bargains. But such participation may have serious disadvantages. When a judge suggests to a defendant, either directly or through his counsel, that he should plead guilty, the coercive effect of this suggestion is likely to be overwhelming.[72] Moreover, the judge may jeopardize his role as an impartial arbiter of justice if he participates in plea negotiating. For example, if a judge urges a defendant to plead guilty in exchange for a two-year sentence and the defendant rejects this arrangement, it would certainly be difficult for the judge to preside over the trial impartially. The judge would be aware of the defendant's probable guilt and would naturally desire to vindicate his initial judgment that the defendant's guilt would be established. At the very least, these factors would tend to sway the judge from his position of neutrality.[73] Finally, active judicial participation in plea bargaining may unfavorably color the defendant's view of the system. To the defendant, the judge becomes an adversary or at least a compromiser rather than an embodiment of his guarantee to a fair trial and an impartial sentence.[74]

III. A Proposal for the Prosecutor's Office

Because courts have been reluctant to impose judicial control on prosecutorial plea bargaining practices,[75] impetus for solving the problems described above must come from the prosecutors themselves.

A. *Suggested Procedure*

One major change in the structure of the prosecutor's office would eliminate many of the problems caused by current plea bargaining practices. Several assistant prosecutors should be given responsibility for negotiating guilty pleas with defense counsel at the earliest possible stage in the proceedings.[76] In Philadelphia, for example, one assistant prosecutor could be chosen to negotiate pleas in homicide cases, one to negotiate pleas in other major cases, and two or three to negotiate pleas in the list room cases.[77] These "executive prosecutors" should be among the most able and experienced in the office. They would have full responsibility for evaluating the facts of all cases assigned to them, deciding what sentence recommendations should be made upon conviction following trial, and determining to what extent a recommendation should be reduced upon the entry of a guilty plea. Their recommendations should be based solely on criteria relating to the defendant's criminal background, the crime committed, and the strength of the state's case. Factors such as the assistant prosecutor's relationship with defense counsel and whether the defendant is free on bail should be completely excluded from consideration.

In cases appropriate for plea bargaining, the executive prosecutor would contact defense counsel at an early stage in the proceedings and either reach a plea agreement immediately [78] or arrange a meeting to explore the possibility of an agreement. In these conversations with defense attorneys, the executive prosecutor should make it clear that he is offering a bargain as good as, if not better than, any he will be likely to offer at a later time. If no plea is negotiated, the executive prosecutor should assign the case to a trial prosecutor with instructions concerning the range of proper sentence recommendations, the range of concessions to be given upon a forthcoming plea, and the reasons for these recommendations.[79] The trial prosecutor would have to state persuasive reasons for any departure from the recommendations.[80]

Implementation of these procedures would produce several improvements over the present system. By devoting himself exclusively to plea bargaining, the executive prosecutor should develop a rich background of experience useful in resolving the more difficult questions. He should prove a more efficient and objective plea negotiator because he will not be engaged in the trial of other cases and because possible conflict between office policies and his personal goals will be minimized. In addition, placing the authority for plea negotiation in fewer, more responsible hands would encourage uniform treatment of defendants. Finally, under the proposed procedure plea discussions would be initiated earlier, thus facilitating quick disposition of cases.[81]

One apparent disadvantage with the proposed procedure is the executive prosecutor's relative inability to examine witnesses and defendants in his assigned cases. Philadelphia major trial prosecutors are expected to interview witnesses prior to trial in all cases,[82] but the executive prosecutor in charge of major trials would be unable to schedule such extensive meetings. In most cases, however, the executive prosecutor's failure to meet with witnesses will not substantially impede evaluation of his cases. Investigation reports prepared by the police generally give a full description of the evidence which can be produced against the defendant. When a witness' statement to the police differs significantly from his testimony at the preliminary hearing, this may be noted on the police report by the assistant prosecutor representing the state at the preliminary hearing.[83] While this information may prove inadequate in some cases,[84] major trial prosecutors agree that, in general, examination of witnesses facilitates litigation but does not significantly affect their determination of appropriate sentence concessions.[85] In any event, the slight impairment of the executive prosecutor's ability to evaluate cases will be more than compensated for by the time savings resulting from reduction of pretrial meetings.[86]

The executive prosecutor's inability to see particular defendants would make it impossible for him to rely on a personal evaluation of the defendant in determining sentence concessions. Elimination of this subjective factor will improve the quality of plea bargaining. Under the present system, a trial prosecutor is particularly unqualified to evaluate the defendant's character because, in addition to lacking any special expertise, his judgment may be distorted by his close personal involvement with the case. Moreover, elimination of personal evaluation of defendants should encourage uniformity of treatment. In any case, the sentencing judge's relative lack of personal involvement in the case, and his probable access to reports compiled by experts who have examined the defendant, places him in a far better position to make judgments about the defendant's character.

At least three other possible objections to the proposed plan may arise. First, it has been suggested that most prosecutor's offices simply do not have sufficient manpower to place several experienced men in primarily administrative positions.[87] But this objection overlooks the savings in manpower the proposed reallocation of prosecutorial resources should achieve. If a substantial percentage of cases can be compromised by executive prosecutors at an early stage in the proceedings, the prosecutor's office will need fewer trial attorneys.

It has also been suggested that the proposed change in the structure of the prosecutor's office would be damaging to office morale. Alan J. Davis, formerly a top assistant in the major trial division of the Philadelphia office, suggests that this would occur in two ways: "First, few capable and experienced prosecutors would be willing to have their work limited exclusively to the tedious job of reviewing cases and negotiating pleas. Second, the trial prosecutors would resent this scheme as an encroachment on their authority." [88] Both of Davis' points are valid to a degree. The increased pay and prestige which should attach to the executive prosecutor positions, however, will provide some incentive for experienced prosecutors. And, at least in Philadelphia, some experienced prosecutors would be willing to assume the administrative positions described, even without additional pay, if they believed doing so would be helpful to the overall operation of the office.[89]

Davis' second point is more difficult. Many trial prosecutors feel that they should have the right to make all decisions concerning disposition of their cases. One Philadelphia major trial prosecutor stated that he would resign from his job if stripped of authority to negotiate guilty pleas in cases assigned to him.[90] But the recalcitrance of some prosecutors should not be allowed to bar an otherwise beneficial change. Major trial prosecutors will naturally be reluctant to give up a portion of their power; but virtually unchecked power has indeed caused many of the problems in the present system of plea bargaining. Moreover, implementation of the executive prosecutor system would enable trial prosecutors to concentrate on litigating cases, which they presently perceive to be their primary function, and release them from their role as "dealers in bargain justice."

Finally, it may be objected that the proposed procedure will necessitate greater prosecutorial concessions to induce guilty pleas. Because negotiations will take place at an early stage in the proceedings, the defendant will not be faced with the prospect of an immediately impending criminal trial and will thus be less willing to enter a plea. This objection should not be overemphasized. According to one prominent

Philadelphia defense attorney, most defendants are guided by their attorneys in deciding whether or not to enter a plea.[91]   In most cases, an experienced defense attorney is able to determine what would be an appropriate plea bargain quite early in the proceedings.[92]   Thus, if the prosecutor's offer is really in the defendant's best interest, an early plea should be forthcoming.

On balance, then, the problems resulting from implementation of the proposed procedure will be more than compensated for by substantial, long-run benefits for both society and the prosecutor's office.

B. *Limits on the Executive Prosecutor's Discretion*

To insure effective plea bargaining, the district attorney must maintain some control over the executive prosecutor's exercise of discretion.   Each office should thus formulate plea bargaining policies [93] and provide executive prosecutors with fairly detailed guidelines of the criteria to be applied in determining appropriate concessions.   While such guidelines should not attempt to cover every conceivable situation, they should give some indication of bargaining priorities.   Among the questions which should be answered are: What cases should not be compromised?   What rules should be applied when the prosecutor's case is weak?   What effect, if any, has a defendant's connection with organized crime?   What criteria should be applied in deciding the sentence concessions a defendant will receive for turning state's evidence?   Since the guidelines would be promulgated only to the executive prosecutors, the district attorney should be relatively free to answer these questions candidly and in some detail.[94]

In applying office policies to new situations, the executive prosecutors must, of course, be afforded some discretion.   Also, if an executive prosecutor perceived that a plea bargaining policy established by the district attorney is not leading to effective utilization of trial resources, he should have some latitude to reinterpret the policy.   But, although the executive prosecutors will often be required to exercise discretion, they should also be required to submit their work to rather close scrutiny in order to safeguard the district attorney's control over plea bargaining.   The executive prosecutor should file a brief report of each case stating what concessions, if any, were offered, and why. More detailed reports would be required only when the executive prosecutor confronted a unique plea bargaining situation or initiated a shift in prosecutorial policy.   Such reports should enable the district attorney to determine both the extent of compliance with the plea bargaining guidelines and the need for modification of the guidelines.

C. *Policies To Be Applied by the Executive Prosecutors
When the State's Case Is Weak*

In formulating plea bargaining guidelines, the district attorney should accord special attention to the rules to be applied when the state's case is weak. The rules should reflect a sensitivity to the probable guilt or innocence of the defendant, and not merely a consideration of relative chances of acquittal or conviction. Four variations of a hypothetical case will illustrate several of the problems which should be considered. In the hypothetical, defendant and an accomplice are charged with robbery and burglary after allegedly breaking into a dwelling house, threatening a babysitter with a gun, and taking a substantial amount of money and valuables.

Variation 1. The defendant's accomplice, after making a full, substantiated confession implicating the defendant, flees the jurisdiction and cannot be found. Without the accomplice's testimony, the state has insufficient evidence to establish a prima facie case. *Variation 2.* The only evidence the state can produce is the babysitter's identification of the defendant. It is undisputed that she saw the robbers only briefly in poor light and that she originally gave the police a rather sketchy description. The prosecutor is not at all sanguine about the chances of a conviction based on this evidence. *Variation 3.* The evidence is the same as that in *variation 2*, except that the defendant confesses, giving a full account of the crime with details only the perpetrator could know. The confession, however, is inadmissible because obtained in violation of the requirements of *Miranda v. Arizona*.[95] *Variation 4.* Two hours after the robbery, police find the stolen goods and the gun in the defendant's apartment. But there is about a sixty percent chance that the evidence will be excluded because obtained in violation of the fourth amendment.

Faced with the problem posed in *variation 1*, most prosecutors would share the view of a Philadelphia major trial prosecutor who said, "In this situation, I'd take a plea to anything I could get." [96] This position is legitimate. Although defendant is clearly guilty, without a plea the case will probably continue to clog the docket until dismissed for failure to prosecute. It is certainly preferable that the defendant be given some rehabilitative treatment, even if only a short period of probation.

In *variations 2, 3*, and *4*, the prosecutor is prepared to try the case but the chances of a conviction are small. As noted earlier, the practice in both New York and Philadelphia is to offer greater concessions in weak cases. The stated policy of the Philadelphia office, however, is against the practice.[97] If the prosecutor does not offer special concessions to induce pleas in weak nonserious cases, many defendants will have a strong incentive to go to trial and their election to do so would seriously burden limited trial resources. Even in weak serious cases, a prosecutor could legitimately offer increased inducements, reasoning that society probably receives better protection if all guilty defendants receive some punishment and rehabilitative treatment than it does if some receive the "appropriate" punishment and rehabilitative treatment while others are allowed to go free.[98]

An objection may be made, on an equal protection theory, to plea bargaining guidelines which give effect to the strength of the state's case. A defendant against whom the state has a strong case may argue that he is discriminated against because he is denied the opportunity to strike an equally favorable guilty plea bargain. But the defendant in the weak case does not receive preferential treatment if the prosecutor's concessions do no more than accurately reflect the uncertainties of litigation. He receives a more attractive offer than the defendant in a strong state case only because he is relinquishing a greater chance of obtaining an acquittal. On balance, a policy of attempting to induce guilty pleas by offering concessions which do no more than accurately discount the uncertainties of litigation seems appropriate.[99]

In applying this policy, however, a sharp distinction should be drawn between cases like *variation 2* and those like *variation 3*. In *variation 2*, the defendant's guilt is truly doubtful because the type of eyewitness testimony involved is notoriously unreliable.[100] Thus, if the prosecutor offers strong concessions to induce a plea, an innocent defendant may be pressured into admitting a crime.[101] To avoid this undesirable result, office policy should prohibit plea discussions in this type of case unless initiated by the defendant. Even then, the executive prosecutor should offer no substantial concessions until the defendant produces evidence which convincingly demonstrates his guilt. For this proposal to work, of course, it will be necessary to preclude use at trial of any statements made by the defendant during plea negotiations.[102] In *variation 3*, the strength of the evidence eliminates any substantial risk that an innocent defendant will be induced to plead guilty.[103] In such cases, the executive prosecutor should be instructed to initiate plea discussions and to offer concessions which accurately reflect the uncertainties of litigation.[104]

It may be argued, however, that since the prosecutor's decision to initiate plea discussions is prompted by an illegally obtained confession, any resulting guilty plea is the unlawful fruit of that confession.[105] But the executive prosecutor is not using the confession to place the defendant at a disadvantage;[106] rather, he is offering the defendant a choice between litigating his case and settling it on favorable terms.[107]

In *variation 4*, the sole evidence against the defendant was obtained as a result of police conduct which is probably illegal. Professor Alschuler has argued that when the prosecution induces guilty pleas in cases of this type, the deterrent impact of the exclusionary rule on illegal police conduct is diminished.[108] He reasons that the police may feel that a search of dubious legality is preferable to no search at all because the evidence obtained, although inadmissible at trial, may be helpful in inducing a guilty plea.[109] But police officers are generally more interested in their arrest record than in the ultimate disposition of their cases.[110] If the officer believes that his choice is between no search and one leading to a successful arrest, his conduct will probably not be affected by the exclusionary rule. Moreover, in most situations the officer, lacking expert legal knowledge, will believe that there is some chance that the evidence obtained can be properly introduced at the defendant's trial. Thus, in the situation posed by Professor Alschuler, the officer has an incentive to make an illegal search regardless of the possibility of a guilty plea. In my judgment, the slight and rather speculative deterrent impact to be gained by prohibiting plea bargaining in this situation would be more than offset by the resulting strain on our system.[111] Therefore, in *variation 4*, the prosecutor may properly offer concessions to induce the defendant to plead guilty rather than assert his search and seizure claim at trial.[112]

IV. THE ROLE OF THE COURTS

The proposals offered thus far have been directed at prosecutorial plea bargaining practices. But the judge's role in plea bargaining must also be examined. To date, the judge's involvement has tended towards one of two undesirable models: either the trial judge actively participates in the bargaining process, or he blinds himself to the realities of plea bargaining and engages in the ritual of asking the defendant whether prosecutorial concessions have played a part in inducing his guilty plea.[113]   Although a judge should remove himself from the bargaining process to protect his role as an impartial arbiter, he should also recognize that many guilty pleas occur as a result of prosecutorial concessions.   When receiving pleas, the judge should impose safeguards which protect defendants without unreasonably jeopardizing the prosecutor's efficiency in disposing of cases.

Limiting the judge's sentencing discretion in cases involving bargained pleas would promote these dual ends.   The trial judge should be bound either to impose a sentence no greater than that recommended by the prosecutor or to permit the defendant to withdraw his plea.   This requirement would protect defendants by assuring them that the prosecutor's recommendation sets an absolute ceiling on the sentence which may be imposed if their plea is accepted; it would promote prosecutorial efficiency because defendants would naturally be more willing to enter into plea agreements.

Trial judges must also minimize the possibility that innocent defendants will enter guilty pleas.[114]   Although all federal judges and most state judges must inquire into the "factual basis" of a guilty plea;[115] many consider this requirement satisfied merely by asking the defendant whether he is in fact guilty of the crime charged.   But an affirmative answer to this question may only be a reaffirmation of the defendant's genuine desire to enter a plea.   Rather than engage in this meaningless ritual, judges should require the defendant to detail the circumstances of his alleged crime.   While this device is not infallible, it should give the judge some insight into the actual guilt or innocence of the defendant. In addition, the judge should examine all of the evidence against the defendant.[116]   If, upon examining this evidence and hearing the defendant, the judge seriously doubts the defendant's guilt,[117] he should either refuse to accept the plea or at least strongly urge the defendant to go to trial.[118]

Judges must also assume greater responsibility for evaluating prosecutorial plea bargaining policies.   Professor Davis has criticized "the complete lack of supervision of the typical city or county prosecutor." [119]

> The top prosecutors of federal, state, and local governments are typically subject to little or no checking either by higher officers or by reviewing courts, no matter how seriously they

have abused their powers and no matter how flagrant the injustice.[120]

He invites courts to reconsider their traditional reluctance to review various aspects of the prosecutorial function, including plea bargaining.[121] To facilitate judicial scrutiny, consideration should be given to requiring the prosecutor to issue publicly a formal statement of his policies.[122] The defendant should have the right to challenge a bargaining standard on the ground that, as applied to him,[123] it is contrary to public policy. Either side should be permitted to appeal the judge's ruling on this claim. Adoption of this proposal would promote the uniform application of plea bargaining rules and would also give the highest courts of a state the opportunity to evaluate prosecutorial policies.[124]

Finally, trial judges should endeavor to assure defendants of uniform plea bargaining treatment.[125] To insure that the prosecutor's policies are being applied uniformly, trial judges, before accepting a plea, should require a fairly detailed statement of the reasons supporting the sentence concessions.[126] If the judge believes that the prosecutor is dealing less leniently than customary with a particular defendant, he may impose a sentence less severe than the prosecutor's recommendation; if he believes the prosecutor is excessively generous, he may refuse to accept the plea.

But how may the judge protect a defendant who refuses to plead guilty because he believes he has not been offered concessions equal to those offered similarly situated defendants? If the defendant is allowed to apply to the court for relief prior to trial, the undesirable consequence will be early judicial intrusion into the bargaining process. But if the defendant does not raise the point until after trial and conviction, the societal benefits from effecting a guilty plea bargain are lost, since trial resources will have been consumed and the uncertainties of litigation put to rest. In my judgment, the appropriate procedure is to allow the defendant to raise the point after trial but prior to sentencing. When a defendant raises a claim of unequal plea bargaining treatment, the judge should require the prosecutor to produce evidence illustrating the policy generally followed in cases similar to the defendant's. If the judge finds that the prosecutor's failure to offer certain sentence concessions was a clear deviation from normal policy, he should impose a sentence in keeping with the prosecutor's normal guilty plea sentence recommendation. This procedure would both provide redress to defendants who can establish unfair treatment and, by providing this redress after a possibly time-consuming trial, give prosecutors an additional incentive to apply their guilty plea bargaining rules uniformly.

CONCLUSION

Guilty plea bargaining will remain integral to the administration of criminal justice. This Article has attempted to identify the major problems with present plea bargaining practices and to propose means for alleviating these problems without sacrificing prosecutorial efficiency.

The plea bargaining practices in New York and Philadelphia are detrimental to society's interests. The wide discretion allowed individual prosecutors leads to disparate treatment of similarly situated defendants and, inevitably, to disrespect for the law. The disadvantaged position of indigent defendants is exacerbated by the practice of offering greater concessions to defendants on bail. And, the individual prosecutor's desire to avoid defeat may lead to offering concessions which induce innocent defendants to enter guilty pleas.

Both the district attorney and the courts must meet these problems. Prosecutors must seriously commit themselves to developing fair plea bargaining policies. The executive prosecutor system proposed herein should facilitate application of plea bargaining policies attuned to the often competing needs of the prosecutor's office and society. Trial judges must recognize that plea bargaining does occur and endeavor both to scrutinze the prosecutor's policies and to guarantee certain minimum safeguards to defendants.

NOTES

[1] *See generally* D. NEWMAN, CONVICTION: THE DETERMINATION OF GUILT OR INNOCENCE WITHOUT TRIAL 78-90 (1966) [hereinafter cited as NEWMAN]; Note, *Guilty Plea Bargaining: Compromises by Prosecutors to Secure Guilty Pleas,* 112 U. PA. L. REV. 865, 866, 898 (1964).

[2] *See* NEWMAN 78-80.

[3] One commentator has estimated that roughly 90% of all convictions result from guilty pleas. NEWMAN 3. Limited statistical information makes a precise calculation difficult. *See* PRESIDENT'S COMM'N ON LAW ENFORCEMENT AND ADMINISTRATION OF JUSTICE, TASK FORCE REPORT: THE COURTS 9 (1967) [hereinafter cited as TASK FORCE REPORT].

4 *See* Alschuler, *The Prosecutor's Role in Plea Bargaining*, 36 U. CHI. L. REV. 50 (1968) ; Note, *The Unconstitutionality of Plea Bargaining*, 83 HARV. L. REV. 1387 (1970).

5 397 U.S. 742 (1970).

6 The federal kidnapping statute, 18 U.S.C. § 1201(a) (1964), provides as follows:

> Whoever knowingly transports in interstate or foreign commerce, any person who has been unlawfully seized, confined, inveigled, decoyed, kidnaped, abducted, or carried away and held for ransom or reward or otherwise, except, in the case of a minor, by a parent thereof, shall be punished (1) by death if the kidnaped person has not been liberated unharmed, and if the verdict of the jury shall so recommend, or (2) by imprisonment for any term of years or for life, if the death penalty is not imposed.

7 *Id.* *See generally* United States v. Jackson, 390 U.S. 570 (1968).

8 397 U.S. at 751, 753.

9 *Id.* at 752.

10 *See* H. LUMMUS, THE TRIAL JUDGE 43-46 (1937) ; TASK FORCE REPORT 80; Polstein, *How to "Settle" a Criminal Case*, 8 PRAC. LAW. 35, 37 (1962) ; Note, *supra* note 1, at 881.

11 *See* Dash, *Cracks in the Foundation of Criminal Justice*, 46 ILL. L. REV. 385, 395-97 (1951) ; Newman, *Pleading Guilty for Considerations: A Study of Bargain Justice*, 46 J. CRIM. L.C. & P.S. 780, 783-85 (1956) ; Comment, *The Influence of the Defendant's Plea on Judicial Determination of Sentence*, 66 YALE L.J. 204, 210 (1956).

12 In response to a questionnaire distributed by the *University of Pennsylvania Law Review* in November 1963, 53 of 62 prosecutors stated that the percentage of guilty pleas would decrease if plea bargaining were eliminated. Note, *supra* note 1, at 899. *But see* Scott v. United States, 419 F.2d 264, 278 (D.C. Cir. 1969) (dictum) ("The arguments that the criminal process would collapse unless substantial inducements are offered to elicit guilty pleas have tended to rely upon assumption rather than empirical evidence.").

13 Enker, *Perspectives on Plea Bargaining*, in TASK FORCE REPORT 108, 112 [hereinafter cited as Enker]. *See also* ABA PROJECT ON MINIMUM STANDARDS FOR CRIMINAL JUSTICE, STANDARDS RELATING TO PLEAS OF GUILTY 2 (Tent. draft 1967) [hereinafter cited as ABA STANDARDS].

14 *See* Enker 112. The existing system already places too great a strain on witnesses and jurors. *See* TASK FORCE REPORT 90-91 (noting inadequate or non-existent facilities for witnesses and jurors; repeated trips to court, unnecessary but for lack of notice of trial postponements; and minimal pay for jurors).

15 *E.g.*, NEWMAN 78-104; Alschuler, *supra* note 4, at 52-85; Note, *supra* note 1, at 866-70, 896-908.

16 In response to the 1963 questionnaire, note 12 *supra*, 47 of 67 prosecutors stated that their office had established no formal procedures. Note, *supra* note 1, at 900.

17 Exceptional circumstances would include, for example, a case in which the prosecution has insufficient evidence to go to trial. For a discussion of this situation, see text accompanying note 25 *infra*.

18 Interview with Arlen Specter, District Attorney of Philadelphia, in Philadelphia, Mar. 25, 1970.

19 *Cf.* Specter, Book Review, 76 YALE L.J. 604, 606-07 (1967).

20 Interview with Richard A. Sprague, First Assistant District Attorney, in Philadelphia, Mar. 25, 1970.

21 This would include all of the "very serious" cases previously discussed, text accompanying notes 17-19 *supra*, as well as a fairly large number of other "major" cases. For the definition of a "major" case, see text preceding note 28 *infra*.

22 Review generally occurs in an office meeting at which assistant prosecutors are asked to give brief descriptions of case dispositions.

23 For most crimes, Pennsylvania judges have discretion to impose any sentence from probation up to the maximum sentence prescribed by the legislature. *See generally* Commonwealth *ex rel.* Lockhart v. Myers, 193 Pa. Super. 531, 540, 165 A.2d 400, 405 (1960), *cert. denied,* 368 U.S. 860 (1961).

24 Dismissal or reduction of charges is a common plea bargaining practice in other jurisdictions. *See* NEWMAN 78-104; Enker 108-10.

25 Assistant prosecutors generally wish to avoid having cases continued at their request. But the methods employed to secure immediate disposition do not always take the form of guilty pleas. Often defense counsel will agree to the stipulation of certain testimony in exchange for prosecutorial concessions. Such stipulations may or may not be equivalent to a "slow plea of guilty."

26 For example, if the defendant has been awaiting trial for 58 days, the judge, pursuant to a "time-in" sentence agreement, may impose a sentence of 58 days to 23 months. Under this sentence, the judge has authority to release the defendant from prison immediately and place him on probation for the remainder of the 23 months.

27 The defender has a more immediate interest in reaching an accommodation than does the prosecutor. Most voluntary defenders agree that their primary objective is to secure the release of their clients as quickly as possible. The assistant prosecutor's desire to dispose of cases is tempered by his responsibility for obtaining appropriate sentences. Also, an assistant prosecutor may feel relatively free to sacrifice the efficient disposal of cases on a given day if he believes this will lead to some future prosecutorial benefit (such as showing defense counsel that he "means what he says").

28 Interviews with various major trial prosecutors, in Philadelphia, Mar. 24-26, 1970 (anonymity requested); interview with former major trial prosecutor Alan J. Davis, in Philadelphia, Mar. 25, 1970.

29 Interview with major trial prosecutor, in Philadelphia, Mar. 24, 1970 (anonymity requested).

30 Interview with assistant prosecutor, in Philadelphia, Mar. 26, 1970 (anonymity requested).

31 As the prosecutor explained, "I don't want to spend two weeks in court with an obnoxious defense counsel." *Id.*

32 Interviews with various major trial prosecutors, in Philadelphia, Mar. 24-26, 1970 (anonymity requested).

33 *Id.*

34 Twelve of 17 Philadelphia major trial prosecutors subscribed to this statement. Only one stated that he would give this factor little or no significance. These results are based on a questionnaire submitted to the major trial prosecutors on Mar. 25, 1970 and returned to me by Michael J. Rotko, Chief of Litigation, on May 12, 1970.

35 The New York Supreme Court Bureau is the branch of the New York district attorney's office which prosecutes felony cases.

36 Interview with William Keenan, Chief of the New York City Homicide Division, in New York City, Apr. 28, 1970 [hereinafter cited as Keenan Interview].

37 *Id.*

38 Defense attorneys' reluctance is explained in part by the fact that the New York prosecutor's office will not reward a defendant for merely waiving his right to a jury trial. To receive significant prosecutorial concessions, the defendant must agree to plead guilty.

39 Keenan Interview. The New York office does have more detailed written rules governing plea bargaining than the Philadelphia office. They are available only to attorneys in the office.

40 *Id.* Homicide cases may be assigned to a prosecutor prior to arraignment. *Id.*

41 *Id.*

[42] *Id.* After a New York assistant prosecutor has disposed of a case (whether by guilty plea or otherwise), he is required to fill out a printed form and submit it to District Attorney Frank S. Hogan. When properly filled out, this form contains information concerning the defendant's age, background, and prior record, the type of crime, the use of force or weapons, the extent of injuries to the victim, and the amount of property taken. Space is also available for additional comments by the assistant prosecutor.

[43] Keenan Interview.

[44] Martin Erdman of the New York Legal Aid Society cites as an example a case where the defendant has killed another man in a barroom altercation, but has a colorable claim of self-defense. In exchange for a plea of guilty, the prosecutor would likely reduce the charge from murder to attempted manslaughter and his sentence recommendation from 15 years to life imprisonment to 2 to 3 years imprisonment. Interview with Martin Erdman, New York Legal Aid Society, in New York City, Apr. 28, 1970 [hereinafter cited as Erdman Interview]. In a comparable case in Philadelphia, the assistant prosecutor would not reduce the charge below manslaughter and would recommend a sentence of 5 to 10 years imprisonment.

[45] Erdman Interview; Keenan Interview; interviews with various defense counsel, in New York City, May 5, 1970 (anonymity requested).

[46] The New York assistant prosecutors formerly relied more on charge reductions than on sentence recommendations in plea bargaining. This was primarily due to restrictions on the judges' sentencing discretion. Today, however, New York judges generally have discretion to impose any sentence from probation to the legislatively prescribed maximum. Current plea bargaining efforts are thus more concerned with sentence concessions. *See generally* Ohlin & Remington, *Sentencing Structure: Its Effect Upon Systems for the Administration of Criminal Justice,* 23 LAW & CONTEMP. PROB. 495 (1958).

[47] Interviews with various defense counsel, in New York City, May 5, 1970 (anonymity requested).

[48] *Id.*

[49] *Id.*

[50] Erdman Interview.

[51] Society at large and the prosecutor's office do not necessarily have conflicting goals, but they may often have conflicting priorities. Society is interested both in securing protection and in providing criminal defendants with fair and even-handed treatment. The prosecutor's primary objective is to provide efficient protection for society. In Professor Packer's terms, society's values will tend more toward those incorporated in the Due Process Model while the prosecutor's will tend more toward those incorporated in the Crime Control Model. *See* H. PACKER, THE LIMITS OF THE CRIMINAL SANCTION 149-73 (1968).

[52] K. DAVIS, DISCRETIONARY JUSTICE: A PRELIMINARY INQUIRY 52-141 (1969).

[53] *Cf. id.* 88 (discussion of the harm done when "policy-making power is exercised by individual policemen").

[54] *See generally id.* 142-44.

[55] [A] real vice in the procedure may be that it often gives the defendant an image of corruption in the system, or at least an image of a system lacking meaningful purpose and subject to manipulation by those who are wise to the right tricks. Cynicism, rather than respect, is the likely result.
Enker 112. Correctional authorities are convinced that defendants who feel that they have not been fairly convicted and sentenced often develop a disrespect for the law which makes it difficult for them to accept responsibility for their actions and begin self-rehabilitation. *See* NEWMAN, *supra* note 1, at 44-47, 226-28; J. BENNETT, *A Prison Director's Views on the Public Defender,* in OF PRISONS AND JUSTICE, S. Doc. No. 70, 88th Cong., 2d Sess. 364, 364-65 (1964).

[56] *See* Comment, *Bail: The Need for Reconsideration,* 59 Nw. U.L. REV. 678, 681 (1964).

[57] Foote, *The Coming Constitutional Crisis in Bail: I,* 113 U. PA. L. REV. 959, 961 (1965).

[58] 351 U.S. 12 (1956). *See also* Douglas v. California, 372 U.S. 353, 355 (1963); Gideon v. Wainwright, 372 U.S. 335, 344 (1963).

[59] For a full discussion of the unequal treatment afforded defendants who are unable to raise bail, see Foote, *The Coming Constitutional Crisis in Bail: II,* 113 U. Pa. L. Rev. 1125, 1126-64 (1965). To deal with the problem of unequal plea bargaining treatment, a major change in the structure of the bail system may be needed.

[60] *See, e.g.,* Brady v. United States, 397 U.S. 742, 752 (1970).

[61] Interview with assistant district attorney, in Philadelphia, Mar. 26, 1970 (anonymity requested).

[62] Erdman Interview.

[63] *See* Alschuler, *supra* note 4, at 72; Enker, *supra* note 13, at 112. Of course, substantial concessions should not be made when the defendant is clearly guilty. In such cases, defendants will probably enter guilty pleas in exchange for relatively minor concessions.

[64] *See* Alschuler, *supra* note 4, at 60-61; Comment, *Official Inducements to Plead Guilty: Suggested Morals for a Marketplace,* 32 U. Chi. L. Rev. 167, 177 (1964); Comment, *supra* note 11, at 220-21.

There have also been strong expressions of judicial concern over plea bargaining which encourages innocent defendants to plead guilty. *See, e.g.,* Parker v. North Carolina, 397 U.S. 790, 809 (1970) (Brennan, J., dissenting); Bailey v. MacDougall, 392 F.2d 155, 158 n.7 (4th Cir.), *cert. denied,* 393 U.S. 847 (1968): "Plea bargaining that induces an innocent person to plead guilty cannot be sanctioned. Negotiation must be limited to the quantum of punishment for an admittedly guilty defendant."

Professor Enker warns that the emotional nature of this problem may lead to overstatement. He points out that we do not have conclusive empirical evidence concerning how often innocent defendants enter guilty pleas, and suggests that "the significant question is not how many innocent people are induced to plead guilty but is there a significant likelihood that innocent people who would be (or have a fair chance of being) acquitted at trial might be induced to plead guilty?" Enker, *supra* note 13, at 113.

[65] Keenan Interview.

[66] Erdman Interview.

[67] *Id.*

[68] *See* Alschuler, *supra* note 4, at 61.

[69] This procedure was discontinued after the Pennsylvania Supreme Court, in Commonwealth v. Evans, 434 Pa. 52, 252 A.2d 689 (1969), held that any judicial participation in plea negotiations is inconsistent with due process.

[70] The meetings were generally called by the judge at the request of defense counsel under rule 311 of the Pennsylvania Rules of Criminal Procedure. This rule provides for a pretrial conference to be held by counsel in the presence of a judge. The ostensible purpose of the pretrial conference is to consider means by which the trial of a criminal case may be simplified.

[71] Interview with Richard Sprague, First Assistant District Attorney, in Philadelphia, Mar. 25, 1970.

[72] *See* United States *ex rel.* Elksnis v. Gilligan, 256 F. Supp. 244, 254 (S.D.N.Y. 1966) (holding that "a guilty plea predicated upon a judge's promise of a definite sentence . . . does not qualify as a free and voluntary act"); United States v. Tateo, 214 F. Supp. 560 (S.D.N.Y. 1963) (holding involuntary a plea of guilty made by defendant after the trial judge communicated to defense counsel the sentence he would impose if the defendant were convicted following jury trial); Commonwealth v. Evans, 434 Pa. 52, 57, 252 A.2d 689, 691 (1969) ("The unquestioned pressure placed on the defendant because of the judge's unique role inevitably taints the plea regardless of whether the judge fulfills his part of the bargain."). *But see* United States *ex rel.* Rosa v. Follette, 395 F.2d 721, 725 (2d Cir.), *cert. denied,* 393 U.S. 892 (1968) (judicial participation does not of itself render the guilty plea involuntary). *See generally* Note, *supra* note 1, at 891-92; Comment, *Official Inducements to Plead Guilty, supra* note 64, at 180-83.

73 Recognizing these problems, Professor Enker has suggested that the trial be scheduled before a different judge. Enker, *supra* note 13, at 117. But even if this suggestion were adopted, the possibility would remain that the second judge would be adversely affected by his knowledge "that the defendant had declined a plea agreement tendered by another judge." ABA STANDARDS, *supra* note 13, at 74.

74 *See generally* Comment, *supra* note 11, at 219-20; 19 STAN. L. REV. 1082, 1089 (1967).

75 *See generally* Enker, *supra* note 13, at 108.

76 In Philadelphia, plea discussions could beneficially take place immediately after the defendant's indictment. By this time, defense counsel has generally been able to investigate the case sufficiently, and the executive prosecutor would possess the police investigation report and any observations made by the assistant district attorney who represented the Commonwealth at the preliminary hearing.

77 The Detroit prosecutor's office apparently has implemented a procedure similar to the one advanced here. One assistant prosecutor's "sole job is to screen cases just prior to arraignment with the express purpose of obtaining guilty pleas to reduced charges." NEWMAN, *supra* note 1, at 80.

78 The executive prosecutor in charge of list room cases should be able to arrange many dispositions by telephone. In many of these cases, he can appropriately agree to a recommendation of probation in exchange for a guilty plea. Most enlightened authorities recommend increased use of probation in cases which are not especially serious. *See, e.g.*, N. MORRIS & G. HAWKINS, THE HONEST POLITICIAN'S GUIDE TO CRIME CONTROL 119-23 (1969).

79 The allowable range of concessions should be sufficiently flexible to enable the trial prosecutor to consider information unavailable to the executive prosecutor. In rare cases, the trial prosecutor should be allowed a wide measure of discretion. For example, if the chief Commonwealth witness is an alcoholic, the trial prosecutor should be permitted to gauge the witness' condition on the day of trial before committing himself to a specific course of action. The trial prosecutor should also be allowed to offer additional concessions to induce a plea in uncompromised list room cases when the state is unable to go to trial. To insure that the trial prosecutor accords equal treatment to similarly situated defendants, however, the executive prosecutor should carefully prescribe the additional concessions to be given in this situation.

80 To justify a bargaining concession not authorized by the executive prosecutor, the trial prosecutor would generally have to demonstrate that he acted on the basis of relevant information unavailable to the executive prosecutor. For example, if a close relationship between the defendant and an alleged rape victim is brought to light, the trial prosecutor would be expected to modify the executive prosecutor's recommendations accordingly.

81 In addition to easing congested dockets, earlier disposition of cases would result in shorter detention of defendants suitable for probation.

82 In many cases, however, Philadelphia major trial prosecutors do not meet their witnesses until the day the case is listed for trial. Whether an extensive pretrial interview takes place at that time will depend on how quickly the trial begins.

83 In Pennsylvania, any defendant charged with commission of a misdemeanor or felony is entitled to a preliminary hearing. *See* PA. R. CRIM. P. 119, 120. In other states, however, the defendant's right to a preliminary hearing is more limited. *See, e.g.*, KAN. STAT. ANN. § 62-805 (1964).

84 For a description of one such case, see Alschuler, *supra* note 4, at 68.

85 Interviews with various trial prosecutors, in Philadelphia, Mar. 24-26, 1970 (anonymity requested).

86 The executive prosecutor's inadequate knowledge should not prejudice the defendant because in most cases defense counsel will be able to bring to his attention any information favorable to the defendant.

87 Interview with Michael J. Rotko, Chief of Litigation, Philadelphia district attorney's office, in Philadelphia, Mar. 23, 1970.

88 Interview with Alan J. Davis, in Philadelphia, Mar. 25, 1970.

[89] Two experienced major trial prosecutors stated that they would be willing to take the position for up to one year. Interview with Victor J. DiNubile, Jr., in Philadelphia, Mar. 24-25, 1970 (second prosecutor requested anonymity). It might be possible for various highly skilled trial prosecutors to assume executive prosecutor positions, on a rotating basis, for a six-month or one-year period. Such a plan would have the added advantage of keeping the executive prosecutors in relatively close touch with the problems confronting trial prosecutors.

[90] Interview with assistant prosecutor, in Philadelphia, Mar. 24, 1970 (anonymity requested).

[91] Interview with defense attorney, in Philadelphia, Mar. 25, 1970 (anonymity requested).

[92] Defense counsel should be able to make this judgment soon after the preliminary hearing. All he need do is investigate his defense and hear the evidence presented by the state at the hearing.

[93] Professor Davis has observed that "the chief hope for confining discretionary power [is] . . . much more extensive administrative rule-making . . . ." K. DAVIS, *supra* note 52, at 55.

[94] The prosecutor should make public, however, a general statement of the office's bargaining policies. *See* text accompanying notes 122-26 *infra*.

[95] 384 U.S. 436 (1966).

[96] Interview with assistant prosecutor, in Philadelphia, Mar. 26, 1970 (anonymity requested).

[97] It may be argued, in support of the Philadelphia position, that litigation is most appropriate in cases where the outcome is uncertain. *See* Alschuler, *supra* note 4, at 72; Enker, *supra* note 13, at 112. But, as noted earlier, the Philadelphia office does have a policy of litigating "very serious" cases regardless of the certainty of outcome.

[98] Uncertainty as to what constitutes "appropriate" punishment or rehabilitative treatment precludes anything more than speculation on this point. Evidence indicates, however, that increased incarceration may be counterproductive. *See* N. MORRIS & G. HAWKINS, *supra* note 78, at 110-44. If this is the case, sacrificing maximum sentences for some offenders to obtain some treatment for all offenders may better protect society's interests.

[99] *Cf.* Scott v. United States, 419 F.2d 264, 276-77 (D.C. Cir. 1969) (dictum).

[100] *See, e.g.*, E. BORCHARD, CONVICTING THE INNOCENT (1961).

[101] This is, of course, different from the situation where a defendant guilty of one crime pleads guilty to a lesser offense of which he is innocent. The latter situation does not present serious problems because the label placed on a defendant's conduct is generally not important; only the sentence he receives is significant.

[102] In some jurisdictions, statutes forbid introduction of evidence pertaining to a defendant's offer to plead guilty. *See, e.g.*, CAL. PENAL CODE § 1192.4 (1970). The ABA study takes the position that such evidence should not be admissible. ABA STANDARDS, *supra* note 13, at § 3.4, at 77.

[103] The problem with this analysis is that it will occasionally be very difficult for the executive prosecutor to determine whether the defendant's guilt is truly doubtful. If the executive prosecutor initiates plea bargaining and is told by defense counsel that the defendant is innocent, the executive prosecutor should cease discussion.

[104] As noted earlier, however, under no circumstances should the prosecutor's concessions do more than reflect the uncertainties of litigation.

[105] *See generally* Pitler, "*The Fruit of the Poisonous Tree" Revisited and Shepardized*, 56 CALIF. L. REV. 579 (1968).

[106] If the police failed to give the defendant the warnings required by *Miranda*, counsel will almost certainly be aware that the confession is inadmissible. If defense counsel is ignorant in this respect, the executive prosecutor should not attempt to induce a guilty plea on the strength of the illegal evidence.

[107] Indeed, the defendant in *variation 2* might have a basis for complaint because, unlike the defendant who confessed, he was not offered a chance to settle his case on favorable terms. The best answer to this complaint is that the proposed procedure is necessary to prevent innocent people from pleading guilty.

[108] Many exclusionary rules are designed, at least in part, to discourage illegal conduct by insuring that this conduct will not contribute to successful prosecution. Under the guilty-plea system, however, unconstitutional behavior frequently does contribute to successful prosecution. Alschuler, *supra* note 4, at 82.

[109]

> Only a thorough-going demonstration that illegal conduct will be unproductive seems likely to influence his [the police officer's] behavior . . . . An officer should be discouraged from thinking, "I know that it is probably illegal to enter this apartment; but the prosecutor may nevertheless be able to make something of the case. He seems able to get some kind of guilty-plea from almost every defendant, and I can therefore be reasonably confident that the defendant will be convicted of something."

Id. 83.

[110] *See* A. NIEDERHOFFER, BEHIND THE SHIELD 53 (1967); J. SKOLNICK, JUSTICE WITHOUT TRIAL 219-20 (1966).

[111] Professor Amsterdam, while acknowledging the basic wisdom of the exclusionary rule, notes that important societal interests may be sacrificed if it is employed "beyond the confines of necessity." Amsterdam, *Search, Seizure, and Section 2255: A Comment,* 112 U. PA. L. REV. 378, 389 (1964) (footnotes omitted):

> In every litigation in which exclusion is in issue, a strong public interest in deterring official illegality is balanced against a strong public interest in convicting the guilty. As the exclusionary rule is applied time after time, it seems that its deterrent efficacy at some stage reaches a point of diminishing returns, and beyond that point its continued application is a public nuisance.

[112] In both New York and Pennsylvania, the defendant may litigate a search and seizure claim in a pretrial hearing. If the defendant loses on this claim, he may then enter a guilty plea. In Pennsylvania, by entering the plea the defendant waives his right to appeal an adverse ruling on the pretrial motion. In New York, however, the defendant may appeal an adverse ruling even after entering a plea. Of course, the prosecutor may offer the defendant special concessions if he will plead guilty and forego his pretrial claim.

[113] *See* United States v. Jackson, 390 F.2d 130, 138 (7th Cir. 1968) (Kiley, J., dissenting):

> "[P]lea bargaining" is commonly practiced covertly. After the guilty plea is negotiated by the prosecutor and defense counsel and agreed to by the defendant, defendant follows the rubric of telling the court no promise has induced the plea, and while this game is played the prosecutor and defense counsel mutely corroborate the defendant's false statement. Often a court knows of the negotiations and yet plays its part in the rubric by asking the question about any promise, knowing that the answer will be false.

[114] *See* Brady v. United States, 397 U.S. 742, 758 (1970) (dictum).

[115] Federal judges are given this responsibility by rule 11 of the Federal Rules of Criminal Procedure, which provides that a court may not enter judgment upon a plea of guilty "unless it is satisfied that there is a factual basis for the plea." Several states have adopted a similar requirement. *See* People v. Perine, 7 Mich. App. 292, 151 N.W.2d 876 (1967); State v. Johnson, 279 Minn. 209, 156 N.W.2d 218 (1968). An Alabama statute requires the trial judge to hear witnesses produced by the prosecutor and the defendant, or those summoned by the judge, and to accept a guilty plea only if he believes the defendant guilty beyond a reasonable doubt. ALA. CODE tit. 15, §264 (1958). VA. CODE ANN. §19.1-192 (1950) provides: "Upon a plea of guilty in a felony case, tendered in person by the accused after being advised by counsel, the court shall hear and determine the case without the intervention of a jury . . . ." For a general discussion of the federal and state law on this issue, and the American Bar Association's recommendation, see ABA STANDARDS, *supra* note 13, at §1.6, at 30-34.

In Boykin v. Alabama, 395 U.S. 238 (1969), the Supreme Court held that it was a violation of due process "for the trial judge to accept petitioner's guilty plea without an affirmative showing [on the record] that [the plea] was intelligent and voluntary." *Id.* at 242. Justice Harlan, dissenting, interpreted this holding to mean that "the prophylactic procedures of Criminal Rule 11 are substantially applicable to the States as a matter of federal constitutional due process." *Id.* at 247. If this is the correct interpretation of *Boykin,* state judges may be required by the Constitution to inquire into the factual basis for a plea.

116 Note, *supra* note 1, at 885, criticizes this approach on the ground that it "ignores the distinction between the guilty plea procedure and the trial procedure, and apparently directs the court to engage in an abridged trial to determine actual guilt, something that even a formal trial only inaccurately accomplishes." But the procedure contemplated would not constitute an "abridged trial" because in most cases the judge could make his determination on the basis of the police report and other material submitted to him by the prosecutor. Only in exceptional cases would witnesses need to be called.

117 A more precise standard should not be attempted. Since the judge is examining the evidence in a relatively informal manner, he is not in a position to make a more concrete determination of guilt. *Cf.* ABA Standards, *supra* note 13, at § 1.6, at 33.

118 If the defendant prefers to plead guilty even though he has a defense which might be successful, the judge should probably not forbid entry of a plea. *See* McCoy v. United States, 363 F.2d 306, 307 (D.C. Cir. 1966) (dictum).

119 K. Davis, *supra* note 52, at 207.

120 *Id.*

121 *Id.* 213.

122 *Cf. id.* 58 (emphasis in original):

The important part of the basic judicial purpose is to protect against unguided discretionary power to decide individual cases, whenever meaningful guides are feasible. From the standpoint of justice to the individual party, guides created by the administrators can be about as effective as guides imposed by a statute. Accordingly, *I propose that the courts should continue their requirement of meaningful standards, except that when the legislative body fails to prescribe the required standards the administrators should be allowed to satisfy the requirement by prescribing them within a reasonable time.*

123 The problem of when a defendant has standing to challenge a particular administrative standard raises intricate issues beyond the scope of this paper. For a general discussion of the problem, see 3 K. Davis, Administrative Law Treatise §§ 22.01-22.18 (1958).

124 One problem with this proposal is that the prosecutor, as the chief law enforcement officer of a city and often an elected official, may believe that he cannot politically afford to acknowledge that he deals leniently with many offenders. Thus, a requirement that he place his sentencing policies on record might lead him to formulate unreasonably tough policies. To avoid this undesirable situation, perhaps the prosecutor should be required to give a general formulation of priorities rather than a concrete delineation of rules. This type of statement would preserve the prosecutor's flexibility while giving the courts some assistance in checking his exercise of discretion.

125 *See* ABA Standards, *supra* note 13, at § 3.1(c), at 68.

126 *Cf.* K. Davis, *supra* note 52, at 103-06.

POWER AND PERSONALITY
IN THE COURTROOM:
THE TRIAL OF THE CHICAGO 7

Arthur Niederhoffer

Alexander B. Smith

W AS THE TRIAL OF THE CHICAGO 7 a travesty, a tawdry circus, a defeat for the integrity of justice, as critics have described it? It is only too easy to pick the bones of the dismal record and to ridicule the cast in the case, but the protagonists of the drama were tragic figures, and none more so than Federal Judge Julius J. Hoffman himself, an average man failing pathetically in a role where he might have achieved greatness. His personal failures, however, only underscore the vulnerability of our criminal justice system under the determined onslaught of confrontation politics.

Can the political trial of the future withstand the attacks upon it and yet retain the guarantee of due process rights that are the cornerstone of our institutions of justice? What are the rules of this dangerous contest where reputation, liberty, career, and life itself are at stake? What are the effects upon the participants when they know that millions of people are devouring every gory detail and panting for unimaginable thrills? Is this why the defendants violated all the courtroom conventions and called the judge a Hitler, a pig, a runt, and a *schande fur die goyim?* Is this why the judge gave the defendants the maximum permissible term of five years in prison to run concurrently with their contempt sentences? Is this why the jury refused to convict the 7 of the major charge of conspiracy to incite a riot during the 1968 Democratic National Convention? Or is there something deeper at work here that insistently determines the rhythm and the substance of the final *denouement?*

The protagonists, or more realistically, the antagonists—the judge and the lawyers—are bound to follow the canons of ethics adopted by the American Bar Association. A knowledge of the canons is absolutely essential in order to discuss this trial objectively.

CANONS OF JUDICIAL ETHICS

2. The Public Interest

Courts exist to promote justice, and thus to serve the public interest. . . . The judge should avoid unconsciously falling into the attitude of mind that the litigants are made for the courts instead of the courts for the litigants.

5. Essential Conduct

A judge should be temperate, attentive, patient, impartial . . . .

10. Courtesy and Civility

A judge should be courteous to counsel. . . .

11. Unprofessional Conduct of Attorneys and Counsel

A judge should utilize his opportunities to criticize and correct unprofessional conduct of attorneys. . . .

15. Interference in Conduct of Trial

A judge . . . should bear in mind that his undue interference, impatience, or participation in the examining of witnesses, or a severe attitude on his part toward witnesses, especially those who are excited or terrified by the unusual circumstances of a trial, may tend to prevent the proper presentation of the cause, or the ascertainment of the truth in respect thereto.

[T]he judge should be studious to avoid controversies which are apt to obscure the merits of the dispute between litigants and lead to its unjust disposition. In addressing counsel, litigants, or witnesses, he should avoid a controversial manner or tone.

He should avoid interruptions of counsel in their arguments except to clarify his mind as to their positions, and he should not be tempted to the unnecessary display of learning or a premature judgment.

21. Idiosyncrasies and Inconsistencies

Justice should not be moulded by the individual idiosyncrasies of those who administer it. A judge should adopt the usual and expected method of doing justice, and not seek to be extreme or peculiar in his judgment, or spectacular or sensational in the conduct of the court.

Though vested with discretion in the imposition of mild or severe sentences he should not compel persons brought before him to submit to some humiliating act or discipline of his own devising, without authority of law, because he thinks it will have a beneficial corrective influence.

36. Conduct of Court Proceedings

Proceedings in court should be so conducted as to reflect the importance and seriousness of the inquiry to ascertain the truth.

Did Judge Hoffman live up to these standards? Was he the impartial *Magister Ludi* that he was required to be? Was he patient? Was he courteous to counsel? Did he avoid the extreme and the sensational? Here is a description of his behavior in court:

Judge Hoffman has lashed the defendants and their attorneys repeatedly with scornful sarcasm and stinging rebukes; interrupted their lawyers in mid-sentence with admonitions not to waste his time; denied virtually all their motions and protests; cited four of the attorneys for contempt of court, and ordered two of them jailed without bond . . .[1]

The arrogance of power became evident in the first minutes of the trial when the judge ordered the arrest of four defense attorneys because they were not in court on time. When, shortly after, he denied the request of defendant Bobby Seale for an adjournment because his lawyer Charles Garry was in the hospital, a new dimension appeared. The adversary relation is central to the criminal trial and the role traditionally falls to lawyers for the opposing sides. Judge Hoffman by his vindictive stance replaced the prosecuting attorney as one of the adversaries, and challenged both the defendants and their attorneys to take up arms against him.

What about the lawyers? Their conduct is equally circumscribed.

CANONS OF PROFESSIONAL ETHICS

1. The Duty of Lawyers to the Courts

It is the duty of the lawyer to maintain towards the Courts a respectful attitude, not for the sake of the temporary incumbent of the judicial office, but for the maintenance of its supreme importance. Judges, not being wholly free to defend themselves, are peculiarly entitled to receive the support of the Bar against unjust criticism and clamor.

5. The Defense or Prosecution of Those Accused of Crime

It is the right of the lawyer to undertake the defense of a person accused of crime, regardless of his personal opinion as to the guilt of the accused; otherwise innocent persons, victims only of suspicious circumstances, might be denied proper defense . . . .

The primary duty of a lawyer engaged in public prosecution is not to convict, but to see that justice is done . . . .

15. How Far a Lawyer May Go in Supporting a Client's Case

The lawyer owes entire devotion to the interest of the client, warm zeal in the maintenance and defense of his rights and the exertion of his utmost learning and ability, to the end that nothing be taken or be withheld from him, save by the rules of the law, legally applied. No fear of judicial disfavor or public unpopularity should restrain him from the full discharge of his duty. In the judicial forum the client is entitled to the benefit of any and every remedy and defense that is authorized by the law of the land, and he may expect his lawyer to assert every such remedy or defense. But it is steadfastly to be borne in mind that the great trust of the lawyer is to be performed within and not without the bounds of the law . . . .

16. Restraining Clients from Improprieties

A lawyer should use his best efforts to restrain and to prevent his clients from doing those things which the lawyer himself ought not to do, particularly with reference to their conduct towards Courts, judicial officers, jurors, witnesses and suitors. If a client persists in such wrongdoing the lawyer should terminate their relation.

Defense counsel certainly showed devotion and warm zeal with no fear of judicial disfavor. They did not succeed in restraining their clients, if indeed they tried. They did not maintain a respectful attitude toward the judge. For this they paid heavily. The sentence of four years and thirteen days in a Federal prison given to defense attorney William M. Kunstler for violation of these canons was the longest sentence ever given a lawyer in America for contempt of court. The other defense attorney Leonard I. Weinglass did a little better, receiving a sentence of one year eight months and three days. The chasm between the viewpoints of the judge and the lawyer looms large in the eloquent response made by Kunstler.

Citing his practice for 22 years before the Supreme Court, United States Courts of Appeal and Federal District Courts, he said:

> Until today, I have never once been disciplined by any judge
> —Federal or state—although a large part of my practice for
> the last decade has taken place in hostile southern courts
> where I was representing black and white clients in highly
> controversial civil rights cases.
>
> I have tried with all of my heart faithfully to represent my
> clients in the face of what I considered and still consider
> repressive and unjust conduct toward them. If I have to pay
> with my liberty for such representation, then that is the price
> of my beliefs and sensibilities . . .[2]

Judge Hoffman striking out in all directions showed his loss of control by oracular, but fatuous explanations of the increase of crime, during his sentencing of Kunstler for contempt. He is quoted as saying that he wanted to express some unorthodox thoughts on the causes of crime.

> If crime is, in fact, on the increase today, it is due in large
> part to the fact that waiting in the wings are lawyers who are
> willing to go beyond professional responsibilities, profession-
> al obligations, professional duty in their defense. The knowl-
> edge that such lawyers were available had a stimulating
> effect on potential criminals.[3]

This reckless statement not only proves his ignorance and lack of control, it is a gratuitous insult to every member of the Bar. The Federal judge saw himself as a judge of all lawyers. It was no longer United States against the Chicago 7. It soon became Judge Hoffman against defense attorney Kunstler. The gravamen of the Judge's case against Kunstler is instructive. The 74-year-old judge said that:

> ... such misconduct—especially in a lawyer—is of so grave a character as to continuously disrupt the administration of justice and sabotage the functioning of the Federal judicial system.[4]

The judge sees himself as the symbol of the United States. The lawyer matches the move. In the grip of a transcendent emotion he reinterprets the loss of the case *sub specie aeternitatis* as a victory, or else as a magnificent defeat that will unleash the Gotterdammerung. Thus Kunstler after being sentenced, declaimed:

> I can only hope that my fate does not deter other lawyers throughout the country who, in the difficult days ahead, will be asked to defend clients against a steadily increasing governmental encroachment upon their most fundamental liberties. If they are so deterred then my punishment will have effects of such terrifying consequences that I dread to contemplate the future domestic and foreign course of this country.[5]

From the time of Demosthenes in Greece, and Cicero in Rome, there have been many illustrations of lawyer-challengers who have met their nemesis. Was Kunstler's four year sentence part of a pattern? Do great lawyers run a high risk?

There is evidence to support this contention. Any list of the outstanding criminal trial lawyers of the last 50 years would contain most of the following names:

F. Lee Bailey	Jake Ehrlich	William Kleinman
Melvin Belli	William Fallon	Samuel Leibowitz
Clarence Darrow	Percy Foreman	Earl Rogers

The record shows that a high proportion of this elite group were accused of misconduct in connection with their law practice. (And now, of course, we must add to this impressive list the name of William M. Kunstler.) This is doubly surprising in view of their mastery of criminal law and procedure.

How is it possible for one of the finest civil rights lawyers in our country to be sentenced to prison for his too zealous defense of his client? How is it possible for a Federal judge to have become so rabid toward the defense that "he upheld prosecutors' objections even when he had not properly heard or understood them,"[6] and turned the proceedings into a judicial disaster? We think the best explanation for these excesses is the classic one of *Hubris*.

Implicit in the classic Greek philosophy of justice was the concept of a divinely decreed social order in which every human being had his particular place and role. *Hubris* was the fatal flaw of character that impelled a man to violate the most cherished mores. Inexorably Nemesis punished the violator who, as Aristotle puts it, "moved from happiness to misery." It was the most compelling theme of Greek tragedy, but there is no hint of this shattering experience in *Webster's Third International*, which defines *hubris* rather prosaically as "overweening pride, self confidence, or arrogance."

In Jewish folklore we find a similar concept—*chutzpa*, which also connotes insolence, audacity, or arrogance. Leo Rosten, an expert in the joys of Yiddish, tells us that *chutzpa* is "gall, brazen nerve, effrontery, incredible 'guts'; presumption-plus arrogance . . ."[7] And he exhibits his own brand of *chutzpa* by remarking that "no other word, and no other language can do justice to *chutzpa* . . ."

If both *hubris* and *chutzpa* are forms of arrogance, what is the distinction between them? *Hubris* is a reflection of a civilization at the peak of its power, on the verge of assuming mastery of the known world. Its heroes hurled challenges to the gods on Mount Olympus. We think immediately of Prometheus, Sisyphus, Agamemnon, and Oedipus. By comparison, *chutzpa* is a relatively modern term rooted in the ghetto existence of a weak, dispersed, and alienated Jewish minority. *Hubris* grows from a sense of power; *chutzpa* is a compensation for the lack of power. *Hubris* is a quality of a great, or noble man, or one, like Judge Hoffman, occupying a position of great power, but the opposite seems to be true of *chutzpa*, whose exemplars are not titans, judges, or kings, but criminals, beggars, waiters, peddlers, and mothers-in-law.

Chutzpa is not tragic, but comic in the Aristotelian sense of the word. It makes for a small triumph, not a great defeat, and it is immediately recognizable and labeled for what it is. *Hubris* may be disguised for a long time. It is often interpreted as evidence of the high standards and integrity that marks a man for honor until the fatal flaw causes him to overreach. *Hubris* carries with it an almost religious aura, but *chutzpa* rarely exceeds the limits of the profane. *Hubris* signifies a potential threat to the institution, whereas *chutzpa* is usually directed against a person.

The temptation toward *hubris* operates with more intensity in the criminal courts than in the civil courts; it is stronger in a more serious or a more controversial case than in a minor trial. When the charge is a serious crime the judge often drops the facade of objectivity and patience. He frequently excoriates the defense, and the jury as well when they bring in a verdict of "not guilty". So zealous is the judge in pressing for a conviction, that his wrath burns the prosecutor who seems to lag in the pursuit. In the Spock conspiracy case Judge Francis J. W. Ford "was heard whispering urgently to his clerk, 'Tell that son of a bitch (the prosecutor) to cut it out! He'll blow the case if he keeps this up, and get us all in trouble.' "8

In a civil suit the injury, if any, is private and personal. The state is usually not deeply involved. Even in a quasi-criminal proceeding, the judge is more likely to act in his ideal role of the impartial referee who remains above the fray. From this position he can be friendly to jury and counsel. In a long, drawn-out anti-trust trial, for example, Federal Judge Harold Medina once took forty lawyers, representing both sides, to a baseball game between the Dodgers and the Giants, and then treated them to a dinner at the Hotel Bossert.9

When a great criminal trial lawyer consistently defends unpopular defendants and unpopular causes and compounds this "crime" by gaining acquittals in case after case, he becomes a threat to the criminal justice system. By a twist of the theme of guilt by association, the guilt that was legally lifted from the defendants by their acquittals is symbolically transferred to the lawyer. That is one reason that Judge Hoffman ascribed to defense attorney Kunstler some of the blame for the increase in crime.

Once this guilt by association process has operated, the odds against the lawyer's continued success grow heavier. The lines of force pit the virtuosity of the defense lawyer against the awesome power of the judge and the system of criminal justice he represents. Even where personal idiosyncrasies determine the judge's conduct, the judge has the advantage; he is protected; his *hubris,* no matter how transparent, is in defense of the criminal justice system, so that his performance is excused as an excess of zeal and may even be applauded. It is especially easy for a Federal Judge like Judge Hoffman to fall prey to *hubris.* He is protected in his position by the United States Constitution Article III, Section 1, which declares that Federal judges shall be appointed for life during good behavior. With few restraints upon him, the weaker and smaller the person filling the role, the more power he covets as a compensation. Thus, when Judge Hoffman was over-shadowed to some degree by defense counsel Kunstler, and ceased to be the cynosure, his remedy was to assert the almost "Godlike"[10] pow-er—a power possessed by a Federal judge by virtue of the rules. His camouflage to cover his conduct is that his motivation is not neurotic aggression, but is an expression of his commitment to protect the sys-tem. Some lawyers analyzing this judicial *hubris* are convinced that Judge Hoffman

> regards himself as the embodiment of everything Federal . . .
> So, in criminal cases at least, he tends to see the defense and
> their attorneys as the enemy.[11]

Beset by contradictions in his duty to his client, to his profession, to society, and finally to himself, the lawyer (in this case Kunstler) is bound to go too far. Instinctively he senses his dilemma, but he is too much committed to withdraw. He has exceeded the limits beyond which loyalty to the client is interpreted as disloyalty to the system of which he is a part. His success has placed him in jeopardy. He is guilty of the sin of *hubris,* and must be humbled for his transgression.

This is not true of the journeyman criminal lawyer who handles stray cases and is held in low esteem by the legal profession. He must conform and submit to the norms and etiquette of the criminal justice system if he wants to make a living. The rare incident of rudeness or non-conformity on his part is not perceived as a threat. At most it is the *chutzpa* of a marginal person and is easily contained by a warning from the judge.

Thus, the majority of lawyers never get into trouble. Their infre-quent misbehavior is interpreted as a form of mere *chutzpa,* and there is a tendency on the part of the criminal justice system, like all other bureaucracies, to protect the inept and the guilty. But this protection disappears when the wrongdoer is a rebel against the bureaucracy it-self. Although the voices of many notable intellectuals are vibrant with praise for this brave outlaw, rarely do they dwell on the terrible cost of this resistance to the lawyer himself, a cost that may prove more dangerous for success than for failure.

For Judge Hoffman this trial was a great ordeal from which he may never fully recover. It was also a magnificent opportunity to prove dignity, to show intelligence and flexibility, to demonstrate that our legal institutions could rise to meet the challenge.

It was obvious that the Chicago 7 planned to make a shambles of the trial. Their position was that the criminal justice system is evil and to be docile would legitimize the procedure. Therefore, they called the judge names: racist, pig, fascist, and Hitler. Judge Hoffman failed the test, he was thrown off balance, and lost control. The trial degenerated into a test of strength between Judge Hoffman and the defendants. It would be easy to sympathize with the judge and excuse his excesses, until it is remembered that society condemns its policemen when they lash out at demonstrators who call them racists, pigs, facists, and Hitlers. Should the standard of control demanded of a judge be lower than that expected from a policeman?

Judge Hoffman's failure came because he lacked the capacity to wear gracefully the robes of power into which he was thrust. This was his unhappy fate: judicial *hubris*.

Using the trial of the Chicago 7 as a model, we have described three typical patterns in which the criminal trial lawyer endangers himself by violating the mores of the game, and he must pay the penalty for his *hubris* even though he has the best of motives. The first is a type of guilt by association. The attorney like Kunstler who consistently accepts as clients the rebels of society: political radicals, *mafiosi*, foreign spies, and black militants is soon condemned as an outsider himself.

The second is the failure of success. The pride in his victories leads the lawyer to the final boast. "I have never lost a case, or a defendant."[12] Inevitably, to keep his record intact he violates a legal taboo and suffers appropriate punishment. A variant on this theme is the success of failure which impelled Kunstler to declare his defeat (really the defeat of the defendants more than of Kunstler) a victory. The refusal to admit defeat is sometimes considered a virtue in American folklore, but it is apparently nothing but an illusion in the criminal court.

The third kind is the display of such individual brilliance in the court that it may be interpreted rightly or wrongly as a form of personal arrogance. This behavior may well infuriate other members of the criminal justice system. Finally, some enemy brings down the man who has refused to submit to the Procrustean bonds of the conventional courtroom role.

Other illustrations of *hubris* are well known, but no one who enters the field of criminal law can claim that he did not know the rules of the game. Every student of the law learns at the start the fundamental

doctrine upon which criminal justice stands: *"Nemo est supra leges"*—
No one is above the law.

If the judge cannot perceive that this principle applies most force-
fully to himself above all others, then he can hardly hope to impose
the rule of law upon those who appear before him.

NOTES

1. N.Y. Times, October 5, 1969, Section IV, at 9.

2. N.Y. Times, February 16, 1970, at 22.

3. *Id.*

4. *Id.*

5. *Id.*

6. N.Y. Times, February 21, 1970, at 30.

7. L. ROSTEN, JOYS OF YIDDISH 92 (1968).

8. J. MITFORD, THE TRIAL OF DR. SPOCK 162 (1969).

9. This incident occurred in the case of United States v. Morgan. *See* N.Y.
Times, May 29, 1952, at 29.

10. N.Y. Times, October 9, 1969, at 30.

11. *Id.*

12. Sometimes this mantle of invincibility is thrust upon a flamboyant criminal
lawyer, whether he likes it or not. "King of the Courtroom" is the title of a book
about Percy Foreman. According to the blurb, he has represented more than 1,000
accused killers, but "has lost only one client to the executioner." *See* N.Y. Times,
Book Review Section, October 26, 1969, at 16.

DELAY IN CRIMINAL APPEALS:
A FUNCTIONAL ANALYSIS OF
ONE COURT'S WORK

Winslow Christian

> More money and more judges alone are not the primary solution. Some of what is wrong is due to the failure to apply the techniques of modern business to the administration or management of the purely mechanical operation of the courts—of modern record keeping and systems planning for handling the movement of cases. Some is also due to antiquated, rigid procedures which not only permit delay but often encourage it.
>
> —Chief Justice Warren E. Burger[1]

Avoidable delay in deciding criminal appeals is costly to society and detrimental to the aims of the judicial system.[2] Delay in affirming a judgment of conviction may decrease the conviction's deterrent value, as well as frustrate rehabilitation.[3] Delay in reversing a judgment of conviction allows evidence to grow stale, thereby threatening the validity of a new trial as a factfinding process. If reversal is followed by the acquittal of the appellant, each day of appellate delay will have been a day of unjust punishment. Yet delay has become a prominent characteristic of the American appellate process[4] and a growing threat to the effective administration of justice.[5]

While much has been written about this problem in recent years,[6] there has been little empirical analysis of delay in order to determine its causes.[7] This Article reports the results of one such effort. A survey was conducted of 253 criminal appeals processed in 1970 by the California Court of Appeal for the First Appellate District.[8] The results confirm the magnitude of the problem: The full course of a criminal appeal in the First Appellate District takes an average of 498 days (457 days median), well over 16 months.[9] In the typical case,[10] appellant filed notice of appeal in the trial court on the same day he was convicted, but the trial record did not reach the court of appeal for 101 days. Although an attorney was appointed 25 days after the record was filed in the court of appeal, he did not complete his opening brief until 145 days later, having spent about 61 hours in preparation. Once this brief was filed, 99 more days passed before the Attorney General filed his brief. The case was then placed on the court's calendar, argued, and submitted for decision. Finally, 128 days after the briefs had been filed, the court issued its decision.

This Article describes the delay that occurs during the four principal stages of the criminal appellate process: preparation of the record, appointment of counsel, preparation of the briefs, and decisionmaking by the court. Specifically, it identifies the major sources of delay during each step and offers recommendations for accelerating the passage of a case through each stage of the criminal appeals system.

I. PREPARATION OF THE RECORD

A. *Preparation of the Transcripts*

When a notice of appeal is filed,[11] the *California Rules of Court* require the trial court clerk to prepare the clerk's transcript and immediately to notify the court reporter to prepare a transcript of the trial testimony.[12] The reporter is to complete his transcript within 20 days after the filing of the notice of appeal;[13] within 25 days the clerk is to deliver the two transcripts to the trial judge for certification.[14] The parties to the action then have 5 days to propose corrections.[15] If no corrections are made, the trial judge certifies the transcripts and returns them to the clerk, who then transmits the entire record to the appellate court.[16] While preparation of the record should normally be completed within 30 days, the appellate court can extend the limit to 80 days from the filing of the notice of appeal if good cause is shown.[17]

The results of the survey[18] demonstrate that court reporters and clerks are not meeting these standards. The average time between the notice of appeal and the first indication that the reporter's transcript was ready was 72 days (54 days median),[19] with only 20 of 233 reporters' transcripts ready within the 20-day limit. Although the appellate court may extend the limit to 80 days, reporters failed to complete their transcripts within this longer period in 59 of the 233 cases surveyed. Moreover, most of the reporters who exceeded the 20-day limit did so without any extension from the appellate court: Reporters requested extensions in only 34 of 138 such cases.[20]

Although no rule expressly sets a maximum time for the preparation of the clerk's transcript, the requirement that the clerk forward the entire record to the trial judge within 25 days of the notice of appeal[21] implies that his transcript is due 5 days after the reporter's transcript is due,[22] assuming no extensions. Trial courts in the survey received the clerk's transcript within 5 days of the reporter's transcript in 87 percent of the cases, with an average delay of 2 days. Thus, while the clerks also have some responsibility for prompt completion of the record, their contribution to delay is far less significant than the court reporters'.

Once the trial judge has received the transcripts, he is to certify them within 5 days unless the parties propose corrections.[23] In the sampled cases, however, the average time between completion of the last transcript and the trial judge's certification was 21 days (15 days median). Furthermore, there was an average delay of 4 days in the transmission of the full record to the appellate court after the trial court's certification.[24] Combining the delays at these three stages—preparation of the transcripts, trial court certification, and transmission of the record to the appellate court—the average time from notice of appeal to filing of the record in the higher court was 99 days (81 days median),[25] considerably longer than the 30 days allowed by the *Rules of Court*.

1. *Supervision of court reporters and clerks.*

Although it is not clear where primary responsibility lies for monitoring the work of court reporters and clerks, both the trial and appellate courts bear some responsibility for exercising control. The trial judge has close contact with both the reporter and clerk and may supervise their daily courtroom activities.[26] The reporter is appointed by the trial judge and serves at his pleasure.[27] Although the 1943 revision of the *Rules of Court* supposedly shifted responsibility for supervising preparation of the reporter's transcript from the trial judge to his clerk,[28] the judge nonetheless retains ultimate control. Furthermore, there are reported decisions suggesting that the trial court has primary jurisdiction over certain remedies for delay.[29]

The notice of appeal transfers jurisdiction over a case from the trial court to the appellate court,[30] and the appellate court assumes some responsibility to supervise the preparation of the record. For example, extension of the time for preparation of the transcripts beyond 25 days theoretically is allowed only by order of the appellate court.[31] This jurisdiction is not being exercised effectively in the First Appellate District because, under present procedures, the filing of a notice of appeal in the trial court does not inform the appellate court that an appeal has been taken.[32] If an appellate court wished to exercise effective control over delay in preparation of the record, it would first have to obtain reliable information about the commencement of all criminal appeals within the district.[33]

The results of the survey show that in the first district the court of appeal has in fact exercised only nominal control over the preparation of records. Court reporters rarely request extensions, and trial court clerks never do so. When a court does grant an extension, it is typically on an *ex parte* application, and in no surveyed case did the court deny such a request. Indeed, contrary to the *Rules*,[34] several extensions allowed delays exceeding 80 days from the notice of appeal.[35] The usual "good cause"[36] offered by reporters seeking extensions is a general reference to the "pressure of court business."[37] Even this meager excuse apparently is not necessary; the appellate court routinely grants extensions on the mere declaration that the transcript cannot be ready on time.

Counsel are also unlikely to oversee preparation of the record. Trial counsel usually considers his work done when the court pronounces judgment.[38] Appellate counsel might be expected to take an interest in expediting the preparation of the record, but the majority of criminal appellants are indigent,[39] and counsel for an indigent is not appointed until after the record has been filed.[40] Typically, then, the indigent appellant has no counsel while the record is being prepared, unless trial counsel voluntarily extends representation.[41] The Attorney General, like appellants' counsel, does not participate effectively in controlling delays in the preparation of records. Although the trial court clerk must send a copy of the notice of appeal to the respondent in criminal cases,[42] the Attorney General never resists applications for extension of the time for preparation of the record, if for no other reason than that he normally does not receive notice of such applications.[43]

2. Sanctions presently available.

It appears that clerks and reporters are, with impunity, regularly violating time limitations on preparation of the record. This gap between law and behavior is probably attributable to three factors: lack of manpower, inefficiency, and simple inattention to the *Rules*. Accordingly, in devising methods to reduce delay, the contributions of each of these factors to the problem must at some point be evaluated. While there are no empirical studies of the adequacy of manpower in preparation of the record, there is reason to believe that this factor is responsible for only a minor part of the overall delay found in the study. For example, most superior court departments have a full-time deputy clerk and a court reporter who may increase his productivity by employing additional transcribers.[44] In any event, given the time and expense necessary to determine the significance of manpower needs and the funds necessary to remedy this problem if it is a cause of delay, it is reasonable to focus first on the contributions of inefficiency and inattention to the *Rules*. If changes in present practices and exercise of existing sanctions could reduce the delay attributable to these two factors, remaining delay could be attributed to lack of manpower, and appropriate remedial action could be undertaken. Hence, this section outlines several available remedies for inefficiency and inattention to the *Rules*.

Appellants may be able to take direct action to compel clerks, reporters, and trial judges to comply with time limitations on preparation of the record. When a full record has not been delivered to the appellate court within the prescribed period, the appellant may move to have the appellate court order immediate completion of this task.[45] There is also authority implying that an appellant may obtain a writ of mandamus from the appellate court to direct compliance.[46] However, the success of either control technique depends upon the appellant's initiative in seeking relief in the court of appeal—a rare event among indigent appellants for whom appellate counsel is appointed only after the record is filed.[47]

The trial and appellate courts may act on their own initiative to apply sanctions of graduated severity to compel timely preparation of the record. The simplest method is to order immediate compliance with the *Rules* or a showing of good cause for failure to comply.[48] Contempt proceedings are authorized for "[m]isbehavior in office, or other wilful neglect or violation of duty by . . . [a] clerk . . . or other person, appointed or elected to perform a judicial or ministerial service."[49]

Furthermore, special sanctions are available to control delay caused by court reporters. First, the *California Government Code* provides that until a reporter has filed transcripts for all cases reported by him in which a notice of appeal has been filed, he "is not competent to act as official reporter in any court."[50] The statute apparently authorizes a trial or appellate court to exclude a delinquent reporter from covering new cases until he has completed preparation of overdue appellate records.[51] While no reported decision has dealt with the statute, one court did use it to secure immediate filing of a delinquent transcript by ordering the reporter to show cause why he should not be declared incompetent.[52]

Vigorous application of existing sanctions might eliminate much of the delay in preparation of appellate records. Under present circumstances, however, the probability of intensive enforcement is quite low. Parties to the action are unlikely to invoke these sanctions: Indigent appellants usually have no counsel during the period of preparation of transcripts;[53] appellants represented by private counsel or by the public defender may be ignorant of established patterns of delay and of existing remedies;[54] and finally, the Attorney General has shown no interest in ensuring the speedy preparation of appellate records.[55] Furthermore, the trial courts cannot be expected to speed up the process on their own initiative. A trial judge who regularly works with the same reporter and clerk may hesitate to apply sanctions for fear of creating strained working relationships. Appellate courts cannot act effectively to prevent delay so long as they remain unaware that an appeal has been commenced.[56] Thus, new methods of control are necessary in order to reduce delay in preparation of the record.

3. *Recommendations.*

Although everyone involved in the preparation of appellate records shares some responsibility for reducing delay, the California courts of appeal are best positioned to prevent unnecessary delay in this first stage of the appellate process. There are two major reasons for placing primary responsibility on the intermediate appellate courts. First, for the reason mentioned above, trial courts are not likely to apply sanctions against their own reporters and clerks. Furthermore, the primary responsibility of trial judges is the trial of cases, and they should not be additionally burdened with duties related to an appellate court function. Second, the appellate courts are more capable of administering extensions and sanctions on a uniform basis. Even though some variations of policy might develop among appellate districts, consistent treatment within an appellate district could readily be obtained by charging the administrative presiding justice[57] with responsibility to exercise control.[58]

A number of reforms should be adopted in order to facilitate assumption of this responsibility by the appellate courts. First, there should be statutory confirmation of the jurisdiction of the courts of appeal both to hear motions for enforcement of time limitations on preparation of appellate records and to entertain contempt proceedings against trial court clerks, reporters, and judges.[59]

Second, the *California Rules of Court* should be amended to require that a copy of the notice of appeal be sent to the appellate court and that the clerk of the court of appeal open a docket page immediately upon receiving such notice. Thereafter, the clerk of the appellate court should investigate the cause of any delay in the filing of appellate records and bring delinquencies to the attention of the court for possible sanctioning.[60]

Third, continuous representation should be provided for the indigent appellant. The appellate court does not need to see the full record to determine whether appointment of counsel is warranted;[61] therefore the court should inform the appellant immediately upon receiving a copy of the notice of appeal that it will entertain a request for appointment of counsel. It would even be possible to require the trial court, after pronouncing judgment, to inform the defendant of his right to appeal and right to appellate counsel and to provide a combined form of notice of appeal, declaration of indigency, and request for appointment of counsel.[62] In order to guarantee continuous representation, trial counsel should not be permitted to withdraw from a case until appellate counsel has been appointed. In addition, trial counsel should be required to perform such preliminary tasks as filing a notice of appeal if so instructed by his client, seeking bail on appeal, and requesting obviously necessary augmentations of the record during the interim.[63] In its appointment letter, the appellate court should mention the time limits for record preparation and emphasize that one of the responsibilities of appointed counsel is to assist in enforcing compliance.[64]

Fourth, appellate courts should examine requests for extensions by court reporters and clerks far more carefully and should exercise discretion to deny such requests when not meritorious. Since trial court clerks and reporters perform the bulk of the work involved in preparing the record on appeal, it is essential that they conform whenever possible to applicable time limitations. The present practice of uncritically accepting claimed pressure of routine work as "good cause" for granting an extension undermines the purposes of the *Rules* and should be ended.

Finally, to avoid placing on the appellate courts the full burden of routine supervision, clerks, reporters, and trial judges should be required to declare that they have completed preparation or certification of all appellate records within the authorized time before receiving their monthly pay or any further per diem pay.[65] Another technique would be to reduce reporters' per page stipend when preparation of the record is delayed without proper extensions.[66] In addition, the *Government Code* should be amended to provide expressly that a reporter may not report any additional hearings if he has an overdue criminal transcript.[67] These proposals, if adopted, would assure maximum efficiency in the process of record preparation and eliminate any need for routine supervision by the appellate courts.

B. *Augmentation of the Record*

The record on appeal normally contains a clerk's transcript of specified papers in the trial court's file and a reporter's transcript of the oral proceedings.[68] Upon filing notice of appeal, appellant may request inclusion in the record of a number of additional items—any written motion and supporting affidavit, any written opinion on any motion to suppress evidence, the voir dire examination of the jury, opening statements, arguments to the jury, and any oral opinion or comments on the evidence by the court.[69] Within 5 days of a request for augmentation, the judge is to order inclusion of any requested additions he thinks "proper to present fairly and fully the points relied on by appellant in his application."[70] Thus, in the interests of economy, the appellant must demonstrate some rational connection between requested additions and the points he desires to raise on appeal.[71]

Once the notice of appeal is filed, later augmentation may come only by order of the appellate court, acting on its own motion or at the request of either party.[72] Appellate courts liberally grant augmentation to avoid determining issues on a fragmentary view of the proceedings below.[73]

A request for augmentation rarely is made on the trial court level, for such a request must accompany the notice of appeal,[74] which is most often given on the same day as the judgment. Since trial counsel customarily do not plan appellate strategy or consider useful additions to the normal record, any thought of augmentation usually is delayed until the record has been filed in the appellate court and appellate counsel has begun work on his brief. Still more time passes while the appellate court acts upon the request for augmentation and, if it is granted, while the appropriate clerk or reporter complies. Since orders for augmentation routinely grant appellant's counsel 30 days from the filing of the augmented record to complete his brief, the later stages of the appellate process are also delayed.

The survey results clearly demonstrate the delay to the appellate process caused by current augmentation procedures. Augmentation occurred in well over one-third of the cases fully appealed.[75] The delay in requesting augmentation varied considerably between private and appointed counsel. Private counsel requested augmentation an average of 142 days (122 days median) after the normal record was filed. Appointed counsel averaged 57 days (68 days median) from the date of their appointment to a request for augmentation. The average delay in requesting augmentation for all appellants was 77 days (72 days median).[76] While in the majority of cases the appellate court ordered augmentation within one day of receiving appellant's request, the time between the order for augmentation and the filing of the augmented record averaged 50 days (36 days median) in cases of major augmentation, which required preparation of new transcripts.

Appellate counsel appear to be taking far too long to request augmentation. It is difficult to believe that a diligent attorney would reasonably require nearly three months to recognize a need for additions to the transcript. Any attempt to reduce this delay, however, must take account of serious due process constraints. For example, to deny a request for augmentation as unseasonably filed would punish the appellant for his attorney's neglect.[77] Likewise, to apply sanctions against counsel might deter a necessary request for augmentation—a result that would be as unfair to the appellant as a denial of the request by the court.

There are, however, at least two ways of reducing delay at this stage within these constraints. First, if appellate counsel were appointed immediately after the filing of a notice of appeal, as recommended above,[78] it would then make sense to allow requests for augmentation to be made in the trial court until the record is certified. In many cases, appellate counsel might determine that the normal record is inadequate simply by examining the court's file and by interviewing the trial attorney. The trial judge would then be able to make a prompt, reasonably informed decision on the request based on his knowledge of the case. Such a procedure should not prejudice either party since a denial of augmentation would be subject to review in the appellate court.[79]

Once the reporter has completed the transcript, appellate counsel should be allowed to request of the trial court any obviously necessary augmentations during the 5-day period allowed for correction of the record.[80] After the record has been certified and filed in the appellate court, requests for additions should be made there as under present practice.[81] By adopting this approach, the functions of preparation and augmentation of the normal record would be made concurrent rather than consecutive, hopefully reducing the time necessary to complete both tasks.

A second method of reducing delays would be to expand the content of the normal record on appeal.[82] While a survey of only 77 requests for augmentation is not sufficient to prescribe the proper content of the normal record, the sample does suggest that some requests are more common than others.[83] Broadening the normal record to include such material involves balancing the expense of including material that will not be relevant in every case against the costly delays of the augmentation process. A proper balancing requires that a full-scale survey of requests for augmentation be undertaken. On the basis of this survey, the costs of inclusion of a particular item in the normal record could be compared to a more accurate measure of expected benefit—elimination of requests for that item via augmentation.

II. Appointment of Counsel

When the record finally is received by the court of appeal, the clerk sends the appellant a notice informing him when his brief will be due and that, if he is indigent, he may submit a request for appointed counsel.[84] Most criminal appellants are indigent,[85] and in most cases an attorney, usually a new member of the bar, is appointed to conduct the appeal. The court permits appointed counsel to withdraw from the case for reasons such as illness, change of state residence, or the demands of other work.[86] If the court grants such a withdrawal, it will appoint substitute counsel immediately.

Appointed counsel conducted 74 percent of the full appeals in the sample. The average time between the filing of the record and the request for appointment of counsel was 22 days (14 days median). In almost half the cases, the court appointed counsel on the same day appellant's request was received; the average time between request and order was three days.

Appointed counsel eventually withdrew in 20 of 130 fully-appealed cases.[87] The average delay from filing of the record to appointment of final counsel for these 20 cases was 166 days,[88] with an average period of inaction between appointment of first counsel and appointment of final counsel of 137 days (81 days median). Thus the average delay in appointing final counsel in appeals involving withdrawal was more than five times the delay in appeals pursued fully by one attorney.[89]

The survey results demonstrate two of the primary sources of delay at this stage of a criminal appeal: the indigent appellant who neglects to request appointment of counsel promptly,[90] and the appointed counsel who, perhaps after prolonged neglect, finally withdraws from the case. A number of approaches are available to reduce these sources of delay. At minimum, the appointment and withdrawal decisions should be accelerated. Under present practice, an indigent appellant does not receive the clerk's letter informing him of his right to counsel until immediately after the record on appeal is filed. If he does not communicate his desire for appointment of counsel within 30 days, he receives notice that his appeal will be dismissed after the passage of 30 more days unless an appellant's opening brief is filed or good cause is shown for relief from default.[91] In practice, the court will, if requested, appoint counsel even though 30 days may have passed since the second notice was mailed to appellant.[92] Thus, although it may not be in his interest to do so, an appellant may, with impunity, delay requesting appointment for 60 days.[93] While there seems to be no practical method of sanctioning indigent appellants for delay in requesting appointment of counsel, it is likely that if the need for speedy appointment of counsel and the possibility of dismissal after 60 days under Rule 17(a) were fully explained in the original letter sent by the clerk of the appellate court, indigent appellants would file their requests for appointment more promptly.

Under existing rules the appellate court may exercise a variety of controls over attorneys who inexcusably delay their requests for withdrawal. At the outset, the court should emphasize in its letter of appointment that it will allow withdrawal only in unusual circumstances and that a request delayed without good cause may be grounds for application of sanctions.[94] An attorney who seeks to withdraw some time after his appointment, perhaps 30 days, could be required to show cause before his request is allowed.[95] If no meritorious cause is shown, he could be ordered to complete the appeal with diligence[96] or be held in contempt[97] or subjected to professional discipline.[98] Occasional application of these remedies would induce appointed counsel to evaluate his ability and willingness to conduct the appeal and, if he decides to withdraw, to do so as promptly as possible.[99]

Delay could be further reduced by adopting a recommendation made earlier in this Article: amendment of the *Rules of Court* to provide for immediate notice to the appellate court of the pendency of an appeal.[100] This minor alteration in appellate procedure would facilitate rapid appointment of counsel by making such appointment and preparation of the record concurrent activities, thus allowing the accelerated appointment and withdrawal functions to begin at an earlier point in the process.

Finally, a more encompassing and promising approach would be to create a state public defender office responsible for representing indigents in criminal appeals. The Judicial Council of California has recommended such action to the legislature,[101] citing such trends as the steadily increasing number of criminal appeals by indigents, the growing difficulty of recruiting counsel for this financially unattractive work, and the prevalence of inexperienced attorneys among appointed counsel.[102] Creation of a state public defender office would make it possible to eliminate delays now caused by late requests for appointment of counsel and late withdrawals by appointed counsel. Under competent administrative direction appellants normally could file briefs within a few days of the filing of the record rather than months later, as is now common.[103] Furthermore, the improved quality of representation likely to come from an office staffed by experts would speed the work of the appellate courts; much time is now lost by the court's research staff as it struggles with substantial issues that have been poorly presented. For these reasons and others to be discussed later,[104] creation of a state public defender office to handle appeals of indigents would be the strongest suitable remedy for delay in the initial stages of the appellate process.

III. PREPARATION OF BRIEFS

A. *Appellant's Opening Brief*

An appellant's opening brief must be filed in the court of appeal within 60 days of the filing of the record.[105] The time for filing briefs in criminal cases cannot be extended by stipulation of the parties;[106] however, the presiding justice of a division may extend the time for filing,[107] and the court may relieve a party from default in failing to file on time.[108]

1. *Survey findings.*

Appellants' counsel consumed an average of 133 days (120 days median) in preparing their clients' briefs.[109] In the few cases where county public defenders continued representation beyond the trial, the results were much better: Public defenders took, on average, 66 days (68 days median) to file their briefs. Private counsel required an average of 105 days (97 days median) for preparation, while appointed counsel filed their briefs an average of 145 days (125 days median) after their appointment.

2. *Sources of delay.*

There appear to be a number of reasons for the significant delay in preparation of appellants' opening briefs. First, appointed counsel often encounter difficulties in obtaining a copy of the trial record. When the record on appeal is filed with the trial court clerk, the appellant's copy is sent immediately to the appellant or his attorney. Because an indigent appellant usually has no attorney at this point, he is the one who receives the record. Thus, before appointed counsel can begin to prepare a brief, he must obtain the record from the appellant, a task that can be time consuming. This procedure, which is required by the *Rules of Court*,[110] is often cited by counsel as a reason for requesting an extension.[111]

Second, most appointed counsel are inexperienced and spend a great deal of time floundering over problems of research and preparation that would be routine to an experienced lawyer.[112] The Clerk of the Court of Appeal, First Appellate District, estimated that half of the attorneys appointed in his district are in their first year of practice and that 90 percent are in their first three years of practice.[113] The committee report on the bill proposing creation of a state public defender office explained the consequences of the inexperience of most appointed counsel:

All too often, these young lawyers lack even the most fundamental knowledge of the criminal law. For many of them an appellate appointment means that they must learn everything from scratch. Untold hours are spent researching the most basic issues and many of them will waste time and effort simply because they are not even aware of the limited issues that can be raised on appeal. It is not at all unusual for a fresh young lawyer to spend hours searching for new evidence because no one ever told him that a criminal appeal must be limited to the issues raised in the trial record. Appeals that should take no more than 10 to 15 hours to prepare are often 40 to 80 hours in preparation. Briefs that should have been filed within a month are often filed five or six months after they are due.[114]

Third, indigent appeals are unlikely to have high priority in the work of most appointed counsel. While the commonly deficient quality of briefs filed in indigent criminal appeals may charitably be attributed to inexperience, the survey results disclose firm evidence of a less easily excused characteristic of appointed counsel. Examination of requests for compensation from appointed counsel indicated they spent an average of 61 hours (50 hours median) on each indigent appeal. Assuming, for example, that 75 percent of this time is devoted to the preparation of the opening brief,[115] appointed counsel spend, on the average, approximately 45 hours over a period of almost five months to complete this task. I suggest that this figure exceeds the time that a competent lawyer would need to brief the average criminal appeal. The fact that these hours are spread over so long a period suggests that many appointed counsel prepare their briefs in a fashion that can hardly be call diligent.

Fourth, appellate courts have established a well-known practice of liberally granting extensions, particularly to appointed counsel. A striking example of this practice is the letter sent by the clerk to appointed counsel at the time of appointment, automatically granting him an unrequested 30-day extension.[116] The survey was able to detect only part of the delay attributable to extensions in the First Appellate District because the clerk normally discards records of extensions once the briefs have been filed.[117] Nonetheless, records of extensions were found in 24 of the 175 full appeals, with one appellant receiving five extensions. Typically, counsel's assertion that he was "pressed" by other business was sufficient to gain him an extension.[118]

Finally, delay in requesting augmentation of the record makes some contribution to the average delay of 133 days in preparing the appellant's opening brief. In those cases in which no augmentation was requested, delay in preparing the brief averaged 119 days. Where augmentation is requested, the deadline for filing the brief is extended; hence delay is compounded by suspending the already sluggish process of briefing until an augmented record has been filed.

3. *Recommendations.*

While the court of appeal bears the principal responsibility for regulating appointed counsel, there are certain limitations on its ability to exercise control. First, the court cannot attempt to accelerate preparation of the brief by employing sanctions that would in reality punish the indigent appellant for his attorney's neglect. Thus, drastic remedies such as dismissal of the appeal,[119] while perhaps appropriate for appellants represented by private counsel over whom they exercise some control,[120] are unacceptable for the indigent appellant[121] who does not select or compensate his attorney and does not have the freedom to dismiss him.[122] Second, there is little that the courts can do to increase the level of diligence of appointed counsel in indigent cases, for this indifference is largely the product of factors beyond the courts' control.[123] Renewed pleas to the Bar for more able and experienced attorneys and for more diligence in preparing appellants' briefs are unlikely to be of consequence because of the disparity between fees charged by private lawyers and those paid to appointed counsel.[124] Increasing the compensation of appointed counsel to compete with fees earned in private practice is probably not feasible.

Finally, any effort to exert greater control over appointed counsel must fully consider the risk that tighter procedures and exposure to sanctions will discourage some attorneys from volunteering for indigent appeals work. Acceleration of the appellate process would be useless if, as a by-product, it were to dry up present sources of indigent representation.

At minimum, certain alterations of present procedures should be made. The present delay in transmitting the record from the appellant to his counsel could be eliminated if, as recommended above, counsel could be appointed before the record has been completed; the record could then be sent directly to counsel as soon as it has been completed and certified. The court should inform newly appointed counsel that it will insist on expeditious filing of the opening brief.[125] In addition, the strange practice of granting an unsolicited 30-day extension should be discontinued, and the courts should refuse to grant extensions unless there is a showing of valid cause. Finally, when an appellant has not filed his brief on time, the court should not hesitate to remove the attorney and appoint substitute counsel.[126] The court should then refer the dismissed attorney to the Bar for discipline,[127] as well as refuse to compensate him for any time spent on the appeal.[128]

While there is some basis for concern that such alterations would discourage volunteer work in criminal appeals, it seems unlikely that these re-forms would turn away significant numbers of volunteer lawyers. First, some portion of present volunteers seek the experience and income provided by indigent appeals and presumably would continue to participate. Second, there is some degree of social pressure within the organized Bar and within some law firms to encourage young attorneys to accept the responsibility of making the system of criminal justice work for indigents as well as for those who can afford to pay legal fees.[129] Finally, one would expect some of the lawyers now serving to recognize the need for increasing the speed of the criminal appellate process and hence to react positively to the court's initiative in requiring better performance.

Adoption of these minimal reforms, however, is unlikely to solve the problem completely. Because courts are ill-suited to carry on a campaign of indefinite duration to obtain volunteer counsel, new responses must be sought to the challenge of providing adequate representation for indigents. As mentioned earlier,[130] one such response would be the creation of a state public defender office charged with the duty of handling all appeals of indigents. Such an agency promises not only increased efficiency through-out the appellate system, but perhaps more importantly, increased quality in the representation received by indigent appellants.[131] While establish-ment of such an organization would not eliminate every source of un-necessary delay in the appellate system, it would make possible the elimi-nation of most delays caused by the inexperience, inefficiency, and indif-ference of attorneys appointed under the present system.

Should the legislature fail to create a state public defender office, the courts should take the initiative to meet their constitutional duty of provid-ing adequate representation for indigent appellants.[132] Through creative use of their powers to appoint and compensate counsel for indigent ap-peals,[133] the courts of appeal could establish, without further legislation, the functional equivalent of a public defender office for criminal appeals.

The State Bar could be invited to sponsor an experimental office in one appellate district that would be staffed by lawyers handling indigent ap-peals on a full-time basis. The court of appeal and a committee of the Bar could consult to create internal controls on recruitment and management and develop a compensation schedule based on productive norms derived from the experience of public law offices.[134] By ordering appointment of the new office in each indigent appeal and by fixing compensation sep-arately in each case, the court could better fulfill its responsibility to provide adequate representation for indigent appellants.

B. *Respondent's Brief*

The Attorney General is required to file his brief within 30 days after the appellant files his opening brief.[135] However, the survey indicates that the average interval between the filing of the appellant's opening brief and the filing of the Attorney General's brief was 100 days (92 days median). This is less than the average time spent by appointed counsel (145 days), about the same as the time spent by private counsel (105 days), and longer than the time required for county public defenders (66 days).[136] Although the office of the Attorney General is more prompt than most appellant counsel, it is, nonetheless, a significant source of delay in criminal appeals.

One cause for this delay may be the prevailing view that because a criminal judgment cannot be reversed without argument,[137] the respondent must file a brief in every criminal appeal.[138] While this requirement guarantees the people representation whenever a convicted criminal might be freed by an appellate court, it also creates unnecessary delay in those cases that could be disposed of by summary affirmance or reversal without waiting for a brief from the Attorney General.[139] Accordingly, the *Penal Code* should be amended to permit the court to take an appeal under submission without opposition, and reverse if necessary, whenever the Attorney General, without good cause, fails to file his brief on time or decides that no respondent's brief is warranted. This amendment would strengthen the court's hand in dealing with delay and would eliminate one unnecessary and time-consuming step in many uncomplicated cases. At the same time, one would expect the Attorney General to file a brief in any case of importance.

A second reason for delay at this stage is the liberal policy of the courts in granting extensions. Courts granted the Attorney General extensions in 35 of 175 full appeals surveyed, with three or more extensions granted in approximately two-thirds of these cases. The Attorney General requests extensions by submitting a form that has been used without substantial change for more than 20 years. The form states, in part, that "due to the stress of business in this section of the Office of the Attorney General" he has been unable to prepare the brief within the time required by law.[140] The survey results indicate that various divisions of the court treat these requests differently, apparently producing varying performance by the Attorney General. Division Three grants the Attorney General only one extension, while other divisions routinely grant three extensions. The average time for preparation of the respondent's brief in Division Three was 64 days, while average times of 114, 112, and 112 days were found in Divisions One, Two, and Four, respectively. These results clearly suggest that the promptness of the Attorney General's office will depend upon the liberality of court policy in granting extensions. Appellate courts should therefore demand more diligent performance by the Attorney General. Some inexperienced lawyers are on the staff of the Attorney General, but these attorneys have access within the office to more experienced deputies, an advantage not shared by appointed counsel.[141] Furthermore, the bulk of criminal appeals handled by the Attorney General are not so complex as to require more than 30 days for briefing, especially where appeals turn on issues that the same office briefs repeatedly. Finally, the application of stricter standards to the Attorney General—unlike application of such standards to appointed counsel—does not risk reduction of the manpower available to provide necessary legal services.

Courts should no longer routinely dispense extensions of time for the preparation of respondents' briefs. Specifically, a court should not grant any extensions except in very difficult cases involving novel legal questions or requiring extensive research. Should the Attorney General find it difficult to comply with these time limitations, the courts at least will have demonstrated that a significant part of the problem is inadequate manpower. If that should be the case, closer control by the courts might actually assist the Attorney General in demonstrating to the legislature his present inability to comply with court rules, and hence his need for staff augmentation.

IV. Decision by the Court

Once the respondent has filed his brief, the clerk calendars the case for oral argument.[142] Criminal cases receive priority in calendaring;[143] therefore backlogs in calendaring such cases have not been extensive.[144] In the First Appellate District, a division hears oral arguments on two days each month—normally on consecutive mornings. Thus, the earliest available calendar opening may be several weeks from the date on which the respondent files his brief. During the period between calendaring and oral argument, the case is assigned to one of the justices.[145] His research clerk then prepares a memorandum that essentially constitutes a nonpartisan brief of the case. The clerk's memorandum is distributed among the judges who are to hear argument and is used by them in preparing for a preargument conference.[146] At the conclusion of oral argument, the case normally is submitted for decision.[147]

After oral argument, the justice to whom the case was tentatively assigned prepares a draft opinion. The other justices indicate their concurrence or dissent. If there is a dissent, a conference is usually held, and further work may be necessary. The California Constitution provides that if a decision is not filed within 90 days after submission, members of the panel considering the appeal do not receive their salaries for that month until the opinion is filed.[148] When two of the judges on the panel finally join in an opinion, it is filed with the clerk of the appellate court.[149] A remittitur is then sent to the trial court after the expiration of time for granting a petition for hearing in the California Supreme Court.[150]

The average elapsed time in the surveyed cases between the filing of the respondent's brief and filing of the decision was 133 days (116 days median). In the average case the court heard argument 97 days (88 days median) after the respondent filed his brief, and came to a final decision after 36 days (19 days median) of deliberation.

The Judicial Council of California already has launched a three-part program of modernization that is likely to have some effect in reducing this delay.[151] First, the 1970–71 budget authorizes additional research staff, which will operate under the direction of a senior research attorney within each affected district.[152] Second, the Council has empowered the Chief Justice to designate one of the presiding justices in each multi-division district to act as administrative presiding judge of that court with extensive powers of management.[153] Third, the Council has recommended increased use of memorandum opinions by the courts of appeal in cases "that raise no substantial issues of law or fact."[154] Implementation of these measures is likely to increase productivity without a loss of quality or a dilution of judicial responsibility.

Despite these reforms, there still will be a need to accelerate the decision-making process of the appellate courts. At least two sources of delay are in need of further attention: court calendaring procedures and efficiency in reaching decisions and writing opinions. Others have adequately analyzed the uses and limitations of oral argument;[155] the relevant observation here is that in proportion to the serious delays found elsewhere in the appellate process, time spent in oral argument is insignificant.[156] However, calendaring for oral argument does cause important and unnecessary delay in two ways. First, under the present practice of automatically calendaring all criminal appeals for oral argument, whether argument will be useful or not, decision of routine appeals is unnecessarily delayed. Second, because argument is heard only twice each month, cases for which research memoranda have been prepared and circulated often lie dormant, sometimes for weeks, awaiting oral argument.

At minimum, courts should hear oral arguments more often—perhaps once each week. Such a change in procedure would not necessarily increase the aggregate amount of time devoted to hearing oral argument, and more frequent but shorter argument periods would reduce delay. A much more effective reform would be to eliminate the automatic calendaring of oral argument in criminal cases,[157] giving the court discretion to determine when argument would be useful.[158] This would free the court from the artificial restraint of the calendar cycle. Staff research could begin immediately upon the completion of briefing, and cases could be decided when they are ready for decision rather than when they have ripened on the calendar for some weeks before argument that is, in most cases, perfunctory and of little use.

While the survey results do not suggest that judges are flagrantly inefficient in rendering their decisions, there is still opportunity for speeding up this process. As mentioned earlier, California already requires that a judge file his opinion within 90 days after submission or cease to receive his salary. Any further incentive to prompt disposition of cases might infringe upon the necessary independence of judges[159] or compel assembly-line treatment of those cases that really do require deliberate consideration and extended research. Nonetheless, there is an additional way in which the 90-day rule could be used to reduce delay. Realistically, a case is "submitted" for decision when the parties complete their briefing rather than when the court "orders" it to be submitted. This reality should be recognized by assigning every criminal appeal to a judge for authorship when it is filed and requiring the case to be submitted for decision as soon as the time for filing an appellant's closing brief has expired.[160] The judge's research assistant could then begin work immediately on a memorandum that, in routine cases, could be made the basis of a draft opinion to be circulated and filed within 90 days after submission. If preliminary work disclosed difficulties in the case, the judge to whom it tentatively was assigned for authorship would be free to ask that the submission be vacated and the case calendared for argument. After argument the case would be resubmitted for decision and a new 90-day period would begin to run. This reform, which could be adopted without any change in the statutes or rules,[161] would accelerate the appellate decisionmaking process with no risk of compromising the independence of the judiciary.

V. Conclusion

Justice in the criminal law demands that appellate courts control the pervasive delay that plagues the appellate process and at the same time continue to reach well-considered decisions. Analysis of survey data suggests that the existing system could be made vastly more efficient by a concerted exercise of powers that the courts already possess. The California Administrative Office of the Courts has estimated that appellate caseload in this state will double within the coming 6 years.[162] Effective response to that challenge demands initiative and planning by the courts as the agency with primary responsibility. Moreover, the legislature, the Bar, and the courts themselves must begin to view the stages of the appellate process as interdependent phases of a single system performing a vital social task. When appellate work is subjected to such analysis, the need for and feasibility of specific reforms are apparent. Adoption of such reforms will bring into prominent view the financial and human needs of an appellate system competent to carry the burdens that will be thrust upon it in the coming generation of conflict and change.

Notes

1. Burger, *The State of the Judiciary—1970,* 56 A.B.A.J. 929, 929 (1970).
2. *See, e.g.,* H. ZEISEL, H. KALVEN & B. BUCHHOLZ, DELAY IN THE COURT xxii (1959).
3. *See* Singer, *Psychological Studies of Punishment,* 58 CALIF. L. REV. 405 (1970). *But cf.* Mosk, *Crime and the Courts,* 4 U.S.F.L. REV. 195 (1970). *See also* H. PACKER, THE LIMITS OF THE CRIMINAL SANCTION 39–48, 228–33 (1968).
4. *See* JUDICIAL COUNCIL OF CALIFORNIA, 1970 JUDICIAL COUNCIL REPORT TO THE GOVERNOR AND THE LEGISLATURE & ANNUAL REPORT OF THE ADMINISTRATIVE OFFICE OF THE CALIFORNIA COURTS 86 (1970) [hereinafter cited as 1970 JUDICIAL COUNCIL REPORT]. *See also* Shafroth, *Survey of the United States Courts of Appeals,* 42 F.R.D. 247, 257–59 (1967).
5. *See generally* J. FRANK, AMERICAN LAW: THE CASE FOR RADICAL REFORM 1–28 (1969); Burger, *supra* note 1; Warren, *Dedicatory Address,* 21 U. FLA. L. REV. 285, 286–88 (1969).
6. *See, e.g.,* Cohn, *The Proposed Federal Rules of Appellate Procedure,* 54 GEO. L.J. 431 (1966); Committee on Appellate Delay in Criminal Cases, Criminal Law Section, American Bar Ass'n, *Appellate Delay in Criminal Cases,* 2 AM. CRIM. L.Q. 150 (1964); Covington & Reese, *Court Delay—Texas Style,* 4 HOUS. L. REV. 92 (1966); Desmond, *The Courts, the Public, and the Law Explosion: A Critique,* 54 GEO. L.J. 777 (1966); Desmond, *Current Problems of State Court Administration,* 65 COLUM. L. REV. 561 (1965); Hufstedler, *Constitutional Revision and Appellate Court Decongestants,* 44 WASH. L. REV. 577 (1969); Mansell, *Conservation of Time in Relation to Civil Judicial Proceedings,* 45 L.A.B. BULL. 23 (1969); Nix, *Civil Court Congestion in the Superior Court of California for the County of Los Angeles,* 55 GEO. L.J. 1018 (1967); Nye, *A New Approach to an Old Problem: Congestion in Our Courts,* 45 L.A.B. BULL. 325 (1970); Stuart, *Iowa Supreme Court Congestion: Can We Avert A Crisis?,* 55 IOWA L. REV. 594 (1970); Wallach, *Seven Simple Steps Toward Judicial Reform,* 45 CAL. ST. B.J. 90 (1970); Wham, *Civil Jury Backlogs: Should We Amend the Constitution?,* 53 A.B.A.J. 643 (1967); Zeisel & Callahan, *Split Trials and Time Saving: A Statistical Analysis,* 76 HARV. L. REV. 1606 (1963); Comment, *Progressive Judicial Administration in the Superior Court for the County of Riverside,* 36 S. CAL. L. REV. 140 (1962); Comment, *Remedies to Court Congestion,* 19 SYRACUSE L. REV. 714 (1968).
7. *But see* Bell, *Expediting the Disposition of Litigation,* 10 TRIAL JUDGES J. 1 (1971); Halpin, *Delay on Appeal,* 38 CAL. ST. B.J. 279 (1963); Wright, *The Overloaded Fifth Circuit: A Crisis in Judicial Administration,* 42 TEX. L. REV. 949 (1964); Note, *The Second Circuit: Federal Judicial Administration in Microcosm,* 63 COLUM. L. REV. 874 (1963). These articles, although containing empirical data, are more general in their approach to the problem of delay than is the present study.
8. The composition of the survey sample was determined as follows: All criminal appeals in which remittiturs were issued by the court of appeal between January 9 and October 28, 1970, were examined. (No special proceedings such as habeas corpus, prohibition, or mandate were considered). Of the 300 cases in this group, the 253 cases that were appeals taken by defendants from judgments of conviction were extracted for further study. The focus was on these 253 cases for two reasons. First, this category of cases makes up the bulk of the criminal workload of the courts of appeal. *See* 1970 JUDICIAL COUNCIL REPORT, *supra* note 4, at 82–83. Second; the other 47 cases involved actions in which records were too brief to indicate how court personnel performed their functions; these included, for example, attempted appeals from nonappealable orders, which were summarily dismissed, and appeals from the trial court's denial of the writ of error coram nobis, which were summarily dismissed by the court of appeal as being wholly without merit.

Of the 253 cases that were the subject of further study, 78 were dismissed before completion of the appellate process; hence only 175 cases went through the full appeal process. With two exceptions— the "typical" case and the section on preparation of the record—all statistics reported in text are based on these 175 full appeals. *See* notes 10 & 18 *infra* and accompanying texts.

One might object that, because only the work of a single court was studied, the survey results have limited significance for other courts; however, this objection would be based on a misunderstanding of the purpose of the study. Our effort has not been to determine, for example, what the average statewide delay is at various stages of the appellate process. Rather, we are interested in the relationships between various court rules and practices and the amount of delay they generate. For these purposes, a detailed study of the workings of one court is an appropriate research technique, and a finding that a particular rule or practice creates delay in this one court is relevant information for other courts operating under similar procedures. This is particularly true for the California appellate courts, since all these courts follow the *California Rules of Court* which are promulgated by the Judicial Council pursuant to the California Constitution. *See* CAL. CONST. art. VI, § 6 (West Supp. 1971); Albermont Petroleum, Ltd. v. Cunningham, 186 Cal. App. 2d 84, 89, 9 Cal. Rptr. 405, 407–08 (2d Dist. 1960); Gibson, *For Modern Courts*, 32 CAL. ST. B.J. 727, 729–31 (1957). *But see* note 33 *infra* and accompanying text.

9. This compares with a statewide range of from 10 months (in Division One of the Fourth District) to 25 months (in Division Five of the Second District). *See* 1970 JUDICIAL COUNCIL REPORT, *supra* note 4, at 86. The 16-month average total delay for the First District found by the survey corresponds almost exactly with the comparable measurement made by the Administrative Office of the California Courts. *See id.* To some degree, this confirms the representative nature of the sample studied.

As this Article went to press, the comparable 1971 statistics on activity, caseloads, backlog, and delay in the California Courts of Appeal were released. JUDICIAL COUNCIL OF CALIFORNIA, 1971 JUDICIAL COUNCIL REPORT TO THE GOVERNOR AND THE LEGISLATURE & ANNUAL REPORT OF THE ADMINISTRATIVE OFFICE OF THE CALIFORNIA COURTS 91–99 (1971). The updated statistics vary only in slight degree from the 1970 figures, and in no way affect the focus or conclusions of this analysis. *Id.*

10. This typical case is based on the 130 defendant appeals from judgments of conviction that were fully briefed and argued by counsel appointed by the court. In other words, these average time delays were computed without regard to either the 78 appeals that were dismissed before completion of the appellate process or the 45 appeals where appellant was represented by private counsel or the public defender. These 130 appeals were selected as most representative of the normal work of the appellate courts in criminal cases because they constituted 74 percent of the 175 full appeals in the survey, and because "[a]t present most indigent defendants are represented in the appellate courts by counsel assigned by the court." 1970 JUDICIAL COUNCIL REPORT, *supra* note 4, at 15. *See* note 39 *infra*.

11. The notice of appeal in a criminal case must be filed within 10 days of the judgment of conviction. CAL. CT. R. 31. However, the notice of appeal is sometimes given effect though filed after 10 days. Rule 31 provides that the clerk is to accept a late notice of appeal and mark it "Received (date) but not filed." CAL. CT. R. 31(a). Appellant may then present verified statements bearing on the circumstances of the late appeal, and the appellate court will determine whether the delay is excusable. Although such cases turn on questions of fact, the policy of deciding appeals on the merits, absent waiver or estoppel due to delay, is liberally applied in favor of criminal defendants. *See* People v. Casillas, 61 Cal. 2d 344, 346, 392 P.2d 521, 522, 38 Cal. Rptr. 721, 722 (1964). *Compare* People v. Bailey, 1 Cal. 3d 180, 460 P.2d 974, 81 Cal. Rptr. 774 (1969) (appellant misunderstood the effect of an appeal), People v. Acosta, 71 Cal. 2d 683, 456 P.2d 136, 78 Cal. Rptr. 864 (1969) (appellant was ignorant of right to appeal), People v. Curry, 62 Cal. 2d 207, 397 P.2d 1009, 42 Cal. Rptr. 17 (1965) (appellant relied on trial counsel who neglected to file timely notice of appeal) *and* People v. Slobodion, 30 Cal. 2d 362, 181 P.2d 868 (1947) (appellant relied on prison authorities who neglected to mail his timely notice of appeal) *with* People v. Sanchez, 1 Cal. 3d 496, 462 P.2d 386, 82 Cal. Rptr. 634 (1969) (appellant, though ignorant of the 10-day limit, had known for several months of his right to appeal but did not request his attorney to appeal, and his attorney did not promise to appeal) *and* People v. Castillo, 71 Cal. 2d 692, 456 P.2d 141, 78 Cal. Rptr. 869 (1969) (appellant's ignorance of the 10-day limit does not excuse his failure to request his attorney to file timely notice of appeal). A survey of the "Clerk's Monthly Report of Business Transacted" in the first district for calendar year 1969 shows that of a total of 418 criminal appeals filed, 70 (17%) were requests for late appeal pursuant to Rule 31(a). Similarly, of a total of 531 appeals in 1970, 78 (15%) were pursuant to Rule 31(a).

12. CAL. CT. R. 35(a)–(b).

13. CAL. CT. R. 35(b).

14. CAL. CT. R. 35(c).

15. *Id.*

16. CAL. CT. R. 35(c), 35(e).

17. CAL. CT. R. 35(d). Rule 35(d) allows the appellate court to extend the time for preparation

of the record for 60 days. The 60 days does not begin until the 20 days permitted for record preparation by Rule 35(b) have elapsed. *See* CAL. CT. R. 35(b). Thus, the maximum time that the appellate court can allow the reporter for preparation of the transcript is 80 days.

18. The study of the preparation of appellate records is based on the 253 cases in which full records were filed. In other words, this section of the survey includes the 175 full appeals and the 78 additional cases that were dismissed before completion of the appellate process. *See* note 8 *supra*. In 20 of the 253 cases, however, no reporter's transcript was filed, and in one case, no clerk's transcript was filed.

19. For purposes of computing this delay, the reporter's transcript was treated as being completed on the date on which the trial court marked it as received. In some cases, there was no trial court stamp on the transcript; these transcripts were treated as being completed on the date on which the reporter certified the transcript as complete.

20. This statistic was derived by examining the 253 cases in which full records were filed and isolating those cases where more than 20 days elapsed between filing of the notice of appeal and filing of the record in the appellate court during 1969. There were 138 such cases, but in only 34 of those cases were requests for extensions by trial court reporters found in the file maintained by the clerk of the court of appeal for recording such requests.

21. *See* CAL. CT. R. 35(c).

22. In a case where the reporter's transcript was ready in less than the 20-day limit, the clerk still would only be required to deliver both transcripts to the trial judge within the 25-day limit. *See* CAL. CT. R. 35(b)–(c). This circumstance occurred in only 20 of the 233 cases examined. *See* text accompanying notes 18–19 *supra*.

23. CAL. CT. R. 35(c). Since the appellate court receives only transcripts that have been completed and certified, it was not possible to determine the number of cases, if any, in which corrections were proposed by the parties. Nonetheless, since Rule 35(c) requires that "[i]f a proposed correction is filed, the judge shall promptly determine the matter," it is reasonable to infer that disputes over corrections of the record do not eliminate the responsibility of trial judges for delay at this stage of the appellate process.

24. Rule 35(e) requires that the trial court clerk transmit the certified record to the appellate court "[p]romptly on receipt" from the judge of the trial court. CAL. CT. R. 35(e).

25. In one case preparation of the record took 653 days. *See* People v. Wilson, 1 Crim. No. 8873 (Cal. Ct. App., 1st Dist., dismissed Aug. 25, 1970).

26. *See* CAL. CIV. PRO. CODE § 128(5) (West 1954). *See also* 28 OP. CAL. ATT'Y GEN. 92 (1956).

27. CAL. GOV'T CODE § 69,941 (West 1964). *See* CAL. CIV. PRO. CODE § 269 (West 1954).

28. *See* CAL. CT. R. 4, 30, 35(b); Witkin, *New California Rules on Appeal*, 17 S. CAL. L. REV. 79, 109 (1944).

29. *See In re* Byrnes, 26 Cal. 2d 824, 828, 161 P.2d 376, 378 (1945) (granting relief from default for failure to file record); Rappaport v. Superior Court, 39 Cal. App. 2d 15, 102 P.2d 526 (2d Dist. 1940) (contempt).

30. *See* Estate of Hanley, 23 Cal. 2d 120, 123, 142 P.2d 423, 425 (1943); People v. Sonoqui, 1 Cal. 2d 364, 367, 35 P.2d 123, 125 (1934); Estate of Davis, 151 Cal. 318, 329, 90 P. 711, 712 (1907); Diesel Const. Equip. Co. v. Neveils, 214 Cal. App. 2d 877, 880–81, 30 Cal. Rptr. 163, 165–66 (App. Dep't, S.D. Super. Ct., 1963). Remedies for delay in filing the record have been regarded as relief from default and thereby within the discretion of the appellate court. *See* People v. Snowdy, 237 Cal. App. 2d 677, 683–84, 47 Cal. Rptr. 83, 87 (2d Dist. 1965); 2 OP. CAL. ATT'Y GEN. 389 (1943). *See also* CAL. CT. R. 45(e).

31. CAL. CT. R. 35(d).

32. Witkin, *supra* note 28, at 273.

33. The Court of Appeal for the Third Appellate District (Sacramento) presently requires the clerks of the superior courts to send a copy of each notice of appeal to the clerk of the court of appeal. The notices enable the appellate court clerk to compute the normal time for transmitting the record in each appeal and, if the record is not received within that time, to take steps necessary to ensure compliance with the statutory requirements. JUDICIAL COUNCIL OF CALIFORNIA, APPELLATE COURT COMMITTEE, REPORT AND RECOMMENDATIONS FOR JUDICIAL COUNCIL ACTION CONCERNING CONTENTS AND PREPARATION OF RECORDS ON APPEAL 23 (1970).

34. *See* note 17 *supra*.

35. *See, e.g.*, People v. Hayward, 1 Crim. No. 7945 (Cal. Ct. App., 1st Dist., Aug. 5, 1970) (82 days); People v. Prewitt, 1 Crim. No. 8207 (Cal. Ct. App., 1st Dist., July 15, 1970) (109 days); People v. Sanchez, 1 Crim. No. 7794 (Cal. Ct. App., 1st Dist., May 21, 1970) (82 days); People v. Quiroz, 1 Crim. No. 8228 (Cal. Ct. App., 1st Dist., Mar. 2, 1970) (83 days).

36. CAL. CT. R. 35(d).

37. This was the reason given in 26 of the 34 requests for extensions that were on file with the clerk of the Court of Appeal for the First Appellate District. *See* note 20 *supra*.

38. Interview with Lawrence R. Elkington, Clerk, California Court of Appeal, First Appellate District, in San Francisco, Cal., Dec. 17, 1970.

39. In the 175 full appeals examined, appellant was represented by counsel appointed by the appellate court in 130 cases and by the public defender in 9 others. Thus, 79% of the appellants in the sampled cases were indigent with 74% represented by appointed counsel. This figure is somewhat higher than the statewide average. "Five years ago there were 1,330 criminal appeals in California. The courts appointed counsel in 734 of these cases. Last year there were 2,120 criminal appeals and counsel had to be appointed in 1,335 cases. Thus, the number of appeals and appointments has almost doubled in the last five years." ASSEMBLY INTERIM COMM. ON CRIMINAL PROCEDURE, REPORT ON PROPOSED STATE-WIDE PUBLIC DEFENDER'S OFFICE, 1970 Reg. Sess. 3 [hereinafter cited as 1970 ASSEMBLY COMM. REPORT]. See generally Note, 55 CORNELL L. REV. 632, 632 n.2 (1970).

40. See note 84 infra and accompanying text.

41. See CAL. GOV'T CODE § 27,706(a) (West 1968). This is an infrequent situation: "[R]elatively few county public defenders handle indigent appeals. Their offices are typically overworked and understaffed, and they have enough difficulties just meeting their primary obligation of representing indigent clients at trial. If they were to try and provide counsel beyond the trial level, it would put an intolerable strain on their already limited resources. Thus, once a client has been convicted and indicates an interest in appealing, they will, except in rare cases, refer him to the appellate courts for appointment of counsel." 1970 ASSEMBLY COMM. REPORT, supra note 39, at 2.

42. CAL. CT. R. 31(c).

43. In none of the cases surveyed did the Attorney General inquire about delay in preparation or a record or request that the court take action to speed preparation.

44. Some court reporters assigned to busy trial courts do not themselves transcribe the notes they have taken in court. Rather, they dictate from their notes into a recording machine; the recording is then transcribed by a typist who is the employee of the court reporter. Thus, some delay at this stage can be eliminated if reporters hire additional or more efficient typists. Hiring additional typists to expedite a particular case should not increase the court reporter's costs, for these typists are normally paid on a per-page basis. The system of electronic court reporting presently used in Alaska may offer a more effective solution to this problem. See Reynolds, Alaska's Ten Years of Electronic Reporting, 56 A.B.A.J. 1080 (1970). See also Madden, Illinois Pioneers Videotaping of Trials, 55 A.B.A.J. 457 (1969). But see Rodebaugh, Sound Recording in Courts: Echoes from Anchorage and Washington, 50 A.B.A.J. 552 (1964); Rodebaugh, Sound Recording in the Courtroom: A Reappraisal, 47 A.B.A.J. 1185 (1961).

Many of the clerks' transcripts examined in the survey were prepared by photographic processes. Such methods are more efficient than typewriting, and a more accurate record usually results. See CAL. CT. R. 40(i) and (l); CAL. GOV'T CODE § 69,844.5 (West 1964).

45. See People v. Slobodion, 30 Cal. 2d 362, 368, 181 P.2d 868, 872 (1947) (by implication) (appellant's motion to compel trial court reporter to prepare transcript deemed abandoned because transcript subsequently filed).

46. See Darcy v. Moore, 49 Cal. App. 2d 694, 122 P.2d 281 (1st Dist. 1942).

47. See note 39 supra; note 84 infra and accompanying text. Appellant is under no legal duty to assist the court in obtaining prompt filing of the record. See People v. Serrato, 238 Cal. App. 2d 112, 117, 47 Cal. Rptr. 543, 546 (5th Dist. 1965). Cf. Norvell v. Illinois, 373 U.S. 420 (1963).

48. See Rappaport v. Superior Court, 39 Cal. App. 2d 15, 102 P.2d 526 (2d Dist. 1940); CAL. CIV. PRO. CODE § 128(5) (West 1954).

49. CAL. CIV. PRO. CODE § 1209(3) (West 1955). See Williams v. Davis, 27 Cal. 2d 746, 751–52, 167 P.2d 189, 192–93 (1946); Rappaport v. Superior Court, 39 Cal. App. 2d 15, 102 P.2d 526 (2d Dist. 1940).

50. CAL. GOV'T CODE § 69,944 (West 1964).

51. See CAL. CIV. PRO. CODE § 128(5) (West 1954); CAL. GOV'T CODE § 69,941 (West 1964). Another possible means of obtaining compliance with statutory requirements would be referral of negligent court reporters to the Certified Shorthand Reporters Board. See CAL. BUS. & PROF. CODE §§ 8008(b), 8025(c) (West 1964).

52. See Cobas v. Reporter, Dep't 6, Alameda Co. Super. Ct., 1 Civ. No. 26,592 (Cal. Ct. App., 1st Dist., Apr. 17, 1969).

53. See text accompanying notes 39–41 supra.

54. Although a great deal has been written about the problem of delay, a review of the literature revealed no information that would inform an attorney how he might assist the court in obtaining prompt filing of the record on appeal. See authorities cited in note 6 supra. Moreover, the survey revealed no case in which an attorney had attempted to inform the court of prolonged delay in filing an appellate record.

55. See notes 42–43 supra.

56. See note 33 supra and text accompanying notes 32–33 supra.

57. The office of administrative presiding justice was created in 1970 to centralize the administration of appellate courts having more than one division. *See* CAL. CT. R. 75–76; 1970 JUDICIAL COUNCIL REPORT, *supra* note 4, at 26–27.

58. Under Rule 76, the administrative presiding justice could be given responsibility for all matters related to preparation of the record on appeal. *See* CAL. CT. R. 76. For example, all requests for extensions by court reporters could be disposed of by him. This centralization of responsibility and authority would require the approval of the chief justice and a majority of the judges of an appellate district. *See* CAL. CT. R. 75–76(2) & (5).

59. This authority probably exists under present statutes. *See* text accompanying notes 30–33 & 48–52 *supra*. *See also* CAL. CIV. PRO. CODE §§ 128(5), 177, 178, 1209(3), 1219, 1222 (West 1954 & Supp. 1955). A new statute specifically vesting this authority and responsibility in the appellate courts would nevertheless be useful to define clearly the scope of the courts' powers in this area as well as to draw the attention of judges, attorneys, and court personnel to the need for effective control by the courts of appeal.

60. *See* note 33 *supra*.

61. The appellate record rarely contains information about an appellant's financial condition. Moreover, the vast majority of appellants who request appointment were represented at trial by either the public defender or appointed counsel, which is prima facie evidence of indigency. Interview with Lawrence R. Elkington, Clerk, California Court of Appeal, First Appellate District, in San Francisco, Cal., Dec. 17, 1970.

62. *See generally* B. WITKIN, CALIFORNIA CRIMINAL PROCEDURE §§ 640–41 (1963); Boskey, *The Right to Counsel in Appellate Proceedings*, 45 MINN. L. REV. 783 (1961); Comment, *Right to Counsel in Criminal Post-Conviction Review Proceedings*, 51 CALIF. L. REV. 970 (1963).

FED. R. CRIM. P. 32(a)(2) provides that after determination of guilt in a contested federal trial, the judge must advise the defendant of his right of appeal and of the assistance that is available to an indigent. The clerk is required to prepare and file a notice of appeal if the defendant so requests. This practice has enabled the federal courts to reject late filing of notices of appeal even in situations where California courts would find delay to be excusable. *See* United States v. Robinson, 361 U.S. 220 (1960). *But see* Berman v. United States, 378 U.S. 530 (1964) (dissenting opinion). The rule has been criticized as tending to invite frivolous appeals. *See, e.g.*, Mobley v. State, 215 So. 2d 90 (Fla. Ct. App., 4th Dist. 1968); Coleman v. State, 215 So. 2d 96 (Fla. Ct. App., 4th Dist. 1968). However, federal court statistics do not establish a relationship between observed increases in the percentage of convictions appealed and Rule 32(a)(2).

63. *See* INSTITUTE OF JUDICIAL ADMINISTRATION, STANDARDS RELATING TO CRIMINAL APPEALS 47–52, 73–83 (1969). In cases involving indigent defendants, such a requirement would come within the duties of the public defender. CAL. GOV'T CODE § 27,706(a) (West 1968). Where an indigent defendant is represented at trial by appointed counsel, continued representation can be viewed as part of his professional duty. CAL. BUS. & PROF. CODE § 6068(h) (West 1962). *See* People v. Massey, 137 Cal. App. 2d 623, 625–26, 290 P.2d 906, 907–08 (2d Dist. 1955). *See generally* Cheatham, *Availability of Legal Services: The Responsibility of the Individual Lawyer and of the Organized Bar*, 12 U.C.L.A.L. REV. 438 (1965).

64. Such a preliminary statement of the appellate court's position on the duties of appointed counsel would facilitate application of sanctions in cases of negligence by an appointed attorney. *See* notes 94–98 *infra* and accompanying text.

65. *Cf.* CAL. CONST. art. VI, § 19 (West Supp. 1970) (prohibiting judge from receiving salary if any case is left pending more than 90 days after submission).

66. *See* CAL. GOV'T CODE § 69,950 (West Supp. 1970) (establishing rates of compensation for reporters).

67. *See* text accompanying notes 50–52 *supra*.

68. *See* CAL. CT. R. 33(a).

69. *See* CAL. CT. R. 33(b).

70. CAL. CT. R. 33(b)(3).

71. This restriction is limited by the constitutional requirement that indigent appellants be given free records of sufficient completeness to permit proper consideration of their claims, even if the trial judge believes the claims to be frivolous. *See* Draper v. Washington, 372 U.S. 487 (1963). In *Rinaldi v. Yeager*, 384 U.S. 305, 310 (1966), the Court stated: "This Court has never held that the States are required to establish avenues of appellate review, but it is now fundamental that, once established, these avenues must be kept free of unreasoned distinctions that can only impede open and equal access to the courts." *See also* Williams v. Oklahoma City, 395 U.S. 458 (1969).

72. CAL. CT. R. 12(a). *See* CAL. CT. R. 30.

73. *See* Walsh v. Walsh, 108 Cal. App. 2d 575, 578–79, 239 P.2d 472, 475 (1st Dist. 1952); Kuhn v. Ferry & Hehsler, 87 Cal. App. 2d 812, 813–14, 197 P.2d 792, 793 (2d Dist. 1948); Stephenson v. Phoenix Wood & Coal Co., 71 Cal. App. 2d 788, 790, 163 P.2d 457, 458 (4th Dist. 1945).

74. CAL. CT. R. 33(b)(3).

75. The record was augmented in 77 of the 175 full appeals. For purposes of the survey, "major" augmentation was considered to have occurred only when counsel requested an addition to the record that had not previously been transcribed by the reporter of the proceedings below. In addition to 50 cases of this type, there were 27 cases in which counsel requested an addition to the record of a portion of the proceedings that had already been transcribed. For example, although augmentation is technically necessary to obtain a transcript of the preliminary hearing, this transcript has been prepared earlier. Thus, when all that is required to augment the record is transmittal of an already prepared document from one place to another, augmentation is rarely a source of delay, except for the delay that may result from the 30-day extension for preparation of the brief that normally follows orders for augmentation.

76. In only one of the nine cases where appellant was represented by the public defender was a request for augmentation filed in the appellate court. Furthermore, this was not a request for major augmentation, but for addition of a transcript that had been prepared earlier. Since the public defender represents the appellant at trial, he may be more likely to recognize the need for augmentation before the record is filed in the appellate court.

77. Denying augmentation solely for counsel's negligence might conflict with the holding in *Draper v. Washington*, 372 U.S. 487 (1963). *See* note 71 *supra. See also* text accompanying notes 119–22 *infra.*

78. *See* text accompanying note 62 *supra.*

79. *See* CAL. PENAL CODE § 1237(2) (West 1970).

80. *See* CAL. CT. R. 35(c).

81. CAL. CT. R. 12(a); *see* CAL. CT. R. 30.

82. *See* CAL. CT. R. 33(a).

83. For example, of the 77 requests for augmentation, 21 were requests for arguments to the jury, 18 for preliminary hearing transcripts, and 12 for opening statements.

84. The notice reads as follows: "If you are indigent and therefore unable to retain an attorney of your own selection, you may submit to this court a request that an attorney be appointed to represent you. Any such request should be submitted promptly." Form letter from Lawrence R. Elkington, Clerk of the California Court of Appeal, First Appellate District, to all appellants appealing from a judgment of conviction (copy on file with the *Stanford Law Review*).

85. *See* note 39 *supra.*

86. 1970 ASSEMBLY COMM. REPORT, *supra* note 41, at 6–7.

87. Three of these cases involved successive withdrawals by two attorneys.

88. In the 17 cases involving only one withdrawal, delay averaged 122 days. In the three involving two withdrawals, delay averaged 413 days.

89. While it is possible that an attorney who was appointed to represent an indigent appellant and later was allowed to withdraw may have done some work that saved time for the second appointed counsel, this is, in fact, quite rare. In most of the surveyed appeals, the attorney who withdrew had done very little toward developing the appeal and usually requested no compensation. Moreover, the second attorney must always read the transcripts and hardly can avoid thinking through the basic issues to be raised on appeal—efforts that may have been made by the negligent predecessor.

90. In some cases, appellants are simply ignorant of the need for speedy appointment of counsel. A file occasionally indicates that appellant expected his trial counsel to pursue an appeal.

91. *See* CAL. CT. R. 17(a); note 105 *infra.*

92. Interview with Lawrence R. Elkington, Clerk, California Court of Appeal, First Appellate District, in San Francisco, Cal., Dec. 17, 1970.

93. The court cannot order dismissal prior to the elapse of 60 days. *See* CAL. CT. R. 17(a). *See also* CAL. CT. R. 30. It has been argued that the only procedural defect that allows dismissal is failure to file a brief. Witkin, *supra* note 28, at 279.

94. *See* note 64 *supra.*

95. *See* CAL. CIV. PRO. CODE § 128(4)–(5) (West 1954); CAL. BUS. & PROF. CODE § 6068(h) (West 1962).

96. *See* CAL. CIV. PRO. CODE § 128(5) (West 1954).

97. *See* CAL. CIV. PRO. CODE §§ 177(2), 178, 1209(3), 1209(5) (West 1954 & Supp. 1955). *See also id.* §§ 1219, 1222 (West Supp. 1955); CAL. PENAL CODE § 166(4) (West 1970).

98. *See* CAL. BUS. & PROF. CODE §§ 6077, 6078, 6086.5, 6100, 6103 (West 1962 & 1970). *See also* CAL. BUS. & PROF. CODE §§ 6067, 6068(h) (West 1962).

99. Use of such sanctions does risk a counterproductive effect: Attorneys might hesitate to accept indigent appeals if the courts required better performance. However, that risk does not outweigh the reductions in delay that stronger sanctions would probably bring. *See* text accompanying notes 128–29 *infra.*

100. *See* text accompanying notes 59–60 *supra.*

101. Bills to implement this proposal were introduced in both the Senate and Assembly in 1970. *See* S.B. 93, 1970 CAL. SENATE JOUR. 88 (daily ed. Jan. 12, 1970); A.B. 497, 1970 CAL. ASSEMBLY JOUR. 407–08 (daily ed. Feb. 2, 1970). After a favorable committee report, the Assembly passed its version. 1970 CAL. ASSEMBLY JOUR. 2038–39 (daily ed. Apr. 14, 1970). However, both bills failed in the Senate after the administration expressed opposition. 1970 CAL. SENATE JOUR. 5657, 5695 (daily ed. Aug. 20, 1970); Judicial Council of California, Minutes of Meeting of Sept. 16, 1970, at 2.

102. *See* 1970 JUDICIAL COUNCIL REPORT, *supra* note 4, at 15–16.

103. *See* text accompanying note 109 *infra*.

104. *See* text accompanying notes 130–31 *infra*.

105. In a criminal case, appellant's opening brief is due in the appellate court 30 days after the filing of the record in that court. CAL. CT. R. 37(a). After 30 days, however, the appeal is not dismissed; rather, appellant is notified that his appeal will be dismissed if a brief is not filed within 30 more days. CAL. CT. R. 17(a); *see* CAL. CT. R. 30. If the appellant is indigent, time for filing the appellant's opening brief is computed from the date of appointment of counsel. *See* note 116 *infra*.

106. CAL. PENAL CODE § 1252 (West 1970); CAL. CT. R. 37(a). In civil cases, the parties may extend the time for filing any brief 60 days by submitting a stipulation to the reviewing court. CAL. CT. R. 16(a).

107. CAL. CT. R. 17(a) 30, 43, 45(c).

108. CAL. CT. R. 45(e).

109. In deriving this figure, private and appointed counsel were treated differently. For private counsel, elapsed time was measured from the filing of the record to filing of the brief, while delay for appointed counsel was measured from the date of their appointment to the filing of their briefs. In other words, time lost as a result of withdrawals by appointed counsel was not included in the latter measurement.

110. *See* CAL. CT. R. 35(c). There is some possibility that this practice is required by the Constitution. *See* Draper v. Washington, 372 U.S. 487 (1963); *cf. In re* Smith, 2 Cal. 3d 850, 471 P.2d 8, 87 Cal. Rptr. 687 (1970).

111. Interview with Lawrence R. Elkington, Clerk, California Court of Appeal, First Appellate District, in San Francisco, Cal., Dec. 17, 1970.

112. *See* 1970 JUDICIAL COUNCIL REPORT, *supra* note 4, at 16.

113. 1970 ASSEMBLY COMM. REPORT, *supra* note 39, at 4.

114. *Id.* at 5–6.

115. Counsel's time may also be spent in interviewing appellant, travel, and oral argument. In some cases, a closing brief is filed, and, in rare instances, supplemental briefs or additional memoranda of points and authorities are filed.

116. The standard order appointing appellate counsel states, "Time for filing the appellant's opening brief is extended to 60 days from the date of this order." Standard order for appointment of counsel by the California Court of Appeal, First Appellate District (copy on file with the *Stanford Law Review*). Included with the order is a letter from the clerk of the appellate court that states, "The opening brief is expected within 60 days from the date of the appointment." Letter from Lawrence R. Elkington, Clerk, California Court of Appeal, First Appellate District, to attorneys appointed to represent indigent appellants (copy on file with the *Stanford Law Review*).

117. These documents are thought to be of no use to the court. Interview with Lawrence R. Elkington, Clerk, California Court of Appeals, First Appellate District, in San Francisco, Cal., Dec. 17, 1970.

118. This same excuse is commonly asserted by court reporters. *See* text accompanying notes 36–37 *supra*.

119. *See* CAL. CT. R. 17(a), 30.

120. Discharge of a private attorney for slowness would probably be a sufficient justification for granting an extension to prepare an appellant's opening brief. *See* CAL. CT. R. 17(a), 30, 43, 45(c), 45(e), 53.

121. *See In re* Smith, 2 Cal. 3d 850, 87 Cal. Rptr. 687, 471 P.2d 8 (1970). Indigent appellants occasionally request appointment of new counsel because of their attorney's slowness. Sometimes a phone call to the lawyer by the clerk of the court inquiring as to the reason for delay solves the problem. In some cases, however, new counsel is appointed. Interview with Lawrence R. Elkington, Clerk, California Court of Appeal, First Appellate District, in San Francisco, Cal., Dec. 17, 1970.

122. *But see In re* Hough, 24 Cal. 2d 522, 528–29, 150 P.2d 448, 451–52 (1944); Mowrer v. Superior Court, 3 Cal. App. 3d 223, 230–31, 83 Cal. Rptr. 125, 129 (2d Dist. 1969); People v. Lewis, 166 Cal. App. 2d 602, 607, 333 P.2d 428, 432 (2d Dist. 1958); People v. Agnew, 114 Cal. App. 2d 841, 845, 250 P.2d 369, 371 (App. Dep't, L.A. Super. Ct., 1952).

123. One writer persuasively argues that, beginning in law school and continuing throughout their careers, lawyers as a class are conditioned to slowness, inefficiency, and delay. *See* J. FRANK, *supra* note 5, at 33–40. *See also* Finley, *Judicial Administration: What is This Thing Called Legal Reform?*, 65 COLUM. L. REV. 569, 574–76 (1965).

124. *See* 1970 ASSEMBLY COMM. REPORT, *supra* note 39, at 3–4.

125. *See* note 64 *supra*.

126. *See* CAL. CIV. PRO. CODE § 128(5) (West 1954).

127. *See* CAL. BUS. & PROF. CODE §§ 6077, 6078, 6086.5, 6100, 6103 (West 1962 & Supp. 1970). *See also id.* §§ 6067, 6068(h) (West 1962).

128. The *Penal Code* prescribes that counsel appointed for a criminal appeal shall be paid a reasonable sum for his work. *See* CAL. PENAL CODE § 1241 (West 1970). Little or no compensation should satisfy the requirements of the statute in a case where appointed counsel was removed for negligent delay.

129. *See generally* Sutro, *OEO and Legal Services to the Poor*, 41 CAL. ST. B.J. 215, 215–18 (1966).

130. *See* text accompanying notes 101–03 *supra*.

131. "[A state public defender office] would create a corps of experienced lawyers who could function with a high degree of skill and efficiency. Vast wastage of time would be eliminated since its attorneys would not have to research every issue fresh. Adequate supervision, training, and assistance could be provided for new attorneys in the office. And regular communication could be established between its personnel and local public defenders. This would allow both to better understand the entire system and more effectively represent their mutual clients." 1970 ASSEMBLY COMM. REPORT, *supra* note 39, at 7–8.

132. *See* Douglas v. California, 372 U.S. 353 (1963).

133. In *Rowe v. Yuba County*, 17 Cal. 62, 63 (1860), the Supreme Court stated: "[I]t is part of the general duty of counsel to render their professional services to persons accused of crime, who are destitute of means, upon the appointment of the Court, when not inconsistent with their obligations to others; and for compensation, they must trust to the possible future ability of the parties." *See* CAL. BUS. & PROF. CODE § 6068(h) (West 1962). Counsel appointed to represent indigents appealing criminal convictions receive "a reasonable sum for compensation and necessary expenses, the amount of which [is] determined by the court and paid from any funds appropriated for that purpose." CAL. PENAL CODE § 1241 (West 1970).

134. For example, the material prepared by the State Department of Finance and the Legislative Analyst with regard to budget requests of the Department of Justice might be relevant information in developing productive norms.

135. CAL. CT. R. 37(a). *But see* People v. James, 179 Cal. App. 2d 216, 221, 3 Cal. Rptr. 648, 651 (4th Dist. 1960) ("examination of rule 37 of the Rules on Appeal reveals that no penalty is provided for late filing of the respondent's brief").

136. *See* text accompanying note 109 *supra*.

137. CAL. PENAL CODE § 1253 (West 1970).

138. The *Penal Code* does not specifically require such a practice. Nonetheless, the survey revealed no instance in which the Attorney General has not responded to an appellant's opening brief in a criminal appeal.

139. It is impossible to estimate the percentage of criminal appeals in which no respondent's brief would be necessary. In another context, the Judicial Council has noted: "Many appeals, particularly in criminal cases, raise no substantial legal issues and the present practice of writing a full opinion in each case, regardless of its merits, is not an optimum use of judicial time." 1970 JUDICIAL COUNCIL REPORT, *supra* note 4, at 27.

140. Letter from the Office of the Attorney General of California to Preston Devine, Presiding Justice, California Court of Appeal, Division Four (copy on file with the *Stanford Law Review*).

141. *See* text accompanying note 114 *supra*.

142. The letter that accompanies the order appointing an attorney as counsel for an indigent in a criminal appeal states: "The filing of an appellant's closing brief is optional. The case will be placed on calendar promptly whether or not such a brief is filed. Notice thereof will be sent to you approximately one month prior to the hearing date." Letter from Lawrence R. Elkington, Clerk, California Court of Appeal, First Appellate District, to attorneys appointed to represent indigent appellants (copy on file with the *Stanford Law Review*).

143. *See* 1970 JUDICIAL COUNCIL REPORT, *supra* note 4, at 87. Only a final order or judgment of the juvenile court receives calendar priority over criminal appeals. *See* CAL. WELF. & INST'NS CODE § 800 (West Supp. 1971).

144. *See* 1970 JUDICIAL COUNCIL REPORT, *supra* note 4, at 84–85.

145. In the First Appellate District, cases are assigned by the clerk according to a confidential system. No one can know prior to assignment which judge will receive the case. Interview with Lawrence R. Elkington, Clerk, California Court of Appeal, First Appellate District, San Francisco, Cal. Dec. 17, 1970. Authority for this procedure is found in Rule 47, which allows, in appellate districts having more than one division, assignment "to the divisions of the court in such manner as to equalize the distribution of business among them" with the assignments being made by one of the presiding

justices "unless a majority of the judges of the court in the district shall otherwise determine." CAL. CT. R. 47(a).

146. The details of these procedures differ among districts. For a general description of the procedures of courts of appeal at this stage in the appellate process see Molinari, *The Decisionmaking Conference of the California Court of Appeal*, 57 CALIF. L. REV. 606, 609–10 (1969).

147. At present, practices regarding submission of cases vary among the courts of appeal. *See* Farley, *Court Survey*, 33 CAL. ST. B.J. 65, 70–71 (1958); Regan, *Court Survey*, 33 CAL. ST. B.J. 138, 141–143 (1958). Neither the Constitution nor statute prescribes when a case must be "submitted"; this decision is left to the discretion of individual courts of appeal.

148. CAL. CONST. art. VI, § 19. *See* CAL. GOV'T CODE § 68,210 (West Supp. 1970). This rule is self-executing and highly effective. The state controller will not issue a judge's salary warrant until he receives an affidavit or declaration under penalty of perjury certifying that the judge has no late case under submission.

149. CAL. CT. R. 24(a).

150. This period is usually 60 days from the filing of the appellate decision. *See* CAL. CT. R. 24, 28.

151. *See* 1970 JUDICIAL COUNCIL REPORT, *supra* note 4, at 24–29.

152. Additional staff has been authorized for the first and second districts, where the caseload is greatest. Although the Administrative Office of the Courts had submitted a budget request that would have provided such staff for all districts, the administration and legislature favored a smaller experiment that would focus on the busiest districts.

153. *See* notes 57–58 *supra* and accompanying text.

154. *See* 1970 JUDICIAL COUNCIL REPORT, *supra* note 4, at 29.

155. *See, e.g.,* Cohn, *supra* note 6, at 465–66; Cutler, *Appellate Cases: The Value of Oral Argument*, 44 A.B.A.J. 831 (1958); Stuart, *supra* note 6, at 609; Note, *supra* note 7, at 888–90. *See also* Steinberg, *The Criminal Appeal*, 22 RECORD OF N.Y.C.B.A. 71 (1967).

156. *See* CAL. CT. R. 22 (oral argument limited to 30 minutes per party).

157. No statute or court rule requires this practice. *See* CAL. CT. R. 21. "This is the only provision on calendars and sessions in the rules, and it supersedes a considerable amount of detailed procedural material, substituting virtually complete discretion in the reviewing courts." Witkin, *supra* note 28, at 239. Whether oral argument is required to satisfy the constitutional guarantees of due process depends upon the situation; in many cases argument submitted in writing alone is sufficient. FCC v. WJR, The Goodwill Station, 337 U.S. 265, 274–77 (1948).

158. The British approach is the opposite. Using no written briefs and relying completely on oral argument, the English appellate courts resolve criminal appeals in an average of one month from filing of the notice of appeal to filing of the decision. D. KARLEN, APPELLATE COURTS IN THE UNITED STATES AND ENGLAND 150–54 (1963). *See also* Wiener, *English and American Appeals Compared*, 50 A.B.A.J. 635 (1964).

159. *See* Meyers v. Kenfield, 62 Cal. 512 (1881); Wyatt v. Arnot, 7 Cal. App. 221, 94 P. 86 (3d Dist. 1907). *Compare* CAL. CONST. art. VI, §§ 18–19, *with* U.S. CONST. art. III, § I.

160. *See* note 147 *supra*.

161. *See id.*

162. California Administrative Office of the Courts, Workshop for Court of Appeal Justices, June 1969 (unpublished pamphlet, copy on file with the *Stanford Law Review*).

IDEAS WHICH HAVE
MOVED CORRECTIONS

Peter P. Lejins

M AKING A STATEMENT at this Centennial Congress of
Correction on the "Ideas Which Have Moved Corrections"
in the course of the past one hundred years of existence of
what is now called the American Correctional Association is a difficult
task. On one hand the limited time available for such a statement
makes it possible to touch only upon the most general ideas. On the
other hand most of these general ideas are well known, and their brief
presentation can hardly be exciting or fertile in the sense of new
facts and insights. Nevertheless, the speaker must tackle the task
assigned to him and hope that at least some of his general observations
will contribute some new thoughts about whence we came, which is
the theme of the first part of this Congress, and should prove to be a
basis for assaying where we go from here.

1870

An analysis of the ideas which moved corrections during the past
hundred years must start with our taking stock of the ideological set
and the corresponding reality at the time of the Association's establishment. This might be done by structuring this inventory under the
following headings:

1. The place or function of corrections within the total system of
   crime control in 1870;

2. The state of correctional techniques in 1870;
3. The immediate goals and aspirations of the correctional leaders at that time;
4. The spirit of the correctional field at the time of the 1870 Congress.

A brief comment on each one of these issues is in order

The place or function of corrections
within the total system of crime control in 1870

By 1870 correctional activity with regard to criminal offenders was a rather generally accepted practice. Still relatively new as a method of crime control, dating back only to the last years of the 18th century, when it appeared for the first time as a legitimate component in public crime control programs in this country, corrections seemed to be safely "in" by 1870, and the bulk of the discussions in the Congress of that year centered only around the futures strengthening of the correctional approach. The first major bid for correcting the criminal by means of religiously inspired penitence in a penitentiary, in solitude or silence, was becoming a thing of the past as the sole and only method, and the model of the progressive correctional system, relying on the plan of gradual rehabilitation of the offender through a network of rewards and penalties for the right or wrong behavior respectively, was gradually capturing the imagination of correctional leaders everywhere the United States included.

The emphasis on corrections at that time should not, however, mislead us into believing that it was *de facto* the main method for handling the criminal offender in 1870. The punitive crime control system still remained the main bastion of society in its struggle with the criminal. The general public was convinced that an individual not only *gets* punished, but also *should* be punished for committing a crime; law enforcement was apprehending criminals in order to deliver them to the courts, where they were to receive their just due; and the courts sentenced the guilty offender to suffer the penalty prescribed by law. It was only the "correctional crowd" that managed to inch its way into the punitive regime with cause-removing activities—the rehabilitative aspects of the program.

Institutional treatment was almost the only method used in dealing with the convicted criminal. Imprisonment, beginning in 1774 with the Simsbury mine, had gradually replaced corporal punishment and the death penalty by 1870. The extramural methods of probation and parole, although already invented—as the dramatic legend has it—by John Augustus and Alexander Machanochie, were hardly in use as yet at all. The long-time name of the new Association—first National and then American Prison Association—was fully justified, because there was nothing but prisons for dealing with offenders.

In terms of an analysis of the ideas that moved the so-called penal reform of the 19th century, this speaker has repeatedly suggested that the phenomenally fast switch from the earlier modes of punishment to the prison in that century was due to three factors: the capacity of the prison to function both as a punitive and as a correctional facility made it especially suitable for satisfying the needs of an ambivalent society that was vacillating between punitive and correctional goals, with some segments of the population strongly sold on the one, and some on the other, but the large majority vaguely accepting both. Secondly, the belief in punishment was sufficiently strong to preclude the wide adoption of extra-mural forms of treatment, which were not punitive enough for those days: probation and parole had to wait for a point of balance between punishment and correction more favorable to the latter before they could develop to any sizable extent and replace incarceration. And, thirdly, imprisonment meant keeping an offender available for being acted upon, which was not the case with corporal or capital punishment. The incarcerated offender is available to be influenced by religious instruction, academic schooling, vocational training, and the development of such habits as cleanliness or good work habits, all of which were perceived as correctional techniques. The inmate is also available for study, which later on led to testing, case study, diagnosis, and treatment prescriptions in terms of the disciplines of psychology, psychiatry, social work, etc. In other words, imprisonment provided an opportunity to work with the offender correctionally.

Summing up, the American Correctional Association was founded at a time in which the prison was almost the exclusive method of dealing with criminal offenders. Imprisonment was primarily punitive in character, with only a small amount of cause-removing or correctional elements injected into it, which were, however, steadily gaining in scope and acceptance.

The state of correctional techniques in 1870

The above remarks about the place and function of corrections in 1870 should already have given a general idea about the state of correctional techniques at that time. In characterizing the state of correctional techniques in the United States at any point in history, one should keep in mind what I once expressed in another paper[1] in the following manner, *viz.* "that the field of correction can be likened to a very long animal, with its progressive head very far removed from its backward tail." I used the simile of a dachshund or a dinosaur. While the head is trying to keep up, for example, with the atomic age, the tail, in some instances, is still wagging in the 18th century. What I meant is that because matters of criminal justice in this country are a local rather than a federal or centralized responsibility, the many systems of correction differ from each other to such an extent in terms of progressiveness or backwardness, that a generalized characterization of the country as a whole is often meaningless without further qualifications. Thus also in 1870 some states were quite progressive, in terms of the time, in handling their offenders, while others were as backward as could be.

As I have indicated, the American Correctional Association was founded at a time when prison was almost the sole tool for both punishment and correction in the United States. Corporal punishment and the death penalty had largely disappeared, although the former was used exceptionally within some prisons for disciplinary purposes; and probation and parole had not yet arrived. As to the prison regimes, they were for the most part various modifications of the so-called Auburn system, with the eastern penitentiary system confined to Pennsylvania. Many states were still at the level of the state prisons, which developed at the turn of the 18th century as the first places for incarceration and did not even reach the somewhat more corrrectionally oriented organizational pattern of the penitentiary. The employment of prisoners received considerable attention, both as a correctional device, intended to develop in the prisoner some skills for earning money and accustoming him to steady work, and as a source of revenue for the state, to help pay for the maintenance of the prison. Some thought was, of course, given to correction, but it should not be forgotten that these were the pre-progressive-system days, and most correctional ideology still centered around work habits, discipline and moral and religious regeneration of the offender. Education was present only in rather elementary forms, primarily as an effort to eradicate illiteracy, and that especially for the purpose of reading the Bible.

The immediate future goals and aspirations
of the correctional leaders at that time

Although many *desiderata* for corrections which were voiced in the course of the first Congress are reflected in the respective *Proceedings* volume, the following might be singled out as those receiving the greatest emphasis.

The progressive system as the organizational principle for the correctional treatment of incarcerated offenders, and the realization of this system in a "reformatory"-type institution unquestionably constituted the focal point of the Congress. The first news of the progessive system or, as it was then popularly known, the Irish system, which had just been developed in England, reached the United States in the late 1850's. It was only in the late 1860's, that is, just a few years before the Congress, that its real impact on American prison leaders can be detected in the writings of the period. The basic ideas of this system—namely stimulating the gradual progress of the offender by means of a system of rewards and penalties for good or bad behavior respectively, out of the pit of antisociality demonstrated by the crime which brought him to prison, to gradual rehabilitation and the status of a law-abiding citizen who can again take his place as a full-fledged member in the free community—captured the imagination of the prison administrators. A carefully devised system of gradually awarded privileges and responsibilities, meticulously keeping track of the progress made by a system of marks or similar device, all this was obviously perceived as a promising tool and perhaps even the finally discovered key to the solution of the crime problem. Undoubtedly the prison administrators of that day discovered, explicitly or implicitly, the opportunities which this correctional device offered at the same time for the maintenance of discipline by placing into the hands of the administrator the powerful tool of awarding or withdrawing privileges, and, in the case of the indeterminate sentence, by shortening or lengthening the period of incarceration. These principles of the progressive system—which was to become the progressive leitmotif of corrections and still remains the basic organizational principle of today's correctional programs—were for the first time clearly envisaged by the correctional community assembled in Cincinnati and were hailed as a panacea. Four of the 37 principles of the Declaration of 1870 deal specifically with the progressive system, and several others are closely related to it. Sir Walter Crofton himself wrote a paper for the Congress on the system bearing his name, and the word "reformatory" appears in the titles of the majority of the more important papers presented at the Congress. Indeed, the reformatory, as the institution which would embody the principles of the progressive system and would be introduced on the basis of the New York law passed just one year earlier, was the concrete program around which the hopes of the Congress were centered.

The second immediate goal for American corrections which occupied the attention of that first Congress was the organization of an international correctional community. This first national gathering of American prison administrators was of a remarkably international orientation. This is manifested both by the large number of foreign invitees, a number of whom actually took part in the Congress, and the extensive discussion of plans for activities on an itnernational scale. It is, of course, a well established historical fact that in making the 1870 Congress a reality, the prime moving spirit of the Congress, Enoch C. Wines, had primarily in mind the need for a national American organization as an instrument for developing an international organization. The latter he managed to accomplish in the form of the first international congress of the International Penal and Penitentiary Commission in London in 1872. The appointment of Mr. Wines by President Grant as the first United States Commissioner and the founding of the National Prison Association were those outcomes of the Congress which provided the base for Mr. Wines' further activities in organizing the London Congress, for the future U.S. role in the activities of the International Penal and Penitentiary Commission and therefore, more recently, U.S. participation in the activities of the United Nations in the area of corrections, inclusive of the convening of the present United Nations Congresses on the Prevention of Crime and the Treatment of Offenders.

One of the less all-encompassing immediate goals of the 1870 Congress deserving to be singled out is the concern about the problems of the inmates released from prison, especially after a prolonged stay in it and in view of the absence of parole and the help it provides. As principle XXII states:

"More systematic and comprehensive methods should be adopted to save discharged prisoners, by providing them with work and encouraging them to redeem their character and regain their lost position in society. The state has not discharged its whole duty to the criminal when it has punished him, nor even when it has reformed him. Having raised him up, it has the further duty to aid in holding him up. And to this end it is desirable that state societies be formed, which shall cooperate with each other in this work."

Improvement of the local jail was another immediate goal set by the Association and expressed in Principle XX, which reads:

"It is the judgment of this congress, that repeated short sentences for minor criminals are worse than useless; that, in fact, they rather stimulate than repress transgressions. Reformation is a work of time; and a benevolent regard to the good of the criminal himself, as well ar to the protection of society, requires that his sentence be long enough for reformatory processes to take effect."

A further immediate issue was the problem of prison labor. With a number of prisons reporting self support and even surplus income from prison labor, and the contract system being the main organizational principle of the day, the Congress felt reasonably confident in this area but nevertheless clearly indicated the need for further exploration.

Still another issue which occupied the Congress was the development of a system of prisons or correctional institutions instead of having a number of disparate institutions which, like ships at sea, were independent of each other and under the total command of the captain-warden. At the time of the 1870 Congress only very few and disconnected steps had been taken in the direction of unifying and centralizing the institutions of a state, but the idea was planted, and its obvious advantages from the point of view of a rational correctional process were quite obvious.

The spirit of the correctional field
at the time of the 1870 Congress

Perhaps the main contribution of the 1870 Congress was its spirit and the very fact that it took place.

Neither the convening of a congress, nor the founding of the National Prison Association were completely new developments. Organizations dealing with prison matters and established for the purpose of helping and reforming offenders began in the United States as early as 1776 with the founding of *The Philadelphia Society for Assisting Distressed Prisoners,* culminating in the activities of such organizations as the New York Prison Society, established in 1844, and similar organizations in Philadelphia, Boston and elsewhere. There were also previous conferences true, of a local nature, but sometimes of considerable scope. In this case, however, we are dealing with the convening of a *national* congress and the founding of a *national* society, and this in itself added emphasis to the idea and the importance of the event. The Congress as well as the founding of the association testified to the existence of what we would nowadays call a professional group, composed of the carriers of certain skills and knowledge, who identify themselves as individuals working on a common task with a unity of purpose and with a service aspect to it. As just stated, the very fact of the convening of a congress and the establishment of a permanent society testified to the existence of such a group, the numbers and capabilities involved, and permanence of the undertaking.

Equally important, or perhaps even more so than the above two developments, was the spirit of the Congress. Perusal of the volume of the *Proceedings* of the Congress leaves no doubt as to the degree of elated enthusiasm, sense of mission and innovation, and hence of progress coupled with deep confidence that the proposed new departures in the handling of offenders are the long-sought keys to the answer of the crime problem.

In analyzing the spirit of the Congress one must note, as I pointed out elsewhere,[2] that the motivation of the participants was partly humanitarian and partly rational-correctional in terms of means-ends schemes. Although humanitarian motives are still detectable to a considerable degree, the impact of the new ways of social science, proposing study and action on the basis of knowledge with regard to social problems, is quite discernible. We should not forget that the year of the Congress and the founding of the society coincides with the pleas, voiced for the first time by Cesare Lombroso in Italy, for the prevention and control of crime through the study of its causes and the methods 'for removing these causes, as he so eloquently requested in his *L'Uomo Delinquente* while promoting a new scientific discipline of criminology.

Such were the ideas that moved the 1870 Congress and the prison leaders of that time.

In many ways it is perhaps justifiable to state the optimism and enthusiasm of the Congress of 1870 was probably the reflection of similar outbursts of optimism and enthusiasm throughout western society, prompted by awareness of the promise contained in the advent of social science for the solution of what formerly appeared to be the eternal problems of humanity. The rational schemes for the correction of the criminal and his return to the society as a law-abiding citizen, which permeate the pages of the Congress *Proceedings,* seem to be the major source of this optimism and enthusiasm just as the new knowledge derived by research and the rational plans based on it, evoked similar elation in other areas of human endeavor.

THE HUNDRED YEARS

THE FOLLOW-UP OF 1870 IDEAS

The criminological proposition:
the removal of causes

First of all let us look at the fate of the idea of correction of the offender, that is the understanding of the reasons for criminal behavior and the removal of these reasons as the major method of crime control. It is quite obvious that this basic idea still holds the imagination of our society and perhaps with the exception of the last five years, when a certain return to punitive criminal justice has made inroads on the national scene in the United States, the gradual evolvement of the cause removing proposal can be claimed for the entire one hundred years of existence of the American Correctional Association, growing steadily in its sophistication with the development of the basic disciplines of sociology and psychology.

The reformatory

The second idea which is closely related to the first one and is actually a concrete manifestation of it is the creation of the reformatory as the tool for correction, especially of young offenders The reformatory stands quite readily as a symbol of the rational-correctional schemes in general. It at first gained a tremendous acclaim and spread all over the nation until practically all states developed one or more institutions of this type, depending on the size of the state. The developers of the reformatories can in many instances be credited with the meticulously rational planning of the program in terms of the best knowledge of the time and readiness to stand the involved expenses almost to the same degree to which the Pennsylvania Quakers, somewhat earlier, were willing not to spare any amount of expenditure in order to develop the costly Eastern Penitentiary. It must also be recognized that while being one of the major bids of the new movement, the reformatory, after its great initial popularity, proved to be one of the great disappointments with regard to this rational approach to corrections. Somehow it just did not develop into a panacea, solving the problem of crime in the sense of interrupting the beginning of criminal careers of the young offenders. Nobody quite established the reason why the reformatories failed. This does not mean that the reformatories did not mean a considerable step ahead. It also does not mean that the reformatories did not do a lot of good to the very many individuals who profited by the academic and vocational educational programs, their diagnostic facilities, and various treatment methods. But the reformatories failed to become the answer to the crime problem. In that sense, it did mean the failure of at least one of the modern rational approaches of social science to solve the crime problem. It would, however, be exaggerated to say that this completely undermined the belief in the possibilities of the means-end schemes of modern social science.

Humanitarian versus rational motivation

It was pointed out that in 1870 American correctional circles found themselves some place about mid-point of the gradual development away from the humanitarian toward rational-correctional motivations in the penal reform under the impact of the advent of social science. An excellent study of this particular aspect of the penal reform, done by Miss Constance M. Turney and entitled "Humanitarian and Correctional Motivations in the Penal Reform in the United States," shows quite conclusively that by 1870 the humanitarian impulse had largely spent itself as a motivational force, and the rational-correctional motivation was beginning to take over. The *Proceedings* of the subsequent decades contain consistently fewer and fewer papers referring to humanitarian motives, while the proposals for rational methods for the integration of the offender into the law-abiding society appear in ever larger numbers.

The progressive system

The study of the *Proceedings* of the Congresses of the American Correctional Association, as well as a general historical study of corrections in the United States, shows quite clearly that the basic principles underpinning the so-called progressive system of prison discipline, or the Irish system, gradually came to constitute more and more of the basis of all correctional theory and practice in this country. What the papers of Sir Walter Crofton and Enoch C. Wines proclaimed in 1870, gradually—and first of all through the reformatory movement—became the backbone of the correctional process: a system of rewards and handicaps for behavior which the correctional program judges to be right or wrong. This can be and was interpreted in terms of the moral evaluation of the behavior of the offender, but it can also be interpreted in terms of the well-known processes of conditioning and reinforcement in human development as discerned by psychology. Whether we are dealing with a reformatory in 1870 or with a community-based treatment program in 1970, even a superficial perusal and analysis show to what extent the correctional plans are dependent on the theory of the progressive system.

Institutional and correctional systems

As already pointed out, the idea of a state-wide system of penal and correctional institutions made a rather feeble appearance in the 1870 Congress. It developed, however, into one of the major issues in the subsequent 100 years. This development can be differentiated into two phases. The first phase consisted in the recognition of the desirability and in the actual realization of a state-wide administration of prisons. The sociologists would see in this a function of specialization, which in turn probably can be interpreted as a function of the growth of population on one hand and the growth of knowledge in the area of the etiology of criminal behavior on the other. Specialization has its natural counterpart, namely, integration of the specialized parts and agencies, and this means, of course, an over-all state system that is managed in terms of the coordinated functioning of separate institutions performing their specialized functions. This resulted in a modification of the role of the warden and emergence of the role of the administrator of the penal and correctional institutions of the state.

The second phase of this development is related to the gradual emergence of extra-mural or community-based treatment, first of all probation and parole. As probation and parole developed into independent agencies and later on into state-wide systems, especially in the case of parole, the next step in the over-all management of the correctional process was the establishment of an over-all administration of all correctional enterprises as a unified system. This led to the creation of the office of the state correctional administrator, who coordinates the activities of all correctional agencies in the state.

Prison labor

The concern of the 1870 Congress with the problem of the employment of the inmate in the institution, the role of his not being idle but working as he would be working in the open community, and the issue of the productivity of his labor both for the state and for himself and his family continued to occupy American corrections throughout the hundred years. A number of fluctuations in the ideas concerning this issue and the corresponding practices should perhaps be singled out, rather than existence of one single linear trend. In the first decades after the 1870 Congress, the development was clear: the earmark of this period was skepticism about the contract labor program which characterized the prison scene in 1870, and its various forms. The organizational principles of the employment of the offenders within the institution; of the relationship of this employment to the vocational preparation for earning a living in the open community; the relationship of this employment to the support of the institution or the public interest in general, as well as the support of the prisoner's dependents and his own future finances; all these issues showed a considerable amount of fluctuation. The issue of remunerating the offender for his work, as well as the issue of his participation in the work enterprises of the open community—the work release programs—are the more recent questions occupying the minds of correctional administrators at the present time.

International organization

One aspect in which the American Correctional Association remained true to itself and to the efforts of the first Congress and its leaders throughout its hundred years of existence is the active support of an international counterpart to itself; first, the International Penal and Penitentiary Commission and, later on, beginning with the 1950's, the Social Defense Section of the United Nations, and the respective Congresses of these two organizations.

The above does not, of course, exhaust the immediate goals and aspirations, which can be gleaned from the *Proceedings* of the 1870 Congress, and their subsequent fate. It seems that those mentioned above were the major ones, but there were certainly many others which undoubtedly moved some members of the Congress even more than those briefly discussed here.

NEW IDEAS
Extra-mural or community based treatment

Although the participants of the 1870 Congress were concerned with the problems of the offender upon his release from the institution, the developments of the next decades considerably modified this problem and gave it a new direction. The emergence of the idea of treating the offender in the community by means of probation and parole, which gradually developed into two major recognized programs in handling the offender, added new aspects to the discussion of the fortunes of the released prisoner.

Perhaps only the employment aspect remained very much the same before and after the advent of parole. Otherwise the planning of the future life of the parolee considerably modified the problem of the released prisoner. The recently taken position that *all* offenders who have been imprisoned for a considerable length of time should be released under parole supervision still further changes this problem.

Otherwise, probation and parole led to the development of a new professional group, which in 1907 separated itself from the American Prison Association and established the American Probation Association. Later the Parole Association was established, and still later the fusion of the two into the American Probation and Parole Association was a subsequent development. Thus, while in 1870 the Congress and the new organization unified the entire field of correctional work, the American Prison Association later became the organization of institutional personnel alone, and for a long time the field was thus divided between two separate associations. It was only in 1954 that the American Correctional Association made a bid for renewed unification of the field by modifying its name from "Prison" to "Correctional." An almost identical move was undertaken by the National Probation and Parole Association, which also used a change of name to indicate the new all-encompassing nature of that organization—the National Council on Crime and Delinquency. It is interesting to note that only after some fifteen years of co-existence of the two organizations there are beginning to appear signs that the two associations may consider having just one professional-membership organization.

The 1960's saw the development of the concept of community-based treatment, which is broader than probation and parole and encompasses such recent programs as community treatment centers and, in general, a number of combined programs of institutional and community-based treatment such as pre-release centers, halfway houses, etc.

Juvenile and youth offender populations

Since 1825 there were separate institutions for juvenile offenders in the United States, and thus at the time of the Cincinnati Congress the correctional circles were fully aware of this development and of some of the specific problems which the juvenile offender represents. It was not, however, until somewhat later—as a matter of fact 29 years after the Cincinnati Congress—that the first juvenile court was established in the United States and the classical American concept of juvenile delinquency came significantly to the fore. With the gradual rise in importance of the specific juvenile field, a certain separation of the personnel dealing with juveniles from the prison personnel of the American Correctional Association began. This separation occurred along two demarcation lines. One was the fact that extra-mural treatment, especially probation and foster placement, rapidly came into much greater use in the juvenile field than in the adult, and the already mentioned break betwen extra-mural and intra-mural personnel, formalized by the organization of the National Probation Association in 1907, was the function of this break. The field was further fragmentized by the feeling on the part of the personnel of the juvenile institutions, that their interests were not adequately represented in the American Correctional Association, composed primarily of workers in adult institutions. This finally led to the formaton of separate organizations for the personnel of juvenile institutions. These organizations went their own way beginning with the early 1950's. The American Correctional Association was reluctant to recognize the separation of the juvenile field and resorted to committees for the juvenile area after the separation of the affiliated organizations representing this specialty. Thus the American Correctional Association, which represented the entire field of correction in 1870, came to be devoid of two major components of the modified field by about the 80th year of its existence: the juvenile agencies and probation and parole workers. To be sure this was never a complete separation as far as individual memberships were concerned, and, as already pointed out, there are presently trends toward the reunification of the field.

As I have suggested elsewhere, the growth of an independent juvenile field and the fringe separatist developments at the upper age bracket of the juvenile court jurisdiction, that is, with regard to the specialized courts, institutions and programs for youthful and young adult offenders, can be interpreted as the gradual advent of the correctional handling of offenders in general. The younger age categories of offenders have been more accessible to cause-removing or correctional handling in terms of the resistance of the general public and the professional field than have adult criminals. Thus the appearance of the juvenile, youth and young adult offender categories can be viewed, as stated, as the gradual inroads of the correctional approach into the heretofore punitive control area.

Research

Principle XXIX of the Declaration of 1870 reads:

"Prison statistics, gathered from a wide field and skillfully digested, are essential to an exhibition of the true character and working of our prison systems. The collection, collation and reduction to tabulated forms of such statistics can best be effected through a national prison discipline society, with competent working committees in every state, or by the establishment of a national prison bureau, similar to the recently instituted national bureau of education."

This request for prison statistics is probably the best illustration of the depth of the impact of the rational-correctional approach to the control of crime already present in the minds of the participants of the Cincinnati Congress. It is disheartening that the same request for criminal statistics in general could be made today, 100 years later, with almost the same cogency. In spite of this remarkable failure of the field with regard to criminal statistics, it is quite obvious that one of the major additions to the field of correction since 1870 is the advent of research and the growing awareness of its crucial significance for the effective control of crime. The idea of re-examining all existent programs for criminal offenders on the basis of true research data regarding their effectiveness, the planning of all new programs on the same basis, and the operation of programs on the basis of feedback of operational data for better decision-making is gradually gaining general acceptance not only in the form of polite lip service, but also in the form of budget dollars for the necessary programs. The recent developments, under the leadership of the American Correctional Association itself, with regard to the evaluation of institutions, agencies and programs, and the setting of standards through the development of a Manual of Correctional Standards, testify perhaps more than anything else to the gradually increasing impact of the scientific methodology of the behavioral and social sciences on the field of corrections.

NOTES

[1] Peter P. Lejins. "An Agenda For Correction," Presidential Address, Proceedings of the Ninety-third Annual Congress of Correction of American Correctional Association, 1963, p. 10.

[2] Peter P. Lejins. "Penal Reform and the American Correctional Association," *Proceedings* of the Eighty-seventh Annual Congress of Correction, 1957, p. 13.

PSYCHOLOGICAL STUDIES
OF PUNISHMENT

Barry F. Singer

Lawyers, criminologists, and penologists have recognized for some time the relevance of scientific studies of human behavior to their concerns. They have turned first to the *social* sciences—sociology, clinical and social psychology—for useful information and ideas. Those in the social sciences have responded eagerly, and this mutual enthusiasm has resulted in such innovations as consideration by the courts of sociological evidence in deciding whether segregated schools can be truly "equal," consideration by legislatures of similar evidence in framing poverty and welfare laws, the introduction into criminal trials of clinical testimony on legal sanity, and the use of social and psychological predictive indices in sentencing and correctional procedures. In some instances the contributions of the social sciences have been substantial, while in others their additions have been of mixed value. In particular, professionals in the fields of law and criminology have often been confused by contradictory testimony from experts in the social sciences and irritated by their inability to state concrete relationships with complete confidence.

In contrast to the relationship between law and the social sciences, there has been very little interchange between law and criminology and the human *biological* sciences—zoology, physiology, ethology, experimental psychology, and behavioral genetics—which study man as one biological entity among many. Their circumscribed subject matter diminishes their surface relevance for social questions. That same limitation of subject matter, however, allows them to state basic relationships more easily than is possible in the social sciences. Insofar as it is wise and expedient for our social planners to treat man as a biological creature, the human biological sciences should have much to contribute.

The relative neglect of the biological sciences is understandable. Biological scientists have shown little interest in social applications. They have not only failed to interpret their often esoterically stated findings to social institutions that might be interested in them, but have not even made a serious attempt to convince such institutions of their science's usefulness, confining their rare statements on the social implications of biological findings to technical scientific journals. This Article, therefore, will have the following features: It will consider at length the relevance of experimental psychology for social issues, detail the facts and ideas of one of the topics of experimental psychology—punishment—in non-technical terms, and discuss concrete applications of these findings in the field of criminal justice administration. Finally, the Article is written by an experimental psychologist for the professional readership of a law review.

I

THE FRAMEWORK· AND ETHICS OF EXPERIMENTAL PSYCHOLOGY

"Experimental" or "biological" psychology, as opposed to the social or clinical branches, is characterized by a concern with relatively simple and basic phenomena. Experimental psychologists study humans as well as animals, usually focusing on those characteristics which humans share with a large number of other organisms, but alloting no special distinction to the human as subject matter. They state their observations in terms of observable behaviors and, like other scientists, attempt to formulate deterministic laws, that is, laws of invariable association between events. Their hypotheses and theories either refer directly to physiological structures and physical events or have a physical-physiological tinge (as in "stimulus" and "response"). Where they mention an organism's perceptions or thoughts about a situation, it is only in abstract and mechanical terms.

There are three questions regarding experimental psychology, important to this Article, which the nonpsychologist often asks but seldom receives satisfactory answers to: Is a deterministic science of behavior plausible? Can animals really tell us anything about human beings? Do explanations of human behavior in terms of stimulus and response really have any validity?

The nonpsychologist often takes exception to the deterministic statement of behavioral laws—for example, the law that punishment effectiveness decreases increasingly rapidly as punishment for an act is delayed. He argues that humans have free will and do not behave automatically as the law would imply and that the law ignores the factors which really count: human attitudes, beliefs, feelings, perceptions, morals, and the human conscience. Both exceptions are well taken in some senses, but for the purposes of this Article they miss the point. In the first place, although scientists enjoy couching their findings in deterministic form, we are not necessarily required to view their positions as ontological. Apart from philosophical disputes about free will, the above law is true as a simple matter of observable fact, and such laws are being used widely and successfully to control human behavior.[1] Second, if we do involve psychological data in philosophical disputes about free will, we find that the free will arguments are losing ground fast.[2]

The second exception—that the law ignores too much—is more important. The law does indeed ignore a great deal, everything, in fact, except the specific, isolated conditions under which it was formulated. Like any scientific law, it is implicitly prefaced by "All else being equal . . . ." While there are no doubt situations where the law does not hold true, or even where it is reversed, in general it is valid. If we want to hone our control, we can either try to make the conditions of application of our law more like the original laboratory conditions or try to find laws about attitudes and morals so that we can regulate them concurrently.

Experimental psychologists and other biological scientists derive many of their generalizations from animals. The layman often questions the biological psychologist's seemingly blind assumption that because something is true for a rat, it is true for a human. The psychologist or biologist, for his part, is so accustomed to observing physiological and behavioral continuities along the evolutionary order that the similarities between men and the lower animals seem much more basic and obvious than the differences, and he is amused by man's disinclination to admit his animal tendencies.[3] Fortunately, even if one remains skeptical about the generality of animal results, this Article should still be meaningful. Scientists have found that most of the results to be described are demonstrable with a wide variety of species, including man. In the punishment literature, rats, cats, dogs, goldfish, pigeons, monkeys, human adults, and children have all been subjects of experimental reports. Psychologists have found few occasions to qualify the basic laws of punishment with species discrepancies, although they are attentive to such possibilities.[4]

We often have no choice about trusting the animal data, since we are dealing with questions on which it is practically impossible or unethical to do research with humans. If in tests on female monkeys a new measles vaccine causes miscarriages, researchers reject it without further testing. Monkeys are not humans, and the vaccine may be safe for humans (although this is unlikely), but we are unwilling to use humans as research subjects to find out. We know from controlled experiments that deprivation of maternal care and of sensory stimulation in infancy will cause underdevelopment of the cortex, poor learning capacities, motor impairments, and severe permanent personality maladjustments in monkeys and rats.[5] Although naturalistic observations suggest that the same is true for human infants,[6] we can never know for certain unless we experimentally control the degree of environmental deprivation for randomly selected groups of infants and at some future time assess their personalities and cortical weights. Hopefully, we will do no such thing. This being the case, parents and child care institutions have no alternative but to pay careful attention to the animal results. Some of the laws of punishment are likewise for the most part "animal laws": for instance, the law that the more severe the punishment, the more effective it is or the law that punishment will elicit aggressive behavior. We cannot experimentally verify these laws with humans to any great extent without performing unethical research. In lieu of such research, we are obliged to take the animal data into account when assigning prison sentences or planning prison plants.

Some of this Article's explanations for punishment phenomena, even though they are translations of a technical language, may yet seem strange and mechanical. The purposes and volitions we associate with our actions and those of our fellow humans are conspicuously missing. Some illustrations may demonstrate why this is appropriate for our purposes and may remove the nonpsychologist's hesitation as to the validity of explanations of human behavior in terms of "stimulus" and "response." Imagine that being from an isolated southern clime, you are unfamiliar with furnaces or with central heating, and you visit a friend in a northern climate who has both. You observe that at irregular intervals, varying with the room temperature, the furnace and the radiator begin to make clanking noises as steam flows through the pipes, and you ask your friend, "Why is the furnace doing that?" He replies, "Because it wants to keep the house warm. It's doing just what you would do if you were a good furnace." Only a few centuries ago you would have found such an answer quite acceptable and thought no more about it. Today you are not so easily satisfied. Having a scientific bent, you might begin taking careful observations of the conditions under which the furnace went on and off, and might vary the room temperature experimentally until you could formulate the precise rules of its operation. You would then consider what type of mechanism could make the furnace behave in precisely this way as a function of the observed conditions. It would not be surprising if you conceived of a thermostat. You would test this hypothesis by doing things which you thought ought to affect thermostats, and thus indirectly furnaces, and observe whether they did in fact produce the effects; or you might begin probing around inside the system, dissecting the house wiring, with the hope that you would discover the thermostat itself. With much ingenuity, patience, and luck, you would verify your theoretical thermostat explanation. You would then have a vastly increased ability to predict and control the operation of the furnace.

Now assume that you visit a laboratory where experimental psychologists are engaged in punishment studies. There you observe the following: An organism is confined in a small space which has an electric grid for a floor and which contains only a light bulb and a lever. At irregular intervals the light goes on, and soon afterwards the organism receives an electric shock. It leaps about frantically and accidentally depresses the lever: the light and shock turn off. Very soon the organism depresses the lever as soon as the light goes on, and it no longer receives a shock. You ask the laboratory technician, "Why is the organism doing that?" He replies, "That's obvious! It doesn't like being shocked, so it presses the lever in order to avoid it. You'd do the same thing if you were in that box." Such a reply might satisfy you, as it would most people—especially if the organism in the box were a fellow human—and you might wonder why you asked such a question. However, excited by your successful experience with the furnace, you might start looking for "thermostats." After many observations, experiments, and false hypotheses, you might hypothesize the following explanatory mechanism: The light, being initially contiguous with shock, comes by a process of Pavlovian conditioning to evoke strong and unpleasant autonomic emotional responses—fear and anxiety—in the organism. When the organism presses the lever and the light disappears, the unpleasant emotional responses also disappear, strengthening the lever pressing response through reinforcement. Thus the organism comes to press the lever more and more frequently when the light comes on. If you test this explanation experimentally and it continues to fit the data, your ability to predict and control the organism's behavior is now far superior to the lab technician's.

In addition to the foregoing remarks addressed to the nonpsychologist's reservations about experimental psychology, a word about science and ethics is here appropriate. Science provides knowledge, which society can then use for good or for ill. A scientist is no more qualified than any other man to place a value judgment on particular applications of his knowledge. He can inform society about the most expedient means to given ends; but he is not particularly qualified to judge whether these expedient means are ethical or whether the ends themselves are good. This Article considers how punishment can be used *effectively* to suppress criminal behavior, which it assumes to be a desirable end. It does not assume that the use of punishment in itself is ethical or unethical. It represents data according to its relevance and importance, with ethical frameworks playing no intentional role in selection or interpretation. The Article recognizes ethical issues only in a few cases where it seems essential and discusses means of eliminating criminal behavior other than by punishment only where the desirability of other means arises naturally from the laboratory evidence. Specific recommendations fall at various points along the political spectrum. This Article does not consider whether it is good or necessary to punish wrongdoers in order to act out a social ethic. There are thorough discussions of all these issues elsewhere;[7] value decisions are therefore left to others.

II.

EXPERIMENTAL STUDIES OF PUNISHMENT

A. *Applicability*

Experimental models of punishment situations are very simple and hence both basic and general. Typically an experimenter uses rewards, usually food, to induce an organism to perform a simple act, such as pressing a bar or running down an alley. When this behavior is well-learned, he punishes the organism by administering some aversive condition during or after the act, and he measures the effects of the punishment by the future frequency or strength of the behavior. Sometimes he withdraws the reward when the punishment is administered. This is termed punishment under "extinction." Information derived from such studies is potentially applicable wherever punishment is used or phenomena resulting from the use of punishment are dealt with. Thus, the information should have applications in such diverse areas as animal training, criminal behavior and penology, child rearing, and clinical psychology. In some respects the laboratory models resemble animal training—since animals are usually used for experimental subjects—and child rearing—since common types of punishing stimuli are used in both situations. With respect to the focus of concern, however, the experimental models are most similar to criminal behavior and penology in that in both instances the focus is on the suppression of behavior, whereas punishment is likely to be used for other purposes in child rearing and animal training. Perhaps the most serious difference between the punishment of criminals and laboratory models of punishment lies in the punishing stimuli used. We punish criminals by fines or by incarceration, whereas laboratory organisms usually receive short, intense stimuli, such as electric shock, slaps, or loud noises. It is difficult to assess the importance of this difference. We do know that different types of punishment generally do not alter the laboratory laws of punishment: Punishing stimuli such as slaps, buzzers, confinement in a box, shocks of different durations and intensities, and removal from the vicinity of reward, which include some fair analogues of incarceration, all produce about the same experimental results even when more than one punishment is used for the same organism in the same experiment.[8] We can probably assume that our present experimental laboratory laws will prove valid for incarceration, although we know little about the dimensions of incarceration itself. Incarceration for six months may be much more potent in its effects than a one-month sentence, but variations in duration of confinement after six months may represent only small changes on a scale of severity; or the reverse may be true. We have no pertinent knowledge.

Experimental studies of punishment are obviously most applicable to criminal behaviors that, like the laboratory behaviors, are acquired through a simple reinforcement process, are repetitive, and are maintained because they are the most accessible routes to material rewards. We need not be directly concerned here with theories of the genesis of criminal behavior. Some theories explain criminal behavior in terms of simple learning-reinforcement models.[9] No doubt some criminal behavior develops in precisely this way; no doubt much of it does not. It seems likely that property crimes, which comprise the bulk of offenses, are more susceptible to learning theory explanations and to applications of information derived from punishment studies than are "crimes of passion," such as assault. What is perhaps more important for our purposes is to recognize that punishments are similarly administered for crimes of passion and property crimes, so that general principles of punishment ought somehow to be relevant to the former as well as to the latter. In some cases the motivation for criminal behavior may interact with the punishment administered.[10]

This Article does not consider the problem of deterrence of crimes. There are experimental analogues to deterrents, in which a child's behavior is affected by witnessing the punishment of another person for a given act,[11] but such research is done in a context different from that presently under consideration. The results discussed here will tell us how to punish a criminal after he has committed the crime so that he will not repeat it, not how to prevent him from committing it in the first place. Of course, insofar as the known conditions of punishment in fact affect deterrence, the principles discussed here will be relevant. This Article also omits, for the sake of argument, the possibility of punishment by life imprisonment for all crimes. This is obviously a completely effective suppressor of recidivism, but it is more interesting as well as more practical to ask what effects punishments other than permanent incarceration might have on postpunishment behavior.

Two general problems encountered in applying scientific findings remain. First, it is sometimes difficult to set up natural conditions sufficiently similar to the controlled laboratory conditions that the laboratory principles can operate effectively without interference. This is an engineering problem especially troublesome in the behavioral sciences, since it is unethical to put a box around human beings in the same manner as we put vacuum tubes around diodes. Second, laboratory principles are framed in general and abstract terms and are derived from simple, abstract laboratory "operations." It requires considerable imaginative insight and experimentation to produce natural conditions comparable to the laboratory operations. Neither of these problems undermines the validity of the laboratory principles; they merely make the principles more difficult to apply. This Article makes a number of concrete interpretations and suggestions, based on what seem to this author to be sound analogues to laboratory operations and what seem to be practical ways of meeting laboratory conditions. Hopefully, these can at least suggest directions to take. The essential decisions on what is ethical and what is viable, however, reside with the public and the professionals in the criminological disciplines.

B. Studies of Punishment

1. Severity of Punishment

The first experimental investigations of punishment by Skinner[12] and Estes[13] in 1938 and 1944 are still among the most important. Skinner and Estes each established a strong habit of bar pressing in rats for a food reward and then extinguished this habit by withdrawing the reward. At the same time the experimenters punished bar pressing in one group of rats by electric shock or a slap on the paws. They found that after an initial reduction in the level of bar presses the punished animals "recovered" and eventually performed· the same total number of unrewarded bar presses as did the unpunished rats. More severe punishments did decrease the total number of unrewarded responses somewhat, but did not decrease the time necessary for complete extinction. Estes and Skinner both concluded that punishment is ineffective in eliminating behavior, and Skinner suggested that it be eliminated as a social instrument.[14]

This conclusion stood unchallenged for 20 years. It is the main, and almost the only, experimental conclusion about punishment that has entered the criminal literature.[15] This is unfortunate, because it is wrong. Recent work has repeatedly shown that both nonrewarded and rewarded behavior can be quickly, completely, and permanently suppressed by punishment, provided it is severe enough.[16] Incrementally increased severity can produce any desired degree of suppression, from negligible to absolute.[17] In fact, an organism can be made to starve to death rather than perform a food-rewarded but punished behavior.[18] In general, the punishment need not be so severe as to traumatize the organism in order to completely suppress behavior.

One wonders how everyone could have been wrong for so long. The answer, as suggested by Solomon[19] and by Holz and Azrin[20] is that psychologists are human; they do not enjoy experimenting with punishment, especially severe punishment, nor is it congenial to them to advocate punishment as a social tool. Therefore psychologists performed very little research on punishment in the two decades following the work of Skinner and Estes, and they accepted their conclusions without too much question. In the early 1960's, however, research on punishment suddenly skyrocketed. The results have already filled three volumes,[21] and research is still accelerating. The new research has modified old beliefs, and new facts are emerging monthly. The reason for this upsurge is not that psychologists have suddenly become hard-boiled; rather, they have become convinced that knowledge about punishment has widespread humanitarian uses.

The brutal fact, then, is that the more severe the punishment, the more effective it is in suppressing behavior. As has already been pointed out, however, this is no reason automatically to assign punishment bad marks. Furthermore, we have a detailed knowledge of what "severe" means in terms of the behavioral effects of electric shock on rats,[22] but we have no knowledge of what "severe" means in terms of the behavioral effects of incarceration on human beings. Under the proper circumstances, a year's imprisonment might be a severe enough punishment to permanently eliminate any criminal behavior.[23]

A second lesson is that, if we administer a mild punishment, we run the risk that suppression will be only temporary and that the undesirable behavior will return in full strength when the effects of punishment have worn off or when the organism is highly motivated to perform the punished behavior.[24] Again, however, we do not know what constitutes a mild punishment for humans. The fact that a mildly punished behavior will regain its strength has caused some psychologists to think that punishment does not act directly to eliminate behavior in the same sense that extinction may be said to weaken or eliminate behavior, but that it merely suppresses behavior, eliminating it indirectly. In some theoretical sense the behavioral tendency is still there, but inhibited. This is a matter of theoretical debate, with both sides at this point just lining up their ammunition.[25] These debates, at any rate, need not cloud the significance of the empirical facts, which are quite clear: Punishment can effectively suppress behavior, provided it is sufficiently severe.

2. The Importance of Extinction

Extinction, or the withdrawal of reward for a behavior, will eventually eliminate that behavior. The behavior will occur with diminishing frequency until it appears only sporadically. Under no circumstances will the behavior regain any substantial strength, unless it is rewarded again. Moreover, a given intensity of punishment will suppress behavior more effectively if the behavior is also under extinction than if it is still being rewarded.[26] Since criminal behavior is almost always rewarded,[27] this suggests that we give some attention to extinguishing criminal behavior as well as punishing it, by withdrawing the rewards or making them inaccessible. Shah[28] was apparently among the first to discuss this in explicit terms:

> To take a more specific aspect of the relationship between social and environmental factors and deviant behavior, it seems evident that the form and frequency of certain criminal acts bears some connection to the environmental structure and opportunities provided. Thus, the relative ease with which checks may be cashed in the United States is undoubtedly related to the frequency of bad check passing and various related offenses. The relative ease with which cars may be broken into and be started without use of ignition keys, clearly affects the frequency of offenses involving 'joy-riding' and automobile theft. . . . It seems obvious that certain changes in community practices, the requirement that the vast technological skills available in the country be utilized more adequately in the manufacturing of automobiles with better door locks and less vulnerable ignition systems . . . could do much to influence the frequency of certain law violations and other undesirable social situations.[29]

Some manufacturers have in fact equipped their cars with buzzers which sound when the ignition is off and the keys are not removed and with steering columns which lock when the keys are removed. Widespread use of these devices may drastically reduce car thefts. The AC Transit Company in the San Francisco Bay Area, in order to prevent bus robberies, has pioneered an exact change fare system, in which the driver carries no cash. This has reduced the incidence of bus robberies to zero.[30] One of the most effective crime fighters of the coming decade may be generalized credit cards. If liquor stores, markets, and gas stations used credit cards exclusively, there would be very few robberies of the same. Uniformly adequate street lights would no doubt reduce muggings. Many other possibilities exist.

If such reforms are, as Shah phrases it, "obvious" and "evident," why are they not more widely instituted? First, they may not really be "obvious." They seem so common sense that it should be unnecessary for learning theorists to cite them. However, articles on behavior theory and crime have provided the context for both Shah and this author to suggest such changes, and it is possible that the obvious sometimes becomes so only from a novel vantage.

Second, those who subscribe to a hydraulic theory of criminal behavior might believe that these changes will not really decrease the total incidence of crime. They would contend that there is a constant total criminal impulse, and suppression of crime in one form will pressure it into increasing somewhere else. We might, for instance, experience a rash of crimes associated with the fraudulent use of credit cards. It seems much more reasonable, however, to assume that crimes are at least in part a function of the ease with which criminal behavior is rewarded and that we can appreciably reduce the total opportunities for successful criminal behavior in our society by a few simple reforms, thereby forcing many would-be car thieves into becoming used-car dealers.

Third, such reforms may seem mechanically inconvenient. They need not be; some may actually be more convenient, and we must balance any inconvenience against the social cost of crime. It is possible, of course, that mere inertia has impeded the institution of such reforms. The liquor store owner may regard an occasional robbery as part of the cost of doing business, just as the armed robber might consider an occasional jail sentence as part of the cost of his business.

3.   Certainty and Delay of Punishment

The results of experiments on certainty of punishment are expected and straightforward: The more certain the punishment, the more effective it is in suppressing behavior.[31]   All else being equal, punishing an act every time it is committed is the frequency condition most effective for suppression.   In his article on criminal behavior and learning theory, Jeffrey[32] maintained, without citing specific evidence, that "the experimental evidence supports the classical school of criminology in its statement that it is the certainty of punishment—not the severity—that deters people from criminal acts."   This is probably a misleading statement.   In the first place, as mentioned above,[33] the conditions of punishment which minimize recidivism may or may not be the conditions which maximize deterrence.   There is no reason to assume, in fact, that punishment is necessarily a determinant of deterrence.   We have little experimental evidence on the subject.   Second, this author is aware of no experimental evidence which directly compares the suppressive powers of certainty with those of severity.   Indeed, such a comparison would be very difficult.   The indirect evidence concerning suppression supports a conclusion different than that of Jeffrey: A sufficiently severe punishment will suppress behavior effectively even if it is only occasional, whereas a mild punishment will permit complete recovery of the punished behavior even if it is administered every time.[34]   Also, Rettig and Rawson[35] found that estimates of the likelihood of unethical behavior were much more influenced by the potential intensity of punishment than by the potential probability.

The moral derived from the basic experimental results concerning certainty is nevertheless straightforward: Catch more criminals more of the time, presumably through increasing the resources or upgrading the quality of law enforcement. Law enforcement officials would then also more quickly apprehend criminals after the commission of crimes. Experimental knowledge of the degree of suppression as a function of the percentage of total responses punished is inexact, and knowledge of how many criminal acts actually get detected and punished is lacking (although indications are that the percentage is small). Therefore, it is not possible to estimate how effective a given increase in law enforcement capacities would be. Almost any increase would be helpful, however.

Extensive experimental investigation of delay of punishment has shown that the effectiveness of punishment diminishes as it is administered from zero to five seconds after a behavior. After this point, its effectiveness in suppressing behavior drops off quite sharply, reaching a minimum at about 30 seconds, where, however, there is still some residual effect.[36] These results seem to hold true for humans as well as for animals.[37] The crucial question for criminological purposes is: Why is punishment less effective after longer delays? Is delaying a punishment similar to decreasing its certainty or to decreasing its severity? Church[38] showed that increasing the "certainty" of a delayed punishment by providing a continuous noise signal bridging the gap from behavior to punishment did not increase its effectiveness, although behavior was suppressed during the signal itself. As we therefore cannot account for the loss of effectiveness of delayed punishment in terms of its similarity to decreased certainty, it is likely that delaying a punishment has an effect equivalent to decreasing its severity. We also know that, as punishment is delayed, it is more difficult to produce effective *differences* in severity.[39] Some of this experimental work needs to be verified and extended, but the above principles are better than tentative guesses.

When the concern is suppression of a behavioral act more complex than simple bar pressing, it is more effective to punish the beginning stages of the act than to punish it when it is well under way or just completed.[40] The former produces an organism that seldom repeats the act, but shows no anxiety after he does, whereas the latter procedure produces an organism that will repeat the act often, even though it will manifest guilt and anxiety thereafter.[41] The former is presumably preferable.

Clearly the above findings indicate that our present system of punishments should be inadequate.[42] We do not usually inflict penalties within seconds of a criminal act, but after months or even years of waiting and legal proceedings. We would predict that such penalties would have little effect on behavior. Moreover, as Eysenck[43] and others have pointed out, the material rewards for crime are usually immediate, in contrast to the punishment's delay, and immediate rewards will influence organisms more than delayed punishments.

At this point we need to consider two objections. First, cannot humans look ahead farther than 30 seconds to plan for rewards or avoid aversive consequences? Second, does not Eysenck's law predict that everyone should become a criminal?

Consequences more remote than 30 seconds can affect human beings and, in fact, other organisms. However, analysis reveals that the mechanism responsible for bridging the gap is probably "secondary reinforcement" (or secondary punishment)—some signal or symbol which has been reliably associated with reward or punishment and which is present during the delay interval.[44] Such a signal will in fact suppress behavior when it is present during the delay interval, but undesirable behavior will return when it is absent.[45] Thus, such signals will not counteract over a long period of time the weakened effect of delayed punishment.

Eysenck's law does not predict that everyone will actually become a criminal, because many other considerations obtain. For instance, most people are probably deterred from criminal acts by the social stigma of "getting caught," a secondary punishment which is relatively immediate and, for most people, quite potent (almost everybody, however, does commit criminal acts at one time or another—albeit infrequently—as would be predicted by Eysenck's law[46]). Who, then will be most disposed toward criminal acts? It seems reasonable to think, as many people have,[47] that those who are relatively unaffected by secondary rewards or punishments and/or who are relatively more affected than most people by immediate rewards and punishments, are more likely to become criminals. In other words, if criminals are people who must have immediate gratification and are unaffected by secondary rewards, they will probably also be people who will be affected only by immediate punishment and unaffected by secondary symbols of punishment. There is some evidence to support this deduction.[48] To the degree this analysis is valid, it implies that immediacy of primary punishment is even more important for the criminal population than for the general population.

The possibly vitiating effect of delay of punishments for criminals has been noted several times in the criminological literature.[49]   It needs to be emphasized. Delay of punishment is of paramount importance and is probably largely responsible for the apparent ineffectiveness of our current punitive systems. There are a number of things that could be done about it. First, there is no reason why the legal process following arrest cannot be speeded up to days and weeks instead of months and years. The principle impediment is lack of judges and court personnel.[50]   It costs from 2000 to 4000 dollars to incarcerate a man for one year.[51]   If just one man were given a sentence four or five years lighter than normal, we would have saved enough money to procure the full services of an additional judge for one year.

Criminologists have known for some time that increased severity of punishments has little effect on incidence of crimes.[52]   Why does severity have little effect, in view of both common sense and the previously mentioned experimental indications that it ought to? Because the punishments are so uncertain and delayed. The effect of delay is to lessen severity, and manipulations of severity have little effect at long delays.[53]   In other words, a five-year sentence beginning a year after the commission of a crime may not be as effective as a six-month sentence administered without delay. The difference between a ten- and fifteen-year sentence, if both are started after a long delay, would not mean as much as the difference between a one- or two-year sentence immediately administered.

As Jeffrey points out,[54] our own social ambivalences exacerbate the problems. We tend to react to failures to stop crime by creating severer sentences, that is, longer sentences which we assume are more severe. However, when our sentences become longer, we also tend to be more careful about assigning them, and assign them less often. With a relatively long sentence, therefore, punishment becomes even more delayed and uncertain. If the objective is to suppress criminal behavior, this is the worst possible course to take. However, new directions seem possible. If we made five years incarceration the maximum sentence for almost any crime, with the most common sentences being one year or less, we would save enough money to multiply the number of judges and legal personnel, not to mention probation and parole officers. This in turn should reduce crime, which would reduce the total incarceration budget still further. We could give each accused maximum attention immediately, and the transition from criminal act to fines or imprisonment could be smooth and rapid. Manipulations of sentence length would have more effect. These changes would not only reduce severity of punishment; they should also reduce crime.

There is yet another route suggested by the experimental results, and that is the administering of secondary, "provisional" symbols of punishment immediately upon apprehension of a suspect, preferably at the scene of the crime. This would be the optimal condition of punishment in terms of immediacy, cutting the delay to seconds, sometimes even allowing the punishment to take place before the completion of the act. Such procedures would have to fit within the limits of our traditional notions of presumed innocence, and should only follow upon substantial public confidence in the police.[55]

4. Sentencing

Experimental results disclose three other phenomena which are relevant to sentencing policies. First, we know that allowing an organism a measure of control over its punishment will decrease the effectiveness of that punishment. A given quantity of punishment which an organism has through its own efforts decreased to that amount will be less effective than that same quantity administered without the organism's having had the possibility of controlling it.[56] This suggests that for maximum punishment effectiveness we should not permit parole or "time off for good behavior." This is not to say that parole under the present penal system is harmful, or that it is not presently effective for some people, or that it may not be desirable for other reasons. It suggests that the general possibility of parole will probably decrease the effectiveness of incarcerative punishments. Thus a five-year sentence commuted to three for good behavior might have less punitive effect than a three-year sentence fully served. Moreover, if the reforms suggested above can shorten sentences, the need for parole should be lessened.

Second, strong habits are more resistant to a given punishment than weak habits. It takes a more severe punishment to produce the same effect on a long-rewarded and hence well-established behavior as would a less severe punishment on a more weakly established behavior.[57] This suggests a standard minimum sentence for a given crime with increases in sentence length depending on the strength of the criminal tendency. While this suggestion hardly seems novel, current sentencing policies base severity of sentence on previous convictions, which is not necessarily the same as strength of criminal behavior. Thus, we should punish the professional car thief[58] with a stiffer sentence than the teenage joyrider even if he and the teenager each had no previous convictions.

Finally, an "exposure effect" accrues upon repeated punishments; a given punishment quantity will become less effective with repetition.[59] Also, experience with mild (or relatively infrequent, short, or delayed) punishments will attenuate the effects of later more severe (or more frequent, of longer duration, or more immediate) punishments, while initial experience with a relatively more severe punishment will accentuate the effects of later milder ones.[60] If a criminal recidivates and receives the same punishment the second time, it will be less effective, merely because of previous exposure. If he receives a more severe punishment, the previous punishment will mitigate its effects, and it will be no more beneficial than the last one unless it is considerably more severe. It is impossible to frame the suggestion quantitatively, but the lesson is clear: Make repeated punishments not only progressively more severe, but progressively much more severe. Alternatively, if the initial punishment is quite severe, it should suppress behavior more in the first place, and subsequent punishments can be milder and still have the same effect. Remember that "severe" under the proper conditions may mean only a year's imprisonment, and if this is so, the second alternative seems the better one.

5. Theories of Punishment

Psychologists have just begun to examine seriously various alternative explanations of punishment, and, as yet, there is no favored explanation. Involved are two basic theoretical issues which in some ways overlap. The first issue is whether the mechanisms involved in punishment are very basic and general, as the processes involved in reward effects are thought to be, or whether the phenomena of punishment will require subtle and complex explanatory mechanisms. At the moment, psychologists more strongly support the first alternative.[61] The second issue concerns the nature of the relationship between Pavlovian conditioning and the production of punishment effects. There is wide agreement that Pavlovian conditioning is involved, but there are divergent views as to precisely how it is involved. Most theorists believe that when environmental stimuli or the kinetic stimuli produced by the incipient movements of the punished act (especially in the human case, we can also conceive of imaginal stimuli) are made contiguous with punishment, they take on some of the aversive properties of the punishment itself. The next time the organism begins the act, particularly in the same environment, it produces stimuli which through classical conditioning have become aversive. It is these aversive stimuli which then prevent the act from occurring. However, disagreements arise as to just how the conditioned aversive stimuli prevent the act. They might simply lessen the organism's positive motivation to perform the act;[62] they might impel the organism to engage in incompatible behaviors;[63] the organism might learn to escape the aversive conditioned stimuli by ceasing to perform the act or leaving the environment (which would reinforce such behavior in the future);[64] or all of these events may be occurring simultaneously. A better understanding of punishment would enhance our control over its application and its effectiveness.

C. Undesirable Consequences of Punishment and Their Prevention

Some psychologists have issued strong general warnings against the use of punishment, because of some of its undesirable side effects.[65] Such general negative recommendations seem more justified in the context of child rearing than in the context of punishment of criminals and actually are not very cogent even for child rearing.[66] However, it will be useful to examine all of the known inexpedient or unpleasant consequences of punishment in order to determine explicitly whether or not they relate to criminal behavior and, if so, to suggest how we might avoid them.

When punishment for an ongoing rewarded behavior is removed, the rate of occurrence of the behavior will suddenly increase. The increase is often so dramatic that the behavior for a time actually occurs at a higher rate than before it was punished. This phenomenon— "compensatory recovery"— will take place even if the punishment was mild and the behavior during punishment had already recovered completely to pre-punishment levels. When the punishment is removed, the behavior will spurt suddenly to an above-normal peak, then gradually return to normal.[67] One is struck by the similarity between the phenomenon of compensatory recovery and the fact that the greatest proportion of recidivism occurs within a year after release from prison.[68] These facts suggest that we should forcibly remind an offender, whether or not he is a parolee, of the possibility of punishment for a time after leaving prison. Punishment or its symbols should not end abruptly. For instance, we could require all offenders to visit a parole officer frequently for the crucial year after prison, or we might employ "half-way houses" to accomplish the same end.[69]

The administration of punishment to an organism for a continuing rewarded behavior will increase that organism's resistance to extinction. That is, it will continue performing the act longer when it is no

longer rewarded or punished than if it had not been punished originally.[70] Apparently the emotional and other consequences of punishment are very similar to the consequences of removal of reward, and
the initial exposure to punishment inures the organism to the later
effects of nonreward under extinction.[71] This suggests that the punished criminal would tend to persist longer in a criminal act when its
benefits were removed than would the nonpunished criminal. This
does not seem to have important practical implications, however, since
extinction is not a commonly employed method of dealing with crime,[72]
since the experimental effects referred to are slight, and since the
phenomenon would occur in any case only when the punishment was
insufficient to suppress the original behavior, a circumstance which we
presumably would be able to prevent.

Judson Brown in 1947 first observed a paradoxical and striking
effect which punishment occasionally causes: If an organism performs
an act in order to avoid or escape punishment, and one removes the
punishment from which it had learned to escape (extinction condition) and punishes the organism instead *only if it performs the now
unnecessary act*, it will persist in performing the act, thereby unnecessarily punishing itself, far longer than an organism from which all
punishment is simply removed. This "self-punitive behavior" or "vicious circle effect" also occurs when the punishment used in extinction is of a different type from the punishment originally used to
motivate the behavior. Furthermore, the more severe the punishment
given for the unnecessary act, the longer the organism persists in performing it.[73] The probable explanation for this effect is that the
punishment in extinction helps to maintain the same anxieties and fears
from which the organism originally attempted to escape. The more
one punishes it, the more the punishment "reminds" the organism of
the aversiveness of the entire situation, and it performs the original
behavior to escape from punishment; this, however, induces further
punishment.[74]

This suggests that if the desire to escape from fears and anxieties
motivates criminal acts, punishment for those acts might only induce
their repetition. Drug addiction and alcoholism seem to be illustrative of this phenomenon. The original motivation for taking drugs or
alcohol may not have been a desire to escape from or avoid tensions
produced by the environment (although in many cases it probably
was). An addict or alcoholic, however, is a person in whom drugs or
alcohol have set up their own recurring physiological tensions, which
the person must then take drugs or alcohol to avoid. His addictive

behavior is entirely motivated by the desire to avoid or escape aversive withdrawal symptoms. Punishing him should make the situation worse, and it seems to. Recidivism rates for alcoholism and drug addiction offenses are very high.[75] The punishment commonly used, incarceration and withdrawal from the drug, sets up exactly the same situation that the addict took drugs or alcohol to escape. Any future signs of such punishment should drive him to further addiction. As an act of humanity, correction officials may give an addict drugs or drug substitutes during his initial stay in jail or before his court appearance. The addict is thus being punished while he is actually performing the formerly criminal act. For the normal reward-motivated criminal behavior, this would be the best possible course; for the addict such treatment may be disastrous. It may only heighten his motivation to perform the act. Therefore punishment of alcoholics or addicts by incarceration may be worse than useless.

Punishment involves fear, anxieties, pain, and unpleasantness. As we have noted, it probably suppresses behavior by conditioning these aversive reactions to situations, people, or incipient acts. For this reason psychologists have warned parents that they should punish their child sparingly and not by physical means.[76] Otherwise, the parent as punisher may become himself a conditioned aversive stimulus for the child. Such an admonition might sensibly pertain to child rearing, but it seems inappropriate for controlling criminal behavior. To be effective in suppressing behavior, punishment must be unpleasant, and it must create some fractional unpleasantness in future situations. If because of the punishment he has received, a punished criminal now feels fearful and uneasy in the presence of parole officers, courts, or police, or feels anxious when he even thinks about committing a crime, we do not believe that we have grievously damaged his social adjustment.

If we place two organisms in an enclosed space and arbitrarily punish them, they will attack each other. This phenomenon—termed "elicited aggression"—occurs with a wide variety of punishments and organisms, including children.[77] In a more common punishment situation, punishment administered for an act such as bar pressing initially results in a brief flurry of bar depressions, which may be interpreted as an aggressive reaction.[78] Elicited aggression is a serious undesirable consequence of punishment and may be an experimental analogue of the prisoner's hatred of society, his desire to get back at it. It may also explain the frequency and level of prison tensions and riots.

However, it may be possible to avoid it by countermeasures discussed below.[79]

In a series of classic demonstrations Maier[80] presented rats with an insoluble problem and forced them to continue to attempt to solve it. He punished the rats for half of their responses no matter what they did by forcing them to jump into a closed door. In this situation the rats "fixated" on one response, such as always jumping to the left side. Maier later made the problem soluble, but the rats persisted in their compulsive responses even though this meant always being punished when a nonpunished, rewarded alternative was readily available. Unavoidable punishment caused compulsive, neurotic behavior, and when the opportunities for more rational behavior became available, punishment was ineffective in helping the rats to overcome their neurotic tendencies.[81]

Recently, Maier, Seligman, and Solomon[82] have reported extensively on a phenomenon termed "learned helplessness." If one inflicts unavoidable, random punishment upon an organism, it appears to learn that escape-oriented behavior is futile, and it will be retarded in learning a later behavior which will allow it to terminate aversive stimulation. This is apparently a phenomenon of wide generality, having been demonstrated with a variety of punishments and species, including man.[83]

A single causal texture is common to all of the adverse side effects of punishment mentioned above: The infliction of punishment on an organism in a situation where it cannot help what it is doing, for a variety of reasons, or where it has no unpunished alternative route to reward. This causes the organism to become aggressive, compulsive, phobic, retarded, or neurotic, depending on slight alterations in the punishment circumstances. This by itself suggests that we should not punish peoples' behavior without providing them with some alternative behavior through which they can escape punishment and/or secure reward. Moreover, a mass of independent evidence suggests that this is not only desirable and necessary, it is more effective as well.

Holz and Azrin[84] report that when presented with two levers, both leading to reward when pressed but one leading also to punishment, the organism—pigeon or human—will quite quickly, without overt signs of emotion, learn to press the nonpunished lever and will seldom if ever return to the punished lever. Hunt and Brady[85] have shown that controllable or avoidable punishment causes less overt emotional behavior than unavoidable punishment. Solomon[86] and Fowler and Wischner[87] report that when one punishes an organism for choosing the wrong (nonrewarded) alternative in a maze, it quickly learns the right alternative, with no apparent adverse effects. In these situations, then, with a rewarded alternative available, punishment is not only a highly effective suppressor of undesirable behavior, with no apparent concomitant ill effects, it is a valuable aid to learning. Rachlin[88] has shown that manipulations of various aspects of punishment, such as severity, have relatively greater effect on behavior when a rewarded alternative is available. In fact, Fowler and Solomon et al.[89] have demonstrated that even delayed punishment will suppress behavior and aid learning when an alternative is available. Various persons have likewise shown that an enforced "time out" from reward as punishment for a behavior, one of the closer experimental analogues to incarceration, is effective in suppressing behavior *only* if a rewarded alternative is present, and then it is very effective.[90]

Some interesting physiological evidence indicates that avoidable punishment has much less severe emotional and psychosomatic consequences than unavoidable punishment. Miller and Weiss[91] found fewer ulcerations and other psychosomatic symptoms in animals receiving avoidable punishment than in animals receiving the same amount of unavoidable punishment. Seligman et al.[92] repeated these observations, with humans as well as animals. In fact, the typical finding is that organisms receiving punishments they know how to avoid, if they so choose, will be more like wholly unpunished control organisms than like the organisms receiving unavoidable punishment.

This cumulative evidence points directly and overwhelmingly to the importance of combining rehabilitation with punishment. Our correctional system *must* provide offenders alternative routes and skills to obtain the rewards that they formerly obtained only, or much more easily, through crime. Notwithstanding the institution of all of the other reforms previously suggested, the prisons would continue to produce powder kegs instead of refurbished citizens unless there were adequate rehabilitation. Furthermore, the combination of rehabilitation and punishment will suppress criminal behavior much more effectively than punishment alone, even when punishing conditions are not optimal. Punishment without rehabilitation may be a dangerous and ineffective course; their combination, however, may diminish hostilities and neuroses while effectively reducing crime.

III

NOVEL FORMS AND USES OF PUNISHMENT

Incarceration, or at least its widespread use, is a relatively recent form of punishment. We do not know whether it is more or less effective than other types of punishment. We think it is relatively humane, at least in theory, but this is also questionable. Experimental studies have demonstrated the plausibility of alternative forms and uses of punishment.

If one rewards an organism with food every time it presses a lever and also sets up a visual counting device which shows it how many rewards it has accumulated, and then instead of administering a directly aversive stimulus every time it presses the lever, one shows on the counter that it loses a reward for every press, the organism quickly stops pressing the lever. Such punishment is as effective as intense electric shock. Psychologists have demonstrated this phenomenon—termed "response cost"—with humans.[93] It suggests that, if the reward is in apples and the punishment in oranges, the punishment will not be as effective as when it is in the same modality as the reward which motivates the act in question. While this principle is perhaps an overgeneralization from the response cost results, some criminological data supports it: it may be for this reason that the revocation of licenses and other driving privileges is more effective than fines in suppressing traffic violations.[94] We currently fine traffic law violators and incarcerate those convicted of property crimes. The response cost results suggest that the reverse might be more effective. Part of the punishment for property crimes might be restitution to the victim and payment of an identical amount to the state. Of course, this would not always be a viable punishment, but we could institute some similar general policy. Speeding is a very exciting and dangerous form of lawlessness. Rather than fining the speeder, we could immediately impound his car, requiring him to walk, and return his car in a month. License suspension would be a similar but probably less effective punishment, since it would be delayed. If response cost methods of punishment are to be used, however, we should keep in mind the importance of rehabilitation and alternative routes to reward.

Aversion therapy is another potentially useful form of punishment. Aversion therapy is a behavioral therapy treatment[95] which uses aversive stimuli or punishments and is based upon Pavlovian conditioning. The therapist joins the stimulus or act which the patient must learn to avoid or suppress contiguously in time and space with some noxious stimulus, such as electric shock or induced nausea. After a few pairings the to-be-avoided conditioned stimulus will evoke reactions similar to those produced by the noxious unconditioned stimulus, so that the patient will have a strong inclination to avoid the conditioned stimulus.[96]

Studies of punishment obviously have much to contribute here. Many attempts at aversion therapy have been unsystematic and without adequate theoretical base in the punishment and learning literature.[97] Recent punishment studies which should be relevant include demonstrations of the importance of punishing the initial stages of an act,[98] findings on the conditions under which aversive reactions conditioned to one stimulus will generalize to other similar stimuli,[99] and a demonstration that such conditioned aversive reactions will persist undiminished for at least four years.[100] Lovaas[101] has dramatically improved the behavior of psychotic children by punishing their aggressive and violent acts. All of these findings pertain to problems often encountered in aversion therapy and should be helpful.[102]

Criminological discussions of aversion therapy have focused almost exclusively on only a few crimes of a "clinical" nature—gambling, sexual aberrations, drug addiction, and alcoholism.[103] This concentration is no doubt due to the fact that so far only clinical practitioners in psychology and psychiatry have performed aversion therapy, and cases involving armed robbery or trespassing would not ordinarily come within their purview or be of much interest to them. However, there is no reason why one could not use aversion therapy to treat armed robbery or any other crime as easily as homosexuality. The only requirement for treatment is that the crime involve some specific stimulus to which an aversion can be conditioned. A large variety of crimes, such as assault, vandalism, arson, pickpocketing, voyeurism, armed robbery, and shoplifting, meet this requirement. One noteworthy example of such treatment could serve as a model.

Kellam[104] describes the case of a woman in Wales who was an habitual shoplifter. She had been shoplifting for years and had served several prison sentences. Neither the prison sentences nor conventional clinical treatments suppressed her shoplifting. The initial aversion therapy—shocking the patient while she removed small items from a table—failed. The woman reported that the situation held little reality for her. The therapist then repeatedly showed the patient a treatment film in which a woman entered a cooperating store while a number of people in the store overtly watched. When the woman then shoplifted several items on a counter, the film showed expressions of horror and disgust on the faces of those watching. At the moment the woman in the film shoplifted the items, the therapist shocked the patient. Hospital personnel (nuns) administered the treatment. This treatment was successful. The patient finally stopped shoplifting, and she reported uneasy feelings of being watched whenever she entered a store. The therapist planned to repeat the treatment every few months.

This example illustrates most of the advantages, problems, and principles of aversion therapy as applied to criminal behavior. First, the therapist had to make the treatment very realistic in order to overcome the patient's difficulty in generalizing from the laboratory treatment to the normal environment. While rules can guide the efficiency of such generalization,[105] the clinical insight of the therapist and the cooperation of the patient are critical here. Second, the concerned sector of the community—the store—cooperated in making the treatment realistic and helpful. Third, the treatment conditioned the incipient stages of the act—entering the store. This was probably an important aspect of treatment. Fourth, the patient's criminally maladjusted behavior was limited in scope. She only shoplifted. Unlike many other criminal offenders, she did not also embezzle or rob grocery stores. Fifth, technical personnel administered the treatment. The procedures of behavior and aversion therapy are very simple. It takes a behavior therapist to set up an effective individual program, but almost anyone can quickly learn to administer it. Sixth, no one really knew how long the treatment would be effective. It might have lasted only a few months[106] or a lifetime. Since stores are such common environmental objects, extinction might soon set in.[107] As a precaution, the therapist scheduled the patient for regular booster sessions. Seventh, after the treatment the patient felt nervous and uneasy when she entered a store, which is certainly a personal handicap, though not as great as her previous affliction. This is part of the price of successful aversion therapy.

One can treat almost any criminal behavior in a similar manner. Particularly when working with a prisoner serving a sentence of a year or more, the behavior therapist would have time to discover the most effective treatment, and having found it, he could make the conditioning thorough. The program might require community cooperation. For example, a large banking enterprise could establish a branch office for the aversive conditioning and testing of bank robbers. Correction personnel could administer most of the program. Given the time and the resources, a behavior therapy program could make a bank robber want to vomit every time he saw a bank, could make an armed robber shudder every time he saw a gun.[108] As experimenters have successfully conditioned verbal and imaginal stimuli,[109] such a program could also induce these reactions whenever the convicted thief even thought or talked about guns and banks. The program could include booster treatments after prison whenever needed. Afterwards, the offender should probably do his banking by mail.

There is one important qualification to the foregoing conclusions: In most aversion therapy cases, including the shoplifting example above, the behavior is of a compulsive nature, and the client genuinely wants to end it. It seems reasonable that aversion therapy would most effectively suppress criminal behavior where the offender genuinely wants to reform but needs help. It should, however, also be a valuable adjunct to other forms of punishment and treatment with less cooperative subjects. While a voluntary aversion therapy program would probably be most effective, involuntary treatment could also work.[110] Such therapy could be part of a regular sentence or an alternative to it.

Aversion therapy is very new and should see some rapid improvements in the next few years. An especially promising development is N.E. Miller's[111] recent demonstration that characteristics of the autonomic nervous system—which controls our emotional reactions—respond in normal fashion to reward and punishment. Miller suggested possible therapeutic uses of his findings,[112] and Johnson and Schwartz[113] demonstrated such uses in conditioning the emotional levels of college students. This has some interesting implications when considered along with Eysenck's analysis of criminal behavior as being characteristic of extroverts, who in turn owe their extroverted-criminal behavior to an overactive autonomic nervous system.[114] If Eysenck's analysis is valid, we can condition criminal behavior out of existence simply by punishing any above-normal activity of the criminal's autonomic nervous system. While this may be an overstatement, it seems probable that many violent crimes are due to bad temper—in technical terms, a hyperactive autonomic nervous system. Miller's results suggest that we may be able to diminish fits of temper and violence simply by punishing their nervous system components and rewarding more suitable nervous activity.

As noted above,[115] theories of punishment postulate that punishment works by conditioning aversive reactions to behavior-produced stimuli or to environmental stimuli. Environmental stimuli become especially important as the punishment becomes delayed, since they are the only stimuli which are always present and therefore always contiguous with punishment. Punishment can be somewhat effective at long delays if a rewarded alternative is present, but the punishment then is probably largely dependent on conditioning to the environment, and if the environment were changed the suppressive effects of punishment could dissipate.[116]   Prison is at present not only a delayed punishment, it is also as removed from and unlike the normal community environment as seems possible.   On this basis alone we would predict that prison would be almost totally ineffective, and there is little if any evidence to contradict this assertion.   As alternatives or adjuncts to shortening the delays between crime and punishment, we could either make prison more like the community or punish criminals in the community rather than in prison.   The second alternative seems far more practical and potentially effective.   There is currently much enthusiasm for community treatment programs,[117] and some evidence of their success.[118]   Their success may be due to the factors discussed here.

What forms should punishment in the community take?   It should be punishment both in and by the community, and the criminal should develop aversive reactions to courthouses, police, symbols of authority, and probably also to the disapproving frowns and moral censure of his fellow citizens.   There are numerous possibilities for specific forms, and it is difficult even to speculate as to which would be most effective or would have the least damaging side effects.   We could severely curtail the offender's liberties and privileges, or require him to report frequently to police and parole officers, or to work in the community during the day but return to prison at night.   We might draw from "primitive" societies and customs, from times and places without prisons.   Thus, we might require the offender to make a public apology to his victim who would then ceremoniously forgive him,[119] or require him to wear a "scarlet letter."   We might revive stocks and dunkings.   Some of these treatments are in many respects more humane than prison, and they might be more effective.

IV

CRIMINOLOGICAL RESEARCH

This Article's general and specific suggestions for improving the effectiveness of criminal punishments are extrapolations from extensive laboratory research, involving both animals and humans, the results of which constitute our current basic scientific knowledge about punishment.   All else being equal, they should indicate the right directions.   If we are unable or unwilling to do actual field research with criminals, we are especially obliged to pay careful attention to the laboratory results.   However, a monkey is not a completely satisfactory analogue of a bank robber, nor is a laboratory experiment, even with humans, infallibly indicative of what will happen when the results are widely applied. Therefore, to the extent that it is ethically permissible and practically possible, we must test and validate these suggestions through empirical applied research, measuring the results of their implementation. Also, where a number of suggestions are available field research is the only means of deciding among the various alternatives.

A strong tradition of research, of rigorous testing of methods, treatments, and ideas, does not exist in the criminological disciplines. As this may be due to sound ethical and practical considerations,[120] critical comments by a member of another discipline, who cannot fully appreciate the research problems in criminology and penology, may be out of order. But an obtuse gaze, which is sometimes more revealing, might result in contribution.

While the criminological literature frequently mentions the importance of research,[121] it does not treat research as seriously as it might. For instance, as to corrections the most important question at present is, "What is the effect of prison (and comparable treatments) on recidivism?" Meyer,[122] writing in a criminological journal, states offhandedly in a footnote that we know nothing about this: "But statistical studies are not completely accurate, for there is no way of measuring the rate of recidivism had there been no punishment, or the number of persons who never entered into the life of crime because of their fear of punishment." While we in fact do know almost nothing about the effect of prison on recidivism, the lack of general dismay at this state of affairs is surprising, since the research questions should have been asked and answered by Hammurabi.

There have been over 100 studies on the effects of prison and other treatments on recidivism.[123] However, nearly all have employed woefully inadequate matching designs, selecting subjects "ex post facto" from different treatments on the basis of their similarity in supposedly relevant characteristics. Although the difficulties involved in extracting causal relationships from such research are immense, if not insuperable,[124] the tendency to use such designs continues.[125] Regardless of how much we match, we cannot match on the presumably non-random factors used by courts in determining which criminal will receive which treatment, and these may be the determinative factors. This is a confounding factor in all such ex post facto research. An additional confounding "subject" factor, however, exists in criminological studies. If the courts may alternatively assign juveniles to a residential group therapy (or forestry camp, etc.) treatment program or to a normal reformatory, the courts will generally assign the more well-behaved juveniles or those from higher socioeconomic classes to the group therapy program. If we solved all the matching problems and discovered lower recidivism rates for the group therapy treatment program, the effect could be due to the treatment per se, or it could very well be due to the fact that the courts did not randomly assign the juveniles; thus, a subject assigned to residential group therapy might be in exclusive contact with a group which was less "criminally inclined"—a factor independent of the treatment itself.[126]

Finally, an unavoidable statistical factor confounds ex post facto matching studies. In effect, these studies measure the differences between pre- and post-treatment tests for two groups. The pre-test is an index of scores on matching variables, such as degree of education or economic status, on the basis of which "equal" subjects will be selected, and the post-test is an index of scores of later success, such as being employed or avoiding arrest. In general, these two tests or indices are significantly correlated, but the correlation is less than perfect. One must therefore expect statistical regression towards the mean of the post-test (criterion) index, independent of any treatment effects, for *any* given sample of subjects. Also, as the two samples are drawn from different populations, one must expect that, as a statistical artifact, regression toward the means of the respective populations will produce apparent differences in the criterion index, independent of any real differences which may or may not exist due to treatments.

If there are really no treatment effects, one would still expect that in matching studies, as a result of statistical regression, the treatment program to which the more promising subjects are assigned would show a higher success rate when matched samples are compared. This is especially true when the two indices used are not very highly correlated (and in such criminological research they usually are not) and when the treatment populations from which the samples are drawn are quite different (they usually are). In summary, the problem of regression means that one could not plausibly conclude a positive effect of treatment from matched sample ex post facto criminological research.[127] Each of the other two problems mentioned above is equally as damaging. Unfortunately, therefore, it seems futile to look to these studies for any useful information on the effects of prison or other treatments.

By far the best, and perhaps the only remedy for these particular methodological problems is to assign subjects to treatments randomly. In an extensive research program, the California Youth Authority has for some time randomly assigned subjects to treatment groups. Their data at this point indicate that 30 percent of the subjects in a community treatment program recidivate within 15 months, compared with 51 percent placed in a normal reformatory or released directly to parole.[128] These are certainly meaningful results which cast doubt on the relative effectiveness of prisons; they indicate that prison may be worse than useless in preventing future crime. However, the research itself suffers from three experimental faults. First, it would be most meaningful if the Youth Authority manipulated time spent in treatments over a wide range. Presently, time is somewhat confounded with treatment.[129] Second, the Youth Authority omitted a small percentage of eligible offenders who were unacceptable to the community from the study. We know nothing about treatment effects for them. Third, the Youth Authority has not used an adequate untreated control group. On occasion it has drawn the offenders released directly to parole from a different population, and at any rate parole does not constitute a "no treatment" condition. The results from a group which is immediately released after conviction with no further supervision or treatment of any kind, save that necessary to keep track of them, can tell us more precisely what the results from our other groups mean.

There are certainly practical, legal, and especially ethical barriers to such extended and rigorous use of randomized group designs in criminological research. However, one can also question whether it is ethical to continue to inflict punitive treatments when we have no knowledge that they help anyone and when we in fact suspect that in their present form they actually harm the offender and society. We should carefully consider the ethical problems involved in such fully randomized research before we reject it as undesirable.[130] Keeping in mind that the best research consists of randomized assignment of all possible types of offenders to all possible treatment conditions, several compromise solutions to the ethical problems are available.

First, researchers could use juveniles, as in the California Youth Authority program. Perhaps because until recently juveniles have had fewer legal rights than adults or simply because we have more concern for the young, we have used juveniles extensively in experimental-manipulative correctional research, whereas adults are seldom research subjects. Whatever the reasons, we do not seem to perceive ethical problems in such research with juveniles. A tradition of rigorous research with juveniles does exist, and we could easily incorporate randomizing research of the type suggested here within this tradition.

Second, we might vary the time of treatment widely enough to achieve an approximation to an untreated control. Two months in a community treatment program with full release may be more effective than two years in a reformatory. If we find this to be true, we can limit the treatment time gradually to a month, a week, two days, until we have functionally assessed the effects of no treatment.

Third, we might use an "operant" method of assessment.[131] We could vary a treatment condition over time for a specified population and determine whether crime statistics vary directly and in a sustained fashion with our treatment manipulations.[132] This method has already been used in a limited way in assessing the effects of manipulations of severity of sentences, as for example when the sentence for rape was increased in Philadelphia,[133] or when the death penalty was eliminated in England for a five-year trial period. One can use it to assess *any* treatment effect. The method requires that researchers use a specified population, preferably in a specified locale, over a period of time when other conditions are relatively stable and manipulate the treatment condition to be tested up and down over its range at least several times. At some point it will be clear that the treatment has an effect or no effect. Since everyone receives the same treatment at any given time, this method seems to involve fewer ethical and legal problems.

Fourth, we could use a "quasi-experimental analysis"[134] to assess the effects of any social change. Such an analysis is essentially an operant method of assessment based upon careful and sophisticated analysis of alternative explanations of index changes following a single instance of social reform, rather than upon gross observations of the results of repeated manipulations of the reform. Repeated manipulations, of course, would enable quasi-experimental analyses to become even more powerful tools, or, contrarily, a quasi-experimental analysis could be fruitfully combined with an operant method of research. Lempert[135] has discussed the application of such an analysis to legal impact, and Campbell and Ross[136] have provided one impressive example of how such an analysis can be used to assess the effects of alterations in speeding sentences. Criminologists have rarely used the quasi-experimental method, but it deserves the most careful attention.

CONCLUSION

This article has considered the implications laboratory studies of punishment might have for punitive treatments of criminals, has drawn parallels between laboratory operations and actual conditions of punishment of criminals, and has suggested reforms based on the experimental results. While generalizing from experimental studies in basic science to an applied field involves risks, the parallels and suggestions made here ought at least to point in proper directions. The suggestions about effective treatments generally have been made without regard for ethical considerations. Professionals in the criminological sciences are most competent to decide the final form of any concrete implementations of the suggested reforms, and both the professionals and the public must decide the ethical issues involved. In addition this Article has stressed the importance of assessing the effectiveness of our present, traditional criminal treatments or of any new, experimental treatments by rigorous field research.

Punishment is clearly an effective means of eliminating behavior; under ideal conditions manipulating severity can provide any desired degree of suppression. We must determine what concrete manipulations of severity are effective for criminal treatments of humans.

The results of laboratory studies of punishment suggest many possible legal and societal reforms that may reduce criminal behavior. First, as certainty and immediacy are among the most important ideal punishment conditions, by accelerating our legal processes we can increase the effectiveness of punishment. Second, considerations of secondary punishment and compensatory recovery suggest that we should provide offenders with reminders of punishment during the pretrial period and after prison, and that we might administer provisional or symbolic punishment immediately at the time and place of the crime. Third, based upon the experimental operation of extinction, the elimination of opportunities to commit or profit from crimes could markedly reduce criminal behavior. Fourth, as the effectiveness of punishment decreases as the control by the organism punished increases, the elimination of parole may be appropriate. Fifth, as the suppression of strongly established behavioral tendencies requires more severe punishment, sentence severity should be a function of the strength of criminal behavior, and we should punish recidivists increasingly more severely. Sixth, as the desire to escape from fears and anxieties may motivate the alcoholic and the drug addict and as incarceration may increase those very fears and anxieties, especially the physiological tensions associated with the addiction itself, punishment of alcoholics and drug addicts by incarceration might actually increase alcoholism and drug addiction. Seventh, the fact that most of the ill effects of punishment arise where the organism receives random and unavoidable punishment, without any possibility of escape or reward through alternative behavior, and the fact that the effectiveness of a given punishment is dramatically increased by the provision of an alternative route to reward, strongly indicate the importance of combining rehabilitation with punishment. Eighth, response cost results and some field evidence suggest that we "make the punishment fit the crime." Ninth, success with clinical aversion therapy indicates that its extension to the treatment of many criminal offenses would be appropriate. Tenth, theories of punishment suggest that punishments should occur in an everyday environment, in and by the community.

Punishment is a burgeoning scientific field. In five or ten years researchers will have fleshed out the experimental results and will have made important theoretical advances. Hopefully, the criminological disciplines will pay careful attention to these contributions. However, they should not limit their inquiries to the field of punishment. They should also consider in detail other pertinent topics from the human biological sciences: Genetics. Is criminal behavior inheritable, and if so, how? What are the criminological implications of Klinefelter's syndrome?[137] Experimental Psychology. How do crowded living quarters affect organisms and how does this bear on the crime problems in our cities? How do the basic mechanisms of conscience, guilt, and remorse operate? What are the developmental causes of abnormal or criminal behavior in animals? How can aggression be learned? Ethology. What mechanisms do animals have to prevent intra-species violence? What do we know about animal aggression? How is human aggression similar or potentially so? Physiology. What parts of the brain control violence and aggression? How can this knowledge help us? What chemicals can suppress anger and violence? How can we best use them? The potential is vast.

NOTES

1. R. ULRICH, I. STACHNIK & J. MABRY, CONTROL OF HUMAN BEHAVIOR (1966).
2. Immergluck, *Determinism-Freedom in Contemporary Psychology*, 19 AM. PSYCHOLOGIST 270 (1964); Grunbaum, *Causality and the Science of Behavior*, 40 AM. SCIENTIST 665 (1952); Boring, *When is Human Behavior Predetermined?*, 84 SCIENTIFIC MONTHLY 189 (1957). There is nothing in this approach which need contradict legal notions of "responsibility" or "diminished capacity." These notions may appropriately have the same heuristic value in law as determinism does in psychology, and may be construed as an attempt to specify the causal determinants of behavior more precisely, as when we decide whether an habitual shoplifter's behavior is determined by greed or by a neurotic compulsion.

3. This topic deserves a more extensive treatment than can be given here. A number of readable current accounts give the flavor of the biologist's view. *See, e.g.,* D. Morris, The Naked Ape (1967); Tinbergen, *On War and Peace in Animals and Man,* 160 Science 1411 (1968); S. Carrighar, Wild Heritage (1965); K. Lorenz, On Aggression (1966).

4. Karsh & Williams, *Punishment and Reward in Children's Instrumental Learning,* 1 Psychonomic Science 359 (1964). *See also* B. Campbell & R. Church, Punishment and Aversive Behavior App. I (1969); Aronfreed, *Aversive Control of Socialization,* 16 Neb. Symposium on Motivation 271, 308-09 (1968).

5. Krech, *The Chemistry of Learning,* 51 Saturday Review, Jan. 20, 1968, at 48; Harlow, *The Heterosexual Affectional System in Monkeys,* 17 Am. Psychologist 1 (1962); Harlow & Harlow, *Social Deprivation in Monkeys,* 207 Scientific American 137 (1962).

6. Spitz, *Anaclitic Depression,* in 2 The Psychoanalytic Study of the Child (1946).

7. K. Menninger, The Crime of Punishment (1968).

8. Church, *Response Suppression,* in B. Campbell & R. Church, *supra* note 4; Wagner, *Frustrative Nonreward,* in *id.*; McMillan, *A Comparison of the Punishing Effects of Response-Produced Shock and Response Produced Time Out,* 10 J. Experimental Analysis of Behavior 439 (1967); Leitenberg, *Is Time-Out from Positive Reinforcement an Aversive Event? A Review of the Experimental Evidence,* 64 Psychological Bull. 428 (1965).

9. H. Eysenck, Crime and Personality (1964); H. Eysenck, *Crime, Conscience and Conditioning,* in Fact and Fiction in Psychology (1965); Jeffrey, *Criminal Behavior and Learning Theory,* 56 J. Crim. L.C. & P.S. 294 (1965).

10. See text accompanying notes 76-77 *infra.*

11. A. Bandura & R. Walters, Social Learning and Personality Development (1964). *See also* Church, *Emotional Reactions of Rats to the Pain of Others,* 52 J. Comparative and Physiological Psychology 132 (1959).

12. B. Skinner, The Behavior of Organisms (1938).

13. Estes, *An Experimental Study of Punishment,* 57 Psychological Monographs 263 (1944).

14. B. Skinner, Science and Human Behavior (1953).

15. J. Conrad, Crime and Its Correction (1965); Appel & Peterson, *What's Wrong with Punishment?,* 56 J. Crim. L.C. & P.S. 450 (1965); Jeffrey, *supra* note 9. In fairness to these authors it must be pointed out that they were writing for the most part just before the current research boom in the field of punishment.

16. Azrin & Holz, *Punishment,* in Operant Behavior (W. Honig ed. 1966); Solomon, *Punishment,* 19 Am. Psychologist 239 (1964).

17. Solomon, *supra* note 16.

18. *Id.;* Appel & Peterson, *supra* note 15.

19. Solomon, *supra* note 16.

20. Azrin & Holz, *supra* note 16.

21. Punishment: Issues and Experiments (E. Boe & R. Church eds. 1968); B. Campbell & R. Church, *supra* note 4; Aversive Conditioning and Learning (F. Brush ed.) (in preparation).

22. Campbell & Masterson, *Psychophysics of Punishment,* in B. Campbell & R. Church, *supra* note 4.

23. Problems of assessing our treatment effects will be discussed later. See text accompanying footnotes 122-37 *infra.*

24. Azrin & Holz, *supra* note 16.

25. Estes, *Outline of a Theory of Punishment*, in B. CAMPBELL & R. CHURCH, *supra* note 4.

26. Azrin & Holz, *supra* note 16.

27. It is seldom that the housebreaker finds nothing to reinforce his efforts.

28. Shah, *Treatment of Offenders: Some Behavorial Concepts, Principles and Approaches*, 30 FED. PROBATION 29 (1966). *See also* the discussion of reducing criminal opportunities in PRESIDENT'S COMM'N ON LAW ENFORCEMENT AND ADMINISTRATION OF JUSTICE, TASK FORCE REPORT: CORRECTIONS 261 (1967).

29. Shah, *supra* note 28, at 32.

30. Personal communication from Dennis J. O'Connor, Manager, Public Information and Advertising Department, AC Transit, Oakland, California, May, 1969.

31. Azrin & Holz, *supra* note 16; Solomon, *supra* note 16.

32. Jeffrey, *supra* note 9.

33. See text accompanying note 11 *supra*.

34. Azrin & Holz, *supra* note 16.

35. J. ARONFREED, CONDUCT AND CONSCIENCE 39 (1968).

36. Church, *supra* note 8. A sole exception to this rule is punishment by induced nausea, which can cause an organism permanently to shun a food eaten hours before the onset of the sickness. See Garcia, Ervin & Koelling, *Learning with Prolonged Delay of Reinforcement*, 5 PSYCHONOMIC SCIENCE 121 (1966). This supports the contention that consummatory behaviors are abnormally sensitive to punishment. See note 83 *infra*.

37. Vogel-Sprott, *Suppression of a Rewarded Response by Punishment as a Function of Reinforcement Schedules*, 5 PSYCHONOMIC SCIENCE 395 (1966).

38. Church, *supra* note 8.

39. Cohen, *Response Suppression as a Function of Delay and Intensity of Punishment*, 28 DISSERTATION ABSTRACTS 1704 (1967).

40. Church, *supra* note 8.

41. Solomon, Turner & Lessac, *Some Effects of Delay of Punishment on Resistance to Temptation in Dogs*, 8 J. PERSONALITY & SOCIAL PSYCHOLOGY, 233-38 (1968).

42. We do not know whether this is true in fact. See text accompanying notes 122-37 *infra*.

43. H. EYSENCK, CRIME AND PERSONALITY (1964). Eysenck's law that immediate rewards will influence an organism much more than a delayed punishment is not quite accurate. In a series of experiments directly comparing the two, Renner (Renner & Specht, *The Relative Desirability or Aversiveness of Immediate or Delayed Food and Shock*, 75 J. EXPERIMENTAL PSYCHOLOGY 568 (1967)) has shown that punishment can reach farther back in time than reward; *i.e.*, punishment's effects do not fall off as steeply with delay as do reward's. We might say that in this respect Nature is on the side of society. However, for criminal behavior, where the rewards are actually immediate and the punishments uncertain and considerably delayed, Eysenck's law is no doubt true.

44. E. WIKE, SECONDARY REINFORCEMENT (1966); G. KIMBLE, HILGARD AND MARQUIS' CONDITIONING AND LEARNING (1961).

45. Church, *supra* note 8, at 136-40. *See also* the literature on "Conditioned Emotional Response" (CER). A brief review may be found in J. DEESE & S. HULSE, THE PSYCHOLOGY OF LEARNING (1967). A more thorough and recent discussion is Hoffman, *Stimulus Factors in Conditioned Suppression*, in B. CAMPBELL & R. CHURCH, *supra* note 4.

46. H. EYSENCK, *supra* note 9.

47. *See, e.g.*, PRESIDENT'S COMM'N ON LAW ENFORCEMENT AND ADMINISTRATION OF JUSTICE, THE CHALLENGE OF CRIME IN A FREE SOCIETY (1967); Wallerstein & Wyle, *Our Law-Abiding Law Breakers*, 25 PROBATION 107 (1947).

48. J. ARONFREED, *supra* note 35, at 169.

49. H. EYSENCK, *supra* note 9; Jeffrey, *supra* note 9.

50. THE CHALLENGE OF CRIME IN A FREE SOCIETY, *supra* note 47.

51. TASK FORCE REPORT: CORRECTIONS, *supra* note 28.

52. Jeffrey, *supra* note 9.

53. See text accompanying note 39 *supra*.

54. Jeffrey, *supra* note 9; Campbell & Ross, *The Connecticut Crackdown on Speeding,* 3 L. & SOC. REV. 33 (1968).

55. We could apply these procedures to highly visible crimes such as assault, looting, breaking and entering, pickpocketing, lewd behavior, purse-snatching, trespassing, theft, etc. One possibility is suggested by the recent experimental innovation by the San Francisco Police Department of "booking" suspects on the spot when apprehended for engaging in crimes such as those mentioned above. Such "bookings" are an indictment and a notice to appear in court and carry no formal punitive implications, but they might come to have punitive effect in the same way that traffic tickets, also secondary punishments, seem to.

56. Leitenberg, *Response Initiation and Response Termination: Analysis of Effects of Punishment and Escape Contingencies,* 16 PSYCHOLOGICAL REPORTS, 569 (1965); Leitenberg, *Punishment Training With and Without an Escape Contingency,* J. EXPERIMENTAL PSYCHOLOGY 393 (1967).

57. Estes, *supra* note 13; Solomon, *supra* note 16.

58. Police records, personal investigation, the offender's own testimony, or the circumstances of the crime itself could serve as independent determinants of the strength of criminal behavior.

59. Azrin & Holz, *supra* note 16, at 393.

60. Church, *supra* note 8.

61. Rachlin & Herrnstein, *Hedonism Revisited,* in B. CAMPBELL & R. CHURCH *supra* note 4.

62. Estes, *supra* note 25.

63. Seward, *The Role of Conflict in Experimental Neurosis,* in B. CAMPBELL, & R. CHURCH, *supra* note 4.

64. Fitzgerald & Walloch, *Resistance to Extinction of a Punished Wheel-Turning Escape Response in Rats,* 68 J. COMPARATIVE & PHYSIOLOGICAL PSYCHOLOGY 254 (1969).

65. E. HILGARD & R. ATKINSON, INTRODUCTION TO PSYCHOLOGY 242-43 (1967); Azrin & Holz, *supra* note 16; Appel & Peterson, *supra* note 15.

66. See Aronfreed, *supra* note 4, for a very thorough review of punishment in child rearing. *See also* J. ARONFREED, *supra* note 35.

67. Azrin & Holz, *supra* note 16.

68. 1967 UNIFORM CRIME REP. 41.

69. P. KEVE, IMAGINATIVE PROGRAMMING IN PROBATION AND PAROLE (1967).

70. Fowler, *Suppression and Facilitation by Response Contingent Shock,* in AVERSIVE CONDITIONING AND LEARNING, *supra* note 21.

71. Wagner, *Frustrative Nonreward: 4 Variety of Punishment,* in B. CAMPBELL & R. CHURCH, *supra* note 4. *See also* Brown & Wagner, *Resistance to Punishment and Extinction Following Training with Shock or Non-Reinforcement,* 68 J. EXPERIMENTAL PSYCHOLOGY 503 (1964).

72. See text accompanying notes 26-30 *supra*.

73. Fowler, *supra* note 70; Brown, *Factors Influencing Self-Punitive Behavior,* in B. CAMPBELL & R. CHURCH, *supra* note 4.

74. Brown, *supra* note 73.

75. *See generally* 1967 UNIFORM CRIME REP.

76. G. KIMBLE & A. GARMEZY, PRINCIPLES OF GENERAL PSYCHOLOGY 252-53 (1963); H. LINDGREN, D. BYRNE & L. PETRINOVICH, PSYCHOLOGY 58-59 (1966).

77. Azrin & Holz, *supra* note 16.

78. Weiss & Strongman, *Shock-Induced Response Bursts and Suppressions,* 15 PSYCHONOMIC SCIENCE 238 (1969); B. SKINNER, *supra* note 12, at 151.

79. See text accompanying notes 86-94 *infra.*

80. N. MAIER, FRUSTRATION (1949).

81. Masserman (J. MASSERMAN, BEHAVIOR AND NEUROSIS (1943)), in another classic series of experiments, showed that various punishments administered to cats and monkeys at the moment before the ingestion of food would traumatize them so severely that they would later panic at the sight of food and would commonly starve to death before eating again. Solomon (Solomon, *supra* note 16) has remarked that such traumas as a result of punishment seem to be surprisingly characteristic of consummatory behaviors and has obtained similar results with dogs (Solomon *et al., supra* note 41). However, Solomon's conclusion has been challenged (Seward, *supra* note 65) and the interaction of punishment with consummatory behavior is presently in doubt (but see note 35 *supra*). In any case, such results seem to have little bearing on treatment of criminal behaviors, since eating or drinking are seldom criminal offenses, and in any case the offender is not punished at the moment of ingestion.

There are some experimental results to the effect that when a habit is very strong, punishment may tend to fixate it and make it difficult to unlearn or reverse when it is desirable to do so (Lohr, *The Effect of Shock on the Rat's Choice of a Path to Food,* 58 J. EXPERIMENTAL PSYCHOLOGY 312 (1959); Farber, *Response Fixation Under Anxiety and Non-Anxiety Conditions,* 38 J. EXPERIMENTAL PSYCHOLOGY 111 (1948)). There are as yet few experimental results showing the phenomenon, so its existence, causal conditions, and importance are still in doubt.

82. Maier, Seligman & Solomon, *Pavlovian Fear Conditioning and Learned Helplessness,* in B. CAMPBELL & R. CHURCH, *supra* note 4; Seligman, Maier, & Solomon, *Unpredictable and Uncontrollable Aversive Events,* in AVERSION CONDITIONING AND LEARNING, *supra* note 21.

83. Maier, Seligman & Solomon, *supra* note 82, at 333-35.

84. Azrin & Holz, *supra* note 16.

85. Hunt & Brady, *Some Effects of Punishment and Intercurrent "Anxiety" on a Simple Operant,* 48 J. COMPARATIVE & PHYSIOLOGICAL PSYCHOLOGY 305 (1955).

86. Solomon, *supra* note 16; Solomon *et al., supra* note 41.

87. Fowler & Wischner, *The Varied Functions of Punishment in Discrimination Learning,* in B. CAMPBELL & R. CHURCH, *supra* note 4.

88. Rachlin, *The Effect of Shock Intensity on Concurrent and Single-Key Responding in Concurrent Chain Schedules,* 10 J. EXPERIMENTAL ANALYSIS OF BEHAVIOR 87 (1967).

89. Solomon *et al., supra* note 41; Fowler, *supra* note 70.

90. Azrin & Holz, *supra* note 16, at 391-92.

91. Miller & Weiss, *Effects of the Somatic or Visceral Responses to Punishment,* in B. CAMPBELL & R. CHURCH, *supra* note 4.

92. Seligman, Maier & Solomon, *supra* note 82.

93. Azrin & Holz, *supra* note 16; Weiner, *Some Effects of Response Cost Upon Human Operant Behavior,* 5 J. EXPERIMENTAL ANALYSIS OF BEHAVIOR 201 (1962); A. BANDURA, PRINCIPLES OF BEHAVIOR MODIFICATION 341-46 (1969).

94. TASK FORCE REPORT: CORRECTIONS, *supra* note 51, at 78. On an anecdotal level, is it more effective to scold or spank a child for abusing his toys, or to temporarily take the toys away from him until he will play with them properly?

95. Behavior or reinforcement therapy is a clinical treatment based on learning

principles. Criminologists and penologists have recognized its potential for some time, and some correctional institutions have begun behavior oriented programs. See Hutchinson, *Behavior Theory, Behavior Science and Treatment*, 10 CANADIAN J. CORRECTIONS 388 (1968); Konietzko, *Psychological Aspects of Institutional Incentive Systems*, 47 PRISON J. 43 (1967); Shah, *Treatment of Offenders: Some Behavioral Concepts, Principles, and Approaches*, 30 FED. PROBATION 29 (1966).

96. An excellent review of aversion therapy may be found in the *Miami Symposium on the Prediction of Behavior 1967*. Bucher & Lovaas, *Use of Aversive Stimulation in Behavior Modification*, in M. JONES, MIAMI SYMPOSIUM ON THE PREDICTION OF BEHAVIOR 1967: AVERSIVE STIMULATION (1968). *See also* S. RACHMAN & J. TEASDALE, AVERSION THERAPY AND BEHAVIOR DISORDERS (1969). Discussions and examples of aversion therapy are also frequent in the criminological literature. Vietor, *Conditioning as a Form of Psychotherapy in Treating Delinquents: Some Data from the Literature*, 7 EXCERPTA CRIMINOLOGICA 3 (1967); Kushner & Sandler, *Aversion Therapy and the Concept of Punishment*, 4 BEHAVIOR RESEARCH AND THERAPY 179 (1966). An interesting aspect of such discussions is the parallel which has been drawn between aversion therapy procedures and the normal processes by which guilt or conscience may be said to develop. *See, e.g.*, Vietor's discussion of Eysenck's ideas about the growth of conscience; Bucher & Lovaas, *supra* note 96. Solomon and Mowrer have also written extensively on the conditioning of guilt and conscience.

97. Bucher & Lovaas, *supra* note 96.

98. Solomon *et al.*, *supra* note 41.

99. Hearst, *Aversive Conditioning and External Stimulus Control*, in B. CAMPBELL & R. CHURCH, *supra* note 4.

100. Hoffman, *supra* note 45.

101. Bucher & Lovaas, *supra* note 96. *See also* Lovaas' motion picture, "Teaching Mute and Echolalic Children to Speak" (Appleton-Century-Crofts 1969).

102. Birnbrauer, *Generalization of Punishment Effects—A Case Study*, 1 J. APPLIED BEHAVIOR ANALYSIS 201 (1968).

103. Treatment consists, for example, of associating shock with pictures of nude males for male homosexuals, or associating alcohol with severe nausea for alcoholics.

104. Kellam, *Shoplifting Treated by Aversion to a Film*, 7 BEHAVIOR RESEARCH & THERAPY 125 (1969).

105. Hearst, *supra* note 99.

106. Bandura (A. BANDURA, *supra* note 93, at 346-48, 508-09) is optimistic about the potential durability of such treatments, given the proper procedures. See also note 100 *supra*.

107. Bucher & Lovaas, *supra* note 96.

108. Very similar proposals have been made by J.V. McConnell in his article *Criminals Can be Brainwashed—Now*, 3 PSYCHOLOGY TODAY 14-18, 74 (1969).

109. Bucher & Lovaas, *supra* note 96.

110. Bandura's (A. BANDURA, *supra* note 93, at 317) comments on the perception of punishment in a treatment context are relevant here, and are also pertinent to the previous discussion of the importance of rehabilitation.

111. Miller, *Learning of Visceral and Glandular Responses*, 163 SCIENCE 434 (1969).

112. *Id. See also* Cara, *Learning in the Autonomic Nervous System*, 222 SCIENTIFIC AMERICAN 30 (1968). An equally promising and related development is Kamiya's demonstration of conscious control over brain waves, which in turn affect serenity of emotions. *See, e.g.*, Kamiya, *Conscious control of brain waves*, 1 PSYCHOLOGY TODAY 56 (1968).

113. Johnson & Schwartz, *Suppression of GSR Activity Through Operant Reinforcement*, 75 J. EXPERIMENTAL PSYCHOLOGY 307 (1967). *See also* Shapiro *et al.*, *Ef-*

fects of Feedback and Reinforcement on the Control of Human Systolic Blood Pressure, 163 SCIENCE 588 (1969).

114. H. EYSENCK, *supra* note 9. For chemical control of criminal neural functioning, see Schacter & Latane, *Crime, Cognition and the Autonomic Nervous System*, NEBRASKA SYMPOSIUM ON MOTIVATION 221-27 (D. Levine ed. 1964). Delgado, in a forthcoming issue of BRAIN, BEHAVIOR AND EVOLUTION, describes how a computer monitored and selectively reinforced the brain activity of chimpanzees so that they became unusually placid.

115. See text accompanying notes 61-64 *supra.*

116. Solomon *et al., supra* note 41.

117. TASK FORCE REPORT: CORRECTIONS, *supra* note 51.

118. *Id.*

119. *See* M. MEAD, COMING OF AGE IN SAMOA (1928).

120. Minutely inadequate research funding and lack of public interest in such research, for instance, are two important variables over which professionals in the criminological fields have no control. Also mentioned by the *President's Commission Report* (*supra* note 47) are defensiveness and inertia on the part of criminological professionals, a simple lack of trained research personnel, and the indifference of higher education to criminological problems. "Technology transfer" is also cited by Kramer in his article *Criminal Justice R & D: New Agency Stresses Police Over Corrections*, 163 SCIENCE 588 (1969), which is an excellent review of the current status of criminological research and·its associated problems.

121. J. CONRAD, *supra* note 15; Shah, *supra* note 28; *Special Issue: Research*, 18 YOUTH AUTHORITY Q. (1965). Cressey has been most emphatic and detailed about the problems discussed below in his article, *The Nature and Effectiveness of Correctional Techniques*, in L. HAZELRIGG, PRISON WITHIN SOCIETY 349-74 (1968).

122. Meyer, *Reflections on Some Theories of Punishment*, 59 J. CRIM. L.C. & P.S. 595 (1968).

123. Bailey, *Correctional Outcomes: An Evaluation of 100 Reports*, 57 J. CRIM. L.C. & P.S. 153 (1966).

124. B. UNDERWOOD, PSYCHOLOGICAL RESEARCH (1957); D. CAMPBELL & J. STANLEY, EXPERIMENTAL AND QUASI-EXPERIMENTAL DESIGNS FOR RESEARCH (1963). An ex post facto matching design attempts to overcome an initial non-random selection of experimental and control groups. Because of known differences in recidivism tendencies among socioeconomic and racial groups, or because of biases along dimensions that we may or may not actually have evidence on, courts will tend to send middle-class, well-educated Caucasians to liberal treatment programs and ghetto juveniles to prison or to a reformatory. Given this initial difference in population, we can not then simply compare the total recidivism rate of prison releases with that of forest camp graduates and imagine that this will tell us something about the effects of the two programs rather than the different tendencies of the two populations who were selected for the programs, tendencies which they possessed to begin with. A matching design attempts a valid comparison in this situation by finding subjects in the two programs who happen to be "equal" on indices such as education, social class, etc., which are known to be related to crime, and assuming that these subjects constitute initially equivalent groups. A serious difficulty with this procedure, however, is that we do not know many of the factors which affect criminal tendencies, and even if we match on numerous relevant indices, we may have missed some relevant ones, and· these may have been just those factors used by the courts in differentially assigning subjects. The courts do not keep explicit records detailing the basis of their assignment, and the basis of assignment may be unknown even to them. Thus a particular judge may unconsciously tend to assign juveniles to different treatments on the basis of personality, appearance, or manners, which would not be expected to come to the researcher's attention. Nor would they

ordinarily match on these factors. Yet these factors may be important determinants of criminal behavior. A matching design in this case, then, would be futile and harmfully misleading. There is no way to completely overcome such difficulties in ex post facto matching designs.

125. Scarpitti & Stephenson, *A Study of Probation Effectiveness*, 59 J. CRIM. L.C. & P.S. 361 (1968).

126. H. EYSENCK, *supra* note 9.

127. A fuller explanation of these statistical problems can be found in the following references: Thorndike, *Regression Fallacies in the Matched Group Experiment*, 7 PSYCHOMETRIKA 85 (1942); D. CAMPBELL & J. STANLEY, *supra* note 124; Campbell & Clayton, *Avoiding Regression Effects in Panel Studies of Communication Impact*, 3 STUDIES IN PUB. COMMUNICATION 99 (1961).

128. CAL. YOUTH AUTHORITY, *The Status of Current Research in the California Youth Authority* (1968). The community treatment program is also less expensive than the reformatory.

129. Sometimes, for instance, offenders averaged less time in the community treatment program than in the reformatory, and time in any sort of treatment may be the actual determining factor.

130. Campbell, *Reforms as Experiments*, 24 AM. PSYCHOLOGIST 409 (1969).

131. M. SIDMAN, TACTICS OF SCIENTIFIC RESEARCH (1960).

132. For example, I am quite certain that traffic tickets effectively deter students from parking in the campus faculty lot outside my window, even though the student lot is a mile from campus, because every semester during a two-day period in which parking stickers are sold and tickets are therefore suspended, the lot is filled with illegally parked student cars. Before and after the two day period, when tickets are assigned, the lot is devoid of student cars.

133. Schwartz, *The Effect in Philadelphia of Pennsylvania's Increased Penalties for Rape and Attempted Rape*, 59 J. CRIM. L.C. & P.S. 590 (1968).

134. Campbell, *supra* note 130; D. CAMPBELL & J. STANLEY, *supra* note 124.

135. Lempert, *Strategies of Research Design in the Legal Impact Study*, 1 L. & SOC'Y REV. 111 (1966).

136. Campbell & Ross, *The Connecticut Crackdown on Speeding*, 3 L. & SOC'Y REV. 33 (1968). In 1955 Governor Ribicoff of Connecticut, concerned about the high incidence of highway fatalities which he believed were due to speeding, increased the sentence for a speeding conviction from an haphazardly enforced loss of "points" to mandatory suspension of license for 30-90 days. Traffic fatalities declined over the next year. It is important to determine whether or not this decline was actually due to the institution of stiffer penalties. Since there was no unchanged, isolated "control group," exactly equivalent to the Connecticut population but not subject to the increase in penalty, we have no direct comparison on which to base a claim. The decrease in fatalities could have been due to any number of uncontrolled factors, such as safer cars being built in 1956, better weather in Connecticut that year, etc. A quasi-experimental analysis attempts to classify all possible alternative hypotheses in a dozen or so general categories, and uses sophisticated, detailed analysis to determine whether a given category could plausibly account for the effect in question. If none can, we can reasonably conclude that the manipulated factor—in this instance the speeding penalty—had the intended effect. For the case in question Campbell and Ross considered the hypotheses of better weather that year, better roads and cars, improved medical care for accident victims, publicizing of the 1955 death rate, a change in record-keeping procedures, chance variance in measurements, and statistical regression effects. Their chief mode of analysis is an "interrupted time series" design, in which indices of the various hypothesized factors above are plotted for several years before and after the sentencing increase and statistical analyses are applied. They use the same pro-

cedures in examining fatalities in neighboring states as an additional check on consistency of analysis. Campbell and Ross conclude that the harsher penalty was enforced to some extent, but that the increase in sentence severity led to a decrease in the willingness of the courts and police to enforce speeding penalties and in the willingness of the convicted offender to obey the sentence. Because of the possibility of statistical regression, they are unable to attribute the decline in fatalities to the increase in sentence severity. Although their analysis is quite comprehensive and detailed, it is meant only to be illustrative of a serious attempt at quasi-experimental analysis.

137. This refers to the possible linkage between chromosomal abnormalities and criminal predilections. *See,* e.g., Montagu, *Chromosomes and Crime,* 2 PSYCHOLOGY TODAY 42 (1968); Telfer *et al., Incidence of Gross Chromosomal Errors Among Tall Criminal American Males,* 159 SCIENCE 1249 (1968).

CLASSIFICATION OF OFFENDERS AS AN AID TO EFFICIENT MANAGEMENT AND EFFECTIVE TREATMENT

Marguerite Q. Warren

Recent years have brought an increased impetus to thinking about classification systems and typologies[1] of criminals and delinquents. Among the several forces contributing to this development, two stand out. One force has come from developing research programs. As in other fields, scientific progress in the field of corrections depends on reducing the infinite variety of problems through conceptualization.

Research efforts attacking the problems of the field systematically have required some sort of theoretical framework, either a framework which focuses on the etiology of criminal and delinquent behavior, or at least a framework which charts in an organized fashion signs, symptoms, or dynamics of patterns covering the universe of offenders.

The second impetus to offender categorization has come with the switch from custody emphasis to treatment emphasis in handling offenders and with the disappointments regarding the total effectiveness of some attempted treatment programs. Like the humanitarian reform movement itself, trade training, increased facilities for socially acceptable outlets of aggression, and individual and group counseling have each been thought of as *the* answer to the crime problem. While movements in behalf of these causes have undoubtedly made important contributions to the field of corrections, they have tended to be viewed as cure-alls, and it is a matter of record that we do not cure all delinquents and criminals.

RATIONALE FOR CLASSIFICATION

One of the few facts agreed upon in the field of corrections is that offenders are not all alike. That is, they differ from each other not only in the form of their offense, but also in the reasons for and the meaning of their crime. Some individuals violate the law because the peer group, upon which they depend for approval, prescribes criminal behavior as the price of acceptance, or because the values, which they have internalized, are those of a deviant subculture. Other individuals break laws because of insufficient socialization, which leaves them at the mercy of all but the most protected environments. Still others delinquently act out internal conflicts, identity struggles, or family crises. This list is of course illustrative, not exhaustive.

Much of the literature in this field is still written as if all offenders are alike. Many causal theories purporting to explain delinquency have described only one segment of the total offender population and have concluded, for example, that delinquency is a peer group phenomenon. Differential association theories,[2] social disorganization theories,[3] role theories,[4] and psychogenic theories[5] all appear to have a certain amount of validity when applied to some segment of the offender population, but none of these theories alone is sufficiently complex to account for the total observable range of causal factors.

Program prescriptions as well have tended to be made in an across-the-board fashion, with increased staff-offender ratios, improved job opportunities, or insight therapy recommended for all. Although some action programs have been aimed at specific segments of the heterogeneous offender population (for example, psychiatric treatment for the emotionally disturbed delinquent), few programs indeed have based their goals for intervention and their treatment and management prescriptions on a specified rationale for handling differentially the varieties of offender problems which appear in a correctional setting.

A comment should perhaps be made with regard to an extreme opposite position taken by some treatment-oriented people who have emphasized the great differences between offenders and have resisted any schematization on the basis of loss of meaningful information about individuals. Although this position guards against the mistake of administering the same kind of treatment to all offenders, it requires an infinite variety of treatments to fit the uniqueness of each case. This position almost precludes conceptualizing the delinquency problem, developing intervention theories and practices, and instigating research investigations. As such, the position must be rejected.

Theoreticians, practitioners and researchers increasingly seek some classification system, some meaningful grouping of offenders into categories, which offers (1) a step in the direction of explanatory theory with the resulting aid to prediction which follows from understanding, (2) implications for efficient management and effective treatment decisions, and (3) greater precision for maximally effective research.

TYPOLOGIES OF CRIMINALS AND DELINQUENTS

Systems of offender classification might be grouped in several ways. One such grouping, based on the nature of the underlying dimensions crucial to the classification system, follows.[6]

1. Prior probability approaches represented by the Borstal studies,[7] the California Youth Authority,[8] the Department of Corrections Base Expectancy studies,[9] the Glueck prediction tables,[10] and the configuration analysis procedures represented by Glaser.[11]

2. Reference group typologies represented by Schrag[12] and Sykes[13] and the social class typologies represented by W. Miller.[14]

3. Behavior classifications (covering a wide range of specificity from offense types to conformity-nonconformity dichotomies) represented by

Roebuck,[15] McCord, McCord and Zola,[16] Ohlin,[17] and Reckless.[18]

4. Psychiatric-oriented approaches represented by the work of Jenkins and Hewitt,[19] Redl,[20] Erikson,[21] Aichorn,[22] Makkay,[23] Reiss,[24] Argyle,[25] Bloch and Flynn,[26] and the Illinois State Training School Treatment Committee.[27]

5. Social perception and interaction classifications of Gough and Peterson,[28] Hunt and Hardt,[29] Sarbin,[30] Peterson, Quay and Cameron,[31] Gibbons,[32] Studt,[33] MacGregor,[34] Sullivan, Grant and Grant,[35] Warren,[36] and Russon.[37]

Several of the investigators listed under social perception and interaction classification systems might be grouped together on the assumption that their typologies all represent developments in ego psychology, with important underlying concepts identified as stage of ego integration, level of psychosocial development, level of interpersonal maturity, complexity of perceptual differentiation, level of cognitive complexity, etc. Such investigators as Hunt, MacGregor, Makkay, Sarbin, and Warren are currently working on typologies of offenders, utilizing primarily ego psychology concepts.

In addition to the five groupings, some investigators, using a more eclectic approach by including measures of several of the above areas of dimensions, have produced empirical-statistical typologies. Among these investigators are Hurwitz,[38] Jesness,[39] and Palmer.[40] In a recent paper, the Gluecks make a case for this approach and appear to be proceeding to develop a typology in this eclectic manner.[41]

Each of the above classification systems is not equally relevant for all purposes. Some systems concern themselves solely with etiology, others solely with treatment. Some consider precipitating factors, others maintenance factors. Some focus on social organization, some on family organization, some on intrapsychic organization. Some are specific to offender population; others have many domains of applicability. Some are empirical-statistical; some are empirical-observational; some are theoretical models. Some systems represent continua or hierarchies; some are developmental. Some have many more direct treatment implications than do others; some are more fruitful than others in producing research hypotheses.

Clearly, the last word on typologies has not been written yet. Sociologists continue to accuse psychological typologists of taking insufficient cognizance of environmental factors; psychologists continue to accuse sociological typologists of having insufficient regard for intra-psychic factors. Nevertheless, it is now possible to find investigators who are attempting to theoretically link the sociological, psychological, and situational variables which are all relevant to a completely satisfactory taxonomy.

Cloward and Ohlin, in their book *Delinquency and Opportunity: A Theory of Delinquent Gangs*,[42] note that, when identifying the cause of failure in the legitimate system, some individuals blame the social order and others blame themselves. Cloward & Ohlin suggest that this differential perception largely determines what the individual does about his failure. These authors note that attributing failure to the social system is supportive of the delinquent subculture, while attributing failure to self is supportive of the legitimacy of conventional norms. Cloward & Ohlin therefore indicate the need to ". . . identify the types of personality that characteristically attribute causality (for failure) to themselves or to the world without."

In a recent article,[43] Cohen notes that anomie theory must establish a more complete and successful union with role theory and theory of the self. He suggests that anomie theory is concerned with only one structural source of deviance and that other deviant behavior is directly expressive of roles. In seeking a general theory of deviance, he asks:

> Is it possible to make any general statements about the kinds of deviance that may be attributed to anomie and the kinds that may be attributed to role validation through behavior culturally significant of membership in the role? Or may two instances of *any* sort of deviant behavior, identical in their manifest or 'phenotypic' content, differ in their sources or 'genotypic' structure?

In a recent paper,[44] Warren has attempted to identify within the delinquent population those subgroups for which sociological factors (social disorganization, differential association, inadequate access to the legitimate opportunity structure, etc.) appear to have the greatest causal significance, those subgroups for which psychological factors (internal conflict, identity struggles, inadequate socialization, etc.) appear to have the greatest relevance, and those subgroups for which situational factors (acute family crisis, etc.) appear most important in leading to the delinquent act.

As in all science, criminological investigators approached the problem by first looking for the simplest explanation of events. However, as our knowledge has grown, it has become necessary to look at the subject matter in an increasingly complex fashion in order to handle the data that has accumulated.

It is a well accepted principle in psychology that a single behavioral event may stem from a number of different causes or motives, and that any single cause or motive may lead to any one of several different behaviors. That is, the delinquent act as a behavioral event may occur because of a strong youth's agitation of a weak youth, because of an adolescent's need to conform to a peer group's prescription for acceptance, because of the anxiety and despair which a family member feels in a family crisis, because of a youth's need for a car to transport his girl friend to the dance, etc. The behavioral event—a car theft, for example—might have risen from any of the listed causes or still others. With regard to the second part of the psychological principle—that is, that any single causal factor may result in different kinds of behavior—it is possible for one to know much about the causal factors in a particular delinquency and still be unable to ascertain with certainty why the individual committed an act which led to his appearance in the delinquent system rather than committing an act which, for example, led to his appearance in a mental hygiene clinic. There are at least two reasons for belaboring this fairly obvious point. First, there are still those who persist in discussing *the* cause for delinquency or who persist in seeking a cause which will explain "most" of delinquency. Secondly, when the focus is on the management and treatment of offenders, distinguishing among the varieties of causal factors becomes crucial to the establishment of differential goals and methods for transforming offenders into non-offenders.

A classification system for offenders need not serve all purposes in order to be adequate for some purposes. However, certain factors are important in all taxonomies. In addition to the usual criteria expected of a good typology, such as complete coverage of the relevant population, clear-cut, non-overlapping categories, internally meaningful and consistent categories, and parsimoniousness, it is especially important to any classification system used for scientific purposes that the types be sufficiently well defined so that the abstractions can be used with high reliability by trained raters. Beyond these general requirements, it is possible for certain purposes to use a classification system which, for example, has no etiological referents, one which has no implications for treatment, or one which is specific to an institutional setting.

Classification systems which are useful solely for management purposes are distinguishable from those which are more relevant for establishing treatment goals. For purposes of this paper, the term "management" means efficient and effective control over the behavior of the offender so that further law violations are not committed during the period of agency responsibility for the offender. In contrast with "management," the term "treatment" refers to attempts to change the individual offender or the relevant aspects of his environment so that long-term non-violation behavior is assured beyond the period of direct agency responsibility for the offender.

CLASSIFICATION FOR MANAGEMENT PURPOSES

Efficient and effective management in an institutional setting involves protecting those who are weak from those who are strong, those with relatively nondelinquent attitudes from those with strong delinquent orientations, those who are easily agitatable from those who agitate, and those who are non-homosexuals from those who are homosexuals. Since a correctional agency has a mandate to protect the community from offenders, inmates with high escape potential must be identified and placed in maximum security facilities. All of these discriminations imply the need for a classification of offenders on a variety of dimensions. Other areas of management decision which require some classification of inmates in an institutional setting include: open versus closed institutions, single versus dormitory rooms, amount and kinds of punishment, job assignment, time in the institution, use of tranquilizers, custody security level.

In a field setting, management primarily involves control of offenders to prevent further law violations in a way that protects both society and the offender at a "reasonable" price. This means, for example, assigning to high surveillance conditions only those who require constant external controls to prevent crime, and assigning to low surveillance conditions individuals who represent low threat in this regard. It also involves decisions regarding extent of the parolee's freedom to determine his own living arrangements, his job, and his obligations.

All of these management decisions require an implicit or explicit classification system. The difficulty, of course, with an implicit grouping is that there is no way of checking the accuracy or the value of the system; there is no built in self-correcting process. Currently, in the reception and diagnostic centers of many correctional programs, decisions are made with regard to "rehabilitating" a particular offender, using the variety of conditions and programs available to the correctional system. Recommendations for decisions are typically made by intake workers using a subjective weighting of numerous opinions, impressions, and perhaps a few educational and aptitude measures. The basis of the intake worker's judgements may be clear or unclear in his own mind. In either case they are likely based on uncorrected personal biases, since he rarely finds out whether or not his recommendations were, in fact, carried out and, if carried out, whether or not they led to a "rehabilitated" offender. Even if feedback to the intake worker were complete with regard to the effectiveness of his recommendations, as long as the basis for judgements remained implicit and intuitive, the correctional system would benefit only when experienced intake workers were on the job. It is only when recommendations are made on explicit dimensions and expectations that the system has the benefit of checking out expected relationships and passing along relevant information to new and inexperienced workers.

The prior probability approaches, *supra* at 240–41 are examples of classification systems useful for management purposes. Decisions regarding whether a particular offender is to be handled in the community or in an institutional setting may most rationally be made by considering, among other things, the offender's risk of parole violation. Surveillance level on parole and related aspects of caseload size may be determined in part by knowledge of probability of violation. In an interesting experiment in the California Department of Corrections,[45] parolees who represented low risk of parole failure (as predicted by Base Expectancy score) were assigned to minimum supervision caseloads (one contact with parole agent every three months). Violation rates of this experimental group were no higher during a 12-month follow-up than violation rates of a comparable control group which received regular parole supervision.[46]

Prior probability classification systems may be used, not only as an aid to administrative decision-making, but also as a check on whether or not management decisions have the desired effect. In a study reported by Gottfredson,[47] a correctional agency planned to release from an institution somewhat earlier than would be expected a group paroled to special reduced caseloads. The goal involved was that of decreased confinement costs for the selected group without any increase in parole violations. Two prediction classification schemes were needed to control known biases in selecting candidates for special parole programs: (1) a classification of offenders by parole violation risk group, and (2) a classification of expected prison terms under an indeterminate sentence law. Using these two classification systems, the study showed that: overall, men selected for the special program *did not* serve shorter terms; first termers selected for the special program tended to serve less time, while recidivists selected for the special program tended to serve more time; for the total selected group, no differences in parole violation were found; first termers selected tended to have markedly fewer violations during the first year on parole, while recidivists selected tended to have more such violations. Provided with these classification and accounting procedures, it was possible for the administrator to test whether or not paroling decisions had been made consistently with policy objectives.

There are a number of studies using prior probability and psychiatric-oriented classification systems which have implications for the kind of setting in which various subgroups of offenders may best be handled. The Borstal studies[48] and Week's study of Highfields[49] are examples of research showing a relationship between kind of inmate and kind of correctional setting. Both studies show the main advantage of open institutions over closed institutions to be for the better risk inmates. A study by Reiss[50] suggests that all delinquents with relatively strong personal controls should be assigned to home and community placement; whereas, assignments to short terms in institutions or to community placement contingent on case progress should be made for delinquents with relatively weak personal controls; and assignment to closed institutions should be made for those with marked social deterioration or very immature personalities. Beck[51] suggests that Socialized type delinquents should be placed in an open, relaxed, institutional atmosphere best suited to the diversion of their delinquent energy. Unsocialized Aggressive type delinquents should be placed in a controlled institutional environment, since permissiveness will only make this group more difficult to handle. Argyle,[52] among his many recommendations, suggests that the Deviant Identification type delinquent should be separated from his peer group and installed in an essentially nondelinquent environment.

Several of the social perception and interaction classification systems have been used in making management recommendations or decisions. Gibbons[53] bases his typologies of juvenile and adult offenders on patterns of social roles as defined by offense behavior and career, and by self concept and attitudes. Among other management recommendations, Gibbons suggests that Predatory Gang Delinquents be segregated from other boys in order to minimize victimization; that Non-Gang, Casual Delinquents be kept out of the correctional system, *i.e.* merely threatened and released in as much as no intervention is required in such cases; that the Automobile Thief—"Joyrider" be diverted from the "tough guy" pose in an institution by recreational and athletic programs; that Heroin Users be placed in protective environments typified by milieu-management programs such as Synanon; that Overly Aggressive Delinquents be forcibly controlled initially in a residential setting; etc.

Using Warren's Interpersonal Maturity Classification System: Juvenile,[54] Jesness conducted a study[55] in which inmates of a boys' training school

were assigned to living units on the basis of delinquent subtype, and an attempt was made to develop and describe the management techniques most useful in dealing with each subtype. Warren and the staff of the Community Treatment Project have developed a treatment model which defines nine delinquent subtypes and prescribes both differential management and treatment techniques in the community for the various subtypes.[56] The nature of controls to be used by the treatment agent, characteristics of a suitable placement, school, job, and leisure time recommendations are described.

CLASSIFICATION FOR TREATMENT

The function of treatment in a correctional program is to modify the characteristics of the offender and/or the aspects of his environment which are responsible for his involvement in deviant activities. From many treatment prescriptions, it is clear that, in addition to the long-term prevention of law violations, there is also the intent to bring about changes in the offender and in his society which will reduce his cost to society in other ways by, for example, decreasing the chances of the individual's depending on welfare or unemployment rolls, or by increasing the individual's responsibility as a family member and as a citizen.

One source of evidence for the importance of a classification system which differentiates among subgroups of the delinquent population is provided by treatment studies. Studies of the impact of treatment of client populations have been generally discouraging. No one has yet empirically answered Eysenck's challenge that the proportion of mental patients improved following treatment is approximately the same as the spontaneous remission rate.[57] Reviews of the correctional literature tell a similar story—some studies showing the treated to be considerably improved following treatment, some showing negative effects, and most showing no difference. Bailey,[58] in a review of one hundred correctional outcome studies conducted between 1940 and 1959, noted that those studies which exhibited the most rigorous experimental designs reported either more harmful effects of treatment or no change. A fairly typical study is the one which produces contradictory evidence about improvement, with the treated subjects looking improved on some measures of change and either unimproved or in worse condition on other behavioral measures (see, for example, O'Brien[59]).

How should these negative and inconclusive studies be viewed? One possibility is that, in our present state of knowledge, treaters simply don't know how to bring about changes in individuals via:.a treatment process. However, another possible explanation is available, an explanation illustrated by the PICO I study and by the Camp Elliott study. Adams[60] reported on a three-year follow-up of youthful offenders who had taken part in the Pilot Intensive Counseling study, a program of individual interview therapy. Subjects in the study were classified as "amenable" and "non-amenable" to treatment; both groups were then randomly assigned to treatment or nontreatment conditions. Parole performance of the four subgroups was compared on many criteria of performance. The treatment amenable group had a significantly better parole record than the non-treated amenable group. Furthermore, the treated nonamenable group had the poorest parole record of the four subgroups, poorer than either the nontreated amenables or the nontreated nonamenables.

The Camp Elliott study by Grant and Grant[61] investigated an experimental living group program with military offenders. Among the several controlled conditions in this study were the interpersonal maturity levels of individual prisoners in the living and treatment groups and the characteristics of the supervisory team. The most important finding from this study was that the interaction between the maturity level of the subjects and the supervisor characteristics significantly affected later success rate of subjects. Not only were the treatment methods of some internally-oriented supervisory teams effective in increasing the success rates of high maturity offenders, but also, the treatment methods were markedly detrimental to the success chances of low maturity offenders. Furthermore, the externally-oriented supervisory team had the reverse effect on high and low maturity subjects. As long as the data of the Camp Elliott program was used as a study of single variables, its findings were comparable to those of many other correctional studies: that is, no demonstrable treatment (supervisory effectiveness) effect, and only a low, though significant, classification (maturity) effect.

In both the Camp Elliott and the PICO I studies, it was only when the interaction of the treatment and classification variables was considered that one found productive relationships with later success/failure rates. Thus, by lumping together all subjects, the beneficial effects of a treatment program on some subjects, together with the detrimental effects of the same treatment program on other subjects, may each mask and cancel out the other.

It is very likely that, in many treatment studies, this masking effect has occurred, either because the data have not been viewed in sufficiently complex fashion, or because the crucial dimension, the classification of subjects in a treatment-relevant way, was missing. If one accepts the notion that offenders are different from each other in the reasons for their law violations, then it appears rather obvious that attempts to change the offender into a non-offender will vary in ways which are relevant to the cause. Ideally, the goals of the treatment will relate in some direct manner to the causes of the delinquency, and the treatment methods will relate specifically to the goals for the various offender subgroups.

Treatment decisions which must be made by a correctional organization involve in part some of the same issues involved in management decisions. For example, the correctional *setting* may be a treatment tool as well as a management tool. Mueller[62] conducted a study in which "treatment" was defined as the setting in which the offender was handled. The "treatments" available were (a) release to direct parole in the community, (b) forestry camp, and (c) training school. Mueller found differential effects of these treatments over kinds of delinquents. Conforming and over-inhibited boys had higher parole success rates when assigned to non-institutional or open institutional programs. Assigning aggressive or insecure delinquents to any program did not lead to greater success. Subjects least like socialized delinquents and most like emotionally disturbed delinquents were more successful on direct parole, almost as successful in and following camp assignment, and more inclined to fail than succeed in and following a training school experience.

Another group of treatment variables which may be differentially prescribed for various subgroups of offenders relates to the *characteristics of the treater*. An excellent study attempting to match types of probation officers with types of youth on probation was carried out by Palmer.[63] Ratings were made from recorded interviews with officers and probationers, and the ratings were cluster-analyzed. The analyses yielded three distinct empirical groupings of officers and eight groupings of youths. The empirical clusters of probationers were labeled: (a) Communicative-alert, (b) Passive-uncertain, (c) Verbally hostile-defensive, (d) Impulsive-anxious, (e) Dependent-anxious, (f) Independent-assertive, (g) Defiant-indifferent, (h) Wants to be helped and liked. As measured by an index of youths' evaluation of the relationship with their officer and view of the overall effectiveness of probation, a number of interactions between officer type and probationer type were shown. For example, Relationship/Self-expression officers achieved their best results with youths who were Communicative-alert, Impulsive-anxious, or Verbally hostile-defensive. Surveillance/Self-control officers had their greatest difficulties with individuals who were Verbally hostile-defensive or Defiant-indifferent. Surveillance/Self-expressing officers seemed uniquely matched with probationers who wanted to be helped and liked.

A third group of treatment variables which may be differentially prescribed for various subgroups of offenders relates to *characteristics of programs* and *specific therapeutic methods.* Many clinical reports can be found in the literature which suggest differential programs for specified kinds of offenders. To date, few programs have offered any supportive research evidence for stated hypotheses. In the line of recommendations, Jenkins and Hewitt[64] have suggested the following treatment program for the Unsocialized Aggressive delinquent. There should be a warm and accepting attitude on the part of the therapist. He should, in small steps, establish and effectively maintain pressure toward required behavior and against certain objectionable types of behavior. Jenkins and Hewitt believe that the methods suitable for use with the Neurotic child will make the Unsocialized Aggressive child worse; for example, the encouragement of free expression of aggression for this type of child does not help because his well of hostility is bottomless. Jenkins and Hewitt's thinking on the treatment of the Socialized or Adaptive delinquent appears to be based on the assumption that, for this child, the delinquent behavior is a function of social status, role, peer associates, group identifications, and the attitudes and values learned through social contacts. The treatment plan, therefore, is based on the child's fundamental socialization, capacity for loyalty, capacity to identify with a masculine, socialized adult. The methods the authors suggest are somewhat similar to those suggested by Clifford Shaw and his associates in the Area Projects in Chicago for use with the group often known as Cultural delinquents.

In their book, *Origins of Crime*, McCord, McCord and Zola[65] suggest six different treatment plans for six offense types—criminals who commit a wide range of anti-social acts, those who commit crimes against property, those who commit crimes against persons, sex criminals, drunkards, and traffic offenders. The recommended treatment for those who commit crimes against property, for example, centers on the giving of attention and recognition, and on the provision of consistent, nonpunitive discipline.

Also in the line of recommendations for treatment, Gibbons[66] offers suggestions for differential therapeutic methods for his various subtypes defined by social role. For the juvenile subtypes, Gibbons recommends group therapy for Gang de-

linquents and Joyriders, intensive individual psychotherapy for Overly Aggressive delinquents, depth psychotherapy for Behavior Problem delinquents, milieu therapy for Heroin Users, group or individual client-centered counseling and family therapy for Female delinquents, and no treatment for Casual delinquents. For the adult subtypes, Gibbons recommends group therapy for Semiprofessional Property Offenders and Violent Sex Offenders, client-centered counseling for Naive Check Forgers and Nonviolent Sex Offenders, intense individual psychotherapy for "psychopathic" Assaultists, no treatment but help with community adjustment for Professional "Fringe" Violators, Embezzlers, Personal Offenders, and "One Time Losers," and, lastly, altering society so that consistent law enforcement is maintained is recommended treatment for White Collar Criminals.

In an attempt to increase the precision and effectiveness of social casework practice, Freeman, Hildebrand and Ayre,[67] working at the Pittsburgh Family and Childrens Service, have developed a typology of clients with corollary treatment techniques. While this typology is not specific to the offender population, it is an excellent example of a treatment model built from clinical experience and clinical need. The underlying dimension relating the types is a continuum of levels of emotional maturity or ego autonomy. The authors suggest "That the treatment techniques most appropriate to the task of strengthening the coping powers of each type are prescribed by the very nature of the ego structure and the particular stage of ego development."[68] This typology has much in common with the typologies of Hunt,[69] MacGregor,[70] and Warren[71] in that they are all also based on an underlying developmental growth continuum.

MacGregor,[72] in a research study of the families of middle class delinquent youth, has developed a typology of family patterns. Products of the study are a set of propositions by which families may be classified for treatment planning. The family diagnosis, labeled in terms of the arrest in development of the nominal patient, are:

Type A Infantile functioning in adolescence (schizophrenia);

Type B Childish function in adolescence or preadolescence (character disorder), the Autocrats;

Type C Juvenile functioning in adolescence or preadolescence (childhood neurosis), the Intimidated Youth;

Type D Preadolescence functioning in adolescence (adjustment reaction of adolescence), the Rebels.

The bases of the diagnosis involves ratings of such factors as family response to crisis, family relationship with community, family leadership and exploitation, sibling interaction, and family communicative style. The general stated therapeutic goal is to help a family allow its youth to advance beyond the developmental arrest in which all participated. The major method for achieving this goal is multiple impact therapy, i.e., two days of concurrent sessions with varying combinations of therapeutic team and family members.

The following are some treatment recommendations made for Type D: The defiant Rebel should not have his responsibilities diminished. Rebellion should not be encouraged, but respect for the Rebel's opinions and standards should be shown by the treatment team. Identification of the child with the father should be pointed out to the father, and he should be encouraged to offer more open support to his wife.

Treatment recommendations for Type B include: Help the mother to turn to the father, rather than the child, for emotional release, and help the father offer the mother emotional support. Help parents get over fear of exposing themselves to competitive evaluation at home. Encourage father to trust himself to intervene more directly to influence the children. Help mother relinquish her aggressive power role and trust husband's leadership. As a model, treatment team members should demonstrate healthy and vigorous interaction for the parents. Mother should be encouraged to develop interests other than child-rearing. Father-child interaction should be encouraged by having them, in the mother's absence, discuss their dealings with her. Ways of decreasing parental dependence on him should be discussed directly with the child. The Autocrat should be made to see that he is being exploited as much as he is controlling others. The Autocrat should be prepared for the changing balance of forces in the family, and the parents should be prepared to meet the tests of the change which the Autocrat will present.

Based on a theory of socialization—Conceptual Systems,[73] Hunt and Hardt have related developmental stage, i.e., Conceptual Level, to delinquent behavior and delinquent orientations, and have speculated about the implications of the theoretical model for differential treatment of delinquents.[74] Five Conceptual Levels are defined, each level characterizing the person's interpersonal orientation, that is, his knowledge about himself and the relation between himself and others. A major application of the Conceptual System model has occurred in the field of education.[75] Diagnoses of Conceptual Level were made on students in a lower class, junior high school population, and students classified at one of three lowest levels were assigned to classrooms which were homogeneous by developmental stage. Differential management and teaching methods were reported by teachers handling the various groups. On the basis of this study, Hunt defined optimal environments for individuals at the three stages. Since research has shown that these stages bear relationships to delinquent behavior and orientation,[76] Hunt and Hardt have drawn implications from the educational study for the differential treatment of delinquents.

The overall change goal in this system is movement from a lower to a higher conceptual stage. In the context of this general aim, specific suggestions are made regarding treatment methods at each level. For example, boys classified as Sub I "require activities (rather than discussions) focused on the present and organized very clearly."[77] The training agent should offer the Sub I boy "controlled experiences in which he is tangibly responsible for outcomes." For the Stage I boy, the training agent initially should exhibit authority clearly, since persons at this stage are very dependent on normative expectations. Eventually the "agent should attempt to encourage greater self-responsibility and an appreciation of alternative solutions." In working with Stage II boys, the training agent should help the boy discuss his behavior and consider alternative solutions to his problems. A long-term goal for this boy would be to acquire empathy by beginning to understand that some of the feelings of others are similar to his own.

The work of Warren and associates at the California Youth Authority's Community Treatment Project is based on the theory of Levels of Interpersonal Maturity, a formulation describing a sequence of personality integrations in normal childhood development.[78] In many ways similar to the Conceptual System theory, the Interpersonal Maturity Level Classification system focuses upon the ways in which the individual is able to perceive himself and the world, and understand what is happening among others as well as between himself and others. According to the theory, seven successive stages of interpersonal maturity characterize psychological development, ranging from the interpersonal reactions of a new born infant to an ideal of social maturity. Every person does not necessarily work his way through each stage, and may become fixed at any particular level. The range of maturity levels found in an offender population is from Maturity Level 2 (Integration Level 2 or I_2) to Maturity Level 5 (I_5). Level 5 occurs with relative frequency in an adult population, but is rare in a juvenile delinquent population, so that Levels 2 through 4 are sufficient to describe the cases in the Community Treatment Project.

An elaboration of the original classification system was developed by Warren in 1961 for use in the Community Treatment Project (CTP). After assuming that a diagnosis of Maturity Level is identified a group of individuals with a common level of *perceptual differentiation*, it became apparent that not all of the individuals in this group responded to this perceptual level in the same way. An attempt was then made to classify types within each Maturity Level according to *response set*. In this manner, nine delinquent subtypes were identified, i.e., two I_2 subtypes, three I_3 subtypes and four I_4 subtypes. In the 1961 elaboration, the nine subtypes were described by means of item definitions characterizing the manner in which the members of each subgroup perceive the world, and are perceived by others. At the same time, management and treatment plans were prescribed for each subtype. These management and treatment prescriptions grew primarily from the theory, but also, to some extent, from previous work with military offenders[79] and with prison inmates.[80]

Based on the 1961 treatment model, the CTP began to treat serious delinquents in a community setting instead of an institutional setting. In the nine years of the Project's existence, the characteristics items for each subtype have increased and become more detailed, and the treatment strategies have become increasingly specific and realistic. Current descriptions of the nine delinquent subtypes, with predicted most effective intervention or treatment plans, combine to make up the 1966 edition of the treatment model.[81] This model is much too lengthy and elaborate to review here. It is possible only to note the various areas covered by the intervention prescriptions. The specific goals of intervention for each subtype follow from the nature of the problem, as defined in the characteristics items. From each goal, a specific intervention method follows. The treatment plan prescribes: the characteristics of an appropriate placement, preferred family treatment, school and/or job recommendations, sources of community support, leisure time activities, recommendations regarding peer group variables, required controls, specific therapeutic methods, characteristics of an appropriate treatment agent, and support required by the treatment agent working with the subtype.

CROSS-CLASSIFICATION OF TYPOLOGIES

During 1966, a conference on typologies of delinquents was sponsored by NIMH and attended by a number of the investigators whose work is reported in this paper— Hunt, Hurwitz, Jesness, MacGregor, Makkay, Reiss, Quay, and Warren. David Bordua, as well as David Twain and Seymour Rubenfeld of the NIMH staff, also participated in the conference. A cross-tabulation of the classification systems[82] was attempted. Three or four broad bands across the classification systems were identified and tentatively agreed upon by the conference participants. A further breakdown into six cross-classification bands seems also possible.[83] Chart A presents a cross-classification of the typologies represented at the NIMH conference plus a tentative cross-tabulation of other classification schemes.[84]

Within the first of these bands, to be called for purposes of this paper the *Asocial* type, are included Hunt's Sub I type, Hurwitz's Type II, Jesness's Immature-aggressive and Immature-passive, MacGregor's Schizophrenic youth, Makkay's Antisocial Character Disorder—Primitive (aggressive and passive-aggressive), Quay's children high on Unsocialized-psychopathic factor, and Warren's I_2 Asocial aggressives and Asocial passives. To this general classification band tentatively[85] can be added: Argyle's Lack of Sympathy type, Gibbon's Overly Aggressive delinquent, Jenkins and Hewitt's Unsocialized Aggressive delinquent, Schrag's Asocial type, and Studt's Isolate. Behavioral and family history characteristics of offenders who fall in this first classification band are generally agreed upon. The offender classified in this band is described as primitive, under-inhibited, impulsive, hostile, insecure, inadequate, maladaptive, concretely negativistic, undifferentiated, demanding of immediate gratification, non-trusting, thoroughly egocentric, alienated, etc. It is generally agreed that this type of offender does not see himself as delinquent or criminal, but rather seems himself as the victim of an unreasonable, hostile and confusing world. Those typologists who have investigated etiological factors have consistently shown extreme emotional deprivation, generalized and continual parental rejection, and frequently, physical cruelty or abandonment. Most investigators who relate to the treatment question for this type recommend a setting which offers a clear and concrete structure of low pressure, warmth, and acceptance from an extremely patient parent substitute, slow and supportive direction toward conformity, and attempts to reduce the fear of abandonment and rejection via teaching rather than psychotherapy.[86]

The second broad classification band which cuts across typologies, the *Conformist* type, includes

CHART A
CROSS-CLASSIFICATION OF OFFENDER TYPOLOGIES

Subtypes	Jeness	Himt	Hurwitz	Mac-Gregor	Makkay	Quay	Reiss	Warren	A P A	Argyle	Gibbons	Jenkins and Hewitt	McCord	Reckless	Schrag	Studt
1. Asocial		Sub I	Type II	Schizophrenic	Antisocial Character Disorder-Primitive	Unsocialized-psychopath		I_2	Passive-aggressive personality	Lack of sympathy		Unsocialized aggressive			Asocial	Isolate
Aggressive	Immature, aggressive				Aggressive			Asocial, aggressive	Aggressive		Overly aggressive					
Passive	Immature, passive				Passive-aggressive			Asocial, passive	Passive-aggressive							
2. Conformist		Stage I			Antisocial Character Disorder-Organized			I_3	Passive-aggressive personality			/Socialized/	Conformist			Receiver
Noodelinquently-oriented	Immature, passive				Passive-aggressive	Inadequate-immature		Conformist, Immature	Passive-dependent	Inadequate supergo	Gang offenders					
Delinquently-oriented	Socialized conformist					/Subcultural/	/Relatively integrated/	Conformist, Cultural							Antisocial	
3. Antisocial-manipulator	Manipulator	Stage II.		Autocrat	Antisocial Character Disorder-Organized Aggressive	Defective	Defective supergo	I_4 Manipulator	Antisocial personality	Inadequate supergo			Aggressive (psychopathic)	Psychopath	Pseudosocial	Manipulator
4. Neurotic			Type III		Neurotic		Relatively weak ego	I_4 Neurotic	Sociopathic personality disturbance	Weak ego control		Overinhibited	Neurotic-withdrawn	Neurotic Personality	Prosocial	Love-seeker
Acting-out	Neurotic, acting-out							Neurotic, acting-out			Joyrider					
Anxious	Neurotic, anxious / Neurotic, depressed			Intimidated		Neurotic-disturbed		Neurotic, anxious			Behavior problems					
5. Subcultural-identifier	Cultural delinquent	Stage II	Type I	Rebel	Subcultural	Subcultural	Relatively integrated	I_4 Cultural identifier	Dyssocial reaction	Deviant identification	Gang offenders	Socialized			Antisocial	Learner
6. Situational		Stage II						I_4 Situational, emotional reaction	Adjustment reaction of adolescence		Casual delinquent			Offenders of the moment		
Types not cross-classified					Mental Retardate Psychotic						Heroin user female delinquent			Eruptive behavior		

Hunt's Stage I group, Jesness's Immature-passive[87] and Socialized conformist, Makkay's Antisocial Character Disorder-Organized (passive-aggressive), Quay's children high on Inadequate-immature factor, and Warren's I₃ Immature conformists and Cultural conformists. To this classification band tentatively can be added: Argyle's Inadequate Superego delinquent, Gibbon's Gang offenders, McCord's Conformists, and Studt's Receiver. Some typologies do not differentiate between delinquent behavior which is imitated or "conformed to" from delinquent behavior which grows out of an internalized value system;[88] thus, it is difficult to know whether Reiss's Relatively integrated delinquent, Schrag's Antisocial type, Jenkins and Hewitt's Socialized delinquent, and children high on Quay's Subcultural factor belong partially in this second classification band, or whether all delinquents classified in these ways belong in the fifth band, described below. The offender classified in this band is described as concerned with power, searching for structure, dominated by the need for social approval, conforming to external pressure, rule-oriented, unable to empathize, cognitively concrete, having low self esteem, conventional and stereotyped in understanding, oriented to short-term goals, having superficial relationships with others, and self-representing as problem-free. This Conformist group has been subdivided further by some investigators into groups consisting of those individuals whose self perceptions are delinquent and who conform primarily to a delinquent peer group and individuals whose self perception is nondelinquent and who conform to the immediate power structure, delinquent or nondelinquent. Investigators who have studied etiological factors for the Conformists have found patterns of family helplessness or indifference (rather than open · rejection), inability to meet the dependency needs of the children, inconsistent structure and discipline, and absence of adequate adult models. Treatment recommendations for offenders in this classification band include use of a clear, consistent external structure in which concern for the offender can be expressed via controls of his behavior, use of group treatment to increase social perceptiveness, use of peer group as a pressure toward nondelinquency, and teaching of skills in order to help change self-definition in the direction of adequacy and independence.

A third clear-cut cross-classification band— ·the *Antisocial-Manipulator*—includes Jesness's Manipulator, MacGregor's Autocrat, Makkay's Antisocial Character Disorder-Organized (aggressive), Reiss's Defective Superego type, and Warren's I₃ Manipulator. To this classification band can tentatively be added: McCord's Aggressive (psychopathic) type, Reckless's Psychopath, Schrag's Pseudosocial type, and Studt's Manipulator. The offender classified in this band is described as not having internalized conventional norms, guilt-free, self-satisfied, power-oriented, counteractive to the authority system, nontrusting, emotionally insulated, cynical, callous and extremely hostile. Those typologists who have investigated etiological factors have found distrustful and angry families in which members are involved in competitive and mutually exploitive patterns, parents who feel deprived and who expect the children to meet their dependency needs, alternating parental patterns of overindulgence and frustration of the children, and inconsistent parental patterns of affection and rejection. In general, investigators report a discouraging picture as far as the treatment of this group of offenders is concerned. Treatment recommendations take two distinct paths—one path being that of encouraging the Manipulator to develop his manipulative skills in a socially-acceptable direction,[89] and the other path being that of attempting to allow the offender to work through his childhood trauma in a treatment relationship which will revive his capacity to depend on and be concerned about others.[90] The first path makes the assumption that it is possible to have a non-destructive, nondelinquent "psychopath," which many consider a contradiction in terms. Treatment recommendations toward the goal of socially acceptable manipulation include increasing the social perceptiveness and ability to predict via group treatment, and increasing opportunities for legitimate accomplishments via training in job, social, athletic, etc. skills. The second path clearly involves a serious and possibly very long-term individual treatment effort, and one which has no guarantees of success. The latter course is a difficult one to fit into most social agency programs.

The fourth classification band—the *Neurotic Offender*—includes Hunt's Stage II group, Hurwitz's Type III, Jesness's Neurotic (acting-out, anxious, or depressed) types, MacGregor's Intimidated youth, Makkay's Neurotic, Quay's children high on Neurotic-disturbed factor, Reiss's Relatively Weak Ego type, and Warren's I₄ Acting-out Neurotic and Anxious Neurotic types. To this classification band can tentatively be added: Argyle's Weak Ego-control type, Gibbon's Joyrider and Behavior Problem types, Jenkins and Hewitt's Over-inhibited type, McCord's Neurotic-withdrawn, Reckless's Neurotic personality, Schrag's Prosocial type, and Studt's Love-seeker. As is indicated by the terms "intimidated," "disturbed," "overinhibited," "anxious," "depressed," and "withdrawn," most investigators have identified an offender type in which symptoms of maladjustment are clearly visible. Some investigators have identified a second subgroup of neurotic offenders whose inner dynamics are quite similar to the visibly disturbed offender, but whose inner conflicts and anxieties are "acted-out" rather than appearing as neurotic symptoms. In addition to Jesness's and Warren's Acting-out Neurotic types, Gibbon's Joyrider and Studt's Love-seeker types appear to be most like the second group of Neurotic offenders. Investigators of etiological factors suggest that this type of offender is often the victim of parental anxiety or neurotic conflicts between the parents, with the offense viewed as a masculine identity striving. Some investigators have found a fairly typical role-reversal phenomenon in which the child, at an early age, finds himself expected to play a mature, responsible role with a child-like parent. It has been suggested by some authors that neurotic delinquency is primarily a middle class pattern. However, figures from the Community Treatment Project show that, although middle class offenders make up a larger proportion of the Neurotic subtypes than of other subtypes, by far the largest proportion of the Neurotic subgroups, as well as other subgroups, is lower class.[91] Treatment recommendations for the Neurotic offender focus on the resolution of the neurotic conflict through insight into family or individual dynamics which lead to the offense behavior. Such conflict resolution is sought through family group therapy and/or by individual or group psychotherapy for the offender.

The fifth classification band—the *Subcultural-Identifier*—includes Hunt's Stage II, Hurwitz's Type I, Jesness's Cultural delinquent, MacGregor's Rebel, Makkay's Subcultural type, Quay's children high on Subcultural factor, Reiss's Relatively integrated delinquent, and Warren's I_4 Cultural Identifier. To this classification band can be tentatively added: Argyle's Deviant Identification type, Gibbon's Gang Offenders, Jenkins and Hewitt's Socialized type, Schrag's Antisocial type, and Studt's Learner. The essential characteristic of this type of offender is that the individual, although developing "normally"[92] in most respects, has internalized the value system of a deviant subculture. Thus violation behavior, for example stealing from representatives of the larger culture, becomes simply an expression of what the Subcultural-Identifier considers "right." Investigators describe this offender type as interpersonally responsive, psychosocially healthy, loyal to his own principles and his own group, adequate, proud, suspicious of the authority system, capable of identifying himself with a mature socialized person, and accessible to new experiences. As was noted in the description of the second classification band, those investigators who focused on offender *behavior* and delinquent *attitudes* have not distinguished between the Subcultural-Identifier and the Subcultural-Conformist. At these levels of observation, the two groups appear similar: highly peer group oriented, distrusting of the authority system, comfortable with "delinquent" label, extensive delinquent histories, problems viewed as "external" rather than "internal," and apparently self-satisfied. In addition, both types include high proportions of minority group members. Striking differences between the two groups appear when the foci of observation are family stability and concern, individual capacity for self-knowledge and self-evaluation and differentiated perception of others, interpersonal relationship ability, goal orientation, concern with status, time perspective, etc. This series of characteristics becomes crucial to assessment of the individual's potential for becoming a contributing citizen and for making management and treatment decisions. Two levels of treatment appear to be recommended for the Subcultural-Identifier, one focused on stopping the violation behavior and one focused on changing the content of his value system. For the former, suggestions for stopping the violation behavior include demonstrating to the offender through use of the "lock up" that "crime does not pay", and teaching the individual how to meet status and material needs in ways acceptable to the larger culture. The second level of treatment involves working through a relationship with a strong identity model who is a representative of the larger culture and thus enlarging the offender's concept of his in-group and broadening his self-definition.

The sixth classification band—the *Situational Offender*—includes Hunt's Stage II, and Warren's I_4 Situational Emotional Reaction type. To these may be tentatively added Gibbon's Casual Delinquent and Reckless's Offender of the Moment. Offenders in this group are represented as normal individuals who give no evidence of long-term psychoneurosis or psychopathy and for whom crime is ego-alien. These individuals have presumably found themselves involved in violation behavior as a result of accidental circumstances or a specific, nonrecurring situation which taxed their normal coping capacities. Treatment is either considered unnecessary or, if offered, is oriented toward helping the individual solve the specific social or personal problem which led to law-breaking.

In summarizing the cross-tabulation chart, it appears that six classification bands can be tentatively identified as cutting across various typologies. The minimum number of identified subtypes within any of the included typologies is three. Of those systems which involve only a three-way breakdown of the offender population, the single agreed-upon subtype is the one referred to in this paper as Neurotic. Of the sixteen systems charted, ten involve either a three-way or a four-way breakdown. Of these ten, the most typical pattern includes counterparts of the following subtypes: Neurotic (10 out of 10), Subcultural-Identifier (8 out of 10), Asocial (7 out of 10) Conformist (5 out of 10) and Antisocial-manipulator (5 out of 10). Classification systems which involve more than a five-way breakdown of the offender population add the Situational type and/or subdivide the Asocial, the Conformist, and the Neurotic categories. Warren's typology involves the largest number of subgroups, defining—in addition to the Antisocial-Manipulator, the Subcultural-Identifier and the Situational—two kinds of Asocial types (aggressive and passive), two kinds of Conformist types (delinquency-oriented and nondelinquency-oriented), and two kinds of Neurotic types (anxious and acting-out), for a total of nine subtypes.

It should be noted that most of the typologies are based on studies of juvenile boys. Only Hunt, Schrag, and Warren have specifically included girls or women, but these investigators have found their typologies to be equally appropriate for the female population. Schrag's typology is based primarily on adult offenders (although institutionalized juveniles have been classified by some of Schrag's followers), and the original form of Warren's typology (Interpersonal Maturity Levels, without subtypes) was found to be as appropriate for an adult as a juvenile population. It is an assumption, albeit justified, that the six-band cross-classification system is an adequate way of subdividing female juvenile offenders as well as adult offenders.

One measure of the appropriateness of cross-tabulation of subtypes from various classification systems might be the degree of similarity between the proportions of offenders placed in each of the various classification bands. Many of the typologies do not report these data. Even for those who do, the major differences in the nature of the populations studied are so great as to make comparisons of questionable meaning. Table I presents the estimated proportions in the six classification bands, using data from five studies of juvenile offenders. The Jesness data are based on a study of young boys (ages 8 to 14) committed to a state training school. The Community Treatment Project (CTP) data are based on boys and girls (ages 9 to 18) committed to the State Youth

Authority from juvenile courts and declared eligible for participation in an intensive community program. The Preston Typology Study (PTS) data are based on older adolescent boys committed to a state training school. All three of these study groups contain a population of serious or habitual delinquents. The Hurwitz data are based on cases appearing before the juvenile court. The Reiss data are based on 46% of a juvenile probation population, the 46% identified as those probationers who were examined by court psychiatrists. These last two study groups may be generally assumed to include less serious delinquents than those in the first three groups.

TABLE I

ESTIMATED PROPORTIONS OF DELINQUENTS IN VARIOUS SUBTYPES

Subtype	Jesness Data N = 210	CTP Data N = 400	PTS Data N = 371	Hurwitz Data N = 198	Reiss Data N = 511
Asocial	18%	10%	10%	34%	
Conformist	30	28	40		
Antisocial-Manipulator	12	15	15		12%
Neurotic	35	40	33	21	22
Subcultural-Identifier	14	5	2	45	12
Situational		3	1		
Total	100%	100%	100%	100%	46%*

* 54% of Reiss's subjects were not classified.

The higher proportion of the Conformist type in the PTS data than in the Jesness data and the CTP data probably reflects the large number of recidivists in the PTS population. Warren and Palmer[98] have shown a high failure rate for Conformists (compared with most other subtypes) following traditional correctional programs. The Hurwitz data in Table I indicate that Hurwitz's Type II (34%) and Type I (45%) probably contain offenders which should more accurately be cross-tabulated in other classification bands. It is likely that some individuals in Type II could be classified as Antisocial-Manipulators, and that some individuals in Type I could be classified as Conformists. Another possibility is that the Subcultural-Identifier group represents a larger proportion of a court-appearance population than it does of the more serious habitual delinquent population committed to a State program. This possibility is in line with Reiss's assumption that a large number of the 54% of the probationers in his study, who were *not* classified by court psychiatrists, belong in his Relatively Integrated subtype (included here in the Subcultural-Identifier group).

Based on descriptive data, a cross-classification of several important offender typologies is apparently possible. In the present state of the science of corrections, this much consistency in the data of various studies is a most encouraging finding, leading us to feel that the identifiable subtypes of offenders reflect at least a partial "truth" about the population rather than simply a convenient fantasy in the mind of the criminologist. The fact that a cross-classification is possible is even more impressive when one considers the varieties of methods of deriving the subtypes—theoretical formulations, empirical-observational methods, multivariate analysis procedures. Additionally, it is important to note that not only is it possible to find similarities in the descriptions of *offender characteristics* across typologies, but also that consistency is evident in descriptions of *etiological* and *background factors* and in *treatment prescriptions* for seemingly similar subtypes.

Having said that typologies are apparently operating on a common ground, it is necessary to add that much crucial information is missing which would be necessary in order to determine whether or not any two subtypes are exact counterparts. The ultimate test of such a cross-classification would come from a study in which a typing of individuals in a single population was conducted by experts in the use of each of the various classification systems. Such a study would not only clarify the extent to which the subtypes in one system are actual counterparts of those in another system, but also lead typologists to increase the precision of their subtype definitions.

Until the matter of classification of offenders is handled in some generally agreed-upon way, it is almost impossible to compare treatment programs being conducted in various parts of the country. If, from the cross-classification study suggested above, a group of the leading typologists could agree on a common taxonomy, the path would be open for a great number of significant studies. The next important step would be the determination of the most efficient diagnostic methods. Once the categories had been agreed upon, a number of scientists in various parts of the country could work on the problem simultaneously. Additionally, interrelated studies of management and treatment methods could be conducted—trying a variety of well-defined treatment approaches to the same category of offender. It would then be realistic to attempt the replication of experimental approaches, suggested by Keith Griffiths in his Correctional Research Model.

There is evidence that both at the theoretician[94] and practitioner[95] levels, the field is ready to move toward treatment programs which are based on categorizing the range of problems represented in the correctional population. Not only is there a

ready ear for such conceptualizing, but it also appears that a time of consensus among typologists may be approaching in which a rational, correctional treatment model may be begun.

To date, little work has been done toward utilizing typologies for building differential treatment strategies. The work which has been done has occurred largely in small experimental programs. It is right and proper for experimental programs to be in the lead and for the rest of the field to be eyeing their exploratory work with hope. But the *size of the gap* between these programs and the generally undeveloped state of correctional practice is crucial in estimating what programmatic utility the typological concensus has in the foreseeable future. Are the classification concepts or the corollary program prescriptions so esoteric that only academicians can understand them? Are the treatment methods which might arise from a rational correctional model such that the average practitioner could not apply them?

While the typologies reviewed here vary considerably in the complexity of their derivation, the essence of the correctional model which follows from a treatment-relevant typology is a rather simple idea. The idea is this: The *goals* of correctional treatment with any offender should relate in some direct manner to the causes or meaning of the law violation, and the *treatment methods* should relate specifically to the goals. This idea, when put forth with examples, makes the greatest kind of sense to the practitioner who is supposed to "do something" about delinquent behavior.

If the idea is simple, what about its implementation? Assuming an agreed-upon taxonomy, what about the methods of individual diagnosis? In order to move easily beyond small experimental programs into large operating programs, it is essential that the classification be done via easy-to-administer-and-score-measures or via an already-established clinical process in the correctional agency. Most correctional programs now have a time and place set aside for intake and classification procedures, so that the machinery for typing offenders may be well available. As for methods of obtaining the diagnosis, work toward simpler procedures should continue after an agreed-upon typology is available. Of the sixteen typologists represented in the cross-classification chart, several do not specify diagnostic methods, since presumably the major concern in the development of the typology was not the classification of individual offenders (Argyle, Gibbons, McCord, Reckless). The Jenkins and Hewitt, Jesness, and Hurwitz typologies grew out of factor analytic procedures, utilizing many tests and clinical judgements and thus do not lend themselves to individual diagnosis. The Reiss typology was based on psychiatric judgements. The Studt types were derived from a series of intensive interviews with offenders and with others who knew the inmates well. Although the diagnosis of Antisocial Character Disorder is well spelled out by Makkay, differentiations of subtypes within that category are based on a fairly lengthy observation period, with the criteria not well defined as yet. The MacGregor diagnosis is based on a series of interviews with the entire family of the delinquent. Thus, at this point in time, none of the above-listed classification systems represents a practical method for the diagnosis of large correctional populations.

In applying the Warren typology, the primary instrument for diagnosing individuals is a tape-recorded interview with the delinquent subject. A disadvantage of this procedure is the training required to achieve rater reliability. The Warren system currently has some advantages over the others in that hundreds of delinquents have been interviewed sequentially over time. Both high interrater agreement[96] and high reliability over time[97] have been shown. In addition, sets of specific characteristics items to be rated have been developed for each delinquent subtype.[98]

The classification systems having the simplest diagnostic methods are those of Hunt, Quay, and Schrag. Hunt's methods involve a simple T/F instrument and a rating made from a set of subject-completed sentences. Although the discriminations made in Hunt's Conceptual Levels system are clearly treatment-relevant, further work in studying offenders with the typology is needed to determine whether or not the three-way classification of the delinquent population is sufficient for prescribing treatment.

As noted earlier, Quay does not view his work as leading to types of individuals, but rather to a classification of behavior dimensions. An individual is represented by a profile of behavior dimension scores. Those individuals who have similar profiles may presumably be grouped together in terms of treatment need. The diagnostic instruments developed by Quay are easy to administer and score, involving check lists and ratings of the individual's behavioral characteristics. The measurements can be shown to have adequate reliability. The difficulty with using profiles is that, since few individuals have a simple profile—i.e., a high score on one factor and low scores on all other factors—a skilled judgement must be made with regard to grouping for intervention purposes in the majority of cases.

Schrag's typology has been used primarily to study subcultures within the prison walls, and Schrag has not wished to claim more general applicability for it in the absence of research data. Within the institutional setting, 50% to 70% of individuals can be typed easily using questionnaire and interview data. The remaining individuals are identified as mixed types. Since the types described by Schrag compare closely with types described by others, it is very likely that the typology has more general applicability than Schrag has claimed.

An optimistic note may be made with regard to our present ability to diagnose meaningful subtypes with realistically simple procedures. In a study previously mentioned (the Preston Typology Study), Jesness classified the intake population of a large California training school for boys, using the Warren typology. Diagnostic procedures include the Jesness Inventory (consisting of 155 T/F items, scored for delinquent subtype using a discriminant analysis formula), a sentence completion and a short interview. The final diagnosis is made using all three instruments, with the hope that eventually the Inventory alone may be scored to produce an accurate diagnosis. Using all of Warren's nine subtypes, the diagnoses on 500 subjects from the *Inventory alone* agrees 62% of the time with the final diagnosis. If, instead of using the nine subtypes, the three larger categories (Interpersonal Maturity Levels) are used, the agreement is 83%. Within the nine subtypes, some of the groups are identified by the Inventory alone much more accurately than other groups. For example, the Neurotic, Anxious subtype is diagnosed accurately from the Inventory alone 84% of the time, and is diagnosed accurately 94% of the time as falling within Maturity Level 4. The accuracy with other subtypes is lower. It is possible that if the Inventory cannot achieve an acceptable level of accuracy for all subtypes it may at least identify that proportion of the population which needs further diagnostic instruments applied.

An important point to be made with regard to treatment prescriptions which follow from offender typologies is that the *intervention strategies* are not by and large made up of new and unusual treatment methods, but rather consist of many of the old alternatives differentially applied to the various categories of offenders. In this sense a typology which leads to differential prescriptions leaves the field no worse off in terms of the need for skilled treaters. In another sense, the field is far better off. If offenders can be classified by differential treatment need, correctional staff can then be assigned differentially. In this way a particular correctional line worker need not have the entire range of specific management and therapeutic skills at his fingertips. Instead, his training can prepare him to handle only those treatment and management methods appropriate for certain types of offenders. Further, since correctional workers can be characterized as having certain "natural" treatment stances, a matching of worker style and offender problem can be accomplished.[99]

If the field were to move toward a correctional model utilizing differential management and treatment of various subtypes of offenders, how would the *training of correctional workers* be affected? Since a differential model calls for training staff who work with some types of offenders to utilize different methods than those working with other types of offenders, the job for the trainers becomes somewhat more complex; however, the job of the trainees is considerably simplified, since the worker must no longer learn how to handle the entire range of problems. Under these conditions, training content can become less vague, less general, and less oriented toward producing that nebulous entity—the "good correctional worker." Instead, the training content can be specific to characteristics of particular types of offenders and precisely relevant to the management and treatment demands of the offender type. Because of the limitation in the range of content that a particular correctional worker needs to learn in order to deal effectively with his assigned offender population, it is likely that whatever training time is now available in various correctional agencies could be more effectively used. This does not imply, of course, that all is now known about how to turn various kinds of offenders into non-offenders. It does not imply that the need for imaginative and creative approaches to the problem is gone. It does imply, however, that treatment and management programs, if based on an offender typology can become more rational by better defining the differential problems leading to offense behavior, by prescribing differential goals for the correctional effort, and by training workers within the differential framework.

A case can be made for the importance of utilizing an offender classification system at each step along the entire correctional continuum. The advantages of using explicit, rather than implicit, classification systems at each correctional decision point has already been made in this paper. To the extent that the correctional system is free to make decisions based, not on retributive justice, but rather on a goal of turning offenders into nonoffenders, i.e., offender need—to that extent it is important to have available at each correctional decision point classification information which will indicate the setting and methods most likely to achieve the overall goal. For example, what is the treatment of

choice when an individual identified in the cross-classification chart as a Conformist first appears in the correctional system? Some data are available from the Community Treatment Project which indicate that such individuals (1) become increasingly oriented toward delinquency in the highly delinquent peer group atmosphere of an institution, and (2) can be satisfactorily managed and treated in certain kinds of community programs.[100]

Beyond the possibility of sorting out at each decision point those individuals who need to move on through the correctional system, there is a further advantage in making the differential diagnosis as early as possible in the correctional career. A typology with its consequent goal specification allows for a unification among the treatment efforts of various segments of the correctional process. At many points in present correctional practice, it is possible to observe the total irrelevance of the goals and methods of treatment in an institutional setting to the goals and methods of treatment in the after-care program. The goals in the two settings may even be at odds with one another—the aim of the institutional time being to achieve conformity to a strict control system and the aim of the parole time being to achieve individual self-responsibility. While it is true that these two aims follow somewhat naturally from the characteristics of the two settings, it is possible to aim for conformity in a community setting and to aim for individual self-responsibility in an institutional setting—should the nature of the problem with particular offenders require one approach or the other. Even assuming that there are institutional administration needs to consider and community safety needs to consider, it seems possible that the determination of a treatment-relevant diagnosis early in an individual's correctional career might well contribute to a more consistent and therefore more effective total intervention program.

SUMMARY[101]

A rationale for classifying the offender population into meaningful subgroups was presented. Various classification approaches were described and their implications for efficient management practices and effective treatment strategies were illustrated with a number of clinical and research studies. A cross-tabulation of sixteen typological systems was presented and six cross-classification bands were identified. The six bands or offender subtypes were entitled: Asocial, Conformist, Antisocial-manipulator, Neurotic, Subcultural-Identifier and Situational offender. It was pointed out that the consistency in the data of several typological studies which made the cross-classification possible is an encouraging sign. However, the importance of taking the next step—an actual cross-classification of offenders from a single population, using the various typological schemes —was noted. It was further suggested that if a common taxonomy could be agreed upon, the way would be open for conducting and replicating numerous interrelated studies of management and treatment methods.

In asking whether a typological concensus has any programmatic utility at the present time, current interest among practitioners in developing differential treatment strategies for various types of offenders was noted. It was suggested that it may be possible in the near future to make differential diagnoses of large populations, and to

simplify the training of correctional workers by teaching management and treatment specialties rather than the entire range of correctional techniques. The use of differential diagnosis in decision-making along the correctional continuum and its potential value as a treatment-unifying influence was discussed.

Typologies of offenders represent an important method of integrating the increasing body of knowledge in the field of corrections. Ultimately, typological approaches will flourish or not depending on their fruitfulness in producing improved management and treatment methods for the practitioner working in this discouraging field. At the moment, the classification studies reported in this paper appear to represent solid steps in the development of a systematic science of corrections.

Notes

[1] The terms "classification system," "typology," and "taxonomy" have been used somewhat interchangeably in this paper, even though a case may be made for differentiating among the terms for some technical purposes.

[2] See generally H. SUTHERLAND & D. CRESSEY, PRINCIPLES OF CRIMINOLOGY (1960).

[3] See generally C. SHAW & H. McKAY, JUVENILE DELINQUENCY AND URBAN AREAS (1942); R. MERTON, SOCIAL THEORY AND SOCIAL STRUCTURE (1957); A. CLOWARD & L. OHLIN, DELINQUENCY AND OPPORTUNITY: A THEORY OF DELINQUENT GANGS (1960).

[4] See generally Gough & Peterson, The Identification and Measurement of Predispositional Factors in Crime and Delinquency, J. CONSULTING PSYCHOLOGY 207-12 (1952); Sarbin, A Preface to the Psychological Analysis of the Self 59 PSYCHOLOGICAL REV. 11-23 (1952); T. PARSONS, THE SOCIAL SYSTEM (1951); Cohen, The Sociology of the Deviant Act: Anomie Theory and Beyond, 30 AM. SOCIOLOGICAL REV. 5-14 (1965).

[5] See generally K. FRIEDLANDER, THE PSYCHOANALYTIC APPROACH TO JUVENILE DELINQUENCY (1947); Formation of the Anti-Social Character, in PSYCHOANALYTIC STUDY OF THE CHILD, (1945); W. HEALY & A. BRONNER, NEW LIGHT ON DELINQUENCY AND ITS TREATMENT (1936); Redl, New Perspectives for Research on Juvenile Delinquency, CHILDREN'S BUREAU PUBLICATION NO. 356 (H. Witmer & R. Kotinsky ed. 1956); E. ERIKSON, CHILDHOOD AND SOCIETY (1950).

[6] Several reviews of the large number of recent contributions in this area are available. See e.g., Moles, Lippitt & Withey, A Selective Review of the Research and Theory on Delinquency, INTER-CENTER PROGRAM OF RESEARCH ON CHILDREN, YOUTH AND FAMILY LIFE (1959); Grant, Interaction Between Kinds of Treatments and Kinds of Delinquents, 2 CALIFORNIA STATE BOARD OF CORRECTIONS MONOGRAPH 5-14 (1961); Glueck & Glueck, Varieties of Delinquent Types, 5 BRITISH J. CRIM. 236-48, 388-405 (1965); Kinch, Continuities in the Study of Delinquent Types, 53 J. CRIM. L. C. & P. S. 323-28 (1962); Lejins, Pragmatic Etiology of Delinquent Behavior, in THE JUVENILE DELINQUENT (C. Vedder ed. 1954); Roebuck, Criminal Typology: A Critical Overview, 9 ALA. CORRECTIONAL J. 34-66 (1962).

[7] MANNHEIM & WILKINS, PREDICTION METHODS IN RELATION TO BORSTAL TRAINING (1955).

[8] Beverly, A Method of Determination of Base Expectancies for Use in The Assessment of Effectiveness of Correctional Treatment, RESEARCH REPORT No. 3, CALIFORNIA YOUTH AUTHORITY, DIVISION OF RESEARCH (1959).

[9] Gottfredson & Bonds, Systematic Study of Experience as an Aid to Decisions, RESEARCH REPORT No. 2, CALIFORNIA DEPARTMENT OF CORRECTIONS (1961).

[10] S. GLUECK & E. GLUECK PREDICTING DELINQUENCY AND CRIME (1959).

[11] D. GLASER, THE EFFECTIVENESS OF A PRISON AND PAROLE SYSTEM (1964).

[12] Schrag, A Preliminary Criminal Typology, 4 PAC. SOCIOLOGICAL REV. 11-16 (1961).

[13] G. SYKES, THE SOCIETY OF CAPTIVES (1958).

[14] Miller, Some Characteristics of Present-Day Delinquency of Relevance to Educators (unpublished paper presented at the 1959 meetings of the American Association of School Administrators).

[15] Roebuck & Cadwallader, The Negroe Armed Robber as a Criminal Type: the Construction and Application of a Typology, 4 PAC. SOCIOLOGICAL REV. 21-26 (1961).

[16] W. McCORD, J. McCORD, & I. ZOLA, ORIGINS OF CRIME (1959).

[17] L. OHLIN, SELECTION FOR PAROLE (1951).

[18] W. RECKLESS, THE CRIME PROBLEM (1961).

[19] Jenkins & Hewitt, Types of Personality Structure Encountered in Child Guidance Clinics, 14 AM. J. ORTHOPSYCHIATRY 84-94 (1944).

[20] REDL, supra note 5, at 42.

[21] ERIKSON, supra note 5, at 42.

[22] A. AICHORN, WAYWARD YOUTH (1935).

[23] Makkay, Delinquency Considered as a Manifestation of: 1) a Serious Disorder of Development in Early Childhood, and 2) Other Delinquency-Prone Disturbances of Emotional Development (unpublished manuscript 1960).

[24] Reiss, Social Correlates of Psychological Types of Delinquency, 17 AM. SOCIOLOGICAL REV. 710-18 (1952).

[25] Argyle, A new approach to the classification of delinquents with implications for treatment, 2 CALIFORNIA STATE BOARD OF CORRECTIONS MONOGRAPH 15-26 (1961).

[26] H. BLOCH & F. FLYNN, DELINQUENCY (1956).

[27] Illinois State Training School for Boys, Treatment Committee (Report on Diagnostic Categories) (1953).

[28] Gough & Peterson, supra note 4, at 42.

[29] Hunt and Hardt, Developmental Stage, Delinquency,

and *Differential Treatment*, J. RESEARCH IN CRIME & DELINQ. 20–31 (1965).

[30] Sarbin, *supra* note 4, at 42.

[31] Peterson, Quay and Cameron, *Personality and Background Factors in Juvenile Delinquency as Inferred From Questionnaire Responses*, 23 J. CONSULTING PSYCHOLOGY 395–99 (1959).

[32] D. GIBBONS, CHANGING THE LAWBREAKER (1965); Gibbons and Garrity, *Some Suggestions for the Development of Etiological and Treatment Theory in Criminology*, 38 SOCIAL FORCES 51–58 (1959); Gibbons and Garrity, *Definition and Analysis of Certain Criminal Types*, 53 J. CRIM. L. C. & P.S. 27–35 (1962).

[33] E. STUDT, S. MESSINGER & T. WILSON, C-UNIT: SEARCH FOR COMMUNITY IN PRISON (1968).

[34] R. MacGregor, Developmental considerations in psychotherapy with children and youth (paper presented at the Annual Conference of the American Psychological Association, St. Louis, 1962).

[35] Sullivan, Grant and Grant, *The Development of Interpersonal Maturity: Application to Delinquency*, 20 PSYCHIATRY 373–85 (1957).

[36] WARREN *et al*, INTERPERSONAL MATURITY LEVEL CLASSIFICATION (JUVENILE): DIAGNOSIS AND TREATMENT OF LOW, MIDDLE, AND HIGH MATURITY DELINQUENTS, (1966).

[37] Russon, *A Design for Clinical Classification of Offenders*, 4 CANADIAN J. CORRECTIONS 179–88 (1962).

[38] Hurwitz, *Three Delinquent Types: A Multivariate Analysis*, 56 J. CRIM. L.C. & P.S. 328–34 (1965).

[39] Jesness, *The Fricot Ranch Study*, RESEARCH REPORT No. 47, California Youth Authority (1965).

[40] Palmer, *Types of Probation Offenders and Types of Youth on Probation: Their Views and Interactions*, Youth Studies Center, Project Report (1963).

[41] Glueck and Glueck, *Varieties of Delinquent Types*, 5 BRITISH J. CRIM. 236–48, 388–405 (1965).

[42] A. CLOWARD AND L. OHLIN, DELINQUENCY AND OPPORTUNITY: A THEORY OF DELINQUENT GANGS 112 (1960).

[43] Cohen, *The Sociology of the Deviant Act: Anomie Theory and Beyond*, 30 AM. SOCIOLOGICAL REV. 5–14 (1965).

[44] Warren, The Community Treatment Project: An Integration of Theories of Causation and Correctional Practice, (Paper presented at the Illinois Academy of Criminology Conference, Chicago, 1965).

[45] Havel, *Special Intensive Parole Unit IV: The High Base Expectancy Study*, Research Report No. 10, Department of Corrections (California) (1963). *See also Interaction Between Treatment Method and Offender Type*, 1 CAL. ST. BD. OF CORRECTIONS MONOGRAPH 27–30 (1960).

[46] Compared with minimal supervision, regular supervision involved one third more office contacts, twice as many field contacts, and more than twice as many collateral contacts.

[47] Gottfredson, A Strategy for Study of Correctional Effectiveness. (Paper presented at the fifth International Criminological Congress, Montreal 1965).

[48] H. MANNHEIM AND L. WILKINS, PREDICTION METHODS IN RELATION TO BORSTAL TRAINING (1955).

[49] H. WEEKS, YOUTHFUL OFFENDERS AT HIGHFIELDS (1958).

[50] Reiss, *Delinquency as a Failure of Personal and Social Controls*, 15 AM. SOC. REV. 196–207 (1951).

[51] Beverly, *A Method of Determination of Base Expectancies for Use in the Assessment of Effectiveness of Correctional Treatment*, Research Report No. 3, California Youth Authority (1959).

[52] Argyle, *A New Approach to the Classification of Delinquents with Implications for Treatment*, 2 CAL. ST. BD. OF CORRECTIONS MONOGRAPH 15–26 (1961).

[53] D. GIBBONS, CHANGING THE LAWBREAKERS (1965).

[54] Warren, *supra* note 36.

[55] C. JESNESS, THE PRESTON TYPOLOGY STUDY (1970).

[56] Warren, *supra* note 36.

[57] H. EYSENCK, THE SCIENTIFIC STUDY OF PERSONALITY (1952).

[58] Bailey, *Correctional Outcome: An Evaluation of 100 Reports*, 57 J. CRIM. L.C. & P.S. 145 (1966).

[59] O'Brien, *Personality Assessment as a Measure of Change Resulting from Group Psychotherapy with Male Juvenile Delinquents*, California Youth Authority (1961).

[60] Adams, *Interaction Between Individual Interview Therapy and Treatment Amenability in Older Youth Authority Wards*, 2 CAL. ST. BD. OF CORRECTIONS MONOGRAPH 27–44 (1961).

[61] Grant and Grant, *A Group Dynamics Approach to the Treatment of Nonconformists in the Navy*, 322 ANNALS OF AMERICAN ACADEMY OF POLITICAL AND SOCIAL SCIENCE 126–35 (1959).

[62] Mueller, *Success Rates as a Function of Treatment Assignment and Juvenile Delinquency Classification Interaction*, 1 CAL. ST. BD. OF CORRECTIONS MONOGRAPH 7–14 (1960).

[63] Palmer, *Types of Probation Offenders and Types of Youth on Probation; Their Views and Interactions*, YOUTH STUDIES CENTER, PROJECT REPORT (1963).

[64] Jenkins and Hewitt, *Types of Personality Structure Encountered in Child Guidance Clinics*, 14 AM. J. ORTHOPSYCHIATRY 84–94 (1944).

[65] W. McCORD, J. McCORD, & I. ZOLA, ORIGINS OF CRIME (1959).

[66] D. GIBBONS, CHANGING THE LAWBREAKER (1965).

[67] Freeman, Hildebrand, and Ayre, *A Classification System that Prescribes Treatment*, 46 SOCIAL CASEWORK 423–29 (1965).

[68] *Id*. at 429.

[69] O. HARVEY, D. HUNT, & H. SCHRODER, CONCEPTUAL SYSTEMS AND PERSONALITY ORGANIZATION (1961).

[70] MacGregor, Developmental Considerations in Psychotherapy With Children and Youth (paper presented at the annual conference of the American Psychological Association, St. Louis, 1962).

[71] Warren, *supra* note 36.

[72] MacGregor, *supra* note 70.

[73] Harvey, *supra* note 69.

[74] Hunt & Hardt, *Developmental Stage, Delinquency, and Differential Treatment*, J. RESEARCH IN CRIME & DELINQ. 20–31 (1965).

[75] Hunt & Dopyera, *Personality Variation in Lower-Class Children*, 62 J. OF PSYCHOLOGY 47–54 (1966).

[76] Hunt & Hardt, *supra* note 74.

[77] *Id*. at 30.

[78] Sullivan, Grant, & Grant, *The Development of Interpersonal Maturity: Applications to Delinquency*, 20 PSYCHIATRY 373–85 (1957).

[79] Grant & Grant, *A Group Dynamics Approach to the Treatment of Nonconformists in the Navy*, 322 ANNALS OF AMERICAN ACADEMY OF POLITICAL & SOCIAL SCIENCE 126–35 (1959).

[80] Grant, A Study of Conformity in a Nonconformist Population (1961). (Unpublished Ph.D. dissertation, University of California, Berkeley.)

[81] *See* Warren, *supra* note 36, at 46.

[82] It should be noted that, of those who presented classification schemes, all but Quay referred to their system as a typology. Quay prefers to view classifications in terms of dimensions of behavior. *See* Quay, The Structure of Children's Behavior Disorders (1965). (colloquia at the University of Minnesota and the

University of Maryland). *See also, Personality Dimensions in Delinquent Males As Inferred From the Factor Analysis of Behavior Ratings*, 1 J. RESEARCH IN CRIME AND DELINQ. 33–37 (1964).

[82] Since the cross-classification presented here is somewhat more complex than the one discussed at the NIMH conference, the responsibility for errors of placement should be viewed as entirely that of the author.

[84] Several of the classification schemes reviewed for this paper were not included in the cross-classification because the typology did not make enough discriminations (Aichorn, Lejins) because the typology purportedly differentiated among disturbance areas within the individual rather than among individuals (Redl), or because the nature of the underlying bases of the system did not relate to those charted (Ohlin, Walter Miller).

[85] These cross-classifications have not been checked with the authors of the classification systems.

[86] The definitions of subtype characteristics, the descriptions of etiological factors, the treatment recommendations—none of these for this subtype nor the following subtypes do justice to the detailed and extensive work of some investigators. The intent here is simply to indicate in very general terms examples of apparently agreed-upon and disagreed-upon descriptions and prescriptions.

[87] According to Jesness, the Immature-passive group splits, with about half of the group most similar to the Asocial, passives in classification band one and the other half most similar to Immature conformists of classification band two.

[88] W. McCORD, W. McCORD & I. K. ZOLA, ORIGINS OF CRIME 195–98 (1959), presents evidence for the importance of this distinction.

[89] D. C. GIBBONS, CHANGING THE LAWBREAKER (1965); Gibbons & Garrity, *Some Suggestions for the Development of Etiological and Treatment Theory in Criminology*, 38 SOCIAL FORCES 51 (1959); Gibbons & Garrity, *Definition and Analysis of Certain Criminal Types*, 53 J. CRIM. L.C. & P.S. 27 (1962).

[90] E. Makkay *et al, Juvenile Delinquency Field Demonstration and Training Project:* Newton-Baker Project of the Judge Baker Guidance Center. Basic Design. Proposal to National Institute of Mental Health, 1961.

[91] M. WARREN & T. PALMER, COMMUNITY TREATMENT PROJECT, RESEARCH REPORT No. 6, 1965.

[92] Some investigators have noted that this type of offender, while having satisfactory mother-child relationship, does *not* have a strong, authoritive, respected father with whom to identify. R. MacGregor, *Middle Class Delinquent Youth, a Study of Families*. Final Report (1965); E. MAKKAY, DELINQUENCY CONSIDERED AS A MANIFESTATION OF: (1) A SERIOUS DISORDER OF DEVELOPMENT IN EARLY CHILDHOOD, AND (2) OTHER DELINQUENCY-PRONE DISTURBANCES OF EMOTIONAL DEVELOPMENT (unpublished manuscript, 1960).

[93] Warren & Palmer, *supra* note 91.

[94] In the July, 1966 issue of CRIME AND DELINQUENCY, vol. 12, no. 3, Glaser, *The New Correctional Era-Implications for Manpower and Training;* Gilman, *Problems and Progress in Staff Training;* and Nelson, *Strategies for Action in Meeting Correctional Manpower and Program Needs*, all point to the importance of developing treatment-relevant classification systems and differential treatment methods.

[95] Demands for training in differential treatment methods come to the California Youth Authority's

[96] Reliability estimates for all subtypes based upon the independent judgments of two different raters (trained research personnel) made at approximately the same point in time have fallen, on the average, in the mid-80's.

[97] Reliability estimates for diagnosis at intake as compared with followup diagnosis (three to six months later for Experimental cases and eight to twelve months later for Control cases) have centered in the mid-80's and low 90's.

[98] Warren, *Interpersonal Maturity Level Classification (juvenile):* DIAGNOSIS AND TREATMENT OF LOW, MIDDLE AND HIGH MATURITY DELINQUENTS, CTP PUBLICATION (1966).

[99] Investigations into these "natural" stances are being conducted at the Community Treatment Project, see Palmer, *Personality Characteristics and Professional Orientations of Five Groups of Community Treatment Project Workers: A Preliminary Report on Differences Among Treaters*, CTP REPORT SERIES, No. 1, CALIFORNIA YOUTH AUTHORITY (1967); C.F. Jesness, THE PRESTON TYPOLOGY STUDY (1970).

[100] In *CTP*, the failure rate for Conformists with 24 months of community exposure time was only 33.3% for delinquents treated in an intensive community program compared with 72.7% for comparable individuals following a period of incarceration.

[101] In addition to the references already cited, the following sources were consulted in the preparation of this paper: Hayner, *Characteristics of Five Offender Types*, 9 ALABAMA CORRECTIONAL J. 75 (1962); Lindesmith and Dunham, *Some Principles of Criminal Typology*, 19 SOCIAL FORCES 309 (1941); Loveland, *The Classification Program in the Federal Prison System: 1934–60*, 24 FEDERAL PROBATION 8 (1960); Peters, *Treatment Needs of Juvenile Offenders*, 1 CALIF. ST. BD. OF CORRECTIONS MONOGRAPH 22 (1960); Topping, *Case Studies of Aggressive Delinquents*, 11 AM. J. OF ORTHOPSYCHIATRY 485 (1941); Vedder, *Theory of Criminal Types*, 9 ALA. CORRECTIONAL J. 1 (1962).

PRISON CONDITIONS:
AN UNCONSTITUTIONAL ROADBLOCK
TO REHABILITATION

Richard G. Singer

The pre-Gothic appearance of many prison buildings is deceptive; the prison system as we know it today is of quite modern origin.[1] Although William Penn had instituted a program of imprisonment for most felonies in 1682,[2] this radical innovation was repealed in 1718, when, in an attempt to obtain English validation of their trials, the Quakers adopted many features of the harsh English Code.[3] Thus, for all practical purposes, until the Pennsylvania Constitution in 1776 declared its determination to "proceed as soon as might be to the reform of the penal laws, and invent punishments less sanguinary and better proportioned to the various degrees of criminality,"[4] prisons were used mainly for pre-trial detention.[5]

The Philadelphia Society for Assisting Distressed Prisoners, formed in that same year, was to change the picture.[6] After the Revolutionary War, the Society renewed its efforts and in 1787 Dr. Benjamin Rush read to the Society a landmark paper which suggested that the purpose of imprisonment was to make the prisoner repent[7]—the original concept behind the word "penitentiary."[8] Three years later the Pennsylvania legislature responded with legislation adopting hard labor in solitary confinement (for the purpose of contemplation and penitence) as a substitute for capital punishment for certain felonies.[9]

In 1790, the Walnut Street Prison in Philadelphia was opened, bringing the concept of reformation of criminals to realization.[10] The prison, however, was a failure. Overcrowding, corruption, lack of vocational training, and substantial mismanagement collapsed the system; by 1810, there was widespread call for a decrease in leniency, and a stronger "law and order" position.

The Pennsylvania legislature responded by requiring the absolute separation of prisoners from each other. Complete and utter silence—thus reducing the possibility of internal strife, or the "teaching of crime"—became the rule. Prisoners were also restrained from any meaningful activity; their entire lives were spent in their small cells, alone and separate from the rest of the prison community. The move toward this isolation surprisingly received support from several outstanding progressive penologists, including Thomas Eddy, whose earlier progressive experiments with the vocational training at Newgate Prison in New York State, like those at the Walnut Street Prison, had ended in disaster and left him somewhat embittered.[11]

Meanwhile, New York State, which had generally been following Pennsylvania's lead, experienced riots during 1818 at several institutions. The legislature immediately legalized flogging both at Newgate and Auburn; the flogging, however, was to be inflicted only under direct supervision of the warden.[12] Soon thereafter, Elam Lynds, a notorious figure in prison history, was appointed warden; Lynds immediately imposed a thorough and strictly enforced rule of silence, the lock-step and the grotesque black and white prison uniform.[13]

Within a short time the system of total silence, total inactivity, and total isolation led to numerous mental breakdowns among the inmates. Soon, work—whether at hard labor or at some kind of industry—was provided for the inmates, and it is with this new system—the "Auburn system"—that the story of modern prisons begins.[14]

The Auburn system, with its enforced silence, its discipline backed by brute force,[15] and its program of inmate labor, might have passed into ignominy without further ado, except for one factor—the prison became self-supporting; the sales of products from the prison, as well as the intra-prison use of the products, lessened the costs so drastically that, in fact, there was a profit. From 1828 to 1833, Auburn prison itself netted over $25,000.[16]

The experiment at Auburn was successful all around; the public was happy to avoid taxation for the purpose of running prisons, businessmen rejoiced at using cheap labor, and prison officials were pleased at the release of volatile energies.[17] Other states, seduced by the prospect of making crime pay, soon followed suit, and within a few years many of the penitentiaries were self-sufficient. If the industries inside the prisons could not sustain them, convicts were "leased" out. Another popular method saw contractors taking over parts of the prison area itself, using convict labor on a contractual basis.

With the focus now on making prisons profitable, no attention was paid to the conditions under which the prisoners lived. If, as in Maine and Connecticut, the cells were pits in the ground, with no ventilation,[18] or small rooms, 7 feet long and 3½ feet wide,[19] or, as in Vermont, cells in which prisoners had to walk all night to keep warm, being given only one blanket to ward off the most vicious New England winters,[20] these abuses were little noticed by the public. If silence, necessary to increased production, had to be enforced by vicious beatings (in some months at Sing Sing Prison in New York, there were as many as 3,000 lashes given out in punishment),[21] this could be tolerated: the prisoner was, after all, the "slave of the state,"[22] and slaves—and others—elsewhere were being beaten with regularity.[23]

In the 1840's and 50's several reform movements began,[24] but there was little success in ameliorating prison conditions.[25] After the Civil War, however, the New York Prison Society, spurred mostly by Zebulon Brockway, called for a national conference on penology. The result was the first meeting of the National Prison Association, held in 1870, in Cincinnati, Ohio. The ideal of prisoner rehabilitation was repeatedly stressed throughout the conference, and finally, in the keynote speech by Brockway himself. MacKelvey describes the reaction:

> In their enthusiasm for the ideal they rose above the monotony of four gray walls, men in stripes shuffling in lock step, sullen faces staring through the bars, coarse mush and coffee made of bread crusts . . . . They forgot it all and voted for their remarkable declaration of principles: Society is responsible for the reformation of criminals; education, religion and industrial training are valuable aids in this undertaking; discipline should build rather than destroy the self-respect of each prisoner; his co-operation can best be secured with an indeterminate sentence under which his discharge is regulated by a merit system; the responsibility of the state extends into the field of preventive institutions and to the aid and supervision of prisoners after discharge; a central state control should be established so as to secure a stable, non-political administration, trained officers, and reliable statistics.[26]

Thus, the principles which Dr. Rush and his Philadelphia Society had enunciated almost 100 years earlier, were now being accepted, in theory at least, by the representatives of most of the state penal systems in the country. A new era for penology began.

But it was not to last. Many of the officials, returned to their own, less idealistic realms, found the goals impossible of attainment. Politics, as it always had, intervened in prison administration, removing wardens and others.[27] Some of the reformers died; others turned to new fields. Despite some victories, such as the building of the first Reformatory for youthful offenders at Elmira, New York, headed by Brockway, the movement faltered and died. It was revived again, briefly, in the 1880's, with former President Rutherford B. Hayes leading the fight, but his death in 1892 saw the end of the first phase of the revived movement.

Meanwhile, other trends were taking place to make the prison reformers wary. After the Civil War, the prisoners returned to production, and industry. But soon, outside labor, becoming organized for the first time in any meaningful sense, began to complain about the unfair competition of cheap convict labor. Some state legislatures, consequently, restricted in various ways the ability of the prisons to sell their output within the states or to make certain kinds of goods.[28] With this turn of events, the prisons were effectively back where they had been in 1820: prisoners, or great portions of them were unable to work; idleness again became the theme of prison life.

Some states responded with the "contract" or "lease" system. Alabama, for example, switched from leasing prison buildings to leasing prisoners. By the latter 1880's more than half of that state's convicts were engaged in mining coal.[29] In most states, however, opposition to that system was successful. As labor power grew, prison industries shrank until finally, during the depression, Congress passed a series of acts ultimately outlawing interstate traffic in prison-made goods. When this legislation was followed by various state laws, profitable prison industry ceased.[30]

But even at that time, in the late 1880's, penologists and legislators alike were looking toward other goals.[31] There was a "widespread stampede"[32] to the ideas which Brockway and the National Prison Association (which had changed its name in the 1880's to the American Prison Association) had heralded:

> The close of the century found reformatory penology triumphant. Not only had its chief tenets been accepted by the responsible leaders of the many official and semiofficial bodies concerned with the prison, but they had been widely recognized in the statute laws of the North.[33]

And yet—in 1968, Dr. Karl Menninger can proclaim that in our prisons occurs the "Crime of Punishment." In 1969, Arkansas state officials were indicted for beating and torturing inmates with unspeakable devices.[34] And a leading penologist could say, in the 1960's:

If penology does not get the lead out of its feet, a moratorium on research could safely be declared for several decades at least without researchers needing to fear that the practice of penology would catch up with them. There is no immediate prospect that the chasm between practice and theory will be bridged.[35]

What *are* prison practices like in the latter half of the twentieth century? What goes on behind that "dark gray wall?" The cases—and other sources—hold at least a partial answer.

The American Prison in 1970.

The typical prison of the last third of the twentieth century has changed relatively little from the institutions of 150 years earlier. The average prisoner is compelled to live in an antiquated building, probably over 50, and perhaps over 100 years old. If he is fortunate he has only one cellmate, in a cell that could barely be called livable, and certainly not comfortable; otherwise, he will room with five or more inmates in a huge sheep-pen type of arrangement, or be given a bed in a large overcrowded general area.[36] His recreation, if any is allowed at all, is minimal. The food is adequate but not enticing,[37] served either on metal trays in a dining room or in his cell. He will be denied contact with women, since heterosexual contact is, of course, strictly forbidden. Yet the chances are quite high that he will be forced into homosexual contacts with his fellow inmates.

Throughout his day, if he is in a typical institution, his life is one of sheer monotony, broken only by staccato orders of discipline or minimal activity. He may be fortunate enough to work all day on a farm, or undergo vocational training or education, but the chances are slim indeed. He will be unable to interest any of the prison officals in him, unless he is hostile in some way, simply because there are not enough professional people to go around; if he is hostile, the only response will be discipline—probably solitary confinement.

The Physical Conditions of Prisons

In 1961, James Bennett, then Director of the Federal Bureau of Prisons, declared: "More than a hundred prisons still in operation today were built before Grant took Richmond."[38] Six years later, a minimum of 11 percent of all prisons in use were said to be at least 80 years old.[39] Since the federal prison system dates from the establishment of the Federal Bureau of Prisons in 1930, most of the antiquated buildings are state prisons.[40]

A setting less prone to encourage rehabilitation than a building which is disintegrating before the very eyes of its inmates is hard to imagine. Moreover, these old buildings were constructed with a view of imprisonment that is no longer accepted or acceptable; they are composed of elements which increase the suffering of the individual and accomplish nothing toward his eventual resocialization. When the Maine State Prison was first opened, its first warden proclaimed that "Prisons should be so constructed that even their aspect might be terrific and appear like what they should be—dark and comfortless abodes of guilt and wretchedness."[41]

One of the most inhuman aspects of prison life is the lack of privacy caused by the almost universal phenomenon of overcrowding, particularly acute in the older prisons. These are generally left with the overflow of inmates which other, more treatment-oriented, institutions will not take, lest the rehabilitation effort there be frustrated by overpopulation and consequent inattention. In 1964, the conditions in federal prisons, generally considered the best penal institutions in the country, were described to a United States Senate Committee by James Bennett, Director of the Federal Bureau of Prisons:

> Although the general public visualizes a prison as a place where each inmate has his own cell, we do not have single-cell capacity for more than 30 percent of the total population of our maximum custody institutions. The rest are housed in multiple cells holding as many as 10 men, or in large dormitories, in basements, and in units originally constructed for other purposes.
>
> . . . You may remember seeing, for instance at McNeil Island, where they have 10 men in an area no more than 15 by 20 feet, men sleeping in double—or triple—decked bunks, as on shipboard during the war, and they have to be there for long hours together.[42]

While inmates of penal institutions are no longer literally sleeping with pigs, as was true in Louisiana prisons a century ago,[43] the situation seems to have improved relatively little.

The terrible overcrowding in the prisons would almost move one to wish for the return of Pennsylvania's solitary cell, where at least the prisoner could have privacy at some point.[44] But the single cells now used almost exclusively on death row are no better. One deathrow inmate at San Quentin described it this way:

> The picture of the condemned man pacing his cell is not good applied to San Quentin. You can't pace a ten-foot cell that is all cluttered up with bed, table, chairs, toilet, and what not. Or you can, in a sort of fashion, by leaving one foot stationary and taking a pace each way with the other. That rests you from sitting, but is not very much as pacing. Nonetheless, men have paced so, and there is a hollow worn in the center of the concrete floor to prove it. Also the paint is worn away above the grating in the door—worn

through several coats of paint down to the bare steel by men's foreheads pressing, rubbing against it while they look out at the garden, and at the hills over the wall.[45]

These, of course, are not the only physical irritants in prisons. As a result of overcrowding, for example, "Men stand in line at the toilets and washbowls. They go to the dining room in shifts; the dining room of the Atlanta (federal) penitentiary is in continuous use throughout the day."[46]

Modern plumbing has only recently come to many prisons,[47] and is still absent in some, so that the malodorous "bucket" adds to discomfort, particularly at night, when the inmates cannot move freely to the restrooms. Despite the many inmates who are assigned to maintenance duty, and depite continuous attempts on the part of all, there are problems with cockroaches and other insects. It has recently been reported that an inmate of the Virginia State Penitentiary sent to segregation for one month spent his time killing cockroaches and piling them in a corner.[48] Moreover, prison authorities have only begun to allow inmates to use articles to brighten their inevitably dreary cells. Items such as photographs, radios, and the like are only now beginning to appear in many places (assuming that there is room for each man to have some personal article in an eight-man cell).

Brutality in the Prison

Violence permeates prison life. Much of it erupts within the inmate community itself—homosexual assaults, assertions of dominance, enforcement against bad debtors. The most vicious violence, however, is that which the prison officers—particularly the guards—employ against the inmates, who cannot complain because they will not be believed.

Part of the problem is endemic to the prison system. Personnel selected for the position of "correctional line officer" (guard) tend' to be custodially oriented, regarding inmates not as humans but as ciphers.[49] The low salary scale (the salary range for guards is $1500—$9000 a year; the median is $4000—$5000)[50] generally forecloses college graduates and others who, on the whole, might be less physically abusive; indeed, over half the institutions in the country, undoubtedly because of low salaries, require no minimum educational qualifications for guards.[51]

The refusal of guards to accept the "treatment-oriented," more humane approach to inmates, even when the warden has endorsed this approach, is a stubborn fact of prison life.[52] And, of course, where the warden shares the opinion that rehabilitation is an illusory goal, the guards have virtually explicit authority to use force wherever and whenever they desire.

The most scandalous example of this kind of system has recently been un-earthed—and that word is used advisedly—by Thomas Murton, a criminolo-gist who was appointed to the Arkansas' state penal system in 1967.[53] Within a year of his appointment, he had exhumed bodies of prisoners allegedly beaten to death by the guards;[54] discovered files indicating the deaths of many more;[55] and revealed a list of torture devices regularly used by the warden, including the "Tucker telephone," in which a prisoner's testicles were shocked by electrical impulses,[56] and the "teeter board," a plank formed by two-by-four boards, nailed together so that the longer board was on top, and the nails holding the two extended toward the prisoner.[57] If the prisoner fell off the board, and could not make it balance, he was beaten with a five-foot long leather strap.[58] Other physical abuses were common-place in the system; when 144 prisoners sat-in to protest food conditions, tear gas was used to break up the demonstration; later, ten of the leaders were beaten.[59]

These beatings were consciously endorsed by the authorities. When asked what his views on penology were, Governor Orval Faubus responded that "Punishment is the greatest deterrent to crime."[60] The legislature indicated its penal philosophy by giving a standing ovation to an ex-prisoner who told them, at the very time the revelations of the abuses were being made, that the prison had created "the finest atmosphere for rehabilitation of anti-social inmates that has ever been developed anywhere in the world."[61] Grand juries, con-vened to hear testimony, dismissed all the evidence as "prisoner talk;"[62] charges against some of the officials were likewise dismissed by local judges.[63] Later, federal grand juries indicted fifteen of these same officials.[64]

Just as saddening as this picture of the Arkansas system was the initial judicial reaction—or lack of it—to these tales of horror. In 1965, a federal district court refused to call excessive beatings and floggings by inmate-guards cruel and unusual punishment.[65] Instead, said the court, the beat-ing "must not be excessive; it must be inflicted as dispassionately as possible and by responsible people; and it must be applied in reference to recognizable standards whereby a convict may know what conduct on his part will cause him to be whipped and how much punishment any given conduct may pro-duce."[66]

Immediately after this decision, the state penitentiary board drew up new rules. Whipping in the fields was forbidden; whippings were limited to ten lashes. Inmates (trustees) were forbidden to whip other inmates. A Board of Inquiry was established to decide how many lashes should be given.[67] But the Board's fundamental attitude toward the problem is probably better expressed by its one reference to rehabilitation in the new prison rules:

The State Board and the Superintendent, acting in compliance with law, have established a rehabilitation system which largely occupies the time of prisoners by engaging in farm enterprise. This sytem is based on the theory that certain crops must be planted . . . *No one shall be permitted to shirk the work that they are (sic) capable of doing. Your prison commitment reads that you shall be confined "at hard labor" and you are expected to perform labor that you are capable of in a diligent and proper manner.*[68]

As the warden at that time expressed it, "Rehabilitation isn't something you can teach a man, it's a state of mind that can come to a man in the strangest places, even in the middle of a cotton field on a prison farm."[69]

The whipping continued, under the new "safe-guards" promulgated by the Board. Soon, another suit was filed, challenging the whipping, the Tucker telephone, the teeter board, and other similar devices. The torture devices were enjoined,[70] but the whipping was restrained only "until additional rules and regulations are promulgated with appropriate safe-guards."[71] Again, the prison system immediately formed new regulations; corporal punishment could not be imposed until after a Board of Inquiry hearing, could not exceed ten lashes with the strap, could not be applied to the bare skin, could not be used in the field, and could not follow, within 24 hours, another beating.[72]

On appeal, the Eighth Circuit reluctantly held that whipping with a leather strap, no matter how applied or imposed, was cruel and unusual punishment, saying "we have no difficulty in reaching the conclusion that the use of the strap . . . is punishment which, in this last third of the 20th century, runs afoul of the Eighth Amendment; that the strap's use . . . offends contemporary concepts of decency and human dignity. . . ."[73]

The court found the punishment invalid because of its potential for abuse; there was no way that a rule or regulation "however seriously or sincerely conceived and drawn, [would] successfully prevent abuse."[74] Pointing to the methods used by the prison system to evade the earlier rulings in *Talley* and *Jackson*, which called for following specific rules, and declaring that "[c]orporal punishment is easily subject to abuse in the hands of the sadistic and the unscrupulous,"[75] the court stopped the beating of inmates.

The Arkansas system is, fortunately, not the typical system. But while its abuses and corruptions are far in excess of those found in the average penal system, the difference is one of degree rather than kind.

Philip Hirschkop has graphically outlined the brutalities of the contemporary Virginia State Penitentiary.[76] Beatings, neglect, solitary confinement, abuses, and simple ignorance of and refusal to follow due process, are all present in that system. In fact, the periodic, arbitrary tear gassings of prisoners have only recently ceased—and then only by court order,[77] a step the Fourth Circuit Court of Appeals was unwilling to take only three years ago.[78]

A review of both the cases and the observations made by outstanding penologists belies the assertion made by A. MacCormick, head of the Osborne Society, that "[s]ome of the most brutal forms of corporal punishment (flogging, for example) have practically disappeared. . . ."[79] Sol Rubin, an outstanding authority in the field, found in 1963, that

> [a]t least twenty-six prisons employed corporal punishment. Whipping with a strap was common. The Virginia "spread eagle" similar to the medieval rack, stretched the body by ropes and pulleys. Men died or came close to death in Florida's sweat box, an unventilated cell built around a fireplace. In Michigan and Ohio prisoners were kept in a standing position and unable to move; in Wisconsin they were gagged; in West Virginia they were subjected to frigid baths. . . .[80]

While corporal punishment has been abolished in Great Britain,[81] it is still officially allowed by Canadian statute,[82] although the actual use is asserted to be quickly diminishing.[83] Indiana, by statute, still allows corporal punishment in prison in some circumstances.[84] Beatings still occur with distressing regularity. Recently, a Louisiana court allowed recovery to the parents of a juvenile beaten to death with leather straps by officials of a state industrial school;[85] suits for beatings by prison guards have been brought under the Civil Rights Act both by prisoners[86] and by federal government officials.[87] Some courts, however, have refused to deal with allegations of beating by guards.[88]

Nor are guards the only persons in the prison willing or ready to hand out corporal punishment. In the Arkansas system, penologists were most deeply concerned about the fact that other inmates ("trusties") kept guard.[89]

In 1969, a federal district court suggested that the use of trusties as guards might, of itself, create an unconstitutional situation in Arkansas.[90] In a later landmark case,[91] the court, finding that under the system then in effect the state could not protect the inmate from the trusties, held the entire prison system unconstitutionally dangerous, and ordered the prison authorities either to produce a workable plan for improving the situation, or to face the possibility of closing down the prison.

Damage suits against officials who appear to have condoned beatings by inmates have not been well received. Thus, in *Henderson v. Pate*,[92] the court affirmed a dismissal of the case because the inmates could not be said to be state agents, or acting under color of state law. In *Bethea v. Crouse*,[93] the Tenth Circuit reversed a summary judgment for the defendant warden, who allegedly watched as one inmate, supposedly a rape victim, beat his attacker.

The court stated that if the warden had allowed merely minor force, *e.g.*, an assault and battery, he could not be held liable; only if excessive force had been allowed (a jury question) could he be held.[94]

Prisons are not the only places where helpless inmates receive beatings. In *Whitree v. State*,[95] for example, the plaintiff stated that

> after a beating administered by the attendants, he was stripped and placed in the "Blue Room". That said room was a small dark room without toilet facilities, without water facilities, and, without a bed or mattress. He stated he was kept in said room for about eight days on bread and water plus a full meal once every three days. This sounds incredible but it was not refuted by any state witness.[96]

The institution at which the plaintiff was kept was not a prison. It was a state mental hospital in New York State. As the court found, the "patient" had been kept in that institution for approximately 12 years longer than necessary, because he had never received the proper medical treatment—in a hospital—that he needed in order to recover.

Psychological Conditions of Prison Life

The effect on a man who has been allowed to stagnate in prison without a creative or constructive work program is devastating. Among prison officials and penologists there is unanimous agreement that prisoners should work.[97] Yet approximately one-third[98] (other estimates run as high as 40 percent[99]) of the nation's prison population are either completely idle or assigned to over-manned maintenance details. Not only is it true that "[f]ew scenes are more discouraging and contradictory than a prison yard full of men leading a life of indolence while waiting for release to a life of work,"[100] but it is further obvious that such idleness "is a waste of taxpayers' money . . . and, if continued long enough, results in deterioration and dependency, bitterness and hostility."[101] Indeed, "in these conditions occasional outbursts and riots are not incomprehensible; only their rarity is surprising."[102]

There are two basic reasons for this enforced idleness. One is the difficulty of funding. But much more oppressive is the Hawes-Cooper Act,[103] which divests prison-made goods of their interstate character, thus allowing the states to put restrictions on their sale; the Ashurst-Sumners Act,[104] passed in 1935, which allows states to forbid the importation of goods made in out-of-state prisons; and a third federal statute which prohibits the interstate transportation of convict-made goods for any purpose.[105] Together with state restrictions on the intrastate sale of these goods, passed, as were the federal acts, after intense and prolonged lobbying by labor unions,[106] the possibility of prisoners working in industrial, profit-making ventures is almost nil.[107]

This continued monotony of idleness is perhaps the single most piercing aspect of prison life. Aside from its obvious role in the teaching of crime, the lack of constructive goals makes the prisoner more an outcast as each day passes; rehabilitation becomes impossible, because there is no work to serve as a catalyst.

Concurrent with this lack of work is a lack of play. The problems described in a 1942 study of the Alabama system, are still typical of prison leisure today:

> Recreational facilities are sorely lacking in all prisons and road camps, except Kilby and Draper. Practically the only recreation in the road camps is simple games, such as dominos and various forms of gambling. Gambling, while not condoned by Alabama's prison administrators, is tacitly acknowledged and permitted within reasonable limits . . . lack of other recreational outlets . . . has brought about this situation perforce.[108]

Today, television is present in many prisons; films are often available. Baseball, and in some few cases, football, teams are created. But in many institutions, the only daily exercise for thousands of men is still a to-and-fro walk in the small prison "yard."

Still other deprivations occur in prison life, but these can only briefly be mentioned. Perhaps the most obvious of these is the forced lack of heterosexual contact. Few American prisons allow conjugal visiting,[109] although the practice is common in most European and other North American penal systems.[110] This, of course, aggravates the main problem of homosexuality which permeates the "prison community."[111] The lack of heterosexual conduct is striking indeed; as Cory suggests:

> [T]he public would be only mildly shocked if it were to learn that there are frequent homosexual contacts in a given prison . . . but just imagine the wave of shock, incredulity, indignation and the lurid headlines if this same public were to learn that men and women cohabitated and copulated together within these same prison walls.[112]

There will probably not be much change in prison practice in the next ten years. Notwithstanding the provocative suggestion by Dr. Menninger that the deprivation of decent sexual relations is "cruel and unusual punishment,"[113] it is most unlikely that the courts will expand the principle of *Griswold v. Connecticut*[114] to hold that the state must show a reason for totally invading the marital relationship.

The total scrutiny to which each prisoner is subjected each moment of his life is also a "condition" of present prison life. An inmate's mail is censored,[115] and his visits monitored. He is required to follow unintelligibly vague rules,[116] and he is often the victim of arbitrary and peremptory discipline if he fails to do so. He is challenged if he wishes outside reading[117] or seeks religious or moral advice not authorized by his warden.[118] He is subject to a surprise search or a whimsical routing without recourse. And if he complains, he is greeted with grimaces and disbelief at best and punishment, both formal and informal, at worst.

Furthermore, the inmate receives little help in resocialization. Despite frequent public complaints that the principle of "less eligibility"[119] is being transgressed, the fact is that there is usually no meaningful professional help at all. Studies indicate that a state and federal inmate population of 201,220, are now served by 1,124 "professionals," 1,654 "educators," 359 "religious leaders," and 12,734 "other" personnel.[120] The remaining 30,809 employees, two-thirds of the staff in the prison, are "custodial."[121] Indeed, the number of trained professional personnel is so low that in almost all institutions the teachers are inmates or, in some cases, "cast-offs" of the public school systems.[122] Salaries, moreover, are abominably low, so that few qualified persons are attracted to work in the correctional system. In October 1969, the Joint Commission on Correctional Manpower and Training reported that less than half of the administrators of adult or juvenile institutions were making more than $14,000 yearly;[123] very few of the "supervisory" staff were making even that much and almost three-fourths of them were earning less than $10,000.[124] Thus, the inmate's general inability to obtain work which might aid him in adjusting to the outside world is aggravated by the almost total lack of qualified counsellors pursuing the same goal.

Two recent investigations have collected some of the material necessary for an evaluation of these same problems in jails.[125] One of these studies reveals that over two-thirds of all "short-term institutions" are 25 years old and more than one-third are over 50 years old.[126] The jails are terribly overcrowded. The county jail for the Cincinnati area was recently forced to close its doors to new prisoners, because it had housed 355 in a building intended for 150.[127] Dr. Karl Menninger cites statistics showing that two dormitories in the District of Columbia jail, each 180 by 120 feet, are used for 500 prisoners.[128]

The N.C.C.D. Report indicated that one New England state had four jails in which there were no sanitary facilities.[129] "Jails are used in many cities," another study reports,[130] "to get skid row drunks off the street . . . to give prostitutes medical checkups, to house the homeless." Moreover, a high percentage, perhaps 80 percent, of all remaining commitments are for failure to pay a fine.[131]

Recently at a conference at New York University Law School, New York State Senator John Dunne stated that 9,000 of the 15,000 inmates of the New York City jails were awaiting trial, having been convicted of nothing. And, as Professor Foote has shown, those who remain in jail for failure to make bail are more likely to be convicted.[132] Furthermore, the N.C.C.D. Report found[133] that less than 30 percent of those detained in three city jails were actually committed after conviction. A 1969 Rand Institute Study of New York City Criminal Court indicated that only 10 percent of those found guilty were committed to jail.[134] This means that at least 70 to 90 percent spent time in jail prior to trial and were then released after conviction without imposition of a jail senence. The jails seem to be used for every purpose but sentencing. And, of course, there are no rehabilitative programs at all.[135]

Moreover, during this pre-trial detention period, all prisoners, whether convicted or not, mix with each other. The appalling result is told well by one inmate: "During my [pre-trial] confinement, I've already learned how to mix nitroglycerin and how to 'peel' a safe, and I've been given some tips on the kind of weaponry to be used during an armed robbery."[136]

Judging the Prison: A Question of Standards

A major difficulty in evaluating prison conditions today and in determining the relief to which an inmate is entitled from adverse conditions is that of articulating a reasonable standard with which to judge the prison. How, for example, does one translate into legal terms the impact of idleness or of unsanitary conditions? In what meaningful language can the dialogue between court and inmate take place?

Most courts have appealed to the eighth amendment's prohibition of "cruel and unusual punishment." Taking their guideline from two Supreme Court decisions almost a half century apart,[137] which held that the test for violations of the eighth amendment looks to the "dignity of man" as recognized in all "civilized" countries, the lower federal courts have, on occasion, found physical conditions so appalling, particularly in solitary confinement cells, that they have ordered the release from those cells of the plaintiff inmates.[138]

But that standard is undesirably vague and relativistic.[139] It places too great a burden upon the inmate to demonstrate that the conditions are, in fact, unbearable by any reasonable man. Recently some courts, purportedly acting under another test derived from the eighth amendment, a test which has never been articulated by the Supreme Court, have begun to ask the correct question: Does the continuation of X condition, or the imposition of Y punishment, serve a valid penal purpose?[140] Thus far, those courts have not really had to confront this standard, since they have found the activity of the prison either justified or unjustified under other tests.[141] In *Glenn v. Wilkerson*, however, the court did find that the segregation of death row inmates from the general prison population was both a generally practiced prison procedure[142] and one which served the valid penal purpose of keeping morale high in the general prison population.[143] Eventually, however, these courts will have to come to terms with the crucial question: what is the purpose of prison? And, if that hurdle is somehow overcome, they will face another: how closely must the challenged practice conform to that purpose in order to be sustained?

It is widely agreed among penologists that, whatever the purpose of imposing the sanction of the criminal law, the purpose of *prison* is rehabilitation.[144] Thus, a common phrase among correctional professionals today is that an offender is sent to an institution *as* punishment, not *for* punishment, and that the institution's goal should not be punishment, but reformation. Moreover, at least nine states have statutes expressly stating that the purpose of the institutionalization of an offender and the goal of the correctional process is reformation and resocialization.[145] In these states, at least, the difficulty of establishing a purpose of prison has been eliminated by the legislature itself; in other states, the statutes are either silent or opposed to the position that the work of the prison is reformation and resocialization. Nevertheless, there is sufficient statutory and judicial support to warrant a broad finding that these are the goals of imprisonment.

If the purpose of prison is rehabilitation, then what conditions may be justified and what restrictions may be placed on inmates' rights? The last two decades have seen innumerable Supreme Court decisions expanding the protection of human freedoms against encroachment by the states. From a "balancing test" in almost every area,[146] the court has moved to a requirement that, wherever human liberties are involved, the state must demonstrate (a) a compelling state interest; (b) that the challenged procedure or law advances that interest in a manner least drastically curtailing the liberty. Thus, for example, Connecticut's birth control law banning the use of contraceptives was struck down as an overbroad attempt to protect what might otherwise be a legitimate state interest—prevention of the sale of contraceptives within the state.[147] Similarly, attempts to limit the franchise to the most "interested" voters in special elections have been struck down on the ground that the statutes involved excluded voters just as "interested" as those included.[148]

There are many other examples;[149] the cases involving marital privacy and voting rights are mentioned specifically only because they do not involve first amendment freedoms, thereby demonstrating that the sweep of the decisions goes beyond the borders of that "preferred" freedom and reaches any state regulation of any basic human liberty.

The basic human liberties, including the use of mails, the enjoyment of movement, the freedom to read, the right to "happiness" and reasonable comforts, should not lightly be banned from prisons. While there is undeniable justification for restrictions on movement from inside the walls of an institution to an area outside those walls, it would seem perfectly reasonable to suggest, as the Sixth Circuit did a quarter-century ago, that a prisoner retains in prison all rights except those inevitably taken from him in pursuit of the goal of incarceration and neutralization.[150] If indeed, every state action restricting an individual must be rationally explained by the state, there is no compelling reason why this requirement should not apply with equal vigor and force to restrictions placed upon men in correctional institutions.[151]

Thus, in short, we reach the following determination: in order to justify any action of a prison official or to rationalize the continuation of a given condition inside a prison, the prison authorities should be called upon to demonstrate that their action, or inaction, is essentially related to the main purpose of incarceration, and that they achieve this purpose with the least possible restriction of his humanity consonant with that purpose and the lesser purpose of neutralization.

Court Litigation Contesting Conditions in Penal Institutions

There are relatively few cases which specifically address themselves to the question of whether conditions in penal institutions infringe prisoners' rights. By far the bulk of those which do consider the physical environment are those dealing with solitary confinement situations. In several instances, the courts have compelled the release of prisoners subjected to demeaning and debauched conditions.[152] The number of cases so holding is small, and the conditions included, almost universally, lack of any sanitary facilities and of personal hygiene materials as well.[153] In several cases, the lack of proper bathing facilities has been mentioned as one ingredient in a finding that conditions transgress the constitutional limitations of punishment.[154]

Several cases have considered challenges to incarceration in overcrowded facilities. The first of these, Ex Parte *Pickens*,[155] involved the crowding of forty jail prisoners into a room twenty-seven feet square. In denying a petition for habeas corpus, brought by an inmate awaiting trial, the court, obviously depressed by the circumstances outlined at length in its decision, stressed two factors: (1) under the then-prevailing concept of habeas corpus, only total release was possible; (2) there were no other jail facilities in the area to which prisoners could be sent. Since many of the inmates were awaiting trial on serious felony charges, the court felt constrained not to release them, but it suggested that the conditions somehow be alleviated. Moreover, the court was operating under attenuated concepts of the eighth amendment; comparing conditions faced by criminal inmates to those faced by American soldiers then fighting in South Korea, the court found that conditions in the jail were not so intolerable as to violate the concepts of human dignity.[156]

The *Pickens* decision stood for almost 20 years as the sole reported instance in which jail conditions were attacked generally. Recently, however, the awakening of poverty lawyers to the plight of the incarcerated inmate has led to several other decisions concerning prison life. In *Curly v. Gonzales*,[157] the court actually found that the conditions were so intolerable as to violate the Eighth Amendment, and ordered the jail not to house more than 60 inmates. The authorities, stunned by the decision, released all inmates over that number, a course of action not necessarily dictated by the decree. In *Inmates of Cook County Jail v. Tierney*,[158] the plaintiffs complained of various physical conditions in the jail. After initial rulings indicating that the plaintiffs might succeed, the case was settled out of court by the attempts of the defendants to remedy some of the more drastic conditions.

Clearly the most far-reaching of the cases dealing with the physical conditions of a prison system is *Holt v. Sarver*,[159] where the district court, finding that the inmates were so quartered as to facilitate homosexual attacks by other inmates, and that the inmate guards did little to prevent such attacks, ordered the prison authorities either to remedy the situation immediately or to shut down the entire prison system. The court's lengthy and detailed opinion listed other aspects of the prison system which further aggravated the general conditions at the camp: the solitary confinement cells were atrocious; the inmates were allowed to gamble, using a kind of scrip for money; tension at the camp was at a nerve-shattering level because of the use of trusties as guards; and sanitary conditions were at an exceptionally low level.

These cases indicate at least a willingness on the part of the courts to consider drastic remedies in the absence of meaningful amelioration of inhuman conditions in a prison setting. They have all been decided under the eighth amendment, although, at least in *Holt*, there were clear implications that rehabilitation, or the lack of it, would figure in any decision generally considering prison conditions and environment.[160]

Several other cases bear mention because of the indication that the courts will investigate every aspect of prison life. In *Krist v. Smith*,[161] while holding that maximum security was reasonable for the inmate in question, given his escape record, the court clearly intimated that lack of exercise might justify court intervention.

In *Glenn v. Wilkinson*,[162] the court took a similar approach. While holding that isolation of death row inmates as a group from the rest of the inmate population was not unconstitutional and, in fact, was a generally accepted correctional practice, the court took the issue very seriously, thereby intimating two things:

(1) individual isolation might be very suspect;

(2) even group isolation might be suspect in some situations.

The direction of these two cases is totally different from that taken by the courts not so many years ago. Both of these decisions, while holding against the particular plaintiff in the case, evidence a concern for the psychological effects which imprisonment, and especially isolation, may have upon an inmate, and suggest that severe mental strain might activate judicial interposition. The trend is an auspiciously happy one and should be continued.

In *Sostre v. Rockefeller*,[163] the court took cognizance of "[t]he physical and psychological harm . . . of continued confinement in the segregation unit"[164] and, in view of the facts there, ordered release of the prisoner on a motion for preliminary injunction. The psychological harm to which the court referred had stemmed not simply from the physical conditions of the cell, which were not appalling when compared to some other solitary confinement cases, but to the methods used to harass the prisoner. In one instance, the court found that a single light bulb, which the inmate could not control, burned in the middle of the cell for 24 hours a day, making sleep impossible. In addition, the prisoner was awakened every half hour by a guard making his rounds; the usual tactic was to run a billy club across the bars of the cell.

While these latter cases treat mainly isolation from the majority of the prison population, their scope is much wider, for they appear to require a definite showing by the state that the imposition of suffering, whether mental or physical, be absolutely mandated by an interest of the state over and above that of mere punishment. Moreover, *Krist* and *Glenn* clearly focus on the mental anguish which is incident to the operation of the isolation; in neither of those cases was the psychological tenseness intended as a direct result of the procedure.

Those cases, and *Sostre* to a lesser extent, would seem to open a new road for judicial review of prison conditions. Like *Johnson v. Avery*,[165] wherein the Supreme Court overrode considerations of discipline to protect a prisoner's right to effective access to the courts, they require prison officials to consider all the ramifications of any rule, regulation, procedure, or practice, and ascertain that their consequences are not so severe as to make life unbearable in prison.[166] This trend, salutary as it is, could be enhanced if the rehabilitation-due process analysis suggested above were more widely adopted, for then prison officials would have to consider (1) the direct, immediate effect intended to result from any given practice; (2) the indirect consequences of the continuation of a practice or procedure; (3) the rehabilitative effects of the practice. If, under any one of those tests, the prison practice remained dubious, it could be invalidated; at the very least, prison authorities could be required to defend the practice on meaningful grounds. The basic rights of prisoners require at least that much protection.

NOTES

1. A. MacCormick, Adult Correctional Institutions in the United States 9 (1967) [hereinafter cited as MacCormick]. Despite the modern origin of the system, MacCormick asserts that 41 prisons are over 80 years old, and of these 20 are 100 to 158 years old. *Id.* at 62.

2. S. Rubin, H. Weihofen, G. Edwards & S. Rosenzweig, The Law of Criminal Correction 27 (1963) [hereinafter cited as Rubin].

3. W. Lewis, From Newgate to Dannemora 2 (1965) [hereinafter cited as W. Lewis].

4. O. Lewis, The Development of American Prisons and Prison Customs, 1776-1845, at 8 (Patterson Smith reprint ed. 1967) [hereinafter cited as O. Lewis]. Intriguingly enough, the English Parliament, in 1778, provided for the creation of a number of "penitentiary houses," the primary purpose of which was to instill in the inmate Christian virtues. A. Babington, The Power to Silence 94 (1968). And Thomas Eddy, a key figure in the American movement for penal reform, convinced the New York State legislature, in 1796, to abolish the death penalty for all but three crimes, substituting lengthy prison sentences as punishment. W. Lewis, *supra* note 3, at 1-2.

5. *Id.* at 7. This is the normally accepted view, and is generally accurate. A recent careful study, however, has demonstrated that some imprisonment of felons in the Middle Ages was primarily punitive rather than custodial in design. *See* R. Pugh, Imprisonment in Medieval England (1968).

6. O. Lewis, *supra* note 4, at 13. The first Society was short-lived, since the British took possession of the Philadelphia jails early in the Revolutionary War. After the war, Dr. Benjamin Rush, along with Benjamin Franklin and other Quakers, organized the Philadelphia Society for Alleviating the Miseries of Public Prisons.

7. *Id.* at 19.

8. Teeters, *State of Prisons in the United States, 1870-1970*, XX 33 Fed. Prob. 18 (Dec. 1969), gives prison reformer John Howard credit for first coining the word. That penitence was the first goal of the Quakers in prison reform is clear; it meant a consequent lack of concern over such pressing problems as mismanagement and overcrowding which eventually led to the collapse of the whole system. It has, in fact, been suggested that the religious influence may have been the chief cause of the hideous conditions of prison life:

> Subsistence upon coarse food or shortened rations; the wearing of distinctve, and in certain cases humiliating, garb; abstinence from sexual and other excitements; the contemplation of past transgressions, accompanied by resolutions to make future amendment; the use of a cellular form of living accommoda-

tion; and the encouragement or absolute requirement of silence—all these were features of monastic life which may conceivably have influenced the thinking of those who built and administered prisons in the late eighteenth and early nineteenth centuries.
W. LEWIS, *supra* note 4, at 8. *See* K. MENNINGER, THE CRIME OF PUNISHMENT 222 (1968).

9. W. LEWIS, *supra* note 3, at 3.

10. O. LEWIS, *supra* note 4, at 119.

11. W. LEWIS, *supra* note 3, at 41-42. Eddy, in his earlier "Account of the State Prison" (1801), had stressed amendment of the reformer as the most important aim of the penitentiary. O. LEWIS, *supra* note 4, at 53.

12. W. LEWIS, *supra* note 3, at 46.

13. *Id.* at 91-92. The system also had a classification of prisoners, according to the possibility of reformation of the inmate. The approach to penology taken by the board of inspectors at Auburn, was formulated in the following manner:

> The end and design of the law is the prevention of crime, through fear of punishment, the reformation of offenders being of minor consideration. . . . Let the most obdurate and guilty felons be immured in solitary cells and dungeons; let them have pure air, wholesome food, comfortable clothing, and medical aid when necessary; cut them off from all intercourse with men; let not the voice or face of a friend ever cheer them; let them walk within gloomy abodes, and commune with their corrupt hearts and guilty consciences in silence, and brood over the horrors of their solitude, and the enormity of their crimes, without the hope of executive pardon.

O. LEWIS, *supra* note 4, at 81.

14. *Id.* at 78.

15. *Id.* at 93. "It was frankly conceded by the administration that the system could not be maintained without prompt, severe and effective punishment." The story of corporal punishment in the New York state prisons of the early nineteenth century has been carefully described by W. LEWIS, *supra* note 3, at 94-98, and he illustrates the way in which even public unhappiness with the prison system may be unable to affect the management of the institution.

The Auburn system was primarily the brainchild of Elam Lynds, an obvious sadist who dealt unmercifully with the prisoners. By the mid-1820's Lynds had dictatorial power in Auburn. Although a New York law of 1819, legalizing flogging in prison, contained safeguards to prevent abuse, chiefly by requiring the presence of a prison inspector while it was administered, these provisions were constantly evaded under the tutelage of Lynds. "With the development of the Auburn system, and particularly after Lynds gained carte blanche authority to handle disciplinary matters, keepers and turnkeys were given wide latitude in the flogging of felons." *Id.* at 94.

A scandal occurred when a female prisoner, Rachel Welch, died in childbirth after severe floggings. Public outcry led to the appointment of a new warden, Gersham Powers, but when it became known that Powers also believed in corporal punishment, a grand jury was impaneled, which found that the turnkeys had been given summary authority to inflict corporal punishment without consulting the warden. *Id.*

A state investigation commission decided that the 1819 law did not prohibit all flogging, a decision validated by a New York court which held that, notwithstanding the explicit language of the 1819 statute, there was a "common law right" of flogging in prison, and the actions of the officials in the prison were otherwise beyond the ken of the court. *Id.* at 95-96. The law of 1819 thus failed to prevent the whipping, or infliction of other corporal punishment, by guards, and it was another decade before any real movement against corporal punishment took hold. Corporal punishment flourished elsewhere in New York. At Newgate, prisoners were flogged or chained to their beds. On some occasions, they were placed in the "Sunday Cell," about 5 feet high and 3½ feet square, in which a man of ordinary stature could neither stand up nor lie down. O. LEWIS, *supra* note 4, at 61. At Sing Sing, "[s]o pronounced was the mania for flagellation that on one or two occasions keepers were permitted to strip and flog inmates who were just entering prison, 'for insults offered to such keepers, or alleged offenses committed previous to conviction.' " W. LEWIS, *supra* note 3, at 151.

16. O. LEWIS, *supra* note 4, at 133.

17. *See* W. LEWIS, *supra* note 3, at 179, 180.

18. The cells at the Maine Prison at Thomaston, built on the Auburn plan, literally consisted of pits into which the inmate lowered himself each night, and which were then covered by an iron grating. O. LEWIS, *supra* note 4, at 147. Similar cells were in use in Connecticut. W. LEWIS, *supra* note 3, at 83.

19. O. LEWIS, *supra* note 18, at 329.

20. *Id.* at 154.

21. *Id.* at 328.

22. *Id.* at 333. Ruffin v. Commonwealth, 62 Va. 790, 796 (1871), used those exact words to describe a convict.

23. "Floggings were customary outside of prison, in the navy, in the schoolhouse, and the home." O. LEWIS, *supra* note 4, at 328. *See also* W. LEWIS, *supra* note 3, at 96-97.

24. *See* B. McKELVEY, AMERICAN PRISONS: A STUDY IN AMERICAN SOCIAL HISTORY PRIOR TO 1915, at 40-47 (Patterson Smith reprint ed. 1968) [hereinafter cited as McKELVEY].

25. *Id.* at 38.

26. *Id.* at 70-71.

27. McKelvey summarizes some of the problems which constant shifting of wardens brought. *Id.* at 150-151. The effect of politics on the one strong drive for penal reform in New York during the 1840's is told in W. LEWIS, *supra* note 3, at 214. Nor is the problem outdated. W. LUNDEN, THE PRISON WARDEN & THE CUSTODIAL STAFF 36 (1965) contains a statistical breakdown of termination of wardenships demonstrating that 35.2 percent of 294 case studies resulted from changes in state administration or political patronage.

28. New York provided that no prison industry should employ more than five percent of the number working at that same occupation in the state; a few industries were further restricted to a given number of workers. Moreover, the convicts were to be divided into three classes, the last of which were to receive no vocational training. *See* McKELVEY, *supra* note 24, at 98-105.

29. M. MOOS, STATE PENAL ADMINISTRATION IN ALABAMA 14 (1942) [hereinafter cited as MOOS]. The Southern States, as a whole, have continued to lag behind prison movements elsewhere, partially because of continued poverty, and partly because of the inheritance of slavery. Thus, for example, the inmates of Alabama's system were leased under three categories: "full hands," "medium hands" and "dead hands," appellations stemming directly from slave days. *Id.* at 14-15; McKELVEY, *supra* note 24, at 176. The wage scale was $18.50 per month for the first category, $9.00-$13.50 for the second, and maintenance for the third. MOOS, *supra* at 14-15. According to McKelvey, the lease camps, which were generally mines, "never saw the development of the paternalism that had been the saving grace of the old plantation system." McKELVEY, *supra* note 24, at 180-81. Mortality rates were almost triple those in the North—41.3 per thousand per year. These facts, and others, lead McKelvey to the harsh declaration that "The southern states from a penological point of view never really belonged to the Union." *Id.* at 172.

The lease system lost some of its popularity by the early 1900's, but was replaced by an ingenious "surety" system, under which an owner in need of men would attend court, and offer to "lend" money to an accused who could not otherwise pay his fine. In exchange, the accused agreed to work. The agreement was supervised by the court, both as to form and amount of the loan and installments, which were sometimes six dollars per month. That system was declared invalid in United States v. Reynolds, 235 U.S. 133 (1914). The use of convicts in mines, however, continued. The state simply bought the mines and worked them publicly; the owner, meanwhile, got a nice price for his property. It was only in 1928 that the last prisoners were removed from the Alabama mines. Moos, *supra* at 171.

30. 18 U.S.C. §§ 1761-62 (1964). Questions of whether prisoners should work, and if so whether they should be competitive with outside labor are too complex to develop here. The author hopes to focus on this and related problems in the near future. *See* L. ROBINSON, SHOULD PRISONERS WORK? (1931).

31. McKELVEY, *supra* note 24, at 221.

32. *Id.* at 161.

33. *Id.* at 143.

34. A federal jury found the warden, J. L. Bruton, not guilty of nine charges of brutality, even though Bruton never testified to rebut the evidence afforded by a "number of inmates" and others. The jury was hung on the question of whether Bruton employed the "Tucker telephone," perhaps the most vicious device of all. N.Y. Times, Nov. 23, 1969, at 32, col. 1. The Arkansas prison system is discussed in notes 58-80 and accompanying text *infra*.

35. Schnur, *The New Penology: Fact or Fiction*, in PENOLOGY 3, 7 (C. Vedder & B. McKay ed. 1964) [hereinafter cited as PENOLOGY].

36. In early 1970, Archibald Alexander, a member of the Board of Managers of the New Jersey State Prisons, described the overcrowding in that state's jails:

> In one wing of the maximum security prison in Rahway . . . 250 men live in a celless dormitory where plumbing facilities are insufficient and double decker beds, by blocking guards' vision make it easy for the strong to terrorize the weak. In a wing of the maximum security prison at Trenton, there are four men in each cell built for one man in the first half of the nineteenth century. In another wing, four men per cell are even more cramped. These men must use the single toilet in their poorly ventilated quarters.

N.Y. Times, Jan. 24, 1970, at 30, col. 6-7.

37. Random selections from answers to a questionnaire the author submitted to several hundred institutions shows that, of those who answered, annual expenditures per capita for food range from $180.00 to $500.00, with an average of 93 cents per prisoner per day. Even allowing for the possibility that some of these institutions raise some of their own food, thereby lowering the cost, the total expenditures for food seem extremely low.

38. Bennett, *Of Prison and Justice*, in PENOLOGY, *supra* note 35, at 20, 26.

39. MacCORMICK, *supra* note 1, at 9.

40. According to RUBIN, supra note 2, at 268, in 1952, only 17 of 152 state penal institutions (11 percent) were less than 50 years old.

41. K. MENNINGER, THE CRIME OF PUNISHMENT 71 (1968).

42. *Hearings before the Subcomm. on National Penitentiaries of the Sen. Comm. on the Judiciary*, 88th Cong., 2d Sess. 6, 7, 26 (1964) [hereinafter cited as *1964 Hearings*]. Mr. Bennett indicated in an earlier article that "[i]n our Atlanta penitentiary eight and ten men are now occupying cells intended for four. The single cells each hold two men. Beds are strung closely together in dingy basement areas. And prisoners still arrive daily." Bennett, *supra* note 38, at 27. As both he and Fred Wilkinson, Deputy Director, Federal Bureau of Prisons, noted this "close, cheek by jowl housing for long-term prisoners naturally creates friction that leads to quarrels, fights, and sometimes rather serious assaults." *1964 Hearings* at 7.

43. *See*, A. DE BEAUMONT & ALEXIS DE TOCQUEVILLE, ON THE PENITENTIARY SYSTEM IN THE UNITED STATES AND ITS APPLICATION IN FRANCE 48-49 (Lantz ed. 1964), where the authors state that at Cincinnatti they found half of the imprisoned chained with irons. "We are unable to describe the painful impression which we experienced when, examining the prison of New Orleans, we found men together with hogs, in the midst of all odors and nuisances." *Id.* The overcrowding of nineteenth century prisons is traced carefully in McKELVEY, *supra* note 24, at 152-55.

44. Recently, some Black Panthers accused of conspiracy to bomb several buildings in New York City, and unable to make the high bond set for them, sued in federal court to obtain better conditions in the jail in which they had been detained for eleven months awaiting trial. When the district court granted the relief of requiring the

city to provide single cells for these presumably innocent inmates, the New York Times reported that the Panthers had obtained "special" jail status, so scarce were single jail cells. N.Y. Times, Feb. 28, 1970, at 1, col. 5.

45. D. LAMSON, WE WHO ARE ABOUT TO DIE 52 (1936).

46. Bennett, *supra* note 38, at 27.

47. Jails, as usual, are worse. In 1967, The National Council on Crime and Delinquency reported that four jails with 899 cells had no sanitary facilities, and that many others used the "bucket." *Correction in the United States, A Survey for the President's Commission on Law Enforcement and the Administration of Justice* (1967), reprinted in 13 CRIME AND DELINQUENCY 1, 153 (1967) [hereinafter cited as *N.C.C.D. Report*].

48. Hirschkop & Milleman, *The Unconstitutionality of Prison Life*, 55 VA. L. REV. 795, 808 (1969). The superintendent of the prison, C.C. Peyton, attempted to evade the issue by indicating that he had cockroaches in his own home. *Id.* at n.74.

49. Grusky, *Role Conflict in Organization: A Study of Prison Camp Officials*, in PRISON WITHIN SOCIETY 455 (L. Hazelrigg ed. 1968).

50. *N.C.C.D. Report, supra* note 47, at 144.

51. *Id. See also* JOINT COMMITTEE ON CORRECTIONAL MANPOWER AND TRAINING, A TIME TO ACT, 19. In 1960, Myrl Alexander concluded:

> It is possible for anyone, regardless of his education, experience, or understanding of institutions, to become the head of a correctional institution. Hospitals must be administered by skilled and trained hospital administrators . . . the managerial head of a mental hospital must be qualified against accepted standards. But in the field of correctional institution administration, no standards are recognized throughout the country.

Alexander, *Correction at the Crossroad*, in 1964 *Hearings, supra* note 42, at 160, 161-62.

52. McClery and corroborative observations have shown that the custodial function can be performed equally well in an authoritarian organization and in one that grants more scope and self-determination to the prisoners. If repressive and more humane methods can serve equally well to safeguard the community and isolate prisoners, then according to the values of our society the more humane system is preferable.

Grosser, *External Setting and Internal Relations of the Prison*, in PRISON WITHIN SOCIETY 9, 19 (L. Hazelrigg ed. 1968).

53. N.Y. Times, Feb. 15, 1967, at 8, col. 1. The entire story is told in Murton's thorough, if somewhat biased book, ACCOMPLICES TO THE CRIME (1970).

54. N.Y. Times, Jan. 30, 1968, at 1, col. 1.

55. *Id.*, Feb. 7, 1968, at 1, col. 6.

> Inmates were murdered, shot "accidentally" and, during what were described as escape attempts, burned to death, poisoned, drowned, run over by farm wagons, and "accidentally electrocuted." On separate occasions, two men were killed by a "falling tree." Many were listed as dying of heart failure. Thirteen died of sunstroke—four on a single day. One report said the inmate died simply "shot four times with a 38-caliber revolver."

Id. at 22, col. 5.

56. *Id.*, Jan. 17, 1968, at 26, col. 3.

57. The description is from the district court's opinion in Jackson v. Bishop, 268 F. Supp. 804 (E.D. Ark. 1967).

58. N.Y. Times, Sept. 6, 1966, at 52, col. 4.

59. *Id.*; Pearman, *The Whip Pays Off*, 203 THE NATION 701, 702 (1966) [hereinafter cited as Pearman].

60. Pearman, *supra* note 59, at 704.

61. N.Y. Times, Feb. 10, 1968, at 22, col. 3.

62. *Id.*, May 20, 1968, at 53, col. 1.

63. *Id.*, May 14, 1968, at 59, col. 4.

64. Tuscaloosa News (Alabama), July 12, 1969, at 1, col. 1. On November 21,

1969, the jury acquitted Bruton of eight of the nine charges and was hung on the ninth. N.Y. Times, Nov. 23, 1969, at 32, col. 1.

65. Talley v. Stephens, 247 F. Supp. 683 (E.D. Ark. 1965).

66. *Id.* at 689.

67. Pearman, *supra* note 59, at 702-03.

68. As quoted in A. MacCormick, *supra* note 1, at 50 (emphasis added). Although the author did not identify the system, the history and details given unmistakably mark it as Arkansas'.

69. Pearman, *supra* note 59, at 704.

70. Jackson v. Bishop, 268 F. Supp. 804 (E.D. Ark. 1967).

71. *Id.* at 816.

72. Jackson v. Bishop, 404 F.2d 571, 575 n.5 (9th Cir. 1968).

73. *Id.* at 579.

74. *Id.*

75. *Id.*

76. Hirschkop & Milleman, *The Unconstitutionality of Prison Life*, 55 VA. L. REV. 795 (1969).

77. Mason v. Peyton, Civ. No. 5611-R (E.D. Va., order entered Aug. 13, 1968), as reported in Hirschkop & Millemann, *supra* note 76, at 796 n.7.

78. Landman v. Peyton, 370 F.2d 135 (4th Cir. 1967).

79. A. MacCormick, *supra* note 1, at 63.

80. K. Menninger, The Crime of Punishment 80 (1968).

81. M. Wolff, Prison 192-93 (1967).

82. *See* Kirkpatrick, *Corporal Punishment*, 10 CRIM. L.Q. 320, 320-21, 324 (1968). Kirkpatrick reports, however, that this statute was rarely used, and the provision was abolished in Ontario in 1960. Corporal punishment is still allowed as punishment for violation of stated institutional regulations and for some crimes such as rape, indecent assault, incest. robbery, and armed burglary, among others. *Id.* at 321.

83. *Id.* at 325. Kirkpatrick's figures, however, are not as positive as his assertions. The figures show that total use of corporal punishment, both by a judicial court and as an institutional disciplinary measure has been as follows since 1954: 1954-46; 1955-92; 1956-77; 1957-58; 1958-49; 1959-35; 1960-26; 1961-75; 1962-25; 1963-74.

84. INDIANA REV. STAT. § 13.242 (1956).

85. Lewis v. State, 176 So. 2d 718, 729-30 (La. App. 1965), *cited in* F. COHEN, LEGAL NORMS IN CORRECTIONS 107 (1967).

86. *See, e.g.,* Wiltsie v. California Dep't of Corrections, 406 F.2d 515 (9th Cir. 1968).

87. *See* United States v. Jones, 207 F.2d 785 (5th Cir. 1953), holding that the federal government could prosecute, under the Civil Rights Act, a prison officer charged with having beaten, bruised, battered, and injured a prisoner for an infraction of prison rules. The prosecutions against the Arkansas officers, *supra* note 34, were brought under the same section of the Act.

88. *See, e.g.,* Glenfall v. Gladden, 241 Ore. 190, 405 P.2d 532 (1965). *But see* Coffin v. Reichard, 143 F.2d 443 (6th Cir. 1944).

89. This was the system, in 1942, in many southern states, including Alabama and Mississippi. M. Moos, STATE PENAL ADMINISTRATION IN ALABAMA 17 (1942). Most states have since rejected the system.

90. Holt v. Sarver, 300 F. Supp. 825 (E.D. Ark. 1969). *See also* Commonwealth *ex rel.* Bryant v. Hendricks, Civil No. 353 (Philadelphia County Ct. C.P., Sept. 1, 1970).

91. Holt v. Sarver, 309 F. Supp. 362 (E.D. Ark. 1970).

92. 409 F.2d 507 (7th Cir. 1969).

93. 417 F.2d 504 (10th Cir. 1969).

94. A similar case, Roberts v. Williams, 302 F. Supp. 972 (N.D. Miss. 1969), held that a warden could be liable when a trusty accidentally discharged a shotgun. The rationale, however, was that the warden had not verified the trusty's ability to handle a shotgun. Had the trusty been Annie Oakley, the court probably would have found no possible cause of action. *See also* Kish v. Milwaukee, No. 69-C-129 (E.D.

Wis., May 28, 1970) (appeal pending).
95. 290 N.Y.S.2d 486 (Ct. Cl. 1968).
96. *Id.* at 502.
97. M. Moos, STATE PENAL ADMINISTRATION IN ALABAMA 86 (1942).
98. McGee, *The Administration of Justice: The Correctional Process,* in *1964 Hearings, supra* note 42, at 166, 175.
99. A. MacCORMICK, *supra* note 1, at 64.
100. *N.C.C.D. Report, supra* note 47, at 199-200.
101. A. McCORMICK, *supra* note 1, at 63.
102. Grosser, *supra* note 48, at 13.   Most prison riots have as their motive neither "control" of the prison, nor escape from it: they are the last resort of prisoners whose complaints about various conditions in the prison have gone unheeded.   J. MARTIN, BREAK DOWN THE WALLS (1953), describes the prison riot at Jackson State Prison in Michigan in 1952, which he calls "the most dangerous prison riot in American history."   But the riot started without any real cause, and the inmates never attempted to escape.   Instead, they used the opportunity to make public their complaints about prison conditions and employees.   Recently, six rioting inmates at the Minnesota State Prison surrendered on the sole condition that their grievances about prison conditions be publicly aired. N.Y. Times, Feb. 23, 1970, at 20, col. 3.   This was also the motivating factor behind the well-publicized riots in the New York City "Tombs" in the summer of 1970.   The Tombs were operating far in excess of capacity, and most of the inmates were awaiting trial—some for as long as two years.   The list of grievances included alleged racism among guards, insults to visiting relatives, and the intolerable wait for trial. *Id.,* August 11, 1970, at 30, col. 3-5.   Some efforts were made in this direction, but there is much left to do in New York City, as elsewhere.
103. 45 Stat. 1084 (1929).
104. 49 Stat. 494 (1935).
105. 18 U.S.C. § 117 (1964).
106. This was obviously a reaction to the profit-making institution of the early nineteenth century.   The story is succinctly told in PRESIDENT'S COMMISSION ON LAW ENFORCEMENT AND THE ADMINISTRATION OF JUSTICE, TASK FORCE REPORT: CORRECTIONS 55 (1967) [hereinafter cited as TASK FORCE REPORT].
107. Work release programs are a potential answer to at least some of this difficulty.   But as of 1967, less than half the states had even authorized such a program, and these are often woefully underfinanced.   A. MacCORMICK, *supra* note 1, at 15.   The federal project is probably the most ambitious, but for some 50,000 federal prisoners, the government had programs for less than 2,000. *Id. See also* Carpenter, *The Federal Work Release Program,* in THE TASKS OF PENOLOGY 185 (1969).
108. M. Moos, STATE PENAL ADMINISTRATION IN ALABAMA 118 (1942).
109. Mississippi now allows the practice. C. HOPPER, SEX IN PRISON (1969).   California has attempted the program in one prison, on a trial basis. *Id.* at 5.
110. Cavans & Zemans, *Marital Relationships of Prisoners in Twenty-Eight Countries,* in PENOLOGY, *supra* note 35, at 94. HOPPER, *supra* note 109, at 5, finds that 21 of 60 countries he surveyed allow some sort of conjugal visiting or furloughs.
111. Cory, *Homosexuality in Prison,* in PENOLOGY, *supra* note 35, at 89.   Hirschkop and Milleman, *supra* note 76 at 814-15, also indicate the alarming frequency of homosexuality in prisons.   Prison officials voluntarily mention it almost immediately to a stranger, so defensive are they about the question. *See also* Davis, *Sexual Assaults in the Philadelphia Prison System and Sheriff's Vans,* 6 TRANSACTION, Dec. 1968, at 8.
112. Cory, *supra* note 111, at 92.
113. K. MENNINGER, *supra* note 80, at 72.
114. Griswold v. Connecticut, 381 U.S. 479 (1965). *But see* NCCD NEWS 7-8 (Nov.-Dec. 1970) reporting a federal court decision holding that there is no constitutional right to conjugal visitation. *Cf.* Payne v. District Comm'rs, 253 F.2d 867 (D.C. Cir. 1958).
115. Mail censorship is justified by prison officials on the grounds that most inmates, if given the chance, will use the mails to further illegal plans, such as escape,

contraband smuggling, or outside illegal businesses. Vogelman, *Prison Restrictions—Prisoner Rights*, 59 J. CRIM. L.C. & P.S. 386, 387-88 (1968). The courts have often upheld, or refused to review, such regulations and censorship, even in ludicrous situations. *See, e.g.*, McCloskey v. Maryland, 337 F.2d 72 (4th Cir. 1964); Kirby v. Thomas, 336 F.2d 462 (6th Cir. 1964) (total ban on any letters critical of prison officials); Ortega v. Ragen, 216 F.2d 561 (7th Cir. 1954), *cert. denied*, 349 U.S. 940 (1955); United States *ex rel.* Wagner v. Ragen, 213 F.2d 294 (7th Cir. 1954), *cert. denied*, 348 U.S. 846 (1954) (no letters to patent office concerning inventions allowed); Numer v. Miller, 165 F.2d 986 (9th Cir. 1948) (English correspondence course disallowed because inmate admitted he intended to use course to write book critical of prisons); Goodchild v. Schmidt, 279 F. Supp. 149 (E.D. Wis. 1968) (letter to Veteran's Administration complaining of insufficient medical treatment disallowed); Fussa v. Taylor, 168 F. Supp. 302 (M.D. Pa. 1958) (correspondence with common law wife disallowed); Green v. Maine, 113 F. Supp. 253 (S.D. Me. 1953); *In re* Ferguson, 55 Cal. App. 2d 663, 361 P.2d 417 (1961) (letter stopped because critical of officials); Brabson v. Wilkins, 45 Misc. 2d 286, 256 N.Y.S.2d 693 (Sup. Ct. 1965) (business mail can be stopped entirely). According to RUBIN, *supra* note 2, at 297 n.134, the Attorney General has found that unlimited correspondence causes no real problem; yet the great preponderance of prisons still limit correspondence privileges and censor all letters. *See generally* Singer, *Censorship of Prisoners' Mail and the Constitution*, 56 A.B.A.J. 1051 (1970).

116. A 1949 study has listed the rules of the official booklet of the Iowa State Penitentiary. Although these rules may have changed slightly, it is unlikely that there has been much change. The breadth of discretion given those who judge the prisoner is apparent. He may be subjected to penalties for: Altering clothing; bed not properly made; clothing not in proper order; communicating by signs; creating a disturbance; crookedness; defaming anything; dilatoriness; dirty cell or furnishings; disorderly cell; disobedience of orders; disturbance in cellhouse; fighting; grimacing; hands in pocket; hands or face not clean, or hair not combed; contraband; impertinence to visitors; insolence to officers, fellow inmates; inattention in line or school; laughing or fooling; loud talking in cell; loud reading in cell; malicious mischief; neglect of study; not out of bed promptly; not wearing outside shirt; not properly out of ceil when brake is drawn; profanity; quarreling; refusal to obey; shirking; spitting on floor; staring at visitors; stealing; trading; talking in chapel; talking in corridor or in line; vile language; wasting food; writing unauthorized letters. Elliott, *Coercion in Penal Treatment, Past and Present*, FED. PROB., June 1949, at 22, cited in, RUBIN, *supra* note 2, at 294, n.113.

117. Jackson v. Godwin, 400 F.2d 529 (5th Cir. 1968); Rivers v. Royster, 360 F.2d 592 (4th Cir. 1966); Hatfield v. Bailleaux, 290 F.2d 632 (9th Cir.), *cert. denied*, 368 U.S. 862 (1961); Parks v. Ciccone, 281 F. Supp. 805 (W.D. Mo. 1968); Piccoli v. Bd. of Trustees & Warden, 87 F. Supp. 672 (D.N.H. 1949).

118. *See, e.g.*, Walker v. Blackwell, 411 F.2d 23 (5th Cir. 1969); Cooper v. Pate, 382 F.2d 518 (7th Cir. 1967); Long v. Katzenbach, 258 F. Supp. 89 (M.D. Pa. 1966); Desmond v. Blackwell, 235 F. Supp. 246 (M.D. Pa. 1964); *In re* Ferguson, 55 Cal. App. 2d 663, 361 P.2d 417 (1961).

119. The principle of "less eligibility" states that no non-prisoner should be less comfortable than a prisoner. Conversely stated, prisoners should suffer worse conditions than the poorest free member of society. H. MANNHEIM, THE DILEMMA OF PENAL REFORM (1939) (passim).

120. *N.C.C.D. Report, supra* note 47, at 193. MACCORMICK, *supra* note 1, at 57-58, states that the equivalent of 150 full-time psychiatrists and 250 psychologists, served approximately 220,000 prisoners in the state and federal system, a ratio of slightly less than one mental health specialist for every 500 prisoners. Edwin Schur, using slightly lower figures, calculated the impact of these extraordinary figures in the state system:

If full-time employment for a psychiatrist means an eight-hour day, and a 160 hour month, it would mean that there is not more than 82 seconds of psychiatric help available for each inmate during a whole month. Little psychiatric time in prison, however, is focused on life after prison. . . . If the sixty-seven psychologists and psychometrists distributed their time evenly, each inmate could secure about four minutes of their time (monthly) for individual attention. The ninety-six institutional parole officers would have about six minutes for each man each month. Less than ten minutes a month could be afforded each prisoner by the 155 chaplains. The 257 employees responsible for individual case work services have less than sixteen minutes for each man. Not over 45 minutes are available from the 739 academic, vocational, and trade teachers. Inmates who consume more than eighty minutes of service in one month from the whole classification, training, and treatment staff are taking more than their fair share.

Schur, *The New Penology: Fact or Fiction* in PENOLOGY, *supra* note 35, at 4.

121. TASK FORCE REPORT, *supra* note 106, at 51; JOINT COMMISSION ON CORRECTIONAL MANPOWER AND TRAINING, A TIME TO ACT 12 (1969) [hereinafter cited as A TIME TO ACT]. The situation is worse in jails, where less than 3 percent of all workers can be called professionals. *N.C.C.D. Report, supra* note 47, at 142.

122. TASK FORCE REPORT, *supra* note 106, at 54.

123. A TIME TO ACT, *supra* note 121, at 19.

124. *Id.*

125. *N.C.C.D. Report, supra* note 47; TASK FORCE REPORT, *supra* note 106.

126. *N.C.C.D. Report, supra* note 47, at 146.

127. Cincinnati Enquirer, Feb. 7, 1970, at 21, col. 1.

128. K. MENNINGER, *supra* note 80, at 39,38.

129. *N.C.C.D. Report, supra* note 47, at 146.

130. TASK FORCE REPORT, *supra* note 106 at 73.

131. The Supreme Court has just held that imprisonment of an indigent beyond the maximum statutory sentence term because of failure to pay an additional fine, or court costs, is unconstitutional. Williams v. Illinois, 399 U.S. 235 (1970). The court specifically declined to pass on the larger question of whether incarceration in cases of non-willful refusal to pay a fine because of indigency violates the Constitution, but has granted certiorari in a case presenting that point. Tate v. Short, 399 U.S. 925 (1970).

132. Foote, *The Coming Constitutional Crisis in Bail*, 113 U. PA. L. REV. 1125, 1149 (1965).

133. *N.C.C.D. Report, supra* note 47, at 119.

134. N.Y. Times, March 28, 1970, at 29, col. 1.

135. TASK FORCE REPORT, *supra* note 106, at 79-80.

136. PLAYBOY, Aug. 1969, at 48.

137. Weems v. United States, 217 U.S. 349 (1910); Trop v. Dulles, 356 U.S. 86 (1958).

138. *See* the cases cited *infra* note 152.

139. *See* Goldberg & Dershowitz, *Declaring the Death Penalty Unconstitutional*, 83 HARV. L. REV. 1773 (1970).

140. Williams v. Fields, 416 F.2d 483 (9th Cir. 1969); Lee v. Tahash, 352 F.2d 970 (8th Cir. 1965); Hancock v. Avery, 301 F. Supp. 786 (M.D. Tenn. 1969); Jordan v. Fitzharris, 257 F. Supp. 674 (N.D. Cal. 1966). *Cf.* Hyland v. Procunier, 311 F. Supp. 749 (N.D. Cal. 1970).

141. *See, e.g.,* Hancock v. Avery, 301 F. Supp. 786 (M.D. Tenn. 1969) (solitary conditions violate the eighth amendment).

142. 309 F. Supp. 411 (W.D. Mo. 1970).

143. Four states allowed intermingling and two others were experimenting. All others responding to a questionnaire prepared and issued for the litigation segregated death row inmates. *Id.* at 418-20.

144. *Cf.* Hart, *Prolegomenon to the Principles of Punishment*, in PUNISHMENT AND RESPONSIBILITY 1 (1966). *See also* ALI, MODEL PENAL CODE 1.02(2) (1962 Proposed Draft); AMERICAN CORRECTIONAL ASSOCIATION, MANUAL OF CORRECTIONAL STANDARDS (3d ed. 1966).

145. Illinois and New Hampshire provide in their constitutions that the aim of punishment "is to reform, not to exterminate mankind." ILL. CONST., art. 8, § 14; N.H. CONST., pt. 1, art. 1. The constitutions of Indiana (Art. I, § 18) and Oregon (Art. I, § 15) declare that "the penal law shall be founded on the principle of reformation, and not of vindictive justice." Texas, by statute (VERNON'S ANN. PENAL CODE, art. 2) and Wyoming, by its constitution (art. 1, § 20) have similar provisions. Montana (CONST. ART. III, § 24) and North Carolina (CONST., art. XI, § 2) declare that the objective of punishment is reformation and prevention. RUBIN, *supra* note 2, at 649-50. Rhode Island has a similar provision in R.I. GEN. LAWS, § 13-3-1 (1904). *Cf.* 18 U.S.C. § 4081 (1964).

146. *See, e.g.*, Cox v. Louisiana, 379 U.S. 536 (1965); Schneider v. Rusk, 377 U.S. 163 (1964); American Communications Ass'n v. Douds, 339 U.S. 382 (1950); Prince v. Massachusetts, 321 U.S. 158 (1944). For a scathing criticism of the balancing test in the first amendment area, see the dissent of Mr. Justice Black in Konigsberg v. State Bar, 366 U.S. 36 (1961).

147. Griswold v. Connecticut, 381 U.S. 479 (1965).

148. Kramer v. Union Free School District No. 15, 395 U.S. 621 (1969); Cipriano v. City of Houma, 395 U.S. 701 (1969).

149. *See, e.g.*, Shapiro v. Thompson, 394 U.S. 618 (1969); Harper v. Virginia Bd. of Elections, 383 U.S. 663 (1966); Sherbert v. Verner, 374 U.S. 398 (1963).

150. Coffin v. Reichard, 143 F.2d 443 (6th Cir. 1944).

151. *See* cases cited *supra* notes 145-50.

152. Wright v. McMann, 387 F.2d 519 (2d Cir. 1967), *on remand*, Civil No. 66-CV-77 (N.D.N.Y. July 29, 1970); Sostre v. Rockefeller, 309 F. Supp. 611 (S.D.N.Y. 1969), (preliminary injunction), 312 F. Supp. 863 (S.D.N.Y. 1970) (on the merits); Hancock v. Avery, 301 F. Supp. 786 (M.D. Tenn. 1969); Holt v. Sarver, 300 F. Supp. 825 (E.D. Ark. 1969); Jordan v. Fitzharris, 257 F. Supp. 674 (N.D. Ga. 1966). Many courts, however, find no difficulty in upholding the imposition of solitary confinement. Courtney v. Bishop, 409 F.2d 1185 (8th Cir. 1969) (assault on fellow inmate), Ford v. Board of Managers of N.J. St. Prison, 407 F.2d 937 (3d Cir. 1969) (threat to blow up prison); Abernathy v. Cunningham, 393 F.2d 775 (4th Cir. 1968) ("trouble maker"); Bowman v. Hale, 302 F. Supp. 1306 (S.D. Ala. 1969); Knuckles v. Prasse, 302 F. Supp. 1036 (E.D. Pa. 1969) (proselytizing Black Muslim); United States *ex rel.* Holland v. Maroney, 299 F. Supp. 262 (W.D. Pa. 1969); Belk v. Mitchell, 294 F. Supp. 800 (W.D.N.C. 1968); Graham v. Willingham, 265 F. Supp. 763 (D. Kan.), *aff'd*, 384 F.2d 367 (10th Cir. 1967) (being "nearby" when two murders occurred in prison); Fallis v. United States, 263 F. Supp. 780 (M.D. Pa. 1967) (refusal to work in noisy machine shop); State v. Doolittle, 22 Conn. Supp. 32, 158 A.2d 858 (1960) (unclear); McBride v. McCorkle, 44 N.J. Super. 468, 130 A.2d 881 (1957) (foul and obscene language); Hughes v. Turner, 14 Utah 2d 128, 378 P.2d 888 (1963).

153. *See* cases cited *supra* note 152. The ACA requires as a minimum the provision of soap, shaving equipment, towels, bedding, mattress, etc. AMERICAN CORRECTIONAL ASSOCIATION, MANUAL OF CORRECTIONAL STANDARDS 457-60 (3d ed. 1966).

154. Ford v. Board of Managers, 407 F.2d 937 (3d Cir. 1969) (one shower every 5 days); Wright v. McMann, 387 F.2d 519 (2d Cir. 1967); Landman v. Peyton, 370 F.2d 135 (4th Cir. 1966) (one bath a week); Hoard v. Smith, 365 F.2d 428 (4th Cir. 1966) (one bath a week as opposed to daily baths for the general prison population); Jordan v. Fitzharris, 257 F. Supp. 674 (N.D. Cal. 1966) (no shower for twenty days).

155. *Ex Parte* Pickens, 101 F. Supp. 285 (D. Alas. 1951).

156. *Id.* at 289-90.

157. Curley v. Gonzales, Civ. No. 8372 (D.N. Mex., Feb. 12, 1970).

158. Inmates of Cook County Jail v. Tierney, No. 68 C 504 (N.D. Ill., 1968) (settled).

159. Holt v. Sarver, 309 F. Supp. 362 (E.D. Ark. 1970).

160. *Id.* at 378-81.

161. 309 F. Supp. 497 (S.D. Ga. 1970).

162. 309 F. Supp. 411 (W.D. Mo. 1970).

163. 309 F. Supp. 611 (S.D.N.Y. 1969).

164. *Id.* at 613. The case is the precursor of the revolutionary holding that imposition of solitary confinement without a hearing violates due process. In Sostre v. Rockefeller, 312 F. Supp. 863 (S.D.N.Y. 1970) (appeal pending) the court awarded $9000 dollars in compensatory damages, and almost $4000 in punitive damages. A court in the northern district of the state soon followed suit. Wright v. McMann, Civil No. 66-CV-77 (N.D.N.Y. July 29, 1970).

165. Johnson v. Avery, 393 U.S. 483 (1969).

166. Only two cases deal with the issue of conjugal visitation and the deprivation of sexual contact. In Payne v. District of Columbia, 253 F.2d 867 (D.C. Cir. 1958), a wife sued to obtain a declaratory judgment that the prison could not deny her access to her husband. The court turned her away. In *In re* Flowers, 292 F. Supp. 390 (E.D. Wis. 1968), the court rejected a contention that compulsory celibacy violated the inmate's right by impairing the obligations of his marriage contract. No reported case has yet faced the issue of whether continued deprivation is an excessive intrusion upon constitutionally protected marital rights.

THE CITY'S ISLAND
OF THE DAMNED

Harvey Swados

> *Far from being inadequate, the programs of the Department of Corrections are exemplary. They reflect an enlightened recognition of all that is desirable to effect the rehabilitation of the deviant. There is no emphasis on punishment. There is an intelligent effort to effect rehabilitation consistent with necessary custody.*
>
> John V. Lindsay at the Adolescent Remand Shelter, Rikers Island, Feb. 28, 1969

> *To put a man behind walls and not try to change him is to deny him his humanity — and ours.*
>
> Chief Justice Warren Burger, Feb. 21, 1970

In a basement room of Encounter House in lower Manhattan, a slim, good-looking, unusually tall young Puerto Rican sits weeping, his curly head in his hands. Hector, who has been into narcotics and burglary, is 21 years old; he has recently been released from his third confinement in the New York City Reformatory, one of three "correctional" institutions on Rikers Island, a 680-acre land-filled oblong in the East River whose very location — to say nothing of its functions — is vague to most New Yorkers, but whose cells are home, for periods ranging from a day to three years, for thousands of boys like Hector. He is haunted by the memory of his long months there.

"Man, I was so lonesome," he mutters, digging his fingers into his scalp. "That was the worst part of it, I didn't have one friend. I had two terrific teachers there, Lucas and Goldstein, when I was getting my high-school equivalency certificate, but I couldn't talk to them about what was bugging me. It would have been breaking the rules. Aside from them there was nobody I could trust. Nobody. Not even the guy in the cell with me. Because if they got something on my roommate, how did I know he wouldn't try to hang it on me?

"You always had to be tough. That was the big thing, to be tough. I didn't *feel* tough, but I couldn't let on. Even when the guys would take off (sodomize) somebody, it would turn my stomach sick, but I'd have to be one of the leaders or get marked chicken. What I'd do, I'd help to make the guy give in, then when it came my turn I'd say, 'Ah, the hell with it,' and I'd head for my cell. Night after night after night, I'd lay there masturbating — that was all there was for me.

"Then I'm out. All of a sudden, bang, I'm standing on Queensboro Plaza, and I say to myself, 'Is this what I was waiting for?' I go back to my street and to the apartment, and everything looks so small, not like I thought about it in the reformatory. I lay down in my room and I say to myself, 'Well, here it is, the same old crap.' And I can't stop thinking about the way they were always counting you, over and over, like animals. Or the Puerto Rican guy that committed suicide. I really liked him, but after he cut up (slashed his wrists), the guard that got him the razor blade laughed and said, 'Well, that's one less.' I cried myself to sleep that night. I really don't know why I didn't cut up myself. Or hang up."

It was a rash of suicides and suicide attempts in New York City jails and police station lockups that brought the correctional system back into the public eye. They disturbed intelligent, sympathetic (and ambitious) politicians like Senator John R. Dunne, a youngish Republican in the Lindsay mold, who is chairman of the State Senate Committee on Crime and Correction, and community figures like Manuel Casiano, director of the Migration Division of the Commonwealth of Puerto Rico (five of last year's eight suicides in city jails were Puerto Ricans), and lawmen like Bronx County District Attorney Burton B. Roberts, who referred to the "God-forsaken Rikers complex."

But the suicide rate for all of New York's young people is higher than for the nation as a whole — partly, as Associate Medical Examiner Michael Baden pointed out to me, because New York's discovery rate is higher. Although there are no hard data, Dr. Baden says that "It is the opinion of our office that Puerto Ricans tend to be more emotional and to commit suicide oftener than indigenous whites." And although the press and the politicians have been playing it up, there does not seem to be any evidence that the suicide problem is worse on Rikers Island than it is on college campuses.

What *is* worse is the condition not of death but of life, for the thousands of boys and young men who are shuffled back and forth like so many head of cattle across the bridge of sighs that connects the island with Queens. Unhappy college students who upon occasion refer to themselves as "niggers" might be given pause if they were to enter the compounds into which the inmates — 80 to 85 per cent of them black and/or Puerto Rican — are herded while they await trial or serve out their sentences.

While the island has problems endemic to most other prisons across the country — archaic facilities, homosexuality, drug addiction and racial conflict — its sorrows are compounded by overcrowding, idleness and language barriers, all of which have made guards and prisoners alike increasingly restless and resentful. Despite Mayor Lindsay's brave words about rehabilitation more than a year ago, a number of professionals working on the island agree that the prisoners receive very little constructive training or medical treatment.

"The deterioration in the past six months has been unbelievable," says one physician who works part-time in the island's infirmary. This view is shared by professor Joel Walker of the New York University Graduate School of Social Work, training supervisor for a team of students who work three days a week with Rikers adolescents. After my own visits to the island, I was not surprised by the rebellious anger of these students or by Professor Walker's warning words to me: "The Department of Corrections doesn't realize that they're sitting on something that is going to blow."

In order to understand why, it is necessary to cope first with some painful statistics. On an average day in March of this year the total census of prisoners held by the New York City Department of Corrections, both those already convicted or sentenced and those detained before trial, was 13,354 human beings. The total capacity of single cells, dormitories, and the infirmary was 7,993. The rate of occupancy on that day: 167 per cent.

Let us break that down for the three institutions on Rikers Island: The New York City Correctional Institution for Men (the penitentiary housing sentenced adult male prisoners serving terms of one year or less) held 2,283 prisoners on that day. The total capacity was 1,204. The rate of occupancy was 190 per cent.

The New York City Reformatory, repository for adolescent offenders between the ages 16 and 21 confined for periods of up to three years, held 1,700 boys on that day. The total single capacity was 992. The rate of occupancy: 171 per cent.

The Adolescent Remand Shelter, established two years ago in the grim old Cagney-style prison on the island, held 2,601 boys from all the boroughs on that day, some awaiting trial, some awaiting sentencing. The total single capacity of the A.R.S.: 2,147. The occupancy rate: 121 per cent.

What does it mean to say that a place is running at more than 100 per cent occupancy? Picture a cell that is roughly eight-feet wide by eight-feet deep by eight feet high. It has room for a metal bunk, wash basin, toilet bowl, shelf. In it a man can sleep, wash, relieve himself, write letters, and store a few paper-backs and the various snacks and other items available at the commissary. Now mount another bunk atop the first and add another man to the same cube. As Warden James A. Thomas of the A.R.S. observes, doubling up has its merits in suicide prevention — but it has its drawbacks for those coping with homosexual problems.

It is in the Adolescent Remand Shelter that one sees in full flower the processing of street kids into candidates for the reformatory, the city pen, and, later, the state and Federal prisons. This monstrous collection of concrete and steel cell blocks (eight of them, three-tiers high, each with a capacity of 240, a dayroom and a community shower) is, in the words of Warden Thomas, "an exact mirror of what happens in the city — racial antagonisms, crimes against each other, suicides and suicide attempts." Nor should we be deceived by the fact that its percentage of overoccupancy is smaller than those of the other facilities on the island: Since efforts are made to segregate not merely the homosexuals but the heavy offenders and the very young, one cell block may be underoccupied while another is bursting at the seams; and since there is nothing for the boys to do anyway, while nameless, powerful strangers determine their fate, even in the under-occupied cell blocks they present a raucous and degrading spectacle. These are all "interior-type" cells, with the three tiers facing out onto long corridors; their windows cannot be opened by the occupants as in the reformatory, for they have no windows. The gloom is relieved only by an overhead bulb which often blows, just as the toilet bowls often stop-up, so that when you walk down the corridor you are assailed from the inner darkness by cries of, "Hey, how about a bulb in here?" or "How about fixing my toilet?"

On one day that I passed through Block 2, reserved for heavy offenders, there were "only" 201 occupants — 78 of them, and an additional 11 who were absent in court, charged with homicide. (On a guess, this roomful of adolescents from the five boroughs of one city represented more murderers than you could find on a comparable day in all of England.) In contrast, Block 5, containing mostly 16 and 17 year olds, held 363 youths jammed together.

What is life like in these cells? Above all, and over all, is the incessant blare of rock music on the loudspeakers. Below it, the sound of the TV in the day-room, or at night outside the cells. The young blacks seem to do somewhat better at keeping themselves entertained than the Spanish-speaking youths. In the rec room of Block 2, on whose bare wall someone had painted the word LOVE, a group intently watched a boy mouth — in impeccable lip-synch — the song coming over the loudspeaker. In the corridor some sat on the floor playing chess, others shadowboxed, yet others stared dully.

You can tell a good deal about a cell's occupant at one swift glance. The cubicle with a Christ or a bleeding heart, framed or fringed-around, and probably occupied by a Puerto Rican, is not likely to have a naked pin-up girl. Some worship neither the Christ nor the nude, but the automobile, and make a small shrine for the latest model performance car. Quite often, wash cloths and face towels are draped like shawls and tablecloths over the bare china toilet bowls and the wall shelves. On the face towel an inmate will mount the snapshots of family and girl friend framed in silver match-folders.

The cells of Block 5, packed with boys awaiting trial on robbery charges, felonies, whatnot, are apt to be less tidied up. "Dope is not where it's at," is scrawled on one: "Give acid a chance." On another, "Make love not war." In the corridor there is more horseplay, finger-snapping to the blaring rock, judo, cardplaying. As you pass, the expressions range from hopefully expectant to sullen. But that is perhaps preferable to the haughty mien and frozen nonchalance of the self-declared homosexuals, who sit in their own ward staring off into space and filing their nails. Or to the cackles, grim glances, withdrawn brooding stares of the boys under M.O. (medical observation), one of who glides along writing invisible words on the wall with his fingertip. These youths are the oddballs that are batted back and forth between Rikers and Bellevue in a game of psychiatric Ping Pong. Every day perhaps a half dozen of them are either on the way to Bellevue, provisionally diagnosed as psychotic, or on the way back from Bellevue to await trial, diagnosed as "not psychotic at this time."

And then there are the addicts, both at the A.R.S. and the reformatory's Dorm 17 (a new facility growing out of last year's suicides), where a boy is sent as soon as medical diagnostic inspection has verified that he is a D.A.T. (drug addict). Seen three times a day by a physician and administered mild sedation to ease withdrawal pains, these boys stay on an average of three to five days before being discharged by the physician to the general population. Rising from the bunks on which they lie wrapped in blankets, they peer at you with their young-old faces and shuffle forward in their laceless sneakers, complaining that the medication does not help them to sleep, or that they need toothpaste (a dentifrice applied to the forearms can lighten heroin track marks and make them appear less recent).

"These kids aren't *real* addicts," claims a deputy at the shelter. "The stuff they get is so adulterated, the only withdrawal symptom they have is some sleeplessness. I haven't seen a real addict in 10 years, since the days in the Tombs [the Manhattan House of Detention for Men] when the stoical old Chinese opium smokers used to kick it cold turkey, lying in their own vomit and their own excrement . . . "

The main activity of all these masses of boys and young men is being "processed," or herded to and from the courts. Starting at 7:15 A.M., 50 in each of four cell blocks are "pedigreed" and then called out of the block a group at a time, heading for the criminal court or the supreme court in each of the five boroughs. Only after four "ID checks" (one kid, giving the wrong name for kicks, can foul the whole process) are they funneled through the temporary receiving room, handcuffed and loaded into the vans and buses that will take them to court. Somewhat later in the day, batches of returnees file into the receiving room and are stripped down to go through the entire processing procedure again.

From the outset, homosexuals are segregated into a detention cell. "Come on girls," says the guard, "let's go." On a bench several strikingly girlish types, held for prostitution, sit giggling and chatting animatedly; when a third is sent to join them, pecks on the cheek are exchanged. Before being photographed and fingerprinted they take down their teased hair and shake it out; they may be concealing razor blades or narcotics. One, with soft smooth cheeks and plump breasts, is asked if he is wearing a brassiere; pouting, he denies it (He may have been taking hormones, like some of those already in detention.) The homosexuals are allowed to disrobe in privacy.

Across the way 14 new arrivals wait glumly in a temporary cell. Some smoke, others huddle dejectedly on benches or on the floor, sniffing, betraying the symptoms of narcotic withdrawal. The deputy shuffles their arrest record, or "rap sheets"; thirteen of them are listed as drug users; five have already had drug arrests.

"I find it hard to work up any pity for them," says the deputy. "Not when I know of old ladies that they've hit over the head, just for kicks. One passed through a little while ago, tiny, he looked no more than 10 — but he'd already killed somebody." He gestures to a black boy who is standing by the open cell door apart from the others, his face clenched with fear and tension. "Come here, son. What's on your mind?"

"I want to make a phone call. Don't I get to make a call?"

"To whom?"

"To my mother. I never done nothing. I never been in trouble before in my life. They put me in a lockup all night and I was in court all morning."

"How old are you?"

"Nineteen. I got a job, I work in a garage. I was on my way home when I met this kid, he had a flute, one of those things you blow," (he gestures with his fingers held before him) "and then another guy came along, and this guy claimed I stole his flute. I didn't take it, I wouldn't know what to do with it."

"All right, get back in there and wait your turn."

I ask the deputy, "What do you think?"

Pipe clamped between his teeth, he mutters, "I think he's innocent."

What do the boys do, week after week, between being shuffled back and forth from court? Only 180 of the 2500-3000 are fortunate enough to attend the A.R.S. annex of Public School 189, one of the only two schools of its kind in the United States. Because the annex is not now equipped to handle larger numbers, priority is given to those still attending school on the outside, with dropouts waiting their turn to enroll as volunteers. Most of the rest spend their time waiting to be exercised (Warden Thomas: "Even if we had the staff, we don't have the physical facilities to give the kids the three or four hours of exercise they ought to have"), card-playing, conniving, talking tough, daydreaming of miracles and love.

The average stay in the A.R.S. is now about four months, more than twice as long as it was five years ago. The average homocide case will stay for at least a year while the slow trial process grinds on. Corrections Commissioner George F. McGrath sees his population explosion and the increased length of detention as stemming from three factors: an increase in actual crime, growing from the narcotics problem; an increase in police effectiveness; and delays in the court calendar. Many youths sit in the A.R.S. simply because they are unable to furnish $50 to $100 bail.

A recently released study of the New York City Criminal Court by the Rand Institute shows that in 1967 four-fifths of the 53,564 felony charges were either dismissed or reduced to misdemeanor or violation charges. Bronx District Attorney Roberts explains: "We're doing it for the most part not because we don't have a case, but to expedite matters."

The vast majority of inmates at the island's Correctional Institution for Men have been just as happy to "cop a plea" — that is, plead guilty to lesser charges in return for a lighter sentence. Not only do they prefer the lesser sentence; they would rather be incarcerated in the city, where they can receive regular visitors, than serve time hundreds of miles from home and family. Under the New York State Penal Code, men convicted and sentenced to terms of one year or less serve their time in city institutions; all others are sent to upstate facilities.

Even more than the youths at the remand shelter, the sentenced adult prisoners have been through the ropes. Although their average age is only 26, with, as Warden Francis R. Buono says, "amazingly few" between 35 and 50, their rap sheets show an average of at least five arrests and/or convictions, and they are anxious to do good time and get out as quickly as possible. Moreover, a substantial proportion of them are kept occupied in five-hour work details. The 1,300 convicts who maintain and operate Rikers Island do everything from running the island's powerhouse to manufacturing its beds and mattresses and producing the Department of Corrections' printed materials. The rest are in the process of either admission or discharge, except for homosexuals, for those in administrative segregation (a high-class euphemism for what is known more succinctly as "the bing") and for an occasional prisoner like the man I saw in a cell with his head in his hands, mourning his newly-dead mother. Three dozen volunteers on a cemetery work detail travel to Hart Island every day to bury the dead in a potter's field, where a 30-foot-high monument to the unbefriended dead, built by inmate-workers who suggested the idea, bears the single word:

PEACE.

In addition to holding adult prisoners, the correctional institution serves as reception and classification center for all sentenced males 16 and over who will be serving 11 days or more, and runs a narcotics addiction diagnostic center to determine whether the subjects of criminal arrests are apparently addicted — in which case they are eligible for a state program. Nearly a third of those processed, screened, interviewed and examined by medical personnel — over 12,000 men were processed in and out in 1969 — are adjudged addicts at the time of the examination, with a larger percentage identified as previous addicts.

The classification center is not a nice place for a visit, even a brief one. The two streams — one of sentenced adolescents and adults, the other of actual or suspected addicts — are continuous, wretched, shambling wherever you look, whether at their naked bodies being peered at by doctors or at their suddenly defenseless figures swathed in issue-bathrobes. In the slow miserable lines there is no horseplay.

Those under 21 are duly shipped off to the reformatory where, again, according to Warden Raymond F. McAlonan, 90 per cent of the inmates have copped a plea. His deputy, Captain Smith, good-humored and philosophical, adds: "Even though we have almost no first offenders, half of them don't know *why* they were arrested, in legal terms. The great majority have no idea what goes on when they're arraigned and assigned legal counsel, who mumbles something to the judge, and they agree to plead guilty to a lesser charge."

In the reformatory the 1,700 boys are segregated according to assignment. All of those enrolled in P.S. 189 are in one quad; all those awaiting classification are in another. Some of the 16 and 17 year olds who must attend school sit on a waiting list for sometimes a month, sometimes longer, before getting in. In yet another quad are the 100-odd homosexuals, only a few of whom are on work details. Besides work assignments, which occupy 1,200 or so, the only other alternative is a special quad to which admission is gained by application.

This is known as the Honor Quad, in which about 120 boys teach themselves and are not locked up during the day. They do remedial reading, science, high-school equivalency, and weed out undesirables themselves. Does it do any good? No one knows, everyone is dubious. "Without the follow-ups, which we don't have," says Captain Smith, "we're wasting our time. Even those few kids who manage to acquire some skills get lost when they get outside."

In the Honor Quad one finds a plant on a window sill and, tacked to a door, these reflections:

SUBJECTS

Knowledge is Recollection of ones thoughts . . .
Perfection! . . . And what it is! . . .
Death or Abeyance of the Conscious Mind . . .
Females . . . There organs and what Motivates them . . .
Homosexuality . . . And how or why it thrives.
The Universe . . . Life . . . Warning
You Conversate with one of the brothers of Knowledge
At your own Risk . . . You've been Warned . . . Except
The Words of a Wise Man . . . PEACE

Here as nowhere else on the island, one finds anthropology texts and paperbacks on philosophy and popular science on the shelves. Strolling along the corridor with Captain Smith, I learn that his high school English teacher in Harlem was poet Countee Cullen. "That reminds me," he says, "there's something I want to show you." He runs into his office and comes back with a pamphlet published by the Fortune Society (an organization of ex-convicts), a collection of poems, "Return to My Mind," by Stanley Eldridge. On the inside cover is a fulsome inscription to Captain Smith by the author.

As I leaf through the collection, a passing inmate greets him. "You know who this is?" the deputy asks. "Coincidence — it's Eldridge."

I congratulate him on his publication, and he ducks his head shyly. He is a tall, handsome black boy who has already served two years and has some months to go before his release.

"What will you do then? Do you want to write?"

"Yes, but I've got to get an education."

"Who's your favorite writer?"

Eldridge hangs his head, shrugs, then finally glances up as if he had decided to take a chance on me. "Well, it's Carson McCullers. My favorite book is 'The Heart is a Lonely Hunter.' "

"She wasn't much older than you when she wrote that." I add, "She was a remarkable person, she was a neighbor of mine," but already he is retreating uneasily.

No one knows how many Stanley Eldridges there are, struggling to find themselves in an atmosphere that seems expressly designed to repress any aspirations toward individuality — or striving to discover a need for their continued existence. Although it is newer and neater than the A.R.S. fortress onto which it has been tacked, the reformatory's problems parallel those of the remand shelter: There is no follow-up, the same boys keep coming back (Warden McAlonan guesses the recidivism rate is at least 50 or 60 per cent) and those who would truly wish to help them are engulfed by the business of containing them. The 1,700 boys in the reformatory enjoy the services of one psychiatrist for two and a half days a week, three social workers, and zero psychiatric social workers.

A group of young physicians who work part-time in the island's infirmary, disturbed by the feeling that "our primary responsibility is to prevent anybody dying while we're there," began to meet during the winter in an effort to make their discontent effective. On an average night these doctors see between 100 and 200 patients; on an exceptional night, perhaps 350. "Under such conditions, giving good medical care is impossible," says one of them, and with no psychiatrist on duty at night, when most sexual or violent episodes occur, some half dozen suicide efforts a night are shipped off to Bellevue.

For the most part these attempts at self-inflicted injury are either attention-getting devices or ways of breaking the monotony, meeting people, making contacts; but one or two of the successful suicides may have begun "unseriously" and ended in tragedy because they were discovered too late by overburdened guards. According to one doctor, relations between medical personnel and inmates involve "a constant manipulative power struggle. When you do give a man a pill, you haven't just treated him. He's succeeded, he feels, in conning you out of something that has a market value. It's impossible to check out a pathology, either. With men streaming past in such numbers you must choose almost instantaneously whether to be arbitrary or to be a bleeding heart. You are continually making character judgments on flimsy evidence."

Mannie Casiano of Puerto Rico's Migration Division believes that language problems, "combined with our people's emotionalism," lead to frustrations that all too often culminate in suicide attempts on the part of the boys shortly after they are locked up. "Aside from the painfully obvious problems of institutional overcrowding and narcotic addiction," Casiano says about his own study of the problem, "we found that a prison population about 40 per cent Spanish-speaking is being run by a Department of Corrections that is 1.8 per cent Spanish-speaking. Censorship, complicated by translation slowness, heightens the feeling that you're completely cut off when it takes a letter up to two weeks to go through."

Casiano's office came up with seven recommendations, all accepted in principle by Corrections Commissioner McGrath. They range from lowering the height requirements for corrections officers to make more Puerto Ricans eligible, to bringing in Spanish-speaking clergy for counseling boys often obsessed with guilt at having violated the ethos of their religious upbringing.

The correctional officers, who work long overtime hours, are also showing the signs of strain. As the wardens of the three institutions attempted to cope with moving masses of men last winter the guards went on a slowdown in transporting, processing, and overseeing the inmates. The job action, undertaken to force the city to hire additional personnel, succeeded in all but paralyzing the cumbrous movement of men under detention to and from the courts, the hospitals, the work details. In mid-March a substantial percentage of the sentenced prisoners of the Correctional Institution for Men went on a hunger strike, stayed in their dorms, and refused to perform their duties. Within a matter of days, the disruption had spread to the Tombs around the corner from Commissioner McGrath's office, when a battle broke out between guards and inmates after several hundred inmates assigned to the kitchen had refused to work.

To be sure, the prisoners have since quieted down. And after an all-night bargaining session, the corrections officers and their administration agreed to place the question of work load before the city's Office of Collective Bargaining, which was empowered to recommend additional manpower to supplement the 100 guards requested by Commissioner McGrath but has not yet made a report. None of this, however, will make the underlying agonies of Rikers Island go away, any more than will the aspirin asked for by inmates relieve their inner malaise.

Those who try to help ought to be recognized. In the reformatory auditorium I ran into Beverly Rich, a dedicated young woman who is associated with the Theatre for the Forgotten, a foundation-assisted company which has since 1967 brought to prisoners, many of whom had never seen live actors, everything from "The Advocate," a play about Sacco and Vanzetti, to Tennessee Williams and Bernard Shaw. Twenty-five inmates are currently involved with the production of their own 45-minute script, with no outside actors.

The reformatory runs a pre-release orientation program (PROP): A month before their release the boys are counseled by volunteers from various New York colleges and given lectures by representatives of such agencies as Harlem Y, Haryou and Herald, a church-supported agency which maintains a counseling service directed by Buford Peterson, a former inmate. There is a Vista Teacher Corps project on the island too, which is helping inmates to teach other inmates. Two separate agencies — Herald and the Youth Development Corporation — are starting post-release programs, and three additional residential half-way houses will be run by the Department of Corrections and funded by the Government under the Model Cities program.

To see all of this in perspective, however, one must refer to Warden McAlonan: "It's all really a drop in the bucket. If they care for 5 per cent of our population, it'll be a lot."

Most depressing of all are the currently abandoned facilities of the Manpower Development Training program, established in 1965 to serve both adolescents and adults on the island. Six trades, from metal fabrication to furniture-refinishing and repair, were taught by a staff of 19 in the course of a six-hour day. About four months before his discharge, the inmate entered a related program of vocational and academic coursework. As soon as he was released, he was turned over to the M.D.T. in his own community and went on salary according to his family's needs until he had established himself in his own trade. Some 900 adolescents and adults went through M.D.T. with excellent results. Thanks to an infectiously ebullient staff and a solid community follow-up, recidivism was cut at least in half; by some accounts, it was down to 25 per cent.

This did not impress those in Washington whose budgetary priorities do not parallel those of slum dwellers and others who suffer from the antisocial behavior of delinquents. Three times now funds for M.D.T. have dried up. Since August, 1969, the rooms have stood empty — offset printing equipment, $30,000 lathes, 15 new typewriters and comptometers, arc and electric welding equipment, woodworking tools — while a few hundred yards away thousands of the frustrated and the embittered mill about, waiting to be released to the streets where nothing awaits them but more of the same and an eventual return to senseless confinement.

Perhaps, though, it is their loved ones who are the worst losers, the greatest sufferers. On an average night some 200 visitors come to see the adolescents. A few are fathers, but for the most part they are mothers, aunts, grandmothers; nine out of ten are Negro or Puerto Rican. It takes them at least an hour to arrive, walking, transferring from subway to bus (few are car owners); some have been waiting since three in the afternoon in order to be first in line (there are no eating facilities). On Fridays, Warden Thomas says, he has to put on an extra captain to keep order — the families bring in the weekly paychecks from the factory to pay their boys' bail. On the evening that I was there, they had been waiting in line outdoors in the bitter raw cold for three-quarters of an hour, while the jet liners roared directly overhead on the flight path to LaGuardia, bearing the shuttle commuters of another world. In batches of 45, they were herded into the visitors' room, where they were to pick up the soiled clothing their boys had left to be taken home, and to have the fresh clothing they were bringing in inspected for contraband.

It cannot be pleasant to have the belongings that you have laundered and packed searched before you. But heroin has been found in shoulder pads, in comic books, under the embossed decorations of greeting cards. In any case, the dumbly waiting mothers and grandmothers do not complain — unless those who cannot keep their eyes from swimming with tears be regarded as complainers.

A long corridor is lined on either side with 40 phone booth-like cubicles. There they can visit for 30 minutes with their boys, looking at them through an oblong of plate glass while they converse by phone. Not wholly satisfactory, but then, neither was it when some wives began undressing, while their mates did likewise, and began a sexual charade before the guards could stop them; nor was it when a wife, during a personal visit at the adult facility, kissed her husband and passed him by mouth a deck of heroin in a balloon which he swallowed and later excreted.

As I left the building that night on the island bus after a long and wearying day I bumped into the boy who had many hours earlier requested a call to his mother. He had been bailed out by his father, who now sat beside him on the bus, wearier than I, and more uneasy. "When the case comes up," he said, "I'm going to get the Legal Aid." "But I didn't take the flute," his son insisted for what must have been the hundredth time. "I didn't do nothing."

Is there any way out of this sea of misery? At a recent conference on "Prisons Today, A Search for Alternatives," sponsored by the Fellowship of Reconciliation and addressed by everyone from Senator Dunne to assorted radicals, social workers and ex-convicts, two things seemed to emerge: First, none of these competing voices could agree, even within their own interest groups, on alternative solutions. Second, even diagnoses that seem mutually exclusive can be, if each is taken on its own terms, separately accurate and mutually clarifying.

Thus Tom Cornell of the Catholic Peace Fellowship, who has been periodically incarcerated as an antiwar activist, insisted that "rehabilitation is an affront and a reproach to the prisoner who knows it to be hypocrisy." According to Mr. Cornell, and I could not agree more, "We must see the prison as part of the larger society in which human resources are used inhumanly. The prison system cannot be reformed — it has to be replaced." On the other hand, I could not disagree with Henry M. Aronson, director of the Manhattan Court Employment project of the Vera Institute of Justice when he said flatly, "The system is not going to be dismantled." The bastilles of Rikers Island are not about to be stormed by the tribunes of the revolution — nor would the ghetto dwellers, the first and worst victims of adolescent depredations, wish them to be. As for the authorities, Mr. Aronson charges that they "go through a litany: 'more people, more money, more facilities.' But they can't tell you what they'd do with them. We must ask them to set out what they're going to do and how they would experiment."

I had much the same feeling when I listened to the differing judgments of Professor Walker of N.Y.U. and Commissioner McGrath. "There is no imaginative program for correction officers and custodial personnel," argues Walker. "Having nowhere to go with the problems of the inmates, the custodial staff are punitive with cases that ought to be handled rehabilitatively. They have an ethos of keeping people in their place: Those who commit crimes are bad people. And the administration has never really tried to deal with those who are resistant to change."

But in the course of two lengthy conversations with Commissioner McGrath, an earnest optimist whose background includes 15 years with the Glueck

Research Project on Delinquency and Crime at Harvard, I was persuaded not only of his decency and his desire to get on with something better than sitting on a volcano, but of his willingness to concede that much of the somber analysis of experts like Professor Walker is basically accurate. Caught between an exploding prison population and a near-bankrupt city, he remains convinced that "the future looks manageable" if the courts will speed up trials, if the state will take more prisoners into its own often half-empty facilities upstate and if the current Rikers Island building program goes forward (a control building to care for visitors is finished and awaits occupancy, a Correctional Institution for Women is nearing completion and a modern A.R.S. campus-type complex will open in 1972). He grants that correction officers have a "very strong" identification with the police, and that "it is a constant running problem. The disease in this business is cynicism — it feeds on their seeing the same boys return again and again — and they succumb to it." On the other hand, he says, "behavioral people are so permissively oriented that they resent *any* controls."

McGrath is devising a psychological test, based on the traits of his best officers, that will help him find good men, and is hopeful of getting money for it and for officer training, as well as for a model classroom program for short-term detainees. "I have very specific plans and we do know where we're going," says McGrath, "My whole thrust is toward community-based facilities, but we can only get on with a decentralized neighborhood correctional program if we succeed in resolving our current crisis situation."

Commissioner McGrath's optimism would be warranted if genuine decentralized rehabilitative programs could be placed on a par with custody and repression in terms of money and priorities, and removed from the control of those who, as McGrath concedes, are cynical about the life-possibilities of the imprisoned. But this would assume a passionate public revulsion against the complacent class justice which permits the sons of the poor to be held in hideous compounds for want of bail, since their parents, unlike those of middle-class kids in trouble, have no real property for collateral, and must raise the bail dollar by dollar at work. It is a melancholy fact that none of our overwhelming urban problems gets anything more than a muckraking once over lightly until — as with narcotics — it hits the homes of the middle class.

WHY PRISONERS RIOT

Vernon Fox

FINDING valid, consistent, and reliable information as to why prisoners riot defies most standard methods of gathering data on human behavior. Official reports and most articles on the subject focus on overcrowding, poor administration, insufficient financial support, political interference, lack of professional leadership, ineffective or nonexistent treatment programs, disparities in sentencing, poor and unjust parole policies, enforced idleness of prisoners, obsolete physical plant, and a small group of hard-core and intractable prisoners.[1] Psychological viewpoints focus on aggression and acting-out personalities in the prison population.[2] Yet, while all the conditions mentioned in the sociological approaches exist in most prisons, the majority have not experienced riot. Further, all major prisons hold aggressive, hostile, and acting-out people. This leads to concern as to why these factors have been identified as causes of riot when riots have occurred in a small minority of prisons.

An examination of official reports following riots discloses a similar propensity for generalities and platitudes regarding causes of riots. These same conditions are consistently identified as causes of riots almost everywhere. The purpose of official reports, of course, is political in the sense that they give assurance to the general public after a riot that the remaining power structure in the prison has analyzed the causes, taken corrective measures, and merits the confi-

dence of the public in that their interests will be protected. Investigating committees from governors' offices, legislatures, or other political directions seek simplistic answers that seem to structure their interpretations in accordance with the best interests of their own identifications. Reinterpretation of the situation has to occur frequently. Sometimes, the focus is on the predisposing causes, such as poor morale among inmates fostered by poor food or injudicious or misunderstood paroling policies. Sometimes, it is more aimed at the precipitating causes, such as a confrontation between an officer and some inmates. Sometimes, it has been explained as an attempted mass escape that the administration successfully contained.

Many consultants who are invited from outside the jurisdiction as impartial experts tend to protect the person or group who invited them, which is ethical and logical. Diplomatic writing is a consultant's art. Other consultants invited from outside generally are not sufficiently well acquainted with the nuances and underlying intricacies of the power structure to understand as well as they might all the factors entering into a local situation. Whether the governor or the legislative committee chairman of an opposite political party was the source of the invitation seems to make a difference in the tone of the report. An impartial investigator must be aware of the political climate and what will and what will not be accepted in some political settings. Some reports have been rejected by political leaders, others have been used for political purposes, while many have just been shelved. In any case, the use of these reports for finding the real causes of riots must be tempered pending corroboration from other sources. Frequently, though, these reports may set the tone for further interpretation by the news media, political leaders, and writers of documentaries.

Identifying the causes of riot, then, is tenuous when official reports or statements *after* the riot are considered alone. Clearer vision can be obtained from news reports written *during* the riot. In decreasing order of validity and reliability, the materials that comprise this presentation are from (1) news stories during 20 serious riots since 1940 as reported in *The New York Times* during the action, (2) this writer's experience during the Michigan prison riot in 1952, (3) lengthy discussions with inmates involved in four prison riots, (4) conversations with prison personnel involved in seven prison riots, (5) literature concerning prison riots, (6) official reports and official statements *after* the riot, and (7) general literature on aggression, civil disturbances, and violence.

Causes must be divided into *predisposing* causes and *precipitating* causes. Just as in civil disobedience, there has to be a "readiness" to riot. Then, there has to be a "trigger." Too frequently, the predisposing causes have been used as causes for prison riots and the precipitating causes have been identified as causes for civil disorder. Neither is a cause, in itself. The total social situation, with emphasis on the interaction or lack of it between dominant people and subjugated people, either in the prison or in the ghetto, must be evaluated to determine why people riot. It cannot be based simplistically in overcrowding, political interference, lack of treatment programs, or any other simple answer.

Patterns of Riot

The way to make a bomb is to build a strong perimeter and generate pressure inside. Similarly, riots occur in prisons where oppressive pressures and demands are generated in the presence of strong custodial containment. Riots are reported more frequently from custodially oriented prisons. Even the riot in 1962 in the progressive and relatively relaxed District of Columbia Youth Center at Lorton, Virginia, involved suppression, real or imagined, of the Black Muslims.

Riots are spontaneous—not planned—detonated by a spontaneous event. The inmates know who has the weapons and who has the force. The inmates know that no administration ever has to negotiate with them. Planned disturbances end in sitdown strikes, slowdowns, hunger strikes, and self-inflicted injury. Escapes do not begin with disturbances unless they are planned as a distraction, though the disturbance may end in escape attempts. The spontaneous event that detonates the riot may be almost anything from a fight in the yard that expands, someone heaving a tray in the dining hall, to a homosexual tricking a new officer to open his cell, as happened in the Michigan riot in 1952. Violent riots must happen spontaneously. Otherwise, they would not happen. There has to be pressure, though, that builds up the predisposition or readiness to riot and a spontaneous precipitating event to trigger or detonate the riot.

Riots tend to pattern in five stages, four during the riot and one afterward. First, there is a period of undirected violence like the exploding bomb. Secondly, inmate leaders tend to emerge and organize around them a group of ringleaders who determine inmate policy during the riot. Thirdly, a period of interaction with prison authority, whether by negotiation or by force, assists in identifying the alternatives available for the resolution of the riot. Fourthly, the surrender of the inmates, whether by negotiation or by force, phases out the violent event. Fifthly, and most important from the political viewpoint, the investigations and administrative changes restore order and confidence in the remaining power structure by making "constructive changes" to regain administrative control and to rectify the undesirable situation that produced the riot.

The first stage of the riot is characterized by an event that triggered the unbridled violence. The first stage is disorganized among the prisoners and, too frequently, among the prison staff as well. It is at this point that custodial force could alter the course of the riot but, in most instances, custody is caught by surprise and without adequate preparation so that there is little or no custodial reaction other than containment. As a result, the riot pattern is permitted by default to move to the second stage.

The second stage is when inmate leaders emerge and the administrative forces become organized. Inmate leaders who emerge from this violence are people who remain emotionally detached sufficiently so that they lend stability to the inmate group. They "don't panic." They "keep their cool." As a result, they attract around them lesser inmate leaders or "ringleaders" who, similarly, do not panic but need to be dependent upon "the boss." In this manner, an inmate leader can gather around him probably two to six "lieutenants," each with some delegated authority, such as watching hostages, preparing demands, and maintaining discipline in the rest of the inmate group. Further, the inmate leader, like most political leaders, takes a "middle-of-the-road" position where he can moderate the extremes and maintain communication. In a prison riot, some inmates want to kill the hostages. Other inmates want to give up and surrender to the administration. The inmate leader controls these two extremes in a variety of ways and stabilizes the group into a position in the center.

The third stage is a period of interaction between inmates and prison officials. It has taken several forms, though they can be classified generally into (1) negotiation and (2) force or threat of force. No administration has to negotiate with prisoners, but the chances for negotiation are greater when the prisoners hold hostages. The chances for force or threat of force are greater when the prisoners do not have hostages. In either case, the decision on the part of the inmates to surrender is subject to the general principles of group dynamics. When the inmate group is cohesive and their morale is good, the prisoners will maintain the riot situation, whether faced with force or negotiation. When the group cohesion begins to disintegrate by some inmates wanting to surrender, others wanting to retaliate, and the leadership wanting to maintain the status quo, the administration may manipulate it for an early surrender. This disintegration of group cohesion may be promoted by negotiation or by force or threat of force, depending upon the situation. In case of negotiation, the group cohesion is diminished by the administration's demonstrated willingness to negotiate and by the personality of the official negotiators who convey a feeling of trust and confidence. The group can be disintegrated, also, by gas, rifle fire, and artillery shelling, all of which have been used recently in American prison riots. The less destructive approach, of course, is to await disintegration of cohesion by periods of inaction that places strain to hold the group together on the leadership by fatigue and impatience. Faced with this situation, the leadership frequently has to look for an honorable way out of a disintegrating situation.

The fourth stage, or surrender, may be the inmates' giving up after being gassed and shot at or they may surrender in an orderly way either after force or threat of force or by negotiation. Political interference at the wrong time in the prison riot can affect the total situation in terms of negotiation, surrender, and subsequent investigations and administrative decisions.

The fifth stage, that of investigations, consolidation of the remaining power structure, personnel and policy changes followed by political fall-out, is really the most important stage, since it sets policy for the prison and the system for years to come. Editorials and news commentators suggest solutions and interpretations. Administrators have to respond satisfactorily to pressures from interest groups. This is why "get tough" policies become important after riots, even though they tend to intensify the problems.

Riots do not occur in prisons or correctional institutions with exceedingly high morale. Neither do they occur in prisons where the morale is so low that the prisoners endure penal oppression in a docile manner or break their own legs and cut their own heel tendons. Riots occur in prisons where inmates have medium to high morale and where some conflict appears in the staff, probably between treatment and custodial philosophies, and probably when the program is in a state of transition from one type of procedures and objectives to another.

Riots occur in prisons where there is a tenuous balance between controlling behavior and changing behavior. If there is a full commitment to either, riots do not occur. The riot itself, however, results in a political decision to *control* behavior. Consequently, the behavior changing in treatment forces always loses in a riot, at least in the immediate future.

There is also a direct relationship between news coverage by the mass media and the incidence of demonstrations, riots, and civil disturbances.[3] This is one reason why riots tend to cluster in terms of time.

One of the factors that contributed to the prison insurrections of 1952 was the decision of the administration to reverse the drift toward greater inmate control.[4] Abuses of official rules were curbed, preferential treatment for favored prisoners was eliminated, and the social system of the prison was "reformed" in the direction of the image of what the free community thought a maximum-security institution should be.

During the Riot

Guidelines for action during the riot are important. The custodial staff is frequently untrained and the administration is just as frequently caught by surprise. Action during the riot has to be planned ahead of time and modified according to the situation.

During the first stage of a riot, the disorganized inmates could well be effectively faced with force. As a matter of fact, most riots appear to have been vulnerable to custodial force in the early stages because of the disorganization on the side of the inmates. If disorganization occurs on both sides, however, then the riot cannot be contained early. Immediate custodial action could have altered the course of several riots. The lack of training, preparation, or even expectation of riot has resulted in disorganization on both sides for hours.

During the second stage, after the inmates have organized and their leadership begins to emerge, there is the question as to whether force should be used. No prison administration ever needs to negotiate with rioting prisoners. The prisoners know this. If hostages are held, then negotiation becomes a real possibility, depending upon other factors. If the inmates holding the hostages are young, reformatory-type people with short sentences and have not already demonstrated their capability to kill, if they are psychiatric patients who cannot organize into a team, or if their majority can see parole sometime in the future, then negotiation is not necessary. In the Michigan riot of 1952, the decision to negotiate was not made until after the files of the inmates holding the hostages in 15-block had been reviewed. In that situation, negotiation was apparently the only way to save the lives of the hostages. This was supported by subsequent reports by inmates, nationally known clincial psychologists, and consultants brought in for impartial investigation.

The third stage of the riot is determined by the nature of the situation. If no hostages are held or if the prisoners holding hostages are not hard-core intractables with nothing to lose, then force or threat of force is appropriate. If the hostages are considered to be in serious danger, the administration is placed in a real dilemma in determining action because lives have to be considered in relation to public and internal reaction and consequences. If waiting for fatigue to reduce the cohesion of the rebellious inmate group will accomplish the objective, then force is not necessary.

The fourth stage of the riot is the surrender. The regaining of custodial control is all that is needed. Any further action beyond the basic need has to be for public consumption or for the satisfaction of the prison administration.

The fifth stage of the riot is the aftermath where investigations, reinterpretations, and scapegoats are involved. There is not much the prison administration can do about this because the real power lies in the political structure. Free movement of newsmen and free access to information, both inmates and staff, is the only logical approach to take during this period. In this way, the administration can demonstrate that it is attempting to hide nothing, that it recognizes it has problems, and is openly and honestly seeking the best solutions.

In summary, official reaction to riot is dependent upon the situation. As in judo, the reaction is determined by the action of the adversary. No negotiation is needed where no hostages are held or where they might be held by short-term prisoners not considered to be dangerous. Out-waiting might be an approach in doubtful situations. An overshow of force is becoming decreasingly effective in American society and it invites unnecessary derision from some segments of the public.

Administrative Do's and Don'ts

Discretion, rather than negotiation or force, is at issue while handling a riot. A basic principle

of police work or any other type of social control in a democratic society is to use the minimum amount of force and destruction needed to accomplish the objectives.[5]

Discretion is based on knowledge. Consequently, the first approach for a correctional administrator to improve his program is to increase the educational level of his staff by more selective recruitment and by inservice training. In modern democratic society, inservice training should be directed toward the social and behavioral sciences. This can be achieved by bringing neighboring junior colleges and universities into the educational program of the prison.[6] An understanding and knowledgeable prison staff from the custodial employee to the warden is important in the discretionary or decision-making process. It is this staff that determines whether a confrontation occurs or is avoided and, if it occurs, how it will be handled or accommodated. This is why they need to know social problems, personality development and problems, criminology and correctional procedures, as well as the law, particularly as it relates to civil rights.

The correctional officer is the key to riot prevention, although a rough and harsh custodial lieutenant, captain, or deputy warden can use policies and behavior to neutralize the good work of a hundred officers. The entire custodial force has to be treatment-oriented, just as the entire treatment staff has to be aware of custodial problems, in order to emerge with an effective correctional program.

Readiness to riot results from the predisposing causes, such as bad food, oppressive custodial discipline, sadistic staff quick to write disciplinary charges against inmates, and general punitive attitude by administration and line personnel. The precipitating cause that "triggers" the riot is very seldom the real cause. As previously mentioned, a bomb is made by constructing a strong perimeter or casing and generating pressure inside. It blows at its weakest point, but it has to be detonated. The detonation is not the "cause" of the explosion, although it "triggered" it.

During the riot, the inmates want to smash the system that keeps them hopeless, anonymous, and in despair, and they will destroy at random.[7] They become so alienated from society that they regard violence as right and proper. Good treatment programs and an accepting custodial staff tend to reduce this problem. A relaxed atmosphere in a prison that avoids this alienation is most important for the eventual correctional objective and to avoid riots.

How to achieve a relaxed atmosphere is sometimes difficult for the administrator because it appears that he is "taking sides." Custodial personnel are generally concerned with good discipline, which is sometimes interpreted as "nipping problems in the bud" and is translated into overreaction to minor offenses and oppressive custodial control. Many treatment personnel, on the other hand, are in a relaxed atmosphere because it tends to lower the inmates' defenses and permit casework and psychotherapy to be better achieved. The inmates, of course, find the relaxed atmosphere more comfortable, so they favor it. This places the treatment staff "on the side of the inmates," although for different reasons. It is sometimes difficult for an administrator to interpret to the custodial staff the reasons for promoting a relaxed atmosphere in the prison. This is another reason for providing education and inservice training in behavior and social problems to all staff.

Good food, plentiful and well prepared, is important to maintaining a prison. Napoleon's famous remark that an army marches on its stomach could be applied to any group of men. Food becomes a primary source of pleasure to men deprived of many of the comforts of normal life. Consequently, the prison administration cannot realistically compute food costs on the basis of nutritional needs alone. The emotional needs are important. An institutional program can make a lot of mistakes if it has a good kitchen that provides plenty of food. Conversely, food is a tangible item on which can be focused all the discontents and deprivations of the prison. Many riots have begun in or near the dining room. Food simply becomes a tangible substitute target for other complaints. Consequently, an administrator should spend a little extra time and effort to find a good steward to handle food services and pay special attention to the food budget.

Despite the other abuses, riots do not occur in prisons that are essentially run by inmates. There are some Southern prisons where selected inmates carry guns and guard other inmates. All the generalities attributed to riot causation exist, but no riots have occurred in these prisons. This is because the inmate leaders have a vested interest in the status quo and will protect it.

Inmate leadership is present in all prisons, as leadership is present in all groups of people. The constructive use of inmate leadership is an obvious way to avoid riots. Some type of inmate self-government that involves honest and well supervised elections of inmate representatives to discuss problems, make recommendations and, perhaps, even take some responsibilities from the administration could be helpful. Possibilities might be some control of those activities related to formalized inmate activities like manuscripts sent to potential publishers, pricing hobbycraft items for sale, or processing inmate activities like Alcoholics Anonymous or chess clubs. In an era when movements to unionize prisoners appear, such as in West Germany and Sweden, and when litigation initiated by inmates result in court rulings that change conditions and procedures within the prisons, it is in the interest of the administration to know the inmates' thinking and their action. In any case, downward communication is not enough.

The pattern could be taken from student government functioning under a university administration. It could be taken from a civilian government operating under military occupation by the victors after a war, such as those civilian governments in Germany and Japan after World War II. The pattern in the Federal Bureau of Prisons and some other systems has been the inmate council, where elected inmates discuss problems and appropriate policies with the prison administration, making recommendations and suggestions. A suggestion box system for inmates might be instituted if other approaches appear to be too innovative. Regardless of how it is organized, it should promote upward and downward communication between inmates and prison administration and it should provide the inmate leadership with a vested interest in the status quo.

In summary, good communication can avoid the predisposing causes of riot. Whether by inmate council, inmate self-government programs, suggestion boxes, or free up-and-down communication of any type, knowledge by the inmate leadership of situations and their reasons can eliminate most predisposing causes. Establishment of the therapeutic community where inmates take responsibility for the improvement of other inmates, such as in the Provo Experiment in Utah in 1958-1964, the Minnesota State Training School at Red Wing, and some other places, would also provide a vested interest for the inmates in the institution and its program, as well as a constructive attitude. Raising the educational level of the prison staff, especially the correctional officers, would reduce the predisposing causes. Their better understanding of personality development and social problems would provide them with the capacity for discretion that would, in turn, reduce the precipitating causes. Prison riots can be eliminated when upward and downward communication, combined with discretionary use of authority, reduces the probability of serious confrontation that should not have to occur in a democratic society.

Notes

1. A succint and comprehensive review of the literature is found in Clarence Schrag, "The Sociology of Prison Riots," *Proceedings of the American Correctional Association, 1960*, New York, 1961, pp. 136-146.
2. For example, see the late Dr. Ralph Banay's excellent articles on causes of riots in *The New York Times*, July 26, 1959, sec. VI, p. 8; August 9, 1959, sec. VI, p.2; August 16, 1959, sec. VI, p. 72.
3. David L. Lange, Robert K. Baker, and Sandra J. Ball, *Violence and the Media*. Washington, D.C.: United States Government Printing Office, November 1969, p. 614.
4. Gresham M. Sykes, *The Society of Captives*. Princeton, N.J.: Princeton University Press, 1958, p. 144.
5. See George E. Berkley, *The Democratic Policeman*. Boston: Beacon Press, 1969.
6. For suggested curricula, see Vernon Fox, *Guidelines for Correctional Programs in Community and Junior Colleges*, American Association of Junior Colleges, Washington, D.C., 1969, and "The University Curriculum in Corrections," FEDERAL PROBATION, September 1959. Also see *Criminology and Corrections Programs*, Joint Commission on Correctional Manpower and Training, Washington, D.C., 1968.
7. "Violence and Corrections," *The Correctional Trainer*, Southern Illinois University, Carbondale, Vol. I, No. 4, Spring 1970, pp. 56-91.

VIII.

FREEDOM,
ORDER
AND JUSTICE

FREEDOM, ORDER AND JUSTICE

Francis A. Allen

USTICE PLAYS A CENTRAL ROLE in the life
of all countries. This is as true of the
United States as of other nations, even
though we have been more neglectful of the
administration of justice than many. The
framers of the Constitution left no doubt
about the importance they accorded the function of justice in the government they were
creating. In the Preamble to the Constitution the framers aspired both to "the blessings
of liberty" and to "domestic tranquility."

This dual theme of freedom and order
emerges again and again throughout our
history. In dedicating the new government
to both objectives, the framers obviously rejected the notion that freedom and order
were irreconcilable; indeed, they believed
each in the long run to be indispensable to
the other. The framers were practical men
and well aware that although private violence
may be the enemy of liberty, liberty may
also be damaged or even destroyed by efforts
of state officials to suppress private violence.
This is the significance of the fact that four
of the amendments in the original Bill of
Rights expressly regulate the administration

of criminal justice and several others have
relevance for the criminal process. The
American constitutional tradition, therefore,
accords high importance to freedom and
order, and recognizes a continuing necessity
for the proper reconciliation of both values
if either is to be fully realized.

Why have the problems of justice produced
such concern and anxiety in recent years?
Why is the criminal law and its administration
important? No very satisfactory response can
be made to these questions without a good
deal of inquiry and discussion. Even so, it
may be useful to attempt some partial answers. The law—particularly the criminal
law—is important, first, because of what it
seeks to accomplish. Surely one of the principal purposes of the criminal law is to prevent or discourage behavior known to be
dangerous to certain basic interests of mankind. What are these interests? They include
matters no less important than the protection
of men from death and physical injury by
unauthorized violence or carelessness. They
include also the security of men in their possessions—their homes, their wealth, their tools

—from misappropriation and destruction. To obtain fuller protection of these and other basic human interests has always been one of the primary goals of organized society.

There are other reasons for regarding the criminal law as important, however. One of these relates to the nature of criminal penalties or sanctions. Apart from international conflict or civil war, it is in the administration of the criminal law that the government subjects individuals to the most drastic exertions of state power. Criminal sanctions may deprive convicted offenders of their property through fines, their liberty through imprisonment, and even their lives through capital punishment.

The severity of these penalties is evidence of the high value organized societies have placed on the security of life, limb and possessions. Yet as history has frequently demonstrated, these great powers are *capable* of being abused and of being exercised for unauthorized and unjustifiable ends. When this occurs, the apparatus of justice not only fails to give protection to the basic interests it was designed to defend, but may become the engine for their destruction. It is no accident, after all, that one of the first objectives of an emerging totalitarian regime is to gain control of the internal police. Another reason for the importance of justice, therefore, is the necessity for continuing vigilance to insure that the drastic powers exercised by the criminal law are not employed to destroy vital human and political values.

THE "SUBSTANTIVE" CRIMINAL LAW

Fundamental to any system of justice is that body of law or custom which defines conduct that is criminal and subject to penalty. Although most persons today think of the criminal law as a product of legislatures, many of the characteristic crimes in the Anglo-American legal system were first defined by judges; and even in jurisdictions like the federal government that have abolished "common-law crimes" many of the general principles actually applied by the courts are not to be found in statutes, but derive from the common law of England and the United States.

The "substantive" criminal law is basic because it determines what conduct is criminal and the penalties that can be lawfully imposed on those who engage in such conduct. Is a man who smokes a marihuana cigarette a criminal? What about the man who bets on the outcome of a college basketball game, who uses deadly force against an assailant without first taking advantage of a reasonable opportunity to retreat, or who offers corporate securities for sale in a prospectus that inaccurately describes the financial condition of the company? None of these questions can be answered without first referring to the substantive criminal law of the state or country in which the conduct occurred. The central questions addressed by the substantive criminal law are, therefore: Who is the criminal? Who *ought* to be the criminal? What penalties shall be authorized for his punishment?

The substantive criminal law performs another function that may at first be overlooked. When the legislature enacts a statute defining larceny, for example, it authorizes the exertion of state power against the person suspected of crime. The individual may be arrested, deprived of his liberty prior to trial (if he is unable to meet bail requirements), placed in jeopardy and required to sustain the expenses of a criminal trial and, if convicted, required to be separated from his friends and family during a prolonged period of imprisonment.

The statute defining larceny does something more, however. It not only unleashes state power; it limits it. This is true because the statute is implicitly saying not only that persons guilty of the defined behavior may be punished, but also that persons whose conduct does not fall within the definition may *not* be convicted and punished for larceny. The familiar principle of "an eye for an eye, a tooth for a tooth," derived from the *lex talionis,* illustrates a related point. However unenlightened its approach for most modern purposes, the formula limits the retaliation authorized for wrongdoing: at least an eye may not be exacted for a tooth or a life for an eye. Thus the principle of *nulla poena sine lege* (no punishment without law), which is one of the cornerstones of our penal law, regulates and contains the power of the state in its relations with individuals and groups within the community.

When one becomes aware of the vital purposes the law of crimes is called upon to serve, he might reasonably expect the drafting and enactment of criminal legislation to be widely recognized as one of the most important functions of government, and to be a subject of unusual interest and concern for legal scholars. Unfortunately, until recently the contrary has been more nearly true. Even today widespread neglect of the statutory criminal law is only beginning to be overcome in a few American jurisdictions. This is not to say that legislatures have been reluctant to enact statutes creating new crimes. All too often legislators have regarded the passing of a criminal law as the remedy for almost any social ill coming to their attention. It has been estimated that the number of crimes for which prosecutions might be brought doubled in the first half of the twentieth century. There is today hardly any human activity that is not the subject of a criminal statute in one aspect or another.

Unfortunately, however, genuine concern for the criminal law is not demonstrated by the number of criminal statutes passed. In fact, the numbers may often reveal a dangerous unconcern. Typically, the criminal "code" of an American jurisdiction consists of an assortment of statutes enacted over a long period, many in response to particular problems that have long since lost all significance. Most American legislatures (including Congress) have failed to enact a thoroughgoing revision of their criminal statutes in the present century. The consequences are serious. Much criminal legislation does not even articulate its basic provisions adequately, thereby failing to give citizens sufficient notice of conduct subject to serious penalties or to provide courts guidelines to govern the trials of criminal cases. Often indefensible incongruities are permitted to continue for decades. A few years ago, a revision committee discovered that the laws of one of the most populous American states provided larger penalties for horse theft than for stealing automobiles. In another instance the penalty for an attempt was greater than for the completed crime. Because of the helter-skelter, unsystematic growth of legisla-

tion, vitally needed provisions are sometimes completely overlooked.

One of the primary reasons the law of criminal conspiracy has been permitted to persist in its present unsatisfactory state is that its vague and amorphous doctrines can be employed to "fill in the gaps" of the criminal statutes. Although urgently needed provisions are often lacking in the "codes," the statutory criminal law is encumbered by provisions having no possible utility for modern problems. There remained on the statute books of the state mentioned above a provision making a misdemeanant of the owner of a saltpeter cave who failed to fence its entrance against wandering cattle. At the same time, no criminal statute in the state spoke to the problems of the abuse of such a common modern device as the credit card.

In 1942, Louisiana adopted a systematic revision of its law of crimes. Wisconsin followed in the 1950's and the Illinois Criminal Code appeared in 1961. These pioneering ventures preceded more recent revisions in a number of states, including New York and Texas. A major recodification of the federal criminal law has been presented for congressional action, and revision projects are going forward in several states. The more recent revisions have been inspired and guided to a considerable extent by the Model Penal Code of the American Law Institute, to which leading legal scholars, judges, lawyers and some laymen contributed in the 1950's and early 1960's. The Model Code is a major intellectual achievement; almost inevitably the form and content of criminal law revision in the next quarter-century will be strongly influenced by it. Nevertheless, criminal legislation in most American jurisdictions remains unprincipled and technically deficient. In those jurisdictions the statutes, themselves, are important obstacles to both efficiency and justice in the administration of the criminal law.

The pervasive deficiency, of which the failures of our criminal legislation are both a cause and a symptom, is the absence of a genuine penal policy in most American jurisdictions. We have typically provided no thoughtful or consistent answers to the question: Who is the criminal? As a result, we have failed to consider or even identify a number of fundamental issues that must be confronted if rational policy is to be created. These questions are many and difficult: What should our policy be toward those who cause disorder and even violence, but who are nevertheless motivated to achieve a more just society? Should a person who commits an act that creates an injury or violates a regulatory statute, but who does so unintentionally and without negligence, be subject to criminal liability and penalties? What should be the position of the criminal law with regard to the offender whose conduct may in some sense be the result of life-long cultural deprivation or of below-normal intellectual or emotional capacities?

Satisfactory answers to these questions do not come easily. Yet there is another area that may present even more insistent problems. Many competent observers believe that a great deal of behavior that is today regarded as criminal could more appropriately be relegated to the domain of private moral choice than to penal regulation. The *withdrawing* of penal sanctions from such conduct is seen as an overriding necessity. What is at issue here are statutes penalizing activities like gambling, sexual relations between consenting adults, the consumption and sale of alcohol, drugs and the like. The case for "de-criminalization" in these areas is a powerful one. Perhaps the real issue is not whether withdrawal of criminal sanctions is desirable, but how far and how rapidly this withdrawal should proceed.

Those arguing for "de-criminalization" point out that many persons today reject the notion that much of this behavior is seriously immoral, and that the authority of the legal order is subverted in the attempt to punish acts widely defended as proper or, at least, as tolerable. Experience with law enforcement in this field has not been reassuring. Much of the behavior condemned by these laws is conducted in private, and because (unlike such crimes as assault or theft) there are no complaining witnesses to give evidence, the enforcement problem is extraordinarily difficult. The police, therefore, are induced, on occasion, to exceed their powers. It is in cases of this kind that the constitutional rights

of suspected persons are most likely to be violated. Here one most often encounters unreasonable searches and seizures, unlawful arrests, electronic eavesdropping and the dubious activities of undercover police agents and informants.

Finally, the point can be made that the large and largely futile efforts to enforce these laws divert the limited public resources of men and money from the tasks of protecting persons from the loss of life, limb and possessions. Consequently, these laws reduce rather than enhance the protection afforded by the criminal law to the most important interests of men in society. Some of the issues in this highly charged field have already been joined. We can anticipate much acrimony and emotion in future discussions. We shall all gain if at least a modicum of rationality is permitted to temper these deliberations.

THE LAW OF CRIMINAL PROCEDURE

"The history of liberty," wrote the late Mr. Justice Felix Frankfurter, "has largely been the history of the observance of procedural safeguards." Certainly some of the fiercest debates on issues of freedom and order have centered, in recent years, on decisions of the Supreme Court of the United States dealing with procedures of state and federal systems of criminal justice. The law of criminal procedure encompasses the full range of the criminal process from arrest to appeal and extends even to certain problems involving the operations of correctional systems. Not all criminal procedure is concerned primarily with the rights of persons charged with or convicted of crime. Some provisions, for example, are intended simply to advance the effectiveness of the machinery of justice.

Nevertheless, the popular identification of the rights of persons with the law of criminal procedure is essentially sound. The United States Constitution contains a few provisions directed to the substantive criminal law; the constitutional definition of the crime of treason provides one example. Most of the provisions dealing with criminal justice, however, speak to procedural requirements and safeguards: trial by jury, rights of counsel, speedy trial, the privilege against self-incrimination and many more.

Because of the obvious concern of the framers of the Constitution for the criminal process and its possible abuse, it may be surprising to discover that most of the constitutional law of criminal procedure was announced less than 40 years ago; some of it, of course, has appeared only in the last decade. Perhaps the primary reason for this is that the provisions in the original Bill of Rights were assumed to be restrictions only on the federal government, not on state systems of justice. Such limitations as were imposed on the states derived primarily from the due process and equal protection clauses of the Fourteenth Amendment. For the first half of the Amendment's life, the Supreme Court interpreted those clauses very narrowly in criminal cases, with the result that the states proceeded with their administration of criminal justice almost totally free from interference by federal judicial power.

The modern era may be said to begin with the decision in the very famous case of *Powell v. Alabama* (287 U.S. 45) in 1932, which grew out of the prosecution of the "Scottsboro Boys" in the early years of the great depression. For the first time the Supreme Court reversed a state conviction on the ground that rights of counsel implicit in the concept of a fair trial had been denied the defendants and that such rights were protected against state action by the due process clause of the Fourteenth Amendment. Although the holding of the Court in the *Powell* case was narrowly stated, it marked the beginning of one of the most rapid and remarkable developments of constitutional doctrine in the history of the Supreme Court.

It may be interesting to ask why these developments began in the early 1930's. No single answer suffices, and it is doubtful that any combination of answers is fully adequate. The country was nearing the end of the prohibition experiment, and had become acutely conscious of both the problems of crime and the abuses of law enforcement that were associated with that period. Technical changes in the nature of the Court's appellate jurisdiction may have emboldened it to experiment with federal judicial supervision of state criminal justice. Perhaps most important of

all, however, was the concern engendered by the loss of liberty and the abuses of governmental power in the criminal process then becoming apparent in the emerging totalitarian regimes of Western Europe. It is interesting to note that 1932, the year of the *Powell* decision, was also the year that Hitler came to power in Germany.

REMARKABLE RULINGS

Whatever the causes, a series of remarkable holdings followed during the next four decades. Although the development was by no means wholly consistent, it generally had the effect of significantly expanding the rights of individuals caught up in the criminal process. A wide variety of problems was canvassed. A series of cases from state courts involving the "coerced confession" was initiated by the decision in *Brown v. Mississippi* (297 U.S. 278, 1936). The law of rights of counsel pursued its tortuous course. There were cases involving search and seizure, wiretapping and electronic eavesdropping, extradition, the constitutional requirements of public trial and trial by jury, and many more. There were also cases of great complexity dealing with questions of how and when the criminal defendant or prisoner might assert the new constitutional rights being given recognition.

Striking as were these developments in the first three decades following *Powell,* the Warren Court brought this history to a climax in the 1960's. A series of decisions of great importance and potential impact were handed down.

It is not possible within the confines of this survey to identify and discuss the difficult legal issues these cases present. Perhaps an attempt should be made, however, to discover some of the general ideas that underlie many of the modern Court's positions in the area of criminal procedure. One of the most striking concerns of the Court, as it approached cases arising from the criminal process, relates to the adverse effects of poverty and racial discrimination on the administration of criminal justice. The poor man, in fact, suffers substantial disadvantages. He may be unable to hire a lawyer. He may be deprived of his liberty in the critical period prior to trial because of his inability to meet the financial requirements for release on bail. His resources may be inadequate to fund an adequate defense: pretrial investigation to locate witnesses in his behalf may be beyond his means, and he may lack funds to pay for the services of experts in psychiatry, handwriting, or accountancy.

These financial incapacities may place a defendant in great peril of conviction or of more severe penalties for reasons unrelated to his culpability. The reaction of the Court to these problems has been to express concern, not only about possible unfairness caused by the poverty of the accused, but for the unequal impact of the system of criminal justice on the man of little means when compared to the man of wealth. The egalitarianism of the modern Court has been noted in many areas of its adjudication, and this tendency can be seen clearly in many of its opinions in criminal cases.

A second important thread in these decisions is the Court's commitment to the adversary system of justice and its impulse to extend the adversary principle into areas where it has not generally prevailed before. By the "adversary system" of criminal justice is meant one in which accusations are made by the state (which bears the burden of proof) and in which the accused enjoys not only a presumption of innocence, but full and fair opportunities to contest the charges and evidence against him by every legitimate means. The right to counsel is almost a corollary of the adversary system, for an untrained and unaided defendant is unable to contest the prosecution on an equal footing. The Court moved, first, to bring the criminal trial closer to the adversary ideal by insisting that the states provide counsel for indigent defendants in trials of serious criminal charges. Subsequently the Court, noting that the ideal of adversary justice was not even approximated in the private, pretrial interrogation of suspects by the police or prosecutors, sought to reconstruct the character of pretrial proceedings by imposing a right of access to counsel and, where necessary, of appointment of counsel for indigent persons subjected to interrogation by the state prior to trial. In other cases, the Court has attempted to impose the image of adversary justice on the juvenile court, in "line-up" procedures conducted to secure identification of suspected persons, and elsewhere.

The commitment of the Court to the adversary model of criminal justice no doubt reflects its conviction that this course is required to give full protection to the basic rights of individuals suspected of or charged with crime. But there may be other reasons. The American institutions of criminal justice are fragmented and decentralized to a remarkable degree. It is said that in Cook County, Illinois, there are approximately 100 police departments, each largely independent of the other. As a result, political responsibility for the decency and effectiveness of the system is widely diffused, if it can be said to exist at all. In no other advanced nation has this fragmentation proceeded so far. The absence of genuine political and administrative responsibility has resulted in the substitution of judicial supervision of criminal justice administration. Judicial supervision, in turn, has been marked by an attempt to recast many aspects of the criminal process into the adversary mold, perhaps in part to render judicial supervision easier and more effective. That the Supreme Court has made invaluable contributions to the decency of the American system of criminal justice cannot be reasonably denied. It is no condemnation of the Court to add, however, that it has provided little guidance toward the solution of many of the most pressing problems of criminal justice that today afflict us.

A GLANCE AHEAD

This brief survey has made no effort to canvass a number of the gravest difficulties that will beset the administration of justice during the years remaining in the twentieth century. One of these is the problem of doing justice under the weight of overwhelming numbers of cases burdening law enforcement agencies, the courts, and correctional facilities in our urban areas. Perhaps our concerns with doing justice in the individual case (which can never be ignored) have diverted us from the increasingly important questions of how justice can operate more reasonably and effectively as a system.

Another of these problems involves our

correctional practices. Sooner or later we shall be forced to recognize that the prison is an anachronism. The sooner this perception becomes widely shared, the sooner we may be induced to give serious and practical thought to alternatives to incarceration in dealing with our serious offenders.

We are facing in the United States a grave loss of legitimacy of the legal order. By "legitimacy" I mean nothing mysterious or mystical. I refer to the capacity of the law to evoke compliance with a minimum of force from the overwhelming portion of the population. To restore legitimacy and to cure the alienation of many Americans from the legal order will require more than the reform of justice, and particularly criminal justice. Yet in this effort justice has a critical role to play, whether for good or ill. It is always the obligation of a liberal society to search, in the words of the late Max Radin, for "a juster justice, a more lawful law." Today that obligation is more than ever imperative, for on the outcome of the search depends the survival of a society whose values include the reconciliation of freedom and order.

DRUG ABUSE

1970 - 1971

An AMS Anthology

Edited, with an Introduction, by

Herbert S. Anhalt, M.D.

and

Jackwell Susman
American University

"Drug abuse . . . has assumed the dimensions of a national emergency," President Nixon stated to Congress in June, 1971, and added, "but despite the increasing dimension of the problem, and despite increasing consciousness of the problem, we have made little headway in understanding what is involved in drug abuse or how to deal with it."

To begin defining drug abuse, the editors of this anthology — a doctor and a sociologist — have reviewed periodical literature in medicine, pharmacology, sociology, law, psychology, police enforcement, social work, and other disciplines. The result of their research is an anthology of over thirty articles from American and British publications, which during the past year attempted to define the scope of drug abuse and which have set forth some workable (and often controversial) approaches to the problem.

Buckrambound (ISBN: 0-404-10301-4): $14.95   Size: 6 x 9
Paperbound   (ISBN: 0-404-10351-0): $8.95 Approx. 600 pages

EDUCATING
THE
DISADVANTAGED

1970 - 1971

An AMS Anthology

Edited by

Russell C. Doll
University of Missouri-Kansas City

and

Maxine Hawkins
Chicago State College

First publication of new essays by Daniel U. Levine, Robert J. Havighurst, and J. McV. Hunt, two previously unpublished reports from the National Study of American Indian Education, a new list of readings on Mexican-Americans and American Indians, and a guide to resource centers highlight the contents of this anthology which is now in its third year of publication. In addition to the new material, thirty-three papers concerned with educating disadvantaged and culturally different children have been selected by the editors. Among the fifty-five contributors are Ivan Illich, Allan Ornstein, Samuel McCracken, Estelle Fuchs, Robert D. Strom, David Larimore, S.M. Miller, Robert Coles, Harold M. Rose, Jean José, Norman A. Johnson, Peggy R. Sanday, and Warren Winkelstein.

Buckrambound (ISBN: O-404-10103-8): $14.95   Size: 6 x 9
Paperbound   (ISBN: 0-404-10155-0): $8.95   616 pages

EDUCATING
THE
DISADVANTAGED

1968 - 1969

An AMS Anthology

Edited by

Allan C. Ornstein

Thirty-five articles and papers, originally published during the school year of 1968-1969, are included in the first volume concerned with educating disadvantaged children. Represented in the volume are forty contributors, including Nathan Glazer, Daniel P. Moynihan, Jonathan Kozol, Doris R. Entwisle, Christopher Jencks, Robert Coles, Max Lerner, Albert Shanker, Marion Blank and Frances Solomon. The anthology is comprised of five parts:

    I.   Socio-Psychological Factors
         Affecting the Disadvantaged
   II.   Perspective for Teaching the Disadvantaged
  III.   Race and the Nature of the Urban Setting
   IV.   Race and Equal Educational Opportunity
    V.   Urban School Organization and Change

Buckrambound: $14.95   Size: 7 x 10   766 pages

EDUCATING THE DISADVANTAGED

1969 - 1970

An AMS Anthology

Edited by

Allan C. Ornstein

Russell C. Doll

Nancy Arnez

Maxine Hawkins

The second volume in the serial publication on the education of disadvantaged children is comprised of thirty-one articles by thirty-six contributors, including Daniel P. Moynihan, Robert J. Havighurst, Virginia Heyer Young, Irwin Katz, Nancy H. St. John, Henri Tajfel, Edgar Z. Friedenberg, Wan Sang Han, Daniel U. Levine, and Stanford M. Lyman. The selections are grouped in three parts:

    I. Who Are the Disadvantaged?
    II. Class, Race and Society
    III. Programs and Prospects

The contents of the buckrambound volume have been published in two parts in paperbound volumes.

Buckrambound: $14.95   Size: 7 x 10
Paperbound (Part I and Part II): $4.95 each   700 pages

HOUSING

1970 – 1971

An AMS Anthology

Edited, with an Introduction, by

George Sternlieb

Rutgers University

"URBAN RENEWAL IS NOT A CIVIC ORGANIZATION" was printed on a placard, carried recently by an evicted tenant whose protest reflects the growing consciousness of the lack of good, reasonably priced housing in America. A growing, mobile population, inflation in construction costs and building maintenance, deterioration of urban residences, taxation, and the need of owners for income and reinvestment funds have all contributed to an increasing number of such protests and to a new effort by cities and states to define housing as a national priority.

Professor Sternlieb, Director of the Center of Urban Policy Research at Rutgers, has selected for this anthology thirty-six papers from journals in business, economics, real estate, banking, industrial relations, law, sociology, and political science. The book is organized into six parts:

Buckrambound (ISBN: 0-404-10401-0): $14.95   Size: 6 x 9
Paperbound   (ISBN: 0-404-10451-7): $ 8.95 Approx. 600 pages